T0418556

C.P.E. Bach

The Late Eighteenth-Century Composers

Series Editor: Simon P. Keefe

C.P.E. Bach

Edited by

David Schulenberg

Wagner College, USA

Routledge
Taylor & Francis Group

LONDON AND NEW YORK

First published 2015 by Ashgate Publishing

Published 2016 by Routledge
2 Park Square, Milton Park, Abingdon, Oxon OX14 4RN
711 Third Avenue, New York, NY 10017, USA

Routledge is an imprint of the Taylor & Francis Group, an informa business

British Library Cataloguing in Publication Data
A catalogue record for this book is available from the British Library.

The Library of Congress has cataloged the printed edition as follows: 2015933525

ISBN 13: 978-1-4724-4337-3 (hbk)

Contents

PART I THE COMPOSER AND HIS WORKS

PART II INDIVIDUAL COMPOSITIONS AND THEIR SOURCES

PART III THE *VERSUCH* AND OTHER WRITINGS

PART IV PERFORMANCE AND RECEPTION

Acknowledgements

Ashgate would like to thank our researchers and the contributing authors who provided copies, along with the following for their permission to reprint copyright material.

Bach-Archiv Leipzig for the essay: Darrell M. Berg (1988), 'Carl Philipp Emanuel Bachs Umarbeitungen seiner Claviersonaten', *Bach-Jahrbuch*, **74**, pp. 123–61. Copyright © 1988 Evangelische Verlagsanstalt, Leipzig.

Cambridge University Press for the essays: Richard Will (2006), 'Reason and Revelation in C.P.E. Bach's Resurrection Oratorio', in Annette Richards (ed.), *C.P.E. Bach Studies*, Cambridge: Cambridge University Press, pp. 84–115. Copyright © 2006 Cambridge University Press, reproduced with permission; Christopher Hogwood (2006), '"Our Old Great Favourite": Burney, Bach, and the Bachists', in Annette Richards (ed.), *C.P.E. Bach Studies*, Cambridge: Cambridge University Press, pp. 221–50. Copyright © 2006 Cambridge University Press, reproduced with permission.

Musica Antica a Magnano for the essay: David Schulenberg (2000), 'When Did the Clavichord Become C.P.E. Bach's Favourite Instrument? An Inquiry into Expression, Style and Medium in Eighteenth-Century Keyboard Music', in Bernard Brauchli, Susan Brauchli and Alberto Galazzo (eds), *De clavicordio IV: Proceedings of the IV International Clavichord Symposium, Magnano, 8–11 September 1999*, Magnano: Musica Antica a Magnano, pp. 37–52.

The Musical Times Publications Limited for the essay: John A. Parkinson and Rodney Baldwyn (1964), 'Two Notes on C.P.E. Bach', *The Musical Times*, **105(1461)**, p. 839.

Oxford University Press for the essays: Eugene Helm (1972), 'The "Hamlet" Fantasy and the Literary Element in C.P.E. Bach's Music', *Musical Quarterly*, **58**, pp. 277–96; Susan Wollenberg (1988), 'A New Look at C.P.E. Bach's Musical Jokes', in Stephen L. Clark (ed.), *C.P.E. Bach Studies*, Oxford: Clarendon Press, pp. 295–314.

Scarecrow Press for the essay: Annette Richards (2011), 'Picturing the Moment in Sound: C.P.E. Bach and the Musical Portrait', in Thomas Donahue (ed.), *Essays in Honor of Christopher Hogwood: The Maestro's Direction*, Lanham, MD: Scarecrow Press, pp. 57–89.

Steglein Publishing Ltd for the essays: Peter Wollny (2010), 'C.P.E. Bach, Georg Philipp Telemann und die Osterkantate "Gott hat den Herrn auferwecket" Wq 244', in Paul Corneilson and Peter Wollny (eds), *'Er ist der Vater, wir sind die Bub'n': Essays in Honor of Christoph Wolff*, Ann Arbor, MI: Steglein, pp. 78–94. Copyright © 2010 Steglein Publishing, Ann Arbor, MI; Paul Corneilson (2010), 'C.P.E. Bach's Evangelist, Johann Heinrich Michel', in Paul Corneilson and Peter Wollny (eds), *'Er ist der Vater, wir sind die Bub'n': Essays in Honor of Christoph Wolff*, Ann Arbor, MI: Steglein, pp. 95–118. Copyright © 2010 Steglein Publishing, Ann Arbor, MI.

University of California Press for the essay: Richard Kramer (1985), 'The New Modulation of the 1770s: C.P.E. Bach in Theory, Criticism, and Practice', *Journal of the American Musicological Society*, **38**, pp. 551–92.

Publisher's Note

The material in this volume has been reproduced using the facsimile method. This means we can retain the original pagination to facilitate easy and correct citation of the original essays. It also explains the variety of typefaces, page layouts and numbering.

Series Preface

The second half of the eighteenth century boasts as rich and diverse a musical culture as any comparable period before or after. The five composers represented in this series capture the abundant variety of late eighteenth-century musical life: in solo, chamber, vocal and orchestral music performed publicly and privately at courts, salons, halls, churches and homes, at informal and formal concerts and other events; and in dramatic music destined for the stage or elsewhere. Scholarly attention directed towards the composers has manifested itself in different ways over time: C.P.E. Bach and J.C. Bach, once regarded primarily as successors to their father J.S. Bach and as 'pre-classical' forerunners to Haydn and Mozart, are now central figures in their own right; Gluck continues to be considered a pivotal contributor to the history of opera; Haydn, the beneficiary of an extraordinary increase in scholarly interest in the last half century or so, now occupies a place in classical music's elite; and Mozart, never out of the public eye since his death, remains a touchstone of musical greatness.

The editors of the books in the series, leading authorities on their composers, have selected important contributions to the secondary literature published for the most part in the last 40 years, shaping volumes to reflect principal areas of scholarly orientation. Extended introductions also situate the contents of individual volumes in broad scholarly contexts. 'The Late Eighteenth-Century Composers' intends both to increase access to the published literature and to provide scholars, students and general music lovers alike with a reliable reference source. Priority has been given to items in English, but a few seminal contributions appear either in a foreign language or in new, previously unpublished translations. It is hoped that reading and rereading essays in the series will not only enhance appreciation of C.P.E. Bach, J.C. Bach, Gluck, Haydn and Mozart, the environments in which they worked and the musical cultures in which they flourished, but also stimulate further engagement with the large secondary literature on these five great musicians.

SIMON P. KEEFE
Series Editor
University of Sheffield, UK.

Introduction

Second son of one of the supreme masters of what we call Baroque music, Carl Philipp Emanuel Bach (1714–88) was an important composer, player and writer on music in his own right, one of the most significant members of a generation of European musicians distinctly more modern than his father's. His earliest compositions, dating from his student years in Leipzig, clearly belong to the late Baroque of J.S. Bach. Yet they already reveal the influence of more *galant* older contemporaries, such as Telemann and Hasse. By 1738, when he moved to Berlin and was about to take his place in the court musical establishment of Prussian King Frederick II ('the Great'), he had begun to create a distinctive repertory of mostly instrumental works – especially keyboard sonatas and concertos, as well as smaller numbers of solo and trio sonatas with basso continuo. In these, over the next 30 years, emerged his personal version, today known as the *empfindsamer Stil*, of an approach to composition and performance shared with his court colleagues Quantz, the two Graun brothers and the king himself. Then, during his last 20 years, he re-defined himself as a vocal composer, producing sacred and secular works of all sorts (except opera) after taking a position as cantor and music director at Hamburg. He continued, too, to compose innovative instrumental works, publishing collections of concertos, symphonies and, in particular, six sets of keyboard pieces dedicated to 'connoisseurs and music-lovers' (*Kenner und Liebhaber*). It was this last above all that kept his name alive during the century after his death – plus his treatise on keyboard playing, known in English as well as German as the *Versuch* (1753–62), which remained almost continuously in print, though often in shortened or altered form.[1]

For much of his lifetime Emanuel Bach was the best-known member of the family, at least in German-speaking Europe. He was also one of the earliest composers for whom we have not only substantial archival documentation (musical manuscripts, employment records and the like) but also significant critical and literary accounts by contemporaries. Personally gregarious, he was a valued member of intellectual circles in Berlin and Hamburg, a friend of poets and philosophers and he and his works received frequent mention in their letters, memoirs, reviews and the like. Thus, alongside musical and biographical documents of the types that survive for members of his father's generation, we have for him a wealth of material that does not exist for earlier composers. So long as he was considered a minor or transitional figure, of primarily historical interest, much of this material lay unexplored. Recent decades, however, have seen growing interest in Emanuel Bach from listeners and musicians as well as scholars. One result has been a burgeoning list of publications about him and his music, including conference proceedings and collections of essays, as well as anthologies of documents comparable to the one edited by David and Mendel (1966 and 1998) for his father; these are listed below.

---

[1]   Woodward (1995) surveys the work's publishing history in the nineteenth and twentieth centuries.

The present volume offers chiefly recent material, reprinting representative publications from several of the principal strands of current C.P.E. Bach research and interpretation. Because most readers are likely to have access to electronic article databases, the volume focuses on items that are not yet available online. It also concentrates on relatively recent writings in English. These limitations may at first appear to constitute serious disadvantages. Yet much of the older literature is based on a spotty familiarity with the entire breadth of the composer's output and its sources, and older writing in German tends towards either general aesthetic considerations or detailed philological studies. Writing of both sorts can be of great value, yet older publications on aesthetics today are of chiefly historical value, especially when based on a narrow understanding of his works. Older text- and source-critical publications are rapidly being rendered obsolete by the critical commentaries included in a new complete edition of the composer's works; the editorial prefaces and introductions from volumes in this edition, all in English, are being made available online (at www.cpebach.org).

The bibliography that follows this introduction is selective, not comprehensive, listing significant publications that are not reproduced in the present volume.[2] As with other composers, there are whole categories of publications that, by their nature, cannot be reprinted or excerpted here. Among these are critical editions of the composer's music, which, apart from their scores, include verbal material that constitutes an essential resource; collections of letters and other documents, especially those assembled by Suchalla (1985, 1993 and 1994), Clark (1997) and Wiermann (2000); and entries in musical encyclopedias from the eighteenth century to the present (such as Gerber, 1790–92, and Leisinger, 2014). Also important, though hardly making for engaging reading, are catalogues of libraries and archives with significant C.P.E. Bach holdings; those published for collections in Berlin and Brussels include significant background material (see Leisinger and Wollny, 1997; Kast, 2003; Fischer and Kornemann, 2009). Contemporary letters and memoirs are more readable, although one often must scan many pages to find relevant matter (see especially Burney, 1772–73 and also Berg, 2009). The same is true of genre studies such as that of Newman (1972) on the sonata and Smither (1987) on the oratorio, not to mention works of criticism and analysis such as Rosen (1971). Naturally, recordings and other non-verbal publications cannot be incorporated into a printed volume, but the liner notes accompanying audio CDs contain sometimes original scholarship and interpretive criticism, and examples of these are included here. On the other hand, excluded from the present volume are original documents, including letters and writings by the composer himself, which have appeared in other compilations.[3]

During his lifetime, Bach (as he will be termed) was already an object of what we can recognize as proto-musicological interest, evident above all in several early efforts to list his numerous compositions in an orderly manner. The task was made difficult by the composer's frequent revision and re-use of many, perhaps most, of his works, which number roughly a thousand; scholars are still sorting out the details. Bach himself evidently maintained a list of his compositions, and this formed the basis for a catalogue of works – including dates and places of composition – published after his death within the printed catalogue of his estate

---

[2]   More complete lists of older publications can be found in Clark (1988b, pp. 315–35) and Powers (2002); the Helm (1989) (H.) and BR thematic catalogues also cite relevant publications in the entries for individual works.

[3]   A selection of documents in English translation is in preparation.

(NV).[4] At least one younger contemporary, J.J.H. Westphal, systematically assembled a nearly complete collection of Bach's works, most of them in manuscript copies obtained directly from the composer or his heirs. Westphal's collection wound up in the library of the Royal Conservatory in Brussels, where his manuscript list of its contents became the basis for the thematic catalogue by the Brussels librarian Wotquenne (1905) (W.). Despite its flaws and omissions, Wotquenne's numbering system remains in use, and Bach's works are now most frequently identified by 'W' (or 'Wq') numbers. Not until 1989 did E. Eugene Helm issue a catalogue intended to fill Wotquenne's many gaps, but although 'H' numbers were briefly employed for all Bach's works, their use now is largely confined to compositions missed by Wotquenne.[5] A new multi-volume catalogue, part of the larger *Bach-Repertorium* (BR), has begun to appear, incorporating information about works and sources that were inaccessible to Helm.

The cataloguing of works, although indispensable, is merely preliminary to editing, performing and interpreting them. Bach himself saw to the publication of a substantial portion of his output, yet for two centuries after his death his music came out only in occasional and often not very critical editions. For this reason, although inquisitive musicians and writers were already noting some of the distinctive features of Bach's music by the turn of the twentieth century, accounts of it tend to be anecdotal or unbalanced, focusing on idiosyncratic features of a small number of compositions. Good editions of selected keyboard works had already been included in Louise and Aristide Farrenc's *Trésor des pianistes* (Paris, 1861–72), and more followed from Carl Krebs (Leipzig, 1895), Heinrich Schenker (Vienna, 1902) and Rudolf Steglich (Hannover, 1927–28); in addition, Herman Roth and Otto Vrieslander published selections of lieder for voice and keyboard (Leipzig, 1921, and Munich, 1922). Additional works, chiefly keyboard and chamber music, continued to appear sporadically, especially after the Second World War. Yet scholarly attention to Bach proved intermittent, despite the publication of several still-useful books and dissertations, notably by Miesner (1929) and Busch (1957) on portions of his vocal output. The nineteenth-century biography by Bitter (1868) had no real successor prior to an effort by Ottenberg (1982), which, as his translator obliquely admitted in the English version (1990), was hampered by his working behind the Iron Curtain. It was only after 1989, following publication of the Helm catalogue, that Bach's works began to appear in a collected critical edition under the editorial leadership of Helm and Rachel W. Wade (the CPEBE). This effort had been preceded by a small burst of activity that produced dissertations on Bach by several American scholars (Berg, Clark, Fox, Stevens, Wade and the present author); most were associated with the editorial project. Yet devastating reviews of the Helm catalogue (Wollny, 1991) and of volumes in the CPEBE

---

[4]   For this and other abbreviations, see the list at the head of the bibliography. Also useful for tracing the history and provenance of individual works and sources is Bach's earlier manuscript catalogue of his keyboard music (1772), as well as later auction catalogues of his books and musicalia (1789, 1805), published in facsimile with commentary by Wolff (1999), Leisinger (1991), and Kulukundis (1995), respectively.

[5]   One problem with the Helm catalogue was that a preliminary list of the composer's works, included in the entry on him in the first edition of the *New Grove* dictionary (1980), gave H numbers that differed from those in the published catalogue. Some publications from the 1980s identified works using numbers from the preliminary list.

(Leisinger, 1993) demonstrated systematic shortcomings in the latter, and the edition ceased after issuing just four volumes.

None of those involved could have known that the time was simply not quite ripe for such a project. The division of Europe after the Second World War had split the Berlin state library collection, containing the greatest number of Bach sources, between east and west. Other collections were essentially inaccessible, and, together with restrictions on travel and expression, these factors seriously hindered Bach scholarship. With the re-opening of eastern Europe in the 1990s, however, came the identification of the archive of the Berlin Sing-Akademie in Kyiv and its return to the reunified German capital. The collection, which included hundreds of C.P.E. Bach sources, had never been properly investigated, and after its disappearance during the Second World War most of the composer's vocal music, as well as many other works, had been assumed lost. Its recovery, described by Wolff (2001) and Grimsted (2003), was one of a number of developments that made possible the establishment of a new editorial project led by Christoph Wolff and the late Christopher Hogwood under the auspices of the Packard Humanities Institute.[6] Ten years after issuing its first volume (in 2005), at this writing the CPEBCW has published more than half of some 115 projected volumes. Although this project, too, has not gone without criticism (see Wollenberg, 2006 and 2011), it has contributed to a resurgence of C.P.E. Bach scholarship, and it has made possible the first modern performances and recordings of several major works.

The present volume includes writings by scholars associated with both editorial projects. Of course, many others have carried out valuable work on Bach and his music. Whereas contributors to the editions have often considered issues of musical philology – identifying manuscripts and their provenances, establishing textual filiation, and the like – a separate strand of C.P.E. Bach scholarship has concentrated on the related but distinct topic of compositional procedure. For Bach the latter included the arts of embellishment and variation, used by the composer and his contemporaries as both performing practices and means of revising existing compositions, even of creating new ones. Interest in this aspect of Bach's music goes back at least to Schenker, whose pupil Otto Vrieslander published a so-called interpretive edition (*Erläuterungsausgabe*) of Bach's pedagogic keyboard pieces with varied reprises (W. 113–14) as early as 1914.[7] Described in Bach's *Versuch*, the provision of written-out embellishments for repeated passages recurs in many of Bach's other keyboard works and is closely related to improvisation over a bass line, the subject of the final chapter of the *Versuch*. Together with the chromatic harmony of Bach's late works (notably the pieces for *Kenner und Liebhaber*), Bach's embellishments and variations have been perennial topics for writers concerned with musical analysis and compositional procedure, including Berg (1983, 2010 and Chapter 6), Kramer (2008, especially pp. 47–70) and the present author (Schulenberg, 1995).

Whereas Schenker and those influenced by him have seen Bach as a composer of exquisitely fashioned variations on simple *schemata*, a much older view that developed by the mid-nineteenth century regarded him as a transitional figure in a history of musical form and style. In this teleological, evolutionary model of history, the music of Emanuel Bach, trained by Sebastian and admired by Haydn, Mozart and Beethoven, became a link between the

---

[6]   The Bach holdings within the Sing-Akademie archive are catalogued in Enßlin (2006), the collection as a whole in Fischer and Kornemann (2009).

[7]   The pieces were re-edited by another Schenkerian, Oswald Jonas, in 1962 (Vienna: Universal).

contrapuntal style of his father, focused on fugue, and what was taken (prior to Schenker) to be a more homophonic later approach to composition, centred on sonata form. Problems with this view of music history were evident to many by the time Newman published the second edition (1972) of his survey of the Classical sonata, including an extensive section on C.P.E. Bach. Yet this view is taken for granted in many earlier studies (including Barford, 1965, and Suchalla, 1968), and it is still detectable, even if as a foil for other approaches, in writings on Bach's instrumental music by Stevens (1965), Davis (1983 and 1988) and Petty (1995). More recently, as music historians have lost interest in analysis and sonata form, a number of music theorists have developed a 'new *Formenlehre*' or 'sonata theory', but this approach has yet to yield much about Bach's work.

Another traditional area of interest for C.P.E. Bach scholars has been his documentation of eighteenth-century performance practices and aesthetics, explicitly in his *Versuch* and implicitly in certain of his compositions. Once viewed as a key to understanding the historical performance of his father's music, or that of Baroque music generally, the *Versuch* is now more accurately seen as codifying Emanuel Bach's own practices and those of mid-eighteenth-century Berlin. It nevertheless continues to be cited as a source for historical performance generally – above all on the ornaments notated in his music and that of his Berlin court colleagues. By the same token, the treatise's second volume, primarily on figured bass realization, is no longer viewed as a guide to continuo playing in the music of Sebastian Bach, as tended to be assumed in older treatments of the subject that relied heavily on the *Versuch*, such as that of Arnold (1931). Even Bach's prescriptions for certain 'refinements' of continuo realization in his own music tend to be neglected by specialists, despite studies by Staier (1995) and the present author (Schulenberg, 2003). These demonstrate that at Berlin, while developing a unique compositional style, Bach was simultaneously codifying a distinctive approach to keyboard accompaniment for music in the *galant* style.

In addition to considering fingering, ornaments and figured bass realization in unprecedented detail, the *Versuch* also discusses more general aspects of performance, notably expression. Two of Bach's famous aphorisms have been taken as declarations of new aesthetic principles: 'a musician cannot move others unless he himself is moved'; and 'one must play from the soul and not like a trained bird'.[8] The classical source of the first of these (Horace) was identified by Dahlhaus (1972), who argued that the second indeed represented something new, contradicting an older 'imitative' aesthetic characteristic of the Baroque. Earlier writers, such as Schering (Chapter 2), had already seen Bach's instrumental music as employing a new 'rhetorical' type of expression.[9] Since then, Bach's relationship to the aestheticians of his day has been a favourite subject especially for Continental scholars, exploring in particular his connections to Moses Mendelssohn, ignored in Schering's Nazi-era essay (see Grimm, 1999; Plebuch, 2006; and Muns, 2008). Bach's approach to musical expression is often regarded as anticipating that of later Classical and even Romantic composers. Schering repeatedly compared him to Beethoven, and Eggebrecht (1955) and Hoffmann-Erbrecht (1957) followed Schering in associating Bach's style with the so-called *Sturm und Drang* also detected in

---

[8]   *Versuch*, vol. 1, ch. 3, paras 13 and 7.

[9]   Since Schering's time it has become fashionable among 'historically informed' performers to regard not Bach's but older Baroque instrumental music as peculiarly rhetorical; this may reflect the same confusion that continues to make Bach a 'Baroque' composer for many non-specialists and his *Versuch* a source for Baroque performance practices.

some of Haydn's early works. Many have likewise found an anticipation of Romanticism in Bach's *Empfindsamkeit* or hyper-expressive manner, although Berg (1975) criticized use of the latter term, preferring to describe the composer as a 'mannerist'. A programmatic trio sonata that Bach published in 1751 (W. 161/1), accompanied by a detailed verbal explanation of how the music represents a discussion or debate between two very different characters, was early taken as a precursor of Romantic programme music (Mersmann, 1917). The fact that Bach never repeated the experiment has not discouraged fascination in this or in his equally brief involvement with little character pieces for the keyboard. Perhaps because they do raise interesting questions of musical meaning and aesthetics, both continue to be subjects of numerous recordings and writings (see Chapter 12).

Since the advent during the 1990s of what was called the new musicology, the traditional areas of musical research considered thus far have excited less interest among Anglophone musicologists than interdisciplinary efforts to relate music to its social and cultural contexts. Composers themselves (and their works) have been downgraded as objects of investigation, rendering volumes such as the present one irrelevant to some approaches. Yet, at least within the tradition of 'classical' music, the individual creative musician remains a nexus that connects a society or a culture at large with specific compositions or performances. Gender studies made their first encroachment on Bach's music with Head (1995a, 1999), whose Yale dissertation on 'fantasy' in Bach's instrumental works (1995b) made for an interesting complement to Petty's Schenkerian thesis from the same institution in the same year.[10] But although Bach's songs (lieder) and other vocal works surely contain potential material for equally sexy topics, a massive, comprehensive book on Bach's songs by Youngren (2003), as well as Rathey's studies (2007, 2009) of the composer's oratorios and serenatas for the Hamburg milita – arguably political works – remains traditional in its interpretive methods. Of currently active scholars, Annette Richards has been the most persistent in examining 'fantasy' and other aspects of Bach's music from an interdisciplinary perspective (2001, 2006a, 2013, 2014 and Chapter 12).

The four parts of the present volume represent several of the main areas of present-day C.P.E. Bach studies. To introduce the composer, Part I opens with two general essays, one recent, one much older, on Bach's musical style. It continues with several recent selections of a primarily biographical nature. Two essays on Bach's compositional process serve as transition towards Part II, containing writings on particular works. Part III focuses on the *Versuch* and analytic studies that have been inspired by it, concluding with an essay on another verbal publication attributed to Bach that casts light on the intellectual politics of his day. The volume closes with several selections devoted to the performance and reception of his music, chiefly the keyboard works for which he is now best known.

The Composer and his Works

Chapter 1 is a short essay by the distinguished early keyboard specialist Miklós Spányi on the problem of presenting Bach's music to the musical public today. Spányi has not only edited several volumes of Bach's keyboard music but since 1994 has been involved in a project, now nearly complete, to record all of the composer's solo keyboard works, keyboard concertos

---

[10] Wollenberg (2007) has also considered 'fantasia elements' in Bach's sonatas.

and ensemble sonatinas on harpsichord, clavichord and other historical keyboard instruments. Here he succinctly questions whether the 'variety of stylistic elements' so often heard in Bach's music is merely a misperception arising out of unfamiliarity with it. Barford (1965), Rosen (1971, p. 44 and *passim*) and Fox (1983 and 1988) are among many previous authors who addressed stylistic 'non-constancy' or 'incoherence' in his music. The present writer attempted to answer Bach's critics in his dissertation (Schulenberg, 1984), subsequently tracing the origin and early development of some of the commonly mentioned features of Bach's style (1988).

Chapter 2 offers an older view of the composer by Arnold Schering, an influential German musicologist of the early twentieth century. Having edited the extraordinary D-minor concerto W. 23 in 1907,[11] in this essay from near the end of his career (1938) he discovers what he calls the composer's 'rhetorical principle'.[12] Schering's assumptions about 'great' artists and their historical 'mission' now seem dated if not uncomfortably close to authoritarian philosophies of his time.[13] His interest in musical symbolism, his distrust of the 'rationalistic' in favour of the intuitive and his unsubstantiated assertions relating Bach's music to dance, acting and the German Shakespeare revival all reflect long-abandoned styles of historical thought. Although he probably knew as much of Bach's music as anyone at the time, his opinions reflect limited acquaintance with the non-keyboard works (as witness his blinkered judgement on the extraordinary string symphonies). Yet Schering's views of music history in general and of Emanuel Bach in particular have been highly influential, and not only in Germany. The significance that he accords to musical rhetoric and gesture remains widely accepted, though now more typically ascribed to somewhat earlier music. He takes for granted the still-customary division of eighteenth-century music between earlier Baroque and later Classical styles, with Emanuel Bach representing a transitional type that incorporates distinct elements of both. Yet although he cites only a single specific composition and provides no musical examples, he articulates what remains a plausible vision of a composer animated by a desire to make instrumental music 'speak' – a wish that, for Schering, Bach shared with Beethoven.

The problem with such formulations is that the metaphor of music as speech or rhetoric means little apart from a detailed account of how specific musical figures or passages express or represent some particular element or elements of speech. Bach himself seems to have sensed this problem, and despite his concern for music to be expressive appears to have grown sceptical of the value of character pieces and other types of instrumental programme music. Not much more can be said about his views on the matter. Yet the fact that we have any remarks at all from him, or from his contemporaries, on the subject is due to the survival of types of documentation that rarely exist for earlier musicians. The relevant literature on Bach begins with his autobiography (Bach, 1773 ; English translation in Newman, 1965) and continues in his letters and those of his contemporaries. Suchalla first edited Bach's letters to Forkel and to his publisher Breitkopf in a rather poorly produced volume (1985), then

---

[11]   In *Denkmäler deutscher Tonkunst*, vols 29–30 (Leipzig: Breitkopf und Härtel).

[12]   I am grateful to my colleague Kathryn Buck in the Department of Modern Languages at Wagner College for many suggestions and corrections in my translation of Schering's difficult and sometimes obscure language.

[13]   Stanley (2013) presents a balanced view of Schering's position in the cultural politics of Nazi Germany, concluding that, like many of his contemporaries, Schering was a 'careerist' but not an ideologue.

issued a more complete and more professionally prepared edition with extensive annotations (1994). Clark, who had already (1988c) discovered and published several additional letters with illuminating commentary, subsequently issued Bach's entire known correspondence in an elegant translation, with useful prefatory material (1997). Unfortunately, the great majority of these letters date from the last two decades of Bach's life, and most deal with mundane business matters, especially relating to Bach's publications. For deeper insights into Bach's thoughts and into how his music was perceived in his own time, one must scour the letters and memoirs of others, such as the poets Claudius, Gerstenberg, Gleim and Lessing; the violinist and music director Reichardt; and above all the travel writings of Burney (1772–73), who devoted close to 30 pages to his visit to Bach in Hamburg. Bach's career coincided with the emergence of music journalism and criticism in the modern sense; concert reviews and reviews of published music therefore constitute another important source of information, again, however, chiefly from his last two decades. Examples are included in the collections edited by Suchalla (1993) and Wiermann (2000).

No biographer has yet sifted through all the available matter to produce a truly comprehensive study of Bach's life and works. The pioneering effort by Bitter (1868), whose account of the four Bach composer sons focuses overwhelmingly on Emanuel, remains impressive for its early date. Much slighter was the popular account by Vrieslander (1923), and even Ottenberg (1990) offered little that was new, although the English translation by Philip Whitmore was of an updated version of the German original of 1982. Two encyclopaedia essays (Leisinger and Wagner, 1999, and Leisinger, 2014) remain the most recent authoritative biographical accounts. Rampe (2014) provides a massive survey of the life and music; the present author's 'compositional biography' focuses on the works (Schulenberg, 2014, with extensive online supplement).

On specific issues and events in Bach's life there is a substantial literature. The investigation into Bach's uncatalogued early compositions by Leisinger and Wollny (1993) uncovered material relevant to his life and training during studies at Leipzig and Frankfurt (Oder). Wollny subsequently (1996) revealed evidence for the repertory of the collegium musicum directed by Emanuel at Frankfurt (Oder), and in 2010 he reported the sensational discovery of a previously unsuspected vocal work from the same early period (Wollny, 2010b).[14]

Bach's three decades at Berlin, although documented by numerous autograph scores, manuscript copies and published compositions, are represented by surprisingly few sources of other types. In Chapter 3, however, Mary Oleskiewicz shows, using archival records neglected by previous researchers, that, far from being undervalued and underpaid by his royal employer, Bach was among the most favoured instrumentalists at Frederick's court.[15] In further archival research (Oleskiewicz, 2011), she sheds light on the minor Hohenzollern courts, which also employed musicians and thus constituted another part of Bach's cultural environment at Berlin. The most prominent musical phenomenon there, however, and one that clearly influenced Bach's Berlin compositions, was the royal opera, which remains little studied. One must turn to a mid-nineteenth-century source for a systematic account (Schneider,

---

[14]   Readers without German will find the salient information about this work, as for so many others, in the introduction to the relevant volume of the CPEBCW (vol. 5/5.2), at: www.cpeBach.org.

[15]   Not cited in Chapter 3 is a letter, subsequently transcribed by Oleskiewicz, in which Crown Prince Frederick mentions auditioning a keyboard player named 'Back' (discussion in Pegah, 2008).

1852), although Henzel (1997) provides essential information for the crucial years 1740–56. Those without German will find relevant background in dissertations by Mangum (2002), Röder (2009) and Exner (2010).[16]

Bach's instrumental compositions from these years must have been heard often in the concert-giving musical 'academies' that proliferated at Berlin after 1740, but detailed information about their activities before the end of the century is hard to come by. Schwinger (2006) provides a massive compilation of data about several archives that probably incorporated music from the repertories of these institutions, cataloguing manuscript copies of Bach's instrumental works alongside those of lesser contemporaries whose music formed a backdrop to his own. Other aspects of Bach's life at Berlin remain obscure; his teaching, for example, is scarcely documented, although Wollny (2005) has reconstructed a circle of pupils, or at least of younger musicians influenced by Bach in some way. The composer's Latin Magnificat, completed in 1749, remains a somewhat mysterious work, its exact date and purpose unclear, although Blanken (2006), in a major study, showed that it must have been performed at Leipzig and traced Bach's later revisions of most of its component movements.

In 1756 Bach composed an Easter cantata, his first German sacred work in nearly two decades. The purpose of this isolated effort, too, has long been unclear, but Peter Wollny, in Chapter 4, makes a strong case for its biographical significance: with this work Bach deepened his personal relationship with his godfather Telemann and laid the groundwork for his eventual call to Hamburg 11 years later. With Bach's arrival there in 1768, documentation of his life improves considerably. Although his formal position changed from that of a part-time court musician to a full-time city cantor and music director, certain activities initiated at Berlin continued unabated. In Chapter 5, Stephen L. Clark discusses Bach as self-publisher of his own music, a role that he commenced at Berlin and maintained with greater intensity at Hamburg. Ottenberg (1993) and Daub (1996) consider the same topic, focusing on the late publications for *Kenner und Liebhaber*. Reviews and notices of Bach's publications and concert activity, the latter first reported selectively by Sittard (1890), are now collected in Wiermann (2000).

Bach's activities as cantor at Hamburg were the subject of a dissertation by Miesner (1929), which from 1945 to 2000 was practically the sole source of information on his annual passions and other works preserved in the missing archive of the Sing-Akademie. Following the recovery of those sources, Hill (2015) has finally provided a thorough study of the passions. But already shortly after the War the Croatian-born musicologist Dragan Plamenac, best known for his work on early Renaissance music, published a perceptive study (1949) that pieced together bits of information from various sources to shed 'new light' on Bach's circumstances at Hamburg. Plamenac's attribution to Emanuel of an anonymous 'Comparison' of Sebastian Bach and Handel is still generally accepted,[17] and he was also the first to discuss Emanuel seriously as a portrait collector.

Bach's Passions and many other of his Hamburg sacred works are pastiches and parodies (*contrafacta*), representing a vocal counterpart to his work as a reviser and embellisher of existing instrumental music and employing techniques related to those that were part of his original compositional process. Chapters 6 and 7 provide an introduction to Bach's methods

---

[16] Helm's frequently cited study of music at Frederick's court (1960) is now seriously out of date.

[17] For an alternative view, see online supplement 2.2 to the author's 2014 study.

of reworking his compositions. In Chapter 6, Darrell M. Berg demonstrates how Bach 'renovated' (*erneuert*) his early keyboard sonatas and revised later works. Readers without German can gain much from Berg's examples alone; the author's own English version of the essay, generously provided to the author, can be found on the latter's website (http://faculty.wagner.edu/david-schulenberg/c-p-e-Bach-from-ashgate/). Rachel W. Wade provided similar material in her study of Bach's concertos (1981), which remains the most thorough published account of Bach's compositional process, complementing the editions of individual concertos in the CPEBCW (especially vols 3/9.1–15). In Chapter 7 she offers a concise account of Bach's Hamburg reworkings of several earlier vocal works, including one of the most beautiful of the 1758 Gellert songs.[18] Wade's earlier essay on various philosophies and procedures for the scholarly editing of music (1988) remains instructive for anyone setting out to edit Bach's music.

Individual Compositions and their Sources

In seeking up-to-date and reliable information about specific works, readers can turn to the introductions of the respective volumes of the CPEBCW, available online. Yet the prefatory matter for a critical edition usually avoids substantial analytical, critical or interpretive commentary.[19] Thus even older literature on individual compositions can prove worthwhile.

Chapter 8 comprises two very brief items by Rodney Baldwyn and John A. Parkinson on Bach's organ sonatas and his so-called 'Solfegietto' (W. 117/2) – still probably his best-known keyboard piece, thanks to its continuing anthologization, typically in the inauthentic form described here.[20] These minuscule notices are typical of the somewhat casual yet often perceptive and somewhat pedagogic writing that was typical of British commentary on C.P.E. Bach during the twentieth century. Reflecting the tradition of Tovey, other examples include Barford (1965) on the keyboard sonatas and Cole (1970) on Bach's modulating or 'improper' rondos. Eugene Helm, now known for his 1989 thematic catalogue, wrote in a similar vein; Chapter 9 is his classic essay on a famous literary 'experiment' that was applied to the final movement from Bach's *Probestücke* of 1753, which is therefore known as the 'Hamlet' fantasia. Plebuch (2006) has updated some of the underlying facts, yet Helm's humane and readable setting of one of Bach's most famous compositions in its cultural context has not been surpassed.

More 'scientific' study of Bach's music could not proceed, however, without careful attention to such details as the dating of his autograph manuscripts. Scholars of C.P.E. Bach's music were late in applying methods that have been used to sharpen the chronology of J.S. Bach sources since the 1950s. Among the first to do so was Pamela Fox, author of Chapter 10. Since its initial publication in 1998, those associated with the CPEBCW have amassed

---

[18]   The choral arrangements that Bach made of his sacred songs for liturgical use at Hamburg are the subject of Leisinger (2006).

[19]   There are of course exceptions. Christopher Hogwood provides useful background to the works for *Kenner und Liebhaber* in the introductions to CPEBCW, vols 1/4.1–2, and Darrell Berg offers similar matter on the songs as well as a translation of Bach's preface to the Gellert Lieder (W. 194) in vol. 6/1.

[20]   Berg (1998) subsequently provided an in-depth discussion of the origins of Bach's organ sonatas; her conclusions are ratified in the edition by Richards and David Yearsley in CPEBCW, vol. 1/9.

far more information on the subject, doubtless correcting some details. Fox's discussion nevertheless remains the most accessible introduction to the subject, with several well-chosen examples.[21]

Another scholar who applied the lessons of J.S. Bach studies to the music of C.P.E. Bach was Jane R. Stevens. Her book on Bach-family keyboard concertos (2001) capped a scholarly career that began with a dissertation on those of C.P.E. Bach (1965).[22] Chapter 11 comprises programme notes for two CD recordings in which Stevens distils essential information on Bach's concertos and ensemble sonatinas. The latter constitute a distinct genre, a sort of divertimento for keyboard orchestra, which Bach invented during the 1760s.

The previous decade had already seen Bach branching out beyond the sonatas and concertos that he had been producing since his student years. His character pieces, which all date from 1754–57, are the subject of Chapter 12. Here Annette Richards relates several of the most distinctive of these pieces to his collection of portraits on canvas and paper, whose importance she has delineated elsewhere.[23] Bach's emphasis on musical expression in his own writings has led to his being regarded as a uniformly serious composer; Rosen (1971, p. 115) asserted that 'his passion lacked wit'. Yet his humour, which emerges in the character pieces, also characterizes a great many of his other compositions; this is Susan Wollenberg's subject in Chapter 13. A prolific writer in the Toveyan tradition on Bach's keyboard music, here Wollenberg extends her purview to the equally witty sinfonias (symphonies) that Bach composed for public concerts during his later Berlin years and at Hamburg.

At Hamburg, where Bach turned to vocal music on a large scale, the annual Passion performances were among his most important responsibilities. In Chapter 14, Paul Corneilson, managing editor of the CPBECW, provides a detailed account of one of the most important of the many musicians who worked for Bach at Hamburg. Johann Heinrich Michel – long known only by his last name, as 'Herr Michel' – was not only a long-serving tenor, singing the Evangelist parts in Bach's passions, but also the composer's principal copyist, continuing to produce manuscript copies of his works for purchasers such as J.J.H. Westphal after the composer's death. Corneilson provides not only a summary of Michel's career but also a general account of Bach's work as a composer and director of church music during his last two decades, drawing on earlier studies by Clark (1984 and 1988a) and Sanders (2001).

At Hamburg Bach continued to compose songs for voice and keyboard, revealing in the process his continuing interest in contemporary literature.[24] Chapter 15, by Christoph Wolff, provides insights into Bach's artistic relationship with one of his younger literary

---

[21]   More extensive illustrations of Bach's handwriting are available in Berg's facsimile edition of his complete keyboard works (New York: Garland, 1989) and in several supplementary volumes to the CPEBCW. The autograph manuscripts mentioned by Fox (Chapter 10) on page 170 have now been recovered as part of the Sing-Akademie archive.

[22]   For a somewhat different view of the 'invention' of the keyboard concerto, see the present author's 2010 study.

[23]   In addition to her catalogue reconstructing Bach's portrait collection (CPEBCW, vols 8/4.1–2), see Richards (2013 and 2014). Further on these pieces in Berg (1988), Walden (2008) and the preface to the edition by Christopher Hogwood (1989). The pieces have subsequently been edited by Wollny in CPEBCW 1/8.2, with an introduction identifying the persons named in the titles of the pieces.

[24]   On this subject see Berg's studies of his clavichord songs (2000a) and of his relationship to Anna Luisa Karsch (2000b), the leading female poet in German of his day.

contemporaries, offering as well (alongside Chapter 7) further illustrations of his working methods. Wolff is best known for his work relating to J.S. Bach and Mozart, but he was instrumental in the return of the Sing-Akademie archive to Berlin, and he has edited C.P.E. Bach's later trio sonatas for the CPEBCW (vol. 2/2.2), of whose editorial board he was a founding member. Songs for voice and keyboard are the most numerous single category of Bach's works, and during his lifetime those which he published in four large collections (W. 194 and 196–98) were among his best-known works. Yet today they are relatively unfamiliar; here Wolff is concerned primarily with a previously unknown collection (published in CPEBCW, vol. 8/2).

In Bach's own eyes, the great works of his Hamburg years were several large vocal works intended chiefly for concert, not liturgical, use. One of these, his setting of Ramler's *Auferstehung und Himmelfahrt Christi*, is the subject of Chapter 16 by Richard Will. Aspects of the work's complicated genesis and generic status – cantata or oratorio? – have been addressed by Smither (1987 and 1990), Clark (1988c), Finscher (1990), Wiermann (1997) and Grant (2011 and 2013). Here Will, who previously (1997) considered the cultural context of the Programme Trio (W. 161/1), addresses the meaning of Bach's self-proclaimed 'masterpiece' within the literary and theological currents of his time. Two of Bach's other major Hamburg vocal works have provoked comparable studies. Richards (2006a) considers the double-chorus *Heilig* as a representation of the 'sublime', an important category in late-eighteenth-century aesthetics.[25] The Litanies (W. 204), a pair of austere exercises in récherché harmony and restrained spiritual expressivity, are the topic of Marx-Weber (2000), who traces their origin, identifying the poet of the 'new' litany as Klopstock.

Despite their sacred character, Bach envisioned the Litanies as a pedagogic composition (see Ringhandt, 1993). Even the Resurrection Cantata was an exemplary concert piece, not a liturgical work. This may be one reason Emanuel's sacred music has not yet been the subject of the type of investigation (familiar from J.S. Bach studies) in which the theology inherent in a work's libretto is related to the composer and his music. Studies of Emanuel's sacred lieder, like those of his larger vocal works, have instead focused on the formal and literary features of the poetry and their translation in the music, as with Youngren (2003). Leisinger (2006), however, touches on what might be termed the popular piety expressed in some of Bach's choral arrangements of his songs for the Hamburg churches, and Hill (2015) considers the neology or rationalist theology embedded in the librettos of Bach's passions.

The *Versuch* and Other Writings

Like his older contemporary Rameau, Bach has been noted almost as much for his writings on music as for his compositions. The *Versuch* is his counterpart to Rameau's *Traité de l'harmonie* (Paris, 1725) – to some degree probably even a response to it, although its immediate model, or rather spur, must have been Quantz's *Versuch* on the flute, published in 1752, a year before the first volume of Bach's similarly titled book. Thomas Christensen argues in Chapter 17 that, despite its fame, *Versuch* was less influential and sold fewer copies than usually thought.[26] The

---

[25]   On the *Heilig*, see also Chapter 19.

[26]   A note of explanation: Christensen's (Chapter 17) discussion on page 326 refers to a chord on F that is indicated only by the custodes ('directs') in example 5b.

work has nevertheless been an essential source not only on historical performance practice but on Bach's thinking about harmony – particularly since its English translation by William J. Mitchell in 1949. Over the years, various errors and misunderstandings in Mitchell's translation have become apparent, and a new translation is reportedly in the works. Yet Mitchell succeeded in finding elegant phrasings for Bach's lively but typically discursive eighteenth-century prose. His introduction to the work, first published separately (1947) and subsequently reprinted together with the translation, still provides useful bibliographic information. In Chapter 18, published more than two decades later (1970), Mitchell reflects on several issues of terminology relating to modulation – a word whose meaning has evolved substantially since Bach's time – demonstrating how essential it is for a translator of a historical treatise to understand the theoretical language of the author's day.

Modulation is also an important topic in Chapter 19. Here Richard Kramer relates Bach's writings on the subject to several late compositions, especially the double-chorus *Heilig*, which are notable for their chromatic modulations and counterintuitive harmony. Kramer subsequently (2008) has offered thought-provoking reflections on Bach's music and, especially, its relation to that of Beethoven.[27] More recently (2012) he has extended his long grappling with Bach's *Versuch* in a review essay about its new edition in the CPEBCW (vols 7/1–3). Kramer is also translator of Chapter 20 by the Austrian theorist Heinrich Schenker (1868–1935), whose reductive analytical technique was inspired in part by Bach's account, in the final chapter of the *Versuch*, of how to improvise a free fantasia.[28] Bach's account is probably less actual instruction than a way of analysing or conceptualizing the composition of a written fantasia. By the same token, Schenker's essay on improvisation, first published in 1925, is more about Schenker's idealized understanding of tonal composition than actual eighteenth-century practice. Nevertheless, Schenker's essay remains an important document for both Bach reception and the history of music theory; Petty has continued to apply Schenkerian analysis to Bach's music in several publications (1995 and 1999) and subsequent conference presentations.

The *Versuch* was not Bach's only published writing. In addition to a number of reviews, notes and the like, he is often regarded as the author of a work published under the pseudonym 'Caspar Dünkelfeind' (1755). Chapter 21, again by Christensen, treats the latter as well as the treatise by Christoph Nichelmann (1755) to which it was a reply. Nichelmann, demonstrating an exceptional lack of tact, had criticized the music of his most important colleagues at the Berlin court, above all Bach. Christensen not only identifies many of Nichelmann's musical examples but provides a good idea of the intellectual ferment and passionate discussion of music that characterized the Berlin of Emanuel Bach and King Frederick 'the Great' on the eve of the Seven Years' War. The debate was the equivalent for Emanuel Bach of the famous controversy provoked when Scheibe criticized the music of J.S. Bach. Once again, an uncomprehending advocate of what was claimed to be a more rational and expressive type of music merely revealed his prejudices, making himself seem even more ridiculous in this

---

[27] The present author is obliged to mention, with gratitude, that Kramer was his dissertation adviser. A chapter in Kramer (2008) on the meaning of Bach's *Empfindungen* appeared in preliminary form in the anthology edited by Richards (2006b).

[28] Omitted from Chapter 20 are the original pages 14–19 on several keyboard works by Handel.

case by rewriting passages from the works of much better composers, among them a complete song by Emanuel ('Die Küsse', W. 199/4).[29]

Performance and Reception

Whatever the merits of his argument, Nichelmann, like Scheibe, provided an example of the contemporary reception of the music of the Bach family. Other examples include reviews by Forkel and writings by Cramer, which have been examined by Kramer (2008 and Chapter 19). In Chapter 22, Christopher Hogwood takes a critical look at a cult of Emanuel Bach that began during his lifetime and continued well after his death.[30] Keyboard player and for many years director of the Academy of Ancient Music, Hogwood was also a prolific editor and writer on music and chaired the editorial board of the CPEBCW from its inception. One of Bach's most persistent advocates in recent times, he made some of the first recordings on period instruments of major works by Bach.[31] Publications relevant to Emanuel Bach include his essay on a keyboard treatise by Bach's younger contemporary Ernst Wilhelm Wolf (Hogwood, 1988) and editions of keyboard music by Bach's Berlin pupil Carl Fasch, his Berlin colleague Georg Benda and others. Chapter 22 provides a wealth of detailed information relevant not only to the dissemination of Bach's music during the last decades of the eighteenth century but to its performance and Bach's legacy into the nineteenth.

Performance is arguably the most important type of reception, and studies of historical performance practice are therefore a closely related field. This writer's 1988 essay raised a number of questions about C.P.E. Bach performance, such as the most appropriate type of keyboard instrument for it and several issues involving the realization of ornament signs. This was followed up 25 years later with another essay considering how scholars and performers had dealt with those questions in the interim (Schulenberg, 2013). It is nevertheless surprising that relatively few writings have specifically addressed performance issues in music by the author of the *Versuch*. Staier (1995) is one of the few who have discussed figured bass realization in specific works, pointing out some of the distinctive ways in which Bach's actual practice differed from the theoretically correct approach illustrated in the earlier chapters of the treatise's second volume. This writer's contribution to the subject (Schulenberg, 2003) aimed to show that Bach's 'refinements' of a literal four-part realization were a creative response to aesthetic preferences at the Berlin court, like the compositional style that he developed there simultaneously.

---

[29]   See online supplement 8.3 to my 2014 book for an argument against identifying 'Dünkelfeind' with Emanuel Bach.

[30]   Chapter 22 is the later, longer version of an essay first published in Bernard Brauchli, Susan Brauchli and Alberto Galazzo (eds), *De clavicordio IV: Proceedings of the International Clavichord Symposium, Magnano, 8–11 September 1999* (Magnano: Musica Antica a Magnano, 2000), reproduced here without the final paragraph and the detailed list of 'Bachists' that originally followed on pages 251–64. Another 'Bach cult' centred in Berlin is the subject of Wollny (2010a), earlier versions of which appeared in 1993 (English) and 1999 (German).

[31]   Notably the three quartets W. 93–95 (1976) and the *Probestücke* W. 63 (1980), as well as a number of the sinfonias (1977); his website (http://www.hogwood.org) continues to provide details.

Performance problems in Bach's vocal music have been particularly neglected, doubtless because of the rarity of performances until recently. Rifkin (1985) considered the vocal scoring of Bach's large sacred works from the point of view of the 1749 Magnificat and its later performances at Hamburg. His argument for essentially one-on-a-part vocal performance of Bach's 'choral' music has been largely confirmed by the subsequent recovery of the original performing parts for Bach's Passions and other Hamburg vocal works.[32] Dellal (2014) offers perspectives on the songs by one of their most accomplished American performers, but crucial questions remain, such as whether the numerous ornament signs in the melodic lines were meant for the singer or only the doubling keyboard instrument.

Most work on C.P.E. Bach performance has focused, understandably, on the keyboard music, in particular the choice of keyboard instrument for particular works. Chapter 23, by the present author, examines the common assumption that the clavichord was the composer's favourite instrument. It followed on an earlier effort by Speerstra (1995) to identify the intended medium of various keyboard works.[33] Chapter 24 comprises four brief essays by Miklós Spányi on performance issues that arose during his superb complete recording of Bach's keyboard concertos. Like Chapter 11, these originally appeared within booklets accompanying the audio CDs; Spányi has also issued a second series of recordings of Bach's solo keyboard music, with equally informative notes. Each of these essays naturally refers to the specific works whose recordings it originally accompanied, but they are of broader relevance, documenting the process by which a distinguished musician has reached decisions about a fundamental aspect of performance.

What Remains?

At this writing C.P.E. Bach studies continue to be dominated by source and textual criticism, if only because most of the scholars now most engaged with the composer's music are also involved in editing it. Yet although the 'new musicology' has now become old, there remains much that could be said about the representation of women in Bach's songs or performative aspects of his concertos and other music for public concerts. Whether the new fields of experimental science, or new approaches to philosophy and theology, that were emerging during Bach's day had any significant effect on Bach or his music must also be worth considering. Surely sophisticated, culturally contextualized accounts could be made of the programmatic trios and keyboard pieces and their relationships to the musical aesthetics of the period. In a more traditional vein of musicology, the influence of composers such as Graun and Hasse (as opposed to J.S. Bach or even Telemann) on Emanuel's Berlin instrumental

---

[32] See especially the critical commentaries in the volumes of CPEBCW, series 4. Sanders (2001) had previously gathered together the available information about Bach's musicians and performance schedule in the Hamburg churches.

[33] Two points in Chapter 23 require correction. First, only one of the six 'Prussian' Sonatas (W. 48) of 1742 contains more than two dynamic levels, with 'pp' occurring only in two bars of Sonata 2; in the 'Württemberg' Sonatas (W. 49) of two years later, only two works have 'pp', in addition to 'p' and 'f'. Second, the sonata for bowed clavier was probably written not for the instrument by Hohlfeld but a later example. The essay mentioned in the last footnote eventually appeared in *The Harpsichord and Clavichord: An Encyclopedia* (New York: Routledge, 2007).

music and his later vocal works – a theme of my 2014 study – is open to refinement, as is the conventional view of eighteenth-century Berlin and Hamburg as closed, provincial places, as far as music was concerned. There is doubtless much to be discovered about intersections between Bach's music and his public with those of Gluck's, Haydn's and Mozart's Vienna; Christian Bach's London; and the Paris of dozens of other composers.

Richards may have mined as much as can be extracted for the time being from Bach's portrait collection. But, for a composer so attuned to the literary and intellectual currents of his time – and one who had an artist son – there must be many further relationships to explore between his music and other media. The unsolved questions of performance raised by the present author are only a sampling of problems involving instrumentation, ornamentation and embellishment, as well as more global aspects of performance, that arise in Bach's music – particularly in early works, and in early versions of subsequently revised works, that predate his codification of his own principles in the *Versuch*. Research undertaken in conjunction with the new edition continues to produce surprises, such as the apparent destination of Bach's last published keyboard rondo (W. 61/6) for a hybrid instrument combining harpsichord and piano actions. Such findings raise further questions that should not go unasked, even if music editors cannot be expected to pursue them immediately.

Bibliography

Abbreviations (Editions and Thematic Catalogues)

BR	*Carl Philipp Emanuel Bach: Thematisch-systematisches Verzeichnis der musikalischen Werke* (2014–), ed. Wolfram Enßlin and Uwe Wolf, Bach-Repertorium, Part 3, Stuttgart: Carus.
CPEBCW	*Carl Philipp Emanuel Bach: The Complete Works* (2005–), Los Altos, CA: Packard Humanities Institute.
CPEBE	*Carl Philipp Emanuel Bach Edition* (1989–95), Oxford: Oxford University Press.
H.	Catalogue number of work listed in E. Eugene Helm (1989), *Thematic Catalogue of the Works of Carl Philipp Emanuel Bach*, New Haven, CT: Yale University Press.
NV	*Verzeichniß des musikalischen Nachlasses des verstorbenen Capellmeisters Carl Philipp Emanuel Bach* (1790), Hamburg; annotated facsimile ed. Rachel Wade (1981) as *The Catalog of Carl Philipp Emanuel Bach's Estate: A Facsimile of the Edition by Schniebes, Hamburg, 1790*, New York: Garland; searchable transcription at: http://www.cpebach.org/pdfs/resources/NV-1790.pdf.
W.	Catalogue number of work in Alfred Wotquenne (1905), *Catalogue thématique des œuvres de Charles Philippe Emmanuel Bach (1714–1788)*, Leipzig: Breitkopf und Härtel (reprinted as *Thematisches Verzeichnis der Werke von Carl Philipp Emanuel Bach*, 1964, 1972).

Collections of Documents, Essays and Other Writings

Clark, Stephen L. (ed.) (1988b), *C.P.E. Bach Studies*, Oxford: Clarendon Press.

Leisinger, Ulrich and Ottenberg, Hans-Günter (eds) (2000), *Carl Philipp Emanuel Bachs geistliche Musik: Bericht über das Internationale Symposium (Teil 1) vom 12. bis 16. März 1998 in Frankfurt (Oder), Żagań und Zielona Góra im Rahmen der 33. Frankfurter Festtage der Musik an der Konzerthalle 'Carl Philipp Emanuel Bach' in Frankfurt (Oder)*, Carl-Philipp-Emanuel-Bach-Konzepte, Sonderband 3, Frankfurt (Oder): Konzerthalle 'Carl Philipp Emanuel Bach'.

Marx, Hans Joachim (ed.) (1990), *Carl Philipp Emanuel Bach und die europäische Musikkultur des mittleren 18. Jahrhunderts: Bericht über das Internationale Symposium der Joachim Jungius–Gesellschaft der Wissenschaften Hamburg 29. September–2. Oktober 1988*, Göttingen: Vandenhoeck & Ruprecht.

Ottenberg, Hans-Günter (ed.) (1998), *Carl Philipp Emanuel Bach: Musik für Europa: Bericht über das Internationale Symposium vom 8. März bis 12. März 1994 im Rahmen der 29. Frankfurter Festtage der Musik an der Konzerthalle 'Carl Philipp Emanuel Bach' in Frankfurt (Oder)*, Carl-Philipp-Emanuel-Bach-Konzepte, Sonderband 2, Frankfurt (Oder): Konzerthalle 'Carl Philipp Emanuel Bach'.

Ottenberg, Hans-Günter and Leisinger, Ulrich (eds) (2005), *Carl Philipp Emanuel Bach als Lehrer / Die Verbreitung der Musik Carl Philipp Emanuel Bachs in England und Skandinavien. Bericht über das Internationale Symposium vom 29. März bis 1. April 2001 in Słubice–Frankfurt (Oder)–Cottbus*, Carl-Philipp-Emanuel-Bach-Konzepte, Sonderband 4, Frankfurt (Oder): Musikgesellschaft Carl Philipp Emanuel Bach.

Poos, Heinrich (ed.) (1993), *Carl Philipp Emanuel Bach: Beiträge zu Leben und Werk*, Mainz: Schott.

Richards, Annette (ed.) (2006b), *C.P.E. Bach Studies*, Cambridge: Cambridge University Press.

Suchalla, Ernst (ed.) (1985), *Briefe von Carl Philipp Emanuel Bach an Johann Gottlob Immanuel Breitkopf und Johann Nikolaus Forkel*, Tutzing: Hans Schneider.

Suchalla, Ernst (ed.) (1993), *Carl Philipp Emanuel Bach im Spiegel seiner Zeit: Die Dokumentensammlung Johann Jacob Heinrich Westphals*, Hildesheim: Olms.

Suchalla, Ernst (ed.) (1994), *Carl Philipp Emanuel Bach: Briefe und Dokumente: Kritische Gesamtausgabe* (2 vols), Göttingen: Vandenhoeck & Ruprecht.

Wiermann, Barbara (ed.) (2000), *Carl Philipp Emanuel Bach: Dokumente zu Leben und Wirken aus der zeitgenössischen hamburgischen Presse (1767–1790)*, Hildesheim: Olms.

References

Arnold, Franck Thomas (1931), *The Art of Accompaniment from a Thorough-Bass as Practised in the XVIIth and XVIIIth Centuries*, London: Oxford University Press.

Bach, Carl Philipp Emanuel (1753–62), *Versuch über die wahre Art das Clavier zu spielen* (2 vols), Berlin; new edition by Tobias Plebuch (2011) in CPEBCW, vols 7/1–3; trans. William J. Mitchell (1949) as *Essay on the True Art of Playing Keyboard Instruments*, New York: Norton.

Bach, Carl Philipp Emanuel (1773), untitled autobiography, in Carl Burney's *der Musik Doktors Tagebuch seiner musikalischen Reise*, vol. 3, trans. Johann Joachim Christoph Bode, Hamburg, pp. 199–209. English translation in Newman (1965).

Barford, Philipp Trevelyan (1965), *The Keyboard Music of C.P.E. Bach Considered in Relation to His Musical Aesthetic and the Rise of the Sonata Principle*, New York and London: Barrie and Rockcliffe.

Berg, Darrell M. (1975), 'The Keyboard Sonatas of Carl Philipp Emanuel Bach: An Expression of the Mannerist Principle', PhD diss., State University of New York at Buffalo.

Berg, Darrell M. (1983), 'C.P.E. Bach's "Variations" and "Embellishments" for His Keyboard Sonatas', *Journal of Musicology*, **2**, pp. 151–73.

Berg, Darrell M. (1988), 'C.P.E. Bach's Character Pieces and His Friendship Circle', in Clark (1988b), pp. 1–32.

Berg, Darrell M. (1998), 'C.P.E. Bach's Organ Sonatas: A Musical Offering for Princess Amalia?', *Journal of the American Musicological Society*, **51**, pp. 477–519.

Berg, Darrell M. (2000a), 'C.P.E. Bach's Songs for Clavichord', in Bernard Brauchli, Susan Brauchli and Alberto Galazzo (eds), *De clavicordio IV: Proceedings of the International Clavichord Symposium, Magnano, 8–11 September 1999*, Magnano: Musica Antica a Magnano, pp. 95–103.

Berg, Darrell M. (2000b), 'Carl Philipp Emanuel Bach und Anna Louisa Karsch', in Leisinger and Ottenberg (2000), pp. 41–68.

Berg, Darrell M. (2009), *The Correspondence of Christian Gottfried Krause: A Music Lover in the Age of Sensibility*, Farnham and Burlington: Ashgate.

Berg, Darrell M. (2010), 'Das "Verändern ... ist ... unentbehrlich": Variation as Invention in C.P.E. Bach's Keyboard Music', in Paul Corneilson and Peter Wollny (eds), *'Er ist der Vater, wir sind die Bub'n': Essays in Honor of Christoph Wolff*, Ann Arbor, MI: Steglein, pp. 20–42.

Bitter, Carl Hermann (1868), *Carl Philipp Emanuel und Wilhelm Friedemann Bach und deren Brüder* (2 vols), Berlin: Wilhelm Müller.

Blanken, Christine (2006), 'Zur Werk- und Überlieferungsgeschichte des Magnificat Wq 215 von Carl Philipp Emanuel Bach', *Bach-Jahrbuch*, **92**, pp. 229–70.

Burney, Charles (1772–73), *The Present State of Music in Germany, The Netherlands, and United Provinces* (2 vols), London; 2nd edn, corrected, 1775.

Busch, Gudrun (1957), *C.Ph.E. Bach und seine Lieder* (2 vols), Regensburg: Gustav Bosse.

Clark, Stephen L. (1984), 'The Occasional Choral Works of C.P.E. Bach', PhD diss., Princeton University.

Clark, Stephen L. (1988a), 'C.P.E. Bach and the Tradition of Passion Music in Hamburg', *Early Music*, **16**, pp. 533–41.

Clark, Stephen L. (1988c), 'The Letters from C.P.E. Bach to K.W. Ramler', in Clark (1988b), pp. 33–41.

Clark, Stephen L. (ed. and trans.) (1997), *The Letters of C.P.E. Bach*, Oxford: Clarendon Press.

Cole, Malcolm Stanley (1970), 'Rondos, Proper and Improper', *Music & Letters*, **51**, pp. 388–99.

Dahlhaus, Carl (1972), 'Si vis me flere ...', *Die Musikforschung*, **25**, pp. 51–52.

Daub, Peggy (1996), 'The Publication Process and Audience for C.P.E. Bach's Sonaten für Kenner und Liebhaber', in George B. Stauffer (ed.), *Bach Perspectives, Volume Two: J.S. Bach, the Breitkopfs, and the Eighteenth-Century Music Trade*, Lincoln, NE and London: University of Nebraska Press, pp. 65–83.

David, Hans T. and Mendel, Arthur (eds) (1966), *The Bach Reader*, New York: Norton.

David, Hans T. and Mendel, Arthur (eds) (1998), *The New Bach Reader: A Life of Johann Sebastian Bach in Letters and Documents*, revised and enlarged by Christoph Wolff, New York: Norton.

Davis, Shelley (1983), 'H.C. Koch, the Classic Concerto, and the Sonata-Form Retransition', *Journal of Musicology*, **2**, pp. 45–61.

Davis, Shelley (1988), 'C.P.E. Bach and the Early History of the Recapitulatory Tutti in North Germany', in Clark (1988b), pp. 65–82.

Dellal, Pamela (2014), 'The Songs of C.P.E. Bach: A Performer's Perspective', *Early Music*, **42**, pp. 363–77.

'Dünkelfeind, Caspar' (1755), *Gedanken eines Liebhabers der Tonkunst über Herrn Nichelmanns Tractat von der Melodie*, Nordhausen (no publisher named).

Eggebrecht, Hans Heinrich (1955), 'Das Ausdrucksprinzip im musikalischen "Sturm und Drang"', *Deutsche Vierteljahrsschrift für Litteraturwissenschaft und Geistesgeschichte*, **29**, pp. 323–49.

Enßlin, Wolfram (ed.) (2006), *Die Bach-Quellen der Sing-Akademie zu Berlin* (2 vols), Leipziger Beiträge zur Bach-Forschung, 8, Hildesheim: Olms.

Exner, Ellen Elizabeth (2010), 'The Forging of a Golden Age: King Frederick the Great and Music for Berlin, 1732 to 1756', PhD diss., Harvard University.

Finscher, Ludwig (1990), 'Bemerkungen zu den Oratorien Carl Philipp Emanuel Bachs', in Marx (1990), pp. 309–32.

Fischer, Axel and Kornemann, Matthias (eds) (2009), *The Archive of the Sing-Akademie zu Berlin: Catalogue / Das Archiv der Sing-Akademie zu Berlin: Katalog*, Berlin: De Gruyter.

Fox, Pamela Mollard (1983), 'Melodic Nonconstancy in the Keyboard Sonatas of C.P.E. Bach', PhD diss., University of Cincinnati.

Fox, Pamela (1988), 'The Stylistic Anomalies of C.P.E. Bach's Nonconstancy', in Clark (1988b), pp. 105–31.

Gerber, Ernst Ludwig (1790–92), *Historisch-biographisches Lexicon der Ton-Künstler* (2 vols), Leipzig.

Grant, Jason B. (2011), 'Die Herkunft des Chors "Triumph! Triumph! des Herrn Gesalbter sieget" aus dem Oratorium "Die Auferstehung und Himmelfahrt Jesu" von C.P.E. Bach', *Bach-Jahrbuch*, **98**, pp. 273–86.

Grant, Jason B. (2013), 'The Origins of the Aria "Ich folge dir, verklärter Held" and the Recurring Chorus "Triumph!" from the Oratorio Die Auferstehung und Himmelfahrt Jesu by Carl Philipp Emanuel Bach', *BACH Journal*, **44(2)**, pp. 6–24.

Grimm, Hartmut (1999), 'Moses Mendelssohns Beitrag zur Musikästhetik und Carl Philipp Emanuel Bachs Fantasie-Prinzip', in Anselm Gerhard (ed.), *Musik und Ästhetik im Berlin Moses Mendelssohns*, Tübingen: Niemeyer, pp. 165–86.

Grimsted, Patricia Kennedy (2003), 'Bach is Back in Berlin: The Return of the Sing-Akademie Archive from Ukraine in the Context of Displaced Cultural Treasures and Restitution Politics', published online by the National Council for Eurasian and East European Research at: http://www.ucis.pitt.edu/nceeer/2003_816_03_Grimsted.pdf.

Head, Matthew William (1995a), '"Like Beauty Spots on the Face of a Man": Gender in 18th-Century North-German Discourse on Genre', *Journal of Musicology*, **13**, pp. 143–67.

Head, Matthew William (1995b), 'Fantasy in the Instrumental Music of C.P.E. Bach', PhD diss., Yale University.

Head, Matthew (1999), '"If the Pretty Little Hand Won't Stretch": Music for the Fair Sex in Eighteenth-Century Germany', *Journal of the American Musicological Society*, **52**, pp. 203–54.

Helm, E. Eugene (1960), *Music at the Court of Frederick the Great*, Norman, OK: University of Oklahoma Press.

Henzel, Christoph (1997), 'Zu den Aufführungen der grossen Oper Friedrichs II. von Preussen 1740–1756', *Jahrbuch des Staatlichen Instituts für Musikforschung Preussischer Kulturbesitz*, pp. 9–57.

Hill, Moira Leanne (2015), 'Carl Philipp Emanuel Bach's Passion Settings: Context, Content, and Impact', PhD diss., Yale University.

Hoffmann-Erbrecht, Lothar (1957), 'Sturm und Drang in der deutschen Klaviermusik von 1753–1763', *Die Musikforschung*, **10**, pp. 466–79.

Hogwood, Christopher (1988), 'A Supplement to C.P.E. Bach's Versuch: E.W. Wolf's Anleitung of 1785', in Clark (1988b), pp. 133–57.

Hogwood, Christopher (ed.) (1989), *Twenty-three pièces characteristiques*, Oxford: Oxford University Press.

Kast, Paul (2003), *Die Bach-Sammlung: Katalog und Register nach Paul Kast: Die Bach-Handschriften der Berliner Staatsbibliothek, 1958, vollständig erweitert und für die Mikrofiche-Edition ergänzt*, ed. Staatsbibliothek zu Berlin–Preußische Kulturbesitz, Munich: Saur.

Kramer, Richard (2008), *Unfinished Music*, New York: Oxford University Press; corrected paperback edn, 2012.

Kramer, Richard (2012), 'Probing the Probestücke', *Keyboard Perspectives*, **5**, pp. 83–94.

Kulukundis, Elias N. (1995), 'Die Versteigerung von C.P.E. Bachs musikalischem Nachlaß im Jahre 1805', *Bach-Jahrbuch*, **81**, pp. 145–76.

Leisinger, Ulrich (1991), 'Die "Bachsche Auction" von 1789', *Bach Jahrbuch*, **77**, pp. 97–126.

Leisinger, Ulrich (1993), Review of CPEBE, vol. 2/23, *Early Keyboard Journal*, **11**, pp. 146–52.

Leisinger, Ulrich (2006), 'C.P.E. Bach and C.C. Sturm: Sacred Song, Public Church Service, and Private Devotion', in Richards (2006b), pp. 116–48.

Leisinger, Ulrich (2014), 'Carl Philipp Emanuel Bach', in Grove Music Online (the electronic version of *The New Grove Dictionary of Music and Musicians*, 2nd edn), at: www.oxfordmusiconline.com.

Leisinger, Ulrich and Wagner, Günther (1999), 'Carl Philipp Emanuel Bach', in *Die Musik in Geschichte und Gegenwart: Allgemeine Enzyklopäde der Musik begründe von Friedrich Blume*, 2nd edn, ed. Ludwig Finscher, Personenteil, vol. 1, Kassel: Bärenreiter, columns 1312–58.

Leisinger, Ulrich and Wollny, Peter (1993), '"Altes Zeug von mir": Carl Philipp Emanuel Bachs kompositorisches Schaffen vor 1740', *Bach-Jahrbuch*, **79**, pp. 127–204.

Leisinger, Ulrich and Wollny, Peter (1997), *Die Bach-Quellen der Bibliotheken in Brüssel: Katalog, Leipziger Beiträge zur Bach-Forschung*, vol. 2, Hildesheim: Olms.

Mangum, John Richard (2002), 'Apollo and the German Muses: Opera and the Articulation of Class, Politics, and Society in Prussia, 1740–1806', PhD diss., University of California at Los Angeles.

Marx-Weber, Magda (2000), 'Carl Philipp Emanuel Bachs Litaneien', in Leisinger and Ottenberg (2000), pp. 181–205.

Mersmann, Hans (1917), 'Ein Programmtrio K.Ph.E. Bachs', *Bach-Jahrbuch*, **14**, pp. 137–70.

Miesner, Heinrich (1929), 'Philipp Emanuel Bach in Hamburg: Beiträge zu seiner Biographie und zur Musikgeschichte seiner Zeit', PhD diss. (Berlin, 1928), Leipzig: Martin Sädig.

Mitchell, William J. (1947), 'C.P.E. Bach's Essay: An Introduction', *Musical Quarterly*, **33**, pp. 460–80.

Muns, Lodewijk (2008), 'C.P.E. Bach, Haydn, and the Art of Mixed Feelings', at: http://lmuns.home.xs4all.nl/CPEMixedfeelings2010.pdf ('postscript' dated 2012).

Newman, William S. (1965), 'Emanuel Bach's Autobiography', *Musical Quarterly*, **51**, pp. 363–72.

Newman, William S. (1972), *The Sonata in the Classic Era*, 2nd edn, New York: Norton.

Nichelmann, Christoph (1755), *Die Melodie, nach ihrem Wesen sowohl, als nach ihren Eigenschaften*, Danzig.

Oleskiewicz, Mary (2011), 'The Court of Brandenburg-Prussia', in Samantha Owens, Barbara M. Reul and Janice B. Stockigt (eds), *Music at German Courts, 1715–1760: Changing Artistic Priorities*, Woodbridge: Boydell and Brewer, pp. 79–130.

Ottenberg, Hans-Günter (1990), *Carl Philipp Emanuel Bach*, trans. Philip J. Whitmore, Oxford: Oxford University Press.

Ottenberg, Hans-Günter (1993), 'Die Klaviersonaten Wq 55 "im Verlage des Autors": Zur Praxis des Selbstverlages bei Carl Philipp Emanuel Bach', in Poos (1993), pp. 21–39.

Pegah, Rashid-S (2008), 'Carl Philipp Emanuel Bach und Kronprinz Friedrich in Preußen: Die erste Begegnung?', *Bach-Jahrbuch*, **94**, pp. 328–32.

Petty, Wayne Christopher (1995), 'Compositional Techniques in the Keyboard Sonatas of Carl Philipp Emanuel Bach: Reimagining the Foundations of a Musical Style', PhD diss., Yale University.

Petty, Wayne Christopher (1999), 'Koch, Schenker, and the Development Section of Sonata Forms by C.P.E. Bach', *Music Theory Spectrum*, **21**, pp. 151–73.

Plamenac, Dragan (1949), 'New Light on the Last Years of Carl Philipp Emanuel Bach', *Musical Quarterly*, **35**, pp. 565–87.

Plebuch, Tobias (2006), 'Dark Fantasies and the Dawn of the Self: Gerstenberg's Monologues for C.P.E. Bach's C-minor Fantasia', in Richards (2006b), pp. 25–66.

Powers, Doris Bosworth (2002), *Carl Philipp Emanuel Bach: A Guide to Research*, New York: Routledge.

Quantz, Johann Joachim (1752), *Versuch einer Anweisung die Flöte traversiere zu spielen*, Berlin; trans. Edward R. Reilly as *On Playing the Flute*, 2nd edn (1985), New York: Schirmer Books.

Rampe, Siegbert (2014), *Carl Philipp Emanuel Bach und seine Zeit*, Laaber: Laaber-Verlag.

Rathey, Markus (2007), 'Celebrating Patriotism: Carl Philipp Emanuel Bach's Compositions for the Militia in Hamburg', *Eighteenth-Century Music*, **4**, pp. 265–83.

Rathey, Markus (2009), *Kommunikation und Diskurs: Die Bürgerkapitänsmusiken Carl Philipp Emanuel Bachs*, Hildesheim: Olms.

Richards, Annette (2001), *The Free Fantasia and the Musical Picturesque*, Cambridge: Cambridge University Press.

Richards, Annette (2006a), 'An Enduring Monument: C.P.E. Bach and the Musical Sublime', in Richards (2006b), pp. 149–72.

Richards, Annette (2013), 'Carl Philipp Emanuel Bach, Portraits, and the Physiognomy of Music History', *Journal of the American Musicological Society*, **66**, pp. 337–96.

Richards, Annette (2014), 'Listening for Likeness, or C.P.E. Bach and the Art of Speculation', *Early Music*, **42**, pp. 347–62.

Rifkin, Joshua (1985), '"... Wobey aber die Singstimmen hinlänglich besetzt seyn müssen ...": Zum Credo der h-Holl-Messe in der Aufführung Carl Philipp Emanuel Bachs', *Basler Jahrbuch für historische Musikpraxis*, **9**, pp. 157–72.

Ringhandt, Ute (1993), 'Die Litaneien von Carl Philipp Emanuel Bach als "musikalische Lehrgedichte"', in Poos (1993), pp. 197–219.

Röder, Matthias (2009), 'Music, Politics, and the Public Sphere in Late Eighteenth-Century Berlin', PhD diss., Harvard University.

Rosen, Charles (1971), *The Classical Style: Haydn, Mozart, Beethoven*, New York: Norton; 'expanded edition', 1997.

Sanders, Reginald LeMonte (2001), 'Carl Philipp Emanuel Bach and Liturgical Music at the Hamburg Principal Churches from 1768 to 1788', PhD diss., Yale University.

Schneider, Louis (1852), *Geschichte der Oper und des Königlichen Opernhauses in Berlin*, Berlin: Duncker und Humblot.

Schulenberg, David (1984), *The Instrumental Music of Carl Philipp Emanuel Bach*, Ann Arbor, MI: UMI Research Press.

Schulenberg, David (1988), 'C.P.E. Bach through the 1740s: The Growth of a Style', in Clark (1988b), pp. 217–31.

Schulenberg, David (1995), 'Composition and Improvisation in the School of J.S. Bach', in Russell Stinson (ed.), *Bach Perspectives*, vol. 1, Lincoln, NE and Omaha: University of Nebraska Press, pp. 1–42.

Schulenberg, David (2003), '"Toward the Most Elegant Taste": Developments in Keyboard Accompaniment from J.S. to C.P.E. Bach', in Christopher Hogwood (ed.), *The Keyboard in Baroque Europe: Keyboard Studies of the 17th and 18th Centuries*, Cambridge: Cambridge University Press, pp. 157–68.

Schulenberg, David (2010), 'J.S. Bach, C.P.E. Bach, and the Invention of the Concerto for Keyboard and Strings', *Early Keyboard Journal*, **25/26**, pp. 29–59.

Schulenberg, David (2013), 'Performing C.P.E. Bach: Questions Answered?', *Early Music*, **41**, pp. 119–22.

Schulenberg, David (2014), *The Music of Carl Philipp Emanuel Bach*, Rochester, NY: University of Rochester Press (online supplement at: http://faculty.wagner.edu/david-schulenberg/the-music-of-carl-philipp-emanuel-bach/).

Schwinger, Tobias (2006), *Die Musikaliensammlung Thulemeier und die Berliner Musiküberlieferung in der zweiten Hälfte des 18. Jahrhunderts*, Beeskow: Ortus.

Sittard, Josef (1890), *Geschichte des Musik- und Concertwesens in Hamburg vom 14. Jahrhundert bis auf die Gegenwart*, Altona and Leipzig: A.C. Reher.

Smither, Howard E. (1987), *A History of the Oratorio, Vol. 3: The Oratorio in the Classical Era*, Chapel Hill, NC: University of North Carolina Press.

Smither, Howard E. (1990), 'Arienstruktur und Arienstil in den Oratorien und Kantaten Bachs', in Marx (1990), pp. 345–68.

Speerstra, Joel (1995), 'Towards an Identification of the Clavichord Repertoire among C.P.E. Bach's Solo Keyboard Music: Some Preliminary Conclusions', in Bernard Brauchli, Susan Brauchli and Alberto Galazzo (eds), *De clavicordio II: Proceedings of the International Clavichord Symposium, Magnano, 21–23 September 1995*, Magnano: Musica Antica a Magnano, pp. 43–81.

Staier, Andreas (1995), 'Der Generalbass bei Carl Philipp Emanuel Bach', *Basler Jahrbuch für historische Musikpraxis*, **19**, pp. 189–219.

Stanley, Glenn (2013), 'Arnold Schering – ein Nazi-Musikologe? Dokumentation und Analyse', *Archiv für Musikwissenschaft*, **70**, pp. 119–33.

Stevens, Jane R. (1965), 'The Keyboard Concertos of Carl Philipp Emanuel Bach', PhD diss., Yale University.

Stevens, Jane R. (2001), *The Bach Family and the Keyboard Concerto: The Evolution of a Genre*, Warren, MI: Harmonie Park Press.

Suchalla, Ernst (1968), *Die Orchestersinfonien Carl Philipp Emanuel Bachs nebst einem thematischen Verzeichnis seiner Orchesterwerke*, Augsburg: Blasaditsch.

Vrieslander, Otto (1923), *Carl Philipp Emanuel Bach*, Munich: Piper.

Wade, Rachel W. (1981), *The Keyboard Concertos of Carl Philipp Emanuel Bach*, Ann Arbor, MI: UMI Research Press.

Wade, Rachel W. (1988), 'Filiation and the Editing of Revised and Alternate Versions: Implications for the C.P.E. Bach Edition', in Clark (1988b), pp. 277–94.

Walden, Joshua S. (2008), 'Composing Character in Musical Portraits: Carl Philipp Emanuel Bach and "L'Aly Rupalich"', *Musical Quarterly*, **91**, pp. 379–411.

Wiermann, Barbara (1997), 'Werkgeschichte als Gattungsgeschichte: Die "Auferstehung und Himmelfahrt Jesu" von Carl Philipp Emanuel Bach', *Bach-Jahrbuch*, **83**, pp. 117–43.

Will, Richard (1997), 'When God Met the Sinner, and Other Dramatic Confrontations in Eighteenth-Century Instrumental Music', *Music & Letters*, **78**, pp. 175–209.

Wolff, Christoph (1999), 'Carl Philipp Emanuel Bachs Verzeichnis seiner Clavierwerke von 1733 bis 1772', in Barbara Steinwachs, Ulrich Leisinger and Peter Wollny (eds), *Über Leben, Kunst und Kunstwerke: Aspekte musikalischer Biographie; Johann Sebastian Bach im Zentrum*, Leipzig: Evangelische Verlagsanstalt, pp. 217–35.

Wolff, Christoph (2001), 'Recovered in Kiev: Bach et al.: A Preliminary Report on the Music Collection of the Berlin Sing-Akademie', *Notes*, **58**, pp. 259–71.

Wollenberg, Susan (2006), 'Reviving C.P.E. Bach', review of CPEBCW I/3, II/8, and III/3, *Early Music*, **34**, pp. 694–96.

Wollenberg, Susan (2007), '"Es lebe die Ordnung und Betriebsamkeit! was hilft das beste Herz ohne Jene!": A New Look at Fantasia Elements in the Keyboard Sonatas of C.P.E. Bach', *Eighteenth-Century Music*, **4**, pp. 119–28.

Wollenberg, Susan (2011), 'C.P.E. Bach for Connoisseurs and Amateurs', review of CPEBCW, vols 1/4.1–2 and 2/3.2, *Early Music*, **39**, pp. 437–39.

Wollny, Peter (1991), Review of Helm (1989), *Bach-Jahrbuch*, **77**, pp. 215–21.

Wollny, Peter (1993), 'Sara Levy and the Making of Musical Taste in Berlin', *Musical Quarterly*, **77**, pp. 651–88.

Wollny, Peter (1996), 'Zur Überlieferung der Instrumentalwerke Johann Sebastian Bachs: Der Quellenbesitz Carl Philipp Emanuel Bachs', *Bach-Jahrbuch*, **84**, pp. 7–22.

Wollny, Peter (1999), '"Ein förmlicher Sebastian und Philipp Emanuel Bach-Kultus": Sara Levy, geb. Itzig und ihr musikalisch-literarischer Salon', in Anselm Gerhard (ed.), *Musik und Ästhetik im Berlin Moses Mendelssohns*, Tübingen: Niemeyer, pp. 217–55.

Wollny, Peter (2005), 'Carl Philipp Emanuel Bachs Berliner Schüler', in Ottenberg and Leisinger (2005), pp. 69–81.

Wollny, Peter (2010a), *'Ein förmlicher Sebastian und Philipp Emanuel Bach – Kultus': Sara Levy und ihr musikalisches Wirken*, Wiesbaden: Breitkopf und Härtel.

Wollny, Peter (2010b), 'Zwei Bach-Funde in Müggeln: C.P.E. Bach, Picander und die Leipziger Kirchenmusik in den 1730er Jahren', *Bach-Jahrbuch*, **96**, pp. 111–47.

Woodward, Beverly (1995), 'The Probestücke and C.P.E. Bach's Versuch über die wahre Art das Clavier zu spielen', in Bernard Brauchli, Susan Brauchli and Alberto Galazzo (eds), *De clavicordio II: Proceedings of the International Clavichord Symposium, Magnano, 21–23 September 1995*, Magnano: Musica Antica a Magnano, pp. 83–93.

Youngren, William H. (2003), *C.P.E. Bach and the Rebirth of Strophic Song*, Lanham, MD and Oxford: Scarecrow Press.

Part I
The Composer and his Works

[1]

Appreciating the Music of C.P.E. Bach Today

Miklós Spányi

A few months ago, my ensemble played a trio sonata by C.P.E. Bach as the first piece in a concert. To our great surprise, the audience did not applaud following the very energetic *Presto* final movement. Just some twenty minutes later, a Quantz trio sonata was an immediate and great success.

What was the difference between these two compositions and their reception? What was the problem, if any, with the C.P.E. Bach sonata?

One possibility is that we did not play the C.P.E. Bach sonata well enough to offer it in an easily understandable manner to the audience as an opening number. On the other hand, we may suspect that some features of Bach's music are too difficult or complex for an inexperienced audience to follow. The Quantz sonata, also an excellent composition, was the direct opposite with its eloquent simplicity and elegance.

What might make CPEB's music seem more complicated than that of many other composers to the ears of today's listeners? First, the stylistic orientation may be difficult. The sonata we performed was one of the early trio sonatas, although Bach revised it radically in his later years. It contains many elements of baroque style, or more precisely, elements we *associate* with baroque music. But take note that it also features melodic and harmonic turns belonging to the later galant idiom. All of this is combined, especially in the middle movement, with a highly subjective dramatic element, neither baroque nor galant, but based in an *empfindsam* style that awakens in many listeners associations with 19th century romantic music. In many of CPEB's compositions the predominating stylistic element may change from movement to movement or even from one bar to the next, or several elements may be present simultaneously.

This may produce confusion in the listener's mind, given the strict categories we have been taught and our strongly conditioned listening habits. Once our ear associates something with "baroque," it waits for additional similar elements. When instead it receives new elements that it associates with other (real or imagined) "styles," it becomes disoriented and loses track of the flow of the music. In many of CPEB's early works the opening is very baroque, but the rest is not, often building up to a real confrontation of styles. In other works, the galant element may dominate. We often associate the galant style with the "Viennese" classical idiom. When Bach mingles it with slightly more baroque patterns the mind becomes confused again.

An additional stylistic layer in CPEB's music is contributed by elements of a more personal character, typically found only in his music. We could collect his most typical melodic and harmonic turns and create a "C.P.E. Bach vocabulary." These melodic and harmonic patterns often differ from what is found in the styles most familiar to us, but are frequently used by Bach, and are often intermingled with elements reminiscent of other styles.

Once we accept the presence of such a variety of stylistic elements, we can become accustomed to their combinations within one piece or even within a single musical phrase. This can lead to the realization that incorporating these elements of seemingly different origin into a logically coherent whole results in a new style, a style particular to C.P.E. Bach. For Bach, they constitute a very personal musical language, which he spoke perfectly, but which is far less well understood today. Once we realize this, we have made a big step forward towards a deeper understanding of Bach's style and music.

Another interesting feature of C.P.E. Bach's music is the organization and "placement" of the various stylistic elements in the flow of time. Even if certain stylistic features are associated with styles with which we are familiar, they may seem different due to their use at a point when we would not expect them. In general, Bach's music is rooted in the same harmonic-tonal system as the music of other 18th century

(Continued on p.4)

(C.P.E. Bach, Continued from P. 1)

composers. Roughly, this implies that the same harmonies and scales are used, resulting to some extent in similar harmonic and melodic progressions. However, harmonies and the notes of a melodic line can be organized in many different ways. CPEB's music is often very personal and, therefore, radically different from that of other composers who seemingly work with the same material.

It is typical, for example, for Bach not to add a harmony to a melody at a time when we would expect it. Another typical feature involves the structure and placement of cadences. I have been working with some students on improvisation exercises in the galant style, or more specifically in what I will call the CPEB style. Due to their association of the galant style with classicism, the students often include very classical cadences in their improvisations, distorting the otherwise successfully imitated CPEB style. In CPEB's music the cadence is often more concise than in the classical style and is therefore included at a somewhat later phase within a musical phrase. An understanding of this may help us to comprehend the way he organized harmonic progressions in general. His harmonic rhythm and logic often differ radically from those of his contemporaries, even though the differences in terms of music theory may often seem to be just tiny details.

Returning to the Quantz sonata that was so successful in our concert, we note that its melodic lines and harmonic turns are for the most part very close to Italian models. This makes it easy for the listener to recognize its resemblances to music like that of Vivaldi and to follow and understand it easily—despite the fact that Quantz' music is never a copy of high baroque, but is a personal and convincing derivative of that and other stylistic elements. However, unlike the music of C.P.E. Bach, the music of Quantz lacks radically new ways of organizing the harmonic or melodic progress.

Perhaps this means that we can (and should) perform more compositions by Quantz. Given the easily understandable qualities of his music, Quantz can be ranked among the most successful, albeit little-known, composers.

Quantz' music is logical, but generally (and I think intentionally) not very complex. C.P.E. Bach's music is also very logical, but in its basic character generally much more complex. Indeed, in my opinion

it can be ranked among the structurally most complex creations in the history of music. Manifold stylistic elements, seemingly extreme formal solutions, and melodic lines that appear strange on first sight, are all organized in a most logical way. Comprehending this omnipresent logic and coherence can guide us in understanding the deepest and often hidden features of the music. In this respect, there is no difference between understanding C.P.E. Bach or his father, or, for example, understanding the structurally very organic and strictly organized works of Beethoven.

How to achieve a general appreciation and acceptance of the music of C.P.E. Bach by the general public is a very difficult problem. His style is highly personal and can be associated with other styles only in its elements, not in its entirety. This new style needs to be learned both by players and listeners. Players who want to understand it have to play as much of his music as possible and must accommodate themselves to this "new" musical language—a process similar to learning and practicing 20th century or contemporary compositions which do not fit in any known musical style.

From our audiences we cannot expect similar efforts. The only way to educate the listener is to include C.P.E. Bach's music more often in our concerts and to perform his most central compositions repeatedly. Were these compositions performed more often, listeners would become accustomed to his musical language and become able to follow this music more easily. In their times, the works of Johann Sebastian Bach, Beethoven and Wagner were all considered very complicated, strange, and impossible to comprehend. As a result of widespread and frequent performances in the last 150 years, few listeners today would find them weird. Such a process with respect to the music of C.P.E. Bach is still ahead of us. This should be the central task of all musicians who care about this composer and who would like to bring his music closer to contemporary listeners. Once this is done, at least to some extent, we can test again to see whether the audience applauds loudly after a C.P.E. Bach sonata.   Ω

[2]

Carl Philipp Emanuel Bach and the 'Rhetorical Principle' in Music*

Arnold Schering

It would be senseless today to offer another laurel wreath in observance of the one hundred fiftieth anniversary of the death of Carl Philipp Emanuel Bach, the great son of Sebastian.[1] Scholars long ago pointed out the place reserved for him based on his key historical position between the Baroque and the Classical, while also recognizing the promise his creations held for the future. Yet the century to which he belonged as one of the leading minds in his field remains so problematical, with regard to general intellectual and artistic movements, that even he has been affected by it. Every new step undertaken in the domain of intellectual history in his century seems significant for understanding Emanuel, even more so than for Haydn and Mozart. His direct descent from a family of artists, which through generations embodied the powerful high-Baroque musical culture, and his own merging into an age which, driven forward by entirely new vital impulses, sought to repudiate the past – these contradictions between entry and exit were bound to lead to special complications for a born genius destined to live through them.

It has often been proclaimed that Philipp Emanuel, standing in this sense between eras, played the role of a great intermediary – and that he thus was deprived of recognition as a 'classic'. Had his life and output been only half as long, this title would probably have easily been his. The fact that his career endured, and that during its second half conflicts that might once have been easily resolved could persist in notable imbalance, has impressed on his collected work a tragic duality.[2] To regret this, or even to see it as a flaw, would indeed be wrong; it signifies good fortune. The historical greatness of the man is not diminished by it. On the contrary, only a chosen one, an artistic giant, could have waged – consciously or unconsciously – these internal battles **[p. 14]** so unswervingly to the end of his life that he not only gained the full reverence of his contemporaries but also served as their highest model. Personalities with such dispositions achieve human greatness, which may not lead to complete perfection yet will always assure them our lively interest. At the same time they join

* English translation of 'C.Ph.E. Bach und das redende Prinzip in der Musik', *Jahrbuch der Musikbibliothek Peters für 1938* (Yearbook of the Music Publisher Peters for 1938). Leipzig: C.F. Peters, 1939, pp. 13–29. Original page numbers are given in square brackets within the text.

[1] *Trans.:* Schering's term *Ruhmeskranz* actually refers to an honorary wreath or crown typically worn by the honoree at a birthday celebration.

[2] *Trans.:* Schering probably refers to the supposed conflict between old and new elements of style in Bach's music, which would not have arisen had he had a shorter career and therefore never developed 'new' stylistic approaches that so sharply contrasted with others inherited from his father.

those of a markedly problematic nature – doubly so if we are dealing with someone who bears the illustrious name of Bach.

The reason why Philipp Emanuel, despite the care taken by biographers and historians of style, continues to be surrounded by riddles may lie in the fact that until now he has been regarded and explained essentially as a purely musical phenomenon. Certainly it makes sense to begin by considering what objectively produces a musician such as he: how he reveals himself musically, what technical means he uses, to what school or tendency he belongs, what is old, new, original in him. Yet the desire for understanding leads to further connections, above all to the questions of what the master wished, what were the most fundamental driving forces of his creativity, and how did he fulfill his historical mission, if it is possible to specify? It is not as if these questions have been overlooked. Yet they continually recede behind the history of style and development and usually are only asked, not answered. It is possible to search more deeply, beginning at the moment the attempt is made to place Emanuel within the contradictory artistic activity of his age and to comprehend his work on the basis of general considerations – not solely on the basis of artistic considerations applicable to music alone. It is sufficient to consider him as a keyboard composer and player, for his real historical significance rests solely on this dual role.[3] It is the one thing that enables him to move beyond the powerful legacy of his father.

At the conclusion of his autobiography in the Burney-Ebeling *Present State of Music,* volume 3 (1773),[4] Emanuel captured something essential to his keyboard art in the sentence: 'My chief study, especially in recent years, has been directed toward playing and composing at the keyboard in as singing a manner as possible, despite the instrument's lack of sustaining power'. This signifies nothing other than the emphasis on a principle instilled in Emanuel since childhood by his father, which Sebastian had expressed in writing in the foreword to the Inventions (1723).[5] This was nothing new, nor anything that concerned only Sebastian himself, excluding [only] those untalented players intent on producing 'crashing, pounding, and arpeggios'. 'It seems to me that music must above all move the heart,' Emanuel states immediately thereafter.[6] This statement too is of no individual personal significance; it expresses an aesthetic commonplace of the later eighteenth century. If one were to take both

---

[3]   *Trans.:* It is surprising that Schering adopts such a narrow view of C.P.E. Bach's real historical role, considering him only as a composer and player on keyboard instruments because that was the sphere of music in which he chiefly worked (in fact this was not true, at least during his last two or three decades).

[4]   *Trans.:* Schering refers to the German translation by Christoph Daniel Ebeling and Johann Joachim Christoph Bode of Charles Burney, *The Present State of Music in Germany, The Netherlands, and United Provinces,* 2 vols (London, 1772–73). Preceded by a volume recounting the author's earlier travels in central and southern Europe, this work appeared in German as the last two of three volumes comprising *Carl Burney's der Musik Doktors Tagebuch seiner musikalischen Reise* (Hamburg, 1773). Volume 3, translated by Bode, incorporated Bach's autobiographical essay (pp. 199–209) – English translation by William S. Newman as 'Emanuel Bach's Autobiography', *Musical Quarterly* 51(2), (1965), pp. 363–72.

[5]   *Trans.:* Schering must have in mind the elaborate title of the Inventions and Sinfonias in J.S. Bach's autograph manuscript (Berlin, Staatsbibliothek, Mus. ms. Bach P 610). This includes the phrase 'am allermeisten aber eine *cantabile* Art im Spielen zu erlangen' (above all to achieve a singing manner of performance).

[6]   *Trans.:* Both quoted phrases are from the last sentence of Bach's autobiography, op. cit. (p. 209).

pronouncements in isolation, as they stand here, one could hardly see them as the summation of more than forty years of struggle **[p. 15]**. Only if they are considered from a broader perspective and in connection with other phenomena intersecting with Emanuel's development do they acquire colour and life.

Let us stay with the expression 'to sing' at the keyboard. It is not easily clarified. This cannot be done with a few general expressions, such as: to play expressively, to connect, to separate, to emphasize tones and phrases, to make them whisper and fade away or to shake, as happens with singers. The crucial point in singing – otherwise musicians would not be reproached with it – is not the sounding element but rather the *speech* that is bound to it. This speech, clad in a grammatically and syntactically appropriate garment, and arousing and joining certain ideas, is to be reproduced. Music is to *speak*. A principle is thus stated which since mid-century, in Germany as well as France, appears among the fundamental concepts of musical aesthetics. Beginning with Mattheson, Scheibe, and Marpurg, and extending to the aesthetics of early Romanticism, 'speaking' music and 'speaking' performance on instruments serve as an ideal – not, however, in the weak, metaphorical sense of a plain 'speaking to the heart', but in the sense of real speech. One spoke of a *rhetorical principle* in music or, with the French, of '*tons parlants* [speaking tones]'. Taken historically, this is related to the idea of an 'original tone language *[Urtonsprache]*', and the aesthetics of imitation has a role in its establishment.[7] But as it appears in writings concerned primarily with practice, this is to designate not an aesthetic insight but a practical rule: the composer is to proceed, literally, as if he intended to speak. Two things are inherent in this insight: an immediate relationship to rhetoric as such, and a possible connection between instrumental music, which in itself lacks meaning, and the world of ideas. Both were now investigated anew with an eager thirst for knowledge.

Musicians had never lost their awareness of the original relationship of music to rhetoric. But until this time rhetoric had carried significance only for the composer of vocal music; without knowledge of certain rhetorical rules the latter could not have managed even the shortest psalm verse. Now, with the rise of pure instrumental music, the rhetorical principle gained greater value. If instrumental music was only the imitation of vocal music (something no one doubted), it too was subject to this principle. Mattheson expressed this most clearly in the second part of his *Vollkommener Capellmeister* (Hamburg, 1739), especially in the twelfth chapter. In the same year the Leipzig instructor *[Magister]* Birnbaum wrote of Sebastian Bach:

> He understands so perfectly the elements and advantages which the working out of a musical composition has in common with rhetoric, that one not only hears him with a fulfilling pleasure when he directs his rigorous discourse toward the similarity and correspondence of both, but one also wonders at the skillful use of the same in his works.[8]

---

[7] *Trans.*: Schering's term *Urtonsprache* refers to a hypothesized, prehistoric form of proto-communication that preceded language and music. 'Imitation' in the sense used here is the employment of musical sounds or motives that supposedly resemble things in the natural world, that is, word painting, a fundamental element of eighteenth-century aesthetics.

[8] [Johann Abraham Birnbaum,] 'Vertheidigung seiner unpartheyischen Anmerkungen [Defense of his unbiased remarks]', reprinted in Scheibe's *Critischer Musikus*, 2d edn., 1745, p. 997.

[p. 16] Forkel repeated in 1802 that Bach 'regarded music completely as speech and the composer as a poet who, regardless of the language in which he writes, must never lack for adequate expression in the portrayal of his feelings.' He was 'the greatest musical poet and the greatest musical orator there has ever been and probably ever will be.'[9]

Studies showing that Sebastian, too, followed the old rules of rhetoric as an instrumental composer remain incomplete. They will correspond to a most surprising degree with studies of Emanuel's musical rhetoric. Despite every boundary that divides the work of the father from that of the son, one glimpses here an important legacy to the next generation. Emanuel seems to have kept the best of this legacy as a creative secret for himself. Yet remarks by those around him attest to the fact that he at least referred to and took part in polemical discussions of this topic. The highly educated literary circle in Hamburg that included not only Emanuel but also Lessing, Klopstock, and Gerstenberg at its head knew nothing more captivating than to occupy itself with problems of musical rhetoric and to identify the multifaceted points of contact that lead from one art form to another. From this it is clear that rhetoric and poetry were considered to be sisters. Most decisively, as is well known, Gerstenberg emerged as one inspired by an ardent sense of fanaticism regarding the general realization of the rhetorical principle. He seems to have been the chief initiator in this area, not only with his texted version of Emanuel's great C-minor fantasy (the soliloquy of Hamlet, later also that of Socrates drinking the poison cup), but also in other remarks and suggestions.[10]

It is entirely inappropriate to marginalize such efforts as 'flat-out rationalistic' and to characterize the entire realm of thought thus constituted as mere imitation of French tendencies.[11] What today seems odd about it is the frequently exaggerated manner of expression: one struggled to achieve insights for which there was no specialized terminology or scholarly training. Forkel in Göttingen was the first to recognize this problem, and in the introduction to the first volume of his *Allgemeine Geschichte der Musik* [General history of music] (Leipzig, 1788) he sketched a scholarly design for a 'musical rhetoric' (§ 68ff.). Despite Mattheson's precedent, he considered this field of music theory to be 'as yet very undeveloped in this respect', writing (p. 38): 'I am the first among my countrymen to have provided at least a sketch of all the components of musical rhetoric, in the 1777 publication "On the theory of music, insofar as it is necessary and useful for dilettantes and connoisseurs."'[12] [p. 17] Forkel distinguished this discipline from the actual theory of composition (musical grammar) and

---

[9]   *Trans.:* Here and below Schering quotes from Johann Nicolaus Forkel, *Ueber Johann Sebastian Bachs Leben, Kunst und Kunstwerke* (Leipzig: Hoffmeister und Kühnel, 1802); English translation in Hans T. David and Arthur Mendel, *The New Bach Reader: A Life of Johann Sebastian Bach in Letters and Documents*, rev. Christoph Wolff (New York: Norton, 1998).

[10]   *Trans.:* The poet Heinrich Wilhelm von Gerstenberg added his own German texts, based on Hamlet's soliloquy and the dying words of Socrates, to the C-minor fantasia that serves as the final movement of Bach's Sonata W. 63/6 (no. 18 of the *Probestücke*). Schering's original footnote at this point cites older literature on the subject; for a modern English-language discussion, see chapter 9 in the present volume.

[11]   *Trans.:* This is one of several passages in which Schering adopts a stance common in early twentieth-century Germany, decrying eighteenth-century rationalism and 'rationalistic' thought (sometimes associated with France, as here).

[12]   *Trans.:* Forkel, quoted by Schering, refers to his own *Über die Theorie der Musik insofern sie Liebhabern und Kennern derselben nothwendig und nützlich ist: Einladungsschrift zu musikalischen*

from the theory of sound (acoustics), assigning to it, as the most important chapters, form *[Periodologie];* varieties of musical notation; the arrangement of musical ideas with respect to the scope of the composition, as well as the theory of rhetorical figures; performance or recitation *[Deklamation]* of compositions; music criticism. Forkel's achievement must someday be considered separately. He places great value on what he considered to be the still unweakened and viable theory of 'figures', with which the Renaissance masters had established a new relationship [of music] to rhetoric as early as the sixteenth century. He describes several of these oldest figures of speech as transferred to music (ellipse, repetition with paronomasia, suspension, epistrophe, gradation, dubitation), remarking (§ 105):

> In many schools of musical rhetoric it will probably become increasingly common to find that speech in tones and real speech resemble one another not merely in their origin and grammar, but also in the aesthetic constitution of their expressions, up to the moment of their greatest effectiveness.

And immediately thereafter:

> Since the impressions of one sense can be transmitted to another, even abstracted from sensuous ideas and impressions, then it follows that the first purpose of speaking in tones, although not the only one, is sentiment *[Empfindung].*

> This transfer of impressions from one mental faculty *[Kraft]* to another happens excellently through the figures. Hence these really are devices that contain the metaphorical form of an impression according to the particular nature of each faculty, and which transmit the impression from one faculty to the other.

> There is no sentiment and no concept of which the faculty of imagination cannot conceive a metaphorical form, for all our concepts are initially nothing but abstractions of corporeal, visible circumstances. The so-called figures thus lie deep within human nature, and in actual speech they are the first things that natural humans, as yet uncivilized, must have understood how to use.

What Forkel sets forth here was the common aesthetic property of the musical world of his day. If one had come to this world with the expression 'absolute music' – a late intellectual product of world-weary Romantic philosophy – the speaker would have been considered not entirely sane. Indeed, it seems as if Forkel's longer discussion in his *Introduction [Einleitung]* had been drafted with constant glances at the work of his friend Philipp Emanuel, thirty-five years his senior. Surely the latter must have thought so. Although not entirely in agreement with the somewhat excessive pedantry of Forkel's preliminary essay of 1777,[13] Bach openly acknowledged the importance of the 1788 *Introduction,* specifically the part concerned with musical rhetoric:

Vorlesungen (Göttingen, 1777). The phrase 'Kenner und Liebhaber' recurs in the titles of Bach's late keyboard publications (1779–87).

   [13]   'In my opinion, *nota bene:* to train an amateur, many things could be left out that many musicians do not know, even ones that a musician might not realize are essential. The most desirable thing, namely analysis, is missing' (letter to Forkel of 15 Oct. 1777). Schering cites the first publication of Bach's letter in Carl Hermann Bitter, *Carl Philipp Emanuel und Wilhelm Friedemann Bach und deren Brüder,* 2 vols (Berlin, 1868); now see Stephen L. Clark, ed. and trans., *The Letters of C.P.E. Bach* (Oxford: Clarendon Press, 1997).

Music has long been called a language of sentiment, from which it follows that one dimly sensed similarities between its own content and that of verbal expressions; but no one has yet developed the idea so clearly or, as far as [this] reviewer is aware, derived such important conclusions for the theory of art as a whole, as the author does in this introduction.[14]

[p. 18] This appreciation by Emanuel, written in the year of his death and thus one of his final literary legacies, gives us reason to view Forkel's declarations as binding, at least for north-German views on music of that time. Whether we can accept them today is not the question; it suffices that they were in agreement with Sulzer, Agricola, Reichardt, and other spokesmen of this persuasion in expressing a tendency that at the time was felt to be compelling. And in fact does not every composition of Emanuel's, even the shortest, speak for this point of view? Are not the first volumes of sonatas from 1742 and 1744 already filled with the passionate impulse to 'speak' at the keyboard, to say nothing of the famous dialogue trio of 1749 between Melancholicus and Sanguinicus?[15] How effervescent are the antecedent-consequent phrases, calls, questions, disjunctions, interjections, fragments, repetitions, intensifications, pauses, sudden interruptions, build-ups, juxtapositions of quick and slow! What an entirely new way of handling pauses, in which everything actually spoken is for the first time made understandable! And what audacity, even to lay out the Andante of the first Prussian Sonata in the form of a lyric soliloquy with undisguised secco recitative! This increases as he progresses to the great sonatas, rondos, and concertos of later years, reaching its highest point in the fantasias, which still today remain astonishingly moving. Here, as in the 1787 fantasy-sonata in F-sharp minor for keyboard and violin – recently published for the first time in a modern edition[16] – any attempt to understand the music from a formal perspective fails. What guided the composer's faculty of imagination here was no incomprehensible, mystic glance into the 'absolute' but rather an emotional arousal by certain extra-musical ideas and experiences. This music, formed from unpredictable antitheses, can be understood only as the reflection of figures of speech taken from passionate monologues or dialogues, in which unusual spiritual states, serious as well as cheerful, provoked by uncommon ideas and directly comparable with Beethoven's eruptions, find their expression. Their origin cannot be mistaken: the father's free preludes and fantasias, above all the Chromatic Fantasy with its great recitatives.[17] Beside that – in the smaller pieces – is the *musique parlante* [speaking music] of the French. Clearly

---

[14]   *Trans.:* From Bach's review of Forkel's *Allegemeine Geschichte*, published in the *Hamburgerische unpartheyische Correspondent* [Hamburg unbiased correspondent], newspaper, 9 Jan. 1788; Schering cites the reprint in Bitter, op. cit.

[15]   *Trans.:* Schering refers to the six Prussian and six Württemberg sonatas for keyboard (W. 48 and 49) and to the trio sonata in C minor for two violins and continuo (or violin and obbligato keyboard) W. 161/1, known as the Program Trio. The two 'characters' represented in the latter are actually named Melancholicus and Sanguineus.

[16]   By C.F. Kahnt, Leipzig. The composition, one of the last musical professions of the great artist, bears at the beginning the inscription 'C. P. E. Bach's Sentiments' and opens 'Very somberly and entirely slow'. *Trans.:* the term 'fantasy-sonata' is Schering's; the work, W. 80, is entitled *C.P.E. Bachs Empfindungen* in the composer's autograph score, with the initial tempo mark *Sehr traurig und ganz langsam*. It comprises Bach's arrangement for violin and obbligato keyboard of a fantasia (W. 67) and a movement from a sonata (W. 65/45) originally composed separately for solo keyboard.

[17]   *Trans.:* the reference is to the second half of Sebastian's Chromatic Fantasia in D minor for harpsichord, BWV 903/1, marked *Recitativ* in contemporary manuscript copies (no autograph survives).

the stylistic level of Sebastian's Baroque style, which was always able to hold itself in check, is not attained. The temperament of the young generation hurtles carelessly onward, has other ideals, embraces other favourite thoughts, knows other ideas of love and worldly pain. Above all, humour, wit, and whimsy, Emanuel's faithful companions over the course of his life, had changed. Even Sebastian's cantatas must be considered. For here the art of musical rhetoric stands at an unattainable height. To one who even as a boy had been familiar with the fullness of the rhetorical devices and artistic strategies gathered here, the many hundreds of ingeniously conceived figures of speech relating to every domain of the soul, such things might have coursed in his blood through his entire life, **[p. 19]** except that now they were in play within entirely new spheres of feeling. The new era possessed no Brockes, no longer a Picander, rather a Wieland, a Klopstock, a Hagedorn.[18] If someday the whole sphere of thought associated with this is ever systematically examined, it will be easy to describe not only Philipp Emanuel's compositions, but also those of Haydn, Mozart, and Beethoven, more precisely from the perspective of the 'rhetorical principle'. It will be clear that this construct, correctly understood, follows a well thought-out logic, and although today decried as rationalistic applies as much to Hans Sachs's 'Wahn' monologue as to any Adagio by Bruckner.[19]

This is also probably the basis of Emanuel's frequently cited new thematic work. It certainly did not arise from grey theoretical considerations – otherwise it would not have become established – but rather from certain inner compulsions. Even if one divests it of the technical terminology customary today, expressive necessity remains recognizable as its core, with all possible tools of musical rhetoric – including above all an abundance of proliferating figures of speech – helping to lend to a particular internal or external event the greatest possible degree of perceptible vitality.[20] Above all, that which is typically called 'fragmentary work' thereby achieves deeper meaning,[21] for rhetoric is not merely monologue but can also be dialogue.

One thing must not be forgotten. Just as anything written or printed becomes speech only when it sounds comprehensibly from the human mouth, so too the 'rhetorical principle' requires – beyond its theoretical existence – completion through musical performance.

---

[18]   *Trans.:* The names are those of poets whose verses were set, respectively, by members of Sebastian's and Emanuel's generations: Barthold Heinrich Brockes and Christian Friedrich Henrici, known as Picander, on the one hand; Christoph Martin Wieland, Friedrich Gottlieb Klopstock, and Friedrich von Hagedorn on the other.

[19]   *Trans.:* Schering refers to 'Wahn! Wahn! allüberall Wahn' in Wagner's music drama *Die Meistersinger von Nürnberg* and to slow movements in the symphonies of Anton Bruckner, viewed in Schering's day as purely instrumental manifestations of Wagnerian expressive impulses.

[20]   [Johann Georg] Sulzer declares in his *Allgemeine Theorie der Schönen Künste* [General theory of the fine arts, 4 vols (Biel, 1777–78)], vol. 1/2, p. 339, that poetry is 'the art of giving ideas that fall under the expression of rhetoric the highest degree of perceptible strength according to the nature of the intention'. If one replaces the word *ideas* with the following clause: 'that which makes it possible for the tone symbols to be included in the expression of instrumental representation', then one would not have a bad parallel explanation for music without words.

[21]   *Trans.:* the German expression *durchbrochene Arbeit* has no commonly used English equivalent. Introduced in the early twentieth century by the musicologists Guido Adler and Hugo Riemann, it referred to the assignment of successive fragments of a melody to different instruments, as in the orchestral works of Haydn and Mozart.

Everything that we know concerning this from Emanuel himself (in the *Versuch*) and from others indicates that his playing achieved the highest level of musical rhetoric.[22] Whoever heard him at the clavichord was astonished by the sensitivity and control of his declamation. We know the technical means by which he accomplished this, yet we lack any idea of the personal freedom, the concept of sound, the breadth of vibrating content with which the tones were combined. Even the most reliable account could not convey such a thing today; a world of feeling separates us from that time and from the particular nature of its devotion to music. Yet even in muted form these tones still arouse and delight us because they – products of unmediated manifestations of life, just like real or imagined or actual speech – bear within them the truth of their origin and reason for being. What Beethoven thought of the 'rhetorical principle' one can glean from Schindler.[23] Schindler considered it sufficiently important that he dedicated an entire section, with examples, to Beethoven's 'art of rhetoric at the piano', pointing directly to the 'patriarch of modern keyboard playing' **[p. 20]**, that is, Philipp Emanuel. Like him, Beethoven pointed to 'the method of trained singers, who in cantilenas do neither too much nor too little, and further advised occasionally underlaying appropriate words in a problematical passage and singing them'. Something of both the material and the concept of the speech that Emanuel sang out at his keyboard will be suggested later.

Emanuel's second artistic principle, that music must above all move the heart, stands in a close relationship to the first. Aesthetics teaches that the purpose of music is to arouse sentiments. This is repeated in the writings of the time with such unanimity and insistence that we must believe it. Everything musical that did not concern the theory of composition was seen and explained as psychological, the mind being understood as something simpler than it is today. Here we are readily inclined to suppose a rationalistic mutilation of reality and to praise the subsequent advance of psychological knowledge. Yet this does not bring one closer to the period and its metaphysical difficulties. It is necessary rather to suppose complete agreement of its theory of the psyche with the facts of psychological life as actually experienced, including musical ones. Lesser contemporaries of Kant would have allowed a contradiction between the two to exist. But the problem emerges that today we have only the psychological doctrine in our grasp, whereas the necessary complement, namely the emotional life of the time as actual primal experience, has been lost. That points to a serious but not irreversible weakening of the full impression originally made by an art that was attuned to the finest of these inner processes. In other words, this music no longer speaks with its original self-evident comprehensibility, as from one kindred spirit to another. What was then, according to serious reports, experienced as a diversely constituted listening experience – melody, harmony, and rhythm, in which the most wonderful spiritual reflections were continuously perceived – strikes us today as monochromatic, not worthy of mention. It is as if the fire of the music has grown cold or at least has sunk to a much lower temperature. Only

---

[22] *Trans.:* Schering refers to Bach's *Versuch über die wahre Art das Clavier zu spielen* (Essay on the true manner of playing keyboard instruments), 2 vols (Berlin, 1753–62), English translation by William J. Mitchell (New York: Norton, 1949).

[23] *Trans.:* Schering's citation of Schindler's Beethoven biography is vague ('II/2, S. 236ff.'); the work appeared in numerous editions. The reference to C.P.E. Bach as 'Erzvater des modernen Klavierspiels' can be found in Anton Schindler, *Biographie von Ludwig van Beethoven*, 3d edn., 2 vols (Münster: Aschendorff, 1860), vol. 2, p. 227.

the major works of the greatest masters have withstood this cooling process, and even here it is often necessary to call attention expressly to their once fiery miracles.

This also applies to Emanuel. His contemporaries doubtless perceived incomparably *more and stronger* things in his works than is possible for us – even in those perfect little pieces, predecessors of Beethoven's bagatelles, that were also accessible to the hands of amateurs. No one will deny that they are full of character. Yet do they really still speak 'to the heart' as they did around 1760, when this language was new? Today do we weep real tears of emotion, as often happened then, over this or that piece? Do these not resemble valuable pearls in which the ear rejoices and the mind perceives the intellect of the creator [**p. 21**], although we ourselves are not reflected in them? That is to say that the psychological realm of modern man has expanded so widely, has so blurred the boundaries between affects and moods, that the isolation of an individual affect, such as the psychology of the Age of Sentiment took for granted, is hardly still possible.[24] Our 'abundance' of emotion, nourished by the art of the nineteenth century, is no longer able to wander easily back into the delicate, discreet, secret 'smallness' of earlier times, which was in every regard endearing; a special [mental] faculty of backward-looking retrospection must intervene. We can cultivate such a faculty. A particular direction of *musical expression research* would offer the necessary means for its development. In itself this would be nothing new. Although not historically oriented, Emanuel's circle of friends in Berlin and Hamburg, so materially conversant with all related problems, had already taken up the issue. In fact, the thinking of European music aestheticians of these decades circled about it. The question *what* is worthy of musical expression followed immediately at the heels of another: *how* is the relevant musical expression to be realized? Third and most difficult was the question of the extent to which anything expressed in music can be recognized and how obligatory this must be. With that, an agenda for endless discussion was introduced.

The great interest that Lessing brought to it indicates the lively manner in which the possibility and realization of musical 'expression research' was now discussed in Hamburg's artistic circles. What this prince of German criticism expressed on this question at the end of chapter 26 of his *Hamburg Dramaturgy* – after permitting Scheibe, with his rules for the construction of dramatic overtures, to have his say – ranks with the best that his peers have expressed.[25] This is where he explains the relationship between instrumental music and poetry and considers the mysterious affinity of music for the expression of emotion. His words are as follows:

> Indeed, the rules themselves were easy to make, but they teach only what should happen without saying how it can happen. The expression of the passions, on which everything depends, is, however, the work of genius alone. For although there are and have been composers who are successful enough at it to win admiration, clearly there still has been no philosopher who might have learned how to

---

[24] *Trans.:* Here Schering alludes to a view of early modern musical expressivity as involving precise 'affects'; these contrast with the less distinctly defined 'moods' of later sensibility. The idea, which is fundamental to twentieth-century notions of Baroque *Affektenlehre* (theory of the affects), can be traced to Descartes and Mattheson; its influence can be detected in assumptions made by later authors about the 'physiological' character of Baroque expression, as in Hans Heinrich Eggebrecht, *Bachs Kunst der Fuge: Erscheinung und Deutung* (Wilhelmshaven: Noetzel, 1998), p. 87.

[25] *Transl.:* Schering compares Johann Adolph Scheibe's *Critischer Musikus* (Leipzig, 1739–40; rev. edn, 1745) unfavourably with Lessing's *Hamburgische Dramaturgie* (Hamburg, 1767–69).

do so from them and derived general principles from their examples. But the more numerous these examples, the greater the amount of material gathered toward this end and the more we can promise to ourselves, and I would err greatly if a large step in that direction could not be taken via the zealous efforts of composers in dramatic symphonies [that is, theatrical overtures].

In *vocal music* the text supports expression all too much: whatever is weakest and shakiest is clarified and strengthened by the words. In *instrumental music,* on the other hand, this assistance is absent, and the music says nothing at all if it does not honestly say what it wants to say. Here the artist must therefore use his greatest power continually to choose only that which expresses things most clearly; we will hear this more often, we will compare vocal to instrumental music more often, and by noticing what they consistently have in common we will gradually discover the secret of expression.

These sentences were written in 1767, the same year in which Philipp Emanuel came to Hamburg.[26] As a whole they are probably nothing other than the product of countless discussions **[p. 22]** during Lessing's Berlin period, when with Ramler, Gleim, Sulzer, Gottfried Krause, Agricola, Quantz, Philipp Emanuel, and [Carl Heinrich] Graun a sort of German Parnassus emerged. They established nothing less than a demand for a *theory of comparative musical expression or symbolism.* With its help, Lessing believed, one could gradually 'discover the secret of musical expression' and document scientifically what until this point had arisen only from inspired intuition. But the task remained unfinished, lacking an adequate method of musical analysis. Although none of the many gifted authors on music of the time failed to recognize the depth of the problem, clever writings on the subject were, for the most part, its sole result, even from Christoph Gottfried Krause, whose book *Von der musikalischen Poesie* (On musical poetics, Berlin, 1752–53) serves as the classic witness to this generation's quest for knowledge. Basic psychological concepts, too, were still not established. As long as the world of affects was grasped only by dividing it up, like an enormous framework comprising countless individual emotions set beside one another, every theory of musical expression became stuck in rationalistic preconceptions. Lessing himself considered it a critical problem that a single piece of music might allow for two contradictory affects. It was the great accomplishment of Emanuel and those about him to contest this view, providing within one and the same piece depictions of a divided spiritual expression that was virtually Romantic. [The music of] Mannheim and Vienna pales by comparison to Emanuel's efforts in this respect as early as the middle of the century, to say nothing of Italy and France.

This manner of seeking a basis for musical psychology seems reasonable enough today. In fact, it was the only one available at that time. One delved into the confusing diversity of mental life, first peeling away character types and general states of mind based on sharply contrasting opposites:[27]

Generosity, majesty, imperiousness, splendor, pride, valour, astonishment, wrath, terror, fury, vengeance, rage, despair, etc. (these are to be expressed through the methods of 'high' writing style);

---

[26]   *Trans.:* Bach actually arrived in Hamburg in early 1768.

[27]   The following examples are taken from Christoph Gottfried Krause's article 'Vermischte Gekdanken' (Miscellaneous thoughts) in Marpurg's *Historisch-kritischen Beiträgen* (Historical-critical contributions), vol. 3/6 (Berlin, 1758), pp. 533ff.

Characters of piety, joyfulness, contentment, virtue, patience, modesty, love, sensuality, etc. (to be described through 'medium' writing style);

Characters of sinners, beggars, slaves, prisoners, cowards, the despondent, the inconsolable, the base, the uncouth, the stupid, the coarse, the simple, the foolish, the clumsy, the fatuous joker, the unwary, the remorseful, the imploring suppliant, the apologetic, the cowering/groveler, the debased, etc. (in 'low' writing style).

He continues with regard to certain highly emotional utterances:

The sigh of the lover, the groan of the unfortunate, the threat of the wrathful, the lament of the bereaved, the prayer of the wretched, the scolding of an abandoned beauty, the praise of the first friendly glance of the beloved, the joy at receiving the first 'yes', the grief of rejection, the anger upon suffering the beloved's disdain, the child's cajoling, etc.

The vocabulary of more specific words to substitute for the imprecise, pale expressions *Allegro, Adagio, Presto* is considered boundless, such as:

[p. 23] swift, cheerful, defiant, furious, pathetic, sweet, pleasing, harsh, contrary, gentle, quiet, steady, serious, slow, weak, soft, strong, powerful, sublime, lively, fresh, delicate, tender, amusing, demure, noble, fervid, eager, wild, athletic, fleeting, ardent, moving, mocking, heroic, warlike, gushing, anxious, peaceful, plaintive, sparkling, trifling, exuberant, soporific, forceful, feeble, skipping, songlike, proud, fondly hopeful, stiff, serious, mocking, joking, moderate, jolly, mournful, consoling, flowing, gliding, blithe, etc.

The following characters are equally available musically:

friendly encounter, dear embrace, warm agreement, games and competitions, a storm alternating with stillness and quiet, complete downfall and loss of courage (by means of long bow strokes that grow gradually weaker and weaker), confusion and frenzy, inconstancy, exuberantly jubilant joy, fragility of the beloved, sudden eager zeal, an open heart, stubbornness, noble goodness, agitation, constancy, etc.

Krause emphasizes that all these sentiments are to be expressed with 'speaking tones':

One must strive to understand precisely the essence of the affect at hand: to what movements the soul is thereby subjected; how the body, too, is affected by it; to what sort of movements it is thereby compelled; which and what types of tones stir the temperament most congenially; what weakness and strength, highness and lowness, rapidity and sluggishness of tones come closest to the movement of the yearning that we ourselves have in the affect. One brings all one's experiences into consideration, and one cannot believe that it is impossible for music to depict all types of sentiments, with their various effects, or that one should be content only to please.

Although Krause here alluded beautifully to the then generally held conviction that nothing in the spiritual world could not be rendered musically, it was useless to counsel that the way of achieving this was through control of one's own emotions – as if these things could be examined, isolated, retained, and had to show the same musical representation for all time. But this view was common. It is explained by the fact that the general awareness at the time – also socially, politically, pedagogically, philosophically – sought to derive absolutely everything from certain simple formulas. The transitions [between different emotions], which were of primary importance later, with the beginning of Romanticism, were disregarded. Music theory and musical aesthetics resembled great categories of learning in which everything was set carefully and rationally into large and small categories. Anything beyond that could be expected only from the intuitive vision of geniuses. Philipp Emanuel was one of them. Inherent in him – as with the young Beethoven – was a compulsion toward extremes of sharpness and of clarity of the tonal language. His keyboard and chamber music represents a true encyclopedia of practical examples of the musical psychology of the time. How did he and others achieve this capability?

The central question for us is: Did this era understand by 'touching the heart' only a general, indistinct running together of feelings? Evidently not. Why else the overwhelming abundance, as we have just seen, of significant and distinguishing modifiers for musical expressions? If it is impossible to arouse specific feelings and move someone's heart without thereby stirring up corresponding ideas, such ideas must have been understood as self-evident in each of these affective words. Of this there can be no question. Indeed, one could read these affects, moods, emotions, vacillations of mental equilibrium [p. 24] in the eyes, expression, gestures, or bodily movements, in a certain behaviour, in a change in the condition of others or that one observed oneself in such circumstances. Since, moreover, all that was expressive reveals itself in particular forms of speech and types of discourse, and these themselves can cover a vast range of sounds, precise acquaintance with musical rhetoric was considered essential for the 'arousal' [of emotions]. Thus says Mattheson in the *Kern melodischer Wissenschaft* (Essence of melodic science, 1737, chap. 4):

> If he [the composer] wishes to move others, he must know how to express all propensities of the heart through plain sounds, and their meaning without words, to such a degree that the listener can fully grasp and understand the impulse, the sense, the argument and the impression, with every phrase and paragraph, as if it were a real speech.

From these sources an astonishing quantity of the most varied emotions became available to those who were sensitive. As a result of a natural talent inherent in every poet for integrating things with the elements of his art, the musician was able to find certain basic formulas for these emotions, formulas of affective musical speech, as it were, with which one person could communicate wordlessly with another. Their essence is not timeless, however, but temporary, and their comprehensibility did not extend beyond a limited period. The eighteenth century achieved in this an unparalleled inexhaustibility, and Philipp Emanuel must be counted one of the greatest coiners of such formulas of affective language. Many of them are still readily understandable to us, whereas the once vibrant symbolic content of others has faded, and their colours must be restored through artificial means. This is why he [Emanuel] would benefit from extensive 'expression research' with regard to these decades.

Emanuel must have had a great deal of expertise not only in people and souls but also in the language of looks and gestures. Study of the language of gesture had been continuously recommended to composers since Mattheson's time. No affect is recognizable without a visible motion of the body or limbs, and music possesses the fortunate gift of boundless types of movement; therefore, it could express the finest traits of this type. It cannot be a coincidence that two important works on this subject were published precisely during the years when Emanuel's great sonatas for *Kenner und Liebhaber* (experts and amateurs) began to appear (from 1779): Lavater's *Physiognomische Fragmente* (Fragments on physiognomy,

1775–78) and the *Ideen zu einer Mimik* (Thoughts on acting, 1785) of Johann Jakob Engel, who had made a name for himself in 1780 with his essay 'On Musical Painting'.[28] Personal connections probably existed only to Engel, who taught at the Joachimsthal Gymnasium [high school] in Berlin. But it can be assumed that Emanuel was also familiar with Lavater's celebrated volumes, not so much because of the rambling text, but on account of the countless silhouettes that the author provided.[29] Apart from the witty and the grotesque, which confronted Emanuel here in dozens of peculiar male and female figures, the affinity of Lavater's area of investigation to the basic direction of his own work may have appealed to him. If he imagined some of the types of countenance **[p. 25]** categorized by Lavater as moving according to temperament and affect, he would surely have been reminded of some of his own elegiac or boisterous compositions.[30] Engel's fundamental and well-written book supplemented that of Lavater. It extends the subject matter beyond physiognomy to acting and gesture. A wealth of informative observations, doubly valuable because the author was not only a brilliant intellect but also had close ties to music and musicians, it should still be read today by anyone concerned with 'expression research' in the sphere of our classics. For the bridges from music to acting and gesture, as Engel described them, are many. Above all, since the 'rhetorical principle' is the basic principle here as well, the 'expression of sentiments' also appears here as the final purpose of imitative representation, and even the classification of the passions according to demeanour, movement, facial expression can be viewed as a parallel to musical aesthetics. The fact that Engel, following an all too conventional prescription, expects actors to make a desired expression immediately and unambiguously recognizable, is among the weaknesses of Enlightenment aesthetics, but this is also detectable in a similar manner in Emanuel's art. With his entirely boundless diversity of invention, certain melodic, rhythmic, and formal types of expression are present and recur again and again whenever the same [expression] is to be depicted. If, by way of example, one compares the previously mentioned fantasia in F-sharp minor from the year prior to his death with one of the greater works from the period *circa* 1750 or 1760, one is astonished to find not even the slightest progress in the essential musical idiom. The amazing, highly versatile gestures already found in the works of his youth – probably a further legacy from his father – are the same as here. This reveals a limitation in his talent but also something revolutionary within these early creations. Mozart was correct to suggest in 1789 that 'how he makes it', not 'what he makes', was the constant model for his art.[31]

---

[28] *Trans.:* 'Ueber die musicalischer Mahlerey', reprinted in *Magazin der Musik* (10 Nov. 1783), pp. 1139–78; English translation in *Contemplating Music: Source Readings in the Aesthetics of Music*, vol. 3, *Essence*, ed. Carl Dahlhaus and Ruth Katz (New York: Pendragon, 1992), pp. 128–40.

[29] *Trans.:* Schering probably alludes here to Emanuel's portrait collection, which included silhouettes; see chapter 12.

[30] Not only Lavater's book, but also other contemporary documents, pictures as well as writings, suggests the idea that both the outer appearance of Europeans of the time and their character are revealed in what would today be impossibly grotesque contrasting figures, and that one could encounter the most wonderful originals in the daily life of the great city. An alert musician could even draw splended ideas from the sketches of Chodowiecki and Hogarth!

[31] *Trans.:* Schering refers to the same (probably apocryphal) quotation in which Mozart allegedly referred to Emanuel Bach as 'the father', himself as one of 'the children', originally in Johann Friedrich Rochlitz, *Für Freunde der Tonkunst*, vol. 4 (Leipzig, 1832), p. 309n.

It is clear that musical expression research in Lessing's sense cannot be overlooked in the construction of opera, for in opera all the arts join hands. Nevertheless its influence on the pure instrumental music of Emanuel's time cannot be overestimated. Indeed, opera's wealth of vocal forms and the serious or comic nature of its types provided many definite indications, yet it corresponded only partially with the impulse of instrumental music toward free expression according to its own rules. Its chief form, the da-capo aria, remained without any impression on instrumentalists, and even recitative, although evident often enough during these years in the passionate urge to speak at the keyboard, was reserved for particular instances. The most fruitful **[p. 26]** influences always came from comic opera. Its light, casual tone, the charm and diversity of its characteristically sharply delineated situations, corresponding to its thematic punchiness and uncomplicated formal plan, could always be transferred to instruments. It can be attributed to the undisguised optimism of music lovers of the time that many feared the decline of serious music. Although Emanuel acknowledged less and less as time went by any indebtedness to the Italians, from whom such comedic humor sprang, he did not disdain it, and the pieces in which it prevails are not his worst. The capricious is as much a part of his character as the sentimental. Yet he was, as friends report, like Beethoven given to jokes and puns in social conversation. There is hardly a keyboard player of this time, with the exception of Domenico Scarlatti, in whose music the 'speaking' line of the melody reveals capricious zigzags as abundantly as with Emanuel. This often extends right to the boundary at which the *cantabile* ends and melodic declamation begins. Is it possible that here impressions of yet another side [of Emanuel's personality] have come to life?

For with an artist such as Philipp Emanuel the question arises, the longer one engages with him, from where did the hundreds upon hundreds of inspirations come to him? The simple 'theory of ideas', according to which a musician suddenly has an 'idea' which he spins out according to the rules of composition until he believes he has done enough, is useless here. One must deliberately place oneself outside the common manner of thinking that prevailed at the time. Certainly something must have occurred to every musician of the time, but only that to which he was receptive at precisely that moment. As Sulzer put it very aptly to those who composed things at random and therefore inevitably lived on nothing but borrowed strung-together clichés:[32]

> One realizes also how a man of genius comes upon ideas when he has something in front of him that he can keep to; yet when he himself cannot say what he wants to do or what the work that he intends to make is really to be, he works only in the hope of good luck. This is why most compositions of this type are nothing but a pleasant-sounding noise that falls harshly or softly on the ear.
>
> To avoid this the composer does well if he always clearly imagines the character of a person or situation, a passion, and engages his imagination until he thinks he hears one of the persons in these situations speaking. He can help himself in this insofar as he seeks out pathetic and fiery, or soft and tender, lines from poets to recite in an appropriate tone, and then designs his composition according to this feeling. In doing this he must never forget that music, in which no passion or idea is expressed in intelligible language, is nothing but a bare sound.[33]

---

[32]   *Theorie der Schönen Künste* [Theory of the fine arts], vol. 2/2 (1778), p. 376.

[33]   Here compare what Richard Wagner said in 'Über das Opern-Dichten und Komponieren im Besonderen [On writing poetry and music for operas, in particular]', *Ges. Schr.* (Collected writings), 2d edn, vol. 10, pp. 172f. It coincides strikingly with the above cited passage in the idea of questioning a

What speaks in these sentences is neither rationalism nor romanticism but rather healthy common sense: music that is to be comprehensible cannot [**p. 27**] give birth to itself but must draw on circumstances from the sphere of human existence. Without first having a tangible idea, every musician falls into useless chatter, according to Sulzer, as in many concertos, trios, solos, and sonatas. With ballets, dances, and marches the composer might have a certain self-evident guideline, likewise with overtures for plays. But if such is lacking, then he must get it from somewhere – preferably, if his own imagination is insufficient, from literature. There can be no doubt that Emanuel's music is fundamentally conditioned by these ideas, in view of all the characteristics of his music and everything that belongs to the concept of the 'rhetorical principle'. If it were otherwise, his music would have not have belonged to his time and would have contradicted what contemporaries heard and felt in it. All speech, gesture, recitative, singing, and churning of the emotions would have to be understood as masks, his own captivating performance as false preciosity. This is impossible.

From what particular spheres of experience Emanuel's music was constructed must be reserved for the findings of later investigations. A comparative glance reveals essentially four large groups: movements in closed form presenting images of character types (varieties of human characters, tendencies, passions, attitudes, frames of mind, as these were already commonly represented by the French in dance forms); movements of lyric content, as they appear as reflections of poetry of serious or cheerful content (either in song- or sonata-like forms, also as rondos, often arranged cyclically); movements of free construction in the style of spoken monologues or dialogues (free fantasias, also possible in rondo form); cyclic structures as reflections of dramatic scenes or plots (three-movement sonatas, concertos, symphonies). Not only the music itself and its changing style point to these conclusions, as has been emphasized, but also what we learn from many valuable discussions by contemporaries of the mutual interaction of the arts. Poetry and music thus go at all times hand and hand, sisters united by the dance. As one art fertilized the other, so one artist drew inspiration from the imaginative world of another, wherever it was possible. Even the genre of pantomime, little appreciated today, may well have imparted a strong impulse to the instrumental music of the time. Precisely during Emanuel's time, Noverre had raised mime to an artistic level and allowed it to become established as an element of melodrama. Mime released not only the descriptive capabilities of instrumental music to a high degree, but also its capability of expressing sentiment through speech. Precisely here, where the composer felt liberated from the schemes of operatic forms and vocal conventions, the wings of many could grow stronger, which then had a marked effect back on the actor.[34] Whether Philipp Emanuel saw Noverre's ballets with music by Deller and Rudolph – in Hamburg, Lessing began a translation of

---

person represented in the imagination until it seems to open the mouth and, as it were, dictates its speech to the musician.

[34] A fine expression of this reverse influence appears in Noverre's *Lettres sur la danse* (Letters on the dance, Paris, 1760, p. 400): 'Expressive music, harmonious and varied, . . . suggests to me a thousand ideas and characteristics; it transports me, it raises me, it enflames me, and to the various impressions that it makes me experience and that pass right to my soul I owe that which is agreeable, harmonious, striking, new, and fiery, as well as that multitude of striking and singular characters that impartial judges have believed themselves able to discover in my ballets: natural effects of music on the dance, and of the dance on music, where the two arts are reconciled and married, unified and mutually bearing charms that seduce and please.' Compare also H. Abert's discussion of Noverre in the *Peters-Jahrbuch* for 1908

Noverre's *Letters* – is unknown. He knew the genre as well as **[p. 28]** melodrama. He, the master of expression, would have had no difficulty creating solo dramatic scenes, like those for Ariadne and Medea by Georg Benda, adapted for the keyboard in the form of a fantasia or a dramatically fashioned rondo. Many of his keyboard pieces, serious as well as comic, would allow the imposition of a pantomime in rococo style. The 'rhetorical principle' and choreographic fantasy, in the view of the eighteenth century, were not opposites.

But why pantomime and melodrama, since Hamburg had one of the leading dramatic theaters in Germany? Could Emanuel, as a member of the Hamburg literary circle and a friend of Lessing, have ignored the performances made famous there by the latter's *Hamburg Dramaturgy*? Could the extraordinary sensation of Schröder's Shakespeare revivals have left no impression on him? This is not credible. These performances set all of artistic Germany on fire. Could Emanuel not have felt flaring up in the early *Sturm und Drang* ('storm and stress') – which the 1770s produced as a consequence of this same Shakespeare craze – the same fire which he had given to German art forty years earlier? At that time there was still no German Shakespeare, and we do not know who kindled the young Emanuel Bach, whether Gottsched and Gellert with their circle, or Rabener and the *Bremer Beiträge*,[35] the Swiss poets, the French or even the ancient tragedians. And now? Why do the sonatas for *Kenner und Liebhaber*, appearing right after 1774, touch upon the most remote regions of the imagination? Why did his performance on the clavichord now become so dreamy, so tumultuous, that Reichardt and Burney could speak of it only with the most awestruck expressions? The likelihood that Hamburg's theaters and the German Shakespeare emerging before the eyes of the Germans played their part in Emanuel's late creations is so great that indications to the contrary would rather have to be sought. His imagination was no more sluggish than that of André, Vogler, Stegmann, Reichardt, Haydn, who had been working on Hamlet, Macbeth, and King Lear since 1778. If he did not already know the poems from Wieland's translation, he must at least have come across them beginning in 1775, in the collected edition of his friend J[ohann] J[oachim] Eschenburg. For Emanuel the stage does not come into question, only the keyboard and perhaps also the orchestral symphony.[36] To represent Hamlet's monologue, Ophelia's songs, Lear's curses, Macbeth's visions of witches, Othello's and Desdemona's emotions **[p. 29]** at the keyboard, without words yet moving the heart: this must have seemed to the sixty-year-old composer as exhilarating an exercise as it did twenty-five years later to one [Beethoven] who at the time had just begun the first days of his life in Bonn. Perhaps Emanuel shared Beethoven's love of Ossian's poems, eagerly read then in the translations by Denis

---

[Hermann Abert, 'J.G. Noverre und sein Einfluß auf die dramatische Ballettkomposition', *Jahrbuch der Musikbibliothek Peters für 1908*, pp. 29–45].

[35]   *Trans.:* Gottlieb Wilhelm Rabener, *Neue Beyträge zum Vergnügen des Verstandes und Witzes* (New contributions for pleasing mind and wit, Bremen, 1744–1759).

[36]   With one exception, the famous symphonies for van Swieten from the year 1773, now all available, are disappointing. They are without doubt pure program music and contain sufficient audacities. But their completely old-fashioned, ineffective orchestral writing and their disintegration into disconnected, isolated ideas does not permit comparison with the keyboard works. *Trans.:* Schering appears to be comparing the six string sinfonias W. 182 of 1773, dedicated to the Dutch diplomat and musical patron Gottfried van Swieten, unfavourably to the four so-called Orchestral Sinfonias W. 183 of 1776. Five of the former set had appeared in modern editions by 1937, whereas the four Orchestral Sinfonias were edited by Rudolf Steglich only in 1942.

and Harold (1775). The best of his contemporaries clearly recognized that Emanuel was, by nature, a 'poetic spirit' deeply dedicated to poetry in his music. Triest declared as much with clear words, writing in the *Allgemeine musikalische Zeitung* in 1801 (column 299) of the keyboard sonatas and fantasias:[37]

> In him there stirred something aesthetic, that is, an *idea* compounded from concept and feeling, which could not be expressed in words even if it could come *close* to the *particular* sentiment which the song can express for us, and of which it is the model, as it were. He transferred this to the keyboard (or into notes), so that his inner familiarity with the mechanics of tones furnished him the necessary forms almost automatically.

> Since his *poetic spirit* held him apart from common ideas when he was able to compose freely, it was inevitable that those whose spirit was not like his failed to understand him and only after repeated practice barely grasped the richness of ideas concealed within. *Bach* was another *Klopstock*, using tones instead of words. Is it the fault of the poet of odes if his lyric efforts appear to the coarse masses to be nonsense?

Research on Philipp Emanuel Bach, with the exception of biography, is still in its infancy. It will expand broadly, and with it the musical view of the entire century must become the subject of new critical examination. At its center, expression research will raise the study of symbols as the axis around which revolves inquiry into the artistic achievement of this man and his personality. Perhaps then admiration of his life work will increase even more, in many respects. Even during his lifetime a contemporary (the anonymous 'Gedanken und Konjunkturen zur Geschichte der Musik' [Thoughts and conjectures on the history of music], 1780) addressed him with words that Forkel later applied similarly to Sebastian. May they on this occasion be snatched from oblivion:

> It was reserved to a man of lively, spirited imagination and real philosophical spirit, such as Carl Philipp Emanuel Bach, to make the quintessence of all European music his own and to form something more perfect from it. Germany, be proud of his name and of his host of worthy pupils!

---

[37]   *Trans.:* Schering quotes from Johann Karl Friedrich Triest, 'Bermunken über die Ausbildung der Tonkunst in Deutschland im achtzehnten Jahrhundert' (Remarks on the history of German music during the eighteenth century), which appeared in serialized form in the *Allgemeine musikalische Zeitung* (General musical times) during 1801; English translation by Susan Gillespie in *Haydn and His World*, ed. Elaine Sisman (Princeton: Princeton University Press, 1997), pp. 321–94.

[3]

LIKE FATHER, LIKE SON?
EMANUEL BACH AND THE WRITING OF BIOGRAPHY

Mary Oleskiewicz

WE LIKE TO THINK THAT BIOGRAPHIES OF EIGHTEENTH-CENTURY COMPOSERS are based on facts or indisputable evidence, such as that contained in personnel lists and other record-keeping documents. Yet objective sources such as court records and pay lists provide only part of the story and rarely tell us what we most want to know. For more intimate information about a composer's personality and routines we must turn to other sources of information, such as letters and accounts by contemporary observers: memoirs, autobiographies, and diaries. These personal accounts vary wildly in their objectivity and may be particularly unreliable if they were rewritten or reworked for publication.

A favorite biographical source of this type was the published anecdote, which offered some colorful insight into the personality of a famous individual; the greater the figure, the more plentiful (and fanciful) the anecdotes. Anecdotes were a way of humanizing figures who were otherwise larger than life, and they became particularly popular in late-eighteenth-century Berlin, where the life of the flute-playing philosopher-king and general Frederick II of Prussia—called "the Great"—offered fertile material. The anecdotal literature about him was supplemented by visual anecdotes, as it were; that is, images that illustrated various stories or events about famous personages. In the nineteenth century, these found their culmination in the work of Adolph Menzel, first in his drawings for Franz Kugler's popular biography of the king,[1] later in his famous painting "Das Flötenkonzert in Sanssouci" (1852).

MARY OLESKIEWICZ

Among the many figures depicted in Menzel's painting are some of the famous musicians who served Frederick, including the composer and keyboard player Carl Philipp Emanuel Bach (1714–1788). The latter spent the greatest part of his career, from 1740 to 1767, in Frederick's service at Berlin and Potsdam. The relationship between the two, musical and otherwise, has fascinated music historians and biographers, but the various anecdotes and assertions concerning the two have not received the careful evaluation they deserve. A critical reading of the documents relevant to Emanuel Bach's Berlin years raises questions about views and perceptions of his life and character that have prevailed since the early nineteenth century.

Recently, the case has been made for a critical re-examination of the biography of Emanuel's father, Johann Sebastian Bach.[2] The lives of the two composers were very different, but some aspects of their careers are equally mysterious. Sebastian Bach's surviving letters are little more than official documents that tell us primarily about certain mundane activities. More telling are a handful of documents that reveal some of the professional aggravations he endured. Beyond this we have only the music. Biographers of J.S. Bach have therefore relied not only on familiar anecdotes but on speculation to personalize their subject. Emanuel Bach left behind considerably more correspondence than his father, but his letters, like Sebastian's, are mostly impersonal business documents, and virtually all date from the last twenty years of his life, at Hamburg. His reputation, however, had been established at Berlin, and it was primarily with his Berlin years that his first biographers were concerned; there he worked for a court whose employment records are remarkably detailed and largely intact, but few other contemporary documents survive, apart from his compositions.[3]

All accounts of Emanuel Bach's life have relied heavily on a handful of sources from the late eighteenth and very early nineteenth centuries:

1: Charles Burney's *Present State of Music in Germany, the Netherlands, and the United Provinces* (London, 1773);

2: The German translation of the latter, undertaken with the author's consent by Christoph Daniel Ebeling and Johann Joachim Christoph Bode and published as *Tagebuch einer musikalischen Reise*, the relevant portions in volume 3 and translated by Bode (Hamburg, 1773);

3: Johann Friedrich Reichardt's *Musikalischer Almanach* for 1796;

EMANUEL BACH AND THE WRITING OF BIOGRAPHY

4: *Karl Friedrich Christian Fasch* (Berlin, 1801), a biography of Bach's court colleague by Carl Friedrich Zelter; and, related to the latter,

5: A memorial lecture given by Zelter at Königsberg on August 17, 1809.[4]

Burney's work contained the first published biography of Emanuel Bach, but this was replaced in the German translation by Emanuel's autobiographical account. Burney later claimed that Bach had supplied the material for this biography, but if so the latter was evidently altered and interwoven with Burney's own commentary, to a degree that Bach no longer recognized it as his own.[5] In a footnote to the German version, the translator dismissed Burney's version of Emanuel's biography, stating that the reader will prefer to learn *die simple Wahrheit* ("the simple truth") from Emanuel himself. Burney had organized his *Present State of Music* by city, including lengthy discussions of music in Berlin, Potsdam, and Hamburg, where he had conversed with Emanuel Bach and heard him play the clavichord at his home. In Berlin and Potsdam, Burney had met with many of Emanuel's former colleagues at the Prussian court; like colleagues everywhere, these would not have been untouched by the spirit of competition and perhaps even jealousy.[6] There is also evidence that Burney was selling Emanuel Bach's music in London, and he thus had good reason for praising it.[7]

As is now generally acknowledged, Burney visited the court at a time when the players, including the king, had grown old and lost some of their facility, and the repertory had grown stale. But independent accounts of the king's playing, including those of the singer La Mara and the violinist Hertel,[8] attest to considerable virtuosity and refinement of execution in earlier years. Further evidence for this can be seen in the difficult repertory of flute works that he is certain to have played. Emanuel Bach, moreover, would have known that Burney, unlike the visitors in Menzel's painting, would not have been able to hear every nuance of the king's performance, to which he could have listened only from outside the room. Burney withholds this point from the reader, but Reichardt confirms, with more than a hint of *Schadenfreude*, that Burney had to listen from the anteroom.[9] The same is evident from accounts of other visitors, including La Mara, who mentions singers entering only when called upon to perform an aria, after the king had finished his solos and concertos.

MARY OLESKIEWICZ

Burney's volume indeed contained errors, embellishments of fact, and idiosyncratic opinions, some of which angered German readers, including Emanuel Bach. Ebeling corresponded with Burney while the translation was in preparation; as published the German version not only took Burney to task in footnotes but eliminated whole passages. One of the largest of these excisions contained the original biographical section on Emanuel Bach, which would have strongly annoyed Emanuel not only because of its negative appraisal of J.S. Bach, but because of what Emanuel Bach evidently regarded as faulty inferences about his Berlin years.[10] Burney writes:

> During his residence at Berlin, M. Bach does not seem to have enjoyed that degree of favour to which his merit entitled him; for though music was extremely cultivated by his Prussian majesty ... he honored the style of Graun and Quantz more with his approbation, than that of any other of his servants, who possessed greater originality and refinement [p. 262]. ... Though M. Bach continued near thirty years at Berlin, it cannot be supposed that he was perfectly contented with his situation. A style of music prevailed, totally different from that which he wished to establish; his salary was inconsiderable, and he ranked below several that were greatly inferior to him [p. 268].

In response, Ebeling wrote to Burney:

> Nothing can be bad music that was good music for 40 years ... fiat applicatio ad Quantzium whom Mr. Bach thinks really to be a Genius, notwistanding [sic] he blames his exclusive taste that admits no other good taste than his own. (*So Mr Bach denies it, that he was misplaced at Berlin as You think he was.*)[11] [emphasis added]

Nevertheless, Burney's version seems to have been the dominant influence on subsequent accounts of the composer's life. A particularly tenacious idea, first put into print by Burney, concerns the supposedly adversarial nature of the relationship between Emanuel and King Frederick. The standard account goes something like this: by comparison with the lesser lights at court, Emanuel Bach was underpaid and undervalued (and, in some more elaborate versions, maltreated). Emanuel's unhappiness was in part attributable to Frederick's lack of appreciation for Emanuel's music, but his sharp tongue and his unwillingness to be subservient contributed to his fall from favor. Emanuel's supposedly recalcitrant personality is, incidentally, something he

EMANUEL BACH AND THE WRITING OF BIOGRAPHY

would have shared with his father.[12] Some authors assume that Emanuel composed his flute sonatas for Frederick; others suggest that Frederick would not
have liked Emanuel's flute sonatas or would not have been a good enough
flutist to play them. The standard conclusion is that Emanuel left Frederick's
court on unhappy terms for a position in Hamburg and, in an effort to make
amends, Princess Amalia offered him the title of *Capellmeister von Haus aus*.
The negative view of Emanuel's relationship to Frederick has become so
generally accepted that Theodor Schieder's standard biography of Frederick
repeats the essential points without reference to any source.[13] We shall take
up each of these elements in turn, beginning with Emanuel's first encounter
with Frederick.

Vagueness is already evident with Burney as to precisely when and in
what capacity Emanuel entered Frederick's service. In 1736, Frederick had
been forced to marry, and his father, King Friedrich Wilhelm I, purchased
the palace at Rheinsberg for the newlyweds. Frederick had the palace expanded and renovated, but because his relationship to his father was strained
he had few available funds. Frederick was thus forced to build his Capelle
discreetly, and filled his payroll with friends and lackeys who were literary
types and musicians. In this manner, and apparently with the covert financial
help of his mother and his sister Wilhelmina, Frederick was able to create a
little arcadia and gradually assembled a Capelle of some sixteen musicians.
Because Frederick's accounts from this period do not survive, it is unclear
how many of them were paid from the crown prince's privy purse and held
official positions at the Rheinsberg court.

The somewhat clandestine nature of Frederick's music-making at Rheinsberg probably accounts for the fact that some of the circumstances surrounding Emanuel Bach's first employment at court remain unclear. According to
Burney:

> In 1738 he went to Berlin, *not without expectation* [italics added] that the
> prince royal of Prussia, who was then secretly forming a band, would invite
> him to Ruppin; he was not disappointed, the fame of his performance soon
> reaching this prince's ears, his royal highness sent for him to his court, and
> heard him with so much satisfaction, that he afterwards frequently com
> manded his attendance; but from the circumscribed power of the prince at
> that time, he did not take him into actual service till his accession to the
> throne, in 1740, and then M. Bach had alone the honour to accompany his

MARY OLESKIEWICZ

majesty upon the harpsichord in the first flute-piece that he played at Charlottenburg, after he was king.[14]

Emanuel Bach's version of the story, in the autobiography inserted into the
German translation of Burney, omits nearly all of this passage (and most of
what follows); Bach instead wrote:

> As I ended my academic years in 1738 and went to Berlin, I received a very
> advantageous opportunity to lead a young man abroad: *an unexpected and
> gracious call* [italics added] to Ruppin, to the then Crown Prince of Prussia,
> now King, caused me to renounce my travel plans. However, due to cer-
> tain circumstances, I did not formally enter his service until 1740, with the
> accession to the throne of his reigning Prussian majesty; at which time his
> majesty also graciously had me accompany, quite alone on the fortepiano,
> in Charlottenburg, the first flute solo that he played as King.[15]

Emanuel Bach in effect denies that he went to Berlin with the expectation of obtaining a court position, implying that this was Burney's elaboration. Oddly, both accounts refer to the first encounter as taking place in
Ruppin, whereas by 1738 Frederick's residence was officially in Rheinsberg.[16]
In addition to this common detail, Emanuel retains the statement (no doubt
proudly shared with Burney during the interview) that Emanuel had had
the sole honor of accompanying Frederick in his first flute sonata as king.[17]
But Emanuel omits virtually everything else found in Burney's biography,
including Burney's remarks about J.S. Bach.

Later biographies fleshed out and elaborated upon one or the other of
these two versions, some with fictionalized dialogue. Those in Germany
tended to follow Emanuel's autobiography, but some even there seem to have
relied upon Burney.[18] The following anecdote appeared in 1800, very loosely
based on Emanuel Bach's version but chronologically distorted and embellished so as to glorify the keyboard virtuoso:

> Bach had been living a long time in Berlin without the King's [!] having
> taken notice of him. Finally Bach was called to play before his highness.
> Friedrich II asked him: "Can you improvise a melody above an unfigured
> Bass?" Bach replied: "I wish to try, your Majesty." The King laid the bass
> part to a Graun symphony before Bach, a piece that he was certain had
> never been in anyone else's possession. Bach set himself at the keyboard,
> turned the music upside down on the music desk, and played in masterly

EMANUEL BACH AND THE WRITING OF BIOGRAPHY

fashion. Frederick replied to this: "Now I see that one has not spoken too highly of him to me, and that he understands his handiwork."[19]

Eduard Fétis created an image of our young virtuoso as even bolder, relating an anecdote in which Emanuel himself solicited the visit to the crown prince: Emanuel is said to have gone to Rheinsberg to request an audience with the crown prince, which was granted only after Emanuel stated that he was a musician and that he was in no way an emissary of the king. Armed with several keyboard pieces that he had composed for the occasion, Emanuel performed them for the prince and explained his motives for coming to Rheinsberg. To this Frederick responded with surprise and pleasure and even complimented Emanuel, having never before heard such a capable harpsichordist. Frederick, however, had to confess that he did not have the financial means to take Emanuel into his service, but that if Emanuel could wait, "a day will come when the place that he requests will be given to him."[20]

Carl Hermann Bitter, who wrote the first critical biography of Emanuel and his brothers, was skeptical of this account and wrote to Fétis to determine its source. Fétis replied that he could remember nothing more about Emanuel than what he had written in his *Biographie universelle des musiciens*, and that he did not recall that Emanuel had ever been in Rheinsberg.[21] But Johann Friedrich Rochlitz previously had offered an account that more plausibly fleshed out Emanuel Bach's version. According to Rochlitz, Sebastian Bach had himself arranged, upon Emanuel's completion of his studies in Frankfurt-an-der-Oder, for the latter to accompany the son of a wealthy family from Livland (now divided between Estonia and Latvia) on a tour through France, Italy, and England; it is implied that this would have been a lucrative venture for Emanuel. Rochlitz follows Emanuel's account in saying that the call from the Crown Prince of Prussia was unexpected, but adds that it came as a relief to Emanuel because it presented an opportunity to be independent of the support of his father; Rochlitz does not account for Emanuel's report that he was already in Berlin by the time he received Frederick's call.[22]

Rochlitz's account seems to confirm a theory that Emanuel was to have traveled with the son of Count Kayserlingk, who was from Courland in the Baltics.[23] It has also been claimed that Emanuel's call to Ruppin "came about through the sons of the Prussian Minister von Happe," who were fellow students at the University in Frankfurt.[24] But it is perhaps no coincidence

MARY OLESKIEWICZ

that, at about the time that J.S. Bach was winning a court title by writing and performing cantatas with his Leipzig collegium in honor of the royal and electoral Saxon family, Emanuel Bach chose to follow his father's model by performing (and presumably composing) cantatas for visits by the Prussian royal family to Frankfurt.[25] One of these was for the crown prince's birthday in 1737, the year before Emanuel's call to Ruppin.[26] Johann Gottlieb Janitsch, Emanuel's colleague at Rheinsberg and later Berlin, had previously conducted similar collegium concerts in Frankfurt for the Prussian royalty, including one in 1731 for the crown prince; Frederick called Janitsch to Ruppin in 1736.[27]

If Emanuel's first contact with Frederick remains mysterious, the same holds for his actual appointment at Berlin. Burney and Emanuel gave the date as 1740, the year of Frederick's accession, which must also have been the year of that first flute solo at Charlottenburg. Yet Emanuel's name apparently did not appear on the court payroll until the next year. Further confusions arise in accounts of Emanuel's position as a member of the newly re-established Capelle. For instance, we read that Emanuel was "hired as *first cembalist* at a salary of three hundred thalers" and that he was:

> somewhat relieved when Christoph Nichelmann ... was appointed *second* cembalist in *1744*, although this appointment was an occasion for Emanuel's *embarrassment*: Nichelmann was given a salary *twice the size* of his. When Nichelmann left in 1756, his place as *second cembalist* was taken by *Karl Friedrich Christian Fasch, who was a bit less stubborn than Bach.*[28] [italics added to show errors]

In fact, being a brilliant keyboard virtuoso did not earn Emanuel Bach the title of "first keyboard player."[29] The *Capelletats*, annual accounts recording the salaries of Frederick's musicians and other personnel, give the names of musicians who had appointments to the royal Capelle and were paid with state funds. Although the earliest one extant dates from the fiscal year 1742–43, a similar list from 1740–41 has been published; Emanuel's name is not yet listed.[30] Possibly he was at first paid out of the new king's privy purse or *Schatoulle* (discussed below). The Capelletat for 1742–43 distinguishes an *erste* ("first") Capelle comprised of players who were in Frederick's service prior to 1740 from groups that arrived in 1741 and 1742, respectively.[31] Christoph Schaffrath, who had been Frederick's keyboard

EMANUEL BACH AND THE WRITING OF BIOGRAPHY

player since 1733, is designated a member of the first Capelle, earning 400 taler annually. Emanuel Bach, one of the arrivals of 1741, earns 300 taler. His group might be termed the "second" Capelle, but it is not so labeled, although the "first" Capelle continues to be distinguished as such until 1747, when all the musicians of both Capelles are presented as a single entity. But in none of these lists are individual players described as "first" or "second"; the hierarchy, if it is one, reflects seniority and, at least for the two keyboard players, their salaries.

Rochlitz claimed that Emanuel was not unhappy with his initial appointment and that the position was honorable.[32] Most accounts, however, treat Nichelmann's hire several years later, replacing Schaffrath but at a salary 200 taler greater than Emanuel's, as an affront to the latter.[33] This view incorrectly assumes, however, that Emanuel was now "first" harpsichordist, and that the two were hired on an equal basis. But whereas Emanuel seems to have been expected to do nothing more than accompany at court and presumably at the opera, Nichelmann was hired not only as a keyboardist but also a composer, like Quantz, Carl Heinrich Graun, and later Johann Friedrich Agricola.[34] Nichelmann was already a published composer, and unlike Emanuel, his credentials included considerable experience composing Italian vocal music and accompanying at the Hamburg opera.[35] These skills must have made Nichelmann especially valuable to Frederick. This hire may or may not have pleased Emanuel, but when Nichelmann left the Capelle in 1755, Emanuel took over Nichelmann's higher annual salary of 500 taler, and his name subsequently appeared in Nichelmann's place on the Capelletats (sixth from the top, instead of near the bottom).[36] Simultaneously, Carl Friedrich Fasch was hired at 300 taler annually to fill Emanuel's former place, and Fasch's name appears at the position in the Capelletat previously occupied by Emanuel. By the same token, when Emanuel Bach resigned from the Capelle, the Capelletat for 1767–68 shows that Fasch moved up as Emanuel's successor, but at a lower salary of only 400 taler; Johann Christian Schramm was hired to fill Fasch's former position at 300 taler. Hence it is also not quite right to say that Schramm succeeded Emanuel.[37]

These considerations of salaries and pay lists might not be necessary if biographers had not repeatedly mistaken Emanuel Bach's position and advanced his poor pay as a reason for unhappiness at court. Hans-Günter Ottenberg, for instance, writes:

MARY OLESKIEWICZ

> The King took *no steps* to improve his *chief harpsichordist's* wages, which
> must surely have been among the reasons for Bach's renewed efforts in 1753
> to find alternative employment.[38] [italics added]

Although it is true that Emanuel Bach, like his father, did seek alternative
employment at various times during his career, his precise motivation for doing so is not documented, and his claim to have received multiple offers that
he did not accept, prior to leaving Berlin for Hamburg, cannot be verified.[39]
It has always been assumed that a low salary was a reason for his seeking other
posts. But at least a contributing factor from 1747 may have been his gout, a
painful condition that made traveling unpleasant. His duties at the Prussian
court required him to travel regularly by carriage between Berlin and Potsdam, and in a letter to one of the Hamburg authorities who eventually hired
him, Emanuel writes that he had sought other work due to his *cörperlichen
Umstände* ("physical condition").[40]

Emanuel's explanation for leaving his Berlin position may be confirmed
by a lengthy anecdote published by Friedrich Nicolai, which indicates that
Bach was fearful of traveling in general, and reports that one of Bach's more
bitter complaints at court concerned the deteriorating condition of the ramp
that led up to Sanssouci from the side of the art gallery. The dispute supposedly led to hostile words between Bach and Quantz, causing the king to
replace his usual palace concerts with chamber music provided by the visiting
Dresden oboist Richter, accompanied solely by fortepiano (needless to say,
Bach was not the player). Nicolai places this incident during the 1760s,[41] but
a previously unknown court document shows a special payment of 50 talers
to an "oboist from Dresden" during April of 1756.[42] Nicolai is a highly reliable source, and claims to have learned all of his "musical anecdotes about
the king ... from Quantz and from his musical contemporaries more correctly and exactly than perhaps anyone still living, with the exception of Carl
Philipp Emanuel Bach in Hamburg."[43] Perhaps Quantz had simply forgotten the exact date. Charles Burney, in one of his contributions to Abraham
Rees's *Cyclopaedia*, alludes to what was possibly the same incident. According
to this article, Emanuel Bach was supposedly banished from court for one
month, during which time he and his colleagues were allegedly replaced by
a visiting oboist from Dresden, whom Burney names as John Christian Fischer (perhaps confusing him with Richter).[44] Though Bitter found the story

EMANUEL BACH AND THE WRITING OF BIOGRAPHY

plausible, he doubted some of its details; in particular, he found no evidence to support the notion that Fischer had ever been hired at court.

But in any case Emanuel did complain about his pay on more than one occasion, as biographers have duly noted. In one famous instance, Emanuel wrote a letter (not extant) requesting a raise, claiming that he cannot live on his salary and that Nichelmann and Agricola, who were his pupils, receive twice his 300 taler. Evidently the king saw not the actual letter but a digest from his *Kammerdiener* Fredersdorf, to whom Frederick wrote back: "Bach is lying ... he played a concert here once and now he's getting cocky."[45] Emanuel had exaggerated the difference in salaries, and his claim to having taught them cannot be verified. Nichelmann's biography names Wilhelm Friedemann Bach (not Emanuel), Quantz, and Agricola among his teachers, and neither the Capelletat nor the *Schatoull-Rechnung* (lists of Frederick's private expenses) records payments to Bach for teaching Nichelmann or other court keyboard players.[46] The background to this exchange, dated 9 May 1755, was a dispute concerning the expense money for the musicians when serving in Potsdam. Both the dispute and its resolution are recorded in correspondence between Frederick and Fredersdorf, who acted as intermediary in all such matters.[47] Emanuel and his colleagues maintained that their main place of business was Berlin, and that they had been promised a per diem expense allowance (*Diäten*) when they traveled to Potsdam for chamber music. Frederick disagreed and explained to Fredersdorf that, as he resided in Potsdam all year, Potsdam was their main place of business; hence, the musicians should only receive a per diem allowance when serving at the opera in Berlin. Frederick nevertheless paid his chamber musicians ½ taler daily for lodging (*Quartiergeld*) during their shifts in Potsdam. These amounts are recorded in receipts and also in the *Schatoull-Rechnung*, albeit without a clear explanation.[48]

Emanuel Bach's petition for the additional per diem allowance apparently was not successful. But although these demands clearly irritated Frederick, he generously accommodated his musician monetarily. After Nichelmann's departure later that year, Emanuel received a raise initially paid from the king's privy purse, and which therefore is not reflected in the Capelletats; from this time he also began to receive a regular monthly supplement to his salary from the king.[49] His annual court income now totalled 800 taler (500 from the Capelletat plus 300 in supplements). Emanuel was also paid considerable additional sums over long periods of time, recorded separately in the

MARY OLESKIEWICZ

Schatoull-Rechnung, for educating young chamber musicians at court who did not yet receive salaries out of state funds, including a harpist and a bassoon player.[50] Emanuel was thus among a handful of favored court musicians who received regular salary augmentations or extra payments for teaching. Others included Franz Benda, Quantz, and the opera singers Antonio Romani and Giovanna Astrua.

Unfortunately, Emanuel's pay raise came shortly before the outbreak of the Seven Years' War. The Capelletats indicate that the musicians went unpaid from the first quarter of 1758 through mid-1759; for the next two years, the salary of the highest-paid musicians (those normally receiving over 400 taler) was reduced by one-fourth. The others received payment in full, but as Emanuel's salary had been set at 500 taler, he was now receiving reduced pay of 375 taler annually, whereas the flutist Neiffe, the court composer Agricola, and others were again being paid at their normal rate of 400 taler. To be sure, Emanuel seems to have continued receiving his monthly supplement of 25 taler, as well as further payments for teaching the harpist Brennessell (from December 1755 through September 1763), resulting in an additional 498 taler per year.[51] The value of money in Berlin, however, drastically depreciated during the war.

The view of the relationship between Frederick and Emanuel Bach as adversarial, first suggested in print by Burney, has taken hold in no small part due to an uncritical reading of Frederick's memo to Fredersdorf. It is not surprising that biographers who have neglected to take account of Bach's true income and duties—as actually documented by court records—have continued to promote to this view. Ottenberg writes:

> C.P.E. Bach's distinction as a composer had long since won him wide acclaim, as his colleagues must certainly have recognized. Frederick, however, preferred the music of Hasse, Quantz, and the Graun brothers. His harpsichordist and resident composer wrote in a style that pleased him less. As Burney later remarked, the King was not particularly "partial" to it. Bach for his part had much to criticize in the King's flute-playing, and did so quite openly. When a guest once gushingly remarked to the august player: "What rhythm," Bach murmured audibly, "What rhythms!"[52]

This famous story has been enthusiastically repeated in the Bach literature without consideration of its provenance or veracity. Ottenberg cited it from

EMANUEL BACH AND THE WRITING OF BIOGRAPHY

Carl Geiringer's *The Bach Family* which, however, gives no citation for the quote.[53] Geiringer might have taken it from William J. Mitchell, whose version of the story, like the one above, implies that the conversation took place in the king's presence:

> As monarch, he retained and exercised the right to bring the ensemble into agreement with his wayward tempos by beating time forcefully. A story goes that a royal admirer on one such occasion exulted, "What rhythm!" To which Bach replied dryly, "What rhythms!"[54]

In fact the story can be traced to an anecdote published in Johann Friedrich Reichardt's *Musikalischer Almanach* for 1796:

> Als jemand, der das seltne Glück gehabt hatte den grossen König auf der Flöte blasen zu hören, dessen vortrefliches Spiel zu Bach, der dabey akkompagnirt hatte, enthusiastisch lobte, und unter vielen wirklich gegründeten Ausdrükken des Lobes, vielleicht durch die Art wie der König selbst pflegte mit Macht Takt zu schlagen, wenn er aber selbst aus dem Takte gekommen war, bewogen, über diesen einzig schwachen Theil des königl. Virtuosen in die Worte ausbrach "und wie viel Takt!" antwortete Bach gelassen: "Ja vierlerley Takt!"[55]

> Someone who had had the rare pleasure to hear the great king blowing the flute praised his excellent performance to Bach, who had accompanied [the king]. Possibly inspired by the way in which the king would beat time strongly, even when his playing was off the beat, [this person] among many justified words of praise hinted at this sole weakness of the royal virtuoso with the exclamation "and how much rhythm!" to which Bach calmly replied "yes, many rhythms."

Reichardt, who became Frederick's Capellmeister in 1775, eight years after Emanuel's departure from court, names no source for the anecdote.[56] In this version, the conversation is a private one between Emanuel and an admirer of Frederick; the king is not present. Evidently the story had evolved over time, growing more vivid and perhaps implying a certain lack of respect by Emanuel for his employer. The difficult German, incidentally, plays on the meaning of *Takt*, which in every-day German means "tact," and as a musical term might be better understood as meaning "measure" or "beat" rather than "rhythm." But even if true, the story, with its joke by one known for his

MARY OLESKIEWICZ

sharp wit, hardly constitutes evidence for the assertion that Emanuel found "much to criticize in the king's playing."

Nevertheless, another expression of the same view occurs in Zelter's biography of Fasch, in which Zelter's agenda is clearly to promote the more "yielding," flexible musician Fasch, who joined Emanuel as chamber accompanist in 1756:

> Der König bemerkte bald, dass er seinen Mann gefunden hatte. Bach war ein grosser Klavierspieler und hatte den König an sein feines Accompagnement gewöhnt; aber das immerwährende Wiederholen der nemlichen Stücke hatte ihm längst Überdruss gemacht, denn der König blies ohne Ausnahme keine andere Konzerte und Solo, als die Quanz für ihn gemacht hatte, und öfter Flöten-Solo von seiner eigenen Arbeit. Die Aufmerksamkeit, mit der Fasch einmal wie das andere seinen Dienst versah, konnte dem Könige nicht entgehen, und er schätzte und liebte ihn deswegen. ... Bach, der die Anforderungen des Koenigs und sein dreistes Urtheil nicht liebte, war hierin weniger nachgiebig, welches der König empfinden musste, und deswegen nicht so viel auf ihn hielt, als es seine grosse Kunst verdiente.[57]

> The king soon recognized that he had found his man [that is, Fasch]. Bach was a great keyboard player and the king had grown accustomed to his fine accompaniment; but the endless repetition of the same pieces had long made him weary, for the king played without exception only those concertos and solos [sonatas] that Quantz had composed for him, and often flute solos the king had composed himself. The attentiveness with which Fasch always rendered his service could not escape the King, and he valued and loved him for it. ... Bach, who did not like the demands of the king and his brazen judgment, was less accommodating. The king must have sensed it, and thus valued him less than his great art deserved.

Zelter would repeat the same idea in his 1809 memorial, which would be echoed by Georg Thouret at the end of the century: "Carl Philip Emanuel Bach was personally much more distant from the King. ... Bach believed that his talent was not appropriately valued, and in 1767 he took his leave for Hamburg, where he enjoyed greater freedom as an artist."[58] Thouret also lifted the following passage from Zelter, in which Emanuel Bach is supposed to have said:

> Der König sei zwar ein gebietender Herr in seinem Lande, doch nicht im Reiche der Kunst, wo Götter walten, von denen alles Talent ausgehe und

EMANUEL BACH AND THE WRITING OF BIOGRAPHY

wieder dahin zurückgehe. Ein Künstler sei ein von höherer Hand ausgest-
atteter Sohn des Himmels, der der Welt angehöre, wie die Welt ihm, und
daher keiner irdischen Beherrschung unterworfen sei.[59]

The King is a ruling lord in his country, but not in the realm of art. There
gods rule, and all talent flows and returns to them. An artist is a son of
heaven, divinely inspired; he belongs to the world as the world belongs to
him, and is thus not subject to worldly rule.

In addition to its romantic view of the artist, the passage draws an implicit
comparison of Emanuel to Orpheus or perhaps Apollo. If Emanuel said anything resembling these words, the statement might originally have been understood or intended as a critique of the king's taste, or even as a statement
to the effect that Frederick's status as king did not mean that he was always
right in artist matters. But Zelter might have given a distinctly romantic spin
to something that had been reported to him; as transmitted by Zelter, the
statement could be interpreted as expressing the view that artistic genius is
more valuable than inherited privilege, or as showing disdain for the king's
reputedly staid and rationalistic musical preferences. What is unclear, given
the uncertain provenance of the statement, is whether it was Emanuel, Zelter,
or an intermediary who was expressing these sentiments. From this romantic
view of Emanuel Bach as an unappreciated, alienated artist at the Berlin court
it is a short step to assuming that a "lacuna (*recte* hiatus) in the number of flute
sonatas [composed by Emanuel] between 1740 and 1746 is easily explain-
able by the less than ideal musical relationship that subsequently developed
between the composer and the king."[60] In fact there could be any number of
reasons why Emanuel might have ceased composing such works for a while.
Frederick was preoccupied with fighting the first Silesian War and establishing his reign (and his new opera house), and Emanuel's new duties as court
and opera accompanist would have kept him busy. But the most plausible explanation for Emanuel's suspension of writing flute sonatas would have been
not some undefined breakdown in his musical relationship with the king, but
the arrival of Quantz in 1741; his chief duty, unlike Emanuel's, was to supply
new flute music to the king.

Nevertheless, by 1740 Emanuel had composed at least seven solos (sonatas)
for flute and continuo, five of them since moving to Berlin in 1738. At least
two more and possibly a third would follow before he left the king's service,

MARY OLESKIEWICZ

not to mention trio sonatas, concertos, and other works for flute.[61] Although no evidence survives to indicate that the solo sonatas were ever in the king's repertory—there are no copies, for instance, alongside the hundreds of works by Quantz and Frederick himself in the remains of the king's manuscript collection[62]—it is odd that these works appear to have had little if any circulation, in manuscript or print, during Emanuel's lifetime. Until recently only a single manuscript copy was known to have survived for each (with one exception), in a collection assembled at least in part after Emanuel's death.[63] Because flute sonatas were a popular genre, it would be surprising that no copies exist elsewhere unless these pieces had in fact been composed for the king, preventing sale to or performance by others. It is also notable that in 1747, Emanuel Bach not only composed two flute solos; he also wrote two trio sonatas at Potsdam for flute and violin as well as revising six earlier trio sonatas for the same instruments. This was of course the year in which Sebastian Bach made the famous visit to Potsdam that led to the composition of the Musical Offering, whose major component is a trio sonata for the same combination.

Certainly Emanuel's earlier flute solos might have been heard at the crown prince's courts at Ruppin and Rheinsberg, where Frederick devoted his free time to conversation, reading, composing, acting out dramas, and holding concerts;[64] as he wrote from Rheinsberg in 1737, "we have music of every kind."[65] Little documentation survives for the repertory from that period, in part because in 1740 the entire town of Rheinsberg burned down, with the exception of the palace; the musicians lost instruments and music manuscripts.[66] Although in his late years the king evidently performed only his own flute works and those of Quantz, the king did not hold to this limited retinue during earlier periods. In any case, Emanuel and his colleagues had vehicles other than the king's private repertory through which to gain appreciation at court. The royal Capelle regularly performed in numerous court concerts given by the Queen Mother Sophia Dorothea, Frederick's Queen Elisabeth Christine, Princess Amalia, Prince Heinrich, and occasionally by Frederick himself, sometimes collaborating with Princess Amalia and other members of the court in performances.[67] The names of individual performers and compositions are rarely recorded, yet Emanuel is mentioned for a special solo appearance in 1753;[68] thus there is no reason to assume that Emanuel or his music was singled out for exclusion, or that he "never won recognition at court as a composer and virtuoso."[69]

EMANUEL BACH AND THE WRITING OF BIOGRAPHY

Whatever affection or respect Frederick had for his keyboard player might have vanished as soon as Emanuel requested his dismissal in 1767. Memoirists made it clear that Frederick valued loyalty above practically all else. The Freiherr von Bielfeld, just before leaving Berlin, is supposed to have said: "A small fault is sufficient to obliterate the memory of twenty years' faithful service."[70] Had Frederick owned anything of Emanuel's in his music collection, he is likely thereafter to have had no use for it. Nevertheless, upon Emanuel's departure for Hamburg, where he would oversee the music at the city's principal churches, he was granted the title of *Capellmeister von Haus aus* to Frederick's sister Amalia. This is unlikely to have happened without the king's permission, at least tacitly, and biographers have interpreted this as a gesture of reconciliation.[71] But Emanuel was already serving the princess before this time.[72] And with his honorary appointment as a princely Capellmeister, Emanuel was following in the footsteps of his father, just as he did in taking his final position as a director of municipal church music and cantor.[73]

It is clear from Frederick's letters that Emanuel Bach was not the only musician at court to have had complaints at one time or another, and he was by no means unique among them in having annoyed the king. Frederick's autocratic manner of handling musicians differed little from his treatment of those in other positions, and he required complete loyalty from all of them. Court documents show that Emanuel's rank and pay were commensurate with his position at each stage of his career at Berlin, and by the mid-1750s he stood among the most favored and well-paid instrumentalists at court. He also earned far more than Fasch (whom Zelter claimed was more valued by the king). Our understanding of Emanuel's position at court may be misled by romantic and modern-day estimations of his music relative to that of his colleagues such as Quantz, and those views are largely based on the opinion of one man—Burney—with whom Emanuel did not agree. The result is a situation that offers yet another parallel with Emanuel's father: we view J.S. Bach as a genius greater than his immediate colleagues and contemporaries, yet he was only third choice for the position at Leipzig, and Sebastian never ranked as highly as Hasse and other colleagues at the Dresden court.

Clearly, mysteries still abound here, as they do in the life of J.S. Bach. Whether Emanuel Bach's music is of sufficient quality for these mysteries to be worth pursuing is a question on which there might be some disagreement.

MARY OLESKIEWICZ

But the question would not have occurred to those who have repeated these anecdotes, some of them since the eighteenth century. It is therefore high time for the deconstruction of those accounts—such as Peter Williams has undertaken for stories about J.S. Bach—to begin.

❧ NOTES ❧

1. Franz Kugler, *Geschichte Friedrichs des Grossen* (Leipzig, 1840).

2. Peter Williams, *The Life of Bach* (Cambridge: Cambridge University Press, 2004), 1–2.

3. To date, the most objective biography of the composer is that of Ulrich Leisinger, "Bach. III. 9. Carl Philipp Emanuel Bach," *Grove Music Online*, ed. Laura Macy, http://www.grovemusic.com (accessed 8 April 2006), which, however, offers only an overview without critically assessing the sources.

4. "Eine Rede, gehalten zu Königsberg in Pr. im Pallaste des Kronprinzen, von Zelter," in Johann David Erdmann Preuß, *Friedrich der Große*, 4 vols. (Berlin, 1832–34), 3:480–83. Zelter was also the effective author of the entry on C.P.E. Bach in Ernst Ludwig Gerber's *Neues historisch-biographisches Lexicon der Tonkünstler* (Leipzig, 1812–14); see Hans-Günter Ottenberg, "C.P.E. Bach and Carl Friedrich Zelter," in *C.P.E. Bach Studies*, ed. Stephen L. Clark (Oxford: Clarendon Press, 1988), 186.

5. Burney made the claim in his *General History of Music* vol. 4 (London, 1789); ed. by Frank Mercer as *Charles Burney, A General History of Music, From the Earliest Ages to the Present Period* (London: G.T. Foulis, 1935), 2:955, repeating it in his article on the composer in Abraham Rees, ed., *The Cyclopedia; or, Universal Dictionary of Arts, Sciences, and Literature* (London: Longman, Hurst, Rees, Orme & Browne, 1820). I am grateful to Paul Corneilson for kindly supplying these references.

6. Frederick complained bitterly of the open rivalry between his musicians, beginning in Rheinsberg; in 1737, he cites Franz Benda as the most unbearable; see the letter from Frederick to his sister Wilhelmina of 10 December 1737, in *Friedrich der Große und Wilhelmine von Baireuth: Jugendbriefe 1728–1740*, ed. Gustav Berthold Volz (Leipzig: K.F. Koehler, 1924), 366.

7. Stephen L. Clark, *The Letters of C.P.E. Bach* (Oxford: Clarendon Press, 1987), 102, 240. Emanuel Bach's letters indicate that Burney ordered multiple copies of Emanuel's published works for subscribers and his biography of

EMANUEL BACH AND THE WRITING OF BIOGRAPHY

Emanuel included a list of works, "for the satisfaction of those who may wish to procure them."

[8.] "Eine Selbstbiographie der Sängerin Gertrud Elisabeth Mara," *Allgemeine Musikalische Zeitung* 10 (1875), nos. 34 and 35, and *Johann Wilhelm Hertel: Autobiographie*, ed. Erich Schenk (Graz: Hermann Böhlaus Nachf., 1957), 34.

[9.] Johann Friedrich Reichardt, *Briefe eines aufmerksamen Reisenden die Musik betreffend*, 2 vols. (Frankfurt, 1774–76. Facs., Hildesheim: Olms, 1977), "Zehnter Brief. An den Herrn C.B. (Potsdam)," 179: "Und wie wenig er [Burney] davon recht ordentlich bemerkt haben kann, das kann sich wohl aus seiner Unruhe erklären. Denn wie ich mir nicht anders vorstellen kann, so muß der Mann, der schon in Entzücken gerath, wenn ihm die Gräfin Thun ein Compliment macht, oder der Graf Sacken zu Tische behält der muß jetzt, *da er sich im Vorzimmer des Königs von Preussen weiß*, und ihn blasen hört, ganz ausser sich gewesen sein. Ach über den Engländer!" (italics added). Elsewhere, Reichardt writes that even he (as court Capellmeister from 1775) had to obtain special permission to attend the king's private concerts, "which were held without any audience"; see Reichardt, *Musikalisches Kunstmagazin*, 5tes Stück, "Musikalische Anekdoten von Friedrich dem Grossen" (Berlin: Im Verlage des Verfassers, 1791), 40.

[10.] David Schulenberg, "C.P.E. Bach and Handel: A Son of Bach Confronts Music History and Criticism," *Bach: The Journal of the Riemenschneider Bach Institute* 23 (1992): 10, points out that Emanuel Bach, already irritated at Burney for the contents of the biography, was further aggravated by Burney's outspoken idolization of Handel, and observed that this "seems to have angered Emanuel Bach the most." Cf. Charles Burney, *An Account of the Musical Performances in Westminster-Abbey, and the Pantheon, May 26th, 27th, 29th, and June the 3d and 5th, 1784: in commemoration of Handel* (London: 1785); trans. [with numerous corrections] by Johann Joachim Eschenburg as *Dr. Karl Burney's Nachricht von Georg Friedrich Händel's Lebensumständen und der ihm zu London im Mai un Jun. 1784 angestellten Gedächtnissfeyer* (Berlin, 1785).

[11.] Letter from Ebeling to Charles Burney, dated Hamburg, 20 June 1773, in Gorden M. Stewart, "Christoph Daniel Ebeling, Hamburger Pädagoge und Literaturkritiker, und Seine Briefe an Charles Burney," *Zeitschrift des Vereins für Hamburgische Geschichte*, 61 (1975): 52. Ebeling, who was a pioneering Americanist, wrote in English; the content of the letter suggests that it was written on Emanuel Bach's behalf.

MARY OLESKIEWICZ

12. As in the Weimar court secretary's report that the reigning Duke of Weimar had J.S. Bach imprisoned "for overpressing his dismissal"; see Williams, *The Life of Bach*, 76–77.

13. "Er [Emanuel Bach] wurde aber in Berlin nicht warm und litt sehr unter der Geschmacksdiktatur, die der König verhängte. Die grosse Begabung Emanuel Bachs wurde von Friedrich in keiner Weise erkannt und gewürdigt, obwohl er ihn ungern nach Hamburg entliess"; see Theodor Schieder, *Friedrich der Grosse: Ein Königtum der Widersprüche* (Munich: Propyläen, 2002), 432.

14. Charles Burney, *An Eighteenth-Century Musical Tour in Central Europe and the Netherlands*, edited by Percy A. Scholes as *Doctor Burney's Musical Tours in Europe*, vol. 2 (London: Oxford University Press, 1959), 216. This is an annotated modern edition, with revised title, of the second corrected edition (London, 1775).

15. My translation. Charles Burney, *Tagebuch einer musikalischen Reise: Vollständige Ausgabe*, 3 vols. in 1, ed. Christoph Hust (Kassel: Bärenreiter, 2004), 3:198.

16. In August 1736, Frederick moved to Rheinsberg but he continued to spend time in Ruppin when conducting military exercises with his regiment. This is confirmed, for example, in a letter from Frederick to Wilhelmina, dated Ruppin, 15 April 1738; see Volz, *Friedrich der Große und Wilhelmine von Baireuth: Jugendbriefe 1728–1740*, 377; and Schieder, *Friedrich der Grosse*, 50.

17. The term "solo" was regularly used in Berlin to designate solo sonatas with basso continuo, as opposed to concertos with string accompaniment. Interestingly, Emanuel's statement suggests the absence of cello or viola da gamba to reinforce the accompaniment.

18. Carl Freiherr von Ledebur, *Tonkünstler-Lexicon Berlins* (Berlin: Ludwig Rauh, 1861), 18–19, avoids the issue by stating that in 1738 Bach went to Berlin as a freelancer ("wo er Anfangs privatisierte"), receiving a court appointment in 1740 as *Kammermusikus und Clavicembalist*. Georg Thouret, *Friedrich der Grosse also Musikfreund und Musiker* (Leipzig: Breitkopf und Härtel, 1898), 124, writes: "bis an seinen Tod blieb es seine stolze Erinnerung, das erste Flötensolo, das Friedrich II. als König blies, am Klaviere begleitet zu haben." His source must be Burney's original version, for he repeats many of the negative assertions that Emanuel removed in his version.

19. My translation. *Allgemeine Musikalische Zeitung* 3 (1800), cols. 71–72: "'Kann Er auch über unbeziffertem Bass aus dem Stegreif eine Melodie her-

EMANUEL BACH AND THE WRITING OF BIOGRAPHY

unterspielen?' Bach habe geantwortet: 'Ich will es versuchen, Majestät.' Nun habe ihm der König die Baßstimme einer Graun'schen Sinfonie vorgelegt, von der er gewiss gewusst habe, dass sie nie in andern Händen als den seinigen gewesen. Bach habe sich an das Clavier gesetzt, die Stimme verkehrt auf das Pult gestellt und meisterhaft gespielt und Friedrich darauf geantwortet: 'Nun sehe ich, dass man mir nicht zu viel von Ihm gesagt hat und dass Er sein Handwerk versteht.'" Cited by Carl Heinrich Bitter, *Carl Philipp Emanuel Bach und Wilhelm Friedemann Bach und deren Brüder*, 2 vols. (Berlin: Wilhelm Müller, 1868), 1:15.

[20.] My translation. Eduard Fétis, "Les princes musiciens: Fréderic le Grand, 3ᶜ article" (1), *Revue et Gazette Musicale de Paris* 32 (6 August 1854): 255. The article "Carl Philipp Emanuel Bach" in *Grove's Dictionary of Music and Musicians*, 5th ed. (London: Macmillan, 1954), 1:324, follows Fétis and Burney.

[21.] Bitter, *Carl Philipp Emanuel Bach* 1:18n1.

[22.] Johann Friedrich Rochlitz, *Für Freunde der Tonkunst*, 3rd ed. (Leipzig: Carl Cnobloch, 1868), 4:185. Rochlitz spells the name of the Baltic region "Liefland." The first edition of 1832 contains the identical biography (4:273–316). Rochlitz's complete biography of Emanuel Bach in the third edition is found on pp. 182–206. On pp. 181–82 the author says he has relied on the autobiography in Bode's translation of Burney, enriched by "mündliche Mittheilungen von vollkommen unterrichteten und in jeder Hinsicht stimmfähigen Männern, welche auf längere oder kürzere Zeit mit Bach freundschaftlich verbunden gelebt haben: von Doles, seinem Vertrauten auf der Schule und Universität, über seine Jugend; von Reichardt, über seinen Aufenthalt in Berlin und seine früheren Jahre in Hamburg; von Oeser und Hiller, über dieselben und seine spätere Lebenszeit."

[23.] First put forth by Heinrich Miesner, "Graf v. Keyserlingk und Minister v. Happe: Zwei Gönner der Familie Bach," *Bach-Jahrbuch* 31 (1934): 110, without reference to Rochlitz's account.

[24.] Hans-Günter Ottenberg, *Carl Philipp Emanuel Bach*, trans. Philip J. Whitmore (Oxford: Oxford University Press, 1987), 34; Ottenberg cites Miesner, "Graf v. Keyserlingk und Minister v. Happe," but the latter provides only circumstantial evidence.

[25.] Bitter gives the texts for several works performed by Emanuel Bach and the collegium on behalf of the university in Frankfurt, to honor visits by King Frederick William of Prussia and Crown Prince Frederick.

MARY OLESKIEWICZ

26. Ottenberg, *Carl Philipp Emanuel Bach*, 27. Ottenberg cites Emanuel Bach's statement that he composed "for all the public concerts on ceremonial occasions" as evidence that he probably composed these works (the music is apparently lost).

27. Pippa Drummond and Tina Dreisbach, "Janitsch, Johann Gottlieb," in *Grove Music Online*, ed. Laura Macy, http://www.grovemusic.com (accessed 12 June 2006).

28. E. Eugene Helm, *Music at the Court of Frederick the Great* (Norman: University of Oklahoma Press, 1960), 174–75. The confusions with respect to Nichelmann go back at least to Bitter, who writes that Carl Friedrich Fasch was appointed in Nichelmann's place in 1756 at Franz Benda's suggestion; see Bitter, *Carl Philipp Emanuel Bach*, 1:27. This mistake has been repeated most recently by Christoph Henzel, who calls Fasch Nichelmann's "Nachfolger" in his "Neues zum Hofcembalisten Carl Philipp Emanuel Bach," *Bach-Jahrbuch* 85 (1999): 175. Ledebur was among the few to avoid the mistake by simply calling Emanuel Bach "Kammermusikus und Clavicembalist," although he names the year of his appointment as 1740, presumably following the autobiography; see Ledebur, *Tonkünstler-Lexicon Berlins*, 18–19.

29. Rochlitz may have been the first to describe him thus: "When Friedrich became king, he took Bach into his service with a considerable salary as chamber musician and first harpsichordist"; see Rochlitz, *Für Freunde der Tonkunst*, 187. Bitter indicates something similar in stating that at the beginning of the king's reign a second cembalist played only in the case of Emanuel Bach's absence or sickness, but that in later years the two alternated every four weeks; see Bitter, *Carl Philipp Emanuel Bach*, 1:27.

30. Heinrich Miesner, "Beziehungen zwischen den Familien Stahl und Bach," *Bach-Jahrbuch* 30 (1933): 75–76.

31. These documents are at the Geheimes Staatsarchiv (GSTA) in Berlin-Dahlem; the shelf mark of the Capelletat for 1742–43 is I. HA Rep. 36 Nr. 2435. Bach's name falls among the thirteen of the second group, headed "Ausgabe die neuen Capell Bediente, so Anno 1741 zugekommen"; Quantz, who left Dresden in December 1741, is listed at the head of group 3, "Ausgabe die neuen Capell Bediente, so Anno 1742 zugekommen."

32. Rochlitz, *Für Freunde der Tonkunst*, 186.

33. Schaffrath's name appears for the last time in the Capelletat of 1743–44; he was subsequently given the position of cembalist and chamber musician

EMANUEL BACH AND THE WRITING OF BIOGRAPHY

to Princess Amalia, serving in this capacity until his death in 1763; see Hart-mut Grosch, "Christoph Schaffrath," in *Die Rheinsberger Hofcapelle von Fried-rich II*, ed. Ulrike Liedtke (Rheinsberg: Musikakademie Rheinsberg, 1995), 203–40.

[34.] Nichelmann, who had studied with Graun, Quantz, and W.F. Bach, among others, first appears on the Capelletat for 1745–46 with an annual salary of 500 taler; his biography in Marpurg, "Lebensläuffe verschiedener Lebenden Tonkünstler," 438, indicates that the king "intended to use him in composition."

[35.] Douglas A. Lee, "Nichelmann, Christoph," *Grove Music Online*, ed. Laura Macy, http://www.grovemusic.com (accessed 30 May 2006).

[36.] By royal order of 20 December 1755, Nichelmann's remaining salary for the fiscal year was divided between Emanuel Bach and Carl Fasch, the former receiving 56 taler for January and February 1756 and 83 taler, 8 groschen for the Trinity quarter (the last three months of the fiscal year); Fasch received 100 taler for February and Trinity together. Emanuel would keep his salary of 500 taler per year through Lucia (the second quarter of the fiscal year) of 1767, when he left the court; Fasch then received some extra payments for the last two quarters of 1767–68 when he advanced to the position formerly held by Emanuel Bach. Schramm, hired by decree of 18 January 1768, assumed Fasch's old position at 300 taler per year.

[37.] GSTA PK, I HA rep. 36, Hof- und Güterverwaltung, Rep. 2472.

[38.] Ottenberg, *Carl Philipp Emanuel Bach*, 56–57.

[39.] "Von dieser Zeit an, bis 1767 im November, bin ich beständig in preuss-ischen Diensten gewesen, ohngeachtet ich ein paarmal Gelegenheit hatte, vortheilhaften Rufen anderswohin zu folgen." (Autobiography, in the Ger-man translation of Burney).

[40.] Letter of 13 November 1767 to Syndicus Faber of Hamburg, no. 51 in *Carl Philipp Emanuel Bach: Briefe und Dokumente: Kritische Gesamtausgabe*, ed. Ernst Suchalla, 2 vols. (Göttingen: Vandenhoeck & Ruprecht, 1994), 1:118.

[41.] Friedrich Nicolai, *Anekdoten von König Friedrich II. von Preussen, und von einigen Personen, die um Ihn waren*, 6 vols. (Berlin und Stettin, 1791), 5:158–60.

[42.] The document is a so-called *Schatoull-Rechnung* listing miscellaneous payments out of the king's privy purse. GSTA PK, BPH, Rep. 47, Nr. 909,

MARY OLESKIEWICZ

fol. 5r (24 March to 24 April 1756); entry no. 29 reads: "*dem Hautboisten aus Dresden reise Geld L*[aut] *Ordre, 50* [Reichstaler]."

⁴³· Nicolai, *Anekdoten von König Friedrich II*, 1:xx–xxi. Nicolai took his reporting seriously: his own volume critically evaluates the merits and errors of previous books of anecdotes on Frederick II.

⁴⁴· Bitter, *Carl Philipp Emanuel Bach*, 1:180. The anecdote, found under the entry "Fischer, John Christian" in Abraham Rees, ed., *The Cyclopaedia; or, Universal Dictionary of Arts, Sciences and Literature* (London: Longman, Hurst, Rees, Orme & Brown, 1820) quotes Emanuel Bach as having exclaimed the following to one of the members of the court: "'tell our master, sir, that no honour or profit will be a sufficient compensation to us for such dangerous service; and unless the roads are rendered safer, we' (speaking in the name of the whole band), 'can come hither no more.'" It should be noted that the articles in the *Cyclopaedia* are generally known to be unreliable.

⁴⁵· "Bac ligt agricola hat nuhr 500 rt er hat ein mahl im consert hier gespilet nuhn krigt er Spiritus." Apparently extracts from longer documents, these were published in *Die Briefe Friedrichs des Grossen an seinen vormaligen Kammerdiener Fredersdorf*, ed. Johannes Richter (Berlin: Klemm, 1926. Reprint, Braunschweig: Archiv Verlag, 1997); the present extracts are quoted in Heinrich Miesner, "Aus der Umwelt Carl Philipp Emanuel Bachs," *Bach-Jahrbuch* 34 (1937): 139. The concert may or may not be the one that Miesner identifies as having been given for the Queen Mother, involving Emanuel Bach's performance on a *Bogenclavier*; Christoph Henzel, "Das Konzertleben der preußischen Hauptstadt," *Jahrbuch des Staatlichen Instituts Musikforschung für Preussischer Kulturbesitz* (2004): 216–91 lists the concert as actually for Queen Elisabeth Christine (p. 249).

⁴⁶· Marpurg, "Lebensläuffe verschiedener lebenden Tonkünstler," 432–33.

⁴⁷· A detailed account of the exchange is provided by Miesner, "Aus der Umwelt C.P.E. Bachs," 137–38.

⁴⁸· Henzel, "Neues zum Hofcembalisten Carl Philipp Emanuel Bach," 172–73, does not note the distinction between these terms, and assumes that all payments recorded as either *Quartiergeld* or *Diäten* indicate that a musician was in Potsdam, as opposed to Berlin. He thus concludes that payments were based on the location of the musician's residence, and that multiple keyboard players were present at Potsdam simultaneously, when the players more likely were alternating in their service to the king. Despite this distinction in prin-

EMANUEL BACH AND THE WRITING OF BIOGRAPHY

ciple, it appears that the account books create confusion by not consistently maintaining the distinction in terminology.

49. GSTA PK, BPH Rep. 47, Nr. 908, fol. 15, no. 15 (24 November to 24 December 1755): "*dem Musico Bach Zulagen a 500 Rthlr. pro December 41,16.*" This indicates that Frederick commenced paying Emanuel's salary increase in December 1755 from his privy purse; beginning in January 1756, Emanuel was paid a monthly supplement of 25 taler from the king's privy purse, amounting to an additional 300 taler per year (the account for the following pay period, 24 December 1755 to 24 January 1756, reads "dem Musico Bach Zulage pro Jan 25 Taler").

50. Franz Brennessell and Marx; see Henzel, "Neues zum Hofcembalisten Carl Philipp Emanuel Bach," 174.

51. Bach was paid 16½ taler each month over 94 months for teaching Brennessell, an amount equivalent to that which the harpist himself received each month as salary; see, for example, GSTA, BPH Rep. 47, Nr. 909, fol. 1r.: "No. 14. demselben [Bach] vor information des jungen Brennessels pro Jan. [1756] 16.16 [Reichstaler]; No. 15. Tractament vor der Harfenisten Brennessel pro Jan. [1756] 16.16 [Reichstaler]."

52. Ottenberg, *Carl Philipp Emanuel Bach*, 62.

53. Karl Geiringer, *The Bach Family: Seven Generations of Creative Genius* (London: Allen & Unwin, 1954), 339.

54. William J. Mitchell, introduction to his translation of Emanuel Bach's *Essay on the True Art of Playing Keyboard Instruments* (New York: W.W. Norton, 1949), 6. Mitchell relates this as an unattributed "story"; Helm cites it from Mitchell in *Music at the Court of Frederick the Great*, 174.

55. Anecdote no. 16 from Reichardt, "X. Anekdoten aus dem Leben merkwürdiger Tonkünstler," *Musikalischer Almanach* (Berlin, 1796), unpaginated. The brief anecdotes concern—in addition to Emanuel Bach—Abel, J.S. Bach, J.C. Bach, W.F. Bach, and others.

56. In this he differs from Nicolai, who stated that he had investigated the anecdotal literature and aimed to print nothing inaccurate. However, Reichardt visited Hamburg around 1774 and heard some of the Wq. 182 symphonies; see *Allgemeine Musikalische Zeitung* 16 (1814), col. 28–29. Perhaps it was this occasion where he met C.P.E. Bach and heard the story, if he did not make it up. I thank Paul Corneilson for this friendly communication.

57. Zelter, *Karl Friedrich Christian Fasch*, 14.

MARY OLESKIEWICZ

⁵⁸· My translation. Thouret, *Friedrich der Grosse als Musikfreund und Musiker*, 124–25: "Carl Philipp Emanuel Bach stand innerlich viel fremder zum Kö-nige. … Bach aber glaubte, sein Talent würde nicht in gebührendem Maße geschätzt, nahm im Jahre 1767 seinen Abschied und ging nach Hamburg, wo er größere Freiheit als Künstler genoß." The latter sentence is nearly identical to one in Zelter's 1809 memorial (in Preuß, 482).

⁵⁹· My translation. Cited in Preuß, *Friedrich der Große*, 3:482; repeated vir-tually verbatim in Georg Thouret, *Friedrich der Grosse also Musikfreund und Mu-siker* (Leipzig: Breitkopf and Härtel, 1898), 124–5. Thouret follows Zelter in the use of the subjunctive II tense, used to report second-hand what someone is supposed to have said, as opposed to direct quotation. Carl Frieherr von Le-debur, *Tonkünstler-Lexicon Berlin's von den ältesten Zeiten bis auf die Gegenwart*, (Berlin: L. Rauh, 1861), citing Zelter, also repeats this passage on pp. 18–19.

⁶⁰· Leta Miller, "C.P.E. Bach's Compositions for Solo Flute," *Journal of Musicology* 11 (1993): 211.

⁶¹· Emanuel Bach's works are listed and dated in a catalog of his estate published after his death; see Rachel W. Wade, ed., *The Catalog of Carl Philipp Emanuel Bach's Estate: A Facsimile of the Edition by Schniebes, Hamburg, 1790* (New York: Garland, 1981). The sonatas Wq. 123–124 were composed at Frankfurt in the 1730s; Wq. 125–129 at Berlin during 1738–40; Wq. 130–131 and possibly also Wq. 134 (undated in the catalog) at Berlin during 1746–47, together with the unaccompanied flute sonata Wq. 132.

⁶²· These are primarily in the Königliche Hausmusik (KHM) section of the Staatsbibliothek zu Berlin, Preußischer Kulturbesitz, Musikabteilung mit Mendelssohn-Archiv.

⁶³· By Johann Jakob Heinrich Westphal (1756–1825); his collection is now housed at the Royal Conservatory Library in Brussels. A second complete set of copies is in the music archive of the Sing-Akademie zu Berlin; details in the author's critical edition, to appear as volume II/1 in *Carl Philipp Emanuel Bach: The Complete Works* (Los Altos, Calif.: Packard Humanities Institute), forthcoming.

⁶⁴· Horst Richter, "'Ich bin Komponist': Friedrich II. von Preußen in sein-en musikalisch-schöpferischen Kronprinzenjahren in Ruppin und Rheins-berg," in *Die Rheinsberger Hofcapelle von Friedrich II*, 37.

⁶⁵· Letter from Frederick to his sister Wilhelmina of 3 February 1737, in *Friedrich der Große und Wilhelmine von Baireuth*, 348. In other letters, Frederick

EMANUEL BACH AND THE WRITING OF BIOGRAPHY

mentions having the violinist Johann Gottlieb Graun perform during a visit of the *Erbprinz* (Friedrich of Bayreuth) to Ruppin (letter of 24 October 1732, p. 105); he mentions how much he enjoys hearing cantatas of Carl Heinrich Graun in Rheinsberg and fancies composing a flute aria (letter of 12 November 1738, p. 387).

[66] Marpurg reported Janitsch's losses; see Thomas Fritsch, "Johann Gottlieb Janitsch," in *Die Rheinsberger Hofcapelle von Friedrich II*, 186. Frederick mentions the fire in a letter of 18 April 1740 to Wilhelmina, *Friedrich der Große und Wilhelmine von Baireuth*, 446.

[67] The Berlin newspapers announced hundreds of court concerts as involving the royal Capelle; these are listed in Henzel, "Das Konzertleben der preußischen Hauptstadt," 229–91.

[68] Emanuel Bach performed on the *Bogenclavier* (see note 43).

[69] Leisinger, "Bach. III. 9. Carl Philipp Emanuel Bach," *Grove Music Online*.

[70] *Frederick the Great: The Memoirs of His Reader Henri De Catt (1758–1760)*, trans. F.S. Flint, 2 vols. (London: Constable, 1916) 1:x–xi.

[71] Thus Leisinger, in *Grove Music Online*, writes: "By appointing [Emanuel] Bach her honorary Capellmeister Princess Amalia brought a note of conciliation to the close of his period in Berlin."

[72] Cf. the letter to Syndicus Faber (see note 38): "I humbly apologize once again that several unavoidable duties at court and at Princess Amalia's completely prevented me from answering obediently and obligingly right away."

[73] J.S. Bach, after serving as Capellmeister to the Prince of Cöthen, retained the title when he became *director musices* at Leipzig and cantor of the Thomasschule; he later was *Capellmeister von Haus aus* to the Duke of Weißenfels. C.P.E. Bach at Hamburg was both director of music in the city churches and cantor of the Johanneum, the city Latin school.

[4]

C.P.E. Bach, Georg Philipp Telemann
und die Osterkantate "Gott hat den Herrn auferwecket" Wq 244

PETER WOLLNY

Carl Philipp Emanuel Bachs Osterkantate aus dem Jahr 1756 ist ein rätselhaftes Werk, das im Schaffen des Komponisten in mehrfacher Hinsicht eine Sonderstellung einnimmt. Die Kantate entstand zu einer Zeit, als der zweitälteste Bach-Sohn sich in der preußischen Metropole und bei Hofe gesellschaftlich fest etabliert, als Claviervirtuose und -pädagoge profiliert sowie schließlich als Komponist kühner Instrumentalwerke (Sonaten, Konzerte, Sinfonien, Kammermusik) durchgesetzt hatte. An groß besetzten geistlichen Kompositionen hatte Bach hingegen lediglich das lateinische *Magnificat* aus dem Jahre 1749 vorzuweisen, zudem war "Gott hat den Herrn auferwecket" seit Beginn seiner professionellen Laufbahn seine einzige Kirchenkantate,[1] und auch bis zu seinem Wechsel nach Hamburg sollte dieser Werkbereich nur um die kleine Trauungskantate "Willst du mit diesem Manne ziehen" H 824a erweitert werden. Bereits Carl Hermann Bitter hob die Sonderstellung des Werks innerhalb von Bachs Berliner Oeuvre hervor und vermutete daher einen konkreten Entstehungsanlass, den er freilich nicht ermitteln konnte.[2] Das wenig günstige künstlerische Urteil, das Bitter und in der Folge auch Heinrich Miesner[3] über die Osterkantate fällten, scheint in nicht geringem Maße aus der Schwierigkeit zu resultieren, das Werk in einen schlüssigen biographischen und musikgeschichtlichen Zusammenhang einzuordnen. Erst Günther Wagner unternahm vor gut einem Jahrzehnt den Versuch, dessen stilistisches Profil und ästhetischen Kontext zu beschreiben, wobei er "die unmittelbare Anregung, den auslösenden Faktor zur Komposition der Osterkantate" in Carl Heinrich Grauns Passionsoratorium *Der Tod Jesu* aus dem Jahr 1755 sah und eine Verbindung zu Prinzessin Anna Amalia von Preußen vermutete.[4]

Die greifbaren Originalquellen—erhalten sind die autographe Partitur aus dem Jahr 1756 (D-B, Mus. ms. Bach P 345) und das unter Aufsicht des Komponisten angefertigte Stimmenmaterial (D-B, Mus. ms. Bach St 182; geschrieben wohl 1757 und bis 1787 mit Revisionen und Zusätzen versehen)—beleuchten zwar die komplexe Bearbeitungs- und Aufführungsgeschichte speziell in Bachs Hamburger Zeit, sagen über den Entstehungsanlass

---

1. Die in Leipzig und Frankfurt an der Oder komponierten Vokalkompositionen sah C.P.E. Bach offenbar nicht als vollgültige Werke an. Zu diesem Repertoire siehe CPEB:CW, V/2.

2. Carl Hermann Bitter, *Carl Philipp Emanuel und Wilhelm Friedemann Bach und deren Brüder*, Bd. 1 (Berlin: Wilhelm Müller, 1868), S. 131–137.

3. Miesner, *Philipp Emanuel Bach in Hamburg. Beiträge zu seiner Biographie und zur Musikgeschichte seiner Zeit* (Heide: Emil Sund, 1929), S. 76.

4. Günther Wagner, "Carl Philipp Emanuel Bachs Osterkantate aus dem Jahre 1756," *Carl Philipp Emanuel Bachs geistliche Musik. Bericht über das Internationale Symposium (Teil 1) vom 12. bis 16. März 1998 in Frankfurt (Oder), Żagań und Zielona Góra*, hrsg. von Ulrich Leisinger und Hans-Günter Ottenberg (Frankfurt/Oder: Konzerthalle, 2001), S. 30–40.

C.P.E. Bach, G.P. Telemann und die Osterkantate Wq 244

und die erste Darbietung des Werks aber nur wenig aus.[5] So geht der gegenwärtige Kenntnisstand nicht über den Wortlaut des von Bach eigenhändig auf der ersten Seite der autographen
Partitur geschriebenen Titel hinaus:

> Oster Cantate, | wovon | Die Poesie vom H. Hof-Prediger | Cochius, | Die Musick
> von C.P.E. Bachen ist | Beydes ist im Jahre 1756 verfertiget.

Die prominente—und für Bach wie auch für seine Zeitgenossen keineswegs selbstver-
ständliche—Nennung des Librettisten auf der Titelseite der Partitur hat die Forschung bislang
nicht zu Erkundungen über dessen Person und über die Rezeption seiner Kantatendichtung
angeregt. Dies soll im Folgenden nachgeholt werden, bevor einige noch nicht ausgewertete
Quellen zu Bachs Vertonung auf neue Indizien zur Entstehungsgeschichte des Werks befragt
werden.

Der Textdichter

Mit dem in Bachs Autograph genannten "Hof-Prediger Cochius" ist der einer angese-
henen und weitverzweigten reformierten Theologenfamilie entstammende Leonhard Cochius
(1718–1779) gemeint—nicht, wie gelegentlich zu lesen ist, Christian Johann Cochius (1688–
1749), bei dem es sich um einen Onkel handelt. Leonhard Cochius wurde im Januar 1718
in Königsberg als Sohn des Hofpredigers und Konsistorialrats Johann Wilhelm (II) Cochius
und seiner Frau Sophie Louise geb. Weier geboren; als Geburtstag werden der 20. und der
28. Januar genannt.[6] Als wichtigste biographische Quelle darf der kurz nach Cochius' Tod
erschienene Artikel in Goldbecks *Literarischen Nachrichten von Preußen* (1781) gelten, der im
Folgenden auszugsweise zitiert sei:

> Er wurde zu Königsberg … gebohren, und studierte daselbst auf der Universität,
> wo er sich zwar vornehmlich der Gottesgelahrtheit widmete, die andere
> Wissenschaften aber, besonders die Philosophie und Mathematik eben so eifrig

---

5. Notizen auf der Titelseite von St 182 zufolge führte Bach seine Osterkantate in Hamburg in
den Jahren 1769, 1776 und 1787 auf. Die Originalstimmen belegen die Einfügung beziehungsweise
den Austausch von Choralstrophen nach dem Eingangschor und nach der zweiten Arie ("Nun ist des
Höchsten Wort erfüllt" und "Herr, dies sind die edlen Früchte"). Diese Veränderungen haben nichts mit
den Werkfassungen um 1756/57 zu tun und werden in der vorliegenden Studie nicht weiter untersucht.

6. Vgl. *Altpreußische Biographie*, hrsg. von Christian Krollmann, Bd. 1 (Berlin: Elwert 1961), S. 198;
und Johann Friedrich Goldbeck, *Literarische Nachrichten von Preußen*, Teil 1 (Berlin, 1781), S. 64–66.
Andere Quellen geben irrtümlich 1717 als Geburtsjahr an, offenbar infolge einer fehlerhaften Auflösung
der häufig zu lesenden Angabe, Cochius sei 1779 in seinem 62. Lebensjahr gestorben. Zur Genealogie
der Familie Cochius siehe speziell Rudolf von Thadden, *Die brandenburgisch-preußischen Hofprediger im
17. und 18. Jahrhundert* (Berlin: Walter de Gruyter, 1959), Anhang (2. Stammtafel).

Er ist der Vater

trieb. Von Königsberg gieng er nach Marburg, wo er noch 3 Jahre lang die Theologie, und unter dem damals zu Marburg lebenden berühmten Wolf die Philosophie und Mathematik studierte. Hierauf wurde er Hofmeister in dem Hause des General von Münchow zu Berlin, bald nachher aber Konrektor, und nach einigen Jahren Prorektor am Friedrichswerderschen Gymnasium daselbst, wo er sich durch eine 1746 öffentlich gehaltene Lobrede auf den König sehr vortheilhaft bekannt machte.[7]

Im J. 1749 ernannte der König ihn durch eine Kabinetsorder zum Hof- und Garnisonprediger in Potsdam. Seine Abhandlung über die Neigungen, welche 1768 von der Akademie der Wissenschaften zu Berlin gekrönt wurde, war die Veranlassung, daß er ein Mitglied derselben wurde.[8] Friedrich … ernannte ihn, obgleich er von Berlin entfernt lebte, zum ordentlichen Mitglied der Akademie. Eine für ihn rühmliche Ausnahme, da sonst alle ordentliche Mitglieder derselben zu Berlin anwesend seyn müssen.

Cochius starb "nach einer halbjährigen und schmerzhaften Krankheit" am 30. April 1779 in Potsdam. Das hohe Ansehen, das er als Theologe, Philosoph und Wissenschaftler genoss, geht aus einem von dem Akademiekollegen Johann Heinrich Samuel Formey verfassten und 1782 veröffentlichten Nachruf hervor.[9] Johann Gottfried Herder lobte ihn in seinen *Briefen zur Beförderung der Humanität*[10] als scharfsinnigen Denker, und noch Immanuel Kant zitiert ihn in seiner *Metaphysik der Sitten* (1797)[11] als Autorität.

Cochius' Wirken hat auch in der musikgeschichtlichen Literatur Spuren hinterlassen. 1749 war er Gründungsmitglied und erster Direktor der Musikübenden Gesellschaft zu Berlin; seine im November des Jahres erfolgte Berufung nach Potsdam bedingte allerdings, dass er dieses Amt bereits nach kurzer Zeit wieder aufgeben musste.[12] Einen Abschied oder gar

---

7. Gemeint ist offenbar: *Panegyricvs Friderico II. Regi Borvssorvm Invicto Felici Die XXVIII Dec. Qvem Post Bellvm Confestvm Servatam Patriam Et Pacem Devictis Gentibvs Datam Gloriosvs Victoris In Patriam Reditvs Sempiternae Hominvm Memoriae Commendavit A. S. R. MDCCXXXVI Berolini In Gymnasio Friderciano Demississimae Mentis Pietate Dictvs* (Berlin, 1746); Exemplar: Universitätsbibliothek Eichstätt.

8. Gedruckte Ausgabe der Schrift: *Untersuchung über die Neigungen, welche von der Königl. Akademie der Wissenschaften in Berlin für d. J. 1767 ausgesetzten Preis erhalten hat* (Berlin: Haude und Spener, 1769).

9. Johann Heinrich Samuel Formey, *Eloge de M. Cochius* (Berlin, 1782); Exemplar in der Bibliothek der Berlin-Brandenburgischen Akademie der Wissenschaften.

10. Siehe Johann Gottfried Herder, *Theoretische Schriften*, Bd. 1 (Berlin und Weimar: Aufbau-Verlag, 1971), S. 346.

11. Siehe Immanuel Kant, *Schriften zur Ethik und Religionsphilosophie*, Werke, hrsg. von Wilhelm Weischedel, Bd. 4 (Darmstadt: Wissenschaftliche Buchgesellschaft, 1956), S. 513.

12. Vgl. Adolf Friedrich Wolff, "Entwurf einer ausführlichen Nachricht von der Musikübenden Gesellschaft zu Berlin," *Historisch-Kritische Beyträge zur Aufnahme der Musik*, hrsg. von Friedrich Wilhelm Marpurg, Bd. I, 5. Stück (Berlin: J.J. Schützens sel. Wittwe, 1755), S. 385–413, speziell S. 388 und 405.

C.P.E. Bach, G.P. Telemann und die Osterkantate Wq 244

eine Entfremdung von der Musik bedeutete dies freilich nicht. Friedrich Wilhelm Marpurg erinnerte in einem auf den 25. August 1759 datierten Brief an Cochius an die gemeinsame Berliner Zeit und bezeichnete seinen Adressaten als ein Exempel dafür, "daß es nicht unmöglich ist, zugleich an den ernsthaftern Wissenschaften, und an den Reitzen der Tonkunst Geschmack zu finden, und in beyden vortreflich zu seyn."[13] Nach Aussage von Ernst Ludwig Gerber war Cochius "ein Dilettant von seltenen musikalischen Kenntnissen und praktischer Geschicklichkeit. Oft pflegte er in seinem Hause große Oratorien von Händel und Hasse aufführen zu lassen, wobey er selbst am Flügel dirigirte."[14]

Einen tieferen Einblick in Cochius' musikalische Interessen vermittelt das Verzeichnis seiner 1779 auf einer Auktion vereinzelten Bibliothek. Ein offenbar singuläres Exemplar dieses Katalogs hat sich in der Bibliothek der Freien Universität zu Berlin erhalten:[15]

> Verzeichniß | der | Bibliothek, | welche | der Hochwürdige, und Hochgelahrte Herr | Leonhard Cochius, | weil. wirklicher Königl. Hofprediger, und Mitglied der | Berlin. Academie der Wissenschaften, | hinterlaßen hat, | und die | … | den 27. Sept. und folgende Tage 1779, | Nachmittag um 2 Uhr | in der Wohnung des Verstorbenen, den Meistbietenden | gegen baare Bezahlung öffentlich zugeschlagen | werden wird. | … | Potsdam, 1779."

Den Hauptteil des 82 Seiten umfassenden Verzeichnisses bildet eine erlesene Sammlung von Theologica sowie natur- und geisteswissenschaftlichen Abhandlungen. In der Aufstellung der gedruckten Schriften finden sich neben zahlreichen Gesangbüchern (S. 57f.) wichtige musiktheoretische Werke vorzugsweise von Berliner Autoren, darunter auch der zweite Teil von C.P.E. Bachs *Versuch über die wahre Art das Clavier zu spielen.* Die praktischen Musikalien sind auf den Seiten 51 und 52 gebündelt aufgeführt. Der folgende Auszug bietet eine kommentierte Aufstellung der musikalisch relevanten Positionen:[16]

[S. 3]
Athanasii Kircheri Musurgia universalis cum tab. æneis,   RISM B VI[1], S. 449
Tomi II, Romæ 650 perg. R. und E. liber rarus.

[S. 13]
171. 72 Marpurgs Abhandlung von der Fuge, Berlin   RISM B VI[2], S. 540
     1753, frzb. mit einem Bande Kupfertafeln.

---

13. Friedrich Wilhelm Marpurg, *Kritische Briefe über die Tonkunst,* Bd. 1 (Berlin: Birnstiel, 1760), S. 73–80.

14. Ernst Ludwig Gerber, *Neues historisch-biographisches Lexikon der Tonkünstler* (Leipzig: Kühnel, 1812–1814), Bd. 1, S. 752–753.

15. Signatur: 38/77/10998(4).

16. Die umfangreiche Gesangbuchsammlung bleibt hier allerdings ausgespart.

Er ist der Vater

173.	Sorgii Anweisung zum Generalbaß, 3 Theile, Lobenstein, frzb.	RISM B VI^2, S. 794
174.	75 Ph. Em. Bach Versuch über die wahre Art das Clavier zu spielen. Berlin 762, hfrzb. mit 26 Kupfertafeln besonders in pappb.	Wq 254–255; RISM B VI^1, S. 105
176a.76b.	Marpurg Handbuch bey dem Generalbaß und der Composition, mit Kupf. 2 Theile, Berlin 1755, geh.	RISM B VI^2, S. 542
177.	Critische Briefe über die Tonkunst von einer musikalischen Gesellschaft in Berlin, Berlin 760.	RISM B VI^2, S. 543f.

[S. 15]

276.	Kirnbergers gleichschwebende Temperatur m. Kupf.	RISM B VI^1, S. 452

[S. 16]

299. Ein Convolut allerhand Cantaten und Gedichte.

[S. 37]

537. 10 Opernbücher.

543. 11 Texte zur Graunschen und 8 zur Bachschen Paßion.

[S. 51]

An musikalischen Instrumenten und Musikalien.

Ein großer Flügel mit zwey Klavieren, von dem berühmten verstorbenen Hildebrandt in Leipzig verfertigt.

1.	Eine Paßions-Musik von C. P. Bach, in Partitur und gebunden.	Wq 233
2.	Der Tod Jesu etc. von Graun, in Partitur und gebunden.	RISM A/I/3: G 3553?
3.	Sei Duetti per 2 flauti. von Quanz, gebunden.	RISM A/I/7: Q 21
4.	Cramers Psalmen, und	Wq 194; RISM A/I/1: B 131
5.	Gellerts geistl. Oden etc. beyde mit Melodien von C.P.E. Bach.	Wq 196 RISM A/I/1: B 122 (oder spätere Auflage)
6.	Oden mit Melodien, 1ster und 2ter Theil.	RISM B II, S. 270
7.	Quanz neue Kirchen-Melodien zu den geistl. Oden von Gellert.	RISM A/I/7: Q 15
8.	9. u. 10. Lieder der Deutschen.	RISM B II, S. 218
11.	Sechs Sonaten Anno 776 herausgegeben, und	RISM A/I/7: R 979
12.	Sechs Sonaten fürs Klavier Anno 778 herausgegeben, beyde von Reichard.	RISM A/I/7: R 981
13.	J.S. Bachs vierstimmige Choral-Gesänge, 1ster Theil.	RISM A/I/1: B 448

C.P.E. Bach, G.P. Telemann und die Osterkantate Wq 244

14.	Desselben musikal. Opfer, nebst einem Trio über das Königl. Thema. (Ist selten.)	BWV 1079; RISM A/I/1: B 520
15.	Sechs Sonaten fürs Klavier von C.P.E. Bach, gebunden.	Wq 50?; RISM A/I/1: B 70
16.	Sechs Sonaten, von ebendenselben.	Wq 51?; RISM A/I/1: B 75?
17.	13 Flöten-Soli von Quanz, Bach, und andern Meistern.	
18.	54 Bogen Klavier-Sachen, worunter viele Sonaten von Bach.	
19.	Vier Klavier-Konzerte und 6 Trii für das Klavier.	
20.	26 Flöten- und Violin-Trii, von Graun, Bach, Quanz und andern.	

[S. 52]

21.	33 Bogen Ouverturen, Parthien, Sinfonien &c.	
22.	18 Bogen obligate Sachen für die Flöte, Violin und Flauto d'Amore.	
23.	Vier Konzerte für die Flöte.	
24.	21 Opern-Arien, im Klavier-Auszug, nebst einer Cantate von Graun.	
25.	18 Italiänische Arien in Partitur oder in Stimmen von Deutschen und Italiänischen Meistern.	
26.	41 Bogen Kirchen-Musiken in Partitur, von sehr guten Meistern, worunter ein Psalm von Kirnberger.	
27.	Das Vater Unser von Homilius.	
28.	Die Israeliten von Bach vollständig mit allen Stimmen.	Wq 238

[S. 59]

110.	Armida, ein musikalisches Schauspiel, Berlin 751, pappb.	Libretto zur Erstaufführung von C. H. Grauns gleichnamiger Oper[17]
114.	Joh. Rist geistliche Lieder, Lüneburg 651, pergb.	vermutlich RISM A/I/7: R 1746

Neben zentralen Schriften der zeitgenössischen Berliner Musiktheoretiker und einem wertvollen Exemplar der Erstausgabe von Athanasius Kirchers *Musurgia universalis* (1650) fällt die repräsentative Sammlung von C.P.E. Bachs Berliner und frühen Hamburger

---

17. *Armida: ein Musicalisches Singespiel welches auf Sr. Königl. Majestät, in Preusse … an dem höchsterfreulichen Geburts-Feste Ihro Majestät der Königlichen Frau Mutter Frau Sophia Dorothea Königin in Preussen, … auf dem Berlinischen Schauplatze soll aufgeführt werden* (Berlin: Haude und Spener, 1751).

Er ist der Vater

Werken ins Auge. In weitaus breiterem Maße, als es das singuläre Auftreten seines Namens auf der Pränumerationsliste der Cramer-Psalmen Wq 196 bislang erkennen ließ,[18] interessierte Cochius sich offenbar für Bachs Liedschaffen—er besaß eine nahezu vollständige Serie von dessen bis 1779 gedruckten Liedsammlungen sowie offenbar auch eine repräsentative Auswahl von dessen Tasten- und Kammermusik. Ein Indiz für die Vielseitigkeit seiner musikalischen Interessen ist der Nachweis eines der seltenen Exemplare des Erstdrucks von J.S. Bachs *Musikalischem Opfer*. Einen Einblick in das Repertoire der von Gerber erwähnten Hauskonzerte geben die Losnummern 1–2 und 24–28. Der freundschaftliche Kontakt zu C.P.E. Bach war anscheinend auch in dessen Hamburger Jahren noch eng, denn in Cochius' Nachlass fanden sich auch Abschriften der Passionskantate Wq 233 und des Oratoriums *Die Israeliten in der Wüste* Wq 238.[19]

Der Verbleib von Cochius' wertvoller Musikaliensammlung ist noch ungeklärt. Stichproben in den Beständen der Staatsbibliothek zu Berlin (einschließlich Depositum Sing-Akademie) ergaben keine eindeutigen Identifizierungen. Es ist allerdings möglich, dass die Losnummern nicht auf den Exemplaren vermerkt wurden. Sollte dies der Fall sein, wäre zu fragen, ob die mit autographen Zusätzen und einem Korrigendazettel versehene handschriftliche Partitur der Passionskantate im Bestand der Amalienbibliothek (Am.B. 85a) mit der an erster Stelle der Musikalien in Cochius' Nachlassverzeichnis genannten Quelle identisch sein könnte. Das der Handschrift beigebundene gedruckte Textheft (ohne Angabe von Ort, Jahr und Drucker) könnte dann aus der Losnummer 543 stammen und mit einer Privataufführung im Hause Cochius in Zusammenhang stehen. Für die verwickelte Entstehungs- und Rezeptionsgeschichte des Werks ergeben sich jedenfalls neue Perspektiven und Ansätze.[20]

Wie die vorstehende Übertragung und die knappen Anmerkungen zeigen, ist das Nachlassverzeichnis von Leonard Cochius eine zentrale Quelle zur Geschichte des privaten Musizierens im friderizianischen Berlin und im Umkreis der preußischen Hofkapelle. Seine vollständige Auswertung kann an dieser Stelle jedoch nicht erfolgen und muss einer späteren Studie vorbehalten bleiben. In unserem Zusammenhang sei noch angemerkt, dass sich unter den "41 Bogen Kirchen-Musiken in Partitur" (S. 52, Los Nr. 26) eigentlich auch eine in Cochius' Besitz zu vermutende Abschrift der Osterkantate von 1756 befunden haben müsste, da anzunehmen ist, dass Wq 244 in einem der Privatkonzerte des Hofpredigers erklungen ist. Es wäre zu prüfen, ob eine der im Berliner Umfeld überlieferten Quellen des Werks auf ihn

---

18. Vgl. *CPEB-Briefe*, S. 1455.

19. Bach erwähnt in einem Brief an Forkel vom 20. April 1774, dass sein Exemplar der Passionskantate "durch das viele Herumschicken sehr zerlumpt" sei. Das Oratorium *Die Israeliten in der Wüste* wurde zwar 1775 gedruckt, doch scheint der etwas unklar formulierte Eintrag in Cochius' Nachlassverzeichnis auf ausschließlich handschriftliches Material zu deuten.

20. Der gegenwärtige Kenntnisstand ist zusammengefasst bei Anette Nagel, *Studien zur Passionskantate von Carl Philipp Emanuel Bach* (Frankfurt: Peter Lang, 1995).

C.P.E. Bach, G.P. Telemann und die Osterkantate Wq 244

zurückgeführt werden kann—in Frage käme etwa die von Bachs Berliner Kopist Anonymus 303 angefertigte Abschrift Am.B. 86.

Angesichts des—an den frühen Biographien ablesbaren—hohen Ansehens, das Cochius als umfassend gebildeter Theologe genoss, sowie seiner vielfältigen literarischen Interessen, die das Verzeichnis seiner Bibliothek anschaulich belegt, darf vielleicht seine für Bach geschaffene dichterische Vorlage nicht so pauschal abgewertet werden, wie dies Bitter und Miesner tun zu können glaubten. Denn eigentlich entspricht die Dichtung in jeder Hinsicht den Forderungen an die (literarische) Gattung der Kantate, die zeitgenössische Berliner Kunsttheoretiker formuliert hatten.[21] Cochius knüpft seine Betrachtungen an das Diktum aus dem ersten Korintherbrief (1 Kor 6,14) an. Der erste Teil, bestehend aus Rezitativ, Arioso und Arie, schildert die Auferstehung Christi, der zweite, gleichartig strukturierte, behandelt die Gewissheit der Auferstehung auch des Menschen. Die rezitativischen und ariosen Abschnitte dienen der Kontemplation und lehrenden Ausdeutung des biblischen Spruchs, während die beiden Arien vor allem dem Ausdruck stark subjektiver Empfindungen dienen. Cochius strebte offensichtlich an, mit seiner Osterdichtung einen im Sinne der empfindsamen Ästhetik exemplarischen Beitrag zur Kirchenmusik zu liefern. Bach wird diesen dankbar aufgegriffen haben.

Ein Hamburger Textdruck

Das Osterfest fiel im Jahr 1756 auf den 18. April, es ist somit anzunehmen, dass die Komposition spätestens Anfang des Monats fertig vorlag; ein entsprechend früherer Termin ist für die Vollendung der Dichtung anzunehmen. Merkwürdigerweise ist die erste öffentliche Aufführung der Osterkantate in Berlin aber erst für den Ostersonntag des folgenden Jahres belegt: unter der Leitung des Kantors Rudolf Dietrich Buchholtz erklang die—nach dem Urteil der Haude- und Spenerschen Zeitung—"vortreffliche Oster-Musick" C.P.E. Bachs am 10. April 1757 in der Berliner Petrikirche, "wobei gedachter Herr Bach selbst accompagnirte, wie sich denn auch die geschickte Sängerin, Mad. Agricola, und verschiedene andere Virtuosen, mit ihren Stimmen, und Instrumenten, zugleich hören liessen."[22] Die der Aufführung von der Presse gewidmete Aufmerksamkeit und die exquisite Besetzung lassen uns dieses Ereignis eindeutig als Premiere erkennen. Möglicherweise ging dieser ersten öffentlichen Aufführung aber eine Darbietung in privatem Kreise im Hause Cochius in Potsdam voraus; diese könnte dann bereits im April 1756 erfolgt sein.

---

21. Vgl. etwa Johann Georg Sulzer, *Allgemeine Theorie der Schönen Künste*, Bd. 2 (Leipzig: Weidmann, 1792), S. 443–449, speziell S. 444.

22. Vgl. Christoph Henzel, "Das Konzertleben der preußischen Hauptstadt 1740–1786 im Spiegel der Berliner Presse (Teil 1)," *Jahrbuch des Staatlichen Instituts für Musikforschung Preußischer Kulturbesitz 2004*, S. 216–291, speziell S. 255. Der Berliner Aufführung von 1757 sind vermutlich das originale Stimmenmaterial (St 182) und ein undatierter Textdruck (DK-Kk, ohne Signatur) zuzuordnen. Auf den Textdruck machte mich freundlicherweise mein Kollege Wolfram Enßlin aufmerksam.

Er ist der Vater

Da Dichter und Komponist beide am preußischen Hof wirkten und vermutlich regelmäßig zusammentrafen, und da Bach zudem im Titel der Niederschrift ihre enge Zusammenarbeit
so ausdrücklich betont, erscheint es merkwürdig, dass sich die Aufführung einer Vertonung
von Cochius' Dichtung noch im Entstehungsjahr 1756 außerhalb Berlins belegen lässt: Nach
Ausweis eines gedruckten Texthefts[23] erklang diese an den Sonntagen Quasimodogeniti
und Jubilate (1. und 2. Sonntag nach Ostern) in den Kirchen St. Katharinen und St. Maria
Magdalena zu Hamburg, und zwar unter der Leitung von Georg Philipp Telemann. Werner
Menke, der im Rahmen seiner 1942 erschienenen Dissertation systematisch die musikali-
schen Quellen und Textdrucke zu den Hamburger Kantatenaufführungen zwischen 1721 und
1767 gesammelt hat,[24] wies—in Unkenntnis von C.P.E. Bachs Vertonung—das Werk auf der
Grundlage des Textdrucks bedenkenlos Telemann zu und nahm es in sein Werkverzeichnis auf
(TVWV 1:651).[25] Seither gilt es als—verschollene beziehungsweise nur textlich erhaltene—
Kantate des Hamburger Musikdirektors.

Ein Vergleich des Hamburger Librettos mit der Textfassung von Bachs autographer
Partitur scheint die These einer Telemannschen Parallelvertonung zunächst zu bestätigen. In
den Rezitativen und Arien finden sich lediglich einige kleinere Varianten, allerdings erscheint
die ursprünglich fünfsätzige Vorlage im Hamburger Textheft wesentlich erweitert:

P 345	Textheft Hamburg
[Chor:] Gott hat den Herrn auferwecket	[Chor:] Gott hat den Herrn auferwecket
	Choral: Jesus, der mein Heiland, lebt
Recit.: So wird mein Heiland nun erhöht	[Recit.:] So wird mein Heiland nun erhöht
Aria: Dir sing ich froh, erstandner Fürst des Lebens	[Aria:] Dir sing ich froh, erstandner Fürst des Lebens
	Choral: Weil du vom Tod erstanden bist
Recit.: So sei nun, Seele, sei erfreut	[Recit.:] So sei nun, Seele, sei erfreut
Aria: Wie freudig seh ich dir entgegen	[Aria:] Wie freudig seh ich dir entgegen
Choral: O süßer Herre, Jesu Christ	Choral: So fahr ich hin zu Jesu Christ

Der von Bach dem Werk als Satz 6 hinzugefügte Schlusschoral wurde durch einen anderen Choral ersetzt, während sich zwei weitere Choräle unmittelbar an den Eingangschor und
die erste Arie anschließen. Telemann behandelte die Dichtung also auf die gleiche Weise wie

---

23. D-B, Beilage zu Mus. ms. 21736/190.

24. Vgl. Werner Menke, *Das Vokalwerk Georg Philipp Telemanns. Überlieferung und Zeitfolge* (Kassel:
Bärenreiter, 1942), S. 25–28 und 70.

25. Menke, *Thematisches Verzeichnis der Vokalwerke von Georg Philipp Telemann*, Bd. 1 (Frankfurt:
Klostermann, 1988), S. 61.

C.P.E. Bach, G.P. Telemann und die Osterkantate Wq 244

er es beispielsweise mit den rein madrigalischen Vorlagen des schlesischen Dichters Benjamin Schmolck tat.[26]

Die Indizien für eine gleichzeitige Vertonung von Cochius' Text durch Telemann und C.P.E. Bach scheinen mithin plausibel. Sie werden sogar durch einen bemerkenswerten Parallelfall erhärtet: Im Jahr zuvor (1755) hatten Telemann und Carl Heinrich Graun in einem freundschaftlichen Wettstreit Carl Wilhelm Ramlers Passionsdichtung "Der Tod Jesu" in Musik gesetzt, ihre Werke an ihren jeweiligen Wirkungsstätten aufgeführt und sie sodann für Darbietungen im folgenden Jahr ausgetauscht.[27] Überhaupt waren Telemanns Verbindungen zu Berliner Musikern in den 1750er Jahren außerordentlich eng. Der Hamburger Musikdirektor verfolgte die künstlerischen Entwicklungen in der preußischen Hauptstadt anscheinend mit großer Aufmerksamkeit—ebenso wie das Telemannsche Spätwerk von den jungen Berliner Komponisten mit wachem Interesse wahrgenommen und rezipiert wurde. Neben zahlreichen anderen dokumentarischen Belegen zeigt sich dies insbesondere an der überaus großen Zahl von Telemann-Quellen im Bibliotheksbestand der Sing-Akademie zu Berlin.

Doch gerade hier tut sich ein Problem auf. Sollte man nicht meinen, dass eine Telemannsche Vertonung einer repräsentativen Berliner Kantatendichtung in den Kreisen der Berliner Musiker und Musikliebhaber auf lebhaftes Interesse gestoßen wäre? Und wäre nicht zu erwarten, dass sich dieses Interesse in noch heute nachweisbaren Abschriften niedergeschlagen hätte? Während Telemanns *Der Tod Jesu* in der Tat in mehreren Berliner Abschriften erhalten und seinerzeit eifrig mit der Graunschen Vertonung verglichen worden ist, enthalten weder das musiktheoretische Schrifttum, noch die Berliner Zeitungen, noch auch die umfangreichen literarischen Briefwechsel (etwa von Johann Wilhelm Ludwig Gleim, Christian Gottfried Krause und Karl Wilhelm Ramler) den kleinsten Hinweis auf eine Telemannsche Osterkantate nach einer Dichtung des preußischen Hofpredigers Cochius.

Diese Lücke schien sich zu schließen, als mit der Wiederentdeckung des Musikarchivs der Sing-Akademie zu Berlin eine anonyme fragmentarische Vertonung von Cochius' Dichtung auftauchte. Unter der Signatur SA 567 (olim ZC 685ᵉ) findet sich eine insgesamt 36 Blätter umfassende Partitur von der Hand Johann Friedrich Agricolas, die folgende Sätze enthält:

---

26. Vgl. die Kantaten "Sei du mein Anfang" TVWV 1:1282 und "Michael, wer ist wie Gott?" TVWV 1:1136.

27. Vgl. die ausführlichen Darstellungen von Wolf Hobohm zur Werkgeschichte der "Donnerode" und des Oratoriums "Der Tod Jesu" in den einschlägigen Bänden der Telemann-Auswahlausgabe: Georg Philipp Telemann, *Der Tod Jesu. Oratorium nach Worten von Karl Wilhelm Ramler TVWV 5:6. Betrachtung der neunten Stunde am Todestage Jesu. Oratorium nach Worten von Joachim Johann Daniel Zimmermann TVWV 5:5*, hrsg. von Wolf Hobohm, Georg Philipp Telemann. Musikalische Werke, Bd. 31 (Kassel: Bärenreiter, 2006); sowie ders., *Die Donnerode. Das befreite Israel, TVWV 6:3. TVWV 6:5*, hrsg. von Wolf Hobohm, Georg Philipp Telemann. Musikalische Werke, Bd. 22 (Kassel: Bärenreiter, 1971).

Er ist der Vater

> Rezitativ (Basso): "So wird mein Heiland nun erhöht"
> Arie (Soprano): "Des Todes Macht hält dich vergebens"
> Rezitativ – Arioso – Rezitativ (Tenore, Soprano): "Auch ich soll, Jesu, mit dir leben"
> Arie (Soprano): "Wie freudig seh ich dir entgegen" (mit Orchesterbegleitung)
> Arie (Soprano): "Wie freudig seh ich dir entgegen" (mit Begleitung von Orgel und
> Violine)

Zum Verständnis der Handschrift ist anzumerken, dass die Partitur offenbar aus mehreren verstreuten Faszikeln zusammengesetzt wurde. Heute sind insgesamt sechs Ternionen vorhanden. Vermerke auf Bl. 7r, 13r, 19r, 25r und 31r belegen die nachträglich in der Sing-Akademie wiederhergestellte Abfolge. Unbemerkt blieb bisher allerdings, dass zwischen Bl. 6 (letztes Blatt des ersten Ternio) und Bl. 7 (erstes Blatt des zweiten Ternio) ursprünglich offenbar eine weitere Lage vorhanden war, die vermutlich ebenfalls drei Bögen bzw. sechs Blätter umfasste. Damit ist ein großer Teil der ersten Arie verloren. Bl. 6v bricht wenige Takte vor dem Schluss des Eingangsritornells ab, Bl. 7r beginnt mit der letzten Periode des Ritornells am Ende des A-Teils der Arie. Bei dem auf Bl. 9r einsetzenden Part der Singstimme handelt es sich bereits um den Beginn des B-Teils. Es fehlt mithin der gesamte Vokalpart des A-Teils (Text: "Dir sing ich froh").

Merkwürdig ist die zweimalige Niederschrift der zweiten Arie in abweichender Instrumentierung. Werner Menke kannte diese Quelle; er nahm aber—aus nicht mehr nachvollziehbaren Gründen—lediglich die zweite, kammermusikalisch besetzte Fassung der Arie als ein Werk zweifelhafter Echtheit in sein Verzeichnis der Vokalwerke Telemanns auf (TVWV 1:1621). Die Verbindung zu dem von ihm ebenfalls ausgewerteten Textdruck aus dem Jahr 1756 (TVWV 1:651) blieb ihm augenscheinlich verborgen.

Menkes Vorbehalte hinsichtlich einer Zuschreibung des in SA 567 überlieferten Werks an Telemann waren durchaus begründet. Denn ein Blick in die Noten zeigt, dass es sich hier zweifellos um eine Komposition von Johann Friedrich Agricola handelt. Dies zeigen nicht nur die zahlreichen Retuschen an der kompositorischen Substanz, die in Agricolas Abschriften fremder Werke niemals zu finden sind. Auch die musikalische Faktur weist eindeutig die Züge seines an den Opern Grauns und Hasses geschulten reifen Stils auf. Typisch für Agricolas Kirchenkantaten sind zudem die Bevorzugung von virtuosen Sopranarien—die offenbar ganz auf die stimmlichen Fertigkeiten seiner Frau, der Berliner Opernsängerin Benedetta Emilia Molteni zugeschnitten sind[28] —, die opulente Besetzung (die erste Arie verlangt 3 Trompeten, Pauken, 2 Hörner, 2 Flöten, 2 Oboen, 2 Fagotte, Streicher und obligate Orgel), die gleichsam

---

28. Zu den stimmlichen Fertigkeiten von B. E. Molteni siehe Charles Burney, *Tagebuch einer musikalischen Reise durch Frankreich und Italien und Holland 1770–1772* (Leipzig: Reclam Verlag, 1975), S. 376.

C.P.E. Bach, G.P. Telemann und die Osterkantate Wq 244

sinfonischen Dimensionen sowie die regelmäßige Verwendung der Orgel als konzertierendes Soloinstrument.[29]

Bedingt durch zahlreiche unbeschriebene Seiten macht die Partitur insgesamt einen noch unfertigen Eindruck.[30] Möglicherweise ist also der fehlende Eingangschor nicht verlorengegangen, sondern wurde nie komponiert. Das Wasserzeichen der Partitur (Buchstaben IFS in Schrifttafel) kommt in einer weiteren unvollendeten Partitur von der Hand Agricolas vor—in seiner ebenfalls torsohaften Abschrift der Frühfassung von J.S. Bachs Matthäus-Passion BWV 244a (D-B, Mus. ms. Bach P 26), die mit ihren zahlreichen leeren Seiten und ungebundenen Lagen ein ähnliches Erscheinungsbild bietet. Da als Agricolas Vorlage für P 26 die um oder kurz nach 1770 entstandene Handschrift Am.B. 6/7 bestimmt werden kann, darf als sicher gelten, dass Agricola das IFS-Papier in seinen letzten Lebensjahren verwendet hat.[31] Mir scheint daher, dass es sich bei SA 567 um ein unvollendetes Spätwerk aus Agricolas Todesjahr 1774 handelt.

Nach diesen Beobachtungen und Überlegungen können wir mit guten Gründen das Oeuvre Agricolas um eine bemerkenswerte neue—wenn auch nur fragmentarisch erhaltene—Komposition erweitern, das Verzeichnis der Vokalwerke Telemanns hingegen von einem unechten Werk (TVWV 1:1621) befreien. Ob Telemann aber trotzdem Cochius' Dichtung "Gott hat den Herrn auferwecket" vertont hat, bleibt noch zu klären.

Eine Hamburger Abschrift in Kopenhagen

Erst die Auswertung einer heute in der Königlichen Bibliothek Kopenhagen aufbewahrten Handschrift bringt die erwünschte Klärung der Frage, welches Werk sich hinter dem Hamburger Textdruck von 1756 mit seinen Textvarianten und zusätzlichen Choralstrophen verbirgt. Unter der Signatur mu 6309.0934 findet sich eine Partiturabschrift der Osterkantate Wq 244, die offensichtlich aus Hamburg stammt (Kopftitel: "Auf Ostern Bach"). Ihr Schreiber ist in zahlreichen um und vor 1770 entstandenen Quellen nachweisbar—darunter einige der Partituren von Kantaten Georg Bendas aus C.P.E. Bachs Besitz (D-B, Mus. ms. 1334), die Dubletten im Stimmensatz zur Matthäus-Passion von 1769 (H 782; SA 18), ein Großteil des originalen Stimmensatzes zu der 1770 komponierten und aufgeführten Huldigungsmusik für den schwedischen Kronprinzen (Wq 216; SA 1239), die Partitur der überarbeiteten Fassung der Sinfonie in e-Moll Wq 178 (D-B, P 351/1) und die frühesten Stimmen zum Oratorium *Die Auferstehung und Himmelfahrt Jesu* Wq 240 (D-B, St 178). Der somit vielfach dokumentierte Kopist wird häufig mit dem Hamburger Tenoristen und professionellen Kopisten

---

29. Verglichen wurden insbesondere die im Bestand der Sing-Akademie zu Berlin erhaltenen Kantaten Agricolas sowie dessen Oratorium *Die Auferstehung und Himmelfahrt Jesu*.

30. Vgl. die Quellenbeschreibung bei Enßlin, S. 119.

31. Vgl. NBA II/5, Kritischer Bericht, S. 62–68.

Er ist der Vater

Johann Heinrich Michel gleichgesetzt,[32] doch sind—trotz unbestreitbarer Ähnlichkeiten—die Abweichungen der Schriftformen so gravierend, dass bis zum Beweis des Gegenteils angeraten ist, von zwei unterschiedlichen Schreibern auszugehen.

Die Provenienz der Kopenhagener Partitur kann dank eines Besitzvermerks auf der ersten Seite genau bestimmt werden. Der etwas undeutlich geschriebene Namenszug unter der Autorenangabe ist eindeutig als "HOCZinck" zu entziffern.[33] Dies deutet auf den aus Husum stammenden Sänger, Flötisten und Komponisten Hardenack Otto Conrad Zinck (1746–1832). Zinck wurde am 2. Juli 1746 in Husum als Sohn des dortigen Organisten Benedix Friedrich Zinck (um 1713–1799) geboren. Nach der Ausbildung durch den Vater wandte er sich nach Hamburg, wo er 1768 als Sänger des hamburgischen Musikchors nachweisbar ist. Aus originalen Aufführungsmaterialen Bachs aus den Jahren 1771–1775 geht hervor, dass Zinck als Altist tätig war und zum Teil mit sehr anspruchsvollen Partien bedacht wurde.[34] Zwischen 1772 und 1776 veranstaltete er im Konzertsaal auf dem Kamp regelmäßig Aufführungen mit Instrumental- und Vokalmusik. Im März 1774 dirigierte er Telemanns *Der Tag des Gerichts* und dessen Passionsoratorium *Betrachtung der neunten Stunde*, in der Fastenzeit 1776 leitete er—in Anwesenheit des Komponisten—C.P.E. Bachs Oratorium *Die Israeliten in der Wüste*.[35] Im Dezember 1777 wurde er erster Flötist in der Hofkapelle des Herzogs von Mecklenburg-Schwerin zu Ludwigslust, wirkte hier zehn Jahre und ließ sich schließlich 1787 als Organist, Musiklehrer und Singmeister des Hoftheaters in Kopenhagen nieder, wo er im Jahre 1800 eine Sing-Akademie nach Berliner Vorbild gründete. Zinck starb in seinem 86. Lebensjahr am 15. Februar 1832; seine Musikaliensammlung ging—offenbar geschlossen—in den Besitz der Königlichen Bibliothek in Kopenhagen über.[36]

32. Vgl. zum Beispiel Enßlin, S. 39 und 174; und Barbara Wiermann, "Werkgeschichte als Gattungsgeschichte: 'Die Auferstehung und Himmelfahrt Jesu' von Carl Philipp Emanuel Bach," *Bach-Jahrbuch* 83 (1997), S. 117–118.

33. Es wäre noch zu prüfen, ob Zinck auch als Kopist der Partitur in Frage kommt.

34. Zinck ist in den Quellen zur Einführungsmusik Klefeker von 1771 (H 821b; SA 714), zur Einführungsmusik Winkler von 1773 (H 821f; SA 713), zur Matthäus-Passion von 1773 (H 786; SA 50) und zur Lukas-Passion von 1775 (H 788; SA 5136) als Sänger genannt. Siehe Enßlin, S. 59f., 141f. und 478. Eine später ausgestrichene Zuweisung an Zinck findet sich auch in Bachs Stimmensatz zu Carl Heinrich Grauns Kantate "Herr, leite mich in deiner Wahrheit" (D-B, Mus. ms. 8290/1); vgl. Tobias Schwinger, "Die Kirchenkantaten der Brüder Graun in der Staatsbibliothek zu Berlin Preußischer Kulturbesitz" (unveröffentlichte Magisterarbeit, Technische Universität Berlin, 1997), S. 74.

35. Siehe Wiermann, S. 447f.; sowie Josef Sittard, *Geschichte des Musik- und Concertwesens in Hamburg vom 14. Jahrhundert bis auf die Gegenwart* (Altona und Leipzig: A.C. Reher, 1890), S. 124f.

36. Zu Zincks Biographie und Schaffensgeschichte siehe auch Barbara Wiermann, "Die 'Bachische Schule'—Überlegungen zu Carl Philipp Emanuel Bachs Hamburger Lehrtätigkeit," *C.P.E. Bach als Lehrer. Die Verbreitung der Musik C.P.E. Bachs in England und Skandinavien. Bericht über das Internationale Symposium vom 29. März bis 1. April 2001 in Słubice – Frankfurt (Oder) – Cottbus*, hrsg. von Hans-Günter Ottenberg und Ulrich Leisinger (Frankfurt/Oder: Musikgesellschaft C.P.E. Bach, 2005), S. 119–134, speziell S. 124–127.

C.P.E. Bach, G.P. Telemann und die Osterkantate Wq 244

Die Partiturabschrift der Osterkantate Wq 244 aus Zincks Besitz stimmt in bemerkenswerter Weise mit dem Hamburger Textheft von 1756 überein: Zwei der dort erwähnten Choralstrophen sind an denselben Stellen interpoliert (nach dem Eingangschor und nach der ersten Arie) und auch im Wortlaut identisch; der abschließende Choral fehlt zwar, musste von Zinck aber nicht eigens notiert werden, da der Satz—mit anderem Text—ja bereits nach der Bassarie erklingt. Bemerkenswert ist überdies der Befund, dass sämtliche sprachlichen Varianten des Hamburger Textdrucks—zu nennen sind hier in erster Linie die kleinen, aber bedeutsamen Abweichungen im B-Teil der ersten Arie —, auch in Zincks Partitur anzutreffen sind. Im Vergleich mit Bachs autographer Partitur P 345 erweisen sich diese Abweichungen durchweg als Lesarten ante correcturam. Da die Veränderungen am Text der Arie von C.P.E. Bach aber offenbar bereits für die Berliner Aufführung von 1757 vorgenommen wurden, sind die Lesarten von Zincks Partitur nicht etwa als nachträgliche Eingriffe—etwas als Angleichung an den Hamburger Textdruck—zu werten, sondern als Zeugen der frühesten, anderweitig nicht mehr geschlossen greifbaren Werkfassung. Da die Originalquellen in Bachs Besitz diese Lesartenschicht seit 1757 nicht mehr enthielten und überdies keine Hinweise auf die eingefügten Choralstrophen erkennen lassen, dürfte Zinck für seine Abschrift eine andere, unabhängig von Bach und vermutlich bereits vor dessen Ankunft in Hamburg kursierende Vorlage benutzt haben.

Der Verdacht, dass Zincks Abschrift tatsächlich die von Telemann zu Quasimodogeniti und Jubilate 1756 aufgeführte Kantate—und damit eine leicht bearbeitete Fassung von Wq 244—überliefert, liegt nahe. Er lässt sich durch eine Betrachtung der eingefügten Choräle noch weiter erhärten: Es handelt sich hierbei nachweislich um Sätze Telemanns. Die nach dem Eingangschor eingefügte zweite Strophe des Liedes "Jesus, meine Zuversicht" ist in nahezu identischer Form in zwei Kantaten des "Engel-Jahrgangs" von 1749 nachweisbar,[37] während die Bearbeitung des nach der ersten Arie (und dann vermutlich in identischem Satz wieder am Schluss der Kantate) erklingenden Liedes "Wenn mein Stündlein vorhanden ist" nahezu wörtlich in Telemanns Lukas-Passion von 1744 auftaucht.[38]

Die vorstehend geschilderten Befunde fügen sich widerspruchsfrei zu einem schlüssigen Bild zusammen: Bach sandte seine Vertonung der Dichtung von Leonhard Cochius (Wq 244, Satz 1–5) unmittelbar nach ihrer Vollendung an Telemann in Hamburg; dies geschah noch vor der ersten Berliner Aufführung und zu einem Zeitpunkt, als die autographe Partitur noch nicht die Textänderungen in der ersten Arie und den nachträglich hinzugefügten Schlusschoral "O süßer Herre Jesu Christ" (BWV 342) enthielt. Telemann fügte in die ihm zur Verfügung

---

37. Es handelt sich um die Kopfsätze der Kantaten "Dennoch bleib ich stets an dir" TVWV 1:225 und "Gottes Liebe gehet weit" TVWV 1:640.

38. Satz 45; vgl. Georg Philipp Telemann, *Lukaspassion 1744*, hrsg. von Felix Schroeder, Die Kantate X, 210 (Stuttgart: Hänssler, 1966), S. 150–151.

Er ist der Vater

gestellte Abschrift an drei Stellen eigene Choralsätze ein und führte das Werk sodann an den beiden Sonntagen nach Ostern in den Hamburger Hauptkirchen St. Katharinen und St. Maria Magdalenen jeweils als erste Musik auf. Das von ihm benutzte Aufführungsmaterial ist zwar nicht mehr nachweisbar, stand dem Sänger und Konzertveranstalter Hardenack Otto Conrad Zinck aber noch nach 1768 zur Verfügung. Es wäre daher denkbar, dass Zinck— beziehungsweise der Schreiber der Partitur—auf eine Quelle aus dem 1769 versteigerten musikalischen Nachlass Telemanns zurückgreifen konnte.[39] Dass Zinck im Rahmen seiner Konzertreihen in Hamburg oder aber später in Ludwigslust und Kopenhagen die Osterkantate in der Bearbeitung Telemanns erneut dargeboten hat, darf als sicher gelten; möglicherweise stehen mit diesen Darbietungen ein heute in Brüssel befindlicher undatierter Textdruck des Werks aus der Sammlung des Schweriner Organisten Johann Jakob Heinrich Westphal und eine in Olbernhau überlieferte Abschrift unbekannter Herkunft in Zusammenhang.[40] Diesen und anderen Fragen der Überlieferungsgeschichte von Wq 244 wird zu gegebener Zeit weiter nachzugehen sein.

Nach den quellenkritischen Untersuchungen sind nun noch die biographischen Hintergründe von Telemanns denkwürdiger Hamburger Aufführung der Osterkantate Wq 244 zu beleuchten. Carl Philipp Emanuel Bachs Brief an seinen Patenonkel Georg Philipp Telemann vom 29. Dezember 1756 ist zu entnehmen, dass zwischen den beiden Musikern ein herzlicher Kontakt bestand, der mit einem offenbar regelmäßigen Austausch von Musikalien verbunden war.[41] Ähnliche Verbindungen pflegte Telemann auch zu anderen Berliner Musikern—etwa zu Johann Friedrich Agricola und Carl Heinrich Graun. Dennoch stellte seine Darbietung der repräsentativen Festmusik eines jüngeren Komponisten im Rahmen der Hamburger Hauptkirchenmusik eine Auszeichnung und Ehre dar, die ohne Parallele gewesen zu sein scheint. Carl Philipp Emanuel Bachs Osterkantate "Gott hat den Herrn auferwecket" ist nicht ohne Grund mehr als einmal mit dem 1749 entstandenen *Magnificat* Wq 215 verglichen worden. Ihre weiträumige Anlage, die opulente Besetzung und die überaus sorgfältige musikalische Ausarbeitung ohne einen offensichtlichen besonderen Anlass suggerieren wie beim *Magnificat* Beweggründe, die auf einer anderen, außermusikalischen Ebene liegen. Der Gedanke an ein Bewerbungsstück oder—vorsichtiger ausgedrückt—an ein Werk zur Beförderung der eigenen beruflichen Perspektiven liegt nahe. Die nunmehr als gesichert anzunehmende Aufführung in Hamburg weist auf einen in Absprache mit dem greisen Telemann

---

39. Vgl. Max Schneider, "Einleitung" zu Georg Philipp Telemann, *Der Tag des Gerichts. Ino*, Denkmäler Deutscher Tonkunst, Bd. 28 (Leipzig: Breitkopf & Härtel, 1907), S. LIII–LIV.

40. Vgl. Leisinger/Wollny, S. 236; und D-OLB, Mus. arch. B. 1:1 (RISM A/II: 230.003.536).

41. Siehe Georg Philipp Telemann, *Briefwechsel. Sämtliche erreichbare Briefe von und an Telemann*, hrsg. von Hans Große und Hans Rudolf Jung (Leipzig: Deutscher Verlag für Musik, 1972), S. 372–373.

C.P.E. Bach, G.P. Telemann und die Osterkantate Wq 244

gefassten Plan, auf dessen Nachfolge Einfluss zu nehmen. Telemann hatte im März 1756 sein 75. Lebensjahr vollendet. Seine Gesundheit scheint in dieser Zeit nicht mehr dauerhaft stabil gewesen zu sein—immerhin hatte er seit Beginn des Kirchenjahres 1754/55 die Zahl seiner Kantatenaufführungen drastisch reduziert.[42] Somit ist der Gedanke nicht von der Hand zu weisen, dass Telemann—ähnlich wie Johann Sebastian Bach um 1749/50 in Leipzig[43]—den Versuch unternahm, die Regelung seiner Nachfolge nicht dem Zufall zu überlassen, sondern umsichtig und entschieden einen ihm geeignet erscheinenden Kandidaten ins Spiel zu bringen und die verantwortlichen Stellen durch die Aufführung eines repräsentativen Werkes von dessen Fähigkeiten zu überzeugen.

Ob C.P.E. Bach anlässlich dieser Aufführung in Hamburg zugegen war, um sich gegebenenfalls auch persönlich vorzustellen, ist nicht bekannt. Immerhin würde ein solcher Aufenthalt gut in das Bild seiner Reisen und auswärtigen Bewerbungen in jener Zeit passen. Bislang können folgende Reisen nachgewiesen werden, die vermutlich durchweg—offen oder verdeckt—mit einer Sondierung neuer beruflicher Perspektiven in Zusammenhang stehen:

1750: Leipzig (Bewerbung um das Thomaskantorat)[44]
1751: Braunschweig, Hamburg (Besuch bei Johann Mattheson)[45]
1753: Bewerbung um die Organistenstelle in Zittau[46]
1754: Rudolstadt, Eisenach, Gotha, Kassel[47]
1755: Leipzig (erneute Bewerbung um das Thomaskantorat)[48]

---

42. Siehe Menke, S. 284–285.

43. Siehe hierzu Christine Fröde, "Zu einer Kritik des Thomanerchores von 1749," *Bach-Jahrbuch* 70 (1984), S. 53–58; Hans-Joachim Schulze, "'Wer der alte Bach geweßen weiß ich wol.' Anmerkungen zum Thema Kunstwerk und Biographie," *Johann Sebastian Bachs Spätwerk und dessen Umfeld. Bericht über das wissenschaftliche Symposium anläßlich des 61. Bachfestes der Neuen Bach-Gesellschaft, Duisburg 28.–30. Mai 1986*, hrsg. von Christoph Wolff (Kassel: Bärenreiter, 1988), S. 23–31, speziell S. 31; sowie Peter Wollny, "Wilhelm Friedemann Bach's Halle Performances of Cantatas by His Father," *Bach Studies 2*, hrsg. von Daniel R. Melamed (Cambridge: Cambridge University Press, 1995), S. 202–228, speziell S. 213–215.

44. Vgl. Arnold Schering, *Johann Sebastian Bach und das Musikleben Leipzigs im 18. Jahrhundert* (Leipzig: Kistner & Siegel, 1941), S. 328; Ulrike Kollmar, *Gottlob Harrer (1703–1755). Kapellmeister des Grafen Heinrich von Brühl am sächsisch-polnischen Hof und Thomaskantor zu Leipzig* (Beeskow: ortus, 2006), S. 313 und 316.

45. Johann Mattheson, *Grundlage einer Ehrenpforte* (Hamburg, 1740; Neudruck, hrsg. von Max Schneider, Berlin: Liepmannssohn, 1910), Anhang, S. 28; siehe auch Miesner, S. VII; und *CPEB-Briefe*, 1:9–12.

46. Vgl. *CPEB-Briefe*, 1:13–39.

47. Vgl. Percy M. Young, *The Bachs 1500–1850* (London: Dent, 1970), S. 175; Claus Oefner, *Die Musikerfamilie Bach in Eisenach* (Eisenach: Bachhaus, 1996), S. 78–81; *CPEB-Briefe*, 1:40–41; sowie *Musik am Rudolstädter Hof. Die Entwicklung der Hofkapelle vom 17. Jahrhundert bis zum Beginn des 20. Jahrhunderts* (Rudolstadt: Thüringer Landesmuseum Heidecksburg, 1997), S. 209.

48. Vgl. Schering, S. 343; Kollmar, S. 339–340.

Er ist der Vater

Gern wüssten wir, wie die Aufführung der Osterkantate in Hamburg aufgenommen wurde; hierzu ließen sich jedoch bislang keine Dokumente ermitteln. Einen schlechten Eindruck dürfte das Werk indes kaum hinterlassen haben, denn C.P.E. Bachs im Herbst 1767 erfolgte Berufung scheint ohne jegliche Komplikationen und ohne seine (wiederholte?) persönliche Anwesenheit erfolgt zu sein. Damit wäre Telemanns Plan von 1756 doch noch aufgegangen; dass dies—bedingt durch sein langes Leben—erst mit solch großer zeitlicher Verzögerung geschehen würde, konnte seinerzeit niemand ahnen. Die Osterkantate "Gott hat den Herrn auferwecket" hat schließlich Bachs berufliche Laufbahn doch entscheidend befördert. Ihre auf den ersten Blick so isolierte Stellung trügt: In Wirklichkeit ist sie ein biographisches Schlüsselwerk.[49]

---

49. Unabhängig von den hier vorgetragenen Überlegungen hat Ralph-Jürgen Reipsch jüngst die Vermutung geäußert, dass der Hamburger Textdruck von 1756 etwas mit C.P.E. Bachs Osterkantate Wq 244 zu tun haben könnte und dass es sich bei dem Kantatenfragment in SA 567 möglicherweise um eine Komposition Agricolas handelt. Siehe *Telemann, der musikalische Maler. Telemann-Kompositionen im Notenarchiv der Sing-Akademie zu Berlin. Bericht über die Internationale Wissenschaftliche Konferenz, Magdeburg, 10. bis 12. März 2004, anlässlich der 17. Magdeburger Telemann-Festtage*, hrsg. von Carsten Lange und Brit Reipsch (Hildesheim: Olms, 2010), S. 275–363, speziell S. 284–285. Ich danke Herrn Reipsch für die Zusendung einer Kopie seines Aufsatzes.

[5]

C. P. E. BACH AS A PUBLISHER OF HIS OWN WORKS

Stephen L. Clark

The way C. P. E. Bach earned a living changed when he moved from Berlin to Hamburg in 1768. In Berlin, he worked for a royal patron, Frederick the Great, who controlled his salary and his schedule. In Hamburg, Bach was employed by the five main churches and the city, who likewise determined his income and responsibilities. And in Hamburg, Bach also took the opportunity to provide himself with a regular supplement to his salary by publishing his own music.

In this essay, I explore Bach's activity as a promoter of his own music during the last fifteen years of his life. My focus will be on the twelve publications listed in Table 1: one collection of songs (CRAMER); three choral works (ISRAELITEN, HEILIG, and MORGENGESANG); two collections of keyboard trios (SONATEN I and II); and the six „Kenner und Liebhaber" collections for solo keyboard.

TABLE 1

C. P. E. BACH'S PUBLICATION „IM VERLAGE DES AUTORS", PRINTED BY BREITKOPF

	dates of composition	date of first plans to publish	# of subscribers: # of copies	total # of copies printed
CRAMER (June, 1774)	1773–74	24 June 1773	326:433	1,050
ISRAELITEN (Sept., 1775)	1769	2 June 1773	no list of subscribers	350
SONATEN I (Aug., 1776)	1775	11 July 1775	362:596	1,050
SONATEN II (Sept., 1777)	1777	30 Dec. 1776	no list of subscribers	1,050
KENNER I (July, 1779)	1758, 1765, 1772–74	21 Feb. 1778	332:515	1,050
HEILIG (July, 1779)	1776	28 July 1778	167:267	555
KENNER II (Oct., 1780)	1774, 1778, 1780	10 Dec. 1779	223:337*	1,050
KENNER III (Oct., 1781)	1763, 1766, 1774, 1779–80	8 March 1781	156:297*	1,050
KENNER IV (Sept., 1783)	1765, 1779, 1781–82	17 Aug. 1782	225:432	1,050

200

	dates of composition	date of first plans to publish	# of subscribers: # of copies	total # of copies printed
MORGENGESANG (Sept., 1784)	1783	4 Nov. 1783	176:255	554
KENNER V (Oct., 1785)	1779, 1782 1784	23 Dec. 1784	181:305	1,050
KENNER VI (June, 1787)	1785–86	28 Feb. 1786	201:289*	1,050

(* „so weit die Nachrichten gehen")

CRAMER – *Herrn Doctor Cramers übersetzte Psalmen mit Melodien zum Singen bey dem Claviere.* Leipzig, Autor, 1774, W. 196/H. 733

ISRAELITEN – *Die Israeliten in der Wüste, ein Oratorium.* Hamburg, Autor, 1775, W. 238/H. 775

SONATEN I – *Claviersonaten mit einer Violine und einem Violoncell zur Begleitung, erste Sammlung.* Leipzig, Autor, 1776, W. 90/H. 522–524

SONATEN II – *Claviersonaten mit einer Violine und einem Violoncell zur Begleitung zweyte Sammlung.* Leipzig, Autor, 1777, W. 91/H. 531–534

KENNER I – *Sechs Clavier-Sonaten für Kenner und Liebhaber, erste Sammlung.* Leipzig, Autor, 1779, W. 55/H. 130, 186 ...

HEILIG – *Heilig, mit zwey Chören und einer Ariette zur Einleitung.* Hamburg, Autor, 1779, W. 217/H. 778

KENNER II – *Clavier-Sonaten nebst einigen Rondos fürs Forte-Piano für Kenner und Liebhaber, zweyte Sammlung.* Leipzig, Autor, 1780, W. 56/H. 246, 260 ...

KENNER III – *Clavier-Sonaten nebst einigen Rondos fürs Forte-Piano für Kenner und Liebhaber, dritte Sammlung.* Leipzig, Autor, 1781, W. 57/H. 173, 208 ...

KENNER IV – *Clavier-Sonaten und freye Fantasien nebst einigen Rondos fürs Forte-Piano für Kenner und Liebhaber, vierte Sammlung.* Leipzig, Autor, 1783, W. 58/H. 188, 267 ...

MORGENGESANG – *Klopstocks Morgengesang am Schöpfungsfeste.* Leipzig, Autor, 1784, W. 239/H. 779

KENNER V – *Clavier-Sonaten und freye Fantasien nebst einigen Rondos fürs Forte-Piano für Kenner und Liebhaber, fünfte Sammlung.* Leipzig, Autor, 1785, W. 59/H. 268, 279 ...

KENNER IV – *Clavier-Sonaten und freye Fantasien nebst einigen Rondos fürs Forte-Piano für Kenner und Liebhaber, sechste Sammlung.* Leipzig, Autor, 1787, W. 61/H. 286–291

These are the editions published by Bach himself in Hamburg and printed by Johann Gottlob Immanuel Breitkopf in Leipzig. There were, of course, many other prints authorized by Bach during his lifetime, including several well-known ones from his tenure in Berlin such as the Prussian, Württemberg und reprise sonatas. But it was not until he moved to Hamburg that Bach began the regular practice of issuing his music „im Verlage des Autors", that is assuming the financial risk and enjoying all the profits himself. The *Versuch* is the only publication from Berlin in this category.

There was one other print issued „im Verlage des Autors" while Bach was in Hamburg that does not appear in the Table, a collection of six keyboard concertos published in 1772.[1] Bach's regular printer from his Berlin years, Georg Ludewig Winter, started producing the concertos, but Winter died before finishing the job, causing Bach several

---

[1] *Sei Concerti per il Cembalo concertato accompagnato [...], in Hamburgo, alle spese dell' Autore* (H. 471–76; W. 43).

problems, including a dispute with Winter's widow over rights to the concertos. The establishment of a regular working relationship with the reliable Breitkopf firm was undoubtedly a factor in Bach's decision to return to the active publication of his own works, after the difficult experience of the concertos.

Fortunately, a large number of documents relating to Bach's activity as a publisher of his own music in Hamburg has survived. The most important of these is the extensive collection of Bach's letters to his printer Breitkopf, most of which are now accessible in the edition by Ernst Suchalla.[2] This edition and Suchalla's recent publication of Johann Heinrich Jacob Westphal's *Gesammlete Nachrichten*[3] bring together many of the announcements and reviews of the music that add to the story. Surviving copies of the prints themselves are informative, particularly those with lists of subscribers.

As Table 1 shows, some of the music Bach published was composed close to the date of release and was clearly intended for publication from the start. In other instances, Bach drew from what Pamela Fox has referred to as his „stockpile" of works.[4] The stockpile was so well organized that in 1775 Bach could identify exactly 173 works he had written for solo keyboard, 99 of which had been published.[5] The first, third, and fourth „Kenner und Liebhaber" collections contain pieces composed some 20 years earlier. Bach did not simply publish the latest thing from his pen, he made calculated decisions about what to print based on what he thought would sell well.

Once Bach had decided what music he wanted to publish, he informed Breitkopf of his plans and asked for suggestions about how

---

[2]*Briefe von Carl Philipp Emanuel Bach an Johann Gottlob Immanuel Breitkopf und Johann Nikolaus Forkel* ed. Ernst Suchalla (Tutzing, 1985); see Stephen L. Clark, review of Suchalla, *Briefe*, in *Bach-Jahrbuch* 75 (1989), pp. 240–50; see also *Carl Philipp Emanuel Bach. Briefe und Dokumente. Kritische Gesamtausgabe,* ed. Ernst Suchalla (Göttingen, 1994) (= *Veröffentlichungen der Joachim Jungius-Gesellschaft der Wissenschaften*; 80) (quoted as *Briefe-Gesamtausgabe*).

[3]Ernst Suchalla, ed., *Carl Philipp Emanuel Bach im Spiegel seiner Zeit. Die Dokumentensammlung Johann Jacob Heinrichs Westphals* (Hildesheim, 1993).

[4]Pamela Fox, 'C. P. E. Bach's Compositional Proofreading,' *Musical Times* 129 (1988), p. 653.

[5]Letter to Forkel dated 10 February 1775, *Briefe-Gesamtausgabe*, vol. 1, p 485.

many copies to print, what paper and typeface to use, and what price to charge. Bach's first two projects of this type in Hamburg were his settings of psalms by Johann Andreas Cramer and the oratorio *Die Is-raeliten in der Wüste*. Bach broached the subject of the psalms and the oratorio in letters to Breitkopf written in June of 1773 (the dates of these letters are noted in the second column of Table 1).

A friend of Bach's, the famous Hamburg poet and author Friedrich Gottlieb Klopstock, was launching a publication project of his own at exactly this time. It ist worth examining Klopstock's procedure, since he seems to have given Bach some ideas about publishing his music. In fact, in the case of his oratorio, Bach specifically followed Klopstock's own marketing plan.

The book Klopstock had decided to publish, *Die deutsche Gelehr-tenrepublik*, is a depiction of an ideal society of poets and philosophers. Klopstock announced his intentions to publish the book in notices he placed in the *Hamburgischer Correspondent* in June and July of 1773.[6] In order to be free of the usual book-publishing bureaucracy and to bring himself the most profit, Klopstock set up an elaborate marketing system using agents (he called them „Corresponden-ten") to collect subscriptions to *Gelehrtenrepublik*. He described the system in the notices and also carefully spelled out the rights and responsibilities of subscriber, agent, and author. For example, the author had to cover packing and mailing costs, and an agent received a slightly higher commission if he lived in a particularly remote area.

Klopstock's experiment was wildly successful. He collected subscriptions for 6,656 copies from 3,609 people in 253 different cities. The list of subscribers was printed at the front of the book and fills 71 pages.

Bach was one of 133 subscribers from Hamburg. Klopstock announced his intention to publish a second volume of his *Gelehrten-republik* in the first volume itself, but the novelty of his experiment had worn off. Not enough subscribers were generated and the second volume never even appeared, quickly closing a small chapter in the history of German book publishing.

[6]*Hamburgischer Correspondent*, 11 June and 30 July 1773.

204

In his original description of the marketing plan, Klopstock offers access to his pool of agents to any interested author. All one needed to do was announce publication plans and the system would be activated. Bach took Klopstock up on his offer. The 71-page list of subscribers to *Gelehrtenrepublik* must have attracted Bach's interest. The announcement of publication plans for the oratorio *Die Israeliten in der Wüste* reads in part as follows:[7] „Wegen der Unkosten wähle ich diesmal den sichern Weg der Subscription. Sämtliche Herren Correspondenten bey des Herrn Klopstocks Deutscher Gelehrten-Republik, von denen ich mir dieselbe Gütigkeit aus Liebe zur Tonkunst erbitte und verspreche, werden von jetzt an, bis 10ten Januar 1775, nach des Herrn Klopstocks Plan und Zureden, Subscription annehmen. Alles, was Herr Klopstock diesen Herren geleistet hat, erfülle ich auch, und hoffe dasselbe auch von ihnen."

Bach also describes his intentions in letters to Breitkopf, Forkel, and Heinrich Wilhelm von Gerstenberg.[8] He writes to Gerstenberg:[9] „Jezt trete ich schon wieder mit beykommendem Avertißemente, aufs Theater. Einige meiner Freunde, besonders unser H. Klopstock sind Ursache. Ich muß seinem Plan genau folgen und bitte also Ew. Hochwohlgeb. ergebenst, meine Absicht gelegentlich bekannt zu machen und der Frau Andersen, der Correspondentin des Herrn Klopstocks, ein Paar hundert Subscribenten zuzuweisen."

Israeliten did not, of course, enjoy the same level of commercial success as *Gelehrtenrepublik*, but Bach used Klopstock's basic system for the remainder of his own publication projects. After the Cramer psalms and *Israeliten*, he produced ten additional publications at his own risk and for his own profit, following the plan of advertising his intentions and collecting subscriptions through agents.

Lists of subscribers are included in all but two of Bach's twelve editions. These lists provide a record of who Bach's patrons were,

---

[7]*Hamburgischer Correspondent*, 14 September 1774; reprinted in Hans-Günter Ottenberg, *Carl Philipp Emanuel Bach* (Leipzig, 1982), p. 167; (Oxford, 1987), p. 123.

[8]See Klaus Hortschansky, 'Pränumerations- und Subskriptionslisten in Notendrucken deutscher Musiker des 18. Jahrhunderts,' *Acta musicologica* 40 (1968), p. 157.

[9]Letter to Gerstenberg dated 15 September 1774; see Rudolf Angermüller, 'Carl Philipp Emanuel Bachiana,' *Jahrbuch des Staatlichen Institutes für Musikforschung Preussischer Kulturbesitz* (1985/86), p. 50; see also *Briefe-Gesamtausgabe*, vol. 1, pp. 444–1.

besides church and state, during the last fifteen years of his life. In fact, Bach refers to subscribers as „Gönner" in his letters and advertisements.[10]

Some of the subscription lists are incomplete. Bach was constantly reminding his agents to get the names of their subscribers to him on time and the agents often did not come through before the publication date. The three „Kenner und Liebhaber" collections marked with an asterisk in the third column of Table 1 have printed notices indicating that the lists are incomplete, apparently to make clear to the public that there was more interest in the edition than the printed list implied. Bach wrote to Breitkopf[11] that he could always count on about 40 additional subscribers at the last minute, which suggests that none of the lists are truly accurate. He often requested copies of a print for individuals who finally came forward long after the deadline for subscriptions had passed.

Bach's concern with the completeness of the subscription lists shows that the number of names printed was important to him. In fact, he may have omitted subscription lists from *Israeliten* and the second collection of keyboard trios to avoid embarassment because the number of subscribers was small. A large list was a testament to the popularity of a publication and enhanced the reputation of Bach's music in the marketplace.

The prestige of those listed was likewise an indication of a publication's importance. Bach would even include the name of someone who had not actually paid for a subscription to enhance the list of subscribers. For example, he wrote to Gerstenberg that he would not accept money from him for a subscription to the Cramer psalms, but that he would list his name among the subscribers.[12] A few subscribers did not consider it an honor to be listed and specifically requested

---

[10]For example, see the letter to Breitkopf dated 18 June 1776; *Briefe-Gesamtausgabe*, vol. 1, p. 578.

[11]Letter dated 26 August 1785; *Briefe-Gesamtausgabe*, vol. 2, p. 1092.

[12]Letter dated 21 April 1774: „Dem ohngeacht werden, zu meiner Ehre und zur besten Empfehlung meiner Psalmen, alle die erhabenen und würdigen Nahmen meiner Gönner und Freunde mit beÿgedruckt." Angermüller, 'Carl Philipp Emanuel Bachiana,' p. 45; see also *Briefe-Gesamtausgabe*, vol. 1, pp. 395–6.

anonymity.[13] The subscription lists also indicate how many copies of a print each subscriber ordered. Dealers often requested a dozen or more to have on hand for later sales. Since the price went up after publication, and Bach included a free copy with larger orders, there was a potential advantage to purchasing multiple copies initially.

While there was a small group of regular subscribers, in general Bach had to work hard to generate new ones for each publication. For example, approximately 850 different names appear on the subscription lists for the six „Kenner und Liebhaber" collections. Over 750 of these names appear on only one or two lists. A mere fourteen names show up on every list: the regular patrons such as Duschek in Prague, van Swieten in Vienna, and Bach's circle of friends in Berlin and Hamburg, including his regular reviewer Joachim Friedrich Leister. In fact, Leister's name is the only one to appear on all surviving subscription lists and he probably never paid for a copy. The large turnover of subscribers indicates that Bach did indeed take some risk when he decided to issue a print. He implies as much in reference to the first collection of keyboard trios, which was heavily supported by subscribers unknown to Bach, prompting him to attribute his success more to luck than to hard-earned solicitations through his agents: „Meine starke Praenumeration rührt nicht von meinen bekannten Freunden hier, diese haben mir noch nicht 100 verschaft. Das meiste thun unbekannte Gönner [...] Ich habe freÿlich mehr Glück als Recht."[14]

Even though the turnover of subscribers was high, the geographical base did not change much between 1773 and 1787. In another frequently cited letter, this one addressed to the Leipzig publisher Engelbert Benjamin Schwickert in 1780, Bach identifies northern regions as the main market for his music, „nehml[ich] Rußland, Liefland, Curland, Schweden, Dänemark, Holstein, Hannover, Mecklenburg u. Lauenburg u. Lübeck".[15] A few copies usually went West to London and South to Vienna as well. After the first collection of keyboard trios, the subscription lists are organized geographically rather than alphabetically,

---

[13]See letter to Breitkopf dated 24 February 1775; *Briefe-Gesamtausgabe*, vol. 1, pp. 488–91.

[14]Letter to Breitkopf dated 18 June 1776; *Briefe-Gesamtausgabe*, vol. 1, pp. 578–9.

[15]Letter dated 10 April 1780; Angermüller, 'Carl Philipp Emanuel Bachiana,' p. 77; see also *Briefe-Gesamtausgabe*, vol. 1. p. 830.

perhaps reflecting the importance of regions rather than individuals in the approach to marketing.

The occupations of some subscribers are noted in the lists, revealing that many of Bach's patrons were from the upper strata of society. Royal patrons were among the steadiest supporters; „Herzog" and „Graf" and „Fürst" are frequently named titles. Musicians of all varieties are listed: Kammercomponist, Kammermusikus, Kantor, Hofkantor, Hofmusikus, Stadtmusikus, Kapellmeister, Concertmeister, Sangmeister, Musikdirector, Organist, and the most common title, simply „Musikus". Judging from the subscription lists, some 20 % of Bach's patrons were women. While individuals and dealers predominate, the Göttingen Universitätsbibliothek did order a copy of Morgengesang for its shelves, and a choir in Lübeck added the Cramer psalms to its collection.

Bach always had Breitkopf print many more copies of an edition than were necessary to satisfy subscribers, as the two last columns in Table 1 show.

Because of Breitkopf's method of printing, Bach was simply paying for the cost of the extra paper. The total run for a print was 1,050, except for the three choral works, *Israeliten, Heilig*, and *Morgengesang*. It is worth noting that in September of 1778 Bach told Breitkopf to print only 650 copies of the first „Kenner und Liebhaber" collection. He was probably nervous because of the weak sales of the second collection of keyboard trios, published in 1777. He also expressed concern to Breitkopf about the difficulty of the „Kenner und Liebhaber" sonatas. Two months later, he increased the order to 1,050 and was glad of it since the sonatas sold, in his words, „wie warme Semlen".[16] The run of 554 for *Morgengesang* was a reduction from an initial order for 1,050, a reluctant admission that there was simply not much of a market for choral works.

In an important unpublished letter to Schwickert from 1783, Bach describes his normal expectations for sales of unsubscribed copies of a print: „Meine gedruckte Sammlungen begreifen alle eine Auflage von 1050 Exemplaren [...] Ordentlich sind ohngefahr in 4 Jahren alle Exemplare fort bis auf etwas weniges über 100. Welcher ansehnliche Pro-

---

[16]Letter to Breitkopf dated 2 November 1779; *Briefe-Gesamtausgabe*, vol. 1, p. 786.

fit!"[17] Bach's scenario was just the ideal one, however. We know there were still over 3,000 copies of the six „Kenner und Liebhaber" collections left in 1788 because he embarassingly offered them to Breitkopf at a greatly reduced price.[18] In 1787 Bach wrote to Breitkopf that he still had copies of *Israeliten* and *Heilig* in stock, although he hoped that the choral works would sell again eventually.[19]

So just how much money did C. P. E. Bach earn from sales of his own publications? The records are incomplete for most of the prints, but the figures for the third „Kenner und Liebhaber" collection can serve as an example. There were probably orders for close to 400 copies at the subscription price of 1 Reichstaler, 16 Groschen. If another 500 were sold at the post-subscription price of 2 Reichstaler, following the ideal scenario, Bach's gross income from the collection was 1,700 Reichstaler. Even if only half the total run was sold, the receipts were well over 1,000 Reichstaler.

Breitkopf apparently charged Bach 190 Reichstaler to print the 1,050 copies.[20] Bach also had to absorb packing and mailing costs himself, although he was an expert at keeping these at a minimum by finding couriers who would deliver a few copies for free. Based on this data, it is not unrealistic to estimate that Bach may have earned over 1,000 Reichstaler from the third „Kenner und Liebhaber" collection.

In a letter to Alexander Reinagle from the end of 1785 Bach wrote: „Ich kann Ihnen versichern, daß 1 Theil von meinen Samlungen [...] nach Abzug aller Kosten, mir wenigstens 1000 Mark hiesiges Geld bisher eingebracht haben, ohne einige 100 Exemplaren zu rechnen, die ich noch vorräthig habe u. welche nach und nach auch verkauft werden."[21] This figure of 1,000 Marks implies less profit than my above estimate since the exchange rate was 1 Reichstaler for 3 Marks. Nonetheless, it was a considerable sum. Bach's annual income from his

[17]Letter (private collection) dated 18 February 1783; *Briefe-Gesamtausgabe*, vol. 2, p. 955.
[18]Letter dated 3 May 1788; *Briefe-Gesamtausgabe*, vol. 2, p. 1264.
[19]Letter dated 21 September 1787; *Briefe-Gesamtausgabe*, vol. 2, 1228.
[20]Letter to Breitkopf dated 21 November 1781; *Briefe-Gesamtausgabe*, vol. 2, p. 907.
[21]Angermüller, 'Carl Philipp Emanuel Bachiana,' p. 118; see also *Briefe-Gesamtausgabe*, vol. 2, p. 1131.

church and state responsibilities was 2,550 Marks, or 850 Reichstaler, according to an account prepared by his daughter just after his death.[22] It is clear, then, that sales of his music provided a significant supplement to his income. As he reflected on his career in one of the last letters to Breitkopf he wrote: „Ich bin nicht arm. [...] Ich habe ansehnlich mit meinen Sonaten gewonnen."[23]

A number of well-known editions of Bach's music, authorized by the composer and dating from the 1770s and 1780s, are missing from the Table, notably the four orchestral symphonies published by Schwikkert in 1780, two collections of songs set to texts by Christoph Christian Sturm and published by Herold in 1780 and 1781, and the oratorio *Auferstehung und Himmelfahrt Jesu*. In the case of these editions, someone besides Bach served as publisher and took the financial risk as well as the lion's share of the profits. Bach received an honorarium and some free copies. His decision not to serve as publisher of an edition himself seems to have rested primarily on questions of timing. As the handout shows, Bach's own publications were fairly evenly spaced between 1774 and 1787. He explained to Breitkopf that he would not publish the *Orchester-Sinfonien* himself because „[...] ich will nicht alle Augenblicke Contribution ausschreiben".[24]

While these other editions were authorized by Bach, he did not want them to compete with his own publications. He was particularly concerned that the release of the first set of Sturm songs might hurt sales of the second „Kenner und Liebhaber" collection, which was issued around the same time. Since there were large subscription lists attached to the two Sturm collections, Bach seems to have misjudged the market and passed up a profitable opportunity, although it could simply be that one job of advertising, proofing, packing, mailing, and collecting per year was all he could take on. Breitkopf's 1784 reprint of Bach's songs to texts by Gellert also had a large subscription list attached. Given the obvious demand for Bach's songs, it is curious that the collection of Cramer psalms was the only set of songs issued „im Verlage des Autors."

---

[22]Heinrich Miesner, *Philipp Emanuel Bach in Hamburg* (Wiesbaden, 1929), p. 16.
[23]Letter to Breitkopf dated 3 May 1788; *Briefe-Gesamtausgabe*, vol. 2, p. 1263.
[24]Letter to Breitkopf dated 30 November 1778; *Briefe-Gesamtausgabe*, vol. 2, p. 712.

In the case of Bach's favorite choral work, *Auferstehung und Himmel-fahrt Jesu*, Bach persuaded Breitkopf himself to publish the edition in 1787. This arrangement was part of Bach's careful planning of his estate and legacy in the last two years of his life. The publication of *Auferste-hung* was unfinished business. Bach was frustrated by his inability to generate subscribers, which had resulted in aborted attempts to publish the oratorio in 1781 and 1784.[25]

Why Breitkopf ultimately agreed to assume the risk remains a mystery. Perhaps he felt an obligation to help Bach get his affairs in order. In any event, Breitkopf clearly lost money on the project. *Auferstehung* was a very large work and there was simply not much of a market for a German oratorio at the end of the 18th century. To his credit, Bach worked hard to find subscribers for Breitkopf. But his true reason for wanting to see the work in print can be interpreted from his explanation for the slow sales:[26] „Diese Ramlersche Cantate ist zwar von mir, doch kann ich ohne närrische Eigenliebe behaupten, daß sie sich viele Jahre erhalten wird, weil sie von meinen Meisterstücken ein beträchtliches mit ist, woraus junge Componisten etwas lernen können. Mit der Zeit wird sie auch so vergriffen werden, wie Grauns Tod Jesu. Anfänglich hapert's mit allen solchen Sachen, die zur Lehre u. nicht für Damen u. musikalische Wind-beutel geschrieben sind."

To return to 1773 and the beginning of Bach's regular collaboration with Breitkopf, I would argue that Klopstock's *Gelehrtenrepublik* pro-ject, and what it represented, provided much of the motivation for Bach to launch his career as a publisher of his own music. The coincidence of Bach's letters to Breitkopf from June of 1773 with Klopstock's announcement of *Gelehrtenrepublik* is too much to ignore. Klopstock took advantage of the exponential growth of journals and newspapers in the third quarter of the 18th century to advertise his project and, in effect, to promote his agenda, namely improved social and economic status for the artist. It is not surprising that Bach followed suit with his own publication projects in Hamburg, a city famous for its entre-preneurial spirit.

---

[25]See Stephen L. Clark, 'The Letters from C. P. E. Bach to K. W. Ramler,' *C. P. E. Bach Studies* (Oxford, 1988), pp. 33–42.
[26]Letter to Breitkopf dated 21 September 1787; *Briefe-Gesamtausgabe*, vol. 2, p. 1228.

[6]

Carl Philipp Emanuel Bachs Umarbeitungen seiner Claviersonaten

Von Darrell M. Berg (St. Louis, Missouri)

Zu verschiedenen Zeiten seines Lebens und aus verschiedenen Gründen sah sich Carl Philipp Emanuel Bach veranlaßt, seine Claviersonaten umzuarbeiten und ihnen neue Fassungen zu geben. Im Vordergrund mag dabei das Interesse gestanden haben, den sich ändernden Ansprüchen einer wachsenden Anhängerschaft von Clavierspielern gerecht zu werden, doch war Bach gewiß auch darauf bedacht, seine eigenen wechselnden Qualitätsvorstellungen zu realisieren. Eine Untersuchung dieser Sonaten-Umarbeitungen gewährt darum einen Einblick in seine stilistische Entwicklung und erlaubt Rückschlüsse auf gewisse Aspekte seiner kompositorischen Arbeitsweise.

Die früheste Nachricht über die Umarbeitungen von Bachs Sonaten bietet das 1790 von seiner Witwe veröffentlichte Nachlaß-Verzeichnis,[1] dessen Informationen offensichtlich auf einem vom Komponisten selbst angelegten Werkverzeichnis beruhen.[2] Das Nachlaß-Verzeichnis zählt die Instrumentalkompositionen innerhalb der Werkkategorien in chronologischer Folge auf, nennt für die meisten Stücke das Entstehungsjahr und für einige auch das Jahr der Umarbeitung.

Genau entsprechende Angaben finden sich in einem Katalog, den sich um 1810 der Schweriner Organist Johann Jacob Heinrich Westphal von seiner Sammlung Emanuel Bachscher Werke anlegte.[3] Westphal ergänzte die Informationen des Nachlaß-Verzeichnisses um Publikationsanzeigen und zitierte bis 1809 erschienene Kritiken von Bachs Werken, stimmt jedoch im übrigen weitgehend mit diesem überein. Offensichtlich beruhen die Daten in Westphals Katalog ebenfalls auf Angaben Bachs, da dieser in den 1780er Jahren mit dem Schweriner Organisten korrespondierte.[4] Bei der Ergänzung seiner Sammlung nach Emanuels Tod fand Westphal dann die Unterstützung der Witwe, Johanna Maria, und der Tochter, Anna Carolina Philippina Bach.[5]

Die Angaben über Bachs Umarbeitungen seiner Claviersonaten im Nachlaß-Verzeichnis und im Westphal-Katalog fanden bislang ebensowenig Beachtung

---

[1] NV (siehe Abkürzungen und Sigel).

[2] Vgl. D. M. Berg, *Towards a Catalogue of the Keyboard Sonatas of C. P. E. Bach*, JAMS 32, 1979, S. 280–285.

[3] Abteilung „*Claviersachen*" in „*Catalogue thematique des oeuvres de Charles Philippe Emmanuel Bach* " (Brüssel, Bibliothèque Royale Albert 1er: *Ms.* II 4140). Zu zwei früheren Katalogen Westphals in der Handschrift „*Gesammelte Nachrichten*" (B-Br: II 4133) vgl. R. W. Wade, *The Keyboard Concertos of Carl Philipp Emanuel Bach*, Ann Arbor 1981, S. 9–12.

[4] Vgl. M. Terry, *C. P. E. Bach and J. J. H. Westphal – A Clarification*, JAMS 22, 1969, S. 106–115; E. R. Jacobi, *Five Hitherto Unknown Letters from C. P. E. Bach to J. J. H. Westphal*, JAMS 23, 1970, S. 119–127; ders., *Three Additional Letters from C. P. E. Bach to J. J. H. Westphal*, JAMS 27, 1974, S. 119–125.

[5] Ich danke Frau Lotte Schmid (Augsburg) für die Gewährung der Einsichtnahme in die unveröffentlichten Briefe J. M. und A. C. P. Bachs an Westphal aus ihrer wertvollen Sammlung und für die Erlaubnis zur Veröffentlichung von Briefauszügen.

wie die musikalischen Quellen, in denen sich die verschiedenen Fassungen dokumentiert finden.[6] Eine vollständige Liste der betreffenden Quellen läßt sich aufgrund der beiden Verzeichnisse allerdings nicht erstellen, da diese sich jeweils nur auf den Komplex einer einzigen Sammlung beschränken. Doch bietet Erich Beurmanns Dissertation über „Die Klaviersonaten Philipp Emanuel Bachs" (Göttingen 1952) eine Übersicht aller Sonaten (einschließlich der verschiedenen Fassungen) unter Angabe sämtlicher Quellen. Beurmanns Nachweise konnten inzwischen ergänzt werden durch Informationen in Eugene Helms „A New Thematic Catalog of the Works of Carl Philipp Emanuel Bach" (New Haven/London 1987).

Im Zusammenhang mit den Arbeiten an der Carl-Philipp-Emanuel-Bach-Gesamtausgabe erscheint es nunmehr an der Zeit, einen Vergleich der verschiedenen Sonatenfassungen mit den Angaben der beiden frühen Verzeichnisse durchzuführen. Diese unterscheiden zwischen drei Arten von Umarbeitungen:

1. Erneuerung – die sechzehn zwischen 1731 und 1738 in Leipzig und Frankfurt (Oder) entstandenen Sonaten (einschließlich der Suite Wq 65/4) werden angeführt als in den Jahren 1743 beziehungsweise 1744 „erneuert" (in Ergänzung der Angaben des Nachlaß-Verzeichnisses und des Westphal-Katalogs sind wahrscheinlich mindestens zwei, vielleicht sogar vier der frühen Berliner Sonaten ebenfalls als „erneuert" anzusehen).[7]

2. Veränderung – zwei spätere Sonaten, Wq 65/32 (1758) und Wq 51/1 (1760), werden beschrieben als „nachher verändert".[8]

3. Veränderung und Auszierung – am Schluß der Instrumentalwerke des Nachlaß-Verzeichnisses findet sich die Erwähnung einer für Schüler gedachten Sammlung von „Veränderungen und Auszierungen" zu gedruckten Sonaten.[9]

Der Unterschied zwischen der zweiten und dritten Art von Umarbeitung ist eher gradueller als prinzipieller Natur. In beiden Fällen handelt es sich um die Auszierung von Melodie und Satzgefüge ohne Veränderung von Periodik oder harmonischer Fortschreitung. Die hierhin gehörigen Sonatenfassungen werden denn auch im Nachlaß-Verzeichnis nicht als Ersatzfassungen geführt und haben als aufführungspraktische Einrichtung der Originalfassungen zu gelten. Die vorliegende Studie läßt diese weitgehend unberücksichtigt[10] und konzentriert sich auf die Umarbeitungsfragen der „erneuerten" Sonaten. Eine den jüngsten Forschungsstand berücksichtigende Übersicht sämtlicher Umarbeitungen bietet Tabelle I (S. 151ff.).

Ein wichtiger Unterschied zwischen Bachs „Erneuerungen" und den übrigen

---

[6] Einige Untersuchungen zu Bachschen Werken anderer Gattungen bieten eine entsprechende Quellenübersicht: E. F. Schmid, *Carl Philipp Emanuel Bach und seine Kammermusik*, Kassel 1931; E. Suchalla, *Die Orchestersinfonien Carl Philipp Emanuel Bachs*, Augsburg 1968; R. Wade, a. a. O.

[7] NV, S. 1–4.

[8] NV, S. 14 und 16.

[9] NV, S. 53.

[10] Vgl. D. M. Berg, *C. P. E. Bach's „Variations" and „Embellishments" for his Keyboard Sonatas*, in: The Journal of Musicology 2, 1983, S. 151–173.

Umarbeitungen besteht anscheinend darin, daß die erneuerten Fassungen die früheren ersetzen sollen. Ein Brief an Johann Joachim Eschenburg vom 21. Januar 1786, in dem Bach vom Verbrennen seiner frühen Werke spricht,[11] bestätigt diese Annahme. Es ist zudem wahrscheinlich, daß die Frühfassungen der Claviersonaten, die im Nachlaß-Verzeichnis als „erneuert" angeführt sind, sich unter den von Bach vernichteten Werken befanden. So überrascht es nicht, wenn für fünf frühe Sonaten (Wq 62/1, 65/2, 64/2, 64/3 und 65/5) nur die späteren Fassungen erhalten sind. Andererseits ist ebensowenig überraschend, daß für die übrigen elf der sechzehn frühen „erneuerten" Sonaten (Wq 65/1 und 3, 64/1 und 4–6, 65/6–10) sowie für vier frühe Berliner Sonaten (Wq 62/2, 65/11, 62/3, 65/12 – nicht als „erneuert" angegeben; vgl. Tabelle I) sämtliche Fassungen überliefert sind. Denn 1786 lag es offensichtlich nicht mehr im Bereich von Bachs Möglichkeiten, die Quellen der Frühfassungen aller dieser Werke zu unterdrücken. Vielleicht diente die Angabe „erneuert" im Nachlaß-Verzeichnis nicht zuletzt dazu, den Besitzern älterer Fassungen bekanntzugeben, daß verbesserte Fassungen verfügbar waren.

I. ZUR CHRONOLOGIE DER FASSUNGEN

Eine kursorische Durchsicht der frühen Sonaten läßt erkennen, daß die am reichhaltigsten ausgearbeiteten Fassungen die spätesten darstellen, die schlichtesten hingegen die frühesten – eine Beobachtung, die sich auch bibliographisch erhärten läßt. Die ausgearbeiteten Fassungen finden sich in Quellen, von denen mit Gewißheit angenommen werden muß, daß sie Bachs spätere Umarbeitungen enthalten: 1. zwei Brüsseler Handschriften (B-Bc: *5881* und *5883*), die von Westphal in den späten 1780er Jahren unter Bachs Anleitung angelegt und dann auf Anregung von Bachs Witwe und Tochter ergänzt wurden; 2. zwei gedruckte Clavier-Sammlungen, die jeweils eine umgearbeitete frühe Sonate Bachs enthalten: *Nebenstunden der Berlinischen Musen in kleinen Clavierstücken*, I (Berlin 1762), und *Clavierstücke mit einem practischen Unterricht*, III (Berlin 1763).

Bei Sonaten, die in nur zwei Fassungen überliefert sind, läßt sich leicht feststellen, daß die von der Spätfassung abweichenden Fassungen die früheren sind. Aber auch hier findet sich eine bibliographische Stütze in dem Sachverhalt, daß viele frühere Fassungen von Kopisten geschrieben sind, deren Aktivitäten mit Emanuel Bachs Frühzeit verbunden sind. Einige dieser Fassungen finden sich in größeren Handschriften-Komplexen mit Frühwerken und Frühfassungen.

Am Beispiel von Wq 65/9–10 läßt sich zeigen, welche unterschiedlichen Gesichtspunkte für eine Chronologie der drei verschiedenen Fassungen zu berücksichtigen sind:

---

[11] Zitiert bei E. F. Schmid, a. a. O., S. 76–77.

126   Darrell M. Berg

Beispiel 1: Incipits der drei Fassungen von Wq 65/9 (zu den Quellen vgl. Tabelle 1)

C. P. E. Bachs Umarbeitungen seiner Claviersonaten   127

Beispiel 2: Incipits der drei Fassungen von Wq 65/10 (zu den Quellen vgl. Tabelle I)

Jeder Quellengruppe der einzelnen Fassungen von Wq 65/9 steht bei Wq 65/10 eine eng korrespondierende Quellengruppe gegenüber: (a) die Abschriften von Müthel und Homilius sowie die Sammelhandschriften in der Bibliothek der Gesellschaft der Musikfreunde und der Library of Congress; (b) der nicht-autorisierte Huberty-Druck und P 673 (wohl Abschrift dieses Druckes); (c) Abschriften aus Westphals Sammlung von zu Bachs Lebzeiten ungedruckten Sonaten (B-Bc: 5883, vermutlich in den 1780er Jahren begonnen), eine Hand-schrift aus der Sammlung des Hamburger Musikalienhändlers Johann Christoph Westphal (P 369) und zwei Quellen mit eigenhändigen Korrekturen Emanuel Bachs (P 775 und P 772).

Es besteht kein Zweifel daran, daß die Quellengruppe c Bachs späteste und bevorzugte Sonatenfassungen enthält. Stilistisch deuten die reichhaltig aus-gearbeiteten Melodien und die subtil ausgefeilte Satzanlage auf die Endfassung. Die zeitliche Folge der andern beiden Fassungen erscheint zumindest bei Wq 65/10 einigermaßen klar. Der Huberty-Druck der Gruppe b enthält eine verzierte Fassung des Andante-Satzes, der sich auch in den Quellen der Gruppe a findet. Unabhängig von der Frage, ob Bach als Autor der Verzierungen in Frage kommt, gebührt der unverzierten Fassung die Priorität. Bei Wq 65/9 hielt Beurmann das Larghetto aus dem Huberty-Druck für den frühesten Mittelsatz, der durch ein Adagio ersetzt wurde, das dann für die Endfassung Verzierungen erhielt. Der Vergleich mit Wq 65/10 legt jedoch die Annahme nahe, daß der unverzierte Adagio-Satz als der ursprüngliche anzusehen ist. Darüber hinaus ergibt sich die Abfolge der Quellengruppen a–b–c aus dem Vorhandensein kleinerer Verbesserungen im ersten Satz in den Gruppen b und c (sie fehlen in a).

II. AUSGEZIERTE FASSUNGEN

Welche Arten der Umarbeitung begegnen in den Sonaten der 1730er Jahre? Die vorherrschende Form der Umarbeitung besteht in der Auszierung – einer Technik, die zu den Grundlagen von Bachs Kompositionsweise gehört und deren Entwicklung zu seinen bedeutendsten Errungenschaften zählt. In einigen zweiteiligen Sätzen reicht die Auszierung kaum über die Eröffnungsphrase eines jeden Teils hinaus. Bach befolgt dieses Schema konsequent etwa im ersten Satz der Sonate F-Dur Wq 64/1, indem er den Themenkopf melodisch-rhythmisch abändert und diese Änderungen im wesentlichen beibehält. (Vgl. Beispiel 3 auf Seite 129.)

Im umgearbeiteten letzten Satz der Sonate D-Dur Wq 64/5, einem frühen Beispiel eines veränderten Reprisensatzes, wurde jeder der beiden strukturellen Hauptabschnitte durchgehend ausgeziert, während die veränderten Reprisen unangetastet blieben (vgl. Beispiel 4 auf Seite 129).

C. P. E. Bachs Umarbeitungen seiner Claviersonaten 129

Beispiel 3: Frühe und spätere Fassungen des Hauptthemas von Wq 64/1/I (frühe Fassung nach *P 1001*, spätere Fassung nach *P 776*)

Beispiel 4: Incipits der frühen und der späteren Fassung von Wq 64/5/III sowie der veränderten Reprise T. 17

130   Darrell M. Berg

In vielen frühen Sonaten arbeitete Bach die Melodien verfeinernd aus und
gestaltete zugleich den Begleitsatz im Sinne des style brisé transparenter und
flüssiger. Dadurch wurde der Typus des continuobegleiteten Solosatzes, wie
er in den frühen Sonaten dominiert, zum idiomatischen Claviersatz umgeformt:

Beispiel 5: Änderungen der Textur in den „Erneuerungen" von zwei Sonaten

C. P. E. Bachs Umarbeitungen seiner Claviersonaten 131

In den komponierten Auszierungen der „erneuerten" frühen Sonatensätze hielt sich Bach im allgemeinen streng an die harmonische Struktur und Periodik des Originals. Doch finden sich auch einige interessante Ausnahmen dieses Prinzips. So suchte er im Mittelsatz von Wq 65/12, einer frühen Berliner Sonate, die ursprünglich sequenzierende Parallelführung der Außenstimmen (T. 45–50) auszumerzen:

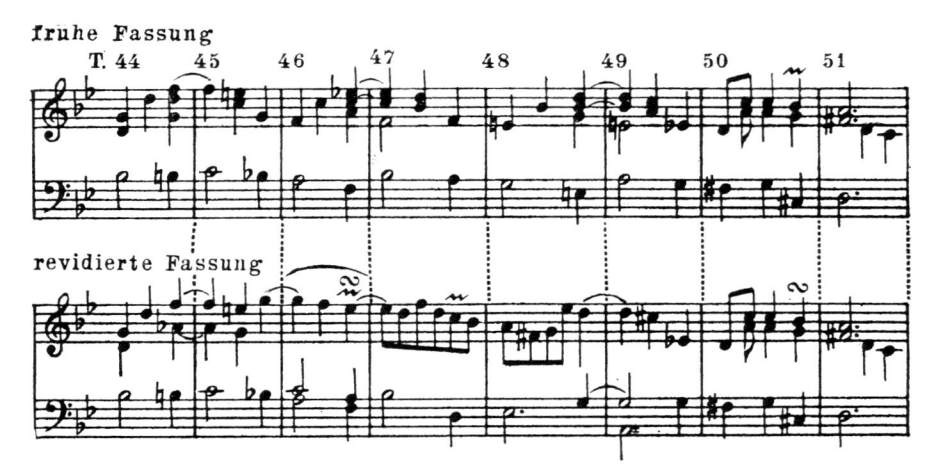

Beispiel 6: Zwei Fassungen von Wq 65/12/II

Die neue Melodie, mit dem oktavierten g der letzten Zählzeit von T. 45 einsetzend, macht Änderungen in der Harmonik erforderlich. Offensichtlich war für Bach die melodische Substanz wichtiger als die ursprüngliche harmonische Sequenz, die er aufgab, um der Melodik eine neue Kontur verleihen zu können. In diesem Falle wie in einigen weiteren Beispielen (siehe unten) löst sich der Verzierungsprozeß von dem Rahmensatz, der normalerweise seinen Verlauf bestimmt.

III. AUSTAUSCH VON SÄTZEN

Eine zweite Art der Umarbeitung besteht in dem Austausch vollständiger Sätze – zumeist Mittelsätze – durch neukomponierte oder entlehnte Stücke. In den sechs Sonatinen Wq 64 wurde dieser Austausch offenbar innerhalb derselben Werkgruppe vorgenommen: (vgl. Tabelle II, S. 160).
Dieses Austauschverfahren scheint sich nach einem symmetrischen Schema vollzogen zu haben, so daß die altmodische suitenähnliche Satzreihung der Frühfassung einer modernen, tonartlich differenzierten Satzfolge Platz machte. Unter Bachs frühen Berliner Sonaten befinden sich zwei Austauschsätze, die im Nachlaß-Verzeichnis nicht aufgeführt werden. So existieren beispielsweise von der Sonate g-Moll Wq 65/11 zwei dreisätzige Fassungen:

132   Darrell M. Berg

Beurmann Nr. 18

Moderato

Andante

Allegretto grazioso

Beurmann Nr. 18a

Moderato

Andante

Presto

Beispiel 7: Incipits der beiden Fassungen von Wq 65/11 (vgl. Abb. 1)

Beurmanns Katalog der Sonaten gibt an, daß das Allegretto grazioso der frühere Schlußsatz sei, das Presto hingegen der spätere. Der stilistische Befund spricht allerdings gegen diese chronologische Folge: das Presto ist kürzer und seine Melodik eher einfältig und kantig; das Allegretto aber ist nicht nur länger, sondern auch von seiner Melodik und Satzfaktur her attraktiver.
Wie bereits erwähnt (siehe oben, S. 128), enthalten die Brüsseler Westphal-Handschriften im allgemeinen die spätesten und bevorzugten Fassungen von Bachs frühen ungedruckten Sonaten. Im Falle von Wq 65/11 jedoch erscheint die Sachlage nicht ganz eindeutig, denn B-Bc 5883 bietet beide Schlußsätze, freilich in der Anordnung einer viersätzigen Sonate[12]:

---

[12] Eine auf dieser Quelle basierende viersätzige Ausgabe von Wq 65/11, hrsg. von E. Bosquet, erschien 1922 bei Senart, Paris.

Abb. 1a–d: Incipits der Sätze von Wq 65/11 in B-Bc: *5883*

134 Darrell M. Berg

Die Problematik der Chronologie der Fassungen dieser Sonate läßt sich jedoch lösen. In einem Brief von Bachs Witwe an Westphal, geschrieben im August 1791, heißt es: „. . . Von den 7 Sonaten hat die 14te der vielen Veränderungen wegen ganz müssen abgeschrieben werden. In der 18ten Sonate ist an die Stelle des Ihrigen ein ganz anderes Andante abgeschrieben, und gehörigen Orts eingeheftet worden, und in der 20ten Sonate ist statt Ihres letzten Presto auf eben die Art ein Allegretto grazioso gekommen. Alles übrige ist scharf durchgesehen, und genau geändert worden, welches insbesondere in der 18ten Sonate sehr zu merken ist."[13] Johanna Maria Bach benutzt für die Sonaten die Numerierung des Nachlaß-Verzeichnisses: NV 14 =

Abb. 2a–c: Incipits der drei ersten von Johanna Maria Bach erwähnten Sätze in B-Bc: *5883* (Satz 4, Andante = Abb. 3d, Satz 5, Allegretto = Abb. 1c)

---

[13] Siehe Fußnote 5.

C. P. E. Bachs Umarbeitungen seiner Claviersonaten 135

Wq 65/6 („ganz müssen abgeschrieben werden"); NV 18 = Wq 65/10 („ganz anderes Andante"); NV 20 = Wq 65/11 („Allegretto grazioso").

Der Brief bezeugt, daß das längere und reizvollere Allegretto grazioso den späteren und bevorzugten Satz darstellt. Der handschriftliche Quellenbefund (siehe Abbildung 1) bestätigt den Sachverhalt: Allegro, Andante und Presto stammen von der Hand Westphals, der neue Satz hingegen von der Hand Michels, der noch nach Bachs Tod für dessen Witwe und Tochter Kopistendienste leistete.[14] Vermutlich hatte Emanuel Bach das Presto zunächst aus der Sonate e-Moll Wq 65/5 (1735) entlehnt, nach g-Moll transponiert und zwischenzeitlich Wq 65/11 beigefügt, bis er der Sonate ihren eigenen neuen Schlußsatz geben konnte.

Bach scheint auch einen anderen Satz aus Wq 65/5 für die Frühfassung der D-Dur-Sonate Wq 62/3 (fast gleichzeitig mit Wq 65/11 entstanden) entlehnt zu haben: der Mittelsatz, ein Siciliano, wurde nach d-Moll transponiert, um Wq 62/3 als Mittelsatz dienen zu können. Doch anders als bei Wq 65/11 kann diese mutmaßliche frühere Fassung von Wq 62/3 weder direkt auf Bach noch auf Westphal zurückgeführt werden; alle erhaltenen Abschriften dieser Fassung sind ungewisser Provenienz. Auf der andern Seite zählen zwei der Abschriften zu den besonders verläßlichen Kopien von Emanuels Claviersonaten.[15] Es läßt sich darum annehmen, daß die Fassung von Wq 62/3 in diesen Quellen (vgl. Tabelle I) durchaus von Bach stammt und daß für die bei Marpurg 1763 veröffentlichte Fassung dieser frühen Berliner Sonate Bach wiederum einen neuen Satz schuf, um den entlehnten zu ersetzen.

Aufschlußreich sind auch Johanna Maria Bachs Bemerkungen zu den andern beiden Sonaten. Abbildung 3 mit den Brüsseler Inzipits der „18ten" Sonate Wq 65/10) zeigt, daß hier ebenfalls vier Sätze vorliegen:

---

[14] Zu Michel vgl. TBSt 1, S. 24. – Michel ist als Sänger in dem gedruckten Programm einer Oratorien- und Serenadenaufführung vom 10. September 1767 aufgeführt (ich danke Walter Steffani für den Hinweis auf diese Quelle). Nach den Archivunterlagen von St. Petri in Hamburg war Michel einer von fünf Sängern, die nach 1793 Zuwendungen aus der Kirchen-Pensionskasse erhielten; seit 1814 erscheint er nicht mehr in den entsprechenden Listen.

[15] P 368 enthält Abschriften des späteren Dresdner Kreuzkantors G. A. Homilius (1735 an der Universität Leipzig immatrikuliert und Schüler J. S. Bachs); P 774 enthält Abschriften von Michel und dem Greifswalder Juristen J. H. Grave, einem Freund C. P. E. Bachs (vgl. hierzu E. F. Schmid, a. a. O., S. 65, und C. H. Bitter, *Carl Philipp Emanuel und Wilhelm Friedemann Bach und deren Brüder*, Berlin 1868, Bd. 2, S. 303f.).

Abb. 3a–d: Incipits der Sätze von Wq 65/10 in B-Bc: 5883 (Zweitschrift des Andante – vgl. Abb. 3d – im Querformat, sonst Hss. im Hochformat)

Das Andante am Fuß der Seite (in Michels Hand) ist identisch mit dem voranstehenden Andante (in Westphals Hand). Offenbar hatte der Schweriner Organist bereits Zugang zu jenem als „ein ganz anderes Andante" bezeichneten Satz. Als er dann aus dem Nachlaß-Verzeichnis erfuhr, daß diese Sonate erneuert worden war, erbat er – im Glauben, das frühere Andante (siehe Beispiel 2) zu besitzen – von Bachs Witwe „ein ganz anderes Andante". Wenn die Angabe „erneuert" bei den sechzehn frühesten Sonaten im Nachlaß-Verzeichnis dazu gedacht war, die Besitzer der älteren Fassungen zur Bestellung der jüngeren zu veranlassen, dann hat sie ihren Zweck erfüllt.

IV. ERWEITERNDE EINSCHÜBE

Umarbeitungen von Bachs eigener Hand im dritten Satz jener „14ten" Sonate, die nach Johanna Maria Bach „der vielen Veränderungen wegen ganz müssen abgeschrieben werden" zeigt Abbildung 4.

Abb. 4: Beginn des 3. Satzes von Wq 65/6 (*P* 772; Hs. Michel, Revision C. P. E. Bach)

Bach notierte seine Veränderungen in die Abschrift seines Hamburger Kopisten Michel. Die ersten beiden Sätze (nicht abgebildet) stammen vollständig
von Michels Hand und berücksichtigen bereits die wohl aus den 1740er
Jahren stammenden Revisionen dieser Sätze. Der dritte Satz jedoch zeigt
eigenhändige Rasuren, Verbesserungen und Eintragungen ausgedehnter
Ersatzpassagen für durchstrichene Stellen, die erst nach der Herstellung von
Michels Reinschrift vorgenommen wurden und damit eine letzte Umarbei-
tungsschicht repräsentieren, von der das Nachlaß-Verzeichnis nicht be-
richtet.

Diese Quelle bringt nicht nur weitere Belege für Bachs übliche Manier der
Ausschmückung von Melodie und Satzfaktur, sondern bietet eine dritte Art
von „Erneuerung", nämlich die Einfügung erweiternder Einschübe. Im
Schlußsatz dieser Sonate finden sich Einschübe hauptsächlich gegen Ende
eines jeden Teiles der binären Struktur, und zwar im Sinne kadenzartiger
Auszierungen der Harmonieschritte. Bach hat hier den Eintritt der Doppel-
dominante von eineinhalb Takten (Beginn der durchstrichenen Stelle in
Abbildung 4) auf zweieinhalb Takte ausgedehnt, ebenso den Eintritt der
Dominante von einem halben Takt (Triller im 2. Takt der ausgestrichenen
Stelle) auf dreieinhalb Takte. Entsprechende Einschübe finden sich im zweiten
Teil (nicht abgebildet).

Zwei weitere Beispiele von Erweiterungen in Bachs frühen Claviersonaten
begegnen in den ersten beiden Sätzen der Sonate Es-Dur Wq 65/7 (zur
komplizierten Quellenlage vgl. Tabelle III, S. 160).

Wahrscheinlich existierten insgesamt nur drei deutlich verschiedene Fassungen
(siehe nachfolgendes Stemma), wenn man berücksichtigt, daß die Handschriften 21a/XI und P 775a (Kolumnen 1 und 3) sich durch zahlreiche Kopier-
fehler „auszeichnen" und somit kaum eigene, geschweige denn autorisierte
Fassungen wiedergeben:

C. P. E. Bachs Umarbeitungen seiner Claviersonaten   139

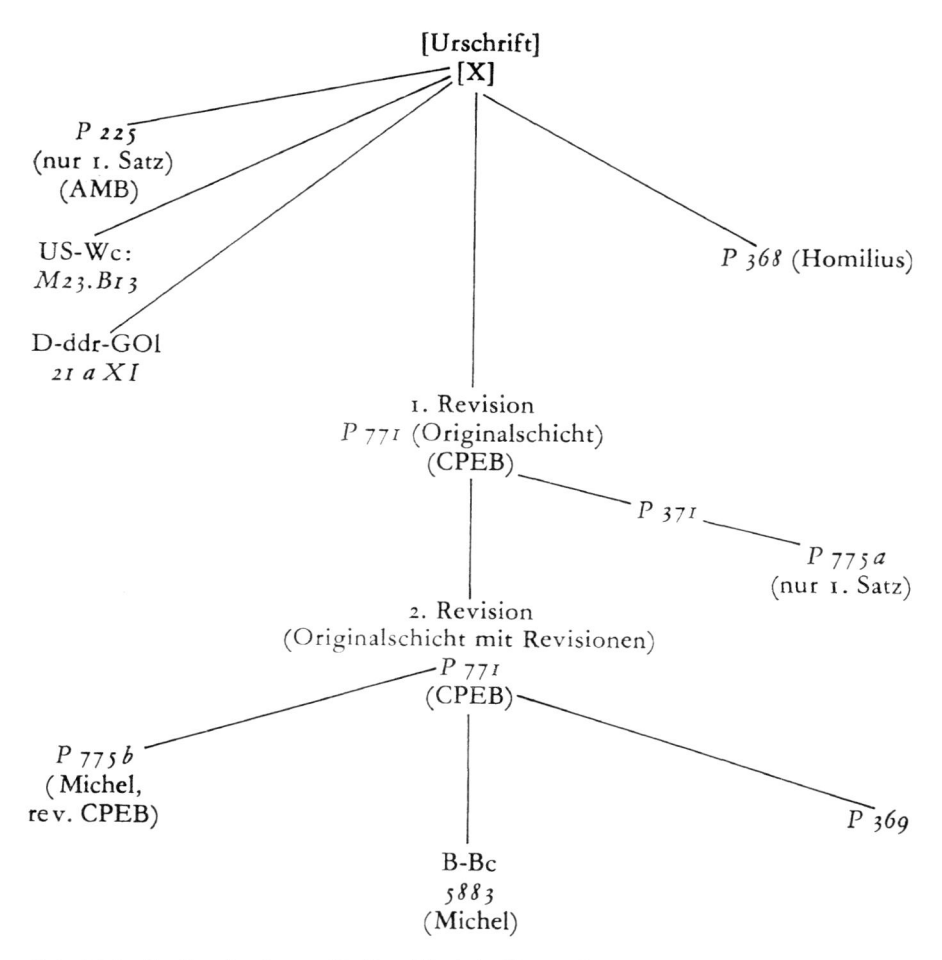

Beispiel 8: Quellen der Sonate Es-Dur Wq 65/7 (Stemma)

Was immer die Anzahl der tatsächlich von Emanuel Bach komponierten verschiedenen Fassungen sein mag, *P 371* und die ursprüngliche Schicht von *P 771* enthalten die erste substantielle Umarbeitung von Wq 65/7. Während sich die Umarbeitung des dritten Satzes (Vivace) im Rahmen der typischen Veränderungen durch Auszierung bewegt, geht Bach im Mittelsatz über das übliche Maß an Verzierungen weit hinaus, so daß das ursprüngliche Siciliano (in Andante umbenannt) kaum mehr erkennbar bleibt. Überdies erweiterte Bach den Satz von 21 auf 32 Takte:

140   Darrell M. Berg

C. P. E. Bachs Umarbeitungen seiner Claviersonaten 141

Darrell M. Berg

C. P. E. Bachs Umarbeitungen seiner Claviersonaten 143

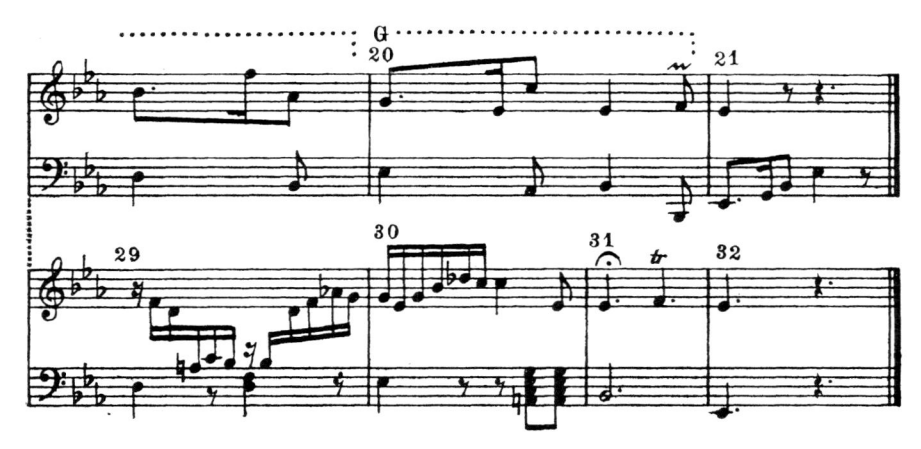

Beispiel 9: Zwei Fassungen von Wq 65/7/II (nach *P 368* bzw. *P 771*)

Erweiternde Einschübe finden sich in den Takten 5 (Modulation: A), 7 (Dominante: B), 12 (Bestätigung der Dominante und Rückleitung zur Tonika: C), 14 (Wiedererreichung der Tonika: D), 15 (aufsteigende Sequenz: E), 19 (Trugschluß: F), 20 (Beginn der Schlußkadenz: G), die jeweils markante Punkte des Satzverlaufs repräsentieren. Bach akzentuiert damit vor allem Kadenzverläufe sowie harmonische Spannungsmomente (T. 5, 12 und 15).[16]
Manche dieser Erweiterungen scheinen der gleichen linearen Auszierungsmethode zu entspringen wie diejenigen in Abbildung 4. Doch führen die erweiternden Einschübe in diesem Siciliano auch darüber hinaus. Die Tonikalisierung des c-Moll in T. 5–8 des Andante erhält einen eigenständigen harmonischen Impetus; die Rückleitung zur Tonika in T. 17–20 zeigt dem Siciliano unbekannte harmonische Brechungen; in T. 21–22 des Andante fügt Bach eine Reprise ein, um gegenüber dem Siciliano die Rückkehr zur Tonika zu akzentuieren.
Die erste Umarbeitung von Wq 65/7 schloß ebenfalls eine Erweiterung des Anfangssatzes von 62 auf 74 Takte ein. Hier richtete Bach seine Aufmerksamkeit in erster Linie auf die Durchführungs- und Reprisenabschnitte. Seine Erweiterung der Durchführung um acht Takte besteht hauptsächlich aus Sequenzen, die diesem Abschnitt zwar kein neues harmonisches Profil verleihen,[17] durch harmonische Abwechslung und schiere Ausdehnung ihre Wirkung jedoch nicht verfehlen.
Die Erweiterung der Reprise dieses Satzes ist für das Studium von Bachs Kompositionsprozeß von größerem Interesse, da sie ein Bemühen um harmonische Symmetrie auf der ganzen Ebene bezeugt. Die Phrase, die die Reprise der Frühfassung einleitet (T. 43–46), scheint eine solche Symmetrie zunächst anzukündigen (die viertaktige Phrase bestätigt die Tonika und enthält sogar

---

[16] Vgl. hierzu C. Rosen, *The Classical Style*, New York 1972, S. 87.
[17] Der einzige harmonische Zusatz in diesem Abschnitt besteht in der neapolitanischen Akkordverbindung (T. 49).

144   Darrell M. Berg

eine Andeutung der Subdominante – ein in vielen Sonatensätzen des 18. Jahrhunderts zu findender Akt der Balance gegenüber der Dominante in der Exposition). Doch die folgenden acht Takte (47–54) widersprechen mit ihrer Betonung der Doppeldominante diesem Balanceakt. Auch ist die Verbindung dieser Takte mit der Schlußwendung (T. 54 ff.) ungeschickt:

Wq 65/7/I (T. 43-58)

Beispiel 10: Wq 65/7/I, T. 43–58

In seiner ersten Umarbeitung dieses Satzes ersetzt Bach diese Takte der Dominantandeutung durch zehn neue Takte, die die Hinwendung zur Tonika deutlicher herausstellen (siehe Abbildung 5 oben, beginnend mit dem Auftakt zu T. 6):

C. P. E. Bachs Umarbeitungen seiner Claviersonaten 145

Abb. 5: Wq 65/7, Satz 1 (P 771; Autograph C. P. E. Bachs)

146   Darrell M. Berg

Bach scheint mit dieser Lösung des Reprisenproblems in Wq 65/7 sich nicht
ganz zufriedengegeben zu haben, denn er nahm später in Hamburg eine
weitere Umarbeitung vor.[18] Diese findet sich auf derselben Seite unten rechts
(siehe Abbildung 5). Hier schuf Bach eine viertaktige Rückleitung (im An-
schluß an die g-Moll-Kadenz = erster gestrichener Takt am Seitenbeginn)
und dehnte zusätzlich den Eintritt der Tonika um vier Takte aus (neuer
Reprisenbeginn = letzter Takt des 1. Systems unten rechts).
Mit den erweiternden Einschüben in diesem Satz sowie im Siciliano tendiert
Bach in gewisser Weise zur Dialektik des klassischen Stils – er hebt das
Moment der Dissonanz auf eine höhere Ebene und erzielt damit eine drama-
tischere Artikulation der Struktur. Freilich tragen nicht alle Einschübe zur
Triftigkeit des dramatischen Zugriffs bei; die flüchtige viertaktige Rückleitung
(Abbildung 5 unten rechts) und die Weitschweifigkeit einiger erweiternder
Abschnitte des Siciliano (siehe Notenbeispiel 9) deuten an, daß die Arbeit an
der Erweiterung Bach nicht leicht von der Hand ging. Es ist die Auszierung
des Siciliano, die die attraktivste und erfolgreichste Seite der Umarbeitung
dieses Satzes bildet.

V. SPÄTE UMARBEITUNGEN

Auszierung – genauer: Veränderung oder Variierung – eines unveränderlichen
Strukturgerüstes ist das vorherrschende Verfahren, nach dem Bach seine
Claviersonaten umarbeitete. Dies gilt nicht nur für die verschiedenen revidier-
ten Berliner Sonaten der 174oer und 175oer Jahre, bei denen er stillschweigend
ältere durch erneuerte Fassungen ersetzte,[19] sondern auch für die späteren
Sonaten: die „Veränderungen und Auszierungen über einige [gedruckte]
Sonaten . . . für Scholaren" und die Veränderung von zwei weiteren gedruckten Sonaten (Wq 65/32 und 51/1). Man mag sehr wohl annehmen, daß
für Emanuel Bach nicht zuletzt ein kaufmännisches Motiv mitspielte, wenn er
die Existenz mehrerer Fassungen bekanntgeben wollte. Andererseits bestand
sein vornehmliches Interesse darin, die Aufmerksamkeit auf seine elegante
Manier und unerschöpfliche Technik der Veränderung zu lenken.
Die erste der beiden späten veränderten Sonaten (Wq 65/32 = Wq 70/1)[20]
zeigt verschiedene Aspekte des Variierungsprozesses. Obgleich man von diesem
Werk nur zwei Fassungen kennt, scheint es Bach in drei Stadien komponiert

---

[18] Die Korrekturen in P 771 zeigen die für Bachs Spätzeit charakteristischen zittrigen Schrift-
züge.

[19] Bach verzierte in unterschiedlichem Ausmaß alle drei Sätze von Wq 65/12 und Wq 65/23
sowie die ersten Sätze von Wq 65/14, Wq 65/15 und Wq 65/30. Unter den Quellen der
Sonaten finden sich auch unverzierte und verzierte Fassungen der Anfangssätze von Wq
62/6 und Wq 65/31. Auch wenn die Quellen der unverzierten Fassungen nicht dem unmittel-
baren Umkreis Bachs angehören, scheinen sie doch authentische Frühfassungen zu über-
liefern, die Bach zu unterdrücken suchte, als er seine eigenen Unterlagen vernichtete.

[20] Wq verzeichnet diese Sonate an zwei Stellen, entsprechend ihrer Bestimmung für Orgel
bzw. besaitete Tasteninstrumente (im NV keine Differenzierung der instrumentalen
Bestimmung).

C. P. E. Bachs Umarbeitungen seiner Claviersonaten 147

zu haben. In einem ersten Stadium (das Nachlaß-Verzeichnis nennt 1758 als Entstehungsjahr) mag das Werk bestimmt worden sein für eine Gruppe von Orgelsonaten, die Bach angeblich für Prinzessin Anna Amalia komponiert hatte.[21] Das zweite Stadium findet sich vertreten in Teil IX von Haffners *Oeuvres melées* (1762–1763), wobei dem letzten Satz einige Auszierungen beigefügt wurden. In ihrem dritten Stadium (nach 1762–1763) erhielt die Sonate eine gründlich erneuerte Fassung, indem Bach dem ersten Satz für jeden Hauptabschnitt eine reich variierte Reprise einfügte und auch den zweiten Satz mit Auszierungen versah.

Vom ersten Stadium an vom Variierungsprinzip beherrscht wird der Schlußsatz dieser Sonate, ein Rondo mit einer nahezu ununterbrochen symmetrischen Phrasenstruktur.[22] Das wesentliche Material für den Satz ist in den ersten vier Takten des Refrains (a^1) enthalten. Diese viertaktige Melodie eröffnet auch das zweite Glied des Refrains und (in die Dominante transponiert) dringt auch in die Couplets (B und B') ein:

	A				B			A'	
a^1	a^2	a^{1v}	a^{2v}	b	a^1/a^2	c		a^{1vv}	a^{2vv}
T. 1–8	9–16	17–24	25–32	33–40	41–48	49–56		57–64	65–72

Tonarten: A-Dur   → E-Dur   A-Dur

(v bedeutet verändert)

	B'			A''		Coda		
b	a^{1vvv}/a^2	c	a^{1vvvv}	a^{2vvv}	d	d^v	a^{1vvvvv}
73–80	81–88	89–96	97–104	105–112			
					113–116	117–120–124	

→ E-Dur   A-Dur

Beispiel 11: Schematische Darstellung der Struktur von Wq 65/32/III (Wq 70/1/III)

---

[21] Vgl. den Westphal-Katalog (Fußnote 3), fol. 31, sowie E. L. Gerber, *Neues Historisch-Biographisches Lexikon der Tonkünstler*, Leipzig 1812–1814, Bd. 1, S. 118.

[22] Dieser sorgfältig ausbalancierte Satz ist ein Vorläufer der rhapsodischen, asymmetrisch modulierenden Rondos der Sammlungen für Kenner und Liebhaber – Stücke, die in beispielloser Weise Rondo- und Variationsprinzip kombinieren.

148   Darrell M. Berg

Die den Satz eröffnende Melodie wird mit jeder nachfolgenden Wiederholung
verändert, so daß sie nie mehr in ihrer ursprünglichen Form erklingt:

Beispiel 12: Incipits des Hauptthemas von Wq 65/32/III (Wq 70/1/III) sowie seiner Varianten
im Verlauf des Satzes

Die eindringlichsten Beispiele für Bachs Variierungstechnik finden sich in den
beiden Sonaten Wq 65/35–36, die auf Wq 51/1 zurückgehen. In jedem Satz
dieser ungedruckten Werke bleibt die Harmonik und periodische Struktur
dieselbe wie in den korrespondierenden Sätzen von Wq 51/1. Infolge von
Bachs strengem Festhalten an dem ursprünglichen Satzgerüst bleibt dessen
Identität in allen veränderten Fassungen unangetastet. Dennoch besitzt jede
einzelne ihre unverwechselbare Satzfaktur und damit einen individuellen
Charakter. In beiden Sonaten läßt sich somit das Zusammenspiel von Konti-
nuität und Wandel erfahren.
Bei drei 1766 komponierten Sonaten nahm Bach Umarbeitungen vor, die das
Nachlaß-Verzeichnis nicht erwähnt. Er fügte dem ersten Satz von Wq 65/44
veränderte Reprisen bei, entfernte den Mittelsatz (Largo) und schrieb statt

C. P. E. Bachs Umarbeitungen seiner Claviersonaten 149

dessen eine kurze Überleitung vom ersten zum letzten Satz.[23] Aus zwei Gründen ist es wahrscheinlich, daß die Änderungen in Wq 65/44 um 1784 vorgenommen wurden: (1) das Largo wird in die 1784 entstandene Sonate Wq 59/3 übernommen; (2) das Kompositionsmanuskript (*St 258 b*), das die veränderten Reprisen für den ersten Satz und die neue Überleitung enthält, zeigt die für Bachs letztes Lebensjahrzehnt typische äußerst zittrige Schrift.

In der Handschrift *St 258 b*, die die Veränderungen ohne zugehörigen Kontext enthält, finden sich auch veränderte Reprisen für die Außensätze der ebenfalls 1766 entstandenen Sonate Wq 65/46. Das ähnliche Erscheinungsbild des Notentextes legt nahe, daß diese Änderungen etwa zur gleichen Zeit wie bei Wq 65/44 vorgenommen wurden.

Während die Umarbeitungen dieser beiden Sonaten (mit Ausnahme der Entfernung des Largo aus Wq 65/44) keine Besonderheiten aufweisen, erscheint bei der ebenfalls aus dem Jahr 1766 stammenden Sonate Wq 65/45 das Ersetzen des Schlußsatzes durch einen neukomponierten durchaus anomal. Ein derartiger Austausch läßt sich in den nach 1740 entstandenen Sonaten nicht mehr nachweisen. Die beiden Schlußsätze finden sich (neben den ersten beiden Sätzen und einem dritten Satz, einem 6/8-Allegro) von der Hand Michels in dem Konvolut *P 771*, dessen Titelblatt von Emanuel Bach mit der Aufschrift „hat noch niemand" versehen ist. In der Tat ist das 6/8-Allegro in dieser Quelle bis heute unbekannt geblieben. Bach scheint an dem Allegro Verbesserungen angebracht zu haben, bevor er es ausschied. Denn er notierte am Ende des Satzes kleinere Zusätze in der Form von Echo-Einschüben.

Zwischen den beiden Seiten dieses Allegro liegt ein Doppelblatt mit dem bekannten 3/8-Allegretto in Bachs zittriger Spätschrift (wohl ebenfalls aus der Zeit um 1784) mit einer Bleistiftnotiz von unbekannter Hand: „Dieses Blatt war auf das vorherige aufgeheftet [sic]. Bach will also, daß statt des 6/8 Allegro der umstehende (autograph) Satz (B-Dur 3/4 [sic]) gespielt wird."

Für die Frühfassung aller drei Sonaten Wq 65/44–46 existiert nur eine Quelle (vgl. Tabelle I), eine Tatsache, die zusammen mit der oben erwähnten Titelblatt-Aufschrift von Wq 65/45 dafür spricht, daß diese Sonaten seinerzeit kaum verbreitet waren. Die Suche nach einem geeigneten Mittelsatz für Wq 59/3 mag Bach um 1784 auf diese vernachlässigten Stücke des Jahres 1766 aufmerksam gemacht und zur Umarbeitung angeregt haben. Es ist möglich, daß diese Werke zu der Gruppe gehören, auf die Bachs Witwe mit der Bemerkung „6 ganz unbekannt und dem Druck bestimmt" in einem Brief vom 5. September 1789 an Sara Itzig-Levy in Berlin anspielt.[24]

*

---

[23] Diese Überleitung kann nicht im Sinne eines erweiternden Einschubes wie bei Wq 65/7 verstanden werden. Sie fungiert als Verbindungspassage, wie sie sich häufig in Bachs Instrumentalmusik findet (schon in Wq 65/16 von 1746 und besonders oft in den Sonaten und Symphonien der 1770er und 1780er Jahre).

[24] Zitiert bei C. H. Bitter, a. a. O., Bd. 2, S. 308.

Gewisse Aspekte von Emanuel Bachs Umarbeitungen seiner Sonaten bleiben
rätselhaft, nichtsdestoweniger läßt sich die Bedeutung dieser kompositorischen Tätigkeit sehr wohl einschätzen. Merkwürdig bleibt, daß im Nachlaß-
Verzeichnis und im Westphal-Katalog penibel auf die Umarbeitungen der
zwischen 1731 und 1738 entstandenen Sonaten hingewiesen wird, daß dort
jedoch eine Reihe weiterer tiefgreifender Umarbeitungen verschwiegen wird.
Dies gilt beispielsweise für die vier frühesten Berliner Sonaten, deren Stil sich
nicht wesentlich von demjenigen der ersten sechzehn unterscheidet. Auch das
Ausmaß der Umarbeitungen jener Berliner Werke (Wq 65/11, Wq 62/3 und
Wq 65/12) entspricht durchaus demjenigen der früheren Sonaten. Die nächst-
liegende und wahrscheinlichste Erklärung für die selektiven Angaben des
Nachlaß-Verzeichnisses zu den Umarbeitungen mag darin zu finden sein, daß
Bach die ersten sechzehn Sonaten als Anfängerwerke ansah. Die frühen Berliner Sonaten wurden geschrieben, nachdem er die Universität in Frankfurt
an der Oder verlassen hatte und in den Kreis der Musiker um den Preußischen
Kronprinzen Friedrich eingetreten war. Damit hatte seine berufliche Laufbahn
begonnen und es scheint, als habe er bei der Vorbereitung seines Werkver-
zeichnisses gleichsam eine Abgrenzung gegenüber den Anfängerwerken vorgenommen.
Die Wahl der Jahre 1743 und 1744 für die Umarbeitungen der sechzehn frühen
Sonaten war logisch, denn er hatte gerade mit den sechs Preußischen Sonaten
(Wq 48) sein erstes größeres Sonatenopus publiziert und war bei der Fertig-
stellung der Württembergischen Sonatensammlung (Wq 49). Die Sätze dieser
Sonaten sind im allgemeinen ausgedehnter als bei den vorigen, auch finden
sich stärkere Kontraste innerhalb eines jeden Zyklus von Sätzen. Die Melodien
sind kunstvoller und zugleich flüssiger, die Satzfaktur eleganter. So erscheint
es verständlich, wenn Bach im Angesicht der gewonnenen Erfahrungen den
Versuch machte, die früheren Werke auf das technische und ästhetische Niveau
der gedruckten Sammlungen aus den 1740er Jahren zu heben.
Laut Nachlaß-Verzeichnis begann Bach zunächst mit den letzten der Anfängerwerke: die Zeitangabe 1743 gehört bis auf eine Ausnahme (Wq 65/7) zu den
Frankfurter Sonaten, 1744 gilt für die Leipziger Werke. Vielleicht glaubte
Emanuel, daß die außerhalb des Bereiches der väterlichen Obhut entstandenen
Frankfurter Sonaten dringender der Revision bedurften. In der Tat zeigen
die Frühfassungen der Frankfurter Sonaten auf der Suche nach einem neuen
und individuellen Stil manche Ungeschicklichkeit.
Obgleich das Nachlaß-Verzeichnis nur das systematische Revisionsprogramm
der 1740er Jahre festhält, nahm Bach – wie gezeigt worden ist – auch darüber
hinaus weitgehende Umarbeitungen seiner Claviersonaten vor. In den letzten
vier oder fünf Jahren seines Lebens entfernte er bei der Sonate Wq 65/44 aus
dem Jahre 1766 einen Satz und verpflanzte ihn in ein Werk aus der fünften
Folge der *Sonaten für Kenner und Liebhaber*, und bei Wq 65/45 ersetzte er einen
prosaisch anmutenden Satz durch einen kapriziösen und witzigen.
Während seiner Hamburger Tätigkeit erweiterte Philipp Emanuel Bach Sätze
früherer Sonaten (Wq 65/6–7) und erweist darin eine gewisse Vorahnung der
dramatischen Tendenzen des klassischen Stils, auch wenn es an zugespitzter
Energie und Zielgerichtetheit noch fehlt. Die erhaltenen Quellen der Clavier-

sonaten deuten an, daß – wenn Bach Sätze größerer Ausdehnung benötigte –
es für ihn leichter war, die alten Sätze durch Neukompositionen zu ersetzen.
Die von Bach am ausgiebigsten gepflegte Umarbeitungsmethode bestand in der
Auszierung: Veränderungen über einem bestehenden Baß und Ausschmückung
eines harmonischen Gerüstes. Bachs Auszierungen zielen zwar nicht selten in
die Richtung linearer harmonischer Ausdehnung, wie sie in den Rondos der
„Sammlungen für Kenner und Liebhaber" auch tatsächlich stattfindet, doch
bleiben sie im ganzen innerhalb der vertikalen harmonischen Gegebenheiten.
Die zweiteilige Satzform dient Bach als Gefäß für Auszierung, nicht aber für
dramatische Entwicklung. Auch findet sich bei Emanuel Bach zu keiner Zeit
die Tendenz, Sonatensätze (im Sinne etwa von Haydn oder Mozart) weiter
auszudehnen und wirklich zu entwickeln. Er bevorzugte letztlich immer wieder
ein und dieselbe Art der prozessualen Ausarbeitung, wie er sie für die veränderten Reprisen seiner Sonaten mustergültig und programmatisch entworfen
hatte. In dieser Hinsicht blieb Bachs Kompositionsart konservativ. Seine
Zeitgenossen konnten ihn kaum fortschrittlich nennen. Da sie jedoch erkann-
ten, wie einzigartig seine Melodien, Satzweisen und Ausdrucksnuancen waren,
bezeichneten sie ihn als Originalgenie.

Tabelle I

Revisionen und „Veränderungen" in C. P. E. Bachs Clavier-Sonaten[25]

Titel	Tonarten	NV Nr.[26]	Wq Nr.	Beur Nr.[27]	Helm Nr.[28]	Entste-hungs-jahr laut NV	Ände-rungs-jahr laut NV	Quellen[29]
Sonate (späte Fassung)	B-g-B	1	62/1	1	2	L.1731	B. 1744	B-Br: II 4094 (Westphal; Ab-schrift nach Druck) P 677 P 727 (nur 1. Satz) P 772 P 775 (An 401) P 790a P 790b P 841

[25] Einige Sonaten mit nachweisbaren oder mutmaßlichen Umarbeitungen werden hier
    ausgelassen: Wq 65/14, Wq 62/6, Wq 65/15, Wq 65/22, Wq 65/23, Wq 65/30, Wq 65/31.

[26] Numerierung des mit „Clavier-Soli" überschriebenen Teils des Nachlaß-Verzeichnisses.

[27] Numerierung des Verzeichnisses der Clavier-Sonaten C. P. E. Bachs von Erich Beurmann
    (siehe S. 124).

[28] Numerierung des Verzeichnisses der Werke C. P. E. Bachs von Eugene Helm (siehe S. 124).

[29] Sofern nicht anders angegeben, handelt es sich um Hss. Erläuterungen der Abkürzungen
    und Sigel im Anhang zu diesem Beitrag.

152   Darrell M. Berg

Titel	Tonarten	NV	Wq	Beur	Helm	EJ	ÄJ	Quellen
								D-ddr-LEb[30]: *Go.S.669* *P 365* (Su III) Druck: *Musikalisches Allerley von verschiedenen Tonkünstlern* (Berlin: Birnstiel, 1761–1762), S. 159–163
Sonate (frühe Fassung)	F-f-F	2	65/1	2	3	L. 1731	B. 1744	*P 758* A-Wgm: *VII 43746* US-Wc: *M 23. B 13.W.65 (1)*
(mit Eigenschaften der frühen Fassung)								DSB: *Ms. Thulemeier 49*
(spätere Fassung)								*P 775* (An 303, rev. CPEB) B-Bc: *5883* (Michel)
Sonate (späte Fassung)	a-e-a	3	65/2	3	4	L. 1732	B. 1744	*P 775* (Michel, rev. CPEB) *P 771* (CPEB) B-Bc: *5883* (Michel)
Sonate (frühe Fassung)	d-B-d	4	65/3	4	5	L. 1732	B. 1744	*P 371* (An 301)
Fspätere (͟assung)								*P 772* (Schlichting, rev. CPEB; sichtbare Änderungen der früheren Fassung) *P 369* B-Bc: *5883* (Michel)

---

[30] Von der Verfasserin nicht eingesehen.

C. P. E. Bachs Umarbeitungen seiner Claviersonaten 153

Titel	Tonarten	NV	Wq	Beur	Helm	EJ	ÄJ	Quellen
Sonatine (frühe Fassung)	F-F-F (derselbe 2. Satz wie spätere Fassung von 64/6)	6	64/1	5	7	L. 1734	B. 1744	*P 1001* (An Palestrina II) D-brd-KIl: *Mb 51/2* US-Wc: *M 23*. *B13.W.64 (1)*
(spätere Fassung)	F-c-F (derselbe 2. Satz wie frühe Fassung von 64/6)			5a				*P 775* (Michel, rev. CPEB) *P 369* A-Wgm: *VII 3872/15* (Michel) B-Bc: *5881* (Michel)
Sonatine (späte Fassung)	G-e-G (derselbe 2. Satz wie frühe Fassung von 64/4)	7	64/2	6a[31]	8	L. 1734	B. 1744	*P 775* (Michel, rev. CPEB) *P 369* A-Wgm: *VII 3872/13* (Michel) B-Bc: *5881* (Michel)
Sonatine (späte Fassung)	a-D-a (ders. 2. S. wie frühe Fassung von 64/5)	8	64/3	7a[32]	9	L. 1734	B. 1744	*P 775* (Michel, rev. CPEB) *P 369* B-Bc: *5881* (Michel)
Sonatine (frühe Fassung)	e-e-e (ders. 2. S. wie späte Fassung von 64/2)	9	64/4	8	10	L. 1734	B. 1744	*P 371* (An 301) US-Wc: *M23*. *B13.W.64 (4)* (An 303)
(spätere Fassung)	e-G-e			8a				*P 775* (Michel, rev. CPEB) *P 369* A-Wgm: *VII 3872/6* (Michel) B-Bc: *5881* (Michel)

---

[31] Mutmaßliche frühe Fassung (von Beurmann irrtümlicherweise als 6 verzeichnet): G-G-G, mit demselben Mittelsatz wie in der späten Fassung von Wq 64/4.

[32] Mutmaßliche frühe Fassung (von Beurmann irrtümlicherweise als 7 verzeichnet): a-a-a, mit demselben Mittelsatz wie in der späten Fassung von Wq 64/5.

154   Darrell M. Berg

Titel	Tonarten	NV	Wq	Beur	Helm	EJ	ÄJ	Quellen
Sonatine (frühe Fassung)	D-D-D (ders. 2. S. wie späte Fassung von 64/3)	10	64/5	9	11	L. 1734	B. 1744	P 789 (An Palestrina II)
(spätere Fassung)	D-a-D			9b[33]				P 775a (Michel) P 775b (Michel) P 369 A-Wgm: VII 3872/17 (Michel) **B-Bc: 5881** (Michel)
Sonatine (frühe Fassung)	c-c-c (ders. 2. S. wie späte Fassung von 64/1)	11	64/6	10	12	L. 1734	P. 1744	D-brd-KII: Mb 61/1 (An 303) P 371 (An 301) DSB Mus. ms. 30385 (An 401)
(spätere Fassung)	c-F-c (derselbe 2. Satz wie frühe Fassung von 64/1)			10a				P 775 (Michel, rev. CPEB) P 369 A-Wgm: VII 3872/3 (Michel) B-Bc: 5881 (Michel)
Sonate (späte Fassung)	e-e-e	13	65/5	11	13	F/O. 1735	B. 1743	P 772 (An 311, rev. CPEB) P 369 B-Bc: 5883 (Michel)
Sonate (frühe Fassung)	G-G-G	14	65/6	12	15	F/O. 1736	B. 1743	US-Wc: M23. B13.W.65 (6) (An 303)
(2. Satz erneuert)								P 772, originale Schicht (Michel)
(letzte Fassung)								P 772 (Michel, rev. CPEB) P 369 B-Bc: 5883 (Michel)

[33] Irrtümlich verzeichnet Beurmann P 371 als Quelle einer Fassung, die er als 9a bezeichnet.

C. P. E. Bachs Umarbeitungen seiner Claviersonaten   155

Titel	Tonarten	NV	Wq	Beur	Helm	EJ	ÄJ	Quellen
Sonate (frühe Fassung)	Es-Es-Es	15	65/7	13	16	F/O. 1736	B. 1744	*P 225* (nur I) (AMB) *P 368* (Homilius) D-ddr-GÖl: *21 a/XI* US-Wc: *M23. B13.W.65 (7)*
(2te Fassung)								*P 371* *P 771*, originale Schicht (CPEB) *P 775 a* (nur I)
(jüngste Fassung)				13 a				*P 771* (CPEB, rev. CPEB) *P 369* *P 775 b* (Michel, rev. CPEB) B-Bc: *5883*
Sonate (frühe „Fassung")	C-F-C	16	65/8	14	17	F/O. 1737	B. 1743	*P 364* A-Wgm: *VII 43747* D-brd-Mbs: *1795* US-Wc: *M23. B13.W.65 (8)*
(spätere „Fassung")								*P 369* *P 771* (CPEB) B-Bc: *5883* (Michel)
Sonate (frühe Fassung)	B-B-B	17	65/9[34]	15 a	18	F/O. 1737	B. 1743	*P 367* (Müthel) *P 368* (Homilius) A-Wgm: *VII 43748* US-Wc: *M23. B13.W.65 (9) a* und *b*
(unautorisierte Fassung)	B-B-B (neuer 2. Satz)			15				*P 673* (wohl Abschrift nach Druck) Druck: *Six Sonates pour le clavecin composées par Mr C. P. E. Bach* (Paris:

---

[34] Nicht eingesehen: SPK (D-brd-B), *Ms. Thulemeier 54.*

156   Darrell M. Berg

Titel	Tonarten	NV	Wq	Beur	Helm	EJ	ÄJ	Quellen
								Huberty [1761], S. 20–24)
(spätere Fassung)	B-B-B (dieselben Sätze wie frühe Fassung)			15b				P 370 (An 401) P 775 (An 311, rev. CPEB) P 369 B-Bc: 5883
Sonate (frühe Fassung)	A-a-A	18	65/10	16	19	F/O. 1738	B. 1743	P 367 (Müthel) P 368 (Homilius) A-Wgm: VII 43749 US-Wc: M23. B13.W.65 (10)a und b
(unauto-risierte Fassung)				16				P 673 (wohl Abschrift nach Druck) Druck: Six Sonates pour le clavecin composées par Mr C. P. E. Bach (Paris: Huberty [1761], S. 8–11)
(spätere Fassung)	A-a-A (neuer 2. Satz)			16a				P 772 (An 301, rev. CPEB) P 369 B-Bc: 5883 (Michel)
Sonate (frühe „Fassung")	G-e-G	19	62/2	17	20		B. 1739	P 772 (rev. CPEB) D-brd-KIl: Mb 48/1 (E. L. Gerber) DSB: Mus. ms. 30385 (An 401)
(spätere „Fassung")								B-Br: II 4094 (Westphal) (Abschrift nach Druck) Druck: Nebenstunden der Berlinischen Musen in kleinen Clavierstücken, I (Berlin, 1762), S. 16–19

C. P. E. Bachs Umarbeitungen seiner Claviersonaten 157

Titel	Tonarten	NV	Wq	Beur	Helm	EJ	ÄJ	Quellen
Sonate (frühe Fassung)	g-B-g (3. Satz aus Wq 65/5)	20	65/11	18a	21	B. 1739		A-Wgm: *VII 43750* B-Bc: *5883* (III) (Westphal) D-brd-KII: *Mb 52/1* und 2
(spätere Fassung)	g-B-g (neuer 3. Satz)			18				P 775 (Michel, rev. CPEB) P 369 A-Wgm: *VII 3872/8* (Michel) B-Bc: *5883* (Westphal, Michel) Posth. Druck: *Trois Sonates pour le clavecin ou le pianoforte* (Berlin: Rellstab, 1792)
Sonate (frühe Fassung?)	D-d-D (2. Satz aus Wq 65/5)	21	62/3	19	22	B. 1740		P 368 P 774 A-Wgm: *VII 43743*
(spätere Fassung)	D-h-D (neuer 2. Satz)			19a				P 772 (rev. CPEB) P 369 B-Br: *II 4094* (Westphal) (Abschrift nach Druck) Druck: *Clavierstücke mit einem practischen Unterricht . . . III*, ed. F. W. Marpurg (Berlin, 1763), S. 10–16 D-brd-BP: *143*[35]
Sonate (frühe Fassung)	G-g-G	22	65/12	20	23	B. 1740		P 368 D-ddr-SWl: *859/1* US-Wc: *M23. B13.W.65 (12)a* und *b*

158   Darrell M. Berg

Titel	Tonarten	NV	Wq	Beur	Helm	EJ	ÄJ	Quellen
(spätere Fassung)								P 772 (Michel, rev. CPEB) P 786 (Schlichting, rev. CPEB) A-Wgm: VII 3872/4 (Michel) B-Bc: 5883 (Michel)
Sonate (frühe Fassung)	A-a-A	100	70/1 (65/32)	79	135 (133)	1758	„nachher verändert"	B-Bc: 5879 (Westphal) (Orgel) P 789 (Grave) (Cembalo) P 365 (Su III) (Cembalo) DSB, Ms. Thulemeier 43 (Cembalo)
(1. veränderte Fassung)							[1762 oder früher]	Druck: Oeuvres mêlées contenant VI sonates pour le clavessin d'autant de plus célèbres compositeurs, IX (Nürnberg: Haffner [1762–1763]), S. 4–9
(letzte veränderte Fassung)							[nach 1763]	P 774 (Michel, rev. CPEB) P 369 (Clavier) D-ddr-LEm: Becker III.8.2 (Cembalo) D-ddr-LEb: Go.S.669[35] B-Bc: 5883 (Michel)
Sonate	C-G-C	119	51/1	94	150	B. 1760	„2 mal durchaus verändert"	Drucke: Fortsetzung von sechs Sonaten fürs Clavier (Berlin: Winter, 1761) (Leipzig: Breitkopf, 1786) Abschriften nach Druck: P 367;

---

[35] Von Verf. nicht eingesehen.

C. P. E. Bachs Umarbeitungen seiner Claviersonaten   159

Titel	Tonarten	NV	Wq	Beur	Helm	EJ	ÄJ	Quellen
								P 674; *P 774* D-ddr-LEm: Becker *III.6.6.* *Poel. Mus. ms. 42*
Veränderung			65/35	94a	156		[1760 oder später]	*P 776* (Michel, rev. CPEB) B-Bc: *5883* (Michel)
Veränderung			65/36	94b	157		[1760 oder später]	*P 776* (Michel) B-Bc: *5883* (Michel)
Sonate (frühe Fassung)	B-Es-B	151	65/44	118	211	E. 1766		*P 1133* (CPEB)
(spätere Fassung)	B--B (VRn zu I; II auf Wq 59/3 über-tragen)						[1766 oder später]	*P 359* (Michel) *P 776* (Michel, rev. CPEB) *P 369* *St 258 b* (nur VRn zu I und Über-gang auf III) (CPEB) B-Bc: *5883*
Sonate (frühere Fassung?)	B-F-B III: 6/8, Allegro	152	65/45	119	212	E. 1766		*P 771* (Michel, rev. CPEB)
(spätere Fassung?)	B-F-B III: 3/8, Allegretto						[1766 oder später]	*P 359* (Michel) *P 369* *P 771* (CPEB) (nur Allegretto) B-Bc: *5883*
Sonate (frühere Fassung)	E-G-E	155	65/46	122	213	P. 1766		*P 364* (CPEB)
(spätere Fassung)	(VRn zu I, III)						[1766 oder später]	*P 369* (Michel) *P 776a* (Michel, rev. CPEB) *P 776b* *P 359* *St 258b* (nur VRn zu I, III) (CPEB) B-Bc: *5883*

160   Darrell M. Berg

Tabelle II

Austausch und Übertragung in den Sonatinen Wq 64
(Mutmaßliche Fassungen in eckigen Klammern, nachweisbare Übertragungen mit Pfeilen,
mutmaßliche Übertragungen mit gestrichelten Pfeilen gekennzeichnet)

Frühe Fassungen			Revidierte Fassungen	
NV Nummer	Tonarten	Übertragungen von Mittelsätzen	Wq	Tonarten
6	F-F-F	→F	64/1	F-c-F
[7	G-G-G]	→G	64/2	G-e-G
[8	a-a-a]	a	64/3	a-D-a
9	e-e-e	e	64/4	e-G-e
10	D-D-D	D	64/5	D-a-D
11	c-c-c	c	64/6	c-F-c

Tabelle III

Fassungen von Wq 65/7

fast identisch:			fast identisch:	
Fassung von 1736 (?)	Fassung von 1736 (?)	Fassung von 1744 (?)	Fassung von 1744 (?)	Fassung nach 1768 komponiert (?)
D-ddr-GOl: 21a/XI	P 225 (nur I) (AMB) P 368 (Homilius) US-Wc: M23. B13.W.65 (7)	P 775a (nur I)	P 371 P 771 (1. Schicht) (CPEB)	P 771 (erneuerte Schicht) (CPEB) P 775b (Michel, rev. CPEB) P 369 B-Bc: 5883 (Michel)
I: Allegro	I: Allegro	I: Allegretto	I: Allegretto (P 771: Allegro moderato)	I: Allegro moderato
60 Takte (37–38 nicht wiederholt)	62 Takte (37–38 wiederholt)	72 Takte (42–43 nicht wiederholt)	74 Takte (42–43 wiederholt)	82 Takte (Fassung der Spalte 4 verziert und erweitert)
II: Siciliano 21 Takte	II: Siciliano 21 Takte (dieselbe Fassung wie in Spalte 1)		II: Andante 32 Takte (Siciliano verziert und erweitert)	II: Andante 32 Takte (dieselbe Fassung wie in Spalte 4)
III: Vivace 26 Takte	III: Vivace 26 Takte (dieselbe Fassung wie in Spalte 1)		III: Vivace 26 Takte (Fassung der Spalte 2 etwas verziert)	III: Vivace 26 Takte (dieselbe Fassung wie in Spalte 4)

C. P. E. Bachs Umarbeitungen seiner Claviersonaten 161

Abkürzungen und Sigel

A-Wgm	Wien, Gesellschaft der Musikfreunde
AMB	Anna Magdalena Bach (Schrift)
An	anonymer Kopist
An 3××	anonymer Kopist, für C. P. E. Bach arbeitend
An 4××	anonymer Kopist, für die Amalienbibliothek arbeitend
B-Bc	Brüssel, Bibliothèque du Conservatoire Royale de Musique
B-Br	Brüssel, Bibliothèque Royale Albert 1er
Beur	Erich Beurmann, *Die Klaviersonaten Ph. E. Bachs* (Dissertation), Göttingen 1952, S. 118–145: Katalog der Klaviersonaten
CPEB	Carl Philipp Emanuel Bach (Schrift)
D-brd-B	Berlin (West), Staatsbibliothek Preußischer Kulturbesitz
D-brd-BP	Sammlung Pretlack, jetzt in D-brd-B
D-brd-Kll	Kiel, Schleswig-Holsteinische Landesbibliothek
D-brd-Mbs	München, Bayerische Staatsbibliothek
D-ddr-Bds	Berlin, Deutsche Staatsbibliothek
D-ddr-Bthu	Sammlung Thulemeier, jetzt in D-brd-B und D-ddr-Bds
D-ddr-GOl	Gotha, Forschungsbibliothek
D-ddr-LEb	Leipzig, Bach-Archiv
D-ddr-LEm	Leipzig, Musikbibliothek der Stadt
D-ddr-SWl	Schwerin, Wissenschaftliche Allgemeinbibliothek
Gorke Slg	Sammlung Gorke, jetzt in D-ddr-LEb
NV	*Verzeichnis des musikalischen Nachlasses des verstorbenen Capellmeisters Carl Philipp Emanuel Bach*, Hamburg 1790; Faks.-Ausgabe, hrsg. von R. Wade, New York 1981
PL-Kj	Krakow, Bibliotéka Jagiellońska
US-Wc	Washington, D. C., Library of Congress
Wq	Alfred Wotquenne, *Thematisches Verzeichnis der Werke von Carl Philipp Emanuel Bach*, Leipzig 1905 (Reprint Wiesbaden 1964)

Der vorliegende Beitrag geht auf ein Referat zurück, das unter dem Titel *Revision in C. P. E. Bach's Keyboard Sonatas* im November 1985 auf dem Annual Meeting der American Musicological Society in Vancouver gehalten wurde.

Publisher's note

An English version of this article updated by the author is available online at: http://faculty.wagner.edu/david-schulenberg/c-p-e-bach-from-ashgate/.

[7]

Carl Philipp Emanuel Bach, the Restless Composer

RACHEL W. WADE

As a composer Carl Philipp Emanuel Bach was restless in the sense that he frequently revised his works. His revisions run the gamut from changing one note to recasting entire movements or substituting one aria for another within a large-scale vocal work. He frequently prepared arrangements or alternate versions, yet another expression of restlessness, and often in the process he altered the musical content of the work as originally conceived. These changes often date from several years after he had finished the work. For example, his monumental Passion Cantata underwent changes of all sorts over nearly twenty years.

Why was Bach so restless? There is no single answer. When it is even possible to guess his motivation, a variety of reasons spring to mind. While for the most part Bach revised on musical grounds, he was also swayed by practical considerations, such as the performing talent at hand, or outside influences that become apparent from studying his biography.

When Bach did revise on musical grounds, he of course occasionally did so because what he had written contained an obvious mistake, but in general he revised out of consideration for the overall structure of a work. It is no accident that time after time his revisions occur at crucial junctures in the form of a piece: in concertos, immediately before the re-entrance of the tutti; in songs, at ends of lines; or in any vocal music, at important dramatic moments as defined by the text. These critical points seemed to remain in his subconscious, and whenever a better solution occurred to him, he did not hesitate to pluck out the score and enter the change. The autograph scores therefore can preserve many layers of revision. The manuscript copies made by his copyists from time to time are very valuable in that they freeze the work as it existed at a given time.

Bach's concern with the large-scale structure of a work is reflected in his treatment of Christian Fürchtegott Gellert's poem "Bitten". For this text he wrote both a solo song and an arrangement for soprano, alto, tenor, bass, and continuo[1]. For his solo song Bach followed the usual procedure of set-

---

1 E. E. Helm, *Thematic Catalogue of the Works of Carl Philipp Emanuel Bach,* New Haven: 1989, in H.686/9 and 826/3; A. Wotquenne, *Catalogue thématique des œuvres de Charles*

176   Rachel W. Wade

ting the melody once, with all verses to be sung to the same melody (Example 1)[2].

For his four-part arrangement, however, he experimented with a more elaborate through-composed setting in which the structure of the whole is closer to that of a theme and variations (Example 2)[3].

If one thinks of Bach's four-part arrangement of "Bitten" as a theme and variations, then the first verse is like the initial straightforward presentation of the theme. The melody is in the top voice and it is harmonized by the three lower voices. Beginning with the second verse the melody shifts from voice to voice, or even momentarily disappears as the variation principle takes over. As might be expected for a theme and variations, the harmonic pattern provides the underlying stability. This gives the listener the basic connection back to the original theme, with only momentary deviations from the basic pattern.

In many cases it remains unclear which version of a work Bach wrote first. For "Bitten" he undoubtedly composed the solo setting first, since it was published in 1758 while Bach was still in Berlin, and the four-part arrangement originated in Hamburg, according to the catalogue of Bach's estate[4]. Even if this chronology of the versions were not known, one might also guess that the solo song had come first purely on musical grounds. Bach originally conceived of "Bitten" in a three-part texture. For the four-voice arrangement he had to add a voice, which was not easy for "Bitten". Its many diminished or augmented chords had to be resolved without creating parallel fifths and octaves. Bach frequently had to double the third of a chord or adopt other tactics he normally avoided in order to have proper part-writing. Thus his many shifts to three-part texture in the choral arrangement of "Bitten" seem entirely natural.

Bach underscored the ends of each verse within his through-composed choral arrangement by assigning the last four bars of each verse to the four vocal parts, *a capella*. This combination of the four voices without continuo accompaniment only occurs at these important points in the structure of the work. In this way Bach settled on a theme-and-variations structure punctu-

---

Philippe Emmanuel Bach, Leipzig 1905; reprinted as *Thematisches Verzeichnis der Werke von Carl Philipp Emanuel Bach*, Wiesbaden 1972, W.1949 und 208/3. Hereafter the abbreviations "H." and "W." stand for these thematic catalogues.

2 As published in *Herrn Professor Gellerts Geistliche Oden und Lieder mit Melodien von Carl Philipp Emanuel Bach*, Berlin 1764.

3 The autograph score is in the Staatsbibliothek Preussischer Kulturbesitz, Berlin, Mus. ms. Bach P 349.

4 *Verzeichnis des musikalischen Nachlasses des verstorbenen Capellmeisters Carl Philipp Emanuel Bach*, Hamburg 1790; facs. ed. annotated by R. W. Wade, *The Catalog of Carl Philipp Emanuel Bach's Estate*, New York 1981, p. 64, item 1.

ated by *a capella* sections. Now he had to write three different four-part harmonizations for the end of each verse, and this task was not any easier considering that "Bitten" was originally conceived in three parts. It is not surprising, then, that by the time he came to the third verse, he crossed out his original idea and wrote a new one on the staff below.

What displeased Bach in the original version was probably the chord progression in bars 81 and 82. The seventh chord across the barline could not be resolved in the usual way and still lead to the cadential 6–4 chord in bar 83. To avoid this problem Bach threw out all four bars and switched to a higher pitch for the soprano melody. The higher soprano part allowed a graceful and more conventional descent in four-part texture to the cadence.

This change shows Bach's habit of revision at crucial points in the structure of a work, such as the imminent return of the primary theme. The revised passage occurs immediately before the last verse, which Bach made into a sort of recapitulation by making it nearly identical to the first verse. When Bach's original plan of unusual chromaticism for this important juncture proved unworkable, he settled for a more conventional transition, but still managed to bring in the striking chromaticism in a dramatic coda of six bars at the very end.

The concern Bach showed for part-writing in setting "Bitten" is typical of his approach. He often quietly tidied up his scores by changing a pitch here and there, in order to follow the conventional rules. A good example of such a change occurs in his oratorio *Die Israeliten in der Wüste,* H.775 (W. 238). Bach submitted his manuscript of this oratorio to his publisher in February 1775, expecting it to come out in June, as is clear from his letters to the publisher Breitkopf[5]. By July, when it had still not appeared, he was able to lament jokingly, "Meine Israeliten bleiben lange auf dem Marsch aus der Wüsten."[6] This long march was fortunate for him, though, for it allowed him to correct a passage near the beginning of the work before its publication. Bach described this change to Breitkopf in a somewhat labored way:

"So, wie es jetzt gedruckt ist, kan der Satz sehr gut defendirt werden, u. ist nicht falsch: aber blos wegen einer naseweisen Critik, denn selten verstehen die H. Critiker etwas gründliches, und um angehenden Componisten nicht zu viel Gelegenheit zu geben, allzugrosse Freyheiten zu brauchen, wünsche ich: dass pag.2, Systm.13, tact 1, die erste note in der Bratsche, statt g lieber d seyn möge."[7]

Here Bach implied that the correctness of this passage was a matter of

---

5 Letter of 24 February 1775, fully transcribed by E.Suchalla, *Briefe von Carl Philipp Emanuel Bach an Johann Gottlob Immanuel Breitkopf und Johann Nikolaus Forkel,* Tutzing 1985, pp.42–5.

6 Ibid., p.47.

7 Ibid.

opinion, but in fact probably few composers of the time wanted to see parallel fifths under their name in print. The parallel fifths are in the order
diminished to perfect and occur across the barline between bars 18 and 19,
between the second violin and viola parts, and also the alto and tenor parts,
which were in unison with the respective string parts. There still exists an
early galley proof for the print of *Die Israeliten,* in a private American collection. In these proofs corrections have been entered in the margins, and
the parallel fifths are present. The print as finally issued corrects the
offending fifths. Not surprisingly, it also bears the telltale signs of alteration in the places Bach requested, for the engraver had to change the pitch,
and in the process he also damaged the staff lines. Ernst Suchalla explained
these fifths in the commentary to his edition of Bach's letters and rightly
observed, "Wenn Bach nur einiger Noten wegen so wortreich schreibt, muß
man hellhörig werden."[8]

The autograph of Bach's drinking song "Ein Leben, wie im Paradies"
shows clearly Bach's restless nature (Example 3)[9].

In this song Bach so heavily revised both treble and bass lines that he had
to clarify many notes of the final version by writing the pitch names above
the staff. Bach altered the last two bars for each line of the text so that both
top and bottom parts would procede in unison. With this revision Bach
highlighted the end of each line and at the same time avoided some awkward voice-leading near the cadences. He also found a way of using a common texture – that of the unison – to unify his setting of this text.

The drinking song is interesting both for the degree of change involved,
and also since the revisions actually result in a different harmonic pattern
for the ends of the first and third lines. Far more commonly, Bach's revisions affect the melody, the texture, or, less frequently, the length of a passage, while the basic chord progression remains the same. This principle is
illustrated in the aria "Wenn sich Einbildungen thürmen," H.796 (Example 4)[10].

Although this aria is not to be found in Wotquenne's catalogue, it can be
judged authentic since there exists an autograph manuscript with signs of
the composer at work. This source is marked "Aria für H. Illert" by Bach.
Illert was a singer in Bach's choir who was paid for his services, according
to the Rechnungsbuch now preserved in the Hamburg Staatsarchiv. The

---

8   Ibid., p. 323.
9   Autograph score in the Staatsbibliothek Preussischer Kulturbesitz, Berlin, Mus. ms. Bach
    P 349; the revised version was the one published in *Neue Lieder Melodien nebst einer
    Kantate zum Singen beym Klavier,* Lübeck 1789, p. 24.
10 Autograph score in the Staatsbibliothek Preußischer Kulturbesitz, Berlin, Mus. ms. Bach
    P 340, p. 65.

name Illert appears from 1763 to 1792, that is, before, during, and after Bach's time as music director in Hamburg[11].

The compositional revision is readily apparent in the first violin part, where Bach crossed out one and a half measures beginning in bar 2, and then again with the repetition of the melody after the singer's entrance. Bach wrote the new violin part on the staff for the second violin. This staff had been left blank since the second violin part doubles the first violin here. At first glance it is not clear why Bach made the change. He did not alter the rhythm, phrase structure, harmony, or harmonic rhythm. Only the pitches differ, with the descending scalar runs in the first version being replaced by an outlining of the triads of the underlying harmony in the second version. The reason for this simple change probably lies in another revision Bach obviously made in this aria sometime after its completion. The score clearly shows that in the original version Herr Illert was accompanied by oboes, violins, viola, and basso continuo. Later Bach added horn parts by drawing staves in blank areas on the page, both above and below the music. Bach probably judged that the new triadic outlining would be more in keeping with the stark and simple horn parts. But even more important were the changes in melodic direction that created contrary motion between these parts. The original version of the string parts brought parallel movement in unison between the second horn part and the violins in bars 3 and 7. One simple change here eliminated some minor dissonance between the horns and violins and also made the passage grammatically correct. Bach's revision of this area may be called a "chain reaction", the term used by Robert Marshall in his study of Johann Sebastian Bach's compositional process[12].

When a revision deviates from Bach's normal type, that is, when the harmonic progression has been changed, one should suspect that the revision is due to practical considerations or outside influences, rather than Bach's innate restlessness. Such a revision is found in *Die Auferstehung und Himmelfahrt Jesu* at the end of the recitative before the bass aria "Willkommen, Heiland!"[13]. Bach's revision was entered in abbreviated form with both vocal part and continuo on a single staff. With this addition Bach redirected the cadence to E-flat, leading to an aria in A-flat. Transposition down a whole step for an aria immediately calls to mind the needs of the singer at hand. We know Bach wrote this aria with Herr Hofmann in mind, for he wrote Herr Hofmann's name at the beginning of the music. Perhaps Bach

---

11 Hamburg, Staatsarchiv, Ms. 462, "Rechnungsbuch der Kirchenmusiken," pp. 5, 9, 25, 29, 49, 53, 69, 75, 78–9, 82–3, 125, 132–3, 151–2, 158, 185–6.
12 R. Marshall, *The Compositional Process of J. S. Bach,* Princeton 1972, I, 34–5.
13 Berlin, Staatsbibliothek Preussischer Kulturbesitz, Mus. ms. Bach P 336.

had second thoughts about requiring Herr Hofmann to sing this rather high part in the key of B-flat, or maybe it was Herr Hofmann who had the second thoughts. Some confirmation of this hypothesis comes from Andreas Holschneider's analysis of the performance parts used by Mozart in Vienna in 1788[14]. Various parts used for this aria were originally copied in A-flat, the key of the revised version in the autograph score. Later, sections of these parts were removed and replaced by the aria in G major. The singer for the Vienna performance, a "Mons. Saal," must have preferred the aria even lower than Herr Hofmann did.

Performers are not the only ones who affect a composers' decisions. In Bach's case the poet of the text also played an important and collaborative role. This is evident in Bach's revision of the end of the tenor recitative "Die frommen Töchter Sions" from *Die Auferstehung*[15]. This alteration is unusual in that Bach inserted one measure in addition to revising the measure following it. In the autograph score half a measure has been crossed out. A symbol above this passage links the old with the new, which is written on the very bottom staff, a staff normally blank. Here each instrumental part appears successively.

In this case the key to understanding the revision lies in the text. The narration concerns the important moment when Mary Magdalene and the others returned to the sepulchre and found the stone rolled away from the door, with a messenger from God announcing that Christ had risen. In the new version a line of text is added, namely, "Es ist erfüllt, was Er zuvor gesagt." Since Bach was not the author of the text, either he merely overlooked one line while setting the poetry, or the line was added later by the poet, Karl Wilhelm Ramler. The correspondence between Ramler and Bach makes it clear that the latter was the case. Sometime after Bach finished the cantata, Ramler revised the text, causing Bach to rethink a work that already pleased him[16]. In fact, the revision was not easy, as Bach observed to Ramler in a letter of 5 May 1778: "Ihre Veränderungen haben Grund. Vielleicht kan ich davon einen Gebrauch machen. So leicht aber, wie Sie, liebster Freund, glauben, wird es nicht angehen."[17] Concerning Bach's partnership with Ramler Stephen Clark observed, "The process of revision was clearly a collaborative one, but it may have been Ramler's interest in tinker-

---

14 A. Holschneider, "C. Ph. E. Bachs Kantate ‚Auferstehung und Himmelfahrt Jesu‘ und Mozarts Aufführung des Jahres 1788," in: *Mozart-Jahrbuch* 1968/70, pp. 264–80, especially 167–8.

15 Staatsbibliothek Preussischer Kulturbesitz, Berlin, Mus. ms. Bach P 336.

16 S. L. Clark, "The Letters from Bach to K. W. Ramler," in: *C. P. E. Bach Studies*, ed. S. L. Clark, Oxford 1988, p. 34.

17 Ibid.

ing with the text as much as Bach's desire for musical improvements that was the source of some changes."[18]

Bach, the restless mind, now had another restless mind as a collaborator, so it comes as no surprise that Bach in turn pressed Ramler for a different text for the aria following this altered recitative. In his letter to Ramler about the new aria text Bach argued tactfully, "So schön Ihre eingesandte Aria ist, so wünschte ich doch, dass sie im ersten Theile gleich mit einem *Zärtlichen* Adagio anfinge, bey dem ich mich, wie bey allen ersten Theilen einer Aria, ausdehnen könnte." Bach then explained exactly what else he desired of the text and concluded, "Von dieser Art Arie haben wir in der ganzen Cantate noch keine: hingegen sind 4 Arien in diesem Stücke, wovon der erste Theil munter, und der 2te Theil langsamer ist."[19] Here again from Bach's comments about varying the types of arias within the cantata we see his concern for large-scale structure. The cantata should not be a loosely-woven amalgam of beautiful arias, recitatives, and choruses, but rather it should hang together as a musical entity, each part contributing something to the whole. Ramler agreed, and the aria "Wie bang" replaced the earlier one, "Sey gegrüsset." Bach did not reject "Sey gegrüsset" for any inherent musical flaws, since he used it later in his 1784 Easter Cantata, H. 807 (W. 243)[20] Rather, he rejected using this aria when its structure was unsuited to the work as a whole.

Of the revisions Bach made due to outside influences or practical considerations, one of the most interesting is found in the sources of his *Sechs Sonaten fürs Clavier mit veränderten Reprisen.* Howard Serwer has recently established that Bach revised this set out of his anger with a publisher who planned to reprint the edition when Bach still had copies of it to sell[21]. This publisher, Johann Carl Friedrich Rellstab, had bought the business of Bach's original publisher, Georg Ludwig Winter, and he claimed that automatically the right to reprint Bach's sonatas was also his. Bach disagreed, but as he had few legal means to enforce his will, he turned to musical means and revised several movements in order to make Rellstab's publication obsolete. Bach then convinced Breitkopf to reissue the sonatas nearly at the same time as Rellstab's. Breitkopf, however, did not include Bach's revisions in his new edition. Serwer concluded, "That Bach's machinations had their effect is evident from the fact that Rellstab had to sell an edition that was

---

18 Ibid.

19 Ibid.

20 S. Clark, *The Occasional Choral Works of C. P. E. Bach,* Ph. D. diss., Princeton University 1984, pp. 168–72.

21 H. Serwer, "C. P. E. Bach, J. C. F. Rellstab, and the Sonatas with Varied Reprises," in: *C. P. E. Bach Studies,* ed. S. Clark, Oxford 1988, pp. 233–44.

more costly to produce than Breitkopf's for a price twenty-five per cent lower than the norm."[22]

When fully traced back to their origins, Bach's revisions reveal much about the nature of his restlessness. As a musician, he wanted to be modern but still strove to obey the laws of partwriting. He also pondered how to improve the most important junctures of a work, that like the arches of a bridge support its structure. As a pratical performer, he bore in mind the needs of performers. As a man, he could become so overcome by anger or other emotions that he abandoned his practicality. All in all, however, these wild episodes must have been fleeting, when one considers his neatly numbered library of scores, the records he obviously kept of when various works were written, and his planning for the income of his wife and unmarried daughter after he died. On the whole Bach was restless because he was a perfectionist, and that is clear from the scores he left behind.

---

22 Serwer, p. 243.

Bitten.

Gott, deine Güte reicht so weit,
So weit die Wolken gehen;
Du krönst uns mit Barmherzigkeit,
Und eilst, uns beyzustehen.
Herr, meine Burg, mein Fels, mein Hort,
Vernimm mein Flehn, merk auf mein Wort;
Denn ich will vor dir beten!

Ich bitte nicht um Ueberfluß
Und Schätze dieser Erden.
Laß mir, so viel ich haben muß,
Nach deiner Gnade werden.
Gieb mir nur Weisheit und Verstand,
Dich, Gott, und den, den du gesandt,
Und mich selbst zu erkennen.

Ich bitte nicht um Ehr und Ruhm,
So sehr sie Menschen rühren;
Des guten Namens Eigenthum
Laß mich nur nicht verlieren.
Mein wahrer Ruhm sey meine Pflicht,
Der Ruhm vor deinem Angesicht,
Und frommer Freunde Liebe.

So gieb ich dich, Herr Zebaoth,
Auch nicht um langes Leben.
Im Glücke Demuth, Muth in Noth,
Das wollest du mir geben.
In deiner Hand steht meine Zeit;
Laß du mich nur Barmherzigkeit
Vor dir im Tode finden.

Example 1. "Bitten", H.686/9 (W.194/9)

184   Rachel W. Wade

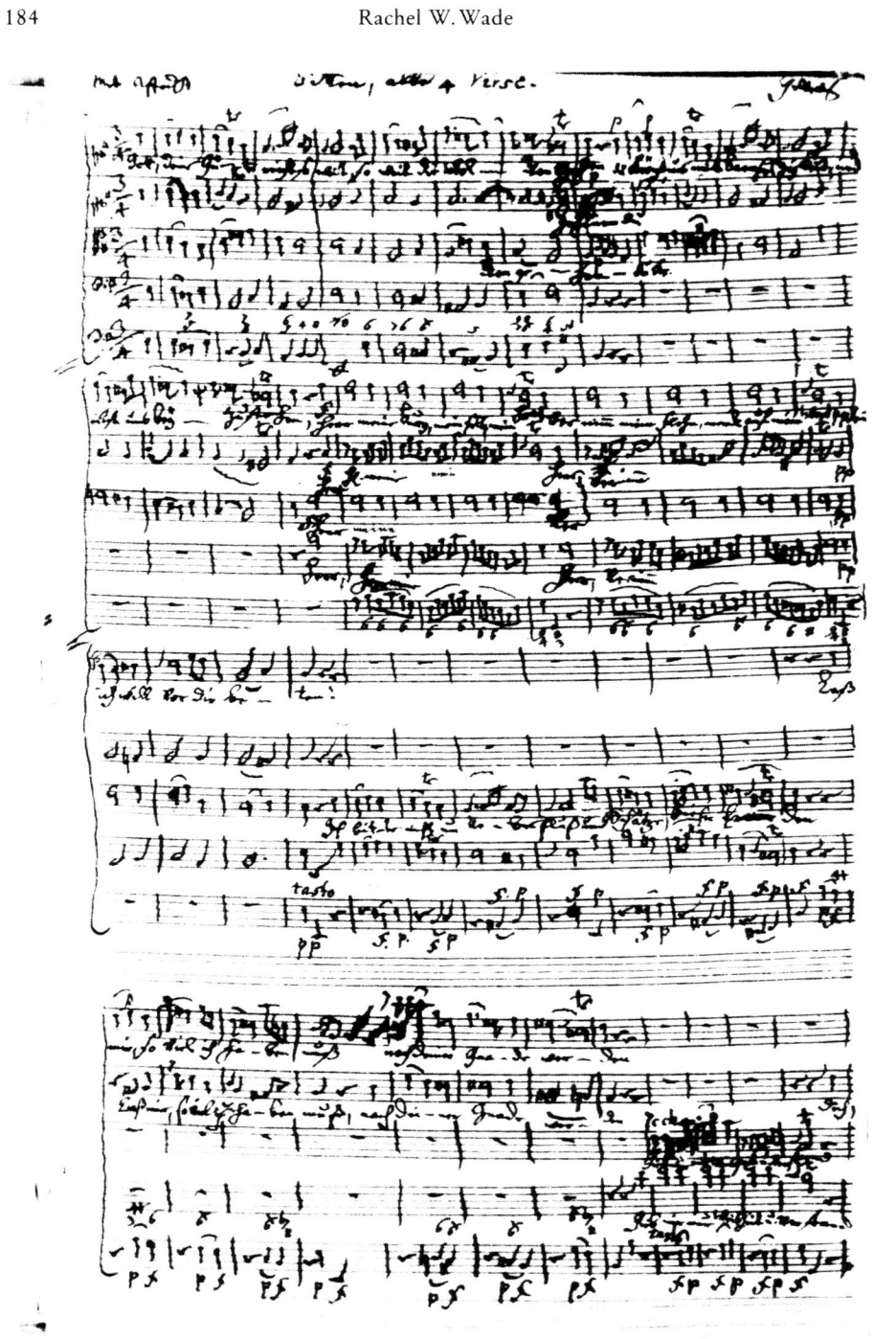

Example 2. "Bitten", H. 826/3 (W. 208/3).

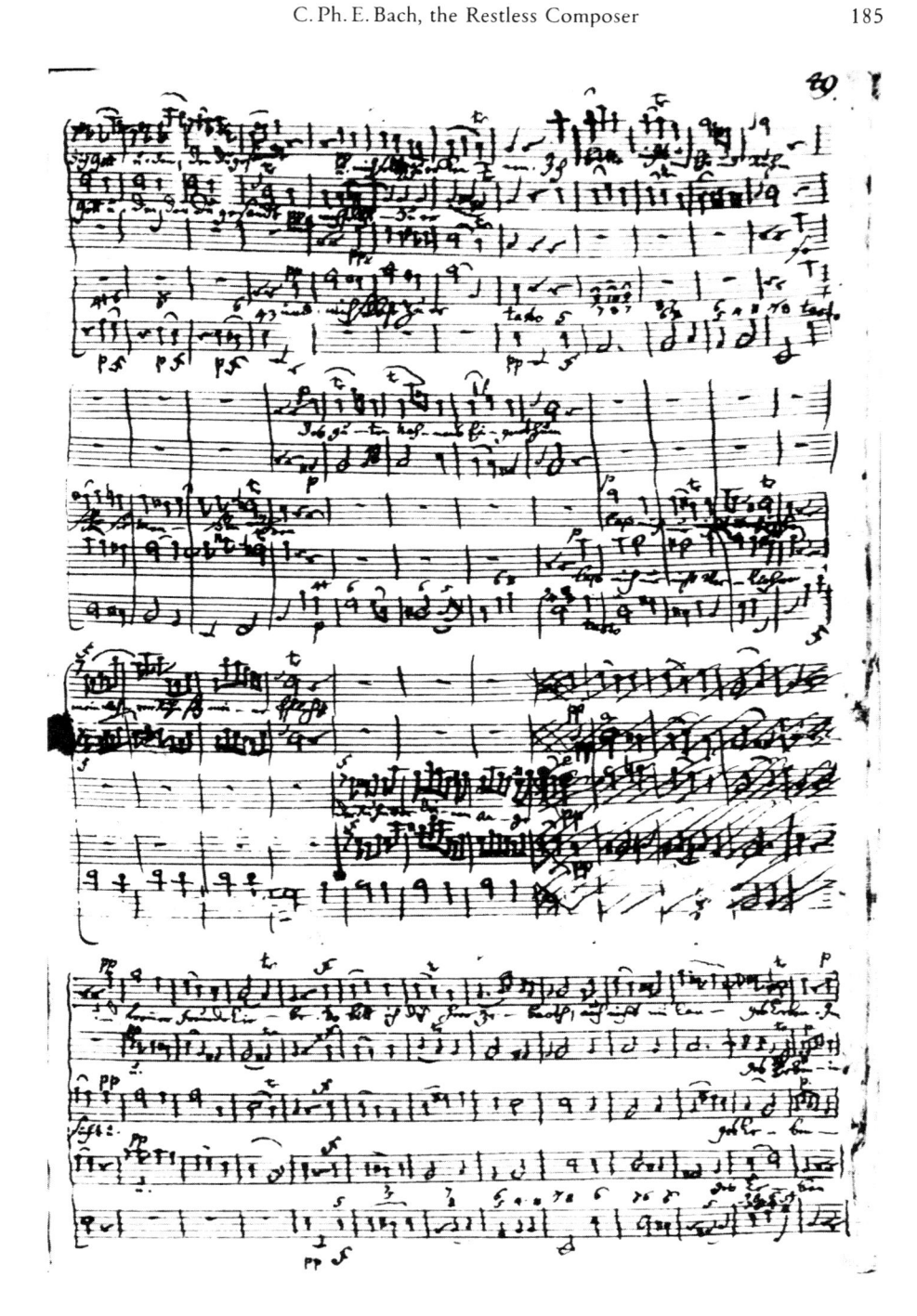

C. Ph. E. Bach, the Restless Composer 187

Example 3. *Trinklied,* H.740 (W.200/13).

188   Rachel W. Wade

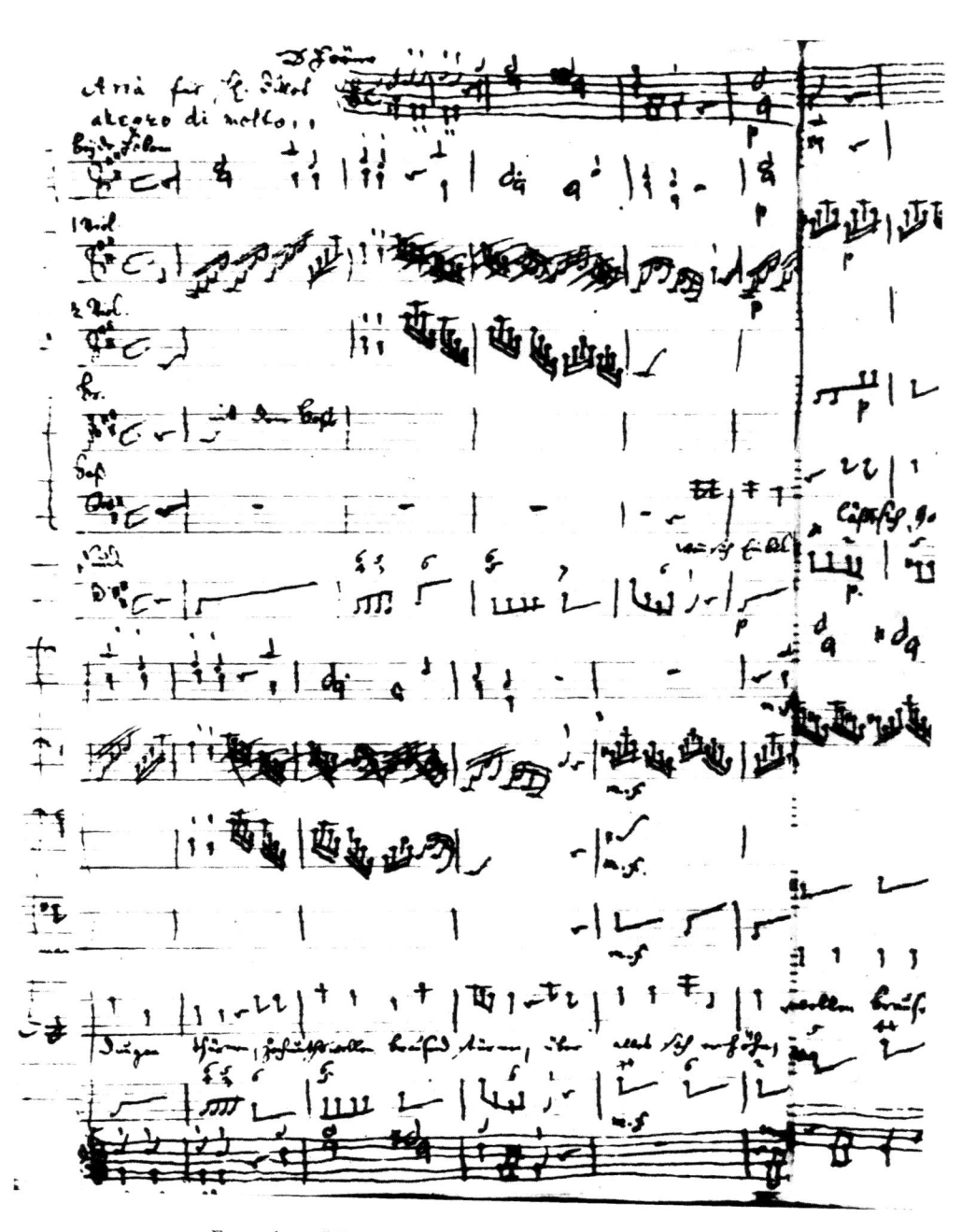

Example 4. "Wenn sich Einbildungen thürmen," H.796.

Part II
Individual Compositions and their Sources

[8]

Two Notes on C.P.E. Bach

John A. Parkinson and Rodney Baldwyn

THE ORGAN SONATAS

Born in 1714 at Weimar, C. P. E. Bach is remembered today as the author of a book on the art of clavier playing, a considerable number of sonatas, and certain stylistic innovations affecting the development of classical sonata form. Most of his music remains unknown, including a set of organ Sonatas written for the Princess Amalia (1723-1787), sister of Frederick the Great of Prussia. Until 1767 C. P. E. Bach was attached to the court of the King as accompanist and composer of the court music. (For convenience, C. P. E. Bach will be referred to as Bach.)

One might have supposed that having been taught music by his father, Bach would have composed in a somewhat similar fashion; as it is, an examination of his keyboard works from the Prussian Sonatas onwards (c1742) reveals a style that foreshadows Mozart and Beethoven, abounding in nervous energy and dramatic tension. He departed from the contrapuntal emphasis of the preceding age in favour of a lighter and more graceful style, laying down the structural outlines from which the classical sonata was to evolve and establishing a link between the sonatas of his father, the Sonata da Chiesa and the Sonata da Camera or Suite, and the sonatas of Haydn.

The Organ Sonatas are of great historical significance because they are among the first examples of the first-movement form based on two themes. They also exhibit a style of writing closer to the clavichord than the organ. Staccato and detached notes abound, and legato is usually confined to the treble line in slow movements. A sustained note is frequently broken up into quavers or crotchets to maintain movement (Ex 1). These slight textures suggest that Bach excluded all but necessities to produce a welcome elegance.

He clearly recognized the interdependence of the vertical and horizontal functions in music, but worked toward a greater freedom of expressiveness and form whilst retaining the essential function of counterpoint to give movement to simple harmonic structures (Ex 2). Ex 3 shows an arpeggiated and melodic extension of a basic one-chord-a-bar harmony, used with greater freedom a few bars further on. The slow movements invariably weave graceful arabesques over straightforward harmonic structures (Ex 4).

Bach's movement sections are not sharply divided, one often flowing naturally out of the other, depending on each other for structural coherence. Several expositions have no real contrasting theme (eg Sonata VI, mvt 1) and recapitulations occasionally omit the contrasting or principal theme, or present it in fragmentary or varied form. Sonata III presents exposition, development and recapitulation in one continuous movement, with an elaborate coda.

These interesting works reward detailed study and are delightful in performance. The 250th anniversary of Bach's birth falls this year, and organists could well grasp the opportunity to restore these works to the repertory. But at the present time, no reliable edition exists. Rellstab's edition of 1790 omitted a Sonata in A in favour of a Harpsichord Sonata in C minor (transposed), and transposed yet

another because of compass difficulties. An edition by Jean Langlais (H. T. FitzSimons of Chicago) is based on Rellstab.

RODNEY BALDWYN

THE 'SOLFEGGIETTO'

Almost the only piece of C. P. E. Bach's keyboard music which has escaped neglect is a certain 'Solfeggietto' in C minor, which is to be found in a great many collections and frequently features as a test piece at music festivals. Unfortunately the version commonly given is a distortion of C. P. E. Bach's original. This may be found in *Musikalisches Vielerley*, published by the composer at Hamburg in 1770, where it is called *Solfeggio*—a title used by Bach on several occasions. Wotquenne lists it on p.45 of his catalogue of C. P. E. Bach's works.

This charming little piece originally ended half way through the final bar on a top C. A century later Berthold Tours issued a version of the piece, in which he renamed it *Solfeggietto* and added a totally unnecessary half-bar which brings the piece to rest on middle C. This glaringly obvious addition has been retained by nearly all later editors, none of whom seems to have taken the trouble to refer to Bach's own edition. An American edition published by Carl Fischer in 1935 ('adapted for teaching purposes by Charles J. Haake') did go so far as to put the offending final notes in small type, but without offering any opinion as to their authenticity.

It grieves me to state that the Associated Board edition of this piece (in Classic and Romantic Pieces, Grade VI) is just as inaccurate as the rest. The only edition currently available which does not distort the author's intentions is that contained in *The Sons of Bach* (Schott), where the piece is correctly titled *Solfeggio* and the spurious ending is relegated to a footnote. But it does not reflect much credit upon all the other editors of this piece that such wide currency has been given to such a vulgar and tasteless addition.

[9]

THE "HAMLET" FANTASY AND THE LITERARY ELEMENT IN C. P. E. BACH'S MUSIC

By EUGENE HELM

MOST musical scholars, if asked to name an important and well-known composition by Emanuel Bach, would perhaps choose the Free Fantasy in C minor for clavichord, first published in 1753 as the last of eighteen *Probestücke* or exhibition pieces (i. e., the last movement in the last of six three-movement sonatas) to accompany Part I of his *Versuch über die wahre Art das Clavier zu spielen*.[1] Like the rest of the *Versuch*, this fantasy was an immediate success in its own time. It became an epitome of Bach's art for the rest of the eighteenth century and well into the nineteenth, a bit of concrete evidence of those legendary clavichord improvisations so admired by Burney and others. When Johann Friedrich Rochlitz wrote the following remark in 1811 on Beethoven's Clavier Fantasy, Opus 77, he was only reflecting a general opinion of Emanuel Bach that had existed for half a century: "The fantasy is truly a free one, and has — in the newness of its several ideas, in daring and surprise of modulation, in learnedness of part-writing, and even in abruptness of style — the most kinship with those of the magnificent Philipp Emanuel Bach. . . ."[2]

Also fairly well-known is the fact that this piece served during Emanuel Bach's lifetime as raw material for a rather strange experiment by the poet and playwright Heinrich Wilhelm von Gerstenberg: the setting of two different texts to it, by which a work

[1] Berlin, 1753 (Part I) and 1762 (Part II); both parts reappeared, singly and together, in reprint, reissue, or revision, in Berlin and Leipzig, through 1797. William J. Mitchell's well-known translation (New York, 1949) combines all these editions. Although the *Probestücke* (issued separately in 1753) are omitted from the Mitchell translation, they are available in a fine edition by Erich Doflein (Schott, 1935, 1963).

[2] *Allgemeine musikalische Zeitung*, XIII (1811), col. 548.

that seemed unequivocally instrumental was transformed into a kind of lied that appears at first glance to belong to a later era.[3] Since Bach's friendship with Gerstenberg was only one aspect of his several ventures into the literary side of composition (I am referring here to his musical compositions per se, not his writings), it seems worthwhile to give an account of Gerstenberg's poetical tinkering with the fantasy and Bach's reaction to, or attitude toward, that tinkering — especially as these exemplify Bach's view of literary or programmatic content in his other works. He is called, often vaguely, both a "Preromantic" and a "Preclassic" composer. There are good reasons for both appellations, and some of the reasons are linked to the rise of literary Romanticism, to *Sturm und Drang* where it might be called such, in the music of his time.

Gerstenberg was undoubtedly the most ardent of that group of north European poets (others were Klopstock, Claudius, Lessing, Voss, Gellert, Uz, Holty, Sturm, Gleim, and Hagedorn) who, together with theorists like Mattheson and Forkel, were caught up in an often obsessive contemplation of the boundary between word and tone, the zone where — as in recitative or melodrama or even program music — word begins to usurp the pre-eminent position of tone, or vice versa.[4] And Emanuel Bach, whose closest friends in

---

[3] The mere addition of words to instrumental pieces was nothing new, of course; both Gerstenberg and Bach undoubtedly knew "Sperontes's" *Singende Muse an der Pleisse* of 1736, for instance, a collection of simple songs adapted from simple clavier pieces. But the idea of adding a text to a work seemingly unperformable in any medium except clavier — and clavichord at that — was distinctly novel.

[4] Some of the better sources of information about this little-understood subject, so important in music of the late eighteenth and early nineteenth centuries, are: Gudrun Busch, *C. Ph. E. Bach und seine Lieder* (Regensburg, 1957); Friedrich Chrysander, "Eine Klavier-Phantasie von Karl Philipp Emanuel Bach mit nachträglich von Gerstenberg eingefügten Gesangsmelodien zu zwei verschiedenen Texten," *Vierteljahrsschrift für Musikwissenschaft*, VII (1891); Matthias Claudius, *Briefe*, ed. Hans Jessen (Berlin, 1938), and a selection from his correspondence with Emanuel Bach in *Allegemeine musikalische Zeitung*, 1881, cols. 577-83; John Wallace Eaton, *The German Influence in Danish Literature in the Eighteenth Century* (Cambridge, 1929), esp. chap. 7; Bernhard Engelke, "Gerstenberg und die Musik seiner Zeit," *Zeitschrift der Gesellschaft für Schleswig-Holsteinische Geschichte*, LVI (1927), 417-48; Ottokar Fischer, "Zum musikalischen Standpunkte des Nordischen Dichterkreises," *Sammelbände der internationalen Musikgesellschaft*, V (1903), 245ff.; Johann Nikolaus Forkel, introd. to the first part of his *Allegemeine Geschichte der Musik* (Leipzig, 1788); H. W. von Gerstenberg, *Gerstenbergs vermischte Schriften in drei Bänden* (Altona, 1815-16), esp. Vol. III; Johann Mattheson, *Der vollkommene Capellmeister* (facsim. reprint of the 1739 ed., Kassel, 1954), esp. the "12. Hauptstück"; Heinrich Miesner, *Philipp Emanuel Bach in Hamburg* (Leipzig, 1929); reprint, Wies-

The "Hamlet" Fantasy 279

Berlin and Hamburg were poets, painters, and professors, was just as completely immersed in this artistic trend as any other leading composer; his and Gerstenberg's paths were bound to cross. Gerstenberg, author of the well-known cantata text *Ariadne auf Naxos*, creator of the powerful *Sturm und Drang* tragedy *Ugolino*, jurist and statesman, was also musically talented — a performer on the violin and gamba, and the founder of a series of *Liebhaberkonzerte* in his house in Lübeck, after the model of his Berlin friend Friedrich Nicolai. He had become Emanuel Bach's friend in Berlin.

In 1767 Gerstenberg, who was then living in Copenhagen, engaged in some musical-poetic experiments with Friedrich Gottlieb Klopstock; Klopstock wrote about these experiments in a letter to his friend Caecilie Ambrosius:

Gerstenberg and his wife sing well, and very much to my taste. . . . We have a delightful little collection of music. We select melodies that particularly please us. We make texts for them when we have none, we change other texts, or we take the text of a melody which we do not like but whose text we like and put it under another melody. . . .[5]

Also in 1767, Gerstenberg wrote this from Copenhagen to Nicolai in Berlin:

Since I am babbling so much today about music, I must tell you that I am engaged in some musical experiments that I should like to have your opinion about. I assume, first, that music without words expresses only general ideas, and that the addition of words brings out its full meaning; second, the experiment is limited to only those instrumental movements in which the expression is very clear and explicit. On this basis I have underlaid a kind of text to some Bach clavier pieces which were obviously never intended to involve a singing voice, and Klopstock and everybody have told me that these would be the most expressive pieces for singing that could be heard. Under the fantasy in the sixth sonata, for instance, that he composed as an example for his *Versuch*, I put Hamlet's monologue as he fantasizes on life and death . . . a kind of middle condition of his shuddering soul is conveyed. . . . Yet I freely admit that one should not extend this experiment too far, since some instrumental movements, though full of feeling, can by no means be sung. . . .[6]

---

baden, 1969); Arnold Schering, "C. Ph. E. Bach und das redende Prinzip in der Musik," *Jahrbuch der Musikbibliothek Peters*, XLV (1938), 13-29, also included in Schering's *Vom musikalischen Kunstwerk*, ed. Friedrich Blume (Leipzig, 1949); Ernst Fritz Schmid, *Carl Philipp Emanuel Bach und seine Kammermusik* (Kassel, 1931).

    [5] Johann Martin Lappenberg, ed., *Briefe von und an Klopstock* (Braunschweig, 1867), no. 98, p. 192.

    [6] Richard Maria Werner, "Gerstenbergs Briefe an Nicolai nebst einer Antwort Nicolais," *Zeitschrift für deutsche Philologie*, XXIII (1891), 56.

Thus it was fourteen years after the fantasy's first appearance in the *Versuch* that Gerstenberg fashioned the *Hamlet* text for it. The experiment was eventually published after another twenty years had passed, in 1787, in Carl Friedrich Cramer's short-lived musical magazine *Flora;*[7] and by this time Gerstenberg had added a second, alternate text — the last words of Socrates as he drinks the cup of poison. The beginning of the experiment and the first few measures of its middle section are quoted here, from *Flora* (preceded by the complete texts alone, with my translations; see pages 281-85, below).

It is easy to see how this fantasy, even so many years later, must have appealed to Gerstenberg's imagination. Consisting of two unmeasured sections separated by a middle section in triple meter and contrasting tempo, it of course fulfills Bach's own specifications for the free fantasia as they are stated in chapter 7, part 2, of the *Versuch*: "It is unmeasured and moves through more keys than is customary in other pieces . . .";[8] "[it] consists of varied harmonic progressions which can be expressed in all manner of figuration and motives"; "the principal key must not be left too quickly at the beginning nor regained too late at the end"; "in a free fantasia modulation may be made to . . . remote . . . keys"; "as a means of reaching the most distant keys more quickly and with agreeable suddenness no chord is more convenient and fruitful than the seventh chord with a diminished seventh and fifth, for by inverting it and changing it enharmonically, a great many chordal transformations can be attained" (a suggestion illustrated perhaps all too well in this fantasy, as far as post-nineteenth-century ears are concerned); "formal closing cadences are not always required"; "it is one of the beauties of improvisation to feign modulation to a new key through a formal cadence and then move off in another direction"; "strange and profuse modulations are not recommended in pieces performed in strict measure . . ." (not a reference to fantasies in general, but applicable here because of the unusual presence of a metrical and tonally conservative middle section).

Gerstenberg did virtually nothing in his experiment but add

---

[7] C. F. Cramer, ed., *Flora,* erste Sammlung (Hamburg, 1787). Cramer prints the experiment on pp. 19-27 and his discussion of it on pp. xii-xiv.

[8] All these specifications are quoted from the Mitchell translation, *op. cit.,* pp. 430-38.

The "Hamlet" Fantasy 281

Sokrates

"Nein, nein, die ernste hohe Gestalt,
Nein, die nahe Stunde soll nicht mich
    schrecken,
Der Verwesung nahe Stunde.
Tod! ich kenne dich.
Geniusgestalt, Geist,
Hoher Himmelsbothe,
Geist, du schwebst den Schwung des
    Lichts,
Unsterblichkeit strahlt von dir aus,
Geist, du bists, der oft im Thal,
Wo ich dich suchte, inbrünstig suchte,
Unsterblichkeit ins Herz mir lispelte.
O du, die in mir jauchzt, O meine
    Seele,
Du bist unsterblich.

Ich soll den Lichtquell trinken
Am himmlischen Gestad:
O heil mir! Unsterblichkeit, Unsterb-
    lichkeit,
Aus seinem vollen Silberstrom!
Ach, wo das Lied der Sterne tönt,
Da, da Unsterblichkeit
Aus seinem Silberstrom.
Gedank, O Strahl des Lichts in mir,
Ach, ich erliege dir!

Todeskelch, Labetrunk,
Mich lechzt, mich lechzt nach dir.
O Rufer durch die Nacht!
O Todesrufer!
Sey mir gesegnet,
Ich folge dir. . . ."
Stirbt! . . . noch bleich vom Gift,
Vom Gift entschwingt sein Geist
Sich, fesselfrey, der Mörderhöhle.

"No, no, the high and serious figure,
No, the approaching hour shall not
    affright me,
The hour of dissolution.
Death, I know thee.
Angelic form, spirit,
High messenger of heaven,
Spirit, thou soarest in shafts of
    light,
Immortality shines forth from thee;
Spirit, thou art he who, oft in vales
Where I sought thee, fervently sought
    thee,
Whispered immortality to my heart.
O thou who exulteth in me, O my soul,
Thou art immortal.

I shall drink the source of light
On heavenly shores:
I am blessed! Immortality, immortal-
    ity
From his full silver stream!
Ah, where the song of stars is heard,
There, there, immortality
From his silver stream.
O beam of light in me, O thought,
Ah, I succumb to thee!

Death chalice, refreshing cup,
I thirst, I thirst for thee.
O summoner across the night!
O death-summoner!
My blessings to thee,
I follow thee. . . ."
Dead! . . . still pale from venom,
From venom his spirit soars
Out of the murderers' den, unfettered.

Hamlet

Seyn oder Nichtseyn, das ist, das ist
    die grosse Frage.
Tod! Schlaf!
Schlaf! und Traum!
Schwarzer Traum!
Todestraum!
Ihn träumen, ha! den Wonnetraum!

To be or not to be: that is the great
    question.
Death! Sleep!
Sleep! and dream!
Black dream!
Dream of death!
To dream it, ah! the blissful dream!

Ins Leben schaun,	To look at life,
Ins Thränenthal,	At the valley of tears
Wo Tücke lauscht,	Where malignity lurks,
Die Bosheit lacht,	Evil laughs,
Die Unschuld weint!	Innocence weeps!
O nein, O nein, erwünschter wärs dir, Seele,	Ah no, ah no, it were better to be wished for thee, soul,
Ins Nichtseyn hinab zu schlummern!	That thou wouldst sink to sleep in oblivion!
Ins Licht zum Seyn erwachen!	To awaken in the light of being!
Zur Wonn' hinaufwärts schaun: O Seele!	To look upward toward joy: O soul!
Die Unschuld sehn, die Dulderinn,	To see the innocent, the patient sufferer,
Wie sie empor ins Leben blüht	How she blooms upward into life
Der Ewigkeit! Sie Alle sehn,	And all eternity! To see all
Die uns geliebt, nicht mehr von uns beweint!	Whom we loved, and to mourn them no more!
Hoch tönts, im Arm der Zärtlichkeit,	Sublimely and in tenderness
Das neue Wiedersehn!	Sounds the new salutation!
Dann stürzt, ach! der Entzückung Fülle,	Then, alas, the great enchantment passes,
Die Himmelsthräne hin!	The heavenly tears are gone!
Wo ist ein Dolch?	A dagger,
Ein Schwert?	A sword. . . .
Ins Grab des Seyns hinab zu fliehn,	To flee existence in the grave,
Zu sterben, ach!	To die, ah!
Den grossen Tod,	Great Death,
Des letzten Seyns!	The last existence!
Wo ist ein Dolch,	A dagger,
Ein Schwert?	A sword. . . .
Vom Thal des Fluchs,	From the valley of malediction
Ins Grab des Seyns,	Into the grave of being,
Hinab zum Leben zu entschlafen!	Down from life into peaceful death!

Ex. 1a

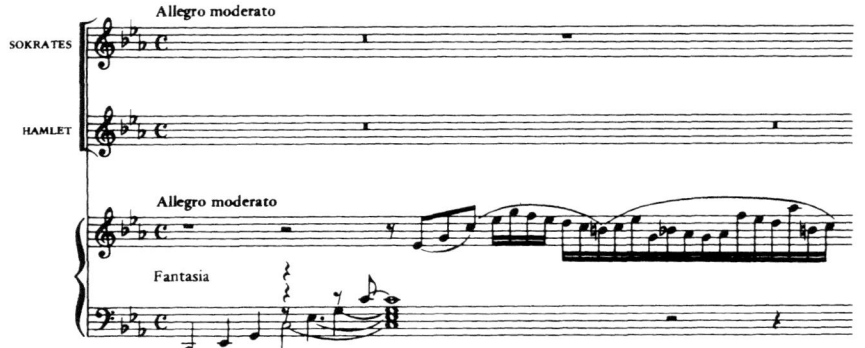

283

"Nein, nein, die ern-ste ho - he Ge -stalt, Nein, die na-heStun-de soll nicht mich

Seyn o-der Nicht-seyn, das ist, das ist die gro - sse

schrec -ken, Der_ Ver-we -sung na - he_ Stun - de.

Fra - ge, das ist die gro - sse_ Fra - ge.

Tod! ich ken -ne dich.

Tod! Schlaf!

284

The "Hamlet" Fantasy 285

words, adjusting only an occasional note here and there[9] in the vocal parts — the "vocal parts" being two different versions of what he thought singable in the fantasy — to make texts and music fit together (not always achieving good accentuation).[10] The natural divisions of sense in the texts correspond fairly well to changes of mood in the music — in the more serene middle section, for in-

[9] The reader might notice that Gerstenberg was a bit casual about time values in a few places; but since few eighteenth-century musicians troubled themselves very much about the minutiae of notated durations once their intentions were clear to the performer, this is not an indication of musical incompetence on the poet's part. In two or three places where the eighteenth-century notation might be misunderstood, I have made a change to twentieth-century practice.

[10] Bach composed the fantasy specifically for the clavichord, of course — his *Lieblingsinstrument*. Although clavichord accompaniment of singing was common at this time, in the present case, where the voice is buried in the instrumental texture, achieving a proper balance between even a light voice and the clavichord is very difficult indeed. Clavichordist Joan Benson and soprano Melinda Hopkins, in the course of producing a fine recording of the experiment for me, finally abandoned the clavichord and used a 1795 Broadwood pianoforte.

stance (see Ex. 1b), where Socrates sings that to drink from the death chalice is to "drink the source of light on heavenly shores," and Hamlet considers the possibility that he might "awaken in the light of being." Unfortunately for Gerstenberg's reputation as a poet, succeeding generations were bound to compare his Hamlet soliloquy to that of Shakespeare, and the effusions of his dying Socrates to the calmness of Plato's classic account in the *Phaedo*. In the Gerstenberg texts — literary style aside — Hamlet's suicidal thoughts lack a dimension of the Shakespeare version, that of "the dread of something after death, the undiscover'd country from whose bourn no traveller returns"; and the tranquil Socrates is transformed into a feverish Teuton. Indeed, Socrates's words are a bit like what the dying Tristan might have sung, and a great deal like the sentiment of the closing scene of Goethe's *Faust*. Perhaps it was partly the German Romantic character of these texts, or rather their character of *Sturm und Drang*, that caused Friedrich Chrysander, in 1891, to point to their immersion in the instrumental web of sound as a prophecy of Wagnerian treatment of the voice.[11]

When Cramer published the piece in 1787, he wrote a careful introduction to it for his readers. Here are some of his remarks:

This musical idea of highest originality requires, perhaps more than any other piece in *Flora*, a commentary. As I have already mentioned in the Musical Magazine (Year 1, part II, p. 1253),[12] the idea originated with one of our greatest composers — I name him: Schulz[13] — like the arrival of a most remarkable meteor; and I dared to ask its originator [Gerstenberg], who perhaps feared that few would be able to digest it, for permission to make it known. This he granted to

11 Chrysander, *op. cit.*, pp. 20f.

12 I. e., in another of his journalistic ventures, the *Magazin der Musik*, 1783, Jahrg. 1, 2. Hälfte, pp. 1238-55, as part of a review of the fourth volume of Bach's *Clavier-Sonaten nebst einigen Rondos fürs Fortepiano, für Kenner und Liebhaber.* On page 1253, having just discussed the two fantasies that close the collection, Cramer mentions that "one of our foremost German poets . . . has even gone so far as to underlay *words for singing* to another no less spendid fantasy by Bach. . . . He chose Hamlet's famous monologue on suicide, and I confess that I know nothing more splendid, in power and original truth, than this underlaying. May I receive his permission to make it kown some day!" Apparently Gerstenberg, who is not mentioned by name in this notice, did grant the desired permission some time between 1783 and 1787, the year the experiment was published in *Flora*. It appears, too, that the Socrates text was added during these four years, since there is no mention of it in the 1783 review. Perhaps being able to add an alternate text helped overcome Gerstenberg's hesitancy about having the piece published.

13 No doubt the famous song composer Johann Abraham Peter Schulz (1747-1800). Schulz is not mentioned in the 1783 review, and apparently had no direct connection with Gerstenberg's experiment other than to commend it to Cramer.

The "Hamlet" Fantasy   287

me, half unwillingly. Its genesis is the following. It had been debated whether pure instrumental music in which an artist had expressed only the dark, passionate conceptions that lay in his soul might also be susceptible to a clear, definite analysis. Gerstenberg . . . made the attempt, and took for the experiment the weightiest [piece] he could think of: the noted Bach clavier fantasy, whose creator had certainly never let himself dream that the unfettered flight of his exalted imagination could be used as the binding thread in a poetical fabric, and for the exhibition of feelings in a piece meant to be sung. . . . From the completely dissimilar phrases of this Fantasy . . . he [Gerstenberg] articulated a double situation for the admiring listener: that of *Hamlet as he contemplates suicide,* and that of *Socrates as he is about to drink the cup of poison.* May the narrow theorists (who up to now have not found out that in heaven and on earth is sung a great deal of song about which not a word is written in their compendia) extract this truth conveyed by experience, and may the discovery, if it can, benefit their souls!

But seriously, I believe very firmly that this eccentric essay belongs among the most important innovations that have ever been conceived by a connoisseur, and that to a *thinking* artist, one who does not always cringe in slavery to tradition, it may be a divining rod for discovering many deep veins of gold in the secret mines of music, in that it demonstrates in itself what can result from this dithyrambic union of instrumental and vocal music: an effect quite different from the customarily confined possibilities of self-willed forms and rhythms. Schulz, who first saw a glimmer here also, and in various songs abolished the bar line and the arbitrarily assumed yoke that went along with it, would be the man to use it [this effect]. . . .

I hardly need mention . . . that the piece is not to be considered a *duet.* . . . The fantasy is to be played on the clavier, and either one or the other poem is to be sung. Hardly will singer or player be versatile enough to perform from these pages on first sight. The fantasy and the song must be *rehearsed.*

C. F. Cramer.[14]

One might argue with Cramer's valuation of the experiment as an isolated work — by pointing out his failure to criticize its lack of an independent voice part, for instance, or by simply trying to perform it! — but his assessment of its importance as a possible touchstone of new freedoms in the lied can hardly be faulted. The novel flexibility of vocal parts and accompaniments in Schulz's songs was indeed a first important step away from the plodding monotony of so many of the songs and odes produced by the "Odenfabrikanten" of the First Berlin School. And Cramer's comment that in "this dithyrambic union of instrumental and vocal music" could be found "an effect quite different from the customarily confined possibilities

14 Cramer, *Flora,* pp. xii-xiv.

of self-willed forms and rhythms" is probably the most important part of his discussion; it sounds as if he is citing a textbook example of what Arthur Koestler, almost two centuries later, was to call "bisociation," or "the perceiving of a situation or idea . . . in two self-contained but habitually incompatible frames of reference,"[15] the two frames of reference being pure keyboard music and pure song. It was essentially this same "bisociation" that Chrysander was driving at in 1891 when he wrote that, in a loose sense, Gerstenberg's relation to Emanuel Bach resembled Wagner's relation to Beethoven:[16] as a literary onlooker — as a poet whose very amateurishness in music gave him an objectivity of view seemingly forbidden to professionally trained musicians — Gerstenberg was able to see the possibility of combining these "two self-contained but habitually incompatible" genres, just as Wagner was able to see the possibility of combining Beethoven's symphonic technique with the traditional procedures and objectives of opera, eventually going so far as to reverse the traditional rule of voice over orchestra. Viewed in this way, the experiment is not a song with an elaborate accompaniment, but is a keyboard fantasy containing its own verbal exegesis; the voice is literalizing the meaning of the music. This was a fine line of distinction, but an important one for Gerstenberg. Obviously he considered the music to "mean" either of the two texts; therefore the process of literalization counted for more than any specific verbal meaning.

Perhaps the most inarguable significance of Gerstenberg's experiment is the light that it casts retrospectively upon Emanuel Bach's music. We do know that Bach made no special objection to it. Many letters passed back and forth between the two;[17] Bach's communications to Gerstenberg are characterized always by cordiality and lively interest, and there is no record, to my knowledge, of his having objected to the experiment's publication in 1787, the year before his death. On the other hand, there is no evidence of strong enthusiasm for such matters on Bach's part, either — which brings us to the documents and the musical evidence that unmistakably demonstrate his real attitude.

15 Arthur Koestler, *The Act of Creation* (London, 1964), p. 35.

16 Chrysander, *op. cit.*, pp. 21f.

17 Most are printed in Busch, Engelke, Fischer, Miesner, and Schmid, *op. cit.* Schmid, pp. 50-59, sets in order much of the Gerstenberg correspondence with Klopstock, Nicolai, Emanuel Bach, and J. C. F. Bach that had previously been published only in scattered sources.

289

Emanuel Bach.

An engraving by Andreas Stöttrup from around 1773.

The Musical Quarterly

Around the middle of 1773, in a rough draft of a letter whose fair copy (now lost) was certainly received by Bach, Gerstenberg mentions a programmatic concerto that he had recently heard, by a certain Tischer,[18] which had been laughed at by the audience. Gerstenberg says that he did not laugh, because, though not much talent was displayed in the piece, there was something to be said for Tischer's efforts, especially since Tischer had tried specifically to evoke particular feelings, and that only a clavier composer of genius (meaning Emanuel Bach) would be needed to transform such good intentions into a new kind of music:

The more I think of it in the meantime, the more evident seem the advantages that the expression of the clavier could win in a collection of sonatas devoted, for example, to some of the most moving Psalms. What would not a beautiful adagio mesto give to this place in the sixth Psalm: "All the night long make I my bed to swim: I water my couch with my tears. Mine eye is consumed because of grief; it waxeth old because of all mine enemies."[19] What an expressive andante patetico would then follow: "Depart from me, all ye workers of iniquity, for the Lord hath heard the voice of my weeping," etc. And how fine it would be if the sonata closed with this allegro: "Let all mine enemies be ashamed and sore vexed: let them return and be ashamed suddenly." . . .

Thus it would remain only to ask whether the clavier is indeed capable of expressing such marked feelings, and whether one can perceive the content of such music when the text is not attached to it. . . . It is in regard to just such questions that I have taken the liberty of writing to you, my admired Herr Capellmeister; only you can answer them.

As far as I as a layman can tell on the basis of a collection of facts, it cannot be impossible to express these marked feelings in keyboard compositions . . . and then why should it be prohibited to distinguish the intended feelings from all similar ones by means of an inscription? . . . Good, the musician sets down an inscription. What does the inscription say? Does it say, "This man with the harp is David"? No less; it says, "What this David sings reads thus in German, and is intended to convey the following feelings." I think even a painter could not do otherwise when he found it necessary to describe the content of his painting just as clearly. . . . Why should one not thank the musician for thus increasing our pleasure by channeling our ideas?[20]

[18] Johann Nikolaus Tischer (1707-1774), town organist in Schmalkalden, formerly thought to have been a pupil of J. S. Bach. See Lilian Pibernick Pruett's article under Tischer's name in *Die Musik in Geschichte und Gegenwart*, XIII, cols. 430-31.

[19] The King James Version is chosen here as the most appropriate translation of Gerstenberg's quotations from the German Bible.

[20] This rough draft was in the Munich Staatsbibliothek at the time of its publication in Fischer, *op. cit.* At the end of this draft, Gerstenberg mentions that "I have already corresponded with your brother in Bückeburg [J. C. F. Bach], . . .

The "Hamlet" Fantasy   291

Most of this was obviously preserved in the letter actually received by Bach, as Bach's answer shows. The answer was cordial and tolerant:

. . . You are, Sir, completely correct when you say that there are earnest feelings which are expressed most properly in music, and I, as a keyboard player, make so bold as to assert that in fact one can say a great deal on our instrument with a good performance. I do not include here a mere tickling of the ears, and I insist that the heart must be moved. Such a keyboard player, especially when he has a highly inventive spirit, can do very much. Meanwhile, words remain always words, and the human voice remains pre-eminent. As long as we can have that which is near, we can ignore that which is further away without depriving ourselves. We should certainly not pour derision on the honest Tischer, who writes under his painting of a bird, "this is a bird," especially when one says nothing about a sickness that offered [me] the opportunity to make certain experiments: I recall when, many years ago, I had my *Sanguineus und Cholericus* printed, and was not exactly insensitive to the jokes made about certain things [in it] by a good friend, who meant no harm but displeased me nevertheless. . . .

All this notwithstanding, Sir, your idea can give occasion for much good thought about our instrument. . . .

If I have more time than presently, I shall certainly dare an attempt of this kind, but simply out of obedience and esteem toward you, Sir, not to be known for it. . . .[21]

---

though with an entirely different motive, on the present subject, expression at the clavier. . . ." A letter from J. C. F. Bach to Gerstenberg dated April 1, 1773, in the old Berlin Staatsbibliothek at the time of Georg Schünemann's publication of it ("Friedrich Bachs Briefwechsel mit Gerstenberg und Breitkopf," *Bach-Jahrbuch*, XII [1916], 20ff.), is almost certainly part of this correspondence: "A composition . . . such as you, Sir, contemplate, on the history of Cleopatra, is not impossible, though on the spur of the moment, only these obstacles occur to me: (1) Every person who wants to play this composition must have a very exact knowledge of the entire history. (2) How many clavier players have the true manner of delivery? (3) Very few . . . would be able to play it. (4) I find the otherwise reasonably adequate clavier not yet sufficient as a means of very perceptibly expressing such a wordless painting. And, finally, such a structure would actually go no further than [any] characteristic fantasy — which, in my humble musical view, is the only name that should be given to it. Admittedly, the clavier can intelligibly convey general character and general passions, in a certain way. I do not know whether you, Sir, would be acquainted with a printed sonata a 3 — two violins and basso — by my Hamburg brother, in which he has tried to convey a discourse between a melancholy and a cheerful man [see the discussion below]. In spite of the great deal of trouble he took with it, one would not feel the meaning of each movement if he had not carefully indicated his intention in words. And I do not believe it would go any better with our Cleopatra. . . ."

21 This reply to Gerstenberg is at present in the Hamburg Staats- und Universitätsbibliothek, Cat. no. 1913/8910. It is published in slightly imperfect transcription in Ernst Bücken, ed., *Musiker-briefe* (Leipzig, 1940), pp. 7-9.

The *Sanguineus und Cholericus* Bach refers to is a programmatic trio sonata published in 1751 by Balthasar Schmid in Wittemberg and entitled *Conversation between a Cheerful Man and a Melancholy Man*.[22] A preface to the music begins by explaining that it is an attempt to express instrumentally that which is usually expressed by voices and words, and then goes into all-too-considerable detail to explain the course of the "conversation," as marked by letters in the music. In the first movement, for instance, consisting of eleven alternations of a "melancholy" allegretto and a "cheerful" presto, " (a) means, because of the half-cadence on the dominant, a question: whether the cheerful man agrees with the melancholy man at this point. That one [the cheerful man], however, at (b), lets it be known clearly enough — through the difference in tempo as well as in the entire content of his answer, and even by beginning in a totally different key [E-flat major instead of the melancholy man's C minor] — that he is of a quite different mind. . . ." And so on through the first two movements, for a total of forty-two points of conversation. Throughout the finale the two "men," though still identifiable, are in "agreement." Needless to say, little is lost if this trio sonata is performed for the sake of the music alone; in fact, it is a rather good piece, in which the quick alternations between "melancholy" and "cheerfulness" are not significantly different in themselves from any of the sudden changes in *Affekt* that characterize many another Emanuel Bach work in *empfindsamer Stil*. One wonders whether the "good friend" who made "jokes" about it might have been Charles Burney. Ironically, it was Burney, one of Emanuel's most enthusiastic admirers, who condemned the work most memorably: "That truly great musician, Emanuel Bach, some years ago, attempted, in a duet [i. e., for two violins and continuo], to carry on a disputation between two persons of different principles; but with all his powers of invention, melody, and modulation, the opinions of the disputants remained as obscure and unintelligible, as the warbling of larks and linnets."[23]

[22] No. 161 in Wotquenne's catalogue of Emanuel Bach's works, the first of *Zwey Trio*. Cf. Hans Mersmann, "Ein Programmtrio Karl Philipp Emanuel Bachs," *Bach-Jahrbuch*, XIII (1917), 137ff.

[23] Book IV, p. 643, in Burney's *General History of Music* (London, 1789); Vol. II, p. 992, in the Dover reprint of 1957. No work other than this one can be meant. Nothing else in Emanuel Bach's production — as gathered throughout Europe and America by the present writer for more than a decade — resembles this piece even slightly. As Bach's reply to Gerstenberg indicates, being burned once was enough; he never again attempted this kind of programmatic writing. The occasion

What did Bach mean by saying in his reply to Gerstenberg, "as long as we have that which is near, we can ignore that which is far away without depriving ourselves"? I believe he meant that two already existing modes of expression were sufficient to convey the kind of poetical meaning Gerstenberg had in mind: namely, the portrayal of the verbal on the one hand by various traditional ways of setting words to music, and the portrayal of the nonverbal on the other hand by means of a sensitive keyboard style. Gerstenberg wanted to find a mode of expression lying between these two, something that rested on the very boundary between word and tone, and that crossed the boundary easily in either direction. Bach was too much the sovereign musician to go that far; he was much more interested in pressing against the boundary as firmly as possible by means of personal "utterances" at the keyboard, setting forth a manner of composition and especially performance that almost spoke, but not quite — or rather, that did in fact speak, but not in words or with reference to words.

Bach's simplest recorded statement recommending the "simple" expedient of setting words to music was made in connection with his character pieces, those two-dozen-plus single-movement keyboard compositions that describe either general character types (having Couperin-like titles, such as "La Complaisante") or actual friends (usually portraying the wives of distinguished Berliners, such as "La Buchholz," wife of the historian Samuel Buchholz).[24] When he ended the Berlin phase of his career he also ended his interest in character pieces.[25] In 1768, soon after he moved to Hamburg — in

---

for Burney's statement was another condemnation, that of a programmatic composition by Geminiani entitled *The Enchanted Forest:* "Music has never had the power, without vocal articulation, to narrate, or instruct; it can excite, paint, and soothe our passions; but it is utterly incapable of reasoning, or conversing, to any reasonable purpose."

[24] Mainly Wotquenne Nos. 117/17-40. The following MSS of character pieces attributed to Emanuel Bach, all very slight works, were not known to Wotquenne: *VI Petites Pièces* ("Le Travagant," "Le Caressant," "Le Contente," "Le Petit Maître," "Le Flegmatique — En colère," "Le Moribant — Il est vive"), all making up MS P 754, now in the Staatsbibliothek der Stiftung Preussischer Kulturbesitz in Dahlem, West Berlin; "La Guillemine" and "La Caroline" (the latter not identical to Wotquenne 117/39), both in the Universitäts- und Stadtbibliothek of Cologne and accessible through Willi Kahl's catalogue of the Ernst Bücken legacy to that library; and "La Juliane," MS 15961 (autograph) in the Nationalbibliothek of Vienna.

[25] See the dates assigned these in *Verzeichnis des musikalischen Nachlasses des verstorbenen Capellmeisters Carl Philipp Emanuel Bach* (Hamburg, 1790; also contributed in H. Miesner, "Philipp Emanuel Bachs musikalischer Nachlass," *Bach-*

fact, while he and his family were still unpacking — he was visited by the poet Matthias Claudius, who was also a new arrival in that city, and who had been primed by Gerstenberg in Copenhagen to pursue the words-and-music theme with Bach. Claudius reported some of their conversation verbatim back to Gerstenberg in a letter, from which the following is quoted:

[Claudius:] "I have just come from Copenhagen, and I bring you greetings from Herr Pastor Resewitz, if you still remember him."

[Bach:] "Oh, yes — how are things musical in Copenhagen?"

Small talk about music follows. Eventually Claudius reports that he "looked him straight in the eye" and said,

"You have written some pieces which are portrayals of characters. Have you not continued this work?"

[Bach:] "No, I wrote the pieces now and again, and have forgotten them."

[Claudius:] "It is, nevertheless, a new path."

[Bach:] "But only a small one. One can come closer to it by setting words to the pieces."[26]

The report could hardly be clearer: better to add words and be done with it, without venturing into the rarefied atmosphere of experiment.

The other already existing mode of expression, a sensitive keyboard style, was, in the end, the only common ground comfortably occupied by both Gerstenberg and Bach. Bach's many fine songs, though Gerstenberg experimented with these too, were no more than tentative material for the poet.[27] Bach was personally uninterested in the melodrama, even though he was virtually present

Jahrbuch, XXXV-XXXVII [1938-48]). Of the character pieces not known to Wotquenne (and not listed in the *Verzeichnis*), MS P 754 (see note 24, above) is a late-eighteenth- or early-nineteenth-century copy of Viennese provenance (see Paul Kast, *Die Bach-Handschriften der Berliner Staatsbibliothek* [Trossingen, 1958], p. 139); I have not been able to date the other MSS. But the trivial nature of these lesser-known pieces, and especially the statement reported by Claudius in the quotation that follows above, make it, clear that after 1767 Bach was uninterested in character pieces.

26 Matthias Claudius, *Briefe,* I, 42-44.

27 In the same letter cited in note 6, above, Gerstenberg tells Nicolai: "I own the following of Bach: . . . The Gellert Lieder [Wotquenne 194-195] (in which I have almost entirely replaced the Gellert texts with Psalms by Cramer or also a song of moralistic content; indeed, in these melodies I have even found a Hagedorn lied to be of use), . . . Phyllis and Thyrsis [Wotquenne 232] (into which I have put a Faun and Diana's nymphs). . . ."

The "Hamlet" Fantasy 295

at the birth of this new genre.[28] He composed no opera. And none of his other music "spoke" to Gerstenberg by verging on the verbal. It was only Bach's most personal keyboard pieces — beginning with the instrumental recitatives in the "Prussian" Sonatas of 1742 and continuing through the great fantasy written in the year before his death[29] — that significantly attracted Gerstenberg-as-experimenter. These compositions, the ones he set aside in his autobiography as being written "merely for myself,"[30] fired Gerstenberg's poetical imagination — and were themselves unaffected by the poet's experiments with them.

These two almost unsingable texts added nothing to the C minor Fantasia itself, resulted in the invention of no new forms, and attracted no special interest from the composer. But what they do amount to is considerable: they are the most striking illustration procurable of what Emanuel Bach meant to his own generation and the next. They proclaim the unparalleled importance that he gave to what has been called the *redende Prinzip*,[31] or principle of expressive musical discourse for instruments, the style that made instruments act out the rapid changes of human emotion, that caused the speechless clavichord to speak. The Emanuel Bach whom we credit with being a major builder of sonata form was less consequential in his immediate influence than the Emanuel Bach who followed this *redende Prinzip* further than any other eighteenth-century composer, and probably further than any major composer in any other era. In making this "proclamation," Gerstenberg was

[28] Georg Benda, who began his career as an associate of Emanuel Bach in the circle of Berlin court musicians, was the chief innovator in this new form during the 1770s, shortly after Rousseau's first productions of melodrama in Paris. Benda's most successful melodrama, *Ariadne auf Naxos*, used a text adapted by Brandes from a cantata text by Gerstenberg. And the air was full of similar innovations: *Musikalisches Mancherley*, for instance, a popular anthology published in Berlin in 1762-63 and featuring the music of Emanuel Bach and his contemporaries, also contains five anonymous little pieces that appear to be program music or melodramas (with the music provided by keyboard only, as in Schubert's "Abschied von der Erde"). One of these, "Ein Compliment" on p. 78, even contains what looks like performance indications for the "reader."

[29] Wotquenne 67, "C. P. E. Bachs Empfindungen," so named in the hand of the composer on the autograph of a slightly different version, for keyboard with violin accompaniment (Wotquenne 80), MS P361 in the Staatsbibliothek der Stiftung Preussischer Kulturbesitz in Dahlem, West Berlin. Wotquenne 67 is ed. by Alfred Kreutz (Schott, 1950) and Wotquenne 80 by Arnold Schering (Kahnt, 1938).

[30] The autobiography, only a few pages long, has been translated by William S. Newman in *The Musical Quarterly*, LI (1965), 363ff.

[31] See Schering, *op. cit.*

only repeating what had already been said many times, and would continue to be said, about this composer;[32] it was his way of saying it that was original.

[10]

TOWARD A COMPREHENSIVE C. P. E. BACH CHRONOLOGY: SCHRIFT-CHRONOLOGIE AND THE ISSUE OF BACH'S „LATE HAND"*

Pamela Fox

Recent scholarship has focused attention on C. P. E. Bach's compositional complexity, particularly his restless penchant for revision and shrewd business acumen.[1] This complexity raises significant questions about the established chronology of Bach's works. Our principal point of departure for answering these questions remains the *Verzeichniß des musikalischen Nachlasses des verstorbenen Capellmeisters Carl Philipp Emanuel Bach.* Published in Hamburg by Schniebes in 1790, the *Nachlaßverzeichnis* was compiled by Bach's family from his own archival record-keeping systems and manuscripts and published as a catalogue of works for sale and as a monument to his compositional legacy. In a letter of 4 March 1789 to Breitkopf, Bach's widow Johanna Maria explained her intent: „Es wird dieser Catalogus eigentlich eine Nachricht enthalten von allen Arbeiten meines seel. Mannes, folglich wird darin aufgenommen werden sowohl was bey mir zu

* Grateful acknowledgment is extended to Miami University, Oxford, Ohio, the American Council of Learned Societies and the International Research and Exchange Board for grant support. Invaluable inspiration and scrutiny was provided through out the entire project by E. Eugene Helm, Rachel W. Wade, and my husband, William Daniel Layman.

[1] Significant recent publications highlighting Emanuel's complexity include (cited in chronological order): *C. P. E. Bach Studies*, ed. Stephen L. Clark (Oxford, 1988); Wolfgang Horn, *Carl Philipp Emanuel Bach: Frühe Klaviersonaten. Eine Studie zur „Form" der ersten Sätze nebst einer kritischen Untersuchung der Quellen* (Hamburg, 1988); *Carl Philipp Emanuel Bach und die europäische Musikkultur des mittleren 18. Jahrhunderts: Bericht über das Internationale Symposium der Joachim Jungius-Gesellschaft der Wissenschaften Hamburg, 29. September–2. Oktober 1988*, ed. Hans Joachim Marx (Göttingen, 1990); and Ulrich Leisinger and Peter Wollny, 'Altes Zeug von mir'. Carl Philipp Emanuel Bachs kompositorisches Schaffen vor 1740', *Bach-Jahrbuch* 79 (1993), pp. 127–204.

haben ist, als was je von ihm verfertigt worden."[2] *The Nachlaß-verzeichnis* does not, however, present a complete nor totally accurate chronology of Bach's works. Bach's records were so complex that his family and friends could not tell his whole compositional story in the *Nachlaßverzeichnis*. Therefore we must return to the sources themselves.

For eight years I have been engaged in a study of Bach's autographs with secondary emphasis on manuscripts in the hands of his copyists, particularly the principal Hamburg copyist Michel.[3] Approximately two hundred of Bach's works exist in autograph or partially-autographic sources, and about fifty autographs bear dates in Bach's own hand.[4] I have systematically studied the evolution of Bach's handwriting within these dated autographs. Subsequently I compiled a general list of *Schriftformen*, differentiated score types (sketches, composing scores, revision and fair copies), and delineated three main phases and ten subperiods of *Schrift-Chronologie* within the broad geographic associations of his career: PHASE 1. LEIPZIG AND FRANKFURT: 1729–1738 (Subperiods: a.1729–31 b.1732-34 c.1734–38) PHASE 2. BERLIN: 1738–1768 (Subperiods a.1738–44 b.1744–49 c. 1749–60 d.1760–68) PHASE 3. HAMBURG: 1768–88 (Subperiods a. 1768–75 b.1775–84 c.1784–88). Within the scope of this paper, these phases cannot be fully explained, but the subperiods are grounded in dated autographs and feature substantial change in calligraphic character.

---

[2]The letter is printed in *Carl Philipp Emanuel Bach. Briefe und Dokumente. Kritische Gesamtausgabe*, ed. Ernst Suchalla (Göttingen, 1994) (= *Veröffentlichungen der Joachim Jungius-Gesellschaft der Wissenschaften*; 80) (quoted as *Briefe-Gesamtausgabe*), vol. 2, pp. 1297–98.

[3]Little biographical information about Bach's principal Hamburg copyist, known to us only by the name Michel, is available. For an insightful initial discussion of Michel's *Schrift-Chronologie* see Joshua Rifkin, „. . . wobey aber die Singstimmen hinlänglich besetzt seyn müssen . . . '' Zum Credo der h-Moll-Messe in der Aufführung Carl Philipp Emanuel Bachs", *Bach Tage* 1986 (Berlin), pp. 104–16. My work on Michel's Schriftchronologie, supporting but expanding Rifkin's conclusions, is not discussed in this paper.

[4]For a list of autograph sources compiled by Rachel W. Wade (though not complete), see E. Eugene Helm, *Thematic Catalogue of the Works of Carl Philipp Emanuel Bach* (New Haven, 1989), p. 242.

A clear understanding of Bach's *Schrift-Chronologie* combines with new knowledge about watermarks and rastrology. Thus it ist now possible to reexamine the dates set forth in the *Nachlaßverzeichnis* and move toward a revised, comprehensive chronology. This new approach suggests that we should revise the dating of more than 25 % of Bach's works. In this paper, part of a much larger study, I will first establish the broad evolution of Bach's handwriting with particular attention to the tremor that afffected C. P. E. Bach from his thirtieth year onward. Secondly, I will submit several examples of my revised chronology and evaluate their ramifications for *Nachlaßverzeichnis* dating and the interpretation of Bach's unique style.

Over a sixty-year period, Bach's handwriting transforms from a large, curvaceous youthful elegance into a minuscule, jagged, painful economy. The autographs function as graphic windows into Bach's creativity. Nikolaus Harnoncourt suggests that a composer's autograph emanates a magical aura. For every musician, Harnoncourt states: „Writing notes is the graphic depiction of a vivid musical event that takes place in his mind. Thus it is only natural that the emotional content communicates itself in the gesture of writing."[5] The exaggerated and meticulous style of a young composer exudes from Bach's autograph of his Polonaise (H. 1, BWV Anh 123; Staatsbibliothek zu Berlin – Preußischer Kulturbesitz, Musikabteilung [= D-B], Mus. ms. Bach P 225), the 17th piece in the *Notenbüchlein* for Anna Magdalena Bach.[6] In the 1740s intense levels of composition and revision are reflected in the hasty Gebrauchsschrift of many concerto, sonata, and chamber autographs.[7] Bach's neat, economical, more uniform

[5]Nikolaus Harnoncourt, *Baroque Music Today: Music As Speech*, translated by Mary O'Neill (Portland/Oregon, 1988), p. 177. Also cited, in similar characterization for the autographs of Johann Sebastian, by Yoshitake Kobayashi, *Die Notenschrift Johann Sebastian Bachs: Dokumentation ihrer Entwicklung* (Kassel/Basel/London, 1989), p. 11.
[6]A facsimile is available in Darrell M. Berg, ed., *The Collected Works for Solo Keyboard by Carl Philipp Emanuel Bach* (New York/London, 1985), vol. 6 pp. 144–45.
[7]See, for example, the facsimile of the first page of the *Concerto per il cembalo concertato accompagnato*, H. 414/W. 11 (Staatsbibliothek zu Berlin – Preußischer Kulturbesitz, Mus. ms. Bach P 354) in „*Er ist Original!" Carl Philipp Emanuel Bach. Sein musikalisches Werk in Autographen und Erstdrucken aus der Musikabteilung der Staatsbibliothek Preußischer Kulturbesitz Berlin. Ausstellung zum 200. Todestag des Komponisten. 14. Dezember 1988 bis 11. Februar 1989*, ed. Hans-Günther Klein (Wiesbaden, 1988), p. 42.

hand of the 1750s and early 1760s mirrors his preoccupation with pedagogical and less experimental works.[8] Finally, the autograph pastiches, fragments, and fair copies in the Hamburg period (particularly the choral works) resonate his manifold day-to-day activities and systematic revisions to many earlier works create juxtaposed calligraphic layers.

Certain features of Bach's writing do remain fairly constant (Figure 1). Bach's braces frequently break in an inelegant attempt to

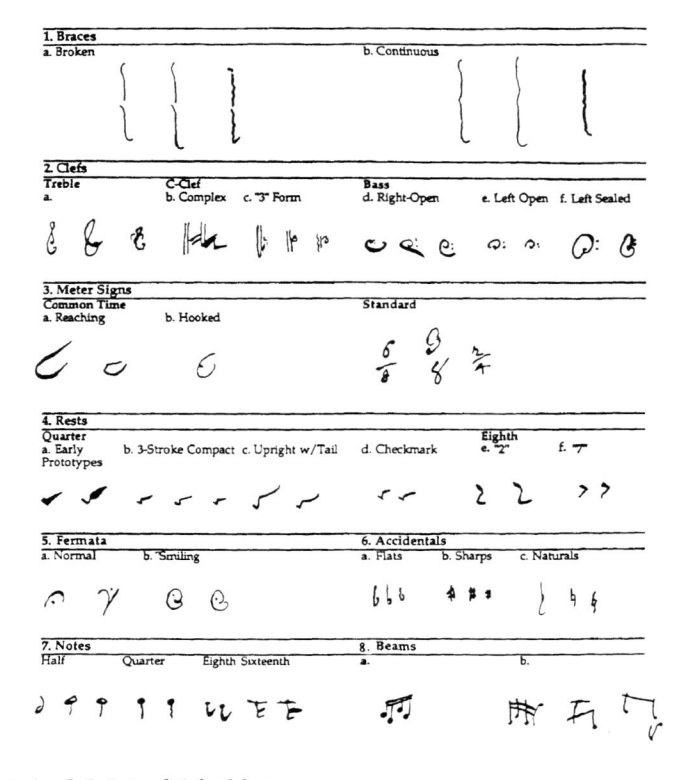

FIGURE 1: *C. P. E. Bach* Schriftformen

[8]See the final page of Bach's autograph for the *Sinfonia*, H. 649/W. 174, dated May 1755 in his hand (Staatsbibliothek zu Berlin – Preußischer Kulturbesitz, Mus. ms. Bach P 351), in „*Er ist Original!*", p. 49.

quickly produce characteristic middle outward flair (1a), though many are also continuous (1b). Treble clefs vary in size, closure, and steadiness, but maintain a similar broken or closed figure 8 formation (2a). The C-clef is not a great aid in dating; the complex, calligraphic model (2b) appears early and in a few later fair copies, but the standard „3-form" (2c) persists throughout most of Bach's career. Common time signs normally appear to reach upward (3a), and a few have distinctive hooked centers (3b). Meter signatures reflect modifications in Bach's numerical formations as observed in his correspondence and Rechnungsbuch entries.[9] One of the more idiosyncratic features of Bach's script is the calligraphic movement-end fermata which resembles a smiling-face, also seen in some of his father's manuscripts (5b). Not shown here is the important evolution of dynamics, ornaments, articulations and changes in letters.

These *Schriftformen* serve as cross-checking controls for validating the authenticity of an autograph and for dating. Some forms become leading indicators within each period of calligraphic development, but others such as quarter rest variants intermingle within single manu-scripts across various subperiods. The eighth rests are more constant: between 1730 and 1744 the „2" form (4e) is common, while a simple „7" (4f) is pervasive for the remainder of Bach's career.[10] Three main types of bass clef appear: the right-opening (distinguished by the degree to which it leans or slants and the thickness of the tail—2d), the left-open (2e), and the left-sealed (2f). Bach abandoned the right-opening bass clef in 1749 for either a left-sealed or left-open form. The *Sonata per il cembalo solo* H. 60/W.

[9]*Rechnungsbuch der KirchenMusiken*, a collection of handwritten bills for composition and performance of choral works in Hamburg from 1740–1800 (Hamburg, Staatsarchiv).

[10]For discussion of Bach's early quarter rests, see Horn, *Carl Philipp Emanuel Bach: Frühe Klaviersonaten*, pp. 155–67. Other discussions of Bach's *Schriftformen* and *Schrift-Chronologie* include: Andreas Glöckner, 'Neuerkenntnisse zu Johann Sebastian Bachs Aufführungskalender zwischen 1729 und 1735', *Bach-Jahrbuch* 67, 1981, pp. 43–75; Georg von Dadelsen, *Bemerkungen zur Handschrift Johann Sebastian Bachs, seiner Familie und seines Kreises* (Trossingen, 1957) (= *Tübinger Bach-Studien*; 1); and Hans-Günter Ottenberg, *Carl Philipp Emanuel Bach* (Leipzig, 1982) (English trans. by Philip J. Withmore, Oxford, 1987), p. 213.

65,24 (D-B, Mus. ms. Bach P 776) and the *Concerto per il cembalo concertato* H. 429/W. 25 (D-B, Mus. ms. Bach P 355), both composed in 1749, illustrate the transformation process mingling left-open and left-sealed types.[11] The change was completed by 25 August 1749, the date entered by Bach at the conclusion of his *Magnificat* score (D-B, Mus. ms. Bach P 341).[12] All bass clefs therein are left-opening, most of the sealed type. This change is definitive and serves as an effective tool for immediately dating Bach's script as pre- or post-1749.

Aside from the definitive change in bass-clef formation after 1749, Bach's gout and tremor is the most critical factor for assessing *Schrift-entwicklung*. Through consultation with a physician at the Mayo Clinic, Eugene Helm was advised that C. P. E. Bach's unsteady hand was caused by „essential tremor".[13] This affected Philipp Emanuel early in life, and we know that he sought treatment at Bad Töplitz in 1743. There is some evidence of tremor between 1742 and 1745, but it is isolated and not in any sense pervasive. For example, the lines Bach added at the bottom of the opening of the third movement of the H. 412/W. 9 in 1742 (D-B, Mus. ms. Bach P 352) shake quite prominently, and Bach's hand also shakes on the long beams in the Helm 348 *Fantasia* (with handwriting dating from 1744–45, D-B, Mus. ms. Nichelmann 1 N). In the 1750s there is very little manifestation of tremor and Bach's hand assumes a more regular and neat appearance.

After 1765 the incidence of tremor escalates and it becomes much more prevalent by 1775. The key factors toward a heightened understanding of Bach's tremor are: (1) what is shaking (clef signs, rests, note stems, beams, etc.) and (2) how frequently the tremor appears (at movement openings only, on isolated symbols, or pervasively throughout a manuscript). Also, the medium (choral versus solo keyboard, etc.) and compositional criteria (composing versus revision or fair copy) must be considered.

---

[11]A facsimile of H. 60 in Berg, *Collected Works*, vol. 4, pp. 33–41.

[12]See facsimiles in *„Er ist Original!"*, pp. 60–61.

[13]Personal correspondece with Eugene Helm.

Yoshitake Kobayashi has stated that the main difference between Johann Sebastian Bach's later tremulous hand and Philipp Emanuel's, is that Philipp Emanuel's shaking was evidenced mainly in vertical lines.[14] This ist true to the extent that the final stage of tremor progession in the 1780s is most visible in the extension of shaking to bar lines, C-clef lines, and note stems. However, the primary consideration is the length of the line, the size of the writing surface itself related to rastrum, complexity of individual shape, and symbol permeation of tremor – or the degree to which tremor pervades an entire manuscript.

One important observation forms a necessary foundation for dating the degree of tremor: the size of score and writing space. It was more difficult for Bach to produce steady, sure writing in small or cramped spaces. In the autograph of the 1781 *Passions-Musik nach dem Evangelisten Matthäus* H. 794 (D-B, Mus. ms. Bach P 340), the aria „Nun sterb ich Sünder nicht'" is crowded into the space at the bottom of the sheet necessitating smaller writing and more shaking than the conclusion of the accompanied recitative's more spacious and sure appearance above. Also, small revisions Bach added after the critical year 1775 (such as the addition of slurs or cautionary accidentals during the process of compositional proofreading) may shake decidedly due to the cramped and uncomfortable need to squeeze details into small spaces. Assessing tremor or dating autographs on the basis of such small, isolated tremulous figures is therefore problematic.

The escalation of tremor after 1775 may be documented through one or more autographs dated in Bach's hand for each year until his death. Musical insertions in Bach's letters and a general study of his non-musical writing offer further evidence. Only the original sources themselves reveal true graphic images. Reductions, excerpts, and microfilm copies are often misleading. My conclusions are based upon examination of the autographs through a magnifiying glass.

All dated examples from 1775–1788 cannot be presented within the scope of this paper. However, three examples serve to demon-

---

[14]Yoshitake Kobayashi, 'Zur Chronologie der Spätwerke Johann Sebastian Bachs. Kompositions- und Aufführungstätigkeit von 1736 bis 1750,' *Bach-Jahrbuch* 74 (1988), pp. 7–72.

strate the transformation. Example 1 (see page 310), *Sonata per il cembalo solo* H. 248/W. 65,47 (Kraków, Biblioteka Jagiellonska [= PL-Kj], Mus. ms. Bach P 771), is dated „1775" in Bach's hand under the title. The noteheads and initial clefs are thick and dark. The treble clef is somewhat smaller than normal to the previous decade and is open and jagged. The bass clef is compact and left-open; the left-sealed bass clef becomes less frequent for the remainder of Bach's life. Unsteadiness is evident on long beams.

All of these manifestations escalate gradually. *The Passions-Musik nach dem Evangelisten Lucas* H. 796, dating from 1782–83, (Example 2; D-B, Mus. ms. Bach P 340; see page 315), illustrates the critical timeframe of permanent deterioration. At the opening of the accompanied recitative „Man riß den Meister hin", the treble clef is barely formed, and the entire C-clef including the „3" tremples, as does the „p" in the second violin. His difficulty in completing complex shapes and the overall impression of dramatic, jagged unsymmetry emerges. Bach seemingly had more trouble beginning this movement than in continuing it, however, since much of the remainder exhibits a surer hand.

After 1785 tremor is no longer limited to movement openings – it pervades entire autographs. From 1785–88 the tremor proceeds metaphorically like a lens that becomes gradually more out of focus while simultaneously shrinking in size. The *Passions-Musik nach dem Evangelisten Matthäus* H. 802/W. 235, (D-B, Mus. ms. Bach P 339), listed in the *Nachlaßverzeichnis* as „die letzte Arbeit des Verfassers", offers the final, poignant testimony. A magnification of the opening of the aria „Erfrecht euch nur" (Example 3; see page 316) shows the unsteady bar lines, short tremulous note stems, jagged clefs and the unfocused character.

Of course we cannot date Bach's hand based solely on the tremor, but this understanding of how tremor escalated after 1775 may be combined with new findings about the paper Bach used in Hamburg to reassess his late compositional activity. We know that in 1788 Bach completed the *Passions-Musik* for 1789 H. 802/W. 235, the *Concerto doppio a cembalo concertato, fortepiano concertato* H. 479/W. 47 (D-B, N. Mus. SA 4), and several key works for which the autographs

EXAMPLE 1, *Sonata per il cembalo solo* H. 248 / W. 65,47 I. Allegro

Kraków, Biblioteka Jagiellonska, P 771

314

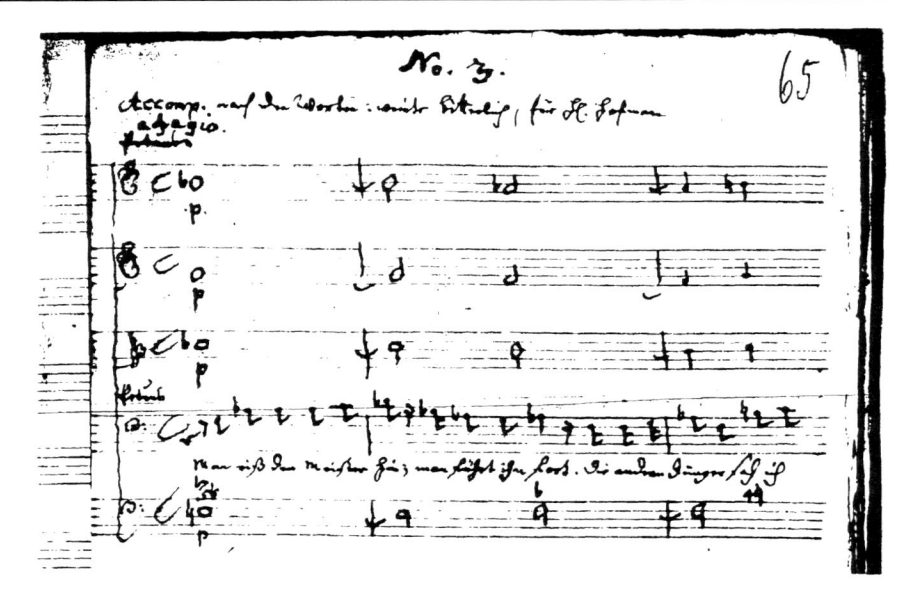

EXAMPLE 2, *Passionsmusik nach dem Evangelisten Lucas,* H. 796: *„Man riß den Meister hin"*

Staatsbibliothek zu Berlin – Preußischer Kulturbesitz, Musikabteilung, P 340

are lost: including the three quartets for clavier, flute, viola and bass (H. 537/W. 93, 538/W. 94, and 539/W. 95) and the two songs composed in the last year of the composer's life on poems by F. von Hagedorn (H. 763). Though dated 1788 in the *Nachlaßverzeichnis*, the *Neue Lieder-Melodien* certainly were not all composed in that year. The song „Ich hoff auch Gott mit festem Muth" H. 760/W. 200,18 is specifically dated „Hamburg, den ersten November 1785" in Bach's hand on an autograph in an American private collection, and several layers of calligraphy and paper are contained in autographs of many of the *Neue Lieder-Melodien* (D-B, Mus. ms. Bach P 349).[15]

[15] The survival of these autographs likely implies that Bach had a copyist prepare a clean copy of the publication's contents. Few autographs of published works are extant, and those that remain are either heavily revised or present texts slightly different from the print. Here, Bach likely instructed his copyists to prepare a clean copy of the songs to send to the publisher with the aid of a list in his hand titled „Liste von Liedern," which provides the order.

EXAMPLE 3, ***Passionsmusik nach dem Evangelisten Matthäus***, *H. 802 / W. 235*
„Jesu, meiner Seelen Licht"
Staatsbibliothek zu Berlin – Preußischer Kulturbesitz, Musikabteilung, P 339

A majority of Bach's Hamburg works are written on a thick unmarked paper with prominent laid lines. While this paper is easily recognized when inserted as a revision folio into a Berlin work, it has not served as a precise dating tool. I have been able to distinguish several common paper types for Hamburg works. One particular paper is frequent within works written between 1787–1788, as found in the *Passions-Musik* for 1789. The paper does not have a watermark, but the uncut sheets are of nearly identical size and thickness with deep 25 mm vertical laid lines. The paper is ruled with a 10 mm rastrum of distinctive light watery brown ink across the gutter with a fairly ragged left edge and features pin holes as guidelines for each single system.

This paper is important for sorting out revisions Bach was conducting in the last years of his life as he extensively reworked many earlier compositions. The Nachlaßverzeichnis lists the *Freie Fantasie fürs*

316

Clavier H. 300/W. 67 as Bach's last keyboard work, numbering it „210". In the autograph (D-B, Mus. ms. Bach P 359), the number „210" and „Hamburg '87" in Bach's hand are consistent with the *Nachlaßverzeichnis* number and date.[16] However, an autograph for the *Sonata per il cembalo solo* H. 49/W. 65,19 (PL-Kj, Mus. ms. Bach P 771) bears the subsequent number „211" in Bach's hand (Example 4, see page 318). Instead of placing this sonata as number 211, the *Nachlaßverzeichnis* enters the sonata as 48, the number in parenthesis on the autograph, and lists the date of composition as 1746.

Most of Bach's instrumental works feature two sets of numbers: the first number is in Emanuel's hand. The second number, usually written below and in parenthesis, is frequently in another hand – a member of Bach's family or a copyist. As here, the second number corresponds to the *Nachlaßverzeichnis* entry. These numbers almost surely derive from one or more thematic catalogues in which Bach indicated dates of composition and revison.[17]

We can now suggest that this autograph was written within the last year of Bach's life on the same distinctive paper as the *Passions-Musik* for 1789, and not in 1746. Whether this activity was recopying or recomposition cannot be determined. The writing is that of Bach's last year – the small, broken clefs, tiny noteheads and stems, shaking crooked bar lines, and pervasive, tremulous lack of clarity.

This same paper and handwriting evidence solve other puzzles. Darrell Berg has uncovered many movement exchanges within the keyboard sonatas, including the insertion of an alternate third movement in Bach's hand for the sonata H. 212/W. 65,45 (PL-Kj, Mus. ms. Bach P 771).[18] I have noticed that this alternate movement is in Bach's very latest hand and is written on the same paper as the Sonata H. 48/W. 65,18 and the 1789 *Passions-Musik*. In addition, it is now clear why Bach wrote this new movement in 1788. The original third movement was later borrowed for the final movement addended to

---

[16] See facsimile in *„Er ist Original!"*, p. 88.

[17] See Darrell M. Berg, 'Towards a Catalogue of the Keyboard Sonatas of C. P. E. Bach,' *Journal of the American Musicological Society* 32 (1979), pp. 276–303.

[18] Darrell M. Berg, 'Carl Philipp Emanuel Bachs Umarbeitungen seiner Claviersonaten,' *Bach-Jahrbuch* 74 (1988), pp. 123–61.

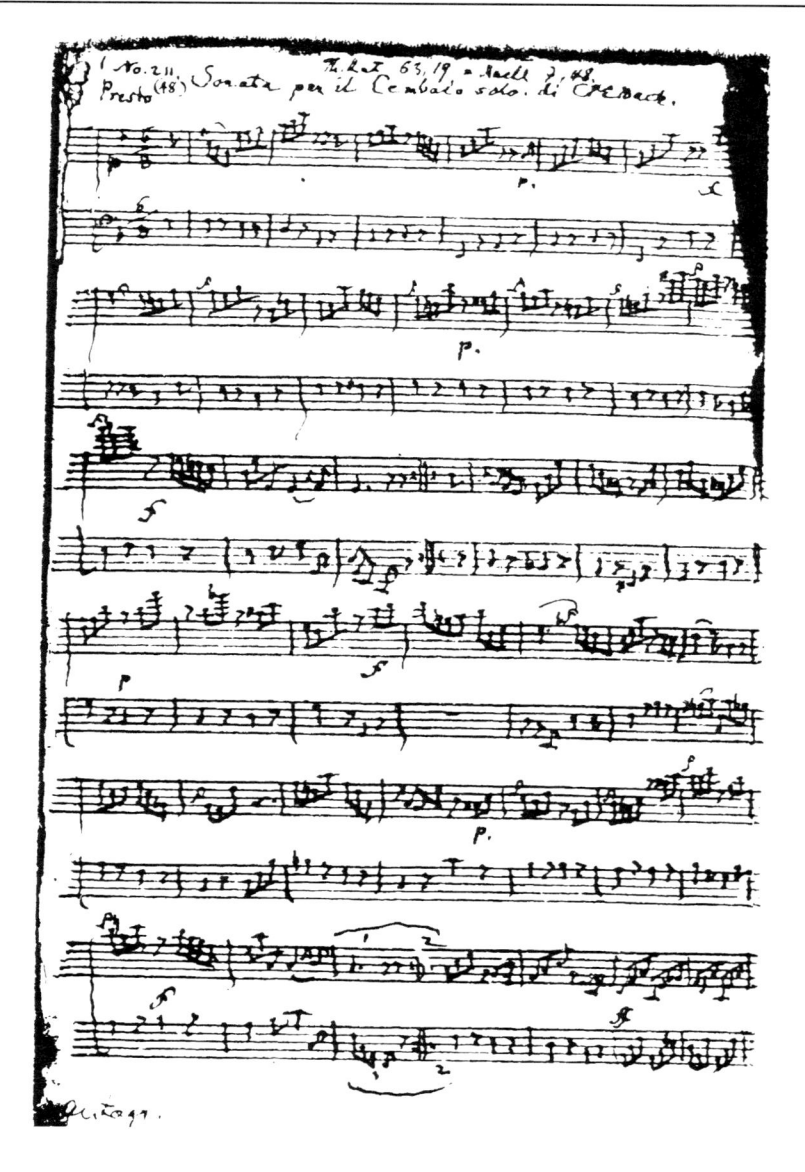

EXAMPLE 4, ***Sonata per il cembalo solo***, *H. 49 / W. 65,19* I. Presto
Kraków, Biblioteka Jagiellonska, P 771

318

Bach's reworking of his last keyboard fantasia into a trio, the *Clavier-Fantasie mit Begleitung einer Violine, "C. P. E. Bachs Empfindungen"* H. 536/W. 80 (D-B, Mus. ms. Bach P 361). He then had to write a new third movement for the sonata.

Our lack of understanding of *Schrift-Chronologie* and the complexity of the *Nachlassverzeichnis* have has forced us to accept certain odd stylistic juxtapositions as Bach's particular brand of schizophrenic flexibility. When reordered, the calligraphic and paper evidence link the movements in similar years and reveal why, in their final forms, some works contain movements so curiously contrastive in style. A final example reinforces these musical and calligraphic combinations.

In 1785 Breitkopf published *Una sonata per il cembalo solo* H. 209/W. 60 that Bach promised to be „ganz neu".[19] Yet, the *Nachlaßverzeichnis* lists this sonata as composed in 1766. Recently I have discovered an autograph which explains the discrepancies between the 1766 date in the *Nachlaßverzeichnis* and Bach's statement that the work was „ganz neu". This autograph (PL-Kj, Mus. ms. Bach P 771) contains the final portion of the first movement of the sonata Breitkopf published in 1785 and two different movements.[20] The watermark and handwriting clearly date this autograph as 1766. When preparing this sonata for publication, Bach kept the first movement from the 1766 work and composed a short transitional second movement and a new third movement, explaining to Breitkopf that ist was „kurz u. beÿnahe ohne Adagio, weil dies Ding nicht mehr Mode ist".[21]

---

[19]Bach to Breitkopf, 23 September 1785; *Briefe-Gesamtausgabe,* vol. 2, p. 1112.

[20]Helm, *Thematic Catalogue,* does not list autograph material for H. 60. Likewise, the useful summary of the Krakow manuscripts by Hans Joachim Marx, 'Wiederaufgefundene Autographe von Carl Philipp Emanuel und Johann Sebastian Bach,' *Die Musikforschung* 41 (1988), p. 155, lists the autograph as pertaining only to H. 298/W. 65,49.

[21]*Briefe-Gesamtausgabe,* vol. 2, p. 1112.

The reason this association has hitherto gone without notice is that only the final portion of the first movement remains – Bach kept the last portion when reworking it for the 1785 publication because the second movement began on the back. Since the Breitkopf sonata's „newness" was its lack of a second movement, and since the third movement of this sonata in its original 1766 form was contrapuntal and rather old-fashioned, Bach saved only the autograph second and third movements for future use. In 1786, when Bach was sorting through his stockpile of potential materials,[22] he retrieved the second and third movements from the 1766 sonata and wrote a new first movement. This layering is visually evident in Example 5A (see page 318) and 5B (see page 319): Bach's late unsteady hand in the first movement (5A) contrasts sharply with the surer hand of 1766 in third movement (5B).

In conclusion, my revised chronology is based upon a new understanding of Bach's *Schrift-Chronologie*, new evidence about watermarks and paper types, and a new interpretation of the *Nachlaß-verzeichnis*. There are two main categories of inconsistencies within the *Nachlaßverzeichnis*: (1) Contradictions, and (2) Omissions. Based upon authoritative evidence of an autographic or documentary nature in conflict with the date of composition provided in the *Nachlaß-verzeichnis*, contradictions normally concern works whose history is too complex to be reflected in the assignment of a single year, such as the *Heilig, mit zwey Chören und einer Ariette zur Einleitung* H. 778/W. 219 and the oratorio *Auferstehung und Himmelfahrt Jesu* H. 777/W. 240.[23] However, the *Nachlaßverzeichnis* does list two years of com-

---

[22]For my theory of Bach's compositional stockpile, see Pamela Fox, 'C. P. E. Bach's Compositional Proofreading,' *The Musical Times* 130 (1989), pp. 651–55.

[23]Bach's *Heilig* was published by Breitkopf in 1779, and the *Nachlaßverzeichnis* lists its date of composition as 1778. The *Heilig* was, however, performed as early as 25 October 1776, according to an announcement in the *Hamburger Correspondenten*. The probable explanation is that when Bach prepared the work for publication, he composed the much-debated Ariette as an introduction. The physical structure of the autograph (Vienna, Österreichische Nationalbibliothek, Musiksammlung, Sign. 15517) supports this sequence of events, since the *Ariette* and *Heilig* are written on paper of two different sizes and display calligraphic variance. The situation is even more involved concerning *Carl Wilhelm Rammlers Auferstehung und Himmelfahrt Jesu*.

position for each Passion (the year of preparation and the year of performance). *Omissions*, or works supported by a high probability of authenticity which are not included in the *Nachlaßverzeichnis*, are more problematic. Even though the *Nachlaßverzeichnis* attempted to convey revisions and alternate versions attendant to many works, it is far from complete in this respect. Movement exchanges between works, further revisions, alternate versions, and even complete authoritative works are unaccounted for.

Both categories of the inconsistency of the *Nachlaßverzeichnis* are signaled by the following: the existence of a wide gap beetween date of *Nachlaßverzeichnis* and date of publication; calligraphic discrepancy; variance between the two sets of authoritative Bach-household numbers written on individual manuscripts; and newspaper announcements or letters which confirm the authentic existence of a work excluded from the *Nachlaßverzeichnis* or which support the performance life of a *Nachlaßverzeichnis*-listed composition prior to ist recorded date.

As a result of a revised chronology we will be able to better understand Bach's stylistic development, particularly his late Hamburg style. Bach was a restless perfectionist, but he was calculatedly systematic as well. The 1780s mix his works reserved from circulation with newly composed movements in the distinctive late style. We are reminded of Bach's own words from a 2 December 1772 letter to Breitkopf: „Es lebe die Ordnung u. Betriebsamkeit! Was hilft das beste Herz ohne jene!"[24]

Although the *Nachlaßverzeichnis* lists the date of composition as 1777 and 1778, the work was performed in some version as early as April 1774. Moreover, Bach made substantial changes to the work between May 1778 and November 1780, after the date listed in the *Nachlaßverzeichnis*. The layered calligraphic complexity of the autograph (D-B, Mus. ms. Bach P 336) supports this intricate history of changes which were likely concluded only with the work's publication in 1787. For insight into both works, see Richard Kramer, 'The New Modulation of the 177s: C. P. E. Bach in Theory, Criticism, and Practice,' *Journal of the American Musicological Society* 38 (1985), pp. 551–92.

[24]*Briefe-Gesamtausgabe,* vol. 1, p. 293.

EXAMPLE 5A, *Sonata per il cembalo solo*, H. 298 / W. 65,49 I. Allegretto
Kraków, Biblioteka Jagiellonska, P 771

322

EXAMPLE 5B, *Sonata per il cembalo solo*, *H. 298 / W. 65,49* III. Allegro
Kraków, Biblioteka Jagiellonska, P 771

[11]

Carl Philipp Emanuel Bach: The Complete Keyboard Concertos and Ensemble Sonatinas

Jane Stevens

3 (Djursholm: Grammofon AB BIS CD-767)

When **Carl Philipp Emanuel Bach** (1714-1788) wrote his very first solo keyboard concerto (H.403 [W.1], recorded in volume 1 of this series [BIS-CD-707]), he was a 19-year-old Leipzig university student ambitious to compose (and perform) the most modern music for keyboard. The project of writing a solo concerto for a principal keyboard instrument, instead of for the more expected violin or oboe, was still rather new and unusual in the 1730s, and one that few composers – apart from Emanuel's father, Sebastian Bach – had pursued. The solo concerto itself, however, had by 1730 established a strong and widely recognized Italianate tradition led most famously by the Venetian violinist Antonio Vivaldi. It was in fact Vivaldi's early concertos from around 1710 that had provided the young Sebastian Bach with his most important models of the modern Italian string concerto, embodying a new concerto manner that exploited the potential excitement of a massed group of stringed instruments by setting them against passages for a single solo instrument supported only by a bass part. And the senior Bach was not alone in his enthusiasm for this new concerto style: from the second decade of the century onward the popularity of Vivaldi's concertos swept through northern Europe.

By 1738, then, when Emanuel Bach took up a position in Berlin as keyboard player in the fledgling court of Frederick II, the Italianate concerto had an accepted role in German chamber music. It was the largest sort of instrumental piece – in terms of both length and ensemble size – that was commonly performed outside the church or the theatre, apart from the fledgling symphony (to which it was closely related); the solo keyboard concerto was, furthermore, the only accepted vehicle outside the church for the ambitious keyboard player who wished to perform for an audience of more than a handful of people. Sebastian Bach seems in fact to have performed his keyboard concertos in their earliest versions as organ concertos that formed part of regular Sunday morning cantatas. But by the 1730s he was apparently performing these pieces on the harpsichord, both at home musical gatherings and at the more public coffee-house meetings of the Leipzig *Collegium musicum*. During the next few decades the number and size of such semi-public musical performances grew steadily in Germany, as in most other countries in Europe, until by the last quarter of the century an institution closely resembling the modern concert became widespread. During the nearly thirty years that Emanuel remained in Frederick's musical establishment in Berlin he may have played his concertos at court; but he most probably performed them much more often in a variety of other private as well as public musical gatherings.

The solo concerto was from the beginning admirably adapted to these new music-making circumstances, and continued to develop within the context of concerts directed toward the serious entertainment of a somewhat knowledgeable but nonetheless relatively large (and steadily growing) audience. When larger audiences prompted the use of larger performing spaces, the string parts could in principle be reinforced by as many instruments as were available; and the solo virtuoso's typical propensity for public display led easily both to increased length and to heightened excitement. The German composers of Emanuel Bach's generation had adopted a rather standardized version of the three-movement concerto plan cultivated by Vivaldi in the 1720s and 1730s. By 1740 the earlier emphasis on frequent timbral juxtapositions of the full string group with the very different sound of a single instrument with bass had given way to the more expansive development of a small number of individual sections: extended sections for the *tutti* strings now alternate with even longer ones dominated by the solo instrument. Thus each of the movements of the three concertos on this disc is divided into a rather small number of large parts defined essentially by timbre. A schematic representation might show quite long *tutti* sections at the beginning and end of each movement, with two or three internal ones that serve to delimit three or four long sections predominantly for the solo keyboard. Yet the oversimplifications of such an abstraction are immediately obvious: the solo keyboard player plays a traditional *basso continuo* part throughout the string passages, and the 'solo sections' are frequently interrupted by brief *tutti* passages and are sometimes accompanied by rather substantial activity.

Despite the deficiencies of this formulation, however, it nonetheless serves as a useful guide to an underlying structural principle of these movements, which are usually said to be in ritornello form, 'ritornello' in this case being predictably returning music played by the string group. It is indeed these ritornellos that commonly provide the most obvious harmonic framework for each movement: the home key is established by the opening *tutti* section and reconfirmed by the closing one, while intermediate ritornellos are typically in other related keys. But this structure neither determines nor restricts the specific musical content of either the string *tutti* or the solo keyboard. Each of the tree pieces on the present disc (like those on the preceding one) is thus free to work out a somewhat different relationship between the strings and the solo keyboard part.

Like the works included in volume 2 of this series (H.406 [W.4], H.410 [W.7], and H.415 [W.12]) the three pieces on the present disc were composed during Emanuel's early years in Berlin, in this case between 1740 and 1745. The concerto that most nearly approaches the smooth integration of solo and strings found in H.406 (W.4) (see volume 2) is H.411 (W.8) in A major, which Emanuel composed in 1741, just three years after his arrival in Berlin. As in that slightly earlier work, all three movements are dominated by graceful, galant melodies first presented by the string *tutti* and then restated by the solo with its own ornamental additions, sometimes even in cooperative alternation with the returning strings. The piece seems largely free from any sense of friction between keyboard and strings: the relatively rapid alterations of the two participants that mark parts of both outer fast movements carry little sense of interruption or of conflict, but seem to project a single musical line in a smoothly balanced, gracious manner.

In both the earliest and latest works on this disc, however, the solo takes on a significant degree of independence, achieved by a variety of means. The fast movements of these concertos, H.409 (W.6) from 1740 and H.421 (W.18) from 1745, open with rather depersonalized and formulaic themes in the strings, but the solo keyboard immediately establishes its own individual character, whether by introducing its own thematic ideas or by transforming bits of *tutti* material into characteristic music of its own. And in both slow movements the solo actually superimposes its own music on the strings' restatement of their opening themes, achieving here an immediately audible claim to its separate identity. The composer seems indeed in these two pieces to have introduced something we might call psychological complexity, in which two self-aware musical personalities confront one another with the eventual aim of achieving some kind of workable relationship.

9 (Djursholm: Grammofon AB BIS CD-868)

During the late 1750s and into the 1760s the city of Berlin was in a state of some unease. Frederick the Great, whose court was located in the city, had begun in 1756 to wage a war against Austria that soon exerted pressure on the Prussian economy and even threatened Berlin itself with possible military invasion. For musicians such as Carl Philipp Emanuel Bach, who had been Frederick's court keyboard player for over twenty years, the war meant not only interruptions in court salary payments but also disruptions in other private musical activity, since many residents of means left the city to avoid the possibility of armed conflict. During the six years between 1755 and 1762, then, Bach composed only one keyboard concerto, the work in E flat major this disc (H.446/W.35).

Yet there are signs that in these years a new sort of opportunity for musical performance was appearing in Berlin, one less dependent on the court and aristocracy and more akin to our own modern concert life. Other cities, most notably London and Paris, had already seen the gradual rise of public concerts, held in rooms large enough to accommodate as many as 100 or more ticket purchasers. We know very little about such concerts in Berlin before 1770; but the one clearly documented earlier instance is especially illuminating. In 1749 J.P. Sachs (about whom we know little or nothing more) founded a 'music-playing society' (Musikübende Gesellschaft) of about 20 mostly amateur musicians who met in his home to play a variety of modern instrumental and operatic works; by 1753 the growing number of guests wishing to hear the music prompted the issuance of tickets to avoid a crush, and a search began for a larger space. In 1755 this group was able to offer a public performance of Carl Heinrich Graun's large (and very popular) oratorio *Der Tod Jesu*.

It was also in 1755 that we have the first signs of Emanuel Bach's possible participation in this new kind of concert. In that year he composed three *Sinfonie*, three-movement orchestral works of genre already associated with relatively large public performance; these three symphonies were followed by one in each of the three following years, and yet another in 1762. All these works include horns together with the string ensemble, and many add flutes, oboes, trumpets, and even timpani as well. The symphony had originated early in the century in the public opera house, as the opera overture; but it quickly took root in the similarly public concert spaces that were springing up in European cities. From the beginning it had been marked by a broad style quite different from that of more intricate chamber works, designed instead for larger ensembles and performance spaces, as well as for larger and more popular audiences. Although most of Emanuel's symphonies could certainly have been performed successfully in the private chambers that typically housed his concerto performance, they would have been at least as effective with larger numbers of instruments in larger halls.

The symphony, or at least its concert venue, seems also to have had an impact on the concerto; most obvious is that beginning with the E flat major concerto of 1759, H.446/W.35, all of Bach's concertos were supplied with parts for two horns, whether as part of the initial composition or as a later addition. This new development did not apparently interfere with continuing performances of earlier concertos, however. The C minor concerto on this disc (H.407/W.5), which was initially composed in 1739, was revised in 1762; clear evidence that it was performed in that year. Moreover, this work seems to have shared with the 1759 concerto in E flat major a particular popularity during the eighteenth century, for it survives in an unusually large number of copies. Yet these two concertos reveal underlying differences that may be attributed to the effect on the later work of Emanuel's intervening experience with the symphony. Rather than the individualized galant melodies of the minor-key H.407/W.5, themes of the E flat major concerto depend, especially in its first movement, less on a distinctive melody than on the relatively straightforward harmonic progression that propels it. This opening theme in fact bears a close resemblance to that of Bach's first symphony of 1755, suggesting that the distance between the two genres was indeed narrowing.

The new kind if concert seems also to lie at the heart if a very different genre, an innovative sort of piece that Emanuel chose to call *Sonatina*. Newly conceived, and never imitated by others, these works seem to have been designed to afford the composer an opportunity to appear as a solo performer in the new kind of public concert. He wrote just twelve of these sonatinas, all within the three-year period from 1762 to 1764, a circumstance that suggests they were intended for a particular but short-lived performance situation. In their instrumentation, for a standard string ensemble with pairs of horns and flutes, the parallel the typical symphony of the times but to that ensemble is now added a solo keyboard (or, in two cases, two keyboards). Thus these pieces appear at first glance to be just like concertos, though with an expanded orchestra; but a closer look at the music itself helps to explain why Bach chose not to label them with a traditional term that clearly had particular significance for him.

The music of the sonatinas has in fact little in common with his earlier works called 'concerto'. Whereas those pieces always conform to a traditional three-movement plan, with two fast movements framing a central slow one, half the sonatinas follow instead a common sonata plan, in which an opening slow or moderate-tempo movement is followed by two faster ones, often concluding with a dance movement. The last piece on this disc, the sonatina in G major, H.451/W.98, for instance, begins with a moderately slow movement that is followed by a faster and more vigorous one, and concludes with a movement 'in the manner of the polacca', a triple-metre 'Polish' dance similar to the minuet. Within these movements the orchestra and solo keyboard share the spotlight, sometimes playing all together (with the solo just one participant among many) but at other times giving special prominence to the more virtuoso soloist. The pattern of alternation corresponds not at all to the ritornello form that is essential to Bach's concertos, but is simply applied to rondo-like or two-part forms associated with smaller genres like the keyboard sonata. Typical is the second movement, which is divided into two large parts, each repeated and each beginning – as is common in Emanuel's solo sonata movements – with the same opening theme; since the first part moves the key to the dominant, however, that theme opens the second part in a different key from the first. The most striking solo passages occur during the changes of key toward the end of each part, to establish and confirm the closing with virtuoso exuberance.

The other sonatina included on this disc, H.449/W.96 in D major, has a looser plan common to the other half of the twelve sonatinas. In this case a perhaps initially confusing series of interlocking parts finally coheres into a single large design in which the opening section, played by all the players together, returns in varied forms in the manner of a refrain, while intervening episodes are dominated by the sometimes rather flashy solo keyboard; this long 'movement' is followed by a concluding, often faster movement of a more conventional kind. The sonatina in D major begins with a graceful, arioso ('song-like') section that returns twice more in varied versions, interspersed with solo sections of a much less singing character. Its concluding movement recalls a lively, jumping dance.

Like all the sonatinas, the two heard here are charming, attractive pieces; at the same time, they are less 'serious' and less difficult to understand on the first hearing than Emanuel Bach's earlier concertos. Those works had been composed for a relatively small, musically educated audience. The sonatinas, however, seem to have been conceived for a much more popular gathering, made up largely of 'amateurs' in the original sense, who enjoyed music but had relatively little musical sophistication. They, like us, cannot but have found these pieces a beguiling entertainment.

[12]

Picturing the Moment in Sound:
C. P. E. Bach and the Musical Portrait

Annette Richards

Carl Philipp Emanuel Bach (1714–88) was a man of many countenances: a virtuosic player on harpsichord, clavichord, and piano; a famed improviser of fantasies; a well-to-do publisher of keyboard music for amateurs and connoisseurs alike; the author of the eighteenth century's standard work on keyboard playing; the composer of symphonies commissioned by Baron van Swieten in Vienna and of monumental choral works disseminated to acclaim across German-speaking Europe; and an artist whose works were already ardently and comprehensively collected during his lifetime. But this is only a partial portrait. For a more complete picture of Bach, one would have to include a larger set of characters: the keen member of northern Germany's premier intellectual and artistic circles; the generous host; the witty joker and maker of puns; the musical melancholic; the proud father of a talented painter; and, not least, the owner of the most famous collection of composer portraits of the age. Many of these characters, especially the last in this list, have faded with time, some quite quickly after Bach's death, others lingering on and gaining unprecedented importance in his later biography. But with the recent rediscovery in Berlin of a large portion of Bach's picture collection, this latter—the man deeply invested financially, emotionally, and musically in the portrait—comes back into focus and demands renewed attention.

While correspondences (and differences) among the arts were the object of intense debate in the eighteenth century, so, in particular, were the challenges associated with the art of portraiture. But discussion of the visual portrait found itself intricately bound up with music, as sound and image intertwined around two fundamental issues: the representation of human emotion in the portrayal of character, and portraiture's engagement with the problem of temporality. Bach's interest in composer portraits has much to tell us about the currency of portraiture in the late eighteenth century, refracting the complex interrelationships among musical and visual portraits as they navigate through feeling and time. Likewise, and this is my focus in this essay, the contemporary critical discourse on portraiture and character study offers important insights into Bach's own exercises in musical portraiture.

This essay is inspired by Christopher Hogwood—like Bach, a collector and polymath—whose talk on "Faces and Fantasies" at the 1999 C. P. E. Bach conference at Cornell University started my own thinking on these topics, and through whose 1989 edition I first encountered C. P. E. Bach's character pieces.[1] It is an honor to dedicate this to Chris.

☙❧

That C. P. E. Bach was a devoted collector of portraits was known to music lovers in German-speaking Europe from reports published in Carl Friedrich Cramer's *Magazin der Musik* in the 1780s.[2] But those readers familiar with Charles Burney's *The Present State of Music* in either its English (1773, 1775) or German (1773) edition, would already have encountered Bach's remarkable collection. When Burney visited C. P. E. Bach in Hamburg in 1772, Bach's first order of business was not music but portraits:

> The instant I entered [the house] Bach conducted me up stairs, into a large and elegant music room, furnished with pictures, drawings and prints of more than a hundred and fifty eminent musicians: among them, there are many Englishmen, and original portraits, in oil, of his father and grandfather.[3]

Only after Burney had spent adequate time inspecting the pictures was he treated to an afternoon and evening of conversation, food, and music.

The collection had increased over the years from about 150 items in 1773 to more than 370 by the time of Bach's death in 1788. Bach's letters during this period to the printer Johann Gottlob Imanuel Breitkopf, to Johann Nikolaus Forkel, and to the Schwerin organist Johann Jacob Heinrich Westphal offer a striking picture of the increasingly obsessive collecting activities of the composer. The letters mostly concern Bach's professional affairs, but they include requests for items for the collection, such as that in a letter to Breitkopf written on 15 April 1775:

> I purchased Herr Hiller's portrait here as soon as it was available and this honest worthy German has already been parading in my picture gallery for a long time. The portrait is in quarto. Herr Ebeling thinks the one in octavo is more realistic. If it is not much trouble, I would also like the latter.[4]

Toward the end of his life, even after his business affairs had been satisfactorily set in order for his heirs, Bach continued with a passion to build his collection. In 1787, the year before his death, he wrote to Westphal, who was amassing a collection of his own on the Bach model:

C. P. E. Bach and the Musical Portrait 59

I have a large collection of engraved portraits of musicians and musical authors. Should you have the opportunity to obtain a few recruits for me, please do so; I will gladly pay for them.[5]

Later that year, only months before his death, he wrote to Westphal in more detail about the portraits in a letter that betrays the extent of the collection (now expanded beyond the available display space on Bach's walls) and conveys the complicated business of portrait exchange:

Now something about the portraits. I will take Kellner's. You have made me very embarrassed by your far too great kindness. I thank you most respectfully for Madame de St. Huberti and Herr Professor Engel. I wanted to keep the latter without a frame since, for lack of space in my hall, I now put my remaining portraits unframed in a portefeuille, and will deal with whatever new ones I receive in the same way. Well, I packed the Engel with the frame, but incompetent packer that I am, I was so unlucky as to break the glass, en fin I had to keep it and I am hereby sending the Engel without the frame back to you. As some compensation for you, I have enclosed seven portraits that you do not yet have. Forgive me, therefore, and make do with them. I am still waiting impatiently for a few recruits who were promised to me, then my catalogue of portraits shall certainly be printed . . .[6]

The printed catalog Bach promised did not appear in his lifetime, but it occupies thirty-six pages of the complete catalog of his estate, printed in 1790.[7] By the time of Bach's death, the collection had achieved an encyclopedic scope. To take merely a selection of sitters whose names begin with the letter A, as they appear with their biographical annotations in the *Nachlassverzeichniss*, is to encounter a varied cast of characters: Carl Friedrich Abel ("viol di gambist in London"), Rudolphus Agricola ("theologian, philosopher, and musician"), Jean d'Alembert ("writer in France"), Alexander the Great ("played the cyther"), Johan André ("director of music in Berlin"), J. H. Anglebert ("French court musician and organist"), Apollo ("inventor of music"), Aretino (Guido), ("Music-Director in Ferrara, was a Benedictine Monk, and the inventor of Solmization"), Aristotle, St. Augustine, and, moving on to B, Bacchus ("God of wine and sponsor of music students").

Bach's collection was not limited to musicians, real or mythological; it included historical and contemporary writers, thinkers, and philosophers, among them Erasmus, Charlemagne, Robert Fludd, Homer, Horace, Milton, Leibnitz, Benjamin Franklin, and the contemporary German poets and men of letters Christoph Daniel Ebeling, Friedrich Gottlieb Klopstock, Gotthold Ephraim Lessing, Moses Mendelssohn, C. F. D. Schubart, and Johan Georg Sulzer. Artists represented included, in originals and engraved prints, some of the most distinguished painters of the time as well as the best of their predecessors. Vast numbers of countenances hung from Bach's walls: great masters of the art of music (or philosophy, aesthetics, theology, poetry), immortalized and accorded their due by inclusion into the great pantheon into which Bach knew that he himself belonged, since his portrait had already been fixed in the public eye in Johann Caspar Lavater's *Physiognomische Fragmente* (1775–78). Yet, the collection also included more intimate portrayals, delicate drawings by artist-friends, of musician-friends who have now been forgotten. One can well imagine Charles Burney, his great project to write a history of music at the front of his mind, excitedly encountering one face after another, and then eagerly scrutinizing them for hour upon hour, while listening to Bach's entrancing after-dinner fantasies at the clavichord.[8]

ය80

In a letter to Breitkopf on 9 August 1777, Bach humorously commented on Lavater's physiognomical reading of his own portrait (figure 1). Surely flattered by Lavater's reading of genius in the lineaments of his face, he wryly noted that the picture on which Lavater based his reading was a poor portrait, adding, with the expertise of a connoisseur, that many others suffer from the same problem:

> . . . And have you seen my Lavater portrait, which it is generally agreed, is any-thing but a good likeness and more resembles someone sleeping than someone awake? The good Lavater reasons so conclusively and certainly, although from what I know and have seen only 2 pieces are characterized fairly well, namely Friedrich [the Great] and Rameau.[9]

Bach had begun collecting in the 1750s, perhaps building on a core collection that he may have inherited from his father.[10] He would have been alert to the difficulties of representing character visually from his own experience with pictures, but he would also have been aware of the active debate on portraiture, whether in paint, prose, or music, carried out in the pages of the German amateur cultural press from the 1750s into the 1780s. Portraiture, and the demands this genre made on the various branches of the arts, was a topic of intense discussion. Running hand-in-hand with the literary genre of biography, it was as much a concern for writers on music as for anyone else. Carl Ludwig Junker's *Zwanzig Componisten: eine Skizze* ("Twenty Composers: A Sketch," Bern, 1776) is a particularly good example. Junker introduces the book as "a small sketch of modern music" and it consists of short character descriptions of twenty famous composers, living and dead. The set includes an effusively generous description of C. P. E. Bach in which the composer is hailed as an original genius. In presenting the book as a mere sketch, Junker borrows from the visual arts to suggest for his account a fashionable fragmentary spontaneity, imputing to his descriptions a timely and unmediated truthfulness. But going further into the

C. P. E. Bach and the Musical Portrait 61

Figure 1. Carl Philipp Emanuel Bach, engraving by Johann Heinrich Lips. In Johann Caspar Lavater, *Physiognomische Fragmente zur Beförderung der Menschenkenntnis und Menschenliebe*, 4 vols. (Leipzig and Winterthur: Weidmanns Erben und Reich, 1777. Reprint, Hildesheim: Weidmann, 2002), III, plate 59 (between pages 200 and 201).

62   Annette Richards

pictorial realm, each account is presented, in breathless prose fragments, as the description of an absent, perhaps imaginary, visual portrait. The entry on Johann Christian Bach is typical:

> Somewhat less of the profundity, depth of vision, force and stature of the previous painting [that of C. P. E. Bach] — somewhat more consistent grace, melody, modernity, flow added — but the full family likeness, same plan, order retained, — mixed together; — thus you have here a painting of the London Bach. *Sublimity* [*Erhabenheit*] is the principal trait with Emanuel, — with the London Bach, *charm* [*Reiz*].[11]

Junker continued his prose-portraiture in the pages of his *Musikalischer und Künstler Almanach* 1782 (Alethinopel) and 1783 (Kosmopolis), confirming an integral relation between the biographical project and visual portraiture. Introducing the 1782 issue, which contained a series of short entries on contemporary musicians and visual artists, Junker referred to his prose *Charakters* as painted portraits:

> Since our paintings are intended as true imitations of nature (and hence we also call them Portraits), we can't be held responsible, if sometimes—a botched, one-eyed, big-nosed, sensuality-obsessed face appears; for so was it in the nature we copied . . .[12]

In the British Library copy of the 1783 issue of the *Almanach*, the short biographical entries occupy single pages that each face a page containing an elaborate engraving of a picture frame: the frame that should surely enclose the portrait discussed (this is the layout in, for example, Lavater's *Physiognomische Fragmente*). Yet no visual image is supplied. The frames are left empty as if to encourage the imagination of the reader to conjure a visual image from the verbal character descriptions.

What made portraiture particularly interesting to musicians and writers on music in this period was the way it engaged with difficult questions of time and temporality, or more particularly, with the play of human feeling across time. Lavater's physiognomical analysis of C. P. E. Bach appeared in a section devoted to the faces of musicians and was prefaced by Lavater's own reflections on the problems of portraiture. Lavater acknowledged the fundamental difficulty in portraying musicians: that the musician is messily immersed in a medium antithetical to painting, that of time. If painting is the art of frozen moments, music, Lavater claims, is that of their fluid succession. As a result, musicians' faces are always more undecided, more fluid, looser (*unbestimmter, flüßiger, lockerer*) than those of painters, "as the nature of [their] susceptibility to emotion and their ability to communicate emotion appears to demand" (*wie's die Natur der Empfindungsempfänglichkeit und der Empfindungsmittheilsamkeit zu erfordern scheint*), and hence far more difficult to capture in all their complex-

C. P. E. Bach and the Musical Portrait 63

ity.[13] Perhaps not surprisingly, the part of the musician's body of greatest interest to the physiognomist is the ear. Unlike the pleasingly symmetrical eye of the painter, the ear is an irregular organ, a grotesque flap with its unruly whorls and cavities, which evokes dynamism rather than stillness (figures 2 and 3).[14]

But as Carl Ludwig Junker explained, the problems created by a musician's portrait were only intensifications of those fundamental to the art of portraiture itself: the art of capturing in an instant a multiplicity of emotional states. In an essay entitled *Charakteristische Vorstellung des einzelnen Menschen Porträt* ("Characteristic Representation in the Portrait of an Individual"), Junker explored the idea that the aim of portraiture is less to represent the subject in the heat of a particular passion than somehow to evoke the transition from one passion to another, the ebb and flow of feeling:

> To make man fully recognizable in his variability and uniformity, in the various manifestations of his abilities and desires, and then, in painterly expression, to be able to bind them fast in a moment! What art! What knowledge![15]

The painter must first observe the subject existing in and moving through time. In so doing, the portraitist watches the play and progression of feeling:

> The painter who wishes to immortalize his art, together with his subject, does not [merely] capture him at that moment at which he commits [his subject] to the canvas. [Rather], he observes the man's happy moments, his joyful lovers' trysts; or perhaps he himself understands the art of setting him in an interesting situation. The man gives himself over to feeling; this emotion animates the dead, stubborn state of his facial features, and the unmeaning stiffness of his body; it rises up, and is active in every muscle; now the man begins to be responsive to the pathetic expression, the painter captures him at this moment, and achieves thereby an eternal guarantee of his good taste.[16]

At its best, a portrait is less a simple visual record of physical appearance than the complex representation of a totality of sensibility, morality, and worldview: an ideal, played out over time, though apprehended immediately.[17] The achievement of this ideal representation of emotional character required a sleight of hand with regard to time that verged on the paradoxical and even the musical.

Music indeed would seem to be the ideal medium for the portrayal of human subjects and their turbulent emotional constitutions. Music, according to Junker, not only arouses and intensifies emotion, but it can depict it, both as a gradual progression towards the height of passion or in a single concentrated moment. Superior to poetry in its ability to represent the inexorable progression of the passions, "climbing rung by rung the whole ladder of the emotions," music shares with painting the ability to represent the ebb and flow of this progression with the subtle gradations that, were it painting (*Farbenkunst*) Junker would call

64   Annette Richards

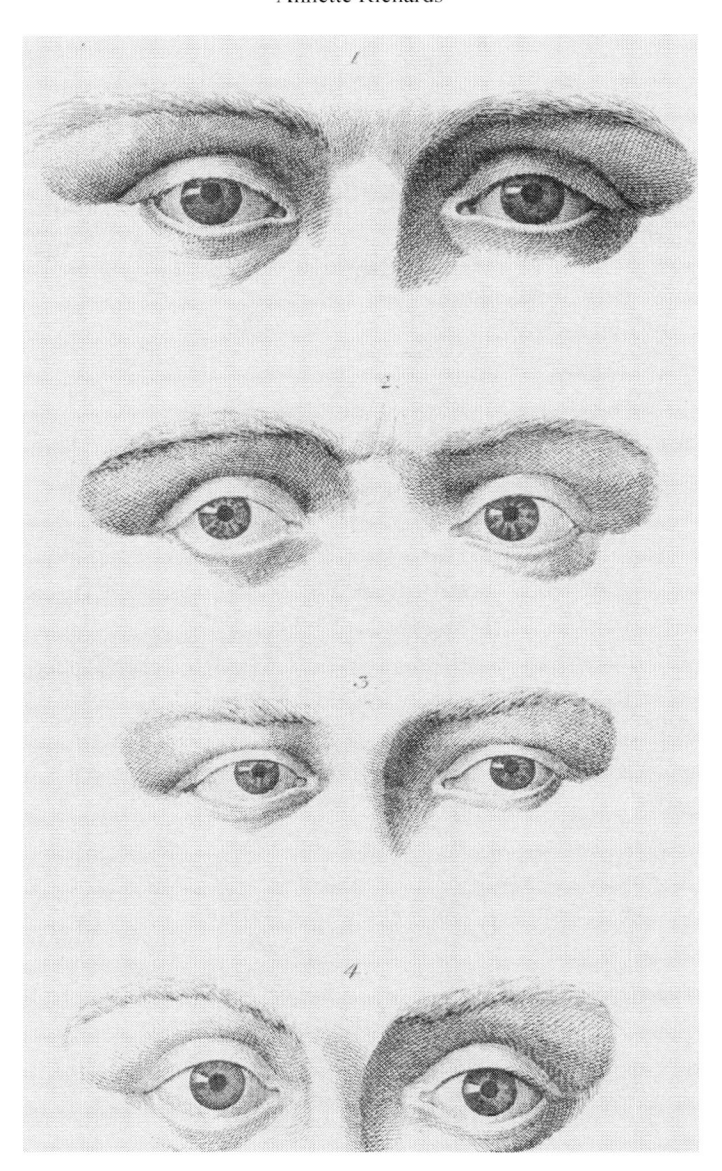

Figure 2. Four Pairs of Eyes. In Johann Caspar Lavater, *Physiognomische Fragmente zur Beförderung der Menschenkenntnis und Menschenliebe*, 4 vols. (Leipzig and Winterthur: Weidmanns Erben und Reich, 1777. Reprint, Hildesheim: Weidmann, 2002), III, plate 29 (between pages 128 and 129).

C. P. E. Bach and the Musical Portrait 65

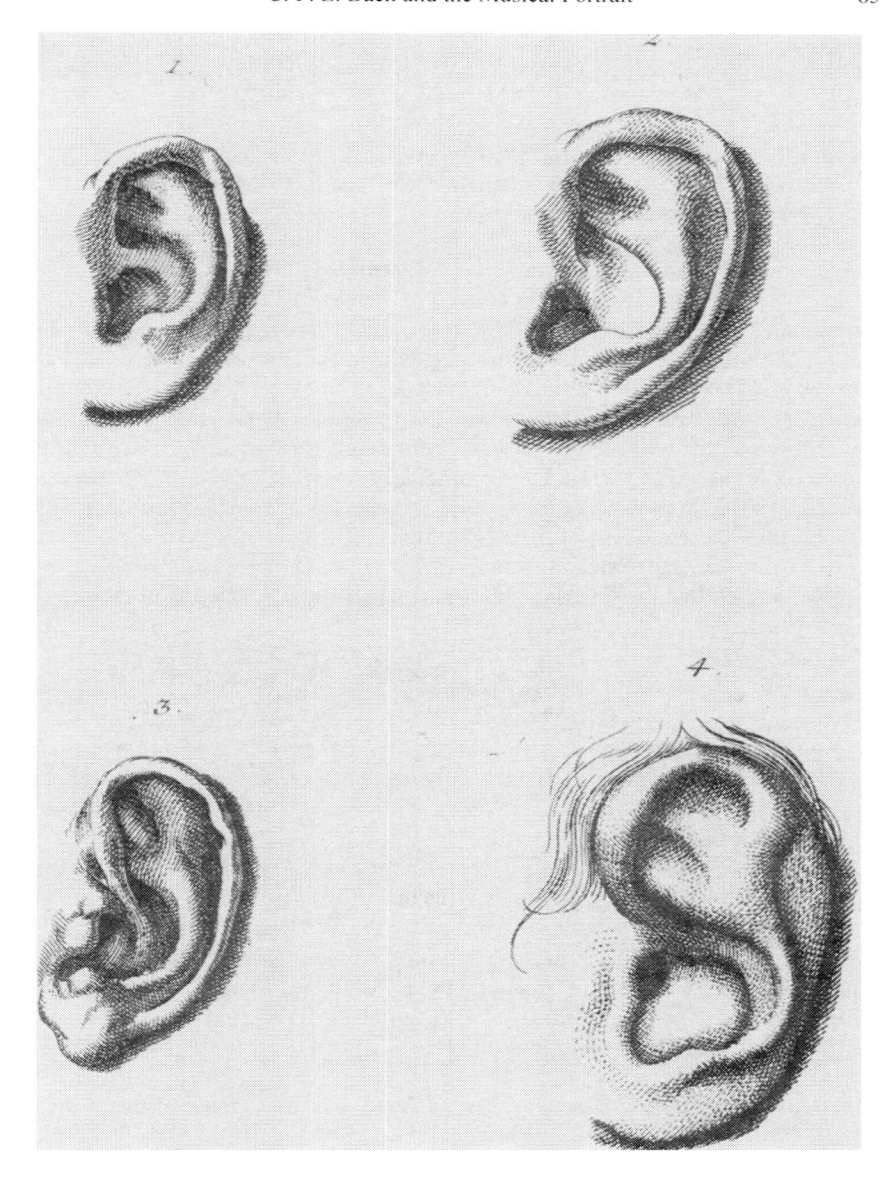

Figure 3. Four Ears. In Johann Caspar Lavater, *Physiognomische Fragmente zur Beförderung der Menschenkenntnis und Menschenliebe*, 4 vols. (Leipzig and Winterthur: Weidmanns Erben und Reich, 1777. Reprint, Hildesheim: Weidmann, 2002), III, plate 28 (between pages 126 and 127).

66   Annette Richards

"mezzotint" (*Mezzotinto*).[18] By the same token, however, Junker, like Lavater, acknowledges that painting and music differ fundamentally in their treatment of time. Junker writes:

> Painting is motionless art, for it is the physical representation of an object, and that object is always perceived instantaneously. Music is progressive, for it is the physical representation of our feelings.[19]

Contemporary readers would have been familiar with this distinction between music and painting. It had been treated at length in Charles Avison's widely circulated *Essay on Musical Expression* (London, 1751) whose discussion of the action of time in the two media was singled out for praise by Johann Nikolaus Forkel in his review of the German translation of Avison in the *Musikalisch-kritische Bibliothek* (1778–79).[20] The notion that a visual image—a painting, say—is perceived all-at-once has since been contested by many art theorists and I will not argue it here. What is crucial to the present discussion is the necessity described by writers such as Junker and Lavater for the painted portrait to push to the limits the fixedness of the visual image. To paint any portrait, especially that of a musician, the artist must magically transcend that fixedness to represent in color and outline the facets of fluidity, change, and the succession of time.

ଓଽଠ

But music suffered its own limitations: fundamentally fluid and expressive, music had the disadvantage of indeterminacy. The question of music's ability to depict particular characters was debated with great interest in the Francophile, art-conscious intellectual circles of Berlin in the 1750s. For music commentators, the discussion focused on a call for the revival of the French character piece, a piece whose subject, however clearly it may be represented in the music, was nevertheless made unambiguous by the addition of a title.[21] According to Friedrich Wilhelm Marpurg, who had recently returned to Berlin from France, music's "characters" could and should be as definite as those of any painting, as proposed by the influential theories of Charles Batteux, from whose *Cours de Belles-Lettres* (1747–50) Marpurg quotes:

> We should judge in the same manner of a piece of music as of a picture, I see strokes, and colors in it whose meaning I understand; the piece strikes, it affects me. But what would be said of a painter, who should content himself with laying on his canvas a parcel of bold strokes and a heap of the most lively colors, without any sort of resemblance to any known object.[22]

Musical character should be explicit, and explicitly indicated.

C. P. E. Bach and the Musical Portrait 67

An essay by Christian Gottfried Krause, which appeared the following year in Marpurg's journal, made the analogy between a musical character piece and contemporary painting in more subtle terms, and pointed to a more modern concept of human feeling as fluid and changeable. Krause, like Marpurg, defended the character piece and called for its revival:

> I have a particular inclination towards so-called character pieces [*characterisierten Stücken*], and very much wish that they were once again fashionable with us. I can not persuade myself that one couldn't also successfully make larger pieces into character pieces, and that we must let ourselves be fobbed off with the ubiquitous heading of Allegro, and Adagio and again Allegro. It would be of especially great use if the small clavichord pieces which are composed for beginners on this instrument (and who in these days doesn't learn to play the clavichord?) were characterized.[23]

But Krause suggested that character pieces might go beyond the depiction of a single affect to evoke past and future feeling enveloped into the present. The resulting complexes of human emotion might include

> the sighs of the love-sick one, the groans of the unhappy one, the threatening gestures of one enraged, the laments of the mourner, the begging of the destitute, the reproaches of an abandoned beauty, praise at the first friendly looks of the beloved, joy on receiving the word "Yes," sorrow over the rejected proposal, anger at suffering the contempt of the beloved, the affection of a child.[24]

To portray "character" in this sense is to retail the quotidian life of the emotions, with its irritations, happinesses, disappointments, and delights in small-scale scenes, whose verbal title or accompanying miniature narrative would allow performer and listener to arrive at precisely the correct complex of emotions represented.

Krause's concept of musical character pieces as small scenes enacted in time—as slices of life—aligned the musical genre closely with the newest French paintings to be seen in Berlin in the 1750s. Paintings by Watteau, Lancret, and Chardin, which were avidly collected by Frederick the Great and displayed at his palaces at Charlottenburg, Berlin, and Potsdam, offered direct representations of emotional character embedded in the stuff of daily life. The small-format French paintings known as *petits sujets* or *petits portraits* were particularly prized, especially those that showed a single individual engaged in a seemingly trivial activity, and that projected a particular emotion or complex of emotions. They were images that concentrated on private human interactions, on the subject captured in an intimate moment; understated, charming encapsulations of a single instant that could point to universal and eternal human emotions and values.[25]

The greatest of all painters of such scenes, and in some sense the inventor or re-inventor of the genre in the early eighteenth century, was Jean-Baptiste-Siméon Chardin, whose work was so comprehensively collected by foreigners—largely Frederick the Great, his sister Friedericke Luise of Sweden, and Catherine the Great of Russia—that French critics lamented that Chardin's paintings hardly ever remained in France.[26] These paintings that so brilliantly "captured attitudes and characters," as one French commentator explained, were already being disseminated in engraved versions by the end of the 1740s:

> The prints that have been engraved after M. Chardin's paintings . . . have become fashionable, which, with those of Teniers, Wouvermans, and Lancret have succeeded in giving the final blow to the serious prints of Le Brun, Poussin, Le Sueur, and even Coypel. The vulgar public takes pleasure in seeing again the activities which take place every day under their eyes at home, and without hesitation gives them the preference over more elevated subjects, whose appreciation demands an element of study. . . . [Chardin] chooses the simplest and most naïve subjects – . . . . He seizes attitudes and character very well, and he is not lacking in expression. I believe this is even what has contributed most until now to encourage the vogue for his pictures . . .[27]

Focusing on a single human figure or face, as a critic wrote in 1753, Chardin

> catches nature in the act. He has the gift of capturing what would escape any other painter; . . . The head of the girl is so expressive that one can almost hear her talk; one can read in her face the sorrow she feels for not knowing her lesson well. . . .[28]

The human face, caught in a single instant, reveals a history of emotion, a complexity of feeling that transcends the fixity of the moment at which it is depicted.

The blurring of the boundary between portrait and genre painting that characterizes Chardin's work marks a moment of fundamental change in portraiture itself: a move from the formal, representative portraits of the Baroque, with their standard gestures and symbolic paraphernalia, to a far more intimate and personal representation of the sitter. Even public figures of great stature—kings, princes, statesmen—could expect a portrait that highlighted the natural over the artificial, and that foregrounded feeling in all its fluidity and sensitivity. As Carl Ludwig Junker noted in the 1770s, portraits were as much private records of a relationship, made for a circle of friends or family members, as they were the immortalization of great men.[29]

Many Chardin masterpieces were bought by the Prussian king. These included *The Return from the Market* (1738) which now hangs in Schloss Charlottenburg in Berlin, as well as its companion piece *Woman Scraping Vegetables*. Paintings such as these convey a sense of a world somehow outside time, "a stopped world (but without surprise), a world at rest, a world of infinite duration."[30] The repetitive action of the stooped vegetable peeler in *Woman Scraping*

Vegetables is suspended as daily occupation and preoccupation transcend the quotidian and are fixed for eternity. The representation of character in paintings such as these is a complex negotiation with time. As René Demoris has commented:

> Though [Chardin's] figures are clearly represented in action, there is no *movement*. They are caught at a timeless moment of their action, which puts them at rest...For the sometimes brief lapse of time recorded in the canvas, the human figure is, in fact, motionless. It is caught at a precise instant, free from activity, in a moment of leisure, no matter how fugitive.... It is a lost moment where time stands still, and the human being, center of activity, is seen for what it is, beyond the grasp of any practical exigency. This still moment of uninhabited time (for we do not know what has caused the servant to look up, and the expression on the mother's face eludes us) transcends the time taken up by the activity depicted: there is a sense of infinity about these human figures which are shown caught in action and yet detached from it.[31]

The remarkable and paradoxical treatment of time in Chardin's work is encapsulated in the painting *Soap Bubbles*, in which a boy leaning on a windowsill blows a magnificent bubble as a small child in the background stretches up to see (figure 4). *Soap Bubbles* was an enormously successful painting of which Chardin himself produced several versions. The picture circulated across Europe in engraved prints and it represents Chardin's central themes: the tension between seriousness and play, the suspension of time in absorbed activity, and, especially, the captured instant, the preservation of the most fragile moment at which the bubble is frozen on the verge of bursting.

The representation of character in paintings such as these is fundamentally concerned with the question of time. What is shown is a constant and careful negotiation between permanence and evanescence. The complex and profound truths engraved in the face indicate a history of feeling as well as feeling's accretion into the complete present character of the sitter. It is a reminder also of the poignant truth of time's limits: to immortalize in a portrait is to recognize the grim truth of mortality.

CЗ80

It was in this context of contemporary interest in the portrayal of character in painting and in music that C. P. E. Bach, who was working as court harpsichordist to Frederick the Great in Berlin and already collecting portrait paintings, drawings, and prints, produced his own series of character pieces and portraits. Between 1754 and 1757, Bach composed twenty-four short pieces for keyboard that ranged from the representation of generalized character traits in the manner of the French *pièce de caractère* with such titles as *La Capricieuse* (the capri-

70   Annette Richards

Figure 4. Jean-Baptiste-Siméon Chardin, *Soap Bubbles*, after 1739. Oil on canvas, 60 × 73 cm. Gift of the Ahmanson Foundation (M.79.251). Los Angeles County Museum of Art, Los Angeles, California. Photo credit: Digital image © 2009 Museum Associates / LACMA / Art Resource, New York. Image reference ART385280. Used by permission.

cious one), *La Complaisante* (the complacent one), *L'Irresoluë* (the irresolute one), to portraits of friends and acquaintances from Bach's Berlin circle of poets, philosophers, courtiers, and music lovers.[32] In the 1772 *Clavierwerkverzeichniss*, as well as in the 1790 *Nachlassverzeichniss* (both prepared by C. P. E. Bach), Bach designated these small works *petites pièces*, a genre designation that echoed contemporary painting's *petits sujets*.[33] They were published in Berlin in anthologies for amateurs in the 1750s and 1760s, and they were well-known and well-liked. Copied and anthologized over the course of the next half century, they circulated widely and retained their fascination for commentators even thirty years after their composition. The majority of Bach's musical portraits depict men, including the poet Wilhelm Ludwig Gleim, privy councilors and amateur musicians Johann Wilhelm Bergius and Ernst Samuel Jakob Borchward, and privy councilor and court physician Georg Ernst Stahl. J. S. Bach stayed in Stahl's home during his visit to Berlin in 1741, and two of Stahl's family members were godparents to C. P. E. Bach's children.

At their most demanding, Bach's musical portraits address many of the questions dealing with the representation of character, emotional complexity, time, and evanescence that concerned contemporary painters and their critics. Georg Ernst Stahl's portrait *La Stahl*, Wq. 117/25 (example 1), is one of these: a work that projects grandeur and pathos, yet instead of consistency or stability of affect, seems concerned rather with the representation of changeability. Many of the hallmarks of Bach's famed fantasy style are to be heard here: grand gestures constituted by dotted rhythms and large chords dissolve into slowly arpeggiated chords, their written-out meterless dissolution perhaps depicting the mercurial temperament of the melancholic, whose changeability music (and especially the fantasia) is uniquely suited to represent.

La Stahl is short enough that its tiny slice of time can "fix" and eternalize its subject, yet even within the sounding moments it plays with the idea of evanescence in the curiously inconclusive fade-out of its ending, a gesture that would be repeated in the final moments of the Fantasia in C major, Wq. 61/6, from the sixth book for *Kenner und Liebhaber* published in 1787 (example 2). In fact, the troubling question of ending in *La Stahl* seems to enter much earlier than the actual end. The "sarabande" half notes midway through the B section at m. 24, followed by the chordal sigh and long rests, recall the opening and seem to signal a sort of recapitulation. But they are followed by the fullest of chords in dominant preparation (m. 26), which vex still further the melancholic mien of the opening. After another long rest with pointed aspirations on the dominant at m. 27, the booming *fortissimo* chords are repeated verbatim before the *piano* quarter notes of m. 29 seem at last to move out of this chordal consternation. Yet in fact all the material that follows, even for its apparent qualities of fantastical exploration, can be heard merely as a prolonged dominant elaboration. That is, with the "recapitulatory" motive at m. 24, the piece seems to demand its own

72   Annette Richards

Example 1. C. P. E. Bach, *La Stahl*, Wq. 117/25 (Berlin, 1755). Published in *Musikalisches Mancherley* (Berlin, 1762).

Example 1 (continued). C. P. E. Bach, *La Stahl*, Wq. 117/25 (Berlin, 1755). Published in *Musikalisches Mancherley* (Berlin, 1762).

74   Annette Richards

Example 2. C. P. E. Bach, Fantasia in C, Wq. 61/6, mm. 201–end. Published in *Clavier-Sonaten und freye Fantasien . . . für Kenner und Liebhaber* VI (Leipzig, 1787).

end, but consumes one-quarter of the total number of measures in the piece before the hot-and-bother of fantasy expire in the resignation of the final two measures. The final gesture, then, extends far beyond the low-register sixths often drawn on by Bach at the close of pieces in his *Kenner*-style, the entire "recapitulation" constituting an expansion of the final cadence until the eventual disappearance into it.

If we are to venture further thoughts on the mercurial character of *La Stahl*, we might turn to Stahl's father, the famous doctor Georg Stahl the elder, who trained his son in Stahlian medicine and its attendant philosophy. The Stahlian approach rejected the received and unyielding post-Cartesian absolute dichotomy between mind and body, and argued, radically, that there was a constant interplay and interdependence between the two.[34] Thus, it might be claimed that the portrayed himself, Georg Stahl the younger, subscribed to a philosophy of medicine which in a sense validated Bach's fluid musical depiction of his character: the fallibility and flux of mind and body in continuous concert that is at the heart of Stahlian medicine is played out before us. Here we have embodied thoughts in all their changeability, in all their propensity for doubt and joy; like Junker's portrait of the man of feeling, this depiction follows Stahl through time, as he thinks and senses. In *La Stahl*, Bach makes the most out of these changes of mind and manner in what appears formally to be a modest piece in binary form of a mere thirty-eight measures,[35] but is in fact a radical new take on the genre, presenting not a single character or affect but rather character as a complex of changing feelings.

Games with time, a reveling in evanescence as much as the frozen moment, take a different form in the obscurely titled *L'Aly Rupalich*, Wq. 117/27 (example 3). This is a bizarre piece, a Turkish-style romp whose murky bass seems to present the musical equivalent of the repetitive work-a-day gestures of Chardin's turnip peeler, yet whose extravagant leaps from harmony to harmony clash loudly with the monotonous two-stroke motor chugging along below. The elaboration of a tonic pedal at the opening of a piece is standard eighteenth-century stuff and one could cite many of Bach's sonatas that do the same. Here, too, one notes the foregrounding of temporality: for all its frenzy of activity, the piece spends a long time going nowhere; it stays where it began. In this case the opening pedal, an even twenty-four measures, symmetrically divisible and subdivisible, is without warning ratcheted up a whole step in the bass (at m. 25), the common tone in the right hand with oddly doubled Cs—the seventh of the seventh chord on D—hardly constituting coherent modulation. Over the next six measures (note the less regular scansion), a serpentine move to the actual dominant (that is, G) at m. 35 brings us back to the pedal point, and the same antic gestures as the opening. This time, at m. 58, after the dominant elaboration, Bach deploys one of his standard tricks: rather than perform an unmediated jump to another harmony, he pulls the plug on the motor altogether and the

76   Annette Richards

Example 3. C. P. E. Bach, *L'Aly Rupalich*, Wq. 117/27, mm. 1–35, 53 (Berlin, 1755). Published in *Musikalisches Mancherley* (Berlin, 1762–63).

C. P. E. Bach and the Musical Portrait   77

Example 3 (continued). C. P. E. Bach, *L'Aly Rupalich*, Wq. 117/27, mm. 54–60, 69–74, 80–84, 93–105 (Berlin, 1755). Published in *Musikalisches Mancherley* (Berlin, 1762–63).

frenzy collides with silence, only for the pause to end with an even bigger side-step than the previous move to D^7, this time to E major.

After a somewhat shorter pedal (now an even more irregular unit of seven measures), the relentless upward motion of the bass teeters back down to C (this time C^7) before a short-lived abandonment of the murky bass for a bit of something that might even be called counterpoint, and is at least "legitimate" two-part writing (mm. 69–73). This snippet recalls another of the character pieces, *La Buchholtz*, Wq. 117/24 (example 4), and would appear again in the slow movement of the Sonata in D major, Wq. 61/2, from Bach's last book for *Kenner und Liebhaber* published some three decades later (example 5), perhaps a kind of internal colloquy in the musical representation of this circle of friends. *L'Aly Rupalich* is full of one-off ideas, as if the constancy of the left hand prompts random outbursts of fancy, as in the eruption of sixteenth-note figures at mm. 80–83 (sixteenth notes being otherwise unexampled in the piece). Then there is a sudden suspension of motion in both hands simultaneously at m. 95 with the sustained diminished octave (F-sharp–F-natural), held for the length of a half note with fermata; this is followed by the *adagio* resolution at mm. 96–97 with another fermata on the dominant. It is as if the music waits there as the murky program reboots, and then the *allegro assai* assault commences once again.

Toward the end, the tonic-subdominant-dominant cadential loop suggests possible conclusion, going through its routine four times from m. 169 onward, until landing for the final tonic pedal at m. 184 (example 6). At the very end of the piece Bach pulls another joke, playing on the abrupt rests heard earlier in the piece, but this time setting up a *pianissimo* echo only to drastically cut off *L'Aly Rupalich* in mid-flow. What began as *forte* high jinks ends with uncertain silence. The end—or perhaps "non-end"—of *L'Aly Rupalich* is quintessentially C. P. E. Bach and leads us to the alternate title for the piece, entered in Bach's own hand in an early copy (and then scratched out), *La Bach*.[36] One cannot be certain to which member of the Bach family this title might refer, but it is tempting to imagine that the exaggeration here of devices so typical of, indeed signature to, C. P. E. Bach's style might present the composer himself in carnivalesque Turkish disguise. In what amounts to more of a caricature than a "character," we might recognize here C. P. E. Bach's famous excursions into *fantasie*, now running amok with dangerously close-to-inept harmonic shocks and temporal jokes, played out over the insistent murkiness that Bach himself had dismissed in the *Versuch* as the refuge of poor composers.[37]

What is particularly characteristic of this Bach's music is its concern with temporality. Indeed, taken as a whole, Bach's oeuvre presents the weakest emphasis on closure and finality of any composer of stature in the eighteenth century, as if, especially in the late rondos, the piece would continue forever if not for some puncturing gimmick that suddenly erases the tableau.[38] Often this involves a verbatim repeat of an opening rondo theme and nothing more, as if the

C. P. E. Bach and the Musical Portrait 79

Example 4. C. P. E. Bach, *La Buchholtz*, Wq. 117/24, mm. 1–10 (Berlin 1755). Published in *Musikalisches Mancherley* (Berlin, 1762–63).

Example 5. C. P. E. Bach, Sonata in D major, Wq. 61/2, Allegretto. Published in *Clavier-Sonaten und freye Fantasien . . . für Kenner und Liebhaber* VI (Leipzig, 1787).

80   Annette Richards

Example 6. C. P. E. Bach, *L'Aly Rupalich* Wq. 117/27, mm. 163–94 (Berlin, 1755). Published in *Musikalisches Mancherley* (Berlin, 1762–63).

piece would or should cycle forever onward, but is prevented from doing so merely because the player stops, as in the Rondo in C minor, Wq. 59/4, from the fifth *Kenner und Liebhaber* book (example 7). The long dying close—as in *La Stahl* and most famously in the later *Abschied von meinem Silbermannschen Clavier* (example 8)—marks a kindred refusal to let go, a lingering in time that ultimately cannot be sustained, but is all the more pathetic, all the more sentimental, for having tried so hard and so sensitively to do so. Both abruptness and reluctance at the ending of a piece reveal an extreme saturation in the temporality of music. The sudden ending, as well as the long fought-against dying echo, both heighten the moment even as they let it go.

C. P. E. Bach puts music to work in his portraits to evoke the spontaneity of emotion, the complexity of character, and the immediacy of (for us) indefinite yet also very vivid personality. While the melancholy of *La Stahl* or the mania of *L'Aly Rupalich* would surely have presented a recognizable portrait to those who knew the dedicatees, for us at a considerable historical remove, the pieces ask that we—as they also asked their original players and listeners—ponder and enjoy the complexity of emotion and of the emotional entity represented.[39] That Bach would depart from his favored lighter style of the 1750s and characterize these people with his fantastical brush, speaks to his cultural investment, and that of his circle, in portraiture. If Bach recognized the validity and importance of capturing the essence, or least part of the essence, of that most basic unit of the Enlightenment—even the despotic Enlightenment of Berlin—the individual, the allusion to the absorptive and constantly changing musical world of the fantasia would suggest that representation of individuality pointed to newly fluid conceptions of the emotions. Generalized affects and enduring heroic postures were no longer satisfactory; instead, Bach portrayed these figures in the moment, exploring their minute and endless possibilities just as Chardin had done in the best of his work.

Let us turn back to Bach's picture collection for a final reflection on the relation between the musical character piece and visual portraiture. In late September 1773, the year that Burney's *Tagebuch* appeared in its German translation, the poet Heinrich Wilhelm von Gerstenberg wrote a long letter to C. P. E. Bach in which he discussed instrumental music and its methods of conveying meaning. Gerstenberg begins by reporting on a recent concert in which Johann Nikolaus Tischer had performed several sonatas composed on the subject of particular biblical texts, sonatas whose "pictorialism" had raised laughter among the audience, but which Gerstenberg sets out to defend: "any attempt to give the clavier expression and meaning appeared to me to be worthy of praise, even if it failed."[40] Gerstenberg suggests that a collection of sonatas might be written that would take as their subject the most moving passages of the psalms:

What precision of expression, otherwise so difficult to attain! Of course, it is the possibility of just this precision, this completely determined significance of

Example 7. C. P. E. Bach, Rondo in C minor, Wq. 59/4. *Top*: mm. 1–4. *Bottom*: mm. 105–end. Published in *Clavier-Sonaten und freye Fantasien . . . für Kenner und Liebhaber* V (Leipzig, 1785).

C. P. E. Bach and the Musical Portrait   83

Example 8. C. P. E. Bach, *Abschied von meinem Silbermannischen Claviere in einem Rondo*, Wq. 66, mm. 77–82 (Hamburg, 1781).

a musical passage, that is always questioned the most. But why impossible . . . ? Indeed, the feelings that a certain admirable man brings forth in me so often in his clavier sonatas are already such marked feelings even without the help of a text . . . [but] Whoever wants to have fixed rather than vague ideas thanks the musician for every means of help, the use of which becomes a widening of pleasure.[41]

છ૪ઝ

Gerstenberg goes on to suggest that painting, too, would benefit from the addition of an explanatory verbal text:

In my view a painter might even add a motto under a praying David, if he truly trusted himself to express the content of the motto well through his painting. It would always be preferable to see in the painting *what* David prays, rather than simply *that* he prays.

At the end of this remarkable letter, the author turns to portrait painting and to Bach's own portrait:

Herr Schörring is thinking of having your portrait engraved. I have composed the inscription to it for him in Danish; it reads (with your permission): "A Rafael in sound, new, multifarious, beyond his time" [*Ein Raffael durch Töne, neu, man-nichfaltig, über ein Zeitalter*]. Herr Schörring, who approves of this inscription, often plays something for me in gratitude for it, from the treasure of sonatinas he brought with him. I hope that Preisler will engrave it, if he has time.[42]

"A Rafael in sound . . . beyond his time." Even the portrait bears an inscription. Indeed, most of the engraved portraits in Bach's own collection bore such verbal texts, ranging from a single line that indicated the subject's most important position or publication, to extended eulogies summarizing a complete career. In the latter case especially, the engraved portrait explicitly announced its concern with time and temporality, with the sitter's relation (usually an exemplary one) to his or her own era, and with the sitter's transcendence of that time as he or she is inscribed into the long trajectory of history. The engraved portrait of C. P. E. Bach, with Gerstenberg's inscription, would not only have confirmed the vision-ary qualities of a composer considered by his contemporaries to be "beyond his time," but it also would have implied that this composer's music would resonate long after his death.

For Bach, as for Carl Ludwig Junker, whose essay on building a print collec-tion Bach must surely have known, portraits were not merely decorative, nor were they simply the culmination of a life-long obsession.[43] Perhaps they were that too, but, crucially for a musician deeply concerned with his own musical lineage and his posthumous reputation, the portrait collection presented a bril-liant visual account of the historical context for Bach's own achievements, de-lineating the past and present of musical culture as he knew it. A history of mu-sic and the other arts pieced together, mosaic-like, from hundreds of individual faces, the collection amounted to nothing less than the physiognomy of eigh-teenth-century European, and especially German, culture.

Famous across northern Germany, Bach's portrait collection spawned nu-merous imitators. Johann Nikolaus Forkel assembled one, as did J. J. H. West-phal. Ernst Ludwig Gerber, too, was a collector of musical portraits, and when he published his influential historical biographical dictionary of music, the *Tonkünstler Lexicon* (1790–92, second expanded edition, 1812–14), Gerber in-cluded a 73-page appendix listing thousands of individual portraits of musicians. In an introductory essay he asserted the tight relation between the writing of historical biography and the collecting of portraits:

Ten years ago my plans consisted of nothing more nor less than to prepare an al-phabetical catalog for my collection of composer portraits, which, in order to aid my memory, would consist of a short biography alongside the principal works of [each of] the composers in this collection.[44]

The impetus for Gerber's seminal work in music history, then, came from the portrait collection. His dictionary was an extended exercise in annotating a picture collection that was itself a much-expanded version of Bach's own.

C. P. E. Bach's musical portraits stand as a remarkable record of his culture's understanding of its historical underpinnings and of Bach's own, often very personal, relation to it. In a portrait collection such as this, the intimate portrayal of the individual that Bach experimented with in his *petites pièces* gives way to a grander vision of musical character: the musical character piece, delineating the shifting emotions of the individual through time, yields to the sweep of history. In Bach's pantheon of great faces, the frozen moment is expanded to an equally timeless eternity of artistic achievement.

Notes

1. Carl Philipp Emanuel Bach, *23 Pièces Characteristiques for Keyboard*, ed. Christopher Hogwood (Oxford: Oxford University Press, 1989).

2. See C. F. Cramer, *Magazin der Musik* II (1:2), 343, 965; and *Magazin der Musik* III (2:1), where a series of letters to the editor by Ernst Ludwig Gerber reports on composer portrait collections. Gerber writes that "To my knowledge, H. Capellmeister Bach possesses the most extensive collection" (1:2, 965). All translations are by the author unless otherwise noted.

3. Charles Burney, *The Present State of Music in Germany, the Netherlands, and United Provinces*, 2 vols., 2nd ed. (London, 1775), II:269.

4. Stephen L. Clark, trans. and ed., *Letters of C. P. E. Bach* (New York: Oxford University Press, 1997), 79. Bach did not acquire the octavo-sized portrait of Hiller, or if he did, he soon passed it on; only the quarto-sized print was listed in the catalog of his estate (see below, note 7).

5. Letter of 5 March 1787 in Clark, *Letters*, 259.

6. Letter of 4 August 1787 in Clark, *Letters*, 267.

7. As early as 1784, the editor of the *Magazin der Musik*, Carl Friedrich Cramer, reported that Bach had promised that he would soon have a complete catalog ready for publication. See note 2 above. For a reprint of the *Nachlassverzeichniss*, see Rachel Wade, *The Catalog of Carl Philipp Emanuel Bach's Estate: A Facsimile of the Edition by Scheibes, Hamburg, 1790* (New York: Garland, 1981). The portrait collection is on pages 92–128. The catalog lists 378 portraits, with details as to whether or not the pictures were framed, and if framed, whether in gold or black and under glass. In addition, the collection included 37 silhouettes and 65 works by C. P. E. Bach's son, J. S. Bach.

8. Long considered lost and dispersed, many items from Bach's collection, including original drawings and pastels as well as prints, recently reappeared in the music department of the Staatsbibliothek zu Berlin. An edition of the collection is in preparation for the *C. P. E. Bach: Complete Works*, ed. Annette Richards (Packard Humanities Institute).

9. Clark, *Letters*, 113.

10. Robin Leaver has surmised that this collection may have been begun by J. S. Bach; see his "Überlegungen zur 'Bildniß-Sammlung' im Nachlaß von C. P. E. Bach," *Bach Jahrbuch* (2007): 105–38.

11. Carl Ludwig Junker, *Zwanzig Componisten, eine Skizze* (Bern, 1776), 14.

12. Carl Ludwig Junker, *Musikalischer Almanach auf das Jahr 1782* (Alethinopel, 1782), 3.

13. Johann Caspar Lavater, *Physiognomische Fragmente zur Beförderung der Menschenkenntnis und Menschenliebe*, 4 vols. (Leipzig and Winterthur: Weidmanns Erben und Reich, 1777. Reprint, Hildesheim: Weidmann, 2002), III:195.

14. Lavater admitted that he had not yet completed his study of musicians' ears, partly because he was working from engraved portraits in which, for the most part, the ear is not sufficiently clearly drawn or is often hidden by hair or a wig. Eyes, by contrast, especially in portraits of artists, tend to be vivid and telling, readily expressing genius. One notes here the considerable limits of Lavater's method, relying as he does on visual images, rather than real faces; see Lavater, *Physiognomische Fragmente*, III:127, 198.

15. Carl Ludwig Junker, "Charakteristische Vorstellung des einzelnen Menschen Porträt," in *Betrachtungen über Mahlerey, Ton- und Bildhauerkunst* (Basel, 1778), 24. Junker was also the author of a widely circulated pamphlet, *Erste Grundlage zu einer ausgesuchten Sammlung neuer Kupferstiche* ("First Fundamentals for a Select Collection of New Engravings"), 1776, advising the art-loving amateur on how to build a collection of reproductive prints; see Anne-Marie Link, "Carl Ludwig Junker and the Collecting of Reproductive Prints," *Print Quarterly* XII (4/1995): 361–74.

16. Junker, "Charakteristische Vorstellung," 33.

17. Framing the portrait within the family circle, Junker suggests that portraits might be motivated by family members' pride, respect, and love, as much as by an individual's desire to project or uphold a lineage or heritage. In either case, what is preserved for eternity in the portrait must transcend the individual's sense of him- (or her-)self, or the affection of the family member commissioning the portrait, and reach for an ideal representation of character. Junker, "Charakteristische Vorstellung," 31.

18. Junker, "Charakteristische Vorstellung," 31.

19. Junker, "Charakteristische Vorstellung," 88.

20. "Karl Avison's Versuch über den musikalischen Ausdruck. Aus dem Englischen übersetzt . . ." in *Musikalisch-kritische Bibliothek*, ed. Johann Nikolaus Forkel, 3 vols. (Gotha, 1778–79), II.

21. The term "Imitative [*nachahmende*] Music," wrote Marpurg, goes so far as to imply "a music in which all the passions are expressed, correctly after their own character, and are then delineated according to the motions of the body that are associated with them." F. W. Marpurg, *Historisch-kritische Beyträge zur Aufnahme der Musik*, 5 vols. (Berlin, 1754), I:32ff.

22. Marpurg, *Historisch-kritische Beyträge*, I:32ff. English translation from Charles Batteux, *A Course of the Belles Lettres: or the Principles of Literature . . . by Mr. Miller*, 4 vols. (London, 1761), I:181. Several of Marpurg's colleagues heeded his call: character pieces appeared in numerous Berlin anthologies in the late 1750s and early 1760s by

C. P. E. Bach and the Musical Portrait 87

composers who included C. P. E. Bach, Marpurg, C. F. C. Fasch, J. P. Kirnberger, C. Nichelmann, C. F. Schale, and J. O. Uhde; see Bernhard R. Appel, "Charakterstück" in *Die Musik in Geschichte und Gegenwart*, 2nd ed., ed. Ludwig Finscher (Kassel: Bären-reiter, 1995–), Sachteil, vol. 2, cols. 636–42; see also Arnfried Edler, "Das Charakterstück Carl Philipp Emanuel Bachs und die französische Tradition," in *Aufklärungen 2. Studien zur deutsch-französischen Musikgeschichte im 18. Jahrhundert: Einflüsse und Wirkungen*, ed. Wolfgang Birtel and Christoph-Hellmut Mahling (Heidelberg: Winter, 1986), 219–35.

23. "Vermischte Gedanken, von dem Verfasser der musikalischen Poesie," in F. W. Marpurg, *Historisch-kritische Beyträge zur Aufnahme der Musik*, vol. III, no. 6 (Berlin, 1758), 533–34.

24. Marpurg, *Historisch-kritische Beyträge*, III/6:534.

25. Contemporary critics used a considerable range of terms for this kind of painting, now normally termed genre painting, including *petits sujets galants*, and *petits sujets naïfs*; see Colin B. Bailey, "Das Genre in der französischen Malerei des 18. Jahrhunderts. Ein Überlick," in *Meisterwerke der Französischen Genremalerei im Zeitalter von Watteau, Chardin und Fragonard*, ed. Colin B. Bailey, Philip Conisbee, and Thomas W. Gaehtgens (Berlin: DuMont, 2004), 2–39.

26. Christoph Martin Vogtherr, "Frédéric II de Prusse et sa collection de peintures françaises. Thèmes et perspectives de recherche," in *Poussin, Watteau, Chardin, David . . .: Peintures françaises dans les collections allemandes XVIIe-XVIIIe siècles* (exhibition catalog, Galeries Nationales du Grand Palais, Paris, 2005), 89–96.

27. Pierre-Jean Mariette, *Abécédario* (1749), quoted in Philip Conisbee, *Chardin* (Lewisburg: Bucknell University Press, 1985), 42. The titles or moralizing verses that accompanied the prints tended to congeal the subtle flux of the *petit portraits* or *petit sujets*—equivocating, as they did, between portraits and genre pieces—into one particular moral or emotional character such as "Industry" or "Idleness," "Folly" or "Innocence."

28. Abbé Jean-Bernard le Blanc, *Observations sur les ouvrages de M.M. de l'Académie . . .* (Paris, 1753), 23–25. In Pierre Rosenberg, *Chardin, 1699–1779* (Cleveland Museum of Art, in cooperation with Indiana University Press, 1979), 82.

29. Junker, "Charakteristische Vorstellung," 31.

30. Rosenberg, *Chardin*, 47–50.

31. René Demoris, "La nature morte chez Chardin," *Revue d'Esthétique* 4 (1969), 369, 377–78, 383–84. Translation from Rosenberg, *Chardin*, 95–96.

32. Darrell Berg's essay is still the standard work on C. P. E. Bach's character pieces; see her "C. P. E. Bach's Character Pieces and His Friendship Circle," in *C. P. E. Bach Studies*, ed. Stephen L. Clark (Oxford: Clarendon Press, 1988), 1–32.

33. As Peter Wollny has pointed out, Bach included other short single-movement pieces under this designation in his catalogs of his works—both the 1772 *Clavierwerkverzeichniss*, and the 1790 *Nachlassverzeichniss*—not confining his use of *petites pièces* to pieces with titles; see Peter Wollny, ed., *Carl Philipp Emanuel Bach: Miscellaneous Keyboard Works II (C. P. E. Bach: Complete Works, I / 8.2)* (Los Altos, CA: Packard Humanities Institute, 2005), xv. Also useful is Ingeborg Allihn, "Die Pièces Caractéris-

tiques des C. P. E. Bach—ein Modell für die Gesprächskultur in der zweiten Hälfte des 18. Jahrhunderts," in *Carl Philipp Emanuel Bach—Musik für Europa. Bericht über das Internationale Symposium vom 8. März bis 12. März 1994 in Frankfurt (Oder)*, ed. Hans-Günter Ottenberg (Frankfurt/Oder: Konzerthalle C. P. E. Bach, 1998), 94–107. For a wider consideration of "characteristic" music see Richard Will, *The Characteristic Symphony in the Age of Haydn and Beethoven* (Cambridge: Cambridge University Press, 2001).

34. Johanna Geyer-Kordesch, *Pietismus, Medizin und Aufklärung in Preußen im 18. Jahrhundert: Das Leben und Werk Georg Enst Stahls* (Tübingen: Niemeyer, 2000).

35. I would not want to say that this is a musical depiction of Stahlian medicine, but rather that if the task of the portrait, according to Junker, is to portray inner feeling, then Stahlian medicine offers a clear and possible metaphysical argument that such an endeavor is indeed possible.

36. Peter Wollny, ed., *Carl Philipp Emanuel Bach: The Complete Works, Volume I/8.2, Miscellaneous Keyboard Works II* (Los Altos, CA: Packard Humanities Institute, 2005).

37. Joshua Walden has reflected on this piece and its title in his "Composing Character in Musical Portraits: Carl Philipp Emanuel Bach and L'Aly Rupalich," *Musical Quarterly* 91 (Fall 2008): 379–411. Darrell Berg has surmised that *L'Aly Rupalich* may have been a cryptic reference to Karl Wilhelm Ramler (see her "Bach's Character Pieces," 31). In the preface to his edition of the character pieces (see note 1), Christopher Hogwood notes the alternative title *La Bach* and draws attention to the possible Turkishness of the name and its characterization. Tom Beghin also addresses the question of "character" and "caricature" in the liner notes to his 2002 compact disc recording "C. P. E. Bach: Pièces de Caractère" (Eufoda 1347).

38. One could cite Haydn as a close second in this.

39. Bach left only one direct clue as to the interpretation of his titles, explaining, according to C. F. Cramer, that *La Pott* was a musical description of the man's manner of walking (*der Gang des Mannes*). From the fine traces of emotion registered in the face, we are presented here with character expressed on the large scale in the motions of the whole body; see C. F. Cramer, *Magazin der Musik* 1/9–10 (Sept.–Oct. 1783), 1179; and Wollny, ed., *Miscellaneous Keyboard Works*, xvi.

40. Clark, *Letters*, 322. Tischer's music, in Gerstenberg's description, strikingly recalls Johann Kuhnau's Six Biblical Sonatas (*Musicalische Vorstellung einiger biblischer Historien*, Leipzig, 1700), although Gerstenberg does not mention these works. Gerstenberg was the author of the now well-known "experiment" to add two poetic texts to C. P. E. Bach's Fantasia in C minor, Wq. 63/6 iii. The letter to the composer discussed here was the culmination of a long-held interest among members of the Gerstenberg circle in Bach's character pieces and the potential for instrumental music to convey specific meanings. This emerges especially clearly in the correspondence between Gerstenberg and the poet Matthias Claudius in the late 1760s and early 1770s; see Eugene Helm, "The Hamlet Fantasy and the Literary Element in C. P. E. Bach's Music," *Musical Quarterly* 58 (1972): 277–96; Annette Richards, *The Free Fantasia and the Musical Picturesque* (Cambridge: Cambridge University Press, 2001); and Tobias Plebuch, "Dark Fantasies

and the Dawn of the Self: Gerstenberg's Monologues for C. P. E. Bach's C Minor Fanta-sia" in *C. P. E. Bach Studies*, ed. Annette Richards (Cambridge: Cambridge University Press, 2006).

41. Clark, *Letters*, 39–40.

42. Clark, *Letters*, 40–41. The original German is to be found in Ernst Suchalla, ed., *Carl Philipp Emanuel Bach: Briefe und Dokumente. Kritische Gesamtausgabe*. 2 vols. (Göttingen: Vandenhoeck & Ruprecht, 1994), I:320–27.

43. On Junker's essay on reproductive prints, see above, note 15.

44. Ernst Ludwig Gerber, *Historisch-Biographisches Lexicon der Tonkünstler* (1790–92). Reprint, Othmar Wessely, ed. (Graz: Akademische Druck und Verlagsanstalt, 1977), "Vorerinnerung," vi.

[13]

*A new look at C. P. E. Bach's Musical Jokes**

Susan Wollenberg

IN writings from his day to the present, the highly personal and characteristic effect of C. P. E. Bach's instrumental works has been generally acknowledged. Reichardt, commenting retrospectively on a first hearing of the symphonies H. 657–62/W. 182 (1773), evoked concepts of boldness, originality, and novelty, as well as humour; Geiringer in the 1950s, synthesizing an account of Bach's character and work, expressed notions of 'ingenuity', 'virtuosity' (in composition) and—in connection with the rondos—the idea of a musical counterpart to Bach's 'witty and spirited conversations', this music revealing 'an exquisite sense of humour'.[1] Such descriptions rightly promote an appreciation of the spirit underlying Bach's compositional processes, rather than a sterile analysis of form. The outmoded 'search for the evolution of sonata form' in his works has been supplanted in recent analytical studies by a readiness to evaluate his personal style on its own terms.[2] Geiringer's choice of the word 'exquisite' provided a significant pointer, suggesting a sense of that attention to precise detail which was essential to Bach's compositional thought.[3] His musical

---

* I should like to thank Dr F. W. Sternfeld (Exeter College, Oxford) and Bernard Harrison (Keble College, Oxford) for some useful discussions; and Susan Orchard (Christ Church, Oxford) for her help with Daniel Weber's treatise, and for providing the reference to Lessing.

[1] J. F. Reichardt, 'Noch ein Bruchstück aus J. F. Reichardts Autobiographie; sein erster Aufenthalt in Hamburg', *AMZ*, 16 (1814), col. 29, quoted in Karl Geiringer, *The Bach Family. Seven Generations of Creative Genius* (London, 1954), 368; see also pp. 358–9.

[2] Pamela Fox, 'Melodic Nonconstancy in the Keyboard Sonatas of C. P. E. Bach', Ph.D. diss., University of Cincinnati, 1983, 8, n. 12. See Fox, 'Melodic Nonconstancy', *passim*; and Darrell Berg, 'The Keyboard Sonatas of C. P. E. Bach: An Expression of the Mannerist Principle' (diss., Ph.D. State University of New York at Buffalo, 1975); Hans-Günter Ottenberg, *Carl Philipp Emanuel Bach* (Leipzig, 1982), trans. Philip Whitmore (1987); David Schulenberg, *The Instrumental Music of Carl Philipp Emanuel Bach* (Ann Arbor, 1984); Rachel Wade, *The Keyboard Concertos of Carl Philipp Emanuel Bach* (Ann Arbor, 1981). Schulenberg, for example, states that his analyses 'might be understood as defining the standards which the works set for themselves' rather than positing absolutes (see Schulenberg, *Instrumental Music*, p. 145).

[3] This, like many of Bach's personal traits, has been seen by some critics as a weakness in relation to the overall structure: see William S. Newman, 'The Keyboard Sonatas of Bach's Sons and their Relationship to the Classic Sonata Concept', *Proceedings for 1949 of the Music Teachers' National Association*, 236–48 (referring to the 'inordinate attention' paid to 'minutiae'; quoted in Fox, *Melodic Nonconstancy*, p. 225, n. 18). Schulenberg (*Instrumental Music*, p. 78) perceives that '. . . the care with which "capricious" details were frequently added to works undergoing revision testifies to planning and calculation at the local level'.

humour often depends for its effect on a single exquisite detail, cleverly manipulated; the possibilities of analysing this manipulation of detail have not yet been exhausted, and indeed may be inexhaustible.

Another important element in the literature has been a recognition of the part played by the listener in the realization of certain compositional effects. Barford has written that 'Composers are not always writing consciously for posterity',[4] but a more pertinent question is whether the composer is writing consciously for the listener, a listener who is expected to be engaged with what is happening in the music from moment to moment. When Barford states that closer examination of the music suggests the importance of the relationship between composer and performer (' . . . performer and composer are to be considered a closely integrated pair')[5] this might valuably be extended to the notion of an intimate triangle of composer, performer, and listener.[6] The effecting of 'musical jokes' in particular exploits such a relationship. Fox has convincingly assumed (and, following Hosler, has documented, for example from C. P. E. Bach, Quantz, and Scheibe) the eighteenth-century composer's wish to maintain the listener in a state of alertness: 'he [C. P. E. Bach] utilized defeat of expectation to arouse the listener's attentiveness'.[7] Marpurg noted that a friend of his, a mere musical amateur, had been gripped by steadily fixed attention in listening to Bach's sonata H. 29/W. 48, 6.[8] Complementary to the idea that Bach's music 'demands attentive listening'[9] is the perception by various writers on Bach of compositional procedures deliberately designed to leave the listener 'in a state of confusion'. Particularly significant for the present paper is Fox's commentary on those movement-openings where 'Bach seems determined to command the listener's immediate attention' by disorientating means or 'expectational defeat'.[10] In Bach's instrumental works (especially those for solo keyboard, and the orchestral symphonies) the listener's attentiveness is heightened not by creating a constant flow of smooth-running ideas but by the use of unexpected or disruptive (Fox's 'non-

---

[4] Philip Barford, *The Keyboard Music of C. P. E. Bach* (London, 1965), 105.

[5] Ibid., p. 100.

[6] This also ties up with ideas of author, text, and reader relationships expounded in modern literary theory.

[7] Fox, 'Melodic Nonconstancy', p. 128. Hosler notes that C. P. E. Bach, Mattheson, L. Mozart, Quantz, and Scheibe 'all point out the pleasurable benefits of playing with the listener's expectations.'; see Bellamy Hosler, *Changing Aesthetic Views of Instrumental Music in 18th-century Germany* (Ann Arbor, 1981), 20; and further, pp. 29, 58 ff.

[8] See Ottenberg, *Bach*, p. 61; Hosler, *Changing Views*, p. 61, quotes Scheibe on the importance of 'uninterrupted . . . attentiveness ' ('ununterbrochene Aufmerksamkeit').

[9] Ottenberg, *Bach*, p. 184 ('Bachs Sinfonien wollen mit wachen Sinnen gehört werden').

[10] Fox, 'Melodic Nonconstancy', pp. 143 and 136 (supported by a quotation from Scheibe, with reference to Hosler, *Changing Views*, p. 58). See also Ottenberg, *Bach*, p. 61, describing the opening of H. 25/W. 48, 2.

A New Look at Bach's Musical Jokes   297

constant') procedures: '. . . it is in this very discontinuity that his [Bach's] individuality is manifested'.[11]

A third important element noted by writers on C. P. E. Bach is the marked stylistic diversity found within his works, indeed often within a single work or movement.[12] What is particularly important here is that this should not be seen as the uncertain vacillation of a composer caught in a 'difficult', 'transitional' period between two distinct style-epochs (another outmoded view), nor, clearly, can it be seen as a personal process of evolution following a neat chronological pattern within his work as a whole, each style supplanting its predecessor. Rather it provides evidence of Bach's stylistic eclecticism and compositional virtuosity, in that he was able to reproduce with facility a wide range of styles (including Baroque motivic-contrapuntal, lightweight *galant* and tear-jerking *empfindsam*, as well as a more regulated 'high Classical' manner); in this respect (as in other respects), like his father, Bach had a lively interest in the diversity of current styles and was able to adopt them as and when he wished, for a few bars or an entire piece.[13] The three, interrelated, elements discussed above: humour, linked with ingenuity and novelty (as manifested in what in Haydn's work we appreciate as 'surprises');[14] the listener's engagement with the work at a detailed level; and stylistic incongruity deriving from the deliberate manipulation of different idioms; all these are further related to the phenomenon which forms one of the central concerns of this paper, the parodistic treatment of material, seen particularly in Bach's solo keyboard sonatas and symphonies.[15]

First I would suggest that in general many of Bach's effects are intended by the composer (and are to be perceived by the performer and the listener—and

[11] Ottenberg, *Bach*, p. 61: '. . . gerade in dieser Diskontinuität liegt das Individuelle begründet'. Hosler discusses with particular reference to Baumgarten and Meier the phenomenon of *Verwunderung*, 'a kind of heightened attentiveness brought on by the perception of "the unexpected, the wonderful, and the pleasantly surprising" ' ('Das Unerwartete, das Wunderbare, und das auf angenehme Art Überraschende'). See Hosler, *Changing Views*, p. 96.

[12] For an extended treatment of Bach's 'Stylistic Mixture of Melodic Procedures' see Fox, 'Melodic Nonconstancy', pp. 184–211.

[13] See Wade, *Keyboard Concertos*, pp. 59 ff.

[14] For a specialized investigation of this topic see Steven Paul, 'Wit, Comedy and Humour in the Instrumental Music of Franz Joseph Haydn' (Ph.D. diss., University of Cambridge, 1981), and 'Comedy, Wit and Humor in Haydn's Instrumental Music', *Haydn Studies: Proceedings of the International Haydn Conference, Washington, DC, 1975* (New York and London, 1981), 450–6. Paul's remark that 'no thorough study of this important aspect of his style' had previously been made with regard to Haydn (*Haydn Studies*, p. 450) applies equally to C. P. E. Bach (whom surprisingly he does not once mention in his article). In his dissertation Paul argues for a view of Haydn as 'the "inventor" of pure, intrinsic musical humour' ('Wit, Comedy and Humour', p. 359) and mentions C. P. E. Bach only *en passant*.

[15] At this point it should be stressed that references to 'parody' here use the term in its humorous sense (cf. Leonard Ratner, *Classic Music: Expression, Form, and Style* (New York and London, 1980), 387–9 and *passim*).

298 *Susan Wollenberg*

conveyed by the performer to the listener) as 'musical jokes' or 'tricks'.[16] This is not to imply that his work is shallow or trivial; rather, his use of procedures creating such 'jokes' adds depth and meaning to an already intense and intellectually lively manner of expression.[17] The selection of examples that follows can be assigned to certain discernible categories.[18] Example 1*a* shows (at measure 16) a typical ploy: a stock cadential phrase with one essential factor omitted. (A useful method of demonstrating the precise unexpected qualities of the originals is to recast passages in a hypothetically 'expected' format. Thus Example 1*b* shows the same phrase in its hypothetical form.) This whole movement is in a musically playful, or 'ludic' style.[19] The B natural at the beginning of measure 16 is clearly an appoggiatura, but by leaving it suddenly and totally unaccompanied at this point the composer thwarts expectations and allows the knowing listener—the *Kenner*—the satisfaction of recognizing and savouring the implications of the moment. It is worth pointing out that the bisectional structures with repeats (whose very repetitiveness has seemed to some writers to be at odds with the essential discontinuity of Bach's thought) give opportunities of intensifying the effect of such 'jokes'. (Because the receptive listener is prepared after a first hearing of a passage, its repetition

[16] Ratner, *Classic Music*, p. 387, comments percipiently on the humour underlying much Classical music: 'Much of the instrumental music of the Classic masters is saturated with comic rhetoric which may be vaguely sensed but is not often fully savoured'. A stimulating treatment of the subject was given in Alfred Brendel's lecture 'Does Classical Music have to be entirely serious?' (8th Darwin Lecture, delivered in the Concert Hall of the Music Faculty, University of Cambridge, 20 Nov. 1984, first broadcast on BBC Radio 3 on 8 Apr. 1985). Quotations from this (as yet unpublished) lecture are taken from the broadcast version.

[17] Hosler, *Changing Views*, in particular pp. 2 and 16–17, usefully draws attention to 18th-century aesthetic problems in accepting the creation of comic effects as an artistically serious endeavour, and to the equating of comic art with triviality and inferiority, and shows that it was with the Romantics that 'music's Tändelei alone was somehow capable of expressing profound and wonderful things' (*Changing Views*, p. 190).

[18] Brendel's examples were taken mainly from Haydn and Beethoven, and he seemed to take C. P. E. Bach's generation as representing utter seriousness: 'For C. P. E. Bach's contemporaries, elevated affections . . . had to be suggested by certain devices of musical style. Haydn applied such devices to the lowest category of poetics [the comic]', and Brendel further adduced Zelter's opinion that Haydn was criticized by his contemporaries because he burlesqued the 'deadly seriousness of his predecessors, J. S. Bach and C. P. E. Bach'. Ottenberg by contrast recognizes throughout his sympathetic discussions of C. P. E. Bach's work the crucial element of 'Spaßlichkeit' (see for example Ottenberg, *Bach*, p. 223, for his comments on the fantasia in C H. 291/W. 61, 6): 'Das Hauptthema ist so recht geeignet, die Dimension des musikalischen Spaßes in ihren mannigfachen Spielarten auszukosten'.

[19] At each stage in the movement, what is 'given' suggests (to the reasonably initiated observer) a particular consequence; an unexpected consequence is then substituted, and this in turn suggests a particular expectation that too is thwarted, and so on. (For example, given the 'Italian sixth' chord at measure 14, itself an unexpected and unexpectedly prolonged event in this harmonic context, the F sharp in the bass at measure 15, intervening (again with some unexpectedness) between the A flat and G, posits the appearance of the diminished seventh often used as intermediary between augmented sixth and Ic or V at the cadence, but an unexpected chromatic chord ($\#IV_7$) is substituted, and other factors add to the effect, such as the melodic leap in the right hand to an unsupported high E in place of the expected G. Dynamics and articulation at the cadence add to the playful effect). On the value of hypothetical recasting see *Essay*, p. 441 n. 8.

A New Look at Bach's Musical Jokes   299

Example 1. Sonata in F major H. 243/W. 55, 5, iii. 'Kenner und Liebhaber',
vol. 1 (Leipzig, 1779)

a mm. 11–16
b 'Expected' format, mm. 15–16

or parallel restatement—and the subsequent repetition of the parallel restatement—offers the chance to enjoy the joke in a more intensely knowing state.)[20]

Another ploy is to omit some crucial factor at the expected moment and then to insert it at the 'wrong' moment as if in (somewhat mocking) compensation for its original omission (see Example 2: Fox has described this passage in terms of its discontinuity.)[21] Here (Example 2, measure 12) Bach typically leaves the

---

[20] There is an element here of Brendel's *faux pas* theory; in Example 1a, the first time it occurs, the listener might think the performer has accidentally omitted to sound the accompanying notes to this appoggiatura, but subsequent recurrences confirm that this was no *faux pas* but a correct rendering of a 'joke'.

[21] Fox, 'Melodic Nonconstancy', p. 84 ('The melodic line resolves down to g^1 in measure 12. The bass, however, does not provide a strong reinforcement to the resolution. No left hand support is provided on the downbeat of measure 12, and only a single accompanying note—the thirty-second note *b*—sounds with the g^1 (of equally short duration) in the right hand. This understated cadence is immediately followed by a unison outburst which arpeggiates the chord of resolution in rapid thirty-seconds. The melodic line expires *pianissimo*, making the *forte* unison interruption even more disruptive.')

Example 2. Sonatina in G major H. 8/W. 64, 2, ii, mm. 11–13. Pamela Fox,
'Melodic Nonconstancy' p. 85, Example 27

double appoggiatura unsupported, but then following the cadence phrase he
introduces a rush of triadic figures in octaves, emphasizing the G which should
have been sounded (and whose omission 'disturbs' the listener) in the bass at
the beginning of the measure: seemingly a compensatory gesture (understatement followed by overstatement), and one with considerable dramatic impact.
Example 3a illustrates the trick of bringing in what would be expected in one
context, in another quite incongruous context (the 'right' thing in the 'wrong'
place). In this example the harmonic progression (over a Baroque chaconne
bass of a type particularly favoured by C. P. E. Bach for movement-openings)
spanning measures 1–4 is apparently established at the outset and at its close
as a straightforward prolongation of the tonic (cf. Handel: Example 3c). But by
introducing the irritant A flat in the fourth chordal component of this phrase,
Bach disturbs the original impression and creates from this point on a
harmonic progression belonging more naturally with a conventional move-
ment-ending, where the subdominant is first approached through its dominant seventh before reasserting its function as IV (enhanced as (II₇b) in the
progression IV (II₇b)–V–I). The irritant effect of the A flat (exacerbated,
typically for this composer, by an ornament on the offending note)[22] is then
intensified by a repetition (in measure 4) of the effect, preceded by a
preposterous leap of a thirteenth. As with other 'eccentric' passages, it is
possible to recompose this extract in an inoffensive manner (see Example 3b).[23]
This passage could almost be interpreted as a brief parodistic portrayal of those
codas where a cadential progression is reiterated, as if the composer were
reluctant to close off the movement.[24] Because the gesture occurs here at the

---

[22] See Ottenberg, *Bach*, p. 61: 'Wenn Bach die Septime zusätzlich mit einem Triller versieht,
dazu noch auf unbetonter Zählzeit, dann ist der Eindruck musikalischer Irregularität offenbar.'

[23] Again Brendel's *faux pas* theory might be relevant here. A good example, in the category of
'false start', is H. 32/W. 49, 4, iii. The music recommences (measure 5) differently, as though now
correcting what was a false start (the use of pauses and irregular phrasing adds to the uncertainty,
while the open-endedness proves useful later).

[24] An example of 'delaying action' at the final cadence occurs at the end of the symphony H.
651/W. 176, iii where it belongs in spirit with the vivacity of the 'hunting-style' finale.

A New Look at Bach's Musical Jokes 301

Example 3. Sonata in B flat major H. 25/W. 48, 2, i. 'Prussian Sonatas' (Nuremberg, 1742/3)

a mm. 1–6.

b 'Hypothetical' version of H. 25/W. 48, 2, i, mm. 1–4.

c G. F. Handel, 'Arrival of the Queen of Sheba' Sinfonia, *Solomon*, pt. III, harmonic reduction

302 *Susan Wollenberg*

very opening of a movement, it has an added degree of eccentricity. Arguably Bach's musical tricks are carefully planned and executed, with all possible levels of the music involved; it is not irrelevant that in his personal life he was known as a 'wit' and a 'practical joker'.[25] In the *Versuch* he recommended the use of 'rational deceptions' when creating an improvised compositional structure:[26] although there the phrase referred specifically to modulatory playfulness, it is a term that serves to evoke the spirit of Bach's musical jokes in general.

The 'rational deceptions' categorized and illustrated in the examples above belong with what Brendel has described as the 'stock-in-trade of the comic': 'breaches of convention, appearance of ambiguity, proceedings that masquerade as something they are not'. And, as Brendel has further noted, 'breaches of order' clearly need a 'framework of order' to be effective. An established musical logic, 'available to the musical layman', creates this framework for musical jokes. In the commentary above on some examples of Bach's jokes, such phrases as 'stock cadential phrase' and 'expected moment' obviously relate to the question of the listener's preparedness. For an ideal listener is not simply required to be alert to the particular piece; he must also possess some preconception of what is 'expected' behaviour in such a piece as a whole, and in individual contexts such as movement-openings and endings. The jokes discussed so far thus make their effect largely by twisting the expected to become the unexpected. It seems a small step from there to the parodistic process referred to earlier, wherein the element of mockery is paramount. A composer so easily able to reproduce the features of various styles could also choose to imitate them 'tongue-in-cheek'. Again, a series of musical examples with commentary will illustrate the point.[27] As a preliminary it is interesting to consider briefly some eighteenth-century ideas of musical humour as set out by Daniel Weber in a short but significant treatise to which Ratner has drawn attention.[28] This document apparently represents a rare (if not ideally lucid) attempt to formulate for music similar theories of comedy to those evolved by literary analysts, in particular C. P. E. Bach's friend Lessing,[29] and it thus helps to set the scene for the present enquiry.

[25] See *Helm/Grove*, p. 845; Geiringer, *The Bach Family*, p. 339; and Reichardt, loc. cit. (n. 1).

[26] *Essay*, p. 434: 'This and other rational deceptions make a fantasia attractive.'

[27] This suggestion of parody (see also n. 15 above) seems new in relation to specific passages and procedures, although Ottenberg has pointed out (in relation to the 'Kenner und Liebhaber' sets generally) that 'Humour is combined with irony.' ('Humor verbindet sich mit ironischem Zungenschlag'; *Bach*, p. 222.)

[28] Weber expressed as his aim 'to fill a gap in the aesthetics of music, which have not yet been systematically treated' ('eine Lücke in der noch nicht systematisch bearbeiteten musikalischen Aesthetik auszufüllen'). See D. Weber, 'Abhandlung: Ueber komische Charakteristik und Karrikatur in praktischen Musikwerken', *AMZ*, 9 (1800), cols. 137–43, 157–62. The quotation above is from col. 138. The treatise was originally written in 1792, with supplementary material added in 1800. See also Ratner, *Classic Music*, pp. 387 ff.

[29] See for example G. E. Lessing, 'Vom Wesen der Komödie. Aus dem 28. und 29. Stück der Hamburgischen Dramaturgie', in *Kritik und Dramaturgie, ausgewählte Prosa*, ed. K. H. Bühner (Stuttgart, 1967), 59–63.

A New Look at Bach's Musical Jokes 303

In spite of his belief that music with text can more easily convey humour, and the fact that his treatise is mainly concerned with music for theatrical comedy, Weber recognizes the possibility of creating 'comic caricature' in working out 'purely instrumental musical humour, without singing or speaking'.[30] Much of his attempt to define and classify comic species is based on his concept of the 'rules'; and the special ways in which the composer may apply or deviate from these rules are essential to Weber's perception of the comic in music.[31] He states that, just as in the visual arts, so also in music, not every comic piece is 'marked with the stamp of caricature'.[32] The comic composer who does not intend to 'descend to the level of caricature, allows himself only cautious deviations from the general rules' (which suggests that the composer who wishes to create caricature may depart more radically from the rules).[33] Weber takes as an example of 'musical depiction, mimicry and caricature' the coachman's aria 'Brillant dans mon emploi' (Philidor). Here the singer strikes up 'a theme which suggests the expectation of a serious bravura aria. A practised ear soon notices in the meantime that it is not meant to be too serious, and the hoped-for bravura aria is not going to turn out as one is accustomed to in grand opera.'[34] Thus besides the idea of bending the rules for comic effect, Weber acknowledges the role of 'defeat of expectation'. Musical reference to the conventions of serious opera, introduced into comic opera in a spirit of caricature (and quite apart from the intrinsic comedy of situation and character contained within the libretto) is a well-recognized feature of eighteenth-century style. The notion of setting up what is apparently a serious piece along conventional lines in order to distort it (to the delight of the knowing listener) into caricature can be shown to be valid also for purely instrumental music.

Weber also uses the term 'parody' and suggests that 'just as poets sometimes parody one another in order to exhibit one another to public ridicule, so too composers often do this',[35] though the parody may not have a specific object; the example Weber offers (from Hiller) parodies in general the style of 'the old-

---

[30] '. . . und die Bearbeitung des Stoffes der lyrischen sowohl als der blos instrumentalen, ohne Gesang und Rede spielenden Farçe, [heisse ich] *komische Karrikatur*.' ('Abhandlung' col. 138; see also col. 140.)

[31] '[Der komische Styl in praktischen Musikwerken] besteht . . . in einer speciellen Anwendung der Regeln der Harmonik und Melodik, wodurch bey dem Zuhörer, dessen Gehör dazu gestimmt ist, ein Gefühl des Lächerlichen erweckt wird.' (Ibid., col. 139.)

[32] '. . . so ist auch nicht jedes lächerliche Tongemählde mit dem Stempel der Karrikatur bezeichnet.' (Ibid., col. 139.)

[33] '. . . so vergönnt sich der komische Tonsetzer, der nicht bis zur Karrikatur herabsinken will, oder muss, nur mässige Abweichungen von der allgemeinen Regel . . .' (Ibid., cols. 139–40.)

[34] '. . . ein Thema . . . , welches eine ernsthafte Bravourarie erwarten lässt. Ein geübter Hörer merkt inzwischen bald, dass es damit so ernstlich nicht gemeynt sey, und die gehoffte Bravourarie nicht so ausfällen werde, wie man's in der hohen Oper gewöhnt ist.' (Ibid., cols. 140–1.)

[35] 'So wie übrigens Dichter einander zuweilen parodiren, um einander im Publikum zum Gelachter auszustellen, so thun es auch manchmal die Tonsetzer.' (Ibid., col. 143.) It is a practice of which Weber evidently disapproves.

fashioned ['altmodisch'] opera arias'. I would suggest that when C. P. E. Bach uses 'old-fashioned' styles (which in fact may mean the idioms of his father) he does so in entire seriousness, and that in his work it is the 'modish' which is parodied. Various writers have suggested that C. P. E. Bach avoids the merely fashionable ('What was criticized in his pieces was their capricious style, often *bizarrerie*, their affected difficulty, eccentric arrangement of notes . . . and their intransigent opposition to the fashion of the moment.')[36] Leaving aside those pieces where Bach adopts a lightly fashionable manner or some conventional formula (such as the 'hunting-style' finale in the symphony H. 654/W. 179) without undue complication,[37] it can be claimed that there are cases where he makes more sophisticated reference to fashionable ideas in order to mock them, and to mock the listener's expectations (in ways which the knowing listener will appreciate). Those same gestures and levels of the music in which, for utterly serious expressive purposes, Bach characteristically invests so much significance (dynamic contrasts, syncopated repetitions, sudden pauses) may elsewhere be exploited for parodistic effect. For example, what Fox describes as 'A full range of dynamic indications, notated with growing exactitude throughout his career, intended to shade subtly the many changes of mood'[38] does indeed serve serious *empfindsam* purposes; but Bach's dynamic indications could also be designed to ridicule such modern conventions as 'symphonic' crescendos and *f–p–f–p* contrast phrases.

Example 4*a* (from the first movement of H. 243/W. 55, 5) demonstrates a play on the use of detailed dynamic indications. This passage could be interpreted as a parody of the stereotyped sequential statement of a motif with progressive dynamics (crescendo effect), often used as a symphonic starting-device.[39] Where the stereotyped version would normally stress the tonic (commonly with a pedal bass underpinning the sequence), Bach's distorted version aims conversely to obscure the tonic (a favourite ploy in his work).[40] Example 4*b* shows the progression in skeleton form, clambering uncertainly up into the tonic key of F,[41] while Example 4*c* gives a hypothetical

[36] 'Unbeugsamkeit gegen den Modegeschmack': C. F. D. Schubart, *Ideen zu einer Ästhetik der Tonkunst*, 1784–5 (Vienna, 1806), 179, translated in Berg, *Keyboard Sonatas*, p. 53.

[37] As in some of the Prussian sonata finales, with their good-natured espousal of a vivacious *buffo* style, using aspects such as register and dynamics entertainingly and carrying off some light-hearted jokes (see especially the finales of sonatas 1, 2, and 5, H. 24, 25, and 28/W. 48, 1, 2, and 5; the finale of sonata 6 (H. 29/W. 48, 6) is perhaps the most unpredictable and imaginative of the set, possibly containing some element of mockery, especially in its opening procedures).

[38] 'Melodic Nonconstancy', p. 5.

[39] For an interesting later manifestation of parody based on sequential presentation of an opening motif with *f–p–f–p* contrasts, see Beethoven, Op. 90, i (also tonally misleading); and compare C. P. E. Bach, H. 142/W. 52, 2, iii).

[40] See Fox, 'Melodic Nonconstancy', pp. 133–4, on the discontinuity of this passage.

[41] In movements subsequent to the first, this kind of opening may relate to—and be explained by—the close of the previous movement (as with the finale of the sonata H. 243/W. 55, 5 or some of the symphonies with linked movements, such as H. 664/W. 183, 2, H. 661/W. 182, 5 and H. 662/W. 182, 6).

A New Look at Bach's Musical Jokes   305

Example 4. Sonata in F major H. 243/W. 55, 5, i. 'Kenner und Liebhaber', vol.
I (Leipzig, 1779)

a mm. 1–3
b Harmonic reduction extracting the basic sequential progression
c 'Hypothetical' version

[outline bass only]

reconstruction possessing the stability and continuity so lacking in Example
4*a*. C. P. E. Bach was perhaps one of the first composers to endow the opening
of an instrumental movement with more than a purely annunciatory
significance. Aspects of his technique such as the impression of 'beginning in
the middle' and the 'non-tonic opening' evoke a sense of subtlety and mystery
more typical of nineteenth-century compositional procedures. The importance
of these enigmatic beginnings relates to the whole movement, not in terms of
establishing the *Affekt* but in terms of the relationship that is established

306   *Susan Wollenberg*

Example 5. Sonata in B minor H. 245/W. 55, 3, i, mm. 1–4. 'Kenner und
Liebhaber', vol. 1 (Leipzig, 1779)

between composer, performer, and listener, and between the composer and his
material.

By definition, the use of another common opening device, the forceful theme
outlining the tonic triad, would seem to be precluded in Bach's 'non-tonic
openings'; but Example 5 shows how in one case a 'non-tonic opening' (H.
245/W. 55, 3, i) contains the three notes of the tonic triad at the start, in an
unaccompanied upbeat scramble—thus tentatively rather than forcefully—
followed by a phrase harmonized in D major, though offering little tonal
stability.[42] Those three introductory notes could be seen as a *reductio ad
absurdum* of the triadic theme, calculated with ironic intent. Straightforward
triadic themes are apparently quite rare in Bach's work. In connection with
the symphonies, Gallagher and Helm have suggested that 'Formula avoidance
is so much in evidence in these works that it seems to be Bach's motto, in the
first movements above all. At the start of a first movement he avoids that triad
in three hammerstrokes that predictably begins many an early Classic
symphony.'[43] This is true to a certain extent. Bach does use formulas (it would
be difficult to evade them entirely) but uses them, not unthinkingly or
mechanically, but with characteristic twists (sometimes a slight detail,
sometimes a more extended treatment), developing various comic usages that
give the standard formulas a remarkable freshness. For example in the opening
of the symphony H. 648/W. 173, which is based, conventionally, on a rising
triad outline, the sixteenth-note scale motif reappears turned upside-down at
measure 5.[44] In Bach's symphonic output as a whole, a humorous context is

---

[42] For commentary on this passage see Fox, 'Melodic Nonconstancy', pp. 135–6, and, on this
and H. 243/W. 55, 5, i, Charles Rosen, *The Classical Style: Haydn, Mozart, Beethoven* (London,
1971), 112–15, partly reviewed and quoted in Fox, 'Melodic Nonconstancy', pp. 134–6.
Interestingly, a full version of the formula, properly establishing the tonic, occurs in Beethoven,
Op. 132 (finale).

[43] See Charles C. Gallagher and E. Eugene Helm, eds., *C. P. E. Bach: Six Symphonies*, The
Symphony, 1720–1840, Series C, vol. 8 (New York and London, 1982), xiii. See also *Helm/Grove*,
p. 853.

[44] Compare the use of the cadential formulas in the sonata H. 136/W. 50, 1, iii—humorously
placed at each of three different registers—where in the varied reprise the third statement turns the

A New Look at Bach's Musical Jokes 307

often established for the simplest of materials, thus transforming them (as with Haydn). To discuss the ramifications of Bach's 'musical jokes' in the symphonies would require a monograph in itself. Here, some selected passages must suffice as examples.

At the opposite extreme to the technique of *reductio ad absurdum* mentioned is the opening of the symphony H. 663/W. 183, 1, where a deceptive and parodistic portrayal of the triadic formula is spread over eighteen measures. The three statements of the arpeggio theme, topped first with repeated Ds, then with F sharps, and then with Bs (separated by pauses to confound the listener),[45] create an extended triadic outline—almost the conventional 'hammerstroke' but altered to outline the 'wrong' triad[46]—drawn out to absurd lengths (see Example 6). That the next event is a diminished-seventh chord mocks the listener's hope of any establishing of a clear key-centre. Only from measure 27 onwards does the arpeggio idea behave with more normal effect in a more continuous and coherent repetition structure and clearly laid-out orchestral texture. It is the juxtaposition of such normal behaviour and the abnormal contexts in which the same material appears initially, that emphasizes the element of parody in the tonally playful opening, in which a variety of musical jokes (such as the false start and restart) is contained. In another case, the first movement of H. 654/W. 179 (see Example 7a), the 'wrong'-note and 'wrong'-triad techniques are applied to a three-note 'hammerstroke' appearing in the wrong place. Further confusion, or enigma, is created by the altered echo of the phrase and by the already unexpected proceedings in measures 3–4 (Example 7b demonstrates the expected progression). The effect of these various proceedings is that by the time the music begins to depart from the tonic it has scarcely been in it, although here again (as in H. 245, first movement) the 'right' notes of the 'right' triad are in fact contained in diminution at the outset of the movement. It is this, taken together with the parodistic form of the 'hammerstroke' in measures 5–6, that constitutes one of the tonal and motivic jokes in the opening bars.

As with the triadic formulas, so with certain conventional textural patterns it is Bach's rejection of the obvious, *per se*, that has attracted comment; Fox refers to the enrichment of his texture by 'the avoidance of stereotypical chord

---

formula upside-down (nicely leading towards the next section as well as providing a little local surprise); and with longer-range repercussions when the inverted version (i.e. the leading-on rather than the closing-off form of the cadence) appears at the corresponding end of the varied reprise of the second section, creating some uncertainty as to whether this is in fact the end of the whole movement.

[45] Note the use of progressive dynamics (*mf, f, ff*), and reservation of the tutti until measure 19. Most pertinently on Bach's symphonic dynamics see E. Suchalla, *Die Orchestersinfonien Carl Philipp Emanuel Bachs* (Augsburg, 1968), 115 ff.

[46] The 'right' triad contained in diminution beneath the Ds is of course turned into V_7 of G major, replacing the possible tonic implications of D by explicit dominant function.

308   *Susan Wollenberg*

Example 6. Sinfonia in D major H. 663/W. 183, 1, i, mm. 1–19. *Vier Orchester-Sinfonien* (Leipzig, 1780); Ed. Steglich (Leipzig, 1942)

A New Look at Bach's Musical Jokes

and Alberti-bass patterns'.[47] A textural rarity in Bach is the Alberti bass, as Fox suggests, but again the familiarity of the device offers possibilities of parody. Example 8 presents a passage remarked on by numerous writers; in choosing to employ the conventional pattern here Bach typically adds a 'twist'. The whole appears as a 'joke' Alberti bass, with its doubling of treble and bass (outlining the characteristic falling chromatic fourth), set rhythmically against the beat in an eccentric and ungainly manner quite alien to the facile elegance of the genuine article.[48]

Such passages as these seem to fulfil the criteria for an interpretation of parodistic intent. For some element of parody to exist, an identifiable original form must be suggested, a degree of distortion must be present, and the original must constitute a recognized device or style-trait. Regarded in this way, the *brisé* textures of, for example, the first movement of H. 59/W. 62, 10 appear as

---

[47] 'Melodic Nonconstancy', p. 5.

[48] Equally Bach could use a similar bass 'straight', with elegant expressive melody above it, as in the symphony H. 650/W. 175, iii, measures 49 ff.

Susan Wollenberg

parody. It should be stressed that this is only one possible interpretation, and that it has only limited application; it can be argued for certain (in fact quite numerous) passages but not at all for others. The richness of reference in C. P. E. Bach's work makes it impossible to uphold any one analysis as the prime one. (At the same time it makes it important to consider all possibly valid ways of looking at his music.) Nor, of course, does the particular meaning that may be assigned to a passage at its first appearance necessarily hold in exactly the same way for subsequent appearances. To take one example: in the first movement of H. 243/W. 55, 5 (see Example 4*a*), the apparent arbitrariness of the key chosen for the opening phrase (C minor) is significantly modified when it returns at the beginning of the repeat of the first section, thus immediately following the C major cadence which closes off the second main key area (strongly established, unlike the first), and forming with it a major–minor contrast. The reappearance of the opening gesture at the head of the second

Example 7. Sinfonia in E flat major H. 654/W. 179, i. Ed. Gallagher and Helm
(New York and London, 1982), 145

a mm. 1–8
b 'Expected' progression

A New Look at Bach's Musical Jokes 311

Susan Wollenberg

312

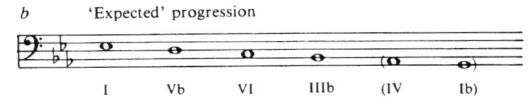

Example 8. Sonata in G major H. 119/W. 62, 19, iii, mm. 1–6. *Musikalisches Mancherley* (Berlin, 1762), 26

A New Look at Bach's Musical Jokes 313

section is used to create further 'surprise' and tonal uncertainty in relation to what preceded it; and to the listener who had (after two hearings) retained in his memory the outline of the original progression, what follows is unexpected in that it remains in the key of the second phrase (see measures 15–17 ff.). These changes of meaning in different contexts ensure that the reuse of a particular gesture does not dull the listener's interest and attentiveness (apart from the fact that the gesture is striking enough, as here, to warrant rehearing). It may also be pointed out that the essence of this kind of opening can have implications beyond the movement where it is introduced. In H. 243/W. 55, 5, the second (Adagio maestoso) and third (Allegretto) movements pick up the tonal ambiguity associated with the first movement (Allegro), as well as being linked together by a unifying long-range progression (see Example 9). Bach's 'eccentricities' are not (*pace* Rosen) isolated events.[49]

There are passages, or whole sections, in C. P. E. Bach's music which if analysed in all seriousness could be regarded as illogical, ill-balanced, even incompetent. But, as Schulenberg has observed in rejecting Rosen's view that Bach's 'passion lacked wit', it is important not to take 'some of Bach's more extreme passages too seriously'.[50] This stricture would apply to a movement such as the first (Allegro) of the sonata H. 29/W. 48, 6. As often in Bach, a promising initial phrase is cut short and never receives the regular continuation that might have been expected (see Example 10a, with hypothetical reconstruction in Example 10b). And when some continuity is restored to the music, it is in such an extreme form as to seem almost to be mocking the use of the conventional materials (scales, arpeggios) with which the keyboard sonata composer might fill out his structure. From measures 6 to 14 there might appear to be some difficulty in departing from the tonic key. But this is surely, like the other irregular and unpredictable aspects of much of Bach's instrumental music, not incompetence but wit, exercised together with a

Example 9. Sonata in F major H. 243/W. 55, 5, reduction to basic progression. 'Kenner und Liebhaber', vol. 1 (Leipzig, 1779)

---

[49] See Rosen, *The Classical Style, passim*, particularly pp. 48 and 79. Commentators on H. 663/W. 183, 1, i, for example, have noted how the eccentric opening progression is developed, not isolated, in the movement.

[50] Schulenberg, *Instrumental Music*, p. 135.

314   *Susan Wollenberg*

Example 10. Sonata in A major, H. 29/W. 48, 6, i. 'Prussian Sonatas'
(Nuremberg, 1742/3)

a measures 1–5
b 'Hypothetical' version

feeling for the long-range effect of passages and proceedings. (The dogged emphasis on the tonic key in measures 6–14 adds all the more freshness to the subsequent adventurous approach to the dominant through its dominant minor (measures 15–23), and there are further repercussions of the passage later in the section, as well as some intriguing connections of events and ideas between the first and second sections.) An appreciation of the cleverness and originality manifest in such music is enhanced by an alertness to its humour.[51] While inevitably the 'irritants', the apparently arbitrary elements, the capriciousness and mockery present in Bach's work, are indeed bound simply to irritate and alienate some listeners, for others they will exert the exquisite and witty effects that the composer surely intended: ' . . . whereby a sense of the comic is aroused in the listener whose hearing is attuned to it.'[52]

[51] Sometimes the joke resides in one particular passage (like the punch line of a verbal joke), or there may be a whole series of antics (like a clown's act) filled with octave displacements, rhythmic displacements, and a variety of surprises; good examples of such sophisticated musical clowning are the finale of the sonata H. 59/W. 62, 10 and the first movement of the sonata H. 286/W. 61, 2. The listener can not afford to let his attention stray in such movements (nor indeed can the performer), nor can assumptions be too readily made (for example at cadence points).

[52] Original given in n. 31.

[14]

C.P.E. Bach's Evangelist, Johann Heinrich Michel

PAUL CORNEILSON

In contrast to Johann Sebastian Bach's tenure at Leipzig, where precious little is known about his church singers, there is ample documentation for C.P.E. Bach's *Kapelle* at Hamburg.[1] One of Bach's most important tenors in Hamburg, Johann Heinrich Michel, also happens to have been Bach's most prolific copyist.[2] Michel normally sang the role of Evangelist in the twenty-one Passions performed between 1769 and 1789, the only exceptions being the St. Luke settings of 1771, 1779, and 1787 which do not call for a tenor Evangelist. In addition, Michel was assigned arias in cantatas and works for special occasions that Bach composed. By analyzing the specific characteristics of arias (range and tessitura, passage work, tonality and affective qualities of the vocal lines), whether written by Bach or another composer, I construct a profile of Michel's voice and attempt to show how Bach employed him as a soloist. Such methodology might be applied to other singers, in Hamburg and perhaps also Leipzig.[3]

When Charles Burney visited Hamburg in 1772 Bach complained that musical standards had declined in the past fifty years.[4]

> He [Bach] offered to accompany me to every church in Hamburg, where a good organ was to be found; said he would look out for me some old and curious things; and told me at my departure, that there would be some poor music of

---

1. Most of the research on J.S. Bach's singers has focused on his ensemble; see the expanding literature by Joshua Rifkin, Andrew Parrott, Christoph Wolff, et al.

2. See Paul Kast, *Die Bach-Handschriften der Berliner Staatsbibliothek* (Trossingen: Hohner, 1958) as well as the more recent survey in Keiichi Kubota, *C.P.E. Bach: A Study of His Revisions and Arrangements* (Tokyo: Academia Music, 2004), appendix 2, 188–190.

3. There is a long tradition of secondary literature on the singers of Handel and Mozart, but relatively little on the singers of J.S. Bach, largely because there is little documentation on their careers. For a recent survey see Andreas Glöckner, "Alumnen und Externe in den Kantoreien der Thomasschule zur Zeit Bachs," *Bach-Jahrbuch* 92 (2006): 9–36; for information on the bass Johann Christoph Samuel Lipsius, see Hans-Joachim Schulze, "Studenten als Bachs Helfer bei der Leipziger Kirchenmusik," *Bach-Jahrbuch* 70 (1984): 45–52.

4. Burney writes, "M. Bach received me very kindly, but said that he was ashamed to think how small my reward would be, for the trouble I had taken to visit Hamburg. 'You are come here, said he, fifty years too late.'" *The Present State of Music in Germany, the Netherlands and United Provinces*, 2 vols., 2nd ed., (London, 1775), 2:246. Although it is possible that something might have been lost in translation, the critique seems at least plausible. Telemann had similarly complained of this decline in the 1730s, following the closing of the Opera. However, Burney knew little German himself, and it is not known how much English Bach knew. When Christoph Daniel Eberling published a German translation of Burney's travels, he substituted the original text of Bach's autobiography, rather than translating Burney's paraphrase. On the other hand, Bach's comments on Hamburg as related in Burney's English are largely repeated in Eberling's German version.

Er ist der Vater

his, performed in St. Catherine's church, the next day, which he advised me not
to hear. His pleasantry removed all restraint without lessening that respect and
veneration for him, with which his works had inspired me at a distance.[5]

Burney appreciated Bach's sense of humor. Undeterred by this warning, on the following
day, Saturday, 10 October 1772,

> … M. Bach accompanied me to St. Catherine's church, where I heard some very
> good music, of his composition, very ill performed, and to a congregation wholly
> inattentive. This man was certainly born to write for great performers, and for a
> refined audience; but he now seems to be out of his element. There is a fluctuation
> in the arts of every city and country where they are cultivated, and this is not a
> bright period for music at Hamburg.
>
> At church, and in the way home, we had a conversation, which was extremely
> interesting to me: he told me, that if he was in a place, where his compositions
> could be well executed, and well heard, he should certainly kill himself, by exer-
> tions to please. "But adieu music! now, he said, these are good people for society,
> and I enjoy more tranquility and independence here, than at a court; after I was
> fifty, I gave the thing up, and said let us eat and drink, for to-morrow we die! and I
> am now reconciled to my situation; except indeed, when I meet with men of taste
> and discernment, who deserve better music than we can give them here."[6]

That same evening, Burney also attended a concert organized by Herr Ebeling that featured
selections from Bach's *Passions-Cantate*, Wq 233 along with other works. Burney explicitly
praises the "pathetic air" depicting Peter's weeping following the denial.

> Several of M. Bach's vocal compositions were performed, in all which great genius
> and originality were discoverable; though they did not receive the embellishments,
> which singers of the first class might have given to them. M. Bach has set to music,
> a Passione, in the German language, and several parts of this admirable composi-
> tion were performed this evening. I was particularly delighted with a chorus in it,
> which for modulation, contrivance, and effects, was at least equal to any one of the
> best choruses in Handel's immortal Messiah. A pathetic air, upon the subject of
> St. Peter's weeping, when he heard the cock crow, was so truly pathetic as to make
> almost every hearer accompany the saint in his tears.[7]

---

5. *Present State of Music*, 2:246–247.

6. Ibid., 2:251–252. The work that Burney probably heard was a Michaelmas cantata, *Ich will den
Namen des Herrn preisen*, Wq 245 (H 810).

7. Ibid., 2:254–255. Burney had written to Eberling in November 1771 and specifically asked him
to send some of Bach's church music and any new harpsichord music. See *The Letters of Dr Charles
Burney*, vol. 1, *1751–1784*, ed. Alvaro Ribeiro (Oxford: Clarendon Press, 1991), 106.

C.P.E. Bach's Evangelist

The aria Burney refers to is "Wende dich zu meinem Schmerze," possibly sung by the tenor (or baritone) "Herr Wreden," for whom it was originally written in the 1769 St. Matthew Passion.[8]

The Hamburg *Kapelle* during C.P.E. Bach's Tenure

In March 1768 Bach arrived in Hamburg, where he succeeded Georg Philipp Telemann as city music director and cantor at the Johanneum. (Technically, it was as cantor, not as music director, that he was responsible for music during worship services at the five principal churches.) Bach was responsible for the preparation and performance of all the *Quartalstücke* ("ganze Musik" or music for high festivals of Christmas, Easter, Pentecost, and Michaelmas) and Sunday cantatas ("halbe Musik").[9] In addition, Passions were presented at the five main churches and many of the lesser churches during Lent and Holy Week. The music director also received additional payment to provide *Einführungsmusiken* (H 821, installation cantatas for which the music director was paid extra based on the amount of new music it contained) and *Bürgercapitainsmusiken* (H 822, music for the irregular meetings of the "captains of the city militia" in 1780 and 1783). Bach led a group of eight "regular" (salaried) singers and a band of fifteen instrumentalists.[10] This means that church music in Hamburg was generally performed with two singers on a part (or one in the case of Bach's double-choir Heilig, Wq 217, a work he frequently inserted in his cantatas).[11] Original performing material, almost all of which descends from Bach's own library and is now located in the Staatsbibliothek zu Berlin, including

---

8. See introduction and critical report to CPEB:CW, IV/4.1. The house copy of the *Passions-Cantate*, D-B, Mus. ms. Bach P 337, p. 44, has "H. Kirchner" for this aria, but he only started singing in Hamburg much later, c. 1786. Michel's name is listed with a few recitatives and the aria "Verstockte Sünder, solche Werke."

9. The meanings of the terms *ganze Musik* and *halbe Musik* were first discussed by Barbara Wiermann, who noticed that the schedule of figural music performances consisted of two independent rotations of *ganze* and *halbe Musiken* in the five principal Hamburg churches. See Wiermann, "Carl Philipp Emanuel Bach Gottesdienstmusiken," *Carl Philipp Emanuel Bachs geistliche Musik. Bericht über das Internationale Symposium (Teil 1) vom 12. bis 16. März 1998 in Frankfurt (Oder), Żagań und Zielona Góra*, ed. Ulrich Leisinger and Hans-Günter Ottenberg (Frankfurt/Oder: Konzerthalle, 2001), 85–103, esp. 87ff. See also Reginald LeMonte Sanders, "Carl Philipp Emanuel Bach and Liturgical Music at the Hamburg Principal Churches from 1768 to 1788" (Ph.D. diss., Yale University, 2001).

10. These forces were occasionally fortified by additional musicians, and at certain times, only seven singers were available to him. This is explained and documented most thoroughly in Sanders, and more recently by Jürgen Neubacher, *Georg Philipp Telemanns Hamburger Kirchenmusik und ihre Aufführungsbedingungen (1721–1767). Organisationsstrukturen, Musiker, Besetzungspraktiken. Mit einer umfangreichen Quellendokumentation* (Hildesheim: Olms, 2009).

11. Paul Corneilson, "Zur Entstehungs- und Aufführungsgeschichte von Carl Philipp Emanuel Bachs 'Heilig'," *Bach-Jahrbuch* 92 (2006): 273–289.

Er ist der Vater

the archives of the Sing-Akademie zu Berlin,[12] identifies many of the specific singers involved in these liturgical "performances."

Surviving calendars and payment records indicate that Bach was responsible for more than a hundred services each year. For most years, however, we have little specific information on exactly what cantatas were performed, with the exception of annual Passions presented on the Sundays of Lent and Holy Week. As is well known by now, Bach mostly borrowed or arranged works of other composers—especially his father and godfather, and a few contemporaries such as Carl Heinrich Graun, Georg Benda, Gottfried August Homilius—occasionally writing choruses, arias, or simple and accompanied recitatives to create new pasticcios for the festival *Quartalstücke*.[13] Notable exceptions are his oratorios (*Die Israeliten in der Wüste, Die Auferstehung und Himmelfahrt Jesu*, and the *Passions-Cantate*) and a number of incidental works or chamber cantatas which, like the oratorios, Bach published (the double-choir Heilig, Wq 217; *Phillis und Thirsis*, Wq 232; *Der Frühling*, Wq 237; and *Klopstocks Morgengesang*, Wq 239). Thus, it seems that what Bach told Burney is essentially true: he did not overexert himself in writing church music, but when he did, the results were successful and many were published to spread his fame.

Sources of Information on Singers

Since the time of Johann Selle, not later than 1643, the Hamburg authorities had supported eight professional singers through a "Convictorium." This was disbanded well before Bach arrived, but there still existed a system of cooperative payment for the singers, including the *Kämmerei*, churches, and other institutions (hospitals and orphanages). As music director, Bach was responsible for hiring and (if necessary) firing the singers and instrumentalists. He also had to provide an accounting of expenses to the *Kämmerei*, for example, in 1788 Bach received 2024 Marks (in quarterly payments of 506 Mk) to distribute among the singers.[14] Pay was determined by seniority and level of responsibility, so that in 1788 the two basses, Illert

---

12. See Enßlin. For a summary of the history of this collection and its importance, see Christoph Wolff, "Recovered in Kiev: Bach et al. A Preliminary Report on the Music Archive of the Berlin Sing-Akademie," *Notes* 58 (2001): 259–271.

13. See Heinrich Miesner, *Philipp Emanuel Bach in Hamburg. Beiträge zu seiner Biographie und zur Musikgeschichte seiner Zeit* (Leipzig: Breitkopf & Härtel, 1929); Stephen L. Clark, "The Occasional Choral Works of C.P.E. Bach" (Ph.D. diss., Princeton University, 1984); Rachel Wade, "Newly Found Works of C.P.E. Bach," *Early Music* 16/4 (1988): 523–532; Ulrich Leisinger, "Neues über Carl Philipp Emanuel Bachs Passionen nach 'historischer und alter Art'," *Jahrbuch des Staatlichen Instituts für Musikforschung Preußischer Kulturbesitz 2002*, 107–119; Uwe Wolf, "Der Anteil Telemanns an den Hamburger Passionen Carl Philipp Emanuel Bachs," *Telemann, der musikalische Maler. Telemann Kompositionen im Notenarchiv der Singakademie zu Berlin*, ed. Carsten Lange and Brit Reipsch (Hildesheim: Olms, 2010), 412–422.

14. For further details, see Sanders, esp. 96–98, 101–103, 146–147.

and Hoffmann, and Michel were the highest paid of the church singers. (Illert, the most senior and hence "first singer," usually sang the role of Jesus in the Passions.) A document in Illert's hand lists the names of eight singers and accompanist Volkers, along with the payment they received in 1788.[15]

Nach dem Bericht des ersten Sängers Jllert hat der verstorbene Kapellmeister Bach, den gewöhnlichen Kirchen Sängern folgende Salaria gegeben

den Bassisten	Jllert jährlich	400 Mk
	Hoffmann	320
den Tenoristen	Michelsen [Michel]	320
	Steinegger	240
den Altisten	Delfert [Delver]	200
	Seidel	200
den Discantisten	Schumacher	264
	Nerich	264
		2208
dem Accompanisten	Volkers	106
		2314 [Mk]

Much information regarding Bach's singers can be gleaned from annotations on the original performing parts. Names of singers are occasionally given as caption headings at the beginning of a part, or more often in the autograph scores and in *Vorlagen* for the pasticcios, where Bach indicated which singer was supposed to sing particular arias, duets, and recitatives, so the copyist would know for which part to copy the music. For instance, figure 1 shows the end of a movement in one of the installation cantatas, followed by the tenor vocal line for an aria (to be copied into Herr Michel's part). In the autograph score of the birthday cantata, *Dank-Hymne der Freundschaft*, H 824e, Bach wrote detailed instructions to his copyist (Michel, in this case) about how to realize the strophic verses in the concluding movement (see CPEB:CW, V/5.1, pp. 142–43). Some of Bach's autograph scores (often incomplete) had been separated from the parts at the time of the 1805 auction. Printed librettos survive for all the Passions and a few of the cantatas, but these do not include the names of the singers and roles they were to sing; however, the librettos for the *Bürgercapitainsmusiken* (H 822a–d) do include names of singers and their allegorical roles. In 1780, Michel sang Der Patriotismus (Patriotism) and Die Eintracht (Concord); in 1783, he sang Die Friede (Peace) and Die Wahrheit (Truth).

---

15. D-Ha, Senat, 111-1, Cl. VII. Lit. He. Nr. 2. Vol. 8b. Fasc. 6, enclosure to fol. 6; transcribed in Sanders, 104, and Neubacher, 214–215.

Er ist der Vater

Figure 1. Autograph score of *Einführungsmusik Winkler*, H 821f, with the cue
"von der dritten Arie, die Singstimme. / H. Michel, poco andante." (D-B, SA 713)

C.P.E. Bach's Evangelist

It was Bach's practice to use boy sopranos, as we know from the *Musikalischen Correspondenz* (Speyer, 1792):

> schon der selige Bach klagte sehr darüber, daß er nichts großes aufführen könnte, und alles gute für diese zwei Stimmen [i.e., basses] geben müsse, weil die 2 Chorknaben selten über zwey oder drei Jahre ihre gute Discantstimme behielten und es denn in verschiedenen Jahren wieder daran fehlte. Die Tenor- und Altsänger sind gute brave Leute, aber ohne gefällige Stimme.[16]

Since the boy sopranos were only able to sing in the group for two or three years, they had a different status than the six adult singers. A few of the boys eventually sang alto or tenor, including Hartnack Otto Conrad Zinck, Friederich Nicolaus Delver, and Hartmann.[17] Others sang soprano for a couple of years then disappeared from the records, including Lüders (1769–1771), Rauschelbach (1773–1774), Ebeling (1776–1777), Johann Christian Lau (1780–1781), Nohrlich (1783–1784), Nerich and Johann Georg Schumacher (1788–1789), who each received 264 Mk in 1788.

Some singers served multiple roles. For instance, Otto Ernst Gregorius Schieferlein (1704–1787) was active from around 1740 as an alto and copyist for Georg Philipp Telemann and C.P.E. Bach. (Schieferlein is probably the scribe known as Telemann A and Anon. 304.)[18] Georg Michael Telemann (1748–1831), grandson of G.P. Telemann, served as his grandfather's accompanist from at least 1765. Together with Schieferlein, he filled in as interim director between the elder Telemann's death and Bach's arrival (June 1767–April 1768).[19] Georg Michael composed music for Bach's introduction on 19 April 1768, and continued to serve as Bach's accompanist until he went to the University of Kiel in 1770. (He eventually became kapellmeister in Riga.) In a letter to Georg Michael, dated 31 January 1771, Bach states that the alto "Herr Holland is no longer able to sing" and that Bach had promised him a position as accompanist "nearly a year ago."[20] Bach was still paying the absent Georg Michael for ac-

---

16. Cited by Sanders, 383, as quoted by Josef Sittard, *Geschichte des Musik- und Concertwesens in Hamburg vom 14. Jahrhundert bis auf die Gegenwart* (Altona and Leipzig: A.C. Reher, 1890), 53.

17. According to Sanders, there was apparently more than one singer by the name of Hartmann, as well as Johann Samuel Hartmann (1748–1830), who played violin, cello, and trumpet.

18. On the possible identity of Anon. 304 and Schieferlein, see Peter Wollny, review of *Georg Philipp Telemann. Autographe und Abschriften*, ed. Joachim Jaenecke, *Bach-Jahrbuch* 81 (1995): 218.

19. See Joachim Kremer, *Das norddeutsche Kantorat im 18. Jahrhundert* (Kassel: Bärenreiter, 1995), 124. See also Neubacher, 454.

20. Stephen L. Clark published an English translation with the German text in "The Letters of Carl Philipp Emanuel Bach to Georg Michael Telemann," *Journal of Musicology* 3 (1984): 188–193; see also *CPEB-Briefe*, 1:132–136; *CPEB-Letters*, 20–22. According to Neubacher, 429, Johann David Holland (1746–1827) became Music Director at the Hamburg Cathedral in 1776 but left Hamburg in 1782 and eventually became a music professor at the University at Vilnius.

Er ist der Vater

companist services he was no longer providing, and Bach said he would not continue to pay him after Easter.

Since Bach does not use alto clef for his altos (modern countertenors), it is sometimes difficult to distinguish between altos and sopranos (both are notated in soprano, C clef). Music for Carl Rudolph Wreden (active between 1760 and 1774)[21] is usually notated in tenor clef but also occasionally in bass clef. There are even times when he (or other tenors) sang music notated in soprano clef, presumably an octave lower than written. Only the organ in St. Michaelis was tuned at *Kammerton* (sounding at the notated pitch). The organs in St. Catharinen and St. Nicolai were tuned a whole step higher than regular pitch, and the organs in St. Petri and St. Jacobi were tuned a minor third higher. But Bach compensated for this by transposing the respective organ parts down to *Kammerton*.

The following are the regular singers (alto, tenor, bass) who were singing in 1788, the final year of C.P.E. Bach's life:[22]

Altos

- Friederich Nicolaus Delver (1759–1847) appeared as a boy soprano in the 1776 Passion, and was singing alto by 1779; he earned 200 Mk in 1788, and received a pension in 1814.
- Johann Matthias Seydel (1755–1792) sang in the *Bürgercapitainsmusik* in 1780, and in 1788 earned 200 Mk.

Tenors

- Johann Heinrich Michel (1739–1810)[23] was active from 1762 until at least 1792, and in 1788 he earned 320 Mk as a church singer.
- Leopold August Elias Steinegger (fl. 1785–1814) performed in 1785 at the Waisenhauskirche (possibly as an instrumentalist) and earned 240 Mk in 1788; he received a pension in 1814.

Two other tenors, Herr Rosenau and Herr Kirchner (their given names are not known), were occasionally used as auxiliary singers between 1785 and 1789.[24]

---

21. See Neubacher, 462–463.

22. For a summary of the entire ensemble of church musicians, see Sanders, appendix 3.2, 148–159; see also Robert von Zahn, *Musikpflege in Hamburg um 1800. Der Wandel des Konzertwesens und der Kirchenmusik zwischen dem Tode Carl Philipp Emanuel Bachs und dem Tode Christian Friedrich Gottlieb Schwenkes* (Hamburg: Verein für Hamburgische Geschichte, 1991), 22, 139, 203.

23. Michel's dates are given in Jürgen Neubacher, "Der Organist Johann Gottfried Rist (1741–1795) und der Bratschist Ludwig August Christoph Hopff (1715–1798): zwei Hamburger Notenkopisten Carl Philipp Emanuel Bachs," *Bach-Jahrbuch* 91 (2005): 121–122. See also Kremer, 300–301.

24. Rosenau's name is listed as one of the tenors for the *Dank-Hymne der Freundschaft*, H 824e (1785); and Kirchner sang in the *Musik am Dankfeste wegen des fertigen Michaelisturms*, H 823 (1786) and the last three Passions.

C.P.E. Bach's Evangelist

Basses

- Friedrich Martin Illert (1738–1811) was active from 1754 until at least 1792,[25] and in 1788 was the "first singer," earning 400 Mk annually.
- Johann Andreas Hoffmann (1752–1832) was singing as a church singer by 1770, and earned 320 Mk in 1788. He received a pension in 1814 and led a performance of Handel's *Messiah* in 1818.[26]

A survey of Bach's vocal music reveals that the two tenor and bass parts are generally quite balanced within each cantata and Passion. This cannot be a coincidence; Bach might have favored certain singers, but for the most part, they were treated equally within the ensemble. What is evident in the performing material from Bach's library is that from time to time adjustments and last-minute substitutions had to be made.

For many years, the tenor Michel was known only by his last name from a reference by Georg Poelchau in a MS copy of BWV 1060.[27] In the last year of his life, Bach only referred to his "busy copyist" in letters to Westphal, who was in the process of acquiring the complete instrumental music of Bach. Bach's widow and daughter continued the correspondence with Westphal, and referred to Michel as their most loyal copyist.[28] Only in 1995 did Stephen Clark find a document, signed by six of Bach's singers, that includes Michel's full name (see figure 2). We can be relatively certain that the copyist Michel and the tenor Michel are one and the same person. It is not entirely clear when Michel became active as a copyist; perhaps as early as 1770, when Bach had to compose, copy, and prepare a work for the visit that year of the Swedish crown prince.[29] However, Michel only became Bach's principal copyist after Anon. 304 declined around 1781.

---

25. Neubacher, 431.

26. Neubacher, 429.

27. D-B, Mus. ms. Bach P 241, p. 34: "Von H. Michels Hand. Tenorist beym Bachschen Kirchenchor in Hamburg 1787." See Georg von Dadelsen, *Bemerkungen zur Handschrift Johann Sebastian Bachs, seiner Familie und seines Kreises* (Trossingen: Hohner, 1957), 24. Rachel Wade also found a similar reference in P 344 (also in Poelchau's hand): "Die Discantstimme hat Herr Michael, Tenorist am Hamburgischen Kirchenchore (Bachs Notist) geschrieben." Wade, *The Keyboard Concertos of Carl Philipp Emanuel Bach* (Ann Arbor: UMI Research Press, 1981), 26, 126.

28. The letters are published in Manfred Hermann Schmid, "'Das Geschäft mit dem Nachlaß von C.Ph.E. Bach.' Neue Dokumente zur Westphal-Sammlung des Conservatoire Royal de Musique und der Bibliothèque Royale de Belgique in Brüssel," *Carl Philipp Emanuel Bach und die europäische Musikkultur des mittleren 18. Jahrhunderts*, ed. Hans Joachim Marx (Göttingen: Vandenhoeck & Ruprecht, 1990), 473–528.

29. According to a note on the wrapper to the parts for "Spiega, Ammonia fortunata," Wq 216 in D-B, SA 1239: "Mit diesem Chor ließ Hamburg anno 70 / den Schwedischen Cron Prinzen und deßen / jüngsten Bruder seine Devotion und Freude / über Ihre hohe Gegenwart bezeugen und / besingen. C.P.E. Bach mußte es in / 12 Stunden componiren. Es wurde 2mahl / gemacht, stark besetzt, copirt, an den / König nach Stockholm geschickt. Sonst hat / es noch Niemand." Two of the three Canto parts and one

Er ist der Vater

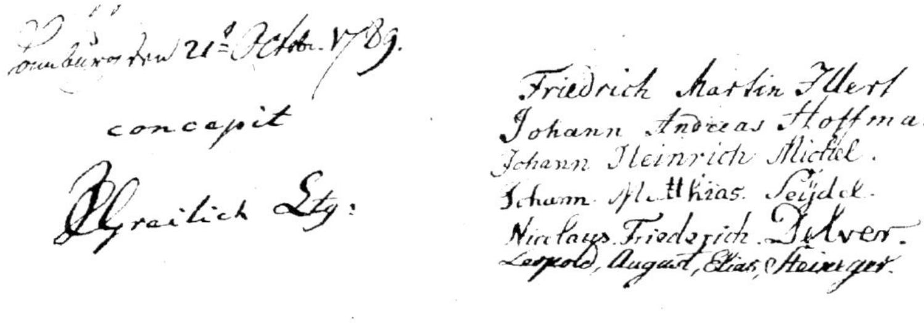

Figure 2. Document extract with signatures of six regular church singers, dated 1789
(D-Ha, Senat Cl. VII. Lit. He. No. 2. Vol. 8b. Fasc. 7, fol. 24)

In a letter dated 7 April 1763, Georg Philipp Telemann informed the Proto-Scholarcha (the chief executive of the Johanneum and Gymnasium) that he had finally hired a suitable tenor for his choir and therefore had to dismiss a less able singer:

> Da, Ew.r Hochweisheiten persönlich meine unterthänige Aufwartung zu machen, durch die zunehmende Schwäche meiner Beine verhindert werde, so habe hiermit gehorsamst anzeigen sollen, daß ich endlich einen tüchtigen Tenorsänger entdeck-et, und ihm bey hiesiger Kirchenmusik einen Platz eingeräumet, dagegen aber einen andern zu verabschieden habe.[30]

This letter almost certainly refers to Michel's appointment, for he is known to have begun singing in Telemann's ensemble as a tenor around 1762. We also know that in 1760 Telemann did not have a reliable tenor, and thus wrote the Evangelist part for bass in the St. Luke Passion that year.[31]

Unlike his godfather and predecessor as music director in Hamburg, Bach did not write operas, either in Berlin or Hamburg. However, there is an account in a review of a staged performance of Dittersdorf's *Hiob* in Berlin, which states that Bach attempted one act of an opera, but it did not succeed:

of the Tenore parts are in Michel's hand; Enßlin tentatively identified some of the other parts as "early Michel?" (fruh Michel?), but these are in a different, otherwise unidentified hand. I am grateful to Peter Wollny for his assistance in evaluating this source; see further discussion in CPEB:CW, V/5.2.

30. *Georg Philipp Telemann. Briefwechsel: sämtl. erreichbare Briefe von u. an Telemann*, ed. Hans Grosse and Hans Rudolf Jung (Leipzig: Deutscher Verlag für Musik, 1972), 45. I am grateful to Jason B. Grant for drawing this letter to my attention. See also Neubacher, 240–241.

31. When C.P.E. Bach used Telemann's 1760 St. Luke Passion as the model for his 1771 Passion (published in CPEB:CW, IV/6.1), he decided to redistribute a portion of the Evangelist part to treble voices.

C.P.E. Bach's Evangelist

> Da der verstorbene Bach in Hamburg mit so vielem Glücke die vortrefflich-
> sten Oden und Oratorii in Music gesetzt hatte; so vermuthete man, daß er auch
> in Opern eben so glücklich seyn würde. Man ersuchte ihn einmahl, sich der
> Tonsetzung eines Singspiels zu unterziehen. Bach that es und lieferte einen Act.
> Man probirte denselben und er mißfiel gänzlich. Der Fehler lag nur darin, weil
> Bach die dramatischen Wirkungen nicht kannte.[32]

One would like to know more about Bach's attempt to write an opera, but no other documentation or music survives, unless of course Bach reused some of it in his cantatas. Some of Bach's
vocal music is quite operatic, and at least one of Telemann's Hamburg church singers, Johann
Friedrich Helmuth, did become an opera singer.[33]

Michel's Voice

Table 1 lists the major works that Michel sang with music either written entirely or arranged by Bach during his tenure at Hamburg: Passions, *Quartalstücke*, *Einführungsmusiken*,
and other works for special occasions. It does not include all of the cantatas he would have
performed from Sunday to Sunday and other occasions (funerals, concerts, etc.). The arias in
boldface type represent pieces by C.P.E. Bach written specifically for Michel. (Arias borrowed
from his own work, e.g., the *Magnificat*, Wq 215, or other arias he borrowed from other
composers, that is, not written for Michel, are not highlighted. Choruses, duets, and recitative—though also written for Michel—are not included in this survey.) Several *Quartalstücke*
were revived and sometimes revised in later years, but the works are only listed at their first
appearance. Thus, the table also provides some sense of the number of "new" vocal works Bach
wrote each year, though his Passions all incorporate music by other composers.

If we examine the range and tessitura of the arias Michel is known to have sung, it is
clear that he was most comfortable singing from F below middle C to the G above (f–g' in the
Helmholtz system). The bottom of his range was around d, though one aria (no. 7 in H 821n,
from 1787) has a low B♭. He could easily sing g' or even a' on occasion (very rarely sustaining
these pitches), but for the most part Bach avoids the highest register, whether in the new music
he wrote for Michel or in choosing music for him by other composers. In the 1772 St. John
Passion, the one aria assigned to Michel (borrowed from Stölzel's 1749 Passion; see CPEB:CW,
IV/7.1) is in E minor with several high a's; this might have been too taxing for Michel, who
was also singing the role of Evangelist in the Passion, and so he copied the aria on a separate

---

32. Quoted in Christoph Henzel, *Quellentexte zur Berliner Musikgeschichte im 18. Jahrhundert*
(Wilhelmshaven: Florian Noetzel, 1999), 205.
33. Jürgen Neubacher, "Von Telemann zu Mozart: ehemalige Hamburger Kirchensänger als
Sängerschauspieler auf Theaterbühnen in der zweiten Hälfte des 18. Jahrhunderts," *Musiktheater in
Hamburg um 1800*, ed. Claudia Mauer Zenck, *Hamburger Jahrbuch für Musikwissenschaft*, 22 (Frankfurt:
Peter Lang, 2005), 29–55.

Er ist der Vater

leaf for one of the boy sopranos to sing (presumably agreed to by both Bach and Michel). It is unclear at what point this change was made, perhaps only after the rotation of Passion performances had begun. It is also possible that Michel alternated with one of the sopranos during Lent 1772; there are no indications in either the tenor or soprano part that one or the other was preferred.

Michel would have been an expert at declaiming simple recitatives as the Evangelist in the Gospel narrative of Passions. Far from generic, the Evangelist's recitatives are quite expressive, as Bach was drawing on his father's Passions for inspiration (primarily in the St. Matthew Passions of 1769, 1781, and 1789). Since C.P.E. Bach borrowed several of J.S. Bach's turbae from the St. Matthew Passion, BWV 244, we can readily see how Emanuel rewrote the vocal lines for the Evangelist to accommodate Michel's lower tessitura. Two examples will suffice: in example 1a (BWV 244, mvt. 38a–38b) the Evangelist has g' on "kleine" followed by a' on "hinzu" in the next measure; in example 1b (H 782, mvt. 17a–17b) the vocal line is a sixth lower, with c♯' on "hinzu" and eventually going as high as f♯' on "zu Petro" (where J.S. Bach has d'). Before the first turba "Lass ihn kreuzigen" (BWV 244, mvt. 45a–45b and H 782, mvt. 24c–24d), the Evangelist's "Sie sprachen alle" has exactly the same notes (b–e'–b–c'), going into the chorus in A minor. In example 2a, before the second turba "Lass ihn kreuzigen," however, Sebastian's Evangelist (BWV 244, mvt. 50a–50b) sings a' on "schrieen" and g's on "sprachen" going to the chorus in B minor, but in example 2b (H 782, mvt. 26a–26b), Emanuel rewrites the line so the Evangelist starts on f♯' on "Sie schrieen" but then descends to g below middle C for "sprachen."

Bach also borrowed and adapted the Gospel narratives of Telemann (1760 St. Luke and 1745 St. John) and Homilius (undated St. Mark, St. Luke, and St. John). Michel frequently sang simple and accompanied recitative in other works, where Bach could rely on him to give a solid performance. For instance, he was given recitatives in the installation cantatas for Pastors Klefeker, Hornbostel, Winkler, Gerling, Sturm, Gasie, Berkhahn, and Willerding. Michel also had only recitatives to sing (in addition to the chorales and choruses) in *Der Frevler mag die Wahrheit schmähn*, Wq 246 (1785), *Wenn Christus seine Kirche schützt*, Wf IV/6 (1778), and *Versammlet euch dem Herrn zu Ehren*, H 823 (1786). (Jason Grant discusses the recitative "O Michael! du, dessen Tritte" elsewhere in this volume.) After 1776, in the years when Michel was singing the Evangelist, he was not given any other arias or duets to sing; only in the St. Luke Passions of 1779 and 1787, when he was not the Evangelist, did Bach assign him arias.

As to be expected in a career lasting more than twenty years, Michel sang a variety of aria types in the Passions and cantatas. One of the first arias that Bach wrote for him is representative: "Verstockte Sünder, solche Werke," no. 20 in the 1769 St. Matthew Passion. (This aria is also discussed by Ulrich Leisinger elsewhere in this volume.) The piece is in F major, with an inclusive range from c to g' but mostly falls within the octave f–f'. There is no opening ritornello, but the tenor begins with an angular motive that defines the key and compass.

C.P.E. Bach's Evangelist

Example 1. Comparison of J.S. Bach's and C.P.E. Bach's recitative
preceeding the turba chorus, "Wahrlich, du bist auch einer von denen"

a. BWV 244, mvt. 38a

b. H 782, mvt. 17a

Example 2. Comparison of J.S. Bach's and C.P.E. Bach's recitative
preceeding the turba chorus, "Lass ihn kreuzigen"

a. BWV 244, mvt. 50a

b. H 782, mvt. 26a

Coming in the Passion right after Judas' betrayal, it is a "rage" aria warning sinners to repent
before it is too late. The setting is marked by Bach's characteristic slippery chromatic harmony,
full of deceptive twists and turns. Michel's ear and musicianship are tested with leaps of minor
7ths (mm. 3, 15, 16), diminished 7ths (mm. 4 and 14), and a diminished 5th (mm. 6–7). (See
example 3.) This is mostly a syllabic setting, though as we shall see Michel was capable of singing passage work as well. Since this aria was also used in the *Passions-Cantate*, Wq 233, a work
sung every Lent at some of the lesser churches in Hamburg, this is the piece Michel probably
sang most frequently during Bach's tenure.

Er ist der Vater

Example 3. Opening of Aria no. 20 (tenor and basso continuo lines)
from the 1769 St. Matthew Passion (CPEB:CW, IV/4.1)

C.P.E. Bach's Evangelist

Two arias from installation cantatas, no. 8 in H 821f (1773) and no. 7 in H 821l (1785), demonstrate a remarkable consistency in expressive details despite contrasting keys (F major vs. G minor) and different formal structures (D.S. vs. two-part aria similar to a sonata).[34] Both are cantabile arias in 3/4 time and moderate tempos (*Poco andante* and *Mäßig und gelassen*, respectively); both arias begin with a leap up a fourth, from scale degree 5 to 8 (see examples 4 and 5), the same interval used to begin many recitatives (see also example 3).

Example 4. Aria no. 8 (tenor and basso continuo lines)
from *Einführungsmusik Winklers*, H 821f

34. For a brief survey of aria forms in works performed by C.P.E. Bach, see Howard E. Smither, "Arienstruktur und Arienstil in den Oratorien und Kantaten Bachs," *Carl Philipp Emanuel Bach und die europäische Musikkultur des mittleren 18. Jahrhunderts*, 345–368.

Er ist der Vater

Example 5. Aria no. 7 (tenor and basso continuo lines)
from *Einführungsmusik Gasie,* H 8211

Neither of these two arias would be out of place in an opera, and it is safe to say that C.P.E. Bach must have absorbed the *galant,* Italianate style of his Berlin colleague Carl Heinrich Graun. Few opera composers of the period were as adventurous harmonically as Bach, especially in the later aria (example 5), with its rising chromatic bass line matched to a certain extent by the tenor.

My last example is the aria no. 9 from the *Dank-Hymne der Freundschaft.* The text has four couplets of hexameter with a dactyl beat (′ ˘ ˘) in the first line that changes to an iamb beat (˘ ′) halfway through the second line, producing a hemiola effect. The couplets, labeled a–d, correspond to the music in example 6.

C.P.E. Bach's Evangelist

a. Schon schimmern durch graulichte Nebel von ferne die güldenen Zinnen, sie leuchten wie Sterne im Rosenlicht der Ewigkeit.
b. Schon weht mir der West paradiesische Düfte sanft lispelnd entgegen, bebalsamt die Luft mit Vorgefühl der Seligkeit.
c. Schon hör ich die Jubel der seligen Chöre, die Hymnen der Andacht, ich höre der Himmelsharfen reinen Klang.
d. Laut schallt es, das Heilig! der Engel, der Brüder, mit Cymbelton hallen die Himmel es wieder, wie Donner hallt in der Hölle der Sang.

Example 6. Aria no. 9 (tenor and basso continuo lines)
from *Dank-Hymne der Freundschaft*, H 824e

Er ist der Vater

Example 6 continued

Bach sets the text in 3/4 meter and rather than setting the couplets in a strictly strophic treat-ment, he composes "varied reprises." The first couplet quickly modulates from the tonic G to dominant D; the second begins in D and modulates to A minor; the third moves from E minor to B minor; and the last begins back in G and closes again on the dominant D. The vocal line becomes more complicated in the first three couplets (a–c), and reaches the highest pitch a' for the tenor on the word "Himmelsharfen" (m. 62). The final couplet begins at the same pitch level as the first, but the "Donner" of the final line makes a dramatic conclusion, setting up the "Chor der Engel" in the double-choir Heilig, Wq 217 with a deceptive cadence (D major to E minor).[35]

In the absence of more definite documentation, it is possible to make educated guesses about the distribution of arias in Bach's other church music. No singers' names are given in the printed libretto for *Die Israeliten* (in D-Hs, A/70012, 13), and the autograph score and performing parts are mostly lost (see CPEB:CW, IV/1). However, the role of Aaron is assigned to a tenor, and given the range of the three solo pieces—accompanied recitative no. 4 (f–f'), aria no. 5 (d–f'), and recitative no. 8 (with only a single ab')—it is plausible that Michel sang the role in the premiere for the opening of the Lazarethkirche in November 1769. Similarly, in *Auf, schicke dich*, Wq 249 (Christmas 1775), Bach reused an aria (no. 8a) that he wrote for Michel in H 821e (no. 11a), so we can assume Michel also sang the aria in the latter work, Wq 249. Although the cantata *Nun danket alle Gott*, Wq 241 (Easter 1780) includes one aria for tenor (no. 3), this was borrowed from the *Einführungsmusik Palm*, H 821a (no. 13) with a different text that was also used in the 1777 St. Matthew Passion (no. 30). Since Michel did not sing this aria in either of the earlier works, it seems unlikely that he would have sung it in Wq 241.

Another curious example is the tenor aria, "Sing ihm, voll Rührung," Wq 212, which as far as we know was written by Bach. The aria was copied out in score and Bach added a new text for the *Einführungsmusik Klefeker*, H 821b, no. 10.[36] This aria was sung by Wreden in November 1771, so when Bach reused it as aria no. 5 in the Michaelmas cantata, *Siehe, ich begehre deiner Befehle*, Wq 247 with the original text ("Sing ihm, voll Rührung") in 1775, Michel probably did not sing it. What work Bach borrowed this aria from is not known, though it seems unlikely he would have written it with one text and substituted another before the original had been performed.

---

35. See the introduction to CPEB:CW, V/5.1, p. xii. See also Corneilson, 279–280.

36. The aria is preserved in the composite MS D-B, Mus. ms. Bach P 349 with the text underlay in Bach's hand. See CPEB:CW, V/3.1 for further information.

Er ist der Vater

Conclusion

Some may well ask, why should we bother to study Michel and the other church singers at Hamburg, especially when very few (if any) modern ensembles will perform Bach's vocal music with exactly the same disposition of singers Bach used in Hamburg? First of all, because we have sufficient documentation to reconstruct Bach's ensemble, it can serve as a case study for liturgical practice in Hamburg at the end of the eighteenth century. This is not to suggest we can say "how it really was" Sunday to Sunday—there are still far too many gaps in our knowledge of the repertory and variables (including sickness and other factors that would have caused Bach headaches, as they did Telemann before him). But we have a good deal more information for C.P.E. Bach's Hamburg than for J.S. Bach's Leipzig. Above all, we can see how the limitations and strengths of his church singers shaped Bach's vocal music. As an overworked church musician, Bach had to deal with the singers and instrumentalists available to him. He secured his reputation for posterity through his *Magnificat*, oratorios, and other published works, especially his late "Kenner und Liebhaber" collections and *Versuch über die wahre Art das Clavier zu spielen*. Nevertheless, the liturgical music for Hamburg provides a glimpse into how he made the most of a less than ideal artistic situation.

On Bach's vocal work, Burney wrote:

> ... for though his genius is equal to every thing in music, yet he has not had the practice, the experience, nor the singers, or orchestra, to write for, which others have had before him: however, each candid observer and hearer, must discover, in the slightest and most trivial productions, of every kind, some mark of originality in the modulation, accompaniment, or melody, which bespeak a great and exalted genius.[37]

---

37. *Present State of Music*, 2:256.

C.P.E. Bach's Evangelist

Table 1. Passions, Oratorios, and Cantatas Sung by the Tenor Michel, 1768–89

Year/ Season or Date	Work	Type/Number (Key, Range)	Documentation
1768			
Easter	Sing Volk der Christen, H 808/3		SA 251; rev. in 1775, 1781
2 July	Meine Seele erhebt den Herrn, H 819		SA 256–257; rev. 1773, 1776, 1780
1769			
Lent	St. Matthew Passion, H 782	**aria no. 20 (F maj., c–g')**[a]	SA 18 and SA 5155
Easter	Gott hat den Herrn auferwecket, Wq 244		P 345 and St 182; originally written in Berlin, 1756; rev. in 1776, 1787
Pentecost	Herr, lehr uns tun, H 817	aria no. 6 (D min., d–e')[b]	SA 257
12 July	Einführungsmusik Palm, H 821a	duet no. 7	SA 711
Michaelmas	Den Engeln gleich, Wq 248	accomp. no. 2	SA 248 and P 373; rev. in 1774
1 Nov.	Die Israeliten in der Wüste, Wq 238	accomp. no. 4; aria no. 5 (D min., d–g')	Performed for the opening of the Lazarethskirche
1770			
Lent	St. Mark Passion, H 783	aria no. 27 (E min., d–a')[c]	SA 22
Michaelmas	Es erhub sich ein Streit, BWV 19 (arr.)	[aria no. 3][d]	St 25b; rev. in 1776, 1781
1771			
Lent	St. Luke Passion, H 784	duet no. 11	SA 23
Easter	Ist Christus nicht auferstanden, H 808/4	[aria no. 5][e]	SA 249
Michaelmas	Wie wird uns werden, Wf XIV/5 (arr.)		St 265
5 Nov.	Einführungsmusik Klefeker, H 821b	**aria no. 9 (D maj., d–a')**	SA 714
8 Nov.	Einführungsmusik Schuchmacher, H 821c	[aria no. 3 (B-flat maj., d–g')]	P 348[f]
1772			
4 Feb.	Einführungsmusik Häseler, H 821d	accomp. no. 2; aria no. 3 (G maj., d–a')[g]	SA 706 and P 346

Er ist der Vater

Table 1 continued

Year/ Season or Date	Work	Type/Number (Key, Range)	Documentation
Lent	St. John Passion, H 785	aria no. 11 (E min., e–a')[h]	SA 4657
23 Sept.	Einführungsmusik Hornbostel, H 821e	**aria no. 11a (E-flat maj., d–f')**	SA 707
Michaelmas	Ich will den Namen des Herrn preisen, Wq 245	[aria no. 2][i]	SA 253; rev. in 1777, 1782, 1786
Christmas	Ehre sei Gott in der Höhe, H 811	[aria no. 5]	SA 247; rev. in 1778, 1782
1773 14 Jan.	Einführungsmusik Winkler, H 821f	**aria no. 8 (F maj., e–a')**	SA 713 and P 340
Lent	St. Matthew Passion, H 786		SA 5136
1774 Lent	St. Mark Passion, H 787		SA 24 and SA 1511
1775 Lent	St. Luke Passion, H 788	trio no. 19	SA 50
Michaelmas	Siehe, ich begehre deiner Befehle, Wq 247		SA 252 and P 349; rev. in 1779, 1783, 1788
12 Dec.	Einführungsmusik Friderici, H 821g	[aria no. 7 (A min., e–a')]	P 347[j]
Christmas	Auf, schicke dich, recht feierlich, Wq 249	aria no. 8a[k]	SA 289; rev. in 1779, 1786
1776 Lent	St. John Passion, H 789	aria no. 11 (E-flat maj., e♭–g')[l]	SA 19
1777 Lent	St. Matthew Passion, H 790		SA 25
28 Nov.	Einführungsmusik Gerling, H 821h	**aria no. 15a (D maj., d–g')**	SA 710
1778 Lent	St. Mark Passion, H 791		SA 26
Easter	Jauchzet, frohlocket, Wq 242	[aria no. 3][m]	SA 255; rev. in 1786
1 Sept.	Einführungsmusik Sturm, H 821i	**aria no. 10 (G maj., f♯–a'); accomp. no. 14**	SA 715
Michaelmas	Wenn Christus seine Kirche schützt, Wf XIV/6 (arr.)		St 266; rev. in 1784

Table 1 continued

Year/ Season or Date	Work	Type/Number (Key, Range)	Documentation
1779			
Lent	St. Luke Passion, H 792	aria no. 22 (B- flat maj., d–g')	SA 21
1780			
Lent	St. John Passion, H 793		SA 27
Easter	Nun danket alle Gott, Wq 241		SA 245; rev. in 1783
7 Sept.	Bürgercapitainsmusiken, Oratorio, H 822a	**aria no. 7** **(G maj., d–g')**	A-Wgm, III 8678 (H 23559)
	Bürgercapitainsmusiken, Serenata, H 822b		A-Wgm, III 29337 (H 27769); D-Hs, Scrin 36
1781			
Lent	St. Matthew Passion, H 794		SA 28 and SA 29
1782			
Lent	St. Mark Passion, H 795		SA 49
15 Jan.	Einführungsmusik Jänisch, H 821k	**aria no. 10** **(A maj., e–a')**	SA 712
Easter	Gott du wirst seine Seele, H 808/1		
1783			
Lent	St. Luke Passion, H 796		SA 30 and SA 717
4 Sept.	Bürgercapitainsmusiken, Oratorio, H 822c		music lost
	Bürgercapitainsmusiken, Serenata, H 822d	duet no. 5	D-Hs, Scrin 37
1784			
Lent	St. John Passion, H 797		SA 31
Easter	Anbetung dem Erbarmer, Wq 243	[accomp. no. 4]	SA 704 and P 339
1785			
Lent	St. Matthew Passion, H 798		SA 32 and SA 269
Jan./Feb.[n]	Dank-Hymne der Freundschaft, H 824e	**aria no. 9** **(G maj., d–g')**	SA 267
3 Aug.	Einführungsmusik Schäffer, H 821m	**aria no. 5** **(A maj., d♮–a')**	SA 708
30 Aug.	Einführungsmusik Gasie, H 821l	**aria no. 7** **(G min., c♯–g')**	SA 709

117

Er ist der Vater

Table 1 continued

Year/ Season or Date	Work	Type/Number (Key, Range)	Documentation
Michaelmas	Der Frevler mag die Wahrheit schmähn, Wq 246		SA 254
1786			
Lent	St. Mark Passion, H 799		SA 33
31 Oct.	Musik am Dankfeste, H 823		SA 243
1787			
Lent	St. Luke Passion, H 800	**aria no. 10** (D maj., d–a′)	SA 34
8 Feb.	Einführungsmusik Berkhahn, H 821n	**aria no. 7** (E-flat maj., B♭–g′)	SA 716
after June	Einführungsmusik Willerding, H 821o	**arioso no. 7** (G maj., g–a′); **aria a 4 no. 9**; **accomp. no. 15b**	SA 705
1788			
Lent	St. John Passion, H 801		SA 35°
1789			
Lent	St. Matthew Passion, H 802		SA 36

a. This aria was also included in the *Passions-Cantate*, Wq 233, as no. 9, a work that was given frequently at Hamburg churches during Lent.

    b. This aria was originally written for alto; cf. no. 7 in the Magnificat, Wq 215, dating from 1749.

    c. This aria was borrowed from the St. Mark Passion by Homilius (see CPEB:CW, IV/5.1).

    d. This aria was borrowed from a cantata by Benda, Lorenz 597.

    e. This aria was borrowed from a cantata by Benda, Lorenz 534.

    f. The original performing material for this work is lost.

    g. This aria was written as no. 3 in Wq 215, with a different text, dating from 1749.

    h. This aria was borrowed from the 1749 Passion by Stölzel (see CPEB:CW, IV/7.1).

    i. This aria was borrowed from a cantata by Benda, Lorenz 603.

    j. The original performing material and libretto for this work are lost.

    k. This is the same aria as H 821e, no. 11a.

    l. This aria was borrowed from the St. John Passion by Homilius (see CPEB:CW, IV/7.2).

    m. This aria was borrowed from a cantata by C.H. Graun, B:III:27, no. 2.

    n. Possibly not performed in 1785 but only later; see introduction to CPEB:CW, V/5.1.

    o. Tenor Evangelist part is lost for this Passion.

[15]

C. P. E. BACH'S UNKNOWN LATE COLLECTION OF SONGS

Christoph Wolff

This paper concerns the older C. P. E. Bach, his songs (an underestimated part of his compositional output), and a completely unknown facet of his late vocal works.

It deals with a man in his late sixties and early seventies, respectively, who suffered from spells of gout and other ailments; with a father who in 1778 had lost his son Johann Sebastian Jr., a promising landscape painter who died prematurely in Rome at age 29.

Bach's compositional activities slowed in his later years, but he continued to pay attention to one of the genres that had been particularly close 'to his heart for most of his life, songs. Thus, it is worth mentioning that at the very end of his life the 74-year old composer published two sets of songs, a group of twelve songs (Wq 202N) for the collection *Freymaurer-Lieder mit ganz neuen Melodien von den Herren Capellmeistern Bach, Naumann und Schulz* (Copenhagen and Leipzig, 1788) as well as a book of twenty-two songs under the title *Neue Lieder-Melodien* (Lübeck, 1789). The latter appeared posthumously, but demonstrated once again his congenial relationship with major literary figures of his time, poets like Lessing, Ebeling, Claudius, and Gleim – all personal friends.

Personal connections with literary figures does not generally play a significant role within the compositional activities of the members of the Bach family. Johann Sebastian Bach, for example, had only a loose working relationship with some of his librettists who lived in the same town, poets like Salomon Franck in Weimar or Christian Friedrich Henrici (Picander) in Leipzig; but we have virtually no detailed information about it. Besides, none of them counts among the major representatives of the German literature of his day. However, the situation is quite different with his son Carl Philipp Emanuel. He appears to be the only one in his family who developed, maintained, and fostered direct, close, and productive relationships with some of the major poets, prominent writers, and literary scholars in mid to late eighteenth-century Germany.

He knew, conversed, corresponded, and in some cases collaborated with Heinrich Wilhelm von Gerstenberg, Johann Heinrich Voss, Johann

Caspar Lavater, Carl Wilhelm Ramler, Christian August Clodius, Johann Joachim Eschenburg, Gotthold Ephraim Lessing, Matthias Claudius, Christoph Christian Sturm, Christian Fürchtegott Gellert, Friedrich Gottlob Klopstock, Carl Friedrich Cramer, Christoph Daniel Ebeling, and others. This took place primarily during his Hamburg years, that is, after 1769. But Bach's literary interests were of earlier origin. His 1753 treatise *Versuch über die wahre Art das Clavier zu spielen* demonstrates considerable literary skill and linguistic elegance that may reflect experiences shaped by his university study at Leipzig and Frankfurt. It is curious, though, that as a musician he grew up as an instrumentalist; he also began as an instrumental composer. After all, his first major vocal composition, the Magnificat of 1749 (Wq 215), was the work of a 35-year old and as such remained for some time an isolated instance.

The bulk of C. P. E. Bach's vocal output, both sacred and secular, belongs to his Hamburg period. A significant exception, however, pertains to the genre of song. Here we find his first published collection in 1758, *Geistliche Oden und Lieder,* based on texts by Gellert, to be followed in 1762 by *Oden mit Melodien,* on texts by various authors. Both collections were preceded by quite a number of individual songs reaching back into the early forties, which – for the most part – were published in various song anthologies. Although song composition in the 1740s seems to have been more of a sporadic activity, from the early 1750s Bach turns to this genre with a consistency matched only by solo keyboard music. Indeed, he remains faithful to the genre of song until the very end of his life, his afore-mentioned *Freymaurer-Lieder* of 1788 and the *Neue Lieder-Melodien* of 1789 representing the closing chapter in his virtually life-long involvement with song.

Bach's production of songs, despite their impressive number (300 plus), generally present no major problems regarding repertory, sources, transmission, and chronology. However, one rather crucial question remained unresolved for a long time. It concerned Bach's association with a project undertaken in the mid-1770s by one of his friends, Carl Friedrich Cramer (1752–1807), professor of classics and oriental languages at the University of Kiel. A highly entrepreneurial and influential man in matters of poetics and music, he announced in 1777 a subscription series in a Hamburg journal (*Altonaischer gelehrter Mercurius*). Under the title *Polyhymnia* (Gr., many hymns or songs) the series was to contain solo and choral songs by the most significant German and foreign composers. The "Avertissement" dated March 20, 1777 specified:

> "Volume 1 will comprise a piano-vocal score of Salieri's [opera] 'Armida,' vol. 2 the complete works of J. J. Rousseau, and the third a collection of scattered song compositions by capellmeister P. E. Bach."[1]

Nothing much happened in the subsequent years; the ambitious project is mentioned again only in September 1782, and on January 15, 1783, a more specific announcement followed that emphasized in particular the importance of Bach's lieder, the songs of "this prolific and unique master of vocal and instrumental art". It then continued:

> "His [Bach's] friends have wished for a long time to own these songs among which there are extraordinary masterpieces in addition to his other compositions. I have compiled a complete collection. I have altered or exchanged the older texts, in high esteem at former times – everything with his permission and under his supervision. Besides, through his friendship (which I pride myself of!) these compositions were supplemented by several completely new works which nobody knows. Because Bach's name says it all, I need not say more."[2]

He concludes with a cautionary note: "I will not specify the date of publication so that I don't run the risk of not keeping my word." But he adds:

> "My manuscript for all three parts is completed (because the idea is not from yesterday); all that matters is your support [i.e., the subscribers'support] and the printer's efficiency."

After six years, in 1783, volume 1 with Salieri's *Armida* was finally published. In 1784 there followed volume 4 with settings of Cramer songs by Friedrich Ludwig Aemilius Kunzen, and in 1785 volume 5 with *Athalia* by Johann Abraham Peter Schulz. Upon publishing volume 5, Cramer apologetically stated in December 1786:

> "As is well known we have previously published volumes 1 and 4 of the Polyhymnia series. The 2nd and 3rd will contain the promised works by Rousseau and Bach."[3]

Yet, despite additional affirmations in subsequent years, the only thing ever published of volumes 2 and 3 were their announcements. Cramer continued by issuing volumes 6–8. However, when volume 8 appeared in 1790 Bach had been dead for nearly two years.

What did happen? – To make a long story short, Bach's scattered and collected songs never appeared in Cramer's *Polyhymnia*. Clearly, the latter's statement of 1783 indicating that his manuscript for the first three volumes had been completed was not quite true. At the same time, the plan to publish a collection of some fifty songs by Bach could hardly have been pure fantasy and must have been worked out in some detail with the composer himself. Fortunately, we can now turn a new page regarding this puzzling project as the carefully prepared manuscript for Bach's contribution to the ill-fated *Polyhymnia* series turned up in the summer of 1999 among the rich collection of Bachiana in the long lost musical archive of the Berlin Sing-Akademie in Kiev, Ukraine.

Along with other museum and library treasures, this important archive disappeared without a trace after World War II since it had been deported as trophy materials by the Red Army. Only two years after its rediscovery, the Sing-Akademie's musical archive was repatriated in December 2001 and can now be consulted at the State Library in Berlin, were it is on deposit.[4]

The Sing-Academie archive that contains the bulk of C.P.E. Bach's estate had previously never been thoroughly researched, not even when the materials were readily available until the early 1940s. Hence, the *Polyhymnia* manuscript, too, had never been identified or described. However, it is now included in the large group of primary sources that finally enables us to undertake a complete works edition for the music of C. P. E. Bach which is currently underway.

The hitherto completely unknown song manuscript turns out to be a particularly fascinating document that demonstrates the great care with which Bach, near the end of his long life, gathered his scattered songs and prepared a collected edition of them. Moreover, it provides new perspectives on Bach's activities regarding the song genre. Finally, it contains some music that has never been performed, not even during Bach's own lifetime because he never gave it away.

The composite manuscript in the Berlin Staatsbibliothek consists of three separate components. Today they bear different shelf marks SA 1689, 1690, and 1691, but in the old Zelter catalogue all three were still kept together under the original number ZC 1305.[5] Table 1 provides a general survey of the contents. Within the principal bound volume SA 1689, units

(1) to (4) and (6) to (7a) are prints of previously published songs whereas units (5) and (7b) are manuscripts of pieces unpublished at the time the collection was gathered. This corroborates Cramer's description from 1777: "in part completely new [unpublished songs], in part from unknown or sold-out collections [published songs]." SA 1690, a separate large fascicle serving as a supplement to the bound volume SA 1689, shows a similar pattern of printed and manuscript songs. SA 1691 is an appendix with lists by Bach's daughter and a much later note by Zelter (Fig. 1) identifying the materials as representing "das Allerletzte was der Componist geschrieben hat" (the very last written by the composer).

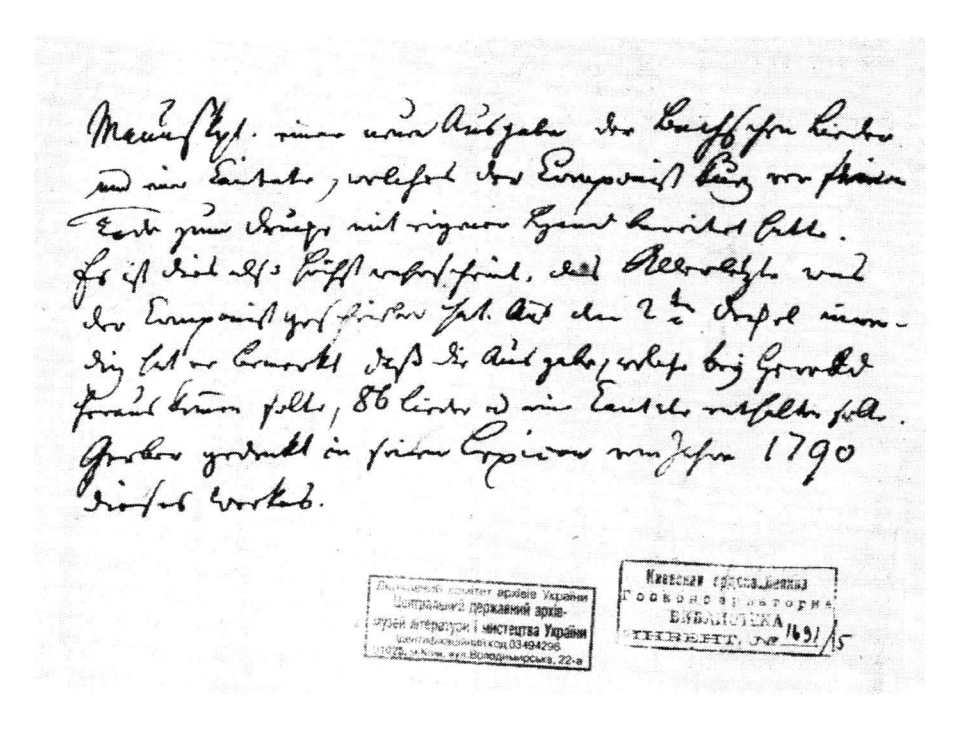

Fig. 1: Note by Zelter, referring to a manuscript of a new edition of Bach's songs which the composer had prepared for publication shortly before his death, Berlin, Sing-Akademie (Depositum in D-B), SA 1691

Table 1: General survey of the contents

D-B: SA 1689

(1) Pages 1–28:
[20] *Oden mit Melodien* (2nd edition, 1774) – CPEB rev.

(2) Pages 29–40:
6 songs from miscellaneous anthologies (1754 and 1768–70) – CPEB rev.

(3) Pages 41–44:
2 songs from *Musen-Almanach* (1782) – CPEB autogr.

(4) Pages 45–54:
6 songs from miscellaneous anthologies (1769–70) – CPEB rev.

(5) Pages 55–67:
Cantata "Die Grazien" (manuscript) – CPEB rev. → publ. 1789 (posthumously)

(6) Pages 68–72:
2 songs from miscellaneous anthologies (1765 and 1770) – CPEB autogr.

(7a/b) Pages 73–122:
20 songs from miscellaneous anthologies (1761–81)
5 songs (manuscripts) → publ. 1789 (posthumously)
3 songs (manuscript by J. H. Michel)

D-B: SA 1690

Supplement (wrapper: original viola part of the harpsichord concerto Wq 1)

1 song from a published anthology (1778)
12 *Freymaurer-Lieder* (1788)
11 songs (manuscript) → publ. 1789 (posthumously);
3 songs – CPEB autogr.

D-B: SA 1691

Appendix: Alphabetical list of 99 songs by ACPB; note by C. F. Zelter

Abbreviations: CPEB autogr. = C. P. E. Bach autograph
                CPEB rev.   = C. P. E. Bach revisions
                ACPB   = Anna Carolina Philippina Bach

As the following sample facsimile pages demonstrate Bach's process of revision shows different ways of dealing with the material at hand, from eliminating entire songs from the selection to smaller and larger manuscript corrections and additions in the printed copies (Figs. 2–4). New works are inserted in manuscript form, either as autographs (Fig. 5) or scribal copies mainly by Bach's principal Hamburg copyist Johann Heinrich Michel (Figs. 6–8).

Fig. 2: The oldest song (*Schäferlied* of 1742) to be deleted ("bleibt weg") from the collection, Berlin, Sing-Akademie (Depositum in D-B), SA 1689

Fig. 3: Autograph addition of a short keyboard introduction, Berlin, Sing-Akademie (Depositum in D-B), SA 1689

Fig. 4: Autograph edits, including a short keyboard postlude.

262

Fig. 5: Autograph song, D-B, SA 1689

Fig. 6: Copy of a song by Michel, with autograph edits by the composer, Sing-Akademie (Depositum in D-B), SA 1689

263

Fig. 7: Scribal copy of the cantata "Die Grazien", with autograph revisions, Berlin, Sing-Akademie (Depositum in D-B), SA 1689

Fig. 8: Cantata "Die Grazien", autograph insert, Berlin, Sing-Akademie (Depositum in D-B), SA 1689

Two short musical examples may serve to illuminate the particular strengths of C. P. E. Bach's songs. They are taken from *Oden mit Melodien* (1762, 2/1774) which opened the *Polyhymnia* Collection and which were included without any change since Bach saw no reason to improve anything there. The strophic form of the songs, the prevailing type among Bach's lieder, requires the musical capturing of the highly differentiated poetic prosody and its expressive intensity. As Bach himself put it in 1758, "the variety of declamatory details, the one- and multi-syllable words, and often the general subject matter as such make a big difference in the musical expression."[6] In Bach's songs, the melody of the singing voice is the decisive element; the restrained, yet pointed keyboard accompaniment has a primarily supporting function.

The poems to be set to music aim in their choice of words and declamatory rhythm (as Bach's friend Ramler put it) at "new, strong, subtle, and moving ideas; at concise, spirited, and appealing expression."[7] C. P. E. Bach's lieder style is characterized by subjectively excited language and a directness of lyric speech in its strictly regulated strophic structure. Goethe, who despised the through-composed song of the later type that Schubert among others preferred, always preferred the specifically lyrical qualities of strophic song that manifested itself in the "steady recurrence of the same sound."[8]

CD Example 1: Die verliebte Verzweiflung (Steinhauer)

Ihr missvergnügten Stunden,
wie groß ist eure Zahl!
So mehret nur Schmerz und Wunden
Und tödtet mich einmal!
Ihr aber, zarte Triebe,
Kommt, schlaft nur mit mir ein:
Denn dieses, was ich liebe,
wird doch nicht meine seyn.

Du Ursprung meiner Plage,
Du rührst mich noch zuletzt.
Die Wollust junger Tage
Hat lange mich ergötzt.
Doch alles wollt ich missen
Mein Herz sucht Grab und Ruh:
O drücke nur dein Küssen
Mein brechend Auge zu!

The subject of the poem is desperation over lost love and the song expresses it primarily in the design of the vocal line – a crucial feature of strophic song. By way of emphatic declamation, the opening lines of both stanzas set the tone. Subtle chromaticism and harmonic shifts (e.g., with the occurrence of d-flat in c minor) in the accompaniment strongly support the vocal line.

CD **Example 2: Der Morgen** (Hagedorn)

Uns lockt die Morgenröte	Die Hügel und die Weyde
In Busch und Wald,	Stehn aufgehellt
Wo schon der Hirten Flöte	Und Fruchtbarkeit und Freude
Ins Land erschallt.	Beblümt das Feld.
Die Lerche steigt und schwirret,	Der Schmelz der grünen Flächen
Von Lust erregt;	Glänzt voller Pracht;
Die Taube lacht und girret,	Und von den klaren Bächen
Die Wachtel schlägt.	Entweicht die Nacht.

This song, extremely different in character from the previous one, also involves metric changes in alternating lines of the poem. As lines 2, 4, 6, and 8 are shorter and have different accents the melody features a regular slowing down in declamatory style, yet without departing from the chosen 6/8 meter. Moreover, the function of the short keyboard introduction serves to set the atmospheric conditions for the song with its subtle hints of a shepherds flute and bird calls. Again, this example demonstrates the principal design elements of strophic song with its clear emphasis on the vocal line and the support character of the accompaniment.

Bach did not date his work on the *Polyhymnia* Collection but the chronology can be determined on the basis of Cramer's advertisements on the one hand, and the publication dates of some of the anthologies included. The first *Avertissement* that appeared in the spring of 1777 sets the absolute terminus post quem, but it is unlikely that Bach started on his part right away. He included songs from the *Musen-Almanach* published in 1782, which indicated that he may have begun his work around that time, if not later. For a later date speaks the fact that volume 1 (*Armida* by Salieri) of Cramer's projected series saw the light of day only in 1783. Moreover, the autograph entries in the composite manuscript show the characteristics of C. P. E. Bach's rather shaky handwriting style of the mid-1780s throughout.

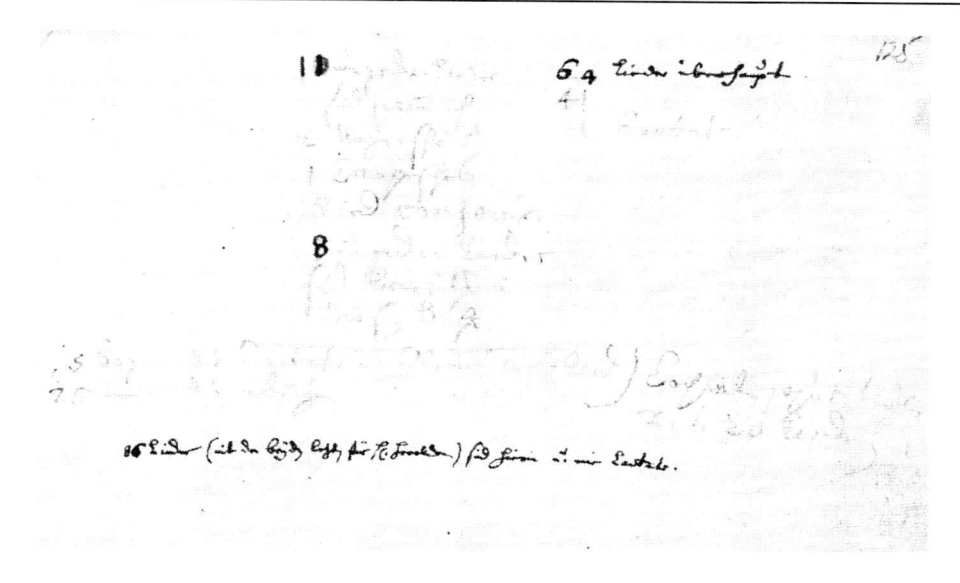

Fig 9: Inside back cover of bound Ms. SA 1689, with autograph annotations in pencil and ink, Berlin, Sing-Akademie (Depositum in D-B), SA 1689

The inside back cover of the bound volume SA 1689 (Fig. 9) shows copious notes in pencil and in ink by Bach. This indicates first of all that Bach himself had the volume bound. Then it shows that the composer was thinking about what to include and what not; his calculations of the number of songs vary and also clearly link the two principal components of the two-part manuscript, the "book" SA 1689 and the supplementary collection SA 1690.

***

Bach's *Polyhymnia* manuscript demonstrates that by the mid to late 1780s his collaborative project with Cramer was virtually completed and basically ready for publication. We don't know what exactly prevented it from being published. After 1782 it could hardly have depended on a lack of subscribers, or else the other *Polyhymnia* volumes could hardly have been financed either. More likely it was the growing number of songs, altogether 87 that Bach eventually planned to include. This certainly made the project unreasonably expensive. After all, Cramer had originally planned to include "some fifty songs." Bach's manuscript exceeded that number by a considerable margin and it seems that he was unwilling to cut back. For there are no signs of any attempt at reducing the contents of the compilation. This then must have been the likely reason for the Cramer-Bach project to fail.

When Bach realized that the project would not materialize in its anticipated form he apparently decided to go his own way and publish at least all newly composed songs from his *Polyhymnia* Collection, the Freemason songs from SA 1690 and the miscellaneous Songs from 1689, but to forgo republishing the scattered songs from the 1770s and 1780s in revised form. Before his death, Bach probably saw the publication of the Freemason songs (Copenhagen, 1788) whereas miscellaneous Songs from the *Neue Lieder-Melodien nebst einer Kantate zum Singen beym Klavier* appeared only posthumously in 1789.

Nevertheless, even if he did not live to see both editions of newly composed pieces they were not lost on his contemporary public. His reputation as a song composer transcended his lifetime.

From a modern perspective as well as from the viewpoint of an aesthetic re-evaluation of the lieder repertoire, the 1788–1789 publications did not make the *Polyhymnia* project superfluous. After all, the *Neue Lieder-Melodien* focused only on a few previously unpublished songs but did not present a complete edition of his scattered songs, many of them in revised versions. Therefore, the two-part manuscript from the Berlin Sing-Akademie serves as a unique document of what Bach considered to be a representative cross-section of his best contributions to the genre of song and, in their revised versions, most certainly songs he was particularly proud of and wanted to be remembered by.

---

[1] CPEB-Dok, II/53. – Trans. author.
[2] Ibid., II/95B.
[3] Ibid., II/95/D.
[4] Christoph Wolff, „Geleitwort" zu Enßlin-Sing-Akademie, 7–10.
[5] Ibid., 184–196.
[6] Preface to Gellerts *Geistliche Oden und Lieder* (Berlin, 1758).
[7] K. W. Ramler, „Vorbericht", in: *Lieder der Deutschen* (Berlin, 1766), fol. 4r – Trans. author.
[8] J. W. v. Goethe, „Lieber die Ballade", in: *Werke. Vollständige Ausgabe letzter Hand* (Stuttgart und Tübingen, 1845), 333. – Trans. author.

[16]

Reason and revelation in C. P. E. Bach's resurrection oratorio

Richard Will

> Although this Ramler cantata is by me, I can nevertheless claim, without ridiculous egotism, that it will wear well for many years, because it is *among* my masterpieces an important one, from which young composers can learn something. In time, it will also sell *as well as* Graun's *Tod Jesu*.[1]

It is disconcerting to find that C. P. E. Bach invested so much significance in *Die Auferstehung und Himmelfahrt Jesu* (The Resurrection and Ascension of Jesus, 1774, revised *c.* 1778–80).[2] As Ludwig Finscher pointed out over a decade ago, Bach's oratorios have been surprisingly little studied given his reputation and the fact that the three works in question, unlike the celebratory cantatas and Passion pastiches he produced in Hamburg, have always been available to scholars.[3] In part, the fame of the keyboard works has overshadowed Bach's achievements in vocal music, but *Die Auferstehung* has also suffered from a general inattention to the eighteenth-century German lyric oratorio. In this distinctive genre, as Howard E. Smither writes, "Rather than presenting the external events of the story in a connected, dramatic or narrative-dramatic text, as the traditional Baroque librettist had done, the poet assumed the listener's knowledge of the story and wrote a contemplative, lyric drama with personages who are usually unnamed and 'idealized,'

[1] Letter of C. P. E. Bach to Johann Gottlob Immanuel Breitkopf, 21 September 1787; Ernst Suchalla, ed., *Carl Philipp Emanuel Bach: Briefe und Dokumente, Kritische Gesamtausgabe*, 2 vols. (Göttingen: Vandenhoeck & Ruprecht, 1994), II: 1228; trans. in Stephen L. Clark, trans. and ed., *The Letters of C. P. E. Bach* (Oxford: Oxford University Press, 1997), 270.

[2] On the composition, revision, and publication history see Barbara Wiermann, "Werkgeschichte als Gattungsgeschichte: Die 'Auferstehung und Himmelfahrt Jesu' von Carl Philipp Emanuel Bach," *Bach-Jahrbuch*, 83 (1997), 117–43.

[3] Ludwig Finscher, "Bemerkungen zu den Oratorien Carl Philipp Emanuel Bachs," in Hans-Joachim Marx, ed., *Carl Philipp Emanuel Bach und die europäische Musikkultur des mittleren 18. Jahrhunderts* (Göttingen: Vandenhoeck & Ruprecht, 1990), 309–10. Finscher's essay interprets the three works (*Die Israeliten in der Wüste*, 1769; the *Passionskantate*, 1770 with later revisions; and *Die Auferstehung*) as "a threefold approach to the search for the 'modern' concert oratorio" (310).

and who express their sentiments about the story's events."[4] Such works became the most popular kind of oratorio in German-speaking Europe in the second half of the century, but modern accounts of the period place them a distant second behind the dramatic and narrative oratorios of Handel and J. S. Bach, and more generally behind developments in opera and instrumental music. As comprehensive a text as Daniel Heartz's recent *Music in European Capitals* devotes several pages to the operas of Carl Heinrich Graun but only a paragraph to his oratorio *Der Tod Jesu* (The Death of Jesus, 1755), the most celebrated example of the lyric genre and the work whose popularity C. P. E. Bach hoped to challenge.[5]

One does not want to exchange neglect for exaggeration. Already in his own day, Bach's keyboard works and performance treatise exerted much more influence than any of his vocal pieces, and while Italian opera and new instrumental genres such as the symphony affected every European musical culture, lyric oratorios made little impression outside German-speaking lands. Still, there are several reasons to look closely at Bach's oratorios, and particularly *Die Auferstehung*. Most obviously, any understanding of the composer that does not engage such ambitious works remains impoverished. With regard to *Die Auferstehung*, it is equally important to recognize that *within* German-speaking musical culture, the significance of the lyric oratorio can hardly be overstated. Graun's *Der Tod Jesu* was performed yearly in many cities throughout the second half of the century (and in some instances through the nineteenth century),[6] and routinely invoked by writers on music as a model of oratorio and of expressive vocal writing. Beyond that, lyric works illustrate the competing demands made on sacred music by an era that subjected religion to Enlightenment critique. German *Aufklärer* typically did not turn to atheism as the corollary of a rational worldview; instead, Protestant intellectuals in particular strove to reconcile the ideals of Enlightened thinking with the tenets of Christianity. Among the results was the mid-century movement known as *Neologie* (i.e., "Neue Theologie," New Theology), which sought to preserve the belief in God and the moral teachings of Jesus while downplaying the "irrational"

---

[4] Howard E. Smither, *A History of the Oratorio*, 4 vols. (Chapel Hill: University of North Carolina Press, 1977–2000), III: 336; his discussion of lyric works encompasses III: 333–9, 361–463. See also Günther Massenkeil, *Oratorium und Passion*, Handbuch der musikalischen Gattungen 10 (Laaber: Laaber-Verlag, 1998), Part I: 220–3, 249–75; Arnold Schering, *Geschichte des Oratoriums* (Leipzig, 1911; reprint Hildesheim: Olms, and Wiesbaden: Breitkopf & Härtel, 1966), 360–81.

[5] Daniel Heartz, *Music in European Capitals: The Galant Style, 1720–1780* (New York: Norton, 2003), 366–73.

[6] Ingeborg König, *Studien zum Libretto des "Tod Jesu" von Karl Wilhelm Ramler und Karl Heinrich Graun* (Munich: Katzbichler, 1972), 5–15. On the critical reception see below.

miracles and revelations through which God, in the Bible telling, educates
and redeems humanity.[7] The librettist of both *Der Tod Jesu* and *Die Auferstehung*, Karl Wilhelm Ramler, was sympathetic to *Neologie* and transformed
the New Testament according to its principles, turning the story of Jesus'
life into a meditation on his human virtues. But he could not avoid the
revelatory elements of his subject entirely, and many other, equally powerful voices resisted any such effort. Whether it was orthodox theologians
demanding respect for traditional doctrine, or aesthetes calling on art to
evoke the sublime, a substantial body of eighteenth-century opinion continued to embrace the association of the sacred with the ineffable. The lyric
oratorio was caught between a tendency to see God working through human
feeling and morality on the one hand, and through miraculous intervention
on the other.

Nowhere is the tension more evident than in *Die Auferstehung*. Text
and music negotiate a middle ground between *Neologie* and a more orthodox religion, striking a precarious balance between the humanly observable
excellence of Jesus' character, and the rationally incomprehensible mystery
of his resurrection and ascension. The result is more difficult to interpret
than *Der Tod Jesu*, where the human clearly wins out over the divine. *Die
Auferstehung* comes closer to equilibrium, which, ironically, may help to
explain why it never supplanted Graun's work in the public's affection, even
after its publication in 1787. Theology is not the only reason its appeal
proved limited, but the simultaneous engagement with conflicting perspectives on the sacred does not make Bach's oratorio an easy work to appreciate.
Die Auferstehung captures the complexity of religious experience in the "Age
of Reason."

REASON

Altogether Ramler wrote three libretti on the life of Jesus, the passion and
resurrection texts already mentioned and a third dealing with the Nativity,
Die Hirten bei der Krippe zu Bethlehem (The Shepherds at the Crib in
Bethlehem). All three consist primarily of original poetic verse. Ramler
quotes and paraphrases the Gospels, and in *Der Tod Jesu* he incorporates
chorale stanzas, but nowhere does he adopt the New Testament wholesale
as do the dramatic and narrative portions of "oratorio Passions" – that
is, libretti based on the text of a single evangelist, such as those set by

---

[7] A helpful account of *Neologie* is Wolfgang Gericke, *Theologie und Kirche im Zeitalter der Aufklärung*
(Berlin: Evangelische Verlagsanstalt, 1989), 95–114; see also König, *Studien zum Libretto des "Tod
Jesu"*, 57–66.

J. S. Bach. *Der Tod Jesu* is what oratorio scholars call a "Passion oratorio," with a story drawn from all four Gospels and told in the author's own words. *Die Auferstehung* and *Die Hirten bei der Krippe* follow the same principles.

Recasting the Gospels in new poetry had a considerable history in Germany, for example in the Passion oratorios written in Hamburg beginning in 1704, most famously *Der für die Sünde der Welt gemarterte und sterbende Jesus* (Jesus Who Suffered and Died for the Sins of the World, 1712) of Barthold Heinrich Brockes, a text set by Telemann and Handel among others.[8] Ramler departs from poets like Brockes in introducing a literary form and an emotional tone reminiscent of the secular fiction of mid-eighteenth-century sentimentalism, or *Empfindsamkeit* as it would be known in Germany. Brockes divides his story between an evangelist and named characters, and his narrator recounts events in the past tense as the Gospel evangelists do. Ramler puts all the narration into the voice of an unnamed witness who speaks in the present tense, and neither his solo nor his choral texts ever explicitly cast the singers in dramatic roles. The witness reports utterances by Jesus and others, and, as we shall see, composers sometimes assigned the quotations to multiple voices, creating dramatic interchanges like those found in more traditional libretti. Read as literary works, however, Ramler's texts have more in common with the epistolary novels of the sentimental writer Samuel Richardson and his German imitators, which likewise forgo a conventional narrator, an omniscient chronicler of things past, in favor of a voice that seems to participate in the story it tells. Like Richardson's Pamela recording her experiences day by day in letters, Ramler's witness reacts to the events of the New Testament step by step in present-tense descriptions. The texts claim to be artifacts of lived experience rather than histories, which enhances the immediacy of their subject matter and, in the oratorios, brings the characters closer than they seem in libretti that assign actual speaking roles. Although mediated through the voice of the witness, the words of the participants belong not to the past but to the present, the time of the reader or listener.

Equally important, witness and characters both speak less of the events of Jesus' life than of the emotions they inspire, and particularly of the compassion that Jesus and his companions feel for one another. Brockes incorporates all the twists and turns of the Passion story, beginning with the Last Supper and including such details as Jesus' prophecy that Peter

---

[8] Stephen L. Clark, "The Occasional Choral Works of C. P. E. Bach" (Ph.D. diss., Princeton University, 1984), 25–6; Smither, *History of the Oratorio*, II: 107–20, 130–8.

will deny him, Judas' kiss of betrayal, and Peter's denial and the subsequent crowing of the cock. While the text is deeply emotional, moreover, its focus is on the feelings of awe and horror occasioned by Jesus' suffering, or, in the cases of Peter and Judas, by traitorous actions. Following their respective betrayals, the latter characters have extended soliloquies in which they imagine themselves experiencing the tortures of hell. Throughout the rest of the libretto, increasingly graphic depictions of Jesus' physical torment cause the onlookers both to recoil and to marvel at the extent of his sacrifice.

Ramler's narratives could hardly differ more. Though it tells the same story as Brockes's text, *Der Tod Jesu* greatly simplifies the action, beginning in the garden of Gethsemane rather than at the Last Supper and omitting numerous episodes and details: one sees Jesus' arrest but not the character of Judas; Peter's denial but not the prophecy or the crowing of the cock; Jesus' trial before a crowd and a "tyrant" but not the earlier questioning by the high priests, or the character of Pilate, or the offer of Barabbas as a substitute for crucifixion – all of which Brockes includes. Nor does Ramler dwell on Jesus' bodily wounds, dispatching the crown of thorns, for example, with a single laconic line ("und [Jesu] trägt sein Dornendiadem") where Brockes spins out a long and gruesome description (culminating with the thorns boring through Jesus' temples to his brain). Plot and external suffering give way to an expression of Jesus' inner states, including doubt, grief, and above all love, which is emphasized at every opportunity. Not only does he forgive the criminal crucified with him and delegate the Beloved Disciple to care for his mother, episodes familiar from the Gospels, he also wakes the sleeping apostles at Gethsemane with a "sweet face" rather than the traditional reproach; he stands before his accusers "full of love"; and he counsels his followers not to weep over his condemnation. The beholders return the sentiment; rather than stand awestruck at his sacrifice, they call on others to share their pity for a character they name the "friend of mankind" ("Menschenfreund").

Die Auferstehung continues in much the same vein, offering further examples of the characters' sentimental attachment. Though an initial, pictorial tableau depicts earthquakes and other upheavals caused by the resurrection (see below), thereafter the story comprises a series of encounters, first between the Daughters of Zion and the archangel Michael, and then between the resurrected Jesus and his followers. In each instance Ramler again simplifies the Gospel telling and expands on its emotional implications. In the Gospel of John, for example, when Mary Magdalene arrives at

Reason and revelation in C. P. E. Bach's resurrection oratorio   89

Jesus' tomb and finds it open, she fetches Peter, who looks in and departs. Magdalene remains and looks in herself, seeing two angels with whom she exchanges brief, substantive questions: "[angels:] Woman, why are you crying? . . . [Magdalene:] You have taken away my Lord, and I do not know where you have laid Him." She then turns and has the same dialogue with Jesus, whom she mistakes for a gardener (John 20: 1–18). Ramler's adaptation of the episode, found in the third recitative of *Die Auferstehung*, eliminates Peter, the angels, and the reference to the gardener – Jesus is simply "unrecognized." The poet then elaborates Magdalene's question into a three-fold, progressively more passionate reiteration of her desire to find Jesus, to which Jesus responds with the same kindness and friendship he shows in *Der Tod Jesu*.

> "O Tochter: warum weinest du?" –
> "Herr: sage, nahmst du meinen Herrn aus diesem Grabe?
> "Wo liegt er? Ach! vergönne,
> "Daß ich ihn hole; daß ich ihn
> "Mit Thränen netze; daß ich ihn
> "Mit diesen Salben noch im Tode salben könne,
> "Wie ich im Leben ihn gesalbt." – "Maria!"
> So ruft mit holder Stimm' ihr Freund
> In seiner eigenen Gestalt: "Maria!" –⁹

"O daughter, why are you crying?" – "Sir, tell me, did you take my Lord from this tomb? Where does he lie? Oh! grant, that I could find him; that I could wash him with tears; that I could anoint him with these ointments in death as I anointed him in life!" – "Mary!" Thus calls, in a sweet voice, her friend in his own form: "Mary!"

The passage instances both the heightened rhetoric and the "sense of intimacy" that scholars cite in linking Ramler's libretti to sentimentalism.[10] Through a language of questions and exclamations, and a setting cleansed of secondary characters, what was originally a prosaic and rather crowded meeting in John 20 becomes a poetic and private moment of recognition.

Equally reminiscent of sentimentalism are narrative strategies which suggest that the scene is unfolding as it is being described, and which require the reader to play an active role in imagining what happens. Beyond using the present tense, Ramler's witness declines to introduce Magdalene, instead beginning the recitative with a description in the form of a question:

---

⁹ Punctuation and orthography from *Karl Wilhelm Ramlers poëtische Werke*, 2 vols. (Vienna: Pichler, 1801; reprint Bern: Lang, 1979), II: 185–98.

¹⁰ Smither, *History of the Oratorio*, III: 365; König, *Studien zum Libretto des "Tod Jesu,"* 68–94.

90   *Richard Will*

> Wer ist die Sionitinn, die vom Grabe
> So schüchtern in den Garten flieht, und weinet?

Who is the woman of Zion, who flees so timidly from the tomb to the garden and cries?

The scripturally well-versed may be able to divine the answer, but veiling Magdalene's identity draws readers into a drama of discovery that they share with the protagonists. In this respect the recitative is typical of the whole oratorio, every scene of which presents fresh mysteries both to the characters, who must struggle to comprehend Jesus' disappearance from the tomb and subsequent reappearances, and to the readers, who must deduce names and events from minimal clues. Thus in the dialogue between Jesus and Magdalene cited above, two recognitions happen simultaneously when Jesus says "Mary": Magdalene sees Jesus for who he is, and readers see her, unveiled at last by the use of her name. While pursuing her identity, furthermore, readers must work to keep track of who is speaking, as the witness alternates without warning between description and quotation. Jesus' initial question is conventionally prepared ("Jesus . . . says to her"), but Magdalene's reply and Jesus' reply to her are separated only by punctuation, whose efficacy in distinguishing their voices diminishes once the text is heard rather than read. The omission of more traditional narrative markers lends urgency to the representation; so intent is the witness on recording the exchange as it happens, that the niceties of story-telling become a hindrance. Their absence transforms readers from observers into creators, partners with the witness in constituting the scene.

Ramler's emotionalism, his elimination of dramatic roles, and his choice of New Testament subjects all found favor with German writers on the oratorio. In 1783, a lengthy essay in Johann Nikolaus Forkel's *Musikalischer Almanach* characterized the lyric oratorio as the goal toward which the genre should strive, citing *Die Hirten bei der Krippe* as evidence.[11] Dramatic oratorios spoke of actions that concert-hall performances could not represent, and when based on the Old Testament they told stories with little relevance to contemporary listeners. The life of Jesus, by contrast, "inspires us . . . to live and act according to [his] deeply felt teachings," and it was also so familiar as to require minimal narration or dramatization.[12] This allowed

---

[11] "Über die Beschaffenheit der musikalischen Oratorien, nebst Vorschlägen zur veränderten Einrichtung derselben," in Johann Nikolaus Forkel, ed., *Musikalischer Almanach für Deutschland auf das Jahr 1783*, 166–206. This essay, Sulzer's *Allgemeine Theorie* (see n. 14 below), and related comments on the oratorio are further discussed in Schering, *Geschichte des Oratoriums*, 364–70; Smither, *History of the Oratorio*, III: 337–9; and Wiermann, "Werkgeschichte als Gattungsgeschichte," 131–3.

[12] "Über die Beschaffenheit der musikalischen Oratorien," 184.

Ramler to satisfy both spiritual and musical needs, for in freeing himself from extensive story-telling responsibilities, he was able to emphasize feeling and thereby to provide the most appropriate subject matter for music, which Forkel like most of his German contemporaries considered to be "only for emotions."[13] The premium placed on emotion figures similarly in the endorsement published a decade earlier in Johann Georg Sulzer's *Allgemeine Theorie der schönen Künste* (1771–4). Ignoring the dramatic tradition altogether, the lexicon defines "Oratorium" wholly in terms of *Empfindsamkeit*: "The oratorio assumes various personages who are strongly moved by the noble religious subject of the feast that is being celebrated and who express their sentiments about it, now singly, now together, in a very emphatic fashion. The purpose of this drama is to penetrate the hearts of the listeners with similar sentiments."[14] Said by the *Theorie* to fulfill this ideal, *Der Tod Jesu* more probably inspired it, for Graun's setting had been a fixture in the musical life of Sulzer's Berlin since its premiere there in 1755. The definition elevates Ramler's lyric conception of the genre to the status of a general principle.

Beyond sentimentality, there is evidence that Sulzer, at least, would also have found the theology of Ramler's texts congenial. In her study of *Der Tod Jesu*, Ingeborg König quotes a revealing letter in which the poet grapples with the mystery at the heart of his subject matter, namely, the ability of Jesus to assume the sins of humanity as his own and redeem them through his death.

Sulzer does not want to suffer even once the passage: "Ah see, He sinks, weighed down with sins," whereas Herr Bergius wishes to hear it several times. I am more of Sulzer's than Bergius's opinion, but even so I cannot cross it out for I see how important it appears to most readers. Otherwise I would greatly desire to put it thus: "Ah see! He sinks, the hero! – His heart in stress." Please decide this battle between orthodoxy and truth or plausibility.[15]

In wanting to attribute Jesus' weariness to emotional distress, rather than to a supernatural transference of others' wrongdoing, Ramler and Sulzer evidence the discomfort with miracles typical of those seeking to reconcile religion and Enlightenment. Miracles did more than disobey the laws of nature: they threatened what was seen as the moral core of Christian teaching, suggesting that redemption depended on divine intervention rather

---

[13] Ibid., 192.

[14] Johann Georg Sulzer, *Allgemeine Theorie der schönen Künste* (Leipzig: 1771–4; 2nd edn. in 4 vols., 1792–4), III: 610; trans. Smither, *History of the Oratorio*, III: 337.

[15] Letter to Johann Wilhelm Ludwig Gleim, 27 October 1754, quoted in König, *Studien zum Libretto des "Tod Jesu"*, 59.

than individual behavior. As Karl Barth put it, "the doctrine of Christ's
vicarious satisfaction . . . contradicts the presupposition that we have to
show ourselves to be true reverers and lovers of God and therefore worthy objects of his love through our own actions."[16] In the Berlin milieu in
which Ramler wrote his libretti, such views were represented by the first
generation of writers associated with *Neologie*, most importantly Johann
Joachim Spalding and August Friedrich Wilhelm Sack, the latter of whom
was pastor of the Berlin court and cathedral throughout the middle decades
of the century. *Neologie* retained an emphasis on individual responsibility stemming from late seventeenth- and early eighteenth-century Pietism,
whose "conviction that spiritual renewal from within was far more important than the purely passive, outward observance of dogmatic principles"
exerted a long-lasting influence on German Protestantism.[17] This privileg-
ing of *Innerlichkeit* is clearly evident in Ramler's texts, although they rely on
descriptions of sentiment to help believers internalize the lessons of Jesus,
rather than the "blood and wounds" imagery favored by Pietist texts such
as the Brockes libretto discussed above. While it accepted that salvation was
individual, however, *Neologie* de-emphasized Pietism's continuing faith in
such inexplicables as the power of Jesus' suffering to redeem. Sack did not
attempt to efface miraculous doctrines as Ramler contemplated doing, but
his teachings on the sacraments, for example, highlighted their "subjective,
human side . . . the Last Supper [is] understood above all as a memorial
drama of the suffering and death of Jesus."[18] It will be remembered that
Ramler omits the Last Supper from *Der Tod Jesu*, no doubt to streamline
the story but surely also to avoid the changing of bread to flesh and wine
to blood. So reluctant to acknowledge an intangible mystery like Jesus'
assumption of human sin, Ramler would hardly have been comfortable
describing the physical miracle of transubstantiation.

On the contrary, in *Der Tod Jesu* Ramler writes a largely "realistic" Passion
consistent with *Neologie*, in which the character of Jesus and his moral
teachings take precedence over his working of miracles. As König shows,
Ramler's Jesus embodies those qualities that Sack most wanted Christians
to learn from his life, a "warm feeling of a generally favorable attitude and
love," and a "sweet and humble spirit."[19] Particularly in the solo numbers,

---

[16] Karl Barth, *Protestant Theology in the Nineteenth Century: Its Background and History*, trans. Brian
   Cozens and John Bowden, 2nd edn. (Grand Rapids, MI: Eerdmans, 2002), 92; see also 106–9.
[17] James Van Horn Melton, "Pietism, Politics, and the Public Sphere in Germany," in James E. Bradley
   and Dale K. Van Kley, eds., *Religion and Politics in Enlightenment Europe* (Notre Dame: University of
   Notre Dame Press, 2001), 298; see also Barth, *Protestant Theology in the Nineteenth Century*, 99–100.
[18] Gericke, *Theologie und Kirche im Zeitalter der Aufklärung*, 98.
[19] König, *Studien zum Libretto des "Tod Jesu"*, 59–67.

Reason and revelation in C. P. E. Bach's resurrection oratorio   93

the oratorio also foregrounds his exemplary virtues, particularly patience, courage, and forbearance; at one point Ramler even writes of an abstract concept of virtue in terms similar to moralizing secular texts such as Mozart's and Schikaneder's later *Magic Flute*: "Klimm' ich zu der Tugend Tempel / Matt den steilen Pfad hinauf" (Wearily I climb the steep path to the Temple of Virtue). Much as Sack and Spalding expected of sermons, the libretto has an "improving, moral character," offering comfort and instruction in place of mystery or dogma.[20]

Needless to say, when Ramler acceded to Telemann's request that he write a sequel to *Der Tod Jesu*,[21] he took on a narrative whose rationally inexplicable elements were much harder to finesse. The crucifixion might survive as a moral drama without the Last Supper or an undue emphasis on doctrine, but what follows cannot happen at all unless Jesus returns miraculously from death. As we shall see, Ramler depicted both the resurrection and the ascension vividly, acknowledging the supernatural in a way that distinguishes *Die Auferstehung* markedly from *Der Tod Jesu*. What makes *Die Auferstehung* such a complex work, however, is the extent to which it preserves the tone and theological orientation of the earlier libretto even in the face of miracle. Most obviously, the resurrected Jesus displays all of his former humility and kindness, not only in his meeting with Magdalene but also in scenes where one might expect him to exercise less restraint. Much as in *Der Tod Jesu*, for example, where he awoke the apostles at Gethsemane with an unexpectedly "sweet face," now he tells the doubting apostle Thomas, "So geh in alle Welt, und sey mein Zeuge!" (So go into the world and be my witness!). This ameliorates the harsher judgment he renders in the Gospel of John (20: 29): "Because thou hast seen me, thou hast believed; blessed are they who have not seen, and yet have believed." Along similar lines, in his final charge to the apostles Jesus first orders them to teach, "Was ihr von mir gehört: / Das ewige Gebot der Liebe!" (What you have heard from me, the eternal message of love!). Only after this reiteration of his emotional commitment to humanity does he add the miraculous gifts God offers, "Versöhnung, Frieden, Seligkeit!" (forgiveness, peace, salvation). Indeed, forgiveness receives surprisingly little attention given the symbolic significance of the resurrection as proof of the redemption of sin. Only one aria explicitly represents Jesus' sacrifice as having been undertaken for the benefit of sinners, while a second addresses believers as "the saved" (Erlöste), and the duet poses the question, "Sagt, wer unserm Gotte

---

[20] Gericke, *Theologie und Kirche im Zeitalter der Aufklärung*, 97.
[21] *Telemann: Musikalische Werke* (Kassel: Bärenreiter, 1950–), XXXII: viii–ix.

94 *Richard Will*

gleicht, / Der die Missethat vergiebet?" (Tell me, who can compare to our God, who forgives misdeeds?) Otherwise the texts concentrate on the affection of Jesus for humanity and his heroism in overcoming death: as in *Der Tod Jesu*, he is "Menschenfreund" (friend of mankind), "Held" (hero), and "Sieger" (victor), but never "Erlöser" (redeemer). He rises from the dead not to deliver the faithful so much as to give further proof of his virtue and compassion. As *Neologie* required, salvation remains primarily in the hands of the individual.

REVELATION

Neither Ramler's texts nor the "Enlightened" religion they express went unchallenged. One of the bitterest theological battles of the century was waged against *Neologie* and related lines of thinking by Johann Melchior Goeze, the orthodox pastor of St. Catherine's in Hamburg from 1755 to 1786, and thus during C. P. E. Bach's tenure in the city.[22] The most famous skirmish occurred during the mid-1770s, the very years in which Bach produced the original version of *Die Auferstehung*, when Gotthold Ephraim Lessing published excerpts from the *Apologie oder Schutzschrift für die vernünftigen Verehrer Gottes* (Apology or Defense of the Rational Worshipper of God) of Hermann Samuel Reimarus. Considerably more radical than anything by Sack or Spalding, the *Apologie* went beyond de-emphasizing miracles and revelations to reject them out of hand, and Reimarus, fearing the indignation it would arouse, refused to publish the work during his lifetime.[23] When Lessing printed the excerpts posthumously the consequences were indeed severe; while he kept the identity of the author secret, Lessing himself was banned by the Hamburg authorities from publishing any further theological writings, including his own.

The most important critique of Ramler himself came from the direction less of orthodoxy than of a *Sturm und Drang* or proto-Romantic enthusiasm for the sublime. Johann Gottfried Herder, who attacked the Neologist Spalding for reducing the minister to a "depository of public morals,"[24] accused Ramler of doing much the same thing to the oratorio – that is, of suppressing the ineffable and epic aspects of his subject matter by relating it in present-tense reports from unnamed witnesses. Herder's criticism

---

[22] Recent accounts include Franklin Kopitzsch, *Grundzüge einer Sozialgeschichte der Aufklärung in Hamburg und Altona* (Hamburg: Hans Christian, 1982), part II: 452–522; Joachim Whaley, *Religious Toleration and Social Change in Hamburg 1529–1819* (Cambridge: Cambridge University Press, 1985), 151–4.

[23] Gericke, *Theologie und Kirche im Zeitalter der Aufklärung*, 84–9.   [24] Ibid., 97.

Reason and revelation in C. P. E. Bach's resurrection oratorio 95

parodies the librettist's fondness for descriptive questions: "Who speaks? who sings? is something narrated in the recitatives? – so cold! so pedantic! As Simon of Cana would hardly have done, when he came in from the fields and wanted to talk of the past. And in between, in arias, in chorales, in choruses – who speaks? who sings? . . . In the entire text there is no point of view!"[25] Herder is not objecting, as even Sulzer did, to the confusion that Ramler's unprepared changes of speaker might cause. What he misses is the linear propulsion and rhetorical intensification that a strong narrating voice could bring to the events. Calling the recitatives "cold and pedantic" seems hardly fair given Ramler's free handling of the Gospels and heightening of their emotional temperature, but the comment occurs at the end of an essay on Ossian, whose epics of medieval Scotland Herder believed to be genuine and also to have been intended for singing. It is in comparison to such works that he condemns "our contemporary musico-poetic structure," with Ramler as his prime example: "How do the sections divide up? Where is mixture? transition? leading forth to rapture? to the illusion of beautiful madness?" ["Unser jetzige Musikalische Poesienbau . . . Wie fallen die Massen aus einander? Wo Verflößung? Übergang? Fortleitung bis zum Taumel? bis zur Täuschung schönen Wahnsinnes?"][26] A true bard generates a forward-driving energy that sweeps listeners beyond the strong but still recognizably human feelings of *Empfindsamkeit*, toward mental states so ecstatic that they surpass the bounds of normal human sentiment.

Among German writers to have approached his ideal Herder singles out Friedrich Gottlieb Klopstock, whose odes and epic poem *Der Messias* famously imbued both emotions and physical events with sublimity. That his *magnum opus* treats the life of Jesus makes it particularly easy to see what Herder found lacking in Ramler. Published in installments between 1748 and 1773, *Der Messias* brackets Ramler's libretti chronologically and resembles them to the extent that Klopstock likewise synthesizes his story from all four Gospels and gives pride of place to feelings. But where Ramler's dramas take place on earth and involve, almost without exception, only Jesus and his followers, Klopstock assembles an enormous cast of both New and Old Testament characters and uses settings on earth, in heaven, and in hell. Similarly, where Ramler streamlines the Biblical versions of Jesus' life, Klopstock complicates them by adding new characters and episodes

[25] Herder, "Briefwechsel über Ossian," in *Von deutscher Art und Kunst* (Hamburg, 1773); quoted from Herder, *Werke in zehn Bänden*, II, ed. Gunter E. Grimm (Frankfurt am Main: Deutscher Klassiker Verlag, 1993), 496–7.
[26] Ibid., 496.

to the Gospels and by having his Old Testament figures play out dramas
of their own. Most importantly, Klopstock magnifies every character and
event with the elaborate syntax, copious repetition, metaphorical imagery,
and imposing hexameter rhythms of his trademark epic style. The meeting
between Jesus and Mary Magdalene after the resurrection makes for a useful point of comparison. At the climax of the scene, Ramler has Jesus say
Mary's name without fanfare, as one "friend" calling softly to another. Klopstock also portrays the moment as an affectionate one, but his preparation
makes it seem as if Jesus must suppress evidence of his divinity – a chorus
of angelic voices praising the resurrection – in order to speak on intimate
terms with Magdalene. He does not naturally inhabit her world, as he does
in Ramler.

> Aber wie Harfen am Throne, wie Jubel der Überwinder,
> Singen sie, ganz in Liebe zerflossen, das Lamm, das erwürgt ward,
> Nicht wie Harfen der Überwinder, und Jubel am Throne,
> Inniger, herzlicher, liebevoller erscholl des Erstandnen,
> Jesus Stimme der Weinenden, Jesus Stimme: Maria![27]

But like harps at the throne, like the jubilation of the conqueror, wholly dissolved in
love, they sing of the lamb who was sacrificed. Not like the harps of the conqueror,
not like jubilation at the throne; more intimately, more warmly, more full of love,
[there] rang out from the resurrected Jesus to the crying one [his] voice, Jesus'
voice: Mary!

For all its lyrical understatement, the final utterance also culminates a narrative that has been building steam for some two dozen lines, and that acquires
even greater momentum from the summoning and dispersing of the musical
metaphor at the end. The heavenly singing not only marks Jesus' presence
as supernatural, it drives his emotion into the realm of the extraordinary.
Borne along by the power of the epic style, human affection turns into the
kind of divine rapture that Herder so desired.

   Ramler never tries to achieve such an exalted tone, which would have
been theologically as well as stylistically foreign to his lyric conceptions.
Yet neither does he remain so determinedly mundane as Herder thought,
at least not in *Die Auferstehung*, which, to repeat, presents a more complicated picture than *Der Tod Jesu*. If Ramler approaches the language of *Der
Messias* at any point, it is in representing the resurrection and ascension,
respectively the first and final scenes. Lacking Klopstock's tortured syntax and metaphorical ebullience, they nevertheless incorporate numerous

---

[27] Klopstock, *Der Messias* (1st edn., Copenhagen, 1768), book 14, lines 115–19; quoted from Klopstock,
   Ausgewählte Werke, ed. Karl August Schleiden (Munich: Carl Hanser, 1962), 549.

spectacular images and a strong sense of linear progression. Both passages consist of a recitative narrating the event, an aria of reaction, and a chorus of celebration. The recitatives and arias are full of miraculous sights: the Jordan flows backwards, angels surround Jesus, Michael descends with flaming face, Jesus ascends in a flaming chariot, the gates of heaven open. Equally striking, they build steadily in excitement toward the choruses, piling up more and more imagery rather than, like the interior scenes of the oratorio, lingering over the emotional bonds between the characters. The resurrection in particular inspires a verbal crescendo that begins, in the recitative, with a series of short exclamations and questions giving way suddenly to a long sentence depicting the miracle itself:

> Judäa zittert! seine Berge beben!
> Der Jordan flieht den Strand! –
> Was zitterst du, Judäens Land?
> Ihr Berge, warum bebt ihr so?
> Was war dir, Jordan, daß dein Strom zurücke floß? –
> Der Herr der Erde steigt
> Empor aus ihrem Schooß, tritt auf den Fels, und zeigt
> Der staunenden Natur sein Leben.

Judea trembles! Its mountains quake! The Jordan flees its banks! – Why do you tremble, land of Judea? Your mountains, why do you quake? What was it, Jordan, that made your current flow backwards? – The Lord of the earth rises out of her womb, steps onto the rock, and shows his life to an astonished Nature.

Michael appears, the Romans flee, and the aria registers wonderment in a text that again follows brief exclamations with a longer final sentence offering at last the image of Jesus' face:

> Mein Geist, voll Furcht und Freude, bebet:
> Der Fels zerspringt: die Nacht wird licht.
> Seht, wie Er auf den Lüften schwebet!
> Seht, wie von seinem Angesicht
> Die Glorie der Gottheit strahlt!

My spirit quakes, full of fear and joy: The rock shatters: Night becomes day. Look, how He floats on the breezes! Look, how the glory of divinity streams from his countenance!

The pattern of short observations followed by major revelation creates a series of interim climaxes that in turn culminate in the following chorus, which proclaims Jesus' "triumph" in equally vivid and emphatic terms. The poetic structure of the scene encourages readers to imagine dimensions beyond the everyday, propelling them toward a chorus whose joy seems truly

98 *Richard Will*

angelic, infused with all the energy of what has preceded and thereby grander, more epochal than the words alone would suggest. Far from limiting the significance of the resurrection, Ramler lets the astonishment of his witnesses surge forth all the way to the sublime.

MUSIC AND SENTIMENT

Bach's setting of *Die Auferstehung* strengthens the contrast between the epic grandeur of the miracle scenes and the sentimental intimacy of the encounters between Jesus and his followers. To the latter he brings an expressive intensity equal to, and in some respects reminiscent of, that which characterizes Graun's *Der Tod Jesu*. For the miracles, however, he summons a rhythmic energy and an orchestral brilliance unlike anything in Graun, while also heightening the atmosphere of wonder with the bold harmonic moves for which his music is renowned. In addition, he expands the narrative directedness of Ramler's opening and closing scenes to encompass the entire oratorio, which now drives in teleological fashion from beginning to end. The moments of greatest human sentiment occur along a trajectory that points clearly toward a larger-than-life, divine culmination.[28]

Bach echoes the emotionalism of Graun most especially in the opening chorus, the first two arias, and the subsequent duet, whose kinship with *Der Tod Jesu* begins with their words. *Die Auferstehung* leads naturally from the earlier libretto in the sense that Ramler preserves, amidst the excitement of his resurrection scene, some of the somberness that pervades the Passion narrative. Thus before the first recitative describes Jesus rising, a chorus implores God to rescue him from hell and decay. Bach's setting is not unlike Graun's of the first chorus of *Der Tod Jesu*, which itself pictures Jesus' weakening and his impending descent into hell: although Graun writes in minor and Bach in major, both have the chorus declaim lyrical phrases over a steadily pulsing accompaniment, and both rely on chromaticism to darken the mood and emphasize the image of hell. Homophonic choral writing suggests beholders reacting together to a prospect marked as poignant by the chromatic harmonies and gently throbbing rhythms, and Bach holds fast

---

[28] Additional discussion of Bach's oratorio, from differing perspectives, is in Smither, *History of the Oratorio*, III: 434–63, and Rainer Cadenbach, "Carl Philipp Emanuel Bachs Vertonung der *Auferstehung und Himmelfahrt Jesu* von Karl Wilhelm Ramler: Beobachtungen zur musikalischen Auslegung einer geistlichen Dichtung," in Cadenbach and Helmut Loos, eds., *Beiträge zur Geschichte des Oratoriums seit Händel: Festschrift Günther Massenkeil zum 60. Geburtstag* (Bonn: Voggenreiter, 1986), 95–122.

to this image, keeping the chorus united throughout where Graun breaks off into fugal imitations. Despite working up to passionate outcries, both choruses also prove unable to dispel the gloom.[29]

The initial arias of the two oratorios have similar texts as well, pairing visions of a glorious or heroic Jesus in their first stanzas (see above) with those of his (or the witness's) punishment in the second. In setting the opening stanzas the composers again proceed along related lines, using brisk dotted rhythms and vocal coloratura to convey Jesus' strength. The central or B sections of the arias, setting the second stanzas, so closely resemble each other that one wonders if Bach meant to pay homage to his predecessor (example 4.1). They share slow tempos, triple meter, and melodic lines filled with lamenting downward half-steps, beginning with an initial descent from the third scale degree. In addition, they are both in Bb minor, a striking and remote choice for Bach given that the surrounding A sections are in C minor: by comparison, Graun's A sections are in the parallel Bb major. Bach may have wanted to play on the remembrance of the Passion embedded in his text, taking the opportunity to recall what was, at the time, the most famous musical treatment of the Passion story.

His determination to sound a depth of feeling comparable to Graun becomes even more evident in the next aria, for which he requested new words from Ramler. The original text, "Sei gegrüßet, Fürst des Lebens!" (Hail, Prince of Life!), called for rejoicing at the sight of Jesus' empty tomb. Telemann, the commissioner of *Die Auferstehung* and composer of its first setting (1760), responded with a quick and majestic aria in D major scored for an orchestra that includes three trumpets. Bach also gave the text an allegro setting when he prepared his own first version of *Die Auferstehung* in 1774. Itself a parody of an aria from an Easter cantata of 1763, his "Sei gegrüßet" remained part of the oratorio through its public premiere in Hamburg in March 1778.[30] By the fall of 1780, however, when Bach initiated what would be a seven-year project of publishing the work, he had decided that other sentiments were needed at this point in the narrative. What he had in mind is suggested by a letter to Ramler written in November of that year, requesting changes to a replacement text that Bach already has before him:

---

[29] As Cadenbach demonstrates, in Bach's chorus the three-fold appeal to God becomes steadily more intense as the movement unfolds; "Carl Philipp Emanuel Bachs Vertonung der *Auferstehung*," 98–100.

[30] Clark, "The Occasional Choral Works of C. P. E. Bach," 168–73.

Example 4.1a C. H. Graun, *Der Tod Jesu* (1755), Aria: "Du Held, auf den die Köcher,"
B section
When I at the brink of this life, see abysses, from which my spirit recoils in vain . . .

Example 4.1b C. P. E. Bach, *Die Auferstehung und Himmelfahrt Jesu*, H. 777 (1774; rev.
1778–80), part I, Aria: "Mein Geist, voll Furcht und Freuden," B section
Did Jesus not struggle with a thousand agonies? Did not his God receive his soul?

Reason and revelation in C. P. E. Bach's resurrection oratorio   101

Beautiful as the aria that you sent is, I would prefer that it begin directly in the first section with a *tender* Adagio, which I could expand as in all initial sections of an aria. The other and shorter part can consist of the last 3 lines and with that the aria is closed *without da capo* . . . We do not yet have arias of this type in the whole cantata, whereas there are 4 arias in this piece in which the first part is lively and the second part slower.[31]

The lines with which Bach wants to begin record the sorrowful memories of a witness to Jesus' death (example 4.2). They have an emotional immediacy exceptional even for Ramler, breaking down twice in despairing exclamations ("Ach!") and putting the performer in the unusual position of enacting the remembrance; the words speak not simply of past events, but of a song that the witness seems at once to recall and to perform again. The largely syllabic declamation of Bach's melody, along with the restrained accompaniment for strings alone, achieve an appropriately song-like directness, within which context he pays close attention to expressive detail. Frequent sigh figures lend the whole melody a lamenting quality, and the two *Achs* cut against the prevailing phrase rhythms to suggest upwellings of emotion too powerful to contain (mm. 2, 9). In addition, as the witness shifts from familiar Ramlerian images of Jesus' kindness ("Unser Trost, der Menschenfreund") to those of his suffering, Bach introduces additional rhythmic instability as well as unsettling chromaticism. The moment is marked by a deceptive cadence to the minor subdominant (m. 5), after which both the vocal line and the accompaniment break into irregular fragments and the harmony wanders in unpredictable progressions through C and F minor before reaching, some eight measures later, a midpoint cadence on F. The journey through the past proves difficult, and it remains so in the second half of the adagio, where Bach fulfills the promise of his letter by writing a varied reprise of the first half, an "expansion" very much in line with those found in the A sections of the other arias. Indeed, he develops the witness's sorrow at such length that it overshadows the expression of joy with which the number concludes. The advancing from darkness to light captures in miniature the emotional structure of the oratorio as a whole, but the bright, coloratura-laden, largely diatonic allegro setting the final verse is one of several passages early in *Die Auferstehung* that sounds as if it comes too soon (see below). Joy awaits, but the emotional aftermath of the crucifixion must first be laid to rest.

---

[31] Letter to Ramler of 20 November 1780; Suchalla, ed., *Briefe und Dokumente*, I: 869–70; Clark, *Letters*, 169. Cf. Stephen L. Clark, "The Letters from C. P. E. Bach to K. W. Ramler," in Clark, ed., *C. P. E. Bach Studies* (Oxford: Clarendon Press, 1987), 34–5; Clark, "The Occasional Choral Works of C. P. E. Bach," 171; Wiermann, "Werkgeschichte als Gattungsgeschichte," 124–5.

102   *Richard Will*

Example 4.2 C. P. E. Bach, *Die Auferstehung und Himmelfahrt Jesu*, part I, Aria: "Wie bang hat dich mein Lied beweint!"

How anxiously my song mourned for you. Oh! Our comfort, the friend of humanity sees no one to comfort him, stands abandoned. He who healed his people bleeds, he who awoke the dead – oh! – must expire. So mourned my anxious song.

Reason and revelation in C. P. E. Bach's resurrection oratorio   103

Example 4.3 C. H. Graun, *Der Tod Jesu*, Recitative: "Da steht der traurige, verhängnisvolle Pfahl"
And Jesus said: My father, my father, Oh! Forgive them, they know not what they do (lit. They do unknowing, what they do).

As one would expect, Bach emphasizes the affective dimensions of Ramler's text in the recitatives as well, where the characters meet and speak. Here, however, he complicates the poet's tableaux by adding an extra dimension to the exchanges between friends. An important decision faced by all composers who set Ramler was how to deal with his unannounced shifts from description to quotation. In *Der Tod Jesu*, Graun gives each recitative to a single voice and indicates quotations by changing texture. During the crucifixion, for example, the witness's description of Jesus being nailed to the cross is sung by a soprano soloist in a rhythmically free recitative accompanied by continuo. When the text reaches the first of Jesus' seven words on the cross – "Father, forgive them, for they know not what they do" – the texture shifts to an arioso characterized by regular rhythmic movement and a more lyrical vocal line than has been heard previously (example 4.3). Typically for such passages throughout the work, the continuo introduces an easily recognized motive that the voice imitates and that the continuo later returns to as it moves in sequence toward the final cadence. Elsewhere Graun uses similar repetitions to link multiple quotations in a single recitative, so that in many cases there is both a change to arioso and the return of a familiar motive to alert listeners that the witness is now recording someone else's words.[32]

With many more quotations than *Der Tod Jesu* as well as dialogue – features that further distinguish the two texts – the recitatives of *Die Aufer-stehung* posed a still greater challenge to composers. Telemann evidently

---

[32] Further examples and discussion in Smither, *History of the Oratorio*, III: 407–16.

decided that Ramler's scenes had become too dramatic to be handled as in Graun (and in Telemann's own setting of *Der Tod Jesu*), and gave the words of different speakers to different voices. In several cases the assignments create roles, as in a dramatic oratorio: Jesus is a bass throughout, Mary Magdalene a soprano, Thomas a tenor. Likewise the setting by Johann Adolph Scheibe (early 1760s) gives all the witness's words to the tenor, creating a part comparable to that of the Evangelist in a traditional oratorio passion.[33] As Barbara Wiermann has shown, Bach approached the recitatives similarly at first, using six soloists to clarify the division of speakers. He did not reduce the witness to a single voice as Scheibe did, preferring to give "the impression that the events are portrayed from ever changing perspectives and from changing persons."[34] He also did not mark every quotation with a new voice; in the exchange between Jesus and Magdalene, the bass sings the words of both the witness and Jesus, and a second soloist enters only with Mary's reply. Nevertheless, the use of multiple voices alters the impact of the scenes considerably, changing the lyrical impressions of a single observer into dramas for multiple figures.

By the time *Die Auferstehung* was published, Bach had revised the recitatives so as to put each one into a single voice. Exactly when he changed his mind is not clear, though it would appear to have been after the premiere of 1778. Wiermann suggests he was inspired by the growing prestige of lyric works like Graun's, whose lack of dramatic parts was among the characteristics that Sulzer and Forkel praised, and by the settings of *Die Auferstehung* by C. P. E. Bach's brother Johann Christoph Friedrich Bach (1771–2) and by Johann Friedrich Agricola (probably 1761), which also use single voices in the recitatives.[35] Whatever Bach's reasons, the results put the burden of distinguishing quotation from description onto the individual singers, who are aided, as in Graun, by textural shifts in the orchestra. Where Bach differs from Graun is in the nature of the textural shifts. When the archangel Michael soothes the daughters of Zion in the second recitative, and thereafter in all but one of the instances when Jesus speaks, the strings enter with sustained chords like those that envelop his voice in a number of seventeenth- and early eighteenth-century works, most famously J. S. Bach's *St. Matthew Passion* (example 4.4, m. 7).[36] C. P. E. Bach's renewal of the tradition lends Jesus more prominence than he enjoys in either Graun's or Telemann's settings of Ramler: enveloped in luminous sound, he stands out against the simpler background of the witness's continuo recitative.

[33] Wiermann, "Werkgeschichte als Gattungsgeschichte," 133–4.   [34] Ibid., 135; see also 128–31.
[35] Ibid., 136–8.   [36] See Smither, *History of the Oratorio*, II: 41; III: 447, 462.

Reason and revelation in C. P. E. Bach's resurrection oratorio   105

Example 4.4 C. P. E. Bach, *Die Auferstehung und Himmelfahrt Jesu*, part I, Recitative: "Wer ist die Sionitin"; translation on pp. 89–90 above.

106   *Richard Will*

Example 4.4 (*cont.*)

To the extent that listeners understand the strings to represent a musical
"halo," as in the conventional interpretation of the *St. Matthew Passion*, he
also gains an aura of divinity largely absent from the texts of the encounter
scenes, where he seems to share the humanity of his followers. Unlike his
father, however, C. P. E. Bach does not use the strings to elevate one voice
above another. When Jesus has his exchange with Thomas near the end,
both are accompanied only by continuo; this is the one recitative where the
strings do not participate. More surprising, in the dialogue with Magdalene
the strings accompany both characters. Indeed, Magdalene's initial words
follow those of Jesus without even a change in harmony, so that the bass must
work hard to project, and the listener to understand, that the witness has
begun to quote her (example 4.4, m. 9). The transition from her voice back
to that of Jesus is more clearly articulated; Bach conveys the rising intensity
of her questions by leading the peaks in the vocal line in a chromatic ascent
from C♯ to E (mm. 11–14), then points up Jesus' calmer response by having
his exclamation, "Maria!" begin at the same high point of E but subside
downward (m. 16). "Maria!" also coincides with a motive in the violins that
returns when Jesus speaks again later (mm. 19 and 23), recalling Graun's
technique for marking his voice. Yet still it does not seem to emanate from
a dimension separate from that of Magdalene; she, too, inhabits the special
musical world created by the strings.

 The effect is to emphasize, on one hand, the intimacy Ramler attributes
to Jesus and his companions. It is as if Jesus embraces Magdalene with
his "halo," signalling his love and his assurance that she will one day take
part in his divinity. At the same time, Bach's setting of both characters'
words in a magical aura recalls Klopstock's rendering of passionate moments
in exalted language. Klopstock's characters experience their feelings in a

landscape made numinous by sublime imagery; Bach's experience theirs in a space separate from that of the mundane witness. And as Klopstock's metaphors elevate the emotions to epic significance, so Bach's shimmering strings endow the inner lives of Jesus and Mary Magdalene with solemnity and grandeur. For all the clarity with which their emotions are delineated, the characters of Bach's recitatives are of grander stature than Graun's or Telemann's, filled with thoughts inexpressible in strictly human terms.

MUSIC AND EPIC

Two additional aspects of Bach's setting emphasize the revelatory rather than the sentimental side of Ramler's text: the harmonic language, and the teleological shape of the work as a whole. As Richard Kramer points out, a paragraph first published in a posthumous edition of Bach's keyboard treatise uses the first vocal phrase of the duet "Vater deiner schwachen Kinder" to illustrate how daring modulations can enrich a tonal palette – "modulation" referring, in this instance, to the movement between chords rather than between large-scale key areas.[37] The passage in question passes from the tonic D minor to the chord of its fifth scale degree, A minor, through a descending sequence that tonicizes the distant chords of C minor and B♭ minor (example 4.5). The progression turns a straightforward description of human frailty into a miniature drama of sin and recovery. The foreign chords set "der Gefallne" (the fallen one) and "der Betrübte" (the sorrower), while the return to a chord with a function in the home key, A minor, comes as the lost souls hear "den ersten Trost" (the best consolation) from God. Of particular importance is that such unusual harmonic motion would occur in a duet. Bach's recitatives include equally radical progressions, such as the move from B minor to G minor just before Mary Magdalene sings of crying over the body of Jesus (example 4.4, m. 12). Yet harmonic surprises abound in eighteenth-century recitatives, including those of Graun and Telemann; Bach's innovation was to extend comparable techniques to set pieces.

   The exotic chords in the duet recall the strings of the recitatives inasmuch as they, too, hint at a world separate from that of Ramler's characters on earth, in this case a shadowland where sinners wander in search of God. Elsewhere Bach associates similar tonal swerves with more explicit references to unearthly dimensions. The final aria, "Ihr Thore Gottes," reacts to the recitative describing the ascension, and as in the opening resurrection scene

---

[37] Richard Kramer, "The New Modulation of the 1770s: C. P. E. Bach in Theory, Criticism, and Practice," *Journal of the American Musicological Society*, 38 (1985), 551–65.

Example 4.5 C. P. E. Bach, *Die Auferstehung und Himmelfahrt Jesu*, part I, Duet: "Vater deiner schwachen Kinder"
Father of your weak children, the fallen one, the sorrower hears from you the best conso-lation.

Ramler's imagery is wholly sublime: the gates of heaven open, Jesus mounts his father's throne, the angels rejoice. Bach uses a brilliant introduction in march style, replete with massive fanfares for the horns and trumpets, to endow the moment with majesty and to reinforce the soloist's demand that heaven welcome the resurrected Jesus. He then offers a vivid picture of the arrival in another realm. After climbing from the tonic B♭ to the dominant F, the bass pauses, goes on to the dominant of the dominant, pauses more briefly, then begins to ascend an F major scale from deep in his register (mm. 17–18; example 4.6). One expects this scale to end on a triumphant high C or F and lead to a definitive cadence in the dominant, but instead the word "throne" brings a stunning diversion to D♭, the altered submediant of F, on which the orchestra and soloist linger for some two-and-a-half measures (mm. 19–21). In the subsequent cadential phrase the vocal line ascends again and does reach both C and F (m. 24), but the D♭ (and the corresponding G♭, in the later, altered reprise of the A section) lingers in the ear as the most significant harmonic event in the aria. Opening up regions of

Reason and revelation in C. P. E. Bach's resurrection oratorio   109

tonal space beyond the normal boundaries of B♭ or F major, the flatted sixth sonority conveys the otherworldliness of the throne to which Jesus ascends.

The triumphant mood of "Ihr Thore Gottes" also represents the penultimate stage in an arduous emotional journey from sorrow to joy. As was noted above, Ramler's libretto begins by imagining Jesus in hell, awaiting redemption, and the second verse of the first aria makes further reference to his suffering and death (see example 4.1b). These dark images are largely obscured by the shining figure of the resurrected Jesus and the excitement over his return. Bach goes to considerable lengths to reverse the emphasis, keeping the mood somber at the beginning and allowing the emotional transformation to happen only gradually. What this requires can best be seen in the contrast between his opening sequence of movements and that of Telemann. Both composers begin with somber orchestral introductions, but Bach achieves an extraordinarily profound gloom by scoring for unaccompanied basses and violas (example 4.7). Significantly, their stark octaves introduce the element of harmonic mystery that breaks out in so many later numbers; after descending through a natural minor scale and then tonicizing the tonic and dominant pitches, the strings prepare to reprise the opening measures by arpeggiating E♭ major, the Neapolitan second (mm. 8–9). Not an uncommon pre-dominant in the minor, the chord still carries the shock of the unfamiliar, especially since its distance from the surrounding harmonies is emphasized by a shift from the governing *piano* dynamic to *mezzo forte*.

The following three numbers are roughly comparable in Bach and Telemann, comprising a sorrowful opening chorus, a pictorial recitative narrating the resurrection, and a minor-key aria expressing fear and joy at the prospect of Jesus' return. Already the B sections of the arias, however, begin to diverge. Where Bach sets the remembrance of Jesus' death as a lament (example 4.1b), Telemann lightens the memory by shifting to the parallel major and a song-like vocal line marked "zärtlich" and accompanied by pizzicato strings. The atmosphere remains bright and confident, and it becomes even more so in the ensuing "Triumph" chorus and the following aria, Telemann's majestic setting, mentioned above, of Ramler's original text: "Sei gegrüßet, Fürst des Lebens!" Bach writes an equally majestic chorus, but since he replaces "Sei gegrüßet" with the mournful "Wie bang hat dich mein Lied beweint" (example 4.2), the triumph of Jesus seems far less secure. Together with the orchestral introduction, the lamenting opening chorus, and the B section of the first aria, the new second aria makes the joy of the "Triumph" chorus sound premature. The impression is reinforced by a small but telling harmonic detail: although the chorus, in E♭

Example 4.6 C. P. E. Bach, *Die Auferstehung und Himmelfahrt Jesu*, part II, Aria: "Ihr Thore Gottes"
He mounts to his father's throne! Make way! The king enters his kingdom!

Example 4.6 (*cont.*)

Example 4.7 C. P. E. Bach, *Die Auferstehung und Himmelfahrt Jesu*, part I, Introduction

major, seems to dispel the shadow of the preceding aria in C minor, the following recitative begins right back in C minor, as if to say that the time for the relative major has not yet come. The witness is not ready to forget the three long days that separated the crucifixion from the resurrection, and indeed the darkness lingers throughout the first half of the oratorio. The duet, which succeeds "Wie bang hat dich mein Lied beweint," never transcends the minor-key pathos of its opening measures (example 4.5), and even the concluding choral fugue, while preceded and followed by

112   *Richard Will*

Example 4.8 C. P. E. Bach, *Die Auferstehung und Himmelfahrt Jesu*, part II, Final chorus "Gott fähret auf mit Jauchzen"

Example 4.8 (cont.)

brief acclamations in G major, is itself primarily in A minor and E minor, with a subject whose predominantly descending contour and emphasis on the minor sixth scale degree (for "Sieg," victory) continue to temper the jubilation.

Ramler incorporates two additional verses of the "Triumph" chorus into the second half of the oratorio, and Bach sets them with the same Eb major music that he used at the beginning. It sounds more convincing with each iteration, its excitement no longer undermined by the surrounding music. The first aria of the second half has a stern but not sorrowful minor-key B section dealing with the victory over hell; the exceptionally long A section, in Ab major, pairs the bass voice with a solo bassoon in a melismatic welcoming of the savior. The second aria likewise combines sternness (a declaration of fealty, in the A section) with lyricism ("Zu dir steigt mein Gesang empor," To you rises my hymn), and the third is "Ihr Thore Gottes" (example 4.6). All the voices are finally beginning to come together in celebration, and when Bach comes to the very last movement he reveals that not only the affect of the recurring "Triumph" choruses but also their key of Eb have been the goal all along. Adumbrated as far back as the Neapolitan chord of the orchestral introduction, in the concluding minutes Eb becomes a point of arrival, heightening the sense of culmination engendered by the drawn-out emotional progression toward joy.[38] Bach also saves for the end a pair of bold modulations that highlight the ultimate settling on Eb as well as point once more toward divine realms. The first recalls the Db of "Ihr Thore Gottes," although in a context where it sounds even more foreign than in the aria (example 4.8). The second section of the last movement, in the relative minor C, has arrived after fifty-four measures at what sounds like a final cadence (m. 112). After a silence, however, the chorus sings "Der Herr ist König" (the Lord is king) on unison Dbs, followed by the orchestra playing Db triads and a vigorous unison melody that confirms the key (mm. 113–29). A shorter pause, and the same music recurs up a step in Eb, as if to restore the original tonic (mm. 129–45). The vision opened up by Dbs, however, is not so easily discarded, and the chorus continues on past Eb to the fifth of C, G minor. The next section returns to Eb but breaks off on a half-cadence, following which a similar group of choral unisons and orchestral affirmations tonicizes first Ab and then Bb. This last, the home dominant, finally resolves the issue, and the ensuing music returns to Eb to prepare a closing fugue that never departs significantly from the home key.

---

[38] Smither also notes Bach's use of Eb major as the key of "joy and triumph"; *History of the Oratorio*, III: 438–9; see also Finscher, "Bemerkungen zu den Oratorien Carl Philipp Emanuel Bachs," 327–8.

Reason and revelation in C. P. E. Bach's resurrection oratorio   115

To drive toward an emotional and tonal goal in this way, imbuing the whole oratorio with an epic force found only in Ramler's opening and closing scenes, again recalls Klopstock. While the characters in *Der Messias* express joy at numerous points between the resurrection and the ascension, Klopstock uses the story of Thomas to invigorate this entire section of the narrative with suspense. First introduced in book 14, Thomas does not finally see Jesus until book 17, and during the interim Klopstock repeatedly shows him questioning his companions and praying for guidance. When his conversion finally resolves the tension, the text melts into ecstasy, giving itself over entirely to celebration and praise. Bach's *Auferstehung* ends similarly inasmuch as the final choruses put the lingering sorrow of the crucifixion to rest. Their joyous music subsumes the witness, the characters, and the listeners into an apotheosis made all the more intense for having been delayed so long.

It was probably a combination of musical and theological considerations that prevented *Die Auferstehung* from achieving the popularity of *Der Tod Jesu*. By the time it was published, some elements of Bach's setting must have seemed outdated: all but one of the arias is in a traditional or modified da capo form,[39] and the trumpet parts are in a clarino style so difficult that Mozart had to rewrite them or give them to other instruments when he directed the piece in Vienna in 1788.[40] The "compound of *Empfindsamkeit* and monumentality," which Ludwig Finscher notes in the work,[41] would have further challenged those whose standard of sacred music was Graun's even more old-fashioned – in musical terms – *Der Tod Jesu*. If Ramler's text insures that *Die Auferstehung* remains as concerned with the human as it is with the divine, Bach's music endows even human participants in the life of Jesus with heavenly auras, and his conclusion disperses all sentiment into the sublime. The oratorio is both Neologist and orthodox, balancing a rational religion of feeling and morality against the irrational power of revelation.

---

[39] One aria is in da capo form, and four others are in what Smither terms "transformed da capo," with an A section that modulates to and cadences in a non-tonic key, a contrasting B section, and a reprise of the A section recomposed so that all the material occurs in the tonic; *History of the Oratorio*, III: 79–80, 439.

[40] Andreas Holschneider, "C. Ph. E. Bachs Kantate *Auferstehung und Himmelfahrt Jesu* und Mozarts Aufführung des Jahres 1788," *Mozart-Jahrbuch* (1968/70), 264–80.

[41] Finscher, "Bemerkungen zu den Oratorien Carl Philipp Emanuel Bachs," 328.

Part III
The *Versuch* and Other Writings

[17]

C. P. E. BACH'S *VERSUCH* AND ITS CONTEXT IN EIGHTEENTH-CENTURY THOROUGH-BASS PEDAGOGY

Thomas Christensen

There is probably no other musical treatise of the eighteenth century that is more esteemed than C. P. E. Bach's manual of keyboard instruction, the *Versuch über die wahre Art das Clavier zu spielen.* From the moment of its appearance, we find the Versuch praised by performers and composers alike – the approbations of Haydn and Beethoven being perhaps the most famous.[1] Musicians of Bach's own time recognized in it the virtues of clarity, completeness, and above all, incomparable musical sensitivity. One might go so far as to say that despite C. P. E. Bach's acknowledged stature as a composer, it was a pedagogical work that did more to secure his reputation in the 18th century than any of his compositions. In the eyes of many German musicians of his day, Bach was first and foremost a pedagogue – the famous author of the *Versuch über die wahre Art das Clavier zu spielen.* Few of Bach's musical publications enjoyed the numerous reprintings and widespread dissemination that his Versuch did. With the possible exception of Jean-Philippe Rameau, there was no composer of the 18th century whose reputation seemed so staked to his pedagogical writings.

Because the *Versuch* was highly praised in the 18th century, however, it does not necessarily follow that all parts of Bach's keyboard treatise were equally influential. As I hope to persuade in this article, such was not the case. The *Versuch*, it will be recalled, is divided into two halves separated in publication date by nine years. The first half published in 1753 deals with performing aspects of the solo keyboard (fingerings, hand position, embellishments, arti-

---

[1]For the respective citations, see the Preface to William Mitchell's translation: *Essay on the True Art of Playing Keyboard Instruments* (New York, 1949), p. 2.

culation, phrasing, and the like), while the second half from 1762 deals with questions of accompaniment (most importantly, the realization of a thorough bass). It was the first half of the treatise which exercised the most influence in the second half of the 18th century. Bach's system of fingering, embellishing, and general advice on playing keyboard instruments laid the foundation for the first generation of piano instruction manuals that were to follow.[2] Part two of the *Versuch* turns out to have had far less resonance, not so much because the practice of thorough bass was in precipitous decline throughout the second half of the century (although this was partly true), but more because Bach's conceptual approach to the practice was rooted in a conservative tradition of compositional pedagogy that was increasingly being displaced by newer developments in harmonic theory emanating from France.

And what were these developments in harmonic theory? It was the system of harmonic generation and syntax articulated by the French composer Jean-Philippe Rameau and his followers. The difference between Bach's and Rameau's approaches to the thorough bass can be simply described. Based upon received traditions of contrapuntal pedagogy, Bach explained the chordal structures encoded in figured-bass signatures as composites of intervals— and hence subject to traditional contrapuntal rules of use. Rameau reversed this relationship by positing chords as the primary constituents of musical practice, while intervals were seen as but a consequence.[3] More audaciously, Rameau enunciated a theory of chordal inversion by which numerous chords could be reduced to two prototypes: the consonant triad and the dissonant seventh chord. By manipulating these two chordal types (primarily through inversion), he was able to generate

---

[2]Among those early piano pedagogues who professed their indebtedness to Bach may be mentioned Marpurg (1765), Rigler (1779), Merbach (1782), Türk (1789), Dusseck (1796), and Clementi (1801).

[3]Rameau first articulated his theory in his *Traité de l'harmonie* of 1722, although he continued to develop and refine his ideas over the next 40 years in another half dozen major publications. A detailed discussion of Rameau's theory may be found in my recently-published book, *Rameau and Musical Thought in the Enlightenment* (Cambridge, 1993).

most every chord listed in the signature tables of traditional figured-bass manuals.

Example 1 offers a simple illustration of these two contrasting perspectives:

Example 1

From a strictly intervallic perspective in which signatures are calculated above the basso continuo, this progression contains three dissonances: the second of the 4#/2 chord, the augmented fourth in this same chord, and the perfect fourth in the 4/3 chord. Of course there is a dissonant major second between the upper voices in the 4/3 chord, but this dissonance is not the one considered in measuring the chord against the basso continuo – it is the fourth. Still, as Bach noted in his discussion of this signature, in practice „the third is treated as a dissonance and the fourth enjoys more freedom than usual".[4] This suggests that the particular value of any interval is determined by its position in a chord. Indeed, Bach goes on to show the reader that there are many ways of employing – and resolving – the 4/3 signature depending upon what scale degree it is played, and what chord follows it. We are thus shown how chordal context can change the abstract value of an interval. As William Mitchell has noted, it is the immediate musical environment of any given interval (i.e. its accompanying intervals and placement within the scale) that determines its ultimate meaning and treatment.[5]

For Rameau and his followers, of course, the paradox of the „dissonant minor third" is easily explained. The 4/3 chord really is an

[4]*Essay*, p. 233.
[5]William J. Mitchell, 'Chord and Context in 18th-Century Theory,' *Journal of the American Musicological Society* 16 (1963), p. 229.

inversion of a dominant seventh chord built on D.[6] The dissonant C, then, is the seventh of the chord (just as the sixth of the preceding 6/3 chord is the true root of that chord). This explains how a normally consonant interval like the minor third can sound like a dissonance in this progression, and must be treated accordingly. Moreover, by Rameau's theory of inversional equivalence, the C4#/2 chord is seen to possess the same root (or „fundamental bass") as the 4/3 chord an A. The „fundamental bass" of this progression would thus be D-D7-G-D7-G. While Rameau would have generally agreed with Bach's strictures concerning the voice-leading of this progression (the voicing of the chords, rules for treating the dissonance, restrictions of parallel motion between perfect consonances, etc.), he would have had a very different explanation of the origins of these strictures, origins that of course lay in the underlying fundamental bass. Whereas Bach's concern was the individual context and behavior of each signature, Rameau's was with their common origins; Bach's approach was rigorously empirical, Rameau's tendentiously reductive.

Now the reductive element in Rameau's theory, it can easily be shown, was born of pedagogical exigency. To see how this is so, we should recall how in the harmonic practice of the early 18th century, thorough-bass realization was not viewed as so daunting a skill that it could not be learnt tolerably well given the knowledge of a limited number of signature types. In his first treatise of accompaniment published in 1711, Johann Heinichen felt it sufficient to identify only twelve signatures for the accompanist to learn:[7]

6   4 3   7 6   7   9 8   9   6/5   6/4-5/3   b7   4/3   4   2

By learning what other intervals normally were to accompany each of these signatures (in most cases a third with the addition of either a

---

[6]Rameau would technically call such a chord a „dominante-tonique" on account of its requisite resolution. He used the more general term „dominant" to designate any minor seventh chord that resolves in imitation of the authentic cadence to some chord whose root lay a fifth below.

[7]Johann David Heinichen, *Neu erfundene und Gründliche Anweisung [...] des General-Basses* (Hamburg, 1711).

fifth, sixth, or octave), the student could expect to produce an acceptable accompaniment to the figured basses of most sacred and chamber pieces. (This was often taught by showing the student where to imagine a triad above a given bass note. For example, in the chord of the sixth, one imagines a triad a third below the bass, while to realize a 4/2 signature, one thinks the triad a second above the bass. Such a heuristic may suggest inversional equivalence to us today, but it was not interpreted as such by pedagogues before Rameau.)

As the more ambitious dissonances and irregular progressions associated with the „stylus theatralus" began to infiltrate the common language of Baroque composers, though, the quantity and complexity of figures facing the continuo player increased concomitantly. It is telling that in his second treatise of 1728, one in which full account of recent developments in Italian operatic practice is taken, Heinichen had expanded his signature table to 32. And when Johann Mattheson came out seven years later with a table of 70 signatures, one organist was reported by Schröter to have exclaimed in despair that the task of continuo playing was now only for the Devil himself.[8]

Clearly, the number and variety of signatures facing the continuo student were creating real pedagogical problems. Various strategies were tried in managing this morass of detail. Most commonly, signatures were grouped and taught on the basis of common interval content. Hence Heinichen arranged his chords based on the ascending order of their characteristic dissonance. After the independent (*ungebundenen*) chords of the „ordinairen Accorde" (major and minor triads) and regular sixth (6/3), Heinichen went on to consider the dissonant chords of the second, followed by those containing the fourth, seventh, and ninth. But even here difficulties arose. Under the category of fourth chords, for example, Heinichen had to consider such disparate signatures as 4/2, 4/3, 4-3, and b4, each demanding different kinds of preparation and resolution. Other thorough-bass pedagogues felt it better to dispense with such signature tables altogether and simply have the student memorize a small number of

---

[8]Quoted in Franck T. Arnold, *The Art of Accompaniment from a Thorough-Bass* (London, 1931), p. 299.

stock mnemonic progressions such as the normative scale har-
monization known as the *règle de l'octave*.[9] But the *règle* was not
much help to the student faced with highly chromatic signatures or
intricate bass lines.

It was precisely on account of the burgeoning number of signatures, then, that Rameau conceived his theory of the fundamental
bass. Through the notion of chordal inversion (as well as ancillary
manipulations such as supposition, suspension, „double employment," etc.), Rameau was able to reduce most chord signatures to the
two fundamental types mentioned above: the triad and seventh. Further, he was by this means able to show how most chord successions
followed a limited number of cadential prototypes (mostly with fifth
motion in the fundamental bass). The fundamental bass thus offered
a clarification and simplification of harmonic practice with immediate
heuristic value. For those thorough-bass theorists who adopted
Rameau's idea, a typical signature table would begin with the common triad and its two inversions (5/3, 6/3, and 6/4), the seventh chord
and its three inversions (7, 6/5, 4/3, and 4/2) and then chords in
which notes were added to the seventh (9, 11, 13), altered chromatic-
ally (diminished and augmented chords of all types), and modified
by anticipations or suspensions (4-3, 9-8, 7/4/2-8/5/3, etc.). Through
this rigorously generative procedure, all figured-bass signatures
could be traced back to the two fundamental chord types the student
needed to keep in mind. All this naturally made the fingering and
memorization of thorough-bass signatures easier for the student.
Rameau, I should add, did not himself fully develop this idea systematically in his own thorough-bass instructors.[10] This was in large
part because he was torn between systematic and pedagogical

[9]This would include the school of „Partimento" instructors discussed in footnote
26 below. For more on the „Rule of the Octave" and its applications, see Thomas
Christensen, 'The *Règle de l'Octave* in Thorough-Bass Theory and Practice,' *Acta
Musicologica* 64 (1992), pp. 91–117.
[10]Rameau's thorough-bass writings are to be found in his *Traité de l'harmonie* (Paris,
1722), Book 4, „Principes de l'accompagnement"; *Dissertation sur les différentes
méthodes d'accompagnement pour le clavecin* (Paris, 1732); and the *Code de musique
pratique* (Paris, 1760).

concerns.[11] Still, his theory offered the means for others to do so. It is not coincidental, then, that the earliest and most widespread adoption of Rameau's fundamental bass is to be found not in practical composition manuals or speculative treatises, but in tutors of the thorough bass.[12] Far from Rameau's theory being antithetical to the spirit of thorough-bass practice, as some theorists today assert, it in fact found there its most fertile application. The fundamental bass was a concept intimately allied to thorough-bass practice. As I have elsewhere argued, the thorough bass „was the chrysalis in which Rameau's theory of the fundamental bass was born; it furnished him with the major pedagogical problems he sought to solve, the notation

[11]As only one example, Rameau vacillated in his writings between accounting for 11th chords as chords of supposition or suspension. (This would incidentally be one of the most contentious issues in the Streit between Rameau's supporters in Germany and his critics.) By the former perspective, the chord was theoretically a seventh chord with a „supposed“ bass placed a fifth below the true fundamental—hence allowing Rameau to subsume the dissonance within his fundamental seventh, as well as maintaining normative root motion of the fifth in the chord resolution. Of course this was purely a theoretical explanation. Practically, it was easier to explain the chord as a simple 4-3 suspension occurring over the same fundamental bass. And in his actual analytic notations, this is exactly what he did. For a more detailed analysis of Rameau's arguments on this topic, see Christensen, *Rameau and Musical Thought*, pp. 123–29.

[12]E.g. Michel Corrette, *Le Maitre de clavecin pour l'accompagnement* (Paris, 1753); Claude de la Porte, *Traité théorique et pratique de l'accompagnement du clavecin* (Paris, 1753); M. Dubugrarre, *Méthode plus courte et plus facile que l'ancienne pour l'accompagnement du clavecin* (Paris, 1754); and Francesco Geminiani, *L'Art de bien accompagner du clavecin* (Paris, 1754). The first German authors to adopt Rameau's fundamental bass also did so in the context of the General Bass: David Kellner, *Treulicher Unterricht im General-Bass* (Hamburg, 1732); Georg Andreas Sorge, *Vorgemach der musicalischen Composition, oder: ausführliche, ordentliche [...] Anweisung zum General-Bass* (Lobenstein, 1747); Hartong (P. C. Humanus), *Musicus Theoretico-practicus* (Nürnberg, 1749); Johann Friedrich Daube, *General-Bass in drey Accorden* (Leipzig, 1756); and Friedrich Wilhelm Marpurg, *Handbuch bey dem Generalbasse und der Composition*, 3 vols. (Berlin, 1755-58). It is revealing Heinichen took belated note of Rameau's fundamental bass at the very end of his 1728 treatise, after the bulk of the work was evidently already written and in press (Joel Lester, *Compositional Theory in the Eighteenth Century* [Cambridge Mass., 1992], p. 56). While Heinichen did not there fully endorse Rameau's ideas, he clearly recognized their relevance and value to the teaching of chord signatures.

and nomenclature to do this, and finally, the practice to which he would continually return in order to test his solutions".[13]

By the time C. P. E. Bach came to publish Part 2 of the *Versuch* in 1762, Rameau's chordal approach to thorough bass had already taken strong hold in German soil. In the circle of musicians surrounding Bach in Berlin, the fundamental bass was adopted in whole or in part by Marpurg, Nichelmann, and Kirnberger (even if not all of Rameau's speculative or acoustical arguments were accepted). On the other hand, theorists who continued to teach thorough-bass skills through the more traditional intervallic approach were on the decline as the century progressed. By 1792 Türk was able to defend his own thorough-bass method by pointing out that the vast majority of music teachers had adopted – like himself – the „Kirnberger" two-chord system. This system,Türk goes on to point out, had proven effective in teaching the thorough bass as well as accounting for the practice of such masters as Johann Sebstian Bach.[14]

Türk was not mistaken concerning the widespread acceptance of Rameau's inversional theory. In a survey of thorough-bass methods published in German between 1762 and 1800, plus a large number of manuscripts I was able to study in the Berlin Staatsbibliothek – Preußischer Kulturbesitz, I found that the vast majority of figured-bass

---

[13]Christensen, *Rameau and Musical Thought*, p. 61. The polarization of Rameau's theory and the thorough bass has been most forcefully propounded in our own century by Schenker and his followers, inspired in no small part by their own political agenda. Mitchell's otherwise admirable article cited in footnote 5 repeats this erroneous dichotomy (p. 228).

[14]Daniel Gottlob Türk, *Beleuchtung einer Recension des Buches Kurze Anweisung zum Generalbaßspielen* (Halle, 1792), p. 23. The „Kirnberger system" refers to Kirnberger's 1781 treatise, *Grundsätze des Generalbasses als erste Linien zur Composition*, which is itself based upon ideas articulated in his *Die Kunst des reinen Satzes in der Musik*, 4 vols. (Berlin, 1771–79). In these works, Kirnberger invokes the generative idea described earlier in this paper, in which two fundamental chord types are posited: the triad and the dissonant seventh; all other signatures are derived from these two prototypes either by inversion, or through the suspension and anticipation of individual chord notes (creating a category of „accidental" dissonances). Few German musicians of the later 18th century who made widespread use of the „Kirnberger system" realized that this was basically Rameau's system (which was mistakenly identified with Marpurg's quite different perversion of that theory).

pedagogues invoke inversional theory in their teachings. Specifically, I have found 24 published treatises in which Rameau's two-chord system (often under the guise of the „Kirnberger system") was either explicitly adopted or implicitly invoked (reflected above all in the groupings of figures based on inversional derivation). On the other hand, I found only eight treatises that seemed to have escaped the juggernaut of inversional theory and maintained a strictly intervallic approach. These two lists are to be found in Tables 1 and 2, respectively.[15] (I might add, too, that if we considered the many genres of composition and harmony treatises, let alone works published in France, England, and Italy, the ratio would be even more heavily weighted toward Rameau.) What is perhaps even more surprising is that in the surviving compositional instructions we have of Mozart and Beethoven, we find the fundamental bass widely used – and this despite their well-known approbations of Bach's *Versuch*. Whether it is Mozart's instructions to Thomas Attwood, or Beethoven's lessons for Archduke Rudolf, we find Rameau's harmonic theories leaving their unmistakable mark.[16] Even counterpoint could be approached harmonically, as Albrechtsberger's *Gründliche Anweisung zur*

---

[15]It should be kept in mind that the „intervallic" tradition did not entirely pass away in the 19th century. Indeed in a few areas of Southern Germany and Austria, it enjoyed something of a revival (although not without betraying influences of Rameau's theory, to be sure). For a good discussion of this literature, see Ulf Thomson, *Voraussetzungen und Artungen der österreichischen Generalbasslehre zwischen Albrechtsberger und Sechter* (Tutzing, 1978).

Still, it was difficult for any 19th-century theorist not to filter Bach's intervallic approach through a more familiar harmonic sieve, as did the editor who brought out a revised edition of Bach's *Versuch* in 1852 and 1856 „im Gewande und nach den Bedürfnissen unserer Zeit." The particular editor in question (Gustav Schilling) there corrupted Bach's text by reordering, revising, and ascribing all figures in terms of inversional derivation. (Walter Niemann arrived at an even easier solution to make Bach's treatise more relevant to his readers in the 1906 reissue of the *Versuch*: He omitted the twenty odd chapters on thorough bass altogether!) It was little wonder that more sensitive musicologists such as Schenker and Otto Vrieslander expessed indignant outrage at such abuse and argued so passionately for a rehabilitation of Bach's original method.

[16]Joel Lester has traced the penetration of Rameau's theory into the compositional pedagogy of the later 18th century in his valuable study, *Compositional Theory in the Eighteenth Century*, especially in Chapter 8, 'Changing Aspects of Harmonic Theory,' pp. 193–230.

Composition (Leipzig, 1790) testifies. In this work, the famous Viennese teacher of Beethoven interprets Fux's species counterpoint from a chordal perspective, describing all intervallic relations and resolutions in terms of their harmonic functional implications (much as did Albrechtsberger's Viennese predecessor, Johann Friedrich Daube).

Now I do not want to explode one set of false polarities (Rameau's theory versus thorough-bass practice) merely to substitute for it another (Bach's „intervallic" approach versus the fundamental bass). There were many ways that the two thorough-bass pedagogies could be mediated, Kirnberger's approach being perhaps the most effective.[17] But it cannot be doubted, too, that in adopting Rameau's fundamental bass, these same composers and pedagogues were assuming a radically new perspective towards the structure and behavior of musical material, a perspective that entailed not only conceptual, but very practical ramifications in how music was taught, performed, and composed.

We can then wonder why Bach was not among those who chose to adopt Rameau's theory in their pedagogy of the thorough bass. It surely cannot have been that Bach was too much of a conservative, as there is little to suggest in his own compositional *oeuvre* that he felt hidebound to tradition. Nor is it likely that Bach was ignorant of Rameau's ideas given in Berlin by Marpurg in his journals. (Although there is no evidence on the other hand that Bach possessed a detailed

---

[17]Kirnberger is often cited as a theorist who bridged the gap between these two traditions. For example, he would distinguish sevenths that were the product of the fundamental bass (*eigentlich*) from those that were products of suspension (*zufällig*), thus showing sensitivity to both vertical and horizontal parameters. Kirnberger, we might also note, based his anthology of keyboard exercises upon Bach's system of fingering: *Clavierübungen mit der Bachischen Applicatur*, 4 vols. (Berlin, 1762–66). According to the Preface, Bach's method „is the easiest, most comfortable, and comprehensive means by which both the student and teacher may achieve [keyboard proficiency] in the shortest time." Still, that Kirnberger would so conspicuously make use of Rameau's fundamental bass in ordering and explaining the behavior of thorough-bass chords suggests that he was quite deliberate in sorting out those parts of the *Versuch* from which he would draw.

understanding of Rameau's theory, despite the single polemical jab he would make at it many years later.)[18]

The most reasonable explanation Bach remained disengaged from Rameau's theory, I think, is simply that it was not useful for his primary goal, which was to elucidate the many contexts in which a given signature may occur. Such variety could not easily be accommodated by the strictures of inversional theory, or at least not in any en-lightening way. Bach's exuberanteven manneristic – employment of dissonant harmonies, appoggiaturas, chromatic figurations, irregular resolutions, and modulations that are illustrated in his *Versuch* defied any easy harmonic codification or reduction. We might say, then, that the empirical riches of the *Versuch* were purchased at the cost of pedagogical efficiency.

To show the trade off most clearly, let us pick one chord—the „chord of the second" (4/2) – and look at how Bach approaches the subject. His discussion of this single figure covers 13 pages and involves almost fifty separate examples.[19] It is the most detailed and nuanced treatment of the 4/2 chord to be found in any thorough-bass treatise hitherto published.

---

[18]In a noisy argument waged between Kirnberger and Marpurg over the value of the fundamental bass, Bach took the side of Kirnberger and proclaimed his and his father's pedagogy to be „antirameauisch" (quoted in Kirnberger's *Die Kunst des reinen Satzes in der Musik*, vol. 4 [Berlin, 1779], p. 188). Such a statement cannot be taken at face value, however, since as I indicated earlier, Kirnberger's own theory was in reality closer to Rameau's theory than was Marpurg's (despite neither of them being aware of the fact). That there was no irreconcilable disjunction between the practice of Johann Sebastian and Rameau's fundamental bass is ironically shown by Kirnberger's own harmonic analysis of Bach's fugues. In any case, as I have argued in a previous paper, a more plausible motivation for Bach's anti-Rameauian posturing may have been political, stemming from Bach's earlier arguments with Christoph Nichelmann, another partisan of Rameau's theory. See Thomas Christensen, 'Nichelmann Contra C. P. E. Bach: Harmonic Theory and Musical Politics at the Court of Frederick the Great,' in: *Carl Philipp Emanuel Bach und die europäische Musikkultur des mittleren 18. Jahrhunderts. Bericht über das Internationale Symposium der Joachim Jungius-Gesellschaft der Wissenschaften Hamburg, 29. September–2. Oktober 1988*, ed. Hans Joachim Marx (Göttingen, 1990), pp. 189–220.
[19]The discussion in the original 1762 edition occurs in Chapter 9, pp. 97–109.

Now the chord of the second, as mentioned earlier, was among the first dissonant signatures to be considered by thorough-bass pedagogues in the traditional „intervallic" school, as the second was the smallest dissonant interval. But whereas Bach's predecessors may have been content to discuss only a few paradigmatic uses of the chord, and then drill the student with lengthy progressions using various transpositions, sequences or textural variants of the chord, Bach is intent upon identifying and illustrating the variety of harmonic contexts and voicings which may apply to the chord. Bach begins by noting that it is the bass voice in the figure which is always to be prepared and resolved as a dissonance. The second is paradoxically to be treated as a consonance. (Rameau, we recall, would easily resolve the paradox by explaining the bass voice as the inversion of a dissonant seventh, while the second represents the stable root of the chord.) As a dissonance, the bass voice should be approached by a passing tone or prepared as a suspension. The most common structure of this chord is a major second and perfect fourth accompanied by a major or minor sixth. These are shown in Examples 2 and 3, respectively.[20]

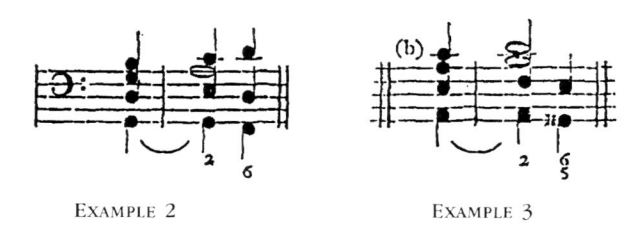

EXAMPLE 2   EXAMPLE 3

Sometimes the second of the chord may be represented by a minor second, shown approached in Example 4 as a passing tone (*transitus*).

---

[20]All of the following examples are taken from Chapter 9 of Book 2, pp. 97–109 (pp. 252–60 in the Mitchell translation).

EXAMPLE 4

Now the normal chord of resolution for this signature is some variety of sixth chord. But other resolutions are possible, too. A few of these are illustrated in Example 5: a) a simple 5/3 chord; b) a 4/3 chord; c) a b7/b5 chord; d) or a 6/b5 chord.

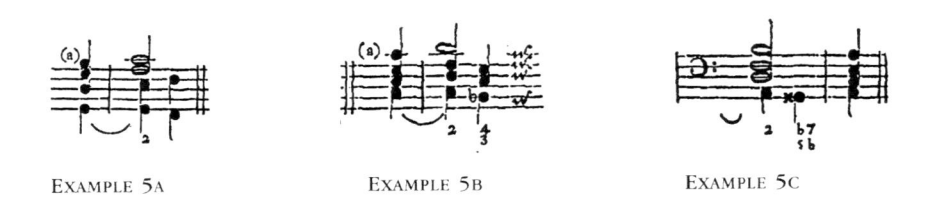

EXAMPLE 5A EXAMPLE 5B EXAMPLE 5C

EXAMPLE 5D

A whole other category of second chords comes about when the augmented fourth is added above the interval of a second. Naturally the dissonant tritone suggests a resolution to a sixth in contrary motion (Example 6a).

EXAMPLE 6A

But other resolutions are also possible when the progression is
allowed to modulate (Examples 6b–d).

EXAMPLE 6B   EXAMPLE 6C   EXAMPLE 6D

Another variant of the chord is the augmented second accompanied
by the augmented fourth and minor sixth (a variety of the diminished-
seventh chord). (Bach offers seven different possibilities of using this
chord, of which Example 7 offers only three).

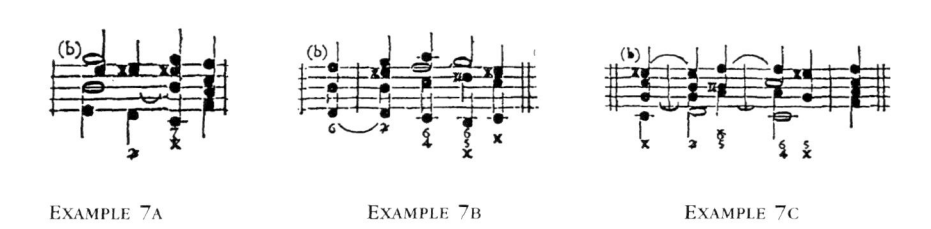

EXAMPLE 7A   EXAMPLE 7B   EXAMPLE 7C

While in all the cases seen so far the bass has resolved *somehow* by
step (although in a few cases this has involved an irregular ascending
resolution), it is possible to leap out of the dissonance as shown in
Example 8.

EXAMPLE 8

365

Other possible uses of the chord are over a pedal note (Example 9),

EXAMPLE 9

or even resolving downwards to another chord of the second (Exemple 10).

EXAMPLE 10

All of these variants, it must be reiterated, are augmented with many more possible resolutions and voicings than those given here. And this is only one chapter. In the following three chapters, Bach goes on to analyze and illustrate the second when coupled with a fifth, a fifth and fourth, and a third, respectively.

The result is one of the most exhaustive and nuanced descriptions of North German *Empfindsam* practice to be found in the entire corpus of pedagogical writings for the time. No other thorough-bass treatise in subsequent generations comes close to the detail and variety Bach offers. The only thorough-bass treatise of greater length – the second volume of Michael Johann Friedrich Wiedeburg's *Der sich selbst informirende Clavierspieler* (Halle, 1767) – is dense only by virtue of the large number of exercises and long-winded commentaries offered by its inept author (who nonetheless stands deeply indebted to Bach). In terms of sheer variety of examples, though, Wiedeburg's work does not approach the number of examples (let alone the musicality) to be found in Bach's *Versuch*.[21]

[21]There is a short, 18-page manuscript of thorough-bass instructions attributed to

Now were we to try and add a fundamental bass to these signa-tures, we would run into difficulties. Let alone the problems in defining the root of many of these chords, the resulting fundamental-bass successions would make havoc of Rameau's normative mo-dels. As one example, the chords in Example 7c resist easy reduction. The diminished-seventh and augmented-sixth chords in the progres-sion do not have unambiguous roots in Rameau's theory. While in one treatise Rameau would have considered the bass of the second chord in Example 7c to be a „borrowed" root (the true root being a half step lower on E), in a later treatise he would simply assign the root to the leading tone (G#). The „German" augmented-sixth chord is one Rameau never discussed in his treatises, although in analyses of related („French") augmented-sixth chords, he seemed inclined to assign a root to the augmented fourth (so in this case the C would be the root „borrowed" from B).

The other problem in applying Rameau's theory to Bach's pro-gressions can be seen in Example 5b. While the designated roots of each chord seem clear, the resulting ascending progression of roots (C, D7, E7/b5, and F) makes little sense within the tonal syntax of fifth motion that Rameau prescribes as the normative motion of the fun-damental bass. The reason, of course, is that not all of the signatures in these perspectives are harmonically functional. Forcing them into such a functional reading, naturally, results in syntactic nonsense. This is not to say, of course, that all fundamental bass readings are uninformative. But Rameau's theory is most insightful when applied to more normative progressions. And this requires disentangling the fundamental harmonies from those chords that are products of line-ar motion between voices. (So to return to Exemple 10, the second

Bach entitled *Kurze Anweisung zum General-Bass* that is in the Brussels conservatory library (B-Bc: MS II, 4165; Ms. Fétis 6487) and listed by Helm als H. 874. Along with Helm, I too am dubious about the accuracy of this attribution (made by Fétis). In both content and style, the manuscript does not at all relate to the *Versuch*: in the scattered ordering of topics, the unsystematic discussion of voice leading, and finally, the rat-her simple-minded exercises prescribed for the student to practice (including simple transpositions, diminutions, and the three [„inversional"] voicings of triads in the right hand).

4/2 chord could be more fruitfully analyzed as a passing chord filling in an arpeggiation of the dominant E Seventh chord.) An intervallic perspective to the thorough bass does not make such distinctions, in that every signature is properly a „chord." This is why Bach feels obliged to delineate all signatures in their manifold contexts in his text, without assigning priority to any one in particular.

One might rightly wonder, because of this, how practical a text Bach's *Versuch* is for learning the thorough bass. And from the above examples, one suspects that it is not. Certainly that seems to have been the general perception in Bach's own day.[22]There are, after all,

---

[22]Many of Bach's own colleagues saw the need for more practical thorough-bass methods despite whatever high regard with which they held the work. The author of the very next *General-Bass* treatise published in Hamburg after the appearance of Part 2 of the Versuch claimed, significantly, to offer the „easiest" method to learn accompaniment without the aid of a teacher: Johann Heinrich Hesse, *Kurze, doch hinlängliche Anweisung zum General-Basse* (Hamburg, 1776). In this light, we should not also be surprised to learn that the most popular method of the thorough bass in Germany during the 18th century was not Bach's, but the little compendium of rules and guidelines written in 1732 by David Kellner, *Treulicher Unterricht im General-Baß* (Hamburg, 1732). Kellner's treatise was precisely geared for wide circulation; it was short, clear and affordable, and employed a variety of helpful mnemonic aids to simplify the learning of the thorough bass: the Rule of the Octave, Rameau's inversional theory, the musical circle, and modulation tables. Kellner's treatise went through nine different editions in the 18th century (the last appaering in 1796) and translations into Swedish, Dutch and Russian. So popular was the work that in the Preface to the second edition of 1737, Georg Philipp Telemann reported with astonishment that the entire first run of 2000 copies had been exhausted in just five years. To put this in perspective, Mitchel estimates Bach's *Versuch* probably had a yearly average sale of 30 to 40 copies between its publication and 1797 (Essay, p. 3). Mitchell tries to argue on the basis of this figure that Bach's *Versuch* was relatively speaking a commercial success. But his argument is unconvincing, especially given the questionable comparison he makes between the sales of the *Versuch* and a much more costly, multi-volumed edition of Goethe's works. When we place Bach's work next to a comparable text of the same genre, such as the keyboard treatises of Kellner, Löhlein, or Türk, its circulation is not at all so impressive. Finally, we might take note of a review of recent thorough-bass methods published in 1797 by the music pedagogue F. G. Drewis, who recommended above all the methods of Kirnberger and Sulzer, and for the theoretically minded, Marpurg – But there was no mention of Bach! (F. G. Drewis, *Freundschaftliche Briefe über die Theorie der Tonkunst und Composition* [Halle, 1797], pp. 73–74. The reference to Sulzer is to the articles on figured bass written by Kirnberger and his student, Johann Abraham Peter Schulz in Sulzer's *Allgemeine Theorie der schönen Künste* [1771–74].)

none of the lengthier exercises and models for the student to practice
that one normally finds in other manuals of the thorough bass.[23]
Indeed, with the exception of the Fantasy written out in the final
chapter, virtually none of Bach's examples exceeds two measures,
with the majority limited to two or three chords. Bach's many illustrations of signatures and their possible voicings, irregular resolutions,
use in modulations, etc. seem less for preparing students for the
kinds of harmonic progressions they may encounter while reading a
figured bass (unlikely except in many of Bach's own *Empfindsam*
experiments), as much as to show a student the *compositional
variety* for which these chords may serve. In other words, Bach seems
to have written as much a composition treatise as he did a thorough-
bass treatise.[24]

   Now the coupling of the thorough bass with composition was
hardly an idea conceived of by Bach. Since at least Friedrich Erhard
Niedt's manual of thorough bass, *Musicalische Handleitung* (published in several volumes between 1700 and 1722), there was an
important tradition in 18th-century German musical thought identifying the skill of the thorough bass with the art of composition. This

---

[23]The *Probestücke* published as an accompaniment to the *Versuch* do not fit the bill,
as they relate to Part 1 on performance skills, and not the figured bass. Otto Vrieslander has suggested, however, that Bach's multiple harmonizations of a chorale
excerpt (*Zwey Litaneyen aus dem Schleswig-Holsteinischen Gesangbuch*, H. 871)
might be seen as practical illustrations of his *Generalbaß-Lehre* (Otto Vrieslander,
Philipp Emanuel Bach [Munich, 1923], p. 130). Illustrations of harmonic invention
they may be, but these chorales hardly constitute practical exercises of thorough bass
for a student to work through.
[24]The refined – we might even say, manneristic – character of Bach's musical
examples has been remarked upon since Bach's own day. Georg Michael Telemann,
the grandson of the famous composer, while an ardent admirer and friend of Bach,
cautioned in the preface to his own thorough-bass manual of 1773 that the musical
examples in Bach's *Versuch* were much too sophisticated and refined to be of value
to beginning harpsichordists, an opinion seconded by Johann Christian Bertram
Kessel in his treatise of 1791. In our own century, the well-known harpsichordist
Ralph Kirkpatrick reassessed the *Versuch* as more a „finishing course" for the
accomplished continuo player (and heavily slanted at that to the practice and taste
of Bach himself) rather than a practical tutor of the figured bass: 'C. P. E. Bach's Versuch Reconsidered,' *Early Music* 4 (1976), pp. 388–89.

is made explicit in the titles of Johann Heinichen's treatise of 1728, *Der Generalbaß in der Composition*, or Marpurg's three-volume manual of thorough bass, *Handbuch bey dem Generalbass und der Composition* (Berlin, 1755–58), and perhaps most explicitly in Kirnberger's treatise, *Grundsätze des Generalbasses als erste Linien zur Composition* (Berlin, 1781). Thorough bass was seen as but a practical form of composition, since the performer must in essence learn how to realize – that is to compose *ex tempore* – appropriate harmonies, melodies, and textures above a given bass line, a bass line that is sometimes figured, but sometimes not.

While Bach was never explicit in connecting the thorough bass with compositional pedagogy, the second half of the *Versuch* could be interpreted as a primer of composition, as Bach covers many topics that one would expect to find in a more complete composition primer: the selection, voicing and connection of chords, requirements for embellishing melodic lines, imitation, cadences, modulation, and various species of non-chord tones: the organ point, appoggiaturas, passing tones, changing notes, etc. Again, the compositional implications of Bach's method were not lost upon contemporaneous observers. Johann Adolf Scheibe noted in 1773 that „whether or not Herr Bach wrote his book for composers, since it is properly about keyboard performance and accompaniment, it nonetheless contains a great quantity of tasteful and sound observations about a large number of harmonic progressions and the proper employment of consonance and dissonance, observations unequaled by any other treatise aimed specifically at the teaching of composition".[25]

The compositional implications of the thorough bass are perhaps made most explicit in the famous last chapter of the work on improvisation in the Free Fantasy. There Bach shows how the figured bass

---

[25]Johann Adolf Scheibe, *Ueber die Musikalische Composition* (Leipzig, 1773), p. 14: „Obschon Herr Bach sein Buch nicht eben für die Componisten geschrieben hat, weil es eigentlich vom Klavierspielen und vom Accompagnement mit dem Klavier handelt: so enthält es doch eine so große Menge geschmackvoller und gründlicher Betrachtungen über eine sehr große Anzahl harmonischer Sätze und über den regelmäßigen Gebrauch der Consonanzen und Dissonanzen, als man wohl in keinem Werke, das von der Satzkunst insonderheit handelt, antreffen wird."

can offer a modulatory skeleton of harmony that forms the basis for melodic and textural elaborations that the keyboardist may improvise. Composition, Bach implicitly shows us, is but the extended realization of some underlying figured-bass structure. (This was the element of Bach's pedagogy, incidentally, upon which Schenker and his followers in our own century have fastened with such enthusiasm).[26]

It is important for us to keep in mind, though, that this linking of thorough-bass and composition was by no means universally made, neither in Bach's own lifetime, nor in subsequent generations. For evidence, we need only look at the writings of Johann Mattheson, one of Bach's Hamburg predecessors. Mattheson – no friend of Rameau's – was a voracious critic of those who would equate thorough bass with the elevated art of composition. For Mattheson, realizing a thorough bass was a utilitarian labor (*Handsachen*) for church organists and members of continuo bands. It consisted of simply playing designated chords in some mechanical fashion – a clear legacy of when organists would accompany by reading tablature – and had nothing in common with the true art of composing music (*Setz-Kunst*), which for Mattheson, consisted above all

---

[26]While it is beyond the scope of this paper to pursue the question further, the equation of improvisation and composition that Bach only suggests (but which Schenker aggressively drew out) raises a host of aesthetic problems over the nature of improvisation and its relation to a written score (to say nothing of the genre of the Fantasy itself). It is questionable whether a truly spontaneous „Free Fantasy" ought be bound by the norms of harmonic coherence, sytax, and modulatory unity one might expect in a fully-composed work. Indeed, one might think that the qualities of unity and cohesion are perhaps the last one would look for in a Fantasy, at least when understood in the context of the more robust strains of German Empfindsam aesthetics. This is partly why Peter Schleuning has argued that improvisation in Bach's eyes was in fact governed by quite differing criteria than those governing his compositions. (See Peter Schleuning, *Die Freie Fantasie* [Göppingen, 1973], p. 95.) In any case, as John Rink has shown, Bach's approach to the teaching of the Fantasy was not necessarily representative in the 18th century, where many pedagogues such as Georg Simon Löhlein and Johann Gottfried Vierling tended to emphasize somewhat more the manipulation of thematic and melodic elements. See John Rink, 'Schenker and Improvisation,' *Journal of Music Theory* 37 (1993), p. 12.

in the writing of melody.[27] Many subsequent pedagogues agreed with Mattheson, including Georg Michael Telemann, who cautioned his readers – with explicit reference to Bach's *Versuch* – that „thorough bass does not deal with composition, but above all, simple accompaniment." It is true, as I noted earlier, that Telemann owes a huge debt to Bach in this treatise, and he acknowledges this debt more than once with cheer and gratitude. (Virtually all of his rules for the realization and resolution of figured-bass signatures are synthesized from the *Versuch*.) But Telemann never placed the compositional burden Bach did upon this skill. As with Mattheson, Telemann saw the realization of the figured bass to be a mechanical trade, one which had no more to do with the composition of music than did a brick-layer's job with the design of a building.[28]

There were of course many teachers who continued to link the thorough bass and composition. Indeed, this was the primary reason the thorough bass survived as a practice to any degree in the 19th century. It is interesting to note, however, that this issue was independent of one's theoretical allegiance. That is, one could accept the thorough bass as the equivalent to composition and reject Rameau's theory in favor of a traditional contrapuntal approach. (Those in this class include, besides Bach, Wiedeburg, Johann Christoph Kellner, and Bühler.) But one could just as well hold the former view and accept Rameau's theory of the fundamental bass (as in the case of Daube, Riepel, Schröter, and Kirnberger,

[27]See Mattheson's comments in his *Kleine General-Baß-Schule* (Hamburg, 1735), pp. 48–51. It is telling that in his own analysis of the chord just discussed – the chord of the second – Mattheson is content to show only one basic variety of resolution (downwards by step to the chord of the sixth). He notes there are at least six other resolutions possible ('Entbindungs-Wege'), but „such instruction belongs more properly to composition than to the thorough bass" (p. 190). Mattheson returned to discuss these additional resolutions in his lengthy book on composition found in *Der Vollkommene Capellmeister* (Hamburg, 1739), pp. 302–07. Characteristically, he describes these additional resolutions of the second – which actually are now ten in number! – in terms of strict two-part counterpoint, not the figured bass.
[28]Georg Michael Telemann, *Unterricht im Generalbaß-Spielen* (Hamburg, 1773), preface. For further evidence documenting the widespread separation accorded thorough-bass realization and compositional/improvisational pedagogy in the 18th century, see Fritz Oberdörffer's fine article, 'Neuere Generalbaßstudien,' *Acta Musicologica* 39 (1967), pp. 182–201.

as well as 19th-century pedagogues such as Sechter). Conversewise, one could reject the compositional implications of the thorough bass and teach it as a purely practical performance skill, and still either accept Rameau's theory (as did Kellner), or remain within the traditional intervallic paradigm. (Besides Mattheson and Georg Michael Telemann, we can probably include in this last category most of the manuals of French and Italian *Partimento exercises*.[29]) Simply put, one's view as to the relation of thorough bass to composition had nothing to do with how one analyzed chord signatures theoretically.

Once we realize the compositional agenda underlying Bach's treatise, we can better understand why it was he was so resistant to Rameau's theory. At the same time, though, we can better appreciate why it was that Bach's method enjoyed relatively little emulation in the later 18th and 19th centuries. In the generations following Bach, a harmonic perspective based upon Rameau's theory of the fundamental bass was inexorably taking hold in Western music theory, and this in turn was effecting both the teaching of the thorough bass and of composition. Türk had enough distance in 1791 to recognize clearly how the topics of chordal construction and succession that had hitherto been included within the discipline of the thorough bass had by now been largely subsummed within an independent pedagogy of harmony – the *Harmonielehre*.[30]

---

[29]The *Partimento* manuals taught the thorough bass through rote practice and memorization of partially-realized figured-bass exercises in increasing orders of difficulty. One would typically begin by learning a very few simple harmonic patterns (such as the 'Rule of the Octave') and then move successively through more complex and lengthy exercises. It was an entirely practical approach to keyboard improvisation, with few subtleties of accompaniment, melody, or form, and with no compositional or theoretical pretenses. The most important *Partimento* tutors were written by French and Italian authors in the late 18th and early 19th centuries, although a few German teachers reflected the spirit of the *Partimento* approach, such as Johann Mattheson's *Exemplarische Organisten-Probe im Artikel vom General-Baß* (Hamburg, 1719). For more on the Partimento school, see my article 'The Règle de l'Octave,' pp. 110–15.

[30]Türk, *Beleuchtung einer Recension des Buches Kurze Anweisung zum Generalbaßspielen*, p. 6.

373

One could lament this historical development, as did Schenker, who believed that the penetration of Rameau's theory into the hallowed practice of German musical thought portended nothing less than the planting of the „seeds of death".[31] But in taking such a myopic view, we would miss the real pedagogical exigencies that drove such a move in the first place. The thorough bass, we must keep in mind, is not a theory; it is a historically flexible and changing practice. But if it is to be codified and taught, this practice can – and indeed demands to be – filtered through some kind of theoretical apparatus. (And make no mistake about it – Bach's *Vesuch* is a theory of the thorough bass no less than Rameau's, even if its theoretical bias is nowhere explicitly articulated.)

The question, then, is not „who got it right: Rameau or Bach?" (Or even more pointedly, as Schenker would demand: „Rameau oder Beethoven? Erstarrung oder geistiges Leben in der Musik?"[32] The question is, rather, to which pedagogical purpose is a given thorough-bass treatise best suited?

It has not been my intention in this paper to cast any aspersions upon Bach's *Versuch*, or to raise suspicion as to the concealed agenda of its author. Its comprehensive musical illustrations and brilliant insights have deservedly stood the test of time. The treatise remains one of the richest troves of knowledge we possess of the musical practice of its author and his contemporaries. We should simply be careful, though, that in our enthusiasm and admiration for the work, we do not unreflecting accept Bach's treatise as the sole legitimate interpretation of this practice. In his rejection of Rameau's inversional theory as well as his equation of the thorough bass with *Setz-Kunst*, Bach assumed a particular view of the thorough bass that was not a common one among his contemporaries and immediate successors. This is by no means to be disparaged, though. Indeed, we might say that there is no more obvious evidence of its worth than precisely in the fact that so few theorists felt the need – or possessed the competence – to imitate it. The work may stand alone among 18th-century through-bass manuals, but in this particular case, that is a testament to the genius of its author, not his failings.

---

[31]Quoted in Harald Krebs, 'Schenker's Changing Views of Rameau,' *Theoria* 3 (1988), p. 59.
[32]Heinrich Schenker, 'Rameau oder Beethoven? Erstarrung oder geistiges Leben in der Musik?,' *Das Meisterwerk in der Musik*, vol. 3 (München, 1930), pp. 9–24.

TABLE 1

GERMAN THOROUGH-BASS MANUALS EMPLOYING RAMEAU'S
FUNDAMENTAL BASS (1762–1800)

*[Die Titelwiedergabe erfolgt nach: Écrits imprimés concernant la musique,
2 Bde., München/Duisburg 1971 (= RISM, B VI)]*

1765.	Georg Simon Löhlein, Clavier-Schule, oder kurze und gründliche Anweisung zur Melodie und Harmonie, Leipzig/Züllichau, 1765 (Later Editions: 1773, 1779, 1782, 1791).
1766.	Georg Friedrich Lingke, Die Sätze der musicalischen Haupt-Sätze in einer harten und weichen Tonart und wie man damit fortschreitet und ausweichet, Leipzig, 1766.
1767.	David Kellner, Treulicher Unterricht im General-Bass, 4. Auflage, Hamburg, 1767 (Later editions: 1773, 1782, 1787, 1796).
1767.	Georg Andreas Sorge, Anleitung zur Fantasie oder zu der schönen Kunst, das Clavier, wie auch andere Instrumente, aus dem Kopfe zu spielen, Lobenstein, 1767.
1767.	Johann Samuel Petri, Anleitung zur practischen Musik, vor neuangehende Sänger und Instrumentspieler, Lauban, 1767.
1767.	Christoph Sasse, „Unterricht vom Generalbass." - D-B: Mus. ms. theor. 770.
1768.	J. C. Schultze, „Drama Per Musica." - D-B: Mus. ms. autogr. theor.
1772.	Christoph Gottlieb Schröter, Deutliche Anweisung zum General-Bass, in beständiger Veränderung des uns angebohrnen harmonischen Dreyklanges, Halberstadt, 1772.
1773.	Johann Christian Carl Töpfer, Anfangsgründe zur Erlernung der Musik und insonderheit des Claviers, Breslau, 1773.
1778.	N. N. Böhmer, „Traktat von der musikalischen Compostion." - D-B: Mus. ms. theor. 115.
1778.	Georg Joseph Vogler, Kuhrpfälzische Tonschule, Mannheim, 1778.

1780.	Johann Michael Bach, Kurze und systematische Anleitung zum General-Bass und der Tonkunst überhaupt, Kassel, 1780.

1781. Johann Philipp Kirnberger, Grundsätze des Generalbasses als erste Linien zur Composition, Berlin, c. 1781.

1782. Johann Gottfried Buchholtz, Unterricht für diejenigen, welche die Musik und das Clavier erlernen wollen, sonderlich für die Aeltern, Hamburg, 1782.

1783. Johann Joseph Klein, Versuch eines Lehrbuchs der praktischen Musik in systematischer Ordnung entworfen, Gera, 1783.

1789. Johann Gottfried Vierling, Kurze Anleitung zum General-Bass, Kassel, 1789.

1789. Georg Friedrich Wolff, Kurzer aber deutlicher Unterricht im Klavierspielen, 3. Auflage, Halle, 1789.

1789. Christian Kalkbrenner, Theorie der Tonsetzkunst, Berlin, 1789.

1789. Johann Friedrich Christmann, Elementarbuch der Tonkunst zum Unterricht beim Klavier für Lehrende und Lernende mit praktischen Beispielen, Bd. 2, Speyer, 1782–1789.

1789. Johann Gottlieb Portmann, Leichtes Lehrbuch der Harmonie, Composition und des Generalbasses, Darmstadt, 1789.

1790. Johann Christian Bertram Kessel, Unterricht im Generalbasse zum Gebrauche für Lehrer und Lernende, Leipzig, 1790.

1791. Daniel Gottlob Türk, Kurze Anweisung zum Generalbaßspielen, Halle/Leipzig, 1791, (Later editions: 1800, 1816, 1822, 1824, and 1841).

1792. Justin Heinrich Knecht, Gemeinnützliches Elementarwerk der Harmonie und des Generalbasses, Augsburg, 1792.

1794. Johann Gottfried Vierling, Versuch einer Anleitung zum Präludiren für Ungeübtere, Leipzig, 1794.

1797. F. G. Drewis, Freundschaftliche Briefe über die Theorie der Tonkunst und Composition, Halle, 1797.

1798. Franz Xaver Rigler, Anleitung zum Gesange, und dem Klaviere, oder die Orgel zu spielen; nebst den ersten Gründen zur Kompositzion, Ofen, 1798.

376

1800. Johann Carl Angerstein, Theoretisch-practische Anweisung, Choral-gesänge nicht nur richtig, sondern auch schön spielen zu lernen, Stendal, 1800.
Also see mansucripts: D-B: Mus. ms. theor. 1165, 1225, and AmB. 678.

TABLE 2

GERMAN THOROUGH-BASS MANUALS EMPLOYING TRADITIONAL „INTERVALLIC" APPROACH (1762–1800)

1765. Gilbert Herr, „Kurtzgefasste Reguln des General-Basses." – D-B: Mus. ms. theor. 380.

1767. Michael Johann Friedrich Wiedeburg, Anderer Theil des sich selbst informirenden Clavier-Spielers oder deutlicher und gründlicher Unter-richt zur Selbst-Information im General-Bass, Bd. 2, Halle/Leipzig, 1767.

1767. Johann Christoph Kühnau, „Die Anfangslehren der Tonkunst." – D-B: Mus. ms. theor. 505.

1768. Georg Joachim Joseph Hahn, Der wohl unterwiesene General-Bass-Schü-ler, oder Gespräch zwischen einem Lehrmeister und Scholaren vom Gene-ral-Bass, 2. Auflage, Augsburg, 1768.

1771. Johann Friedrich Hering, „Regeln des Generalbasses." – D-B: Mus. ms. theor. 348.

1773. Georg Michael Telemann, Unterricht im Generalbass-Spielen, auf der Or-gel oder sonst einem Clavier-Instrumente, Hamburg, 1773.

1774. Henrich Laag, Anfangsgründe zum Clavierspielen und Generalbass, Osna-brück, 1774.

1776. Johann Heinrich Hesse, Kurze, doch hinlängliche Anweisung zum Gene-ral-Basse, wie man denselben aufs allerleichteste, auch ohne Lehrmeister, erlernen kann. Hamburg, 1776.

1783. Johann Christoph Kellner, Grundriss des Generalbasses, eine theoretisch-praktische Anleitung für die ersten Anfänger entworfen, Kassel, 1783.

1791. Johann Georg Albrechtsberger, Kurzgefasste Methode den Generalbass zu erlernen. Wien, c. 1791. (Authorship questionable)

1793. Franz Bühler (Bihler), Partitur-Regeln in einem kurzen Auszuge für Anfän-ger, Donauwörth, 1793.

[18]

MODULATION IN
C. P. E. BACH'S *VERSUCH*

WILLIAM J. MITCHELL

In his *Versuch*,[1] C. P. E. Bach uses two complementary terms, *die Modulation* and *die Ausweichung* in a differentiated manner. In order to describe the differences accurately, it will be well to start with a review of the senses in which one of the terms, modulation, has been applied to music over a fairly inclusive span of time. This will be done without any desire to conduct a philological or semantic exercise, but simply to remind the reader of periodic shifts in the meaning of the word.

Probably all contemporary students of the theory of music learn the meaning of modulation early in life. Depending on the views of their instructors or textbooks they may particularize its sense, distinguishing or not between transient and enduring modulation, employing such terms as applied dominant or secondary dominant, classifying keys as closely, intermediately, or remotely related, or refining the broad structural implications of the technique. But in the end they know, as expressed by Willi Apel,[2] that modulation is solely, 'the change of key within a composition'. In brief, the term has acquired a single definition which all but obliterates its generic sense. In fact, it had become so sharply delimited by the beginning of the twentieth century that Max Reger,[3] in his widely used study of modulation, did not bother to define it. It was in the nineteenth century that the reduction in meaning became normal.

It was quite different in the seventeenth and earlier centuries. The one thing that modulation did not mean in the overwhelming number of cases was 'change of key' or mode. Rather, it referred in the main to proper musical shape, conduct, or context. The best that Thomas Morley[4] could offer was, 'going out of key' and, 'the bass is brought in out of

STUDIES IN EIGHTEENTH-CENTURY MUSIC

key'. About seventy years later, in 1673, Matthew Locke[5] wrote: 'I have annexed an example or two by way of Transition, or passing from one key to another.' Somewhat earlier, Christoph Bernhard[6] had written: 'One should not repeat *einerley Modulation*, although fugues and imitations retain their value', using modulation in the sense of figure or succession. It seems reasonably clear that 'modulation' had not come into more than isolated use to denote 'change of key' or mode.

During the eighteenth century the term began to include change of key among its meanings. It was still unavailable in Germany when Friderich Erhard Niedt[7] in 1700 introduced the subject as: '*Wie man manierlich aus einem Thon in den andern fallen sol.*' (How to move properly out of one key into another.) However, in France at about the same time, modulation had come into use in a new as well as the older sense. Of the older sense, going back to modal theory, Sebastien de Brossard[8] wrote: 'To modulate or modulation has been nothing more than to cause a melody to move between these two extremes [formed by the octave] in such a manner as to pass more frequently through the *essential sounds* than through the others and this always *diatonically.*' Elsewhere,[9] however, he wrote: 'To modulate is also to leave the mode at times, but in order to re-enter it properly and naturally.'

Modulation, now defined with two meanings, appears with increasing frequency throughout the remainder of the eighteenth century. Perhaps the case is most extensively treated by Jean Jacques Rousseau[10] who writes at the beginning of his entry on modulation: 'This is properly the method of establishing and treating the mode; but this word, at present, is more generally taken for the art of conducting the harmony and the air successively in several modes, by a method agreeable to the ear, and comfortable to rules.' Five pages are given over to an explanation of the newer meaning.

An historian's critical approach to the technique, now expressly described as modulation, and his summary description of its operating principles can be found when Charles Burney[11] turns his attention to the Fitzwilliam Virginal Book. He writes: 'In the . . . tune, called Dr Bull's Jewel . . . the modulation from C natural to B flat, and from B flat to C, is sudden and violent in the first part. . . . And in the last strain . . . the modulating instantly into F, is such a violation of all present rules, as seems rude and barbarous.' Indeed, Bull seems to have had a bad taste in modulation. He then cites 'an Allemand by old Robert Johnson as a proof how much secular modulation was governed by ecclesiastical, and

MODULATION IN C. P. E. BACH'S *VERSUCH*

how undetermined the keys were, at this time, by any rules in present use. This short air begins in D minor; but in the first bar, we have the chord of C natural, as fifth of the key of F; then at the third bar, the author returns, in no disagreeable manner, to D minor, ending in the church style, with a sharp third.'

In uneasy summary, then: During the seventeenth century and earlier, modulation, for the musician, meant not 'change of key' but rather, among many other things, 'affirming or sustaining the key' or mode; in the nineteenth and twentieth centuries it has meant essentially 'change of key' and few other things, certainly not 'affirming or sustaining the key'; but in the eighteenth century it meant 'change of key' *and* other things, among which was 'affirming or sustaining the key'.

The modern theorist, working with eighteenth-century materials, encounters disturbing challenges when he comes face to face with the term. He must be prepared to forsake the tight later meaning, yet to bring it into play when it seems called for. He must be prepared also to search for an appropriate different word or expression when 'change of key' is not meant.

In the case of Emanuel Bach's *Versuch*, the modern reader will receive a degree of welcome assistance from the author, for as noted earlier, Bach uses *die Modulation* and *die Ausweichung* in perceptibly differentiated senses. When discussing the technical aspects of 'key change',[12] *die Modulation* is not once used. Rather he relies on *die Ausweichung*, a term in general use which can be taken to mean yielding or shunting, and its verb form, *ausweichen*, along with less formal expressions, such as: '*in andere Tonarten versteigen*'; '*die Haupttonart verlassen . . . wieder ergreifen*'; '*in entlegenere Tonarten gehen*'; or '*die Tonarten berühren*'. Yet in the remainder of the *Versuch*, *die Modulation* is employed quite frequently, and *die Ausweichung* only rarely.

This separation in use suggests a distinction in meaning: *Die Ausweichung* and its related forms stand exclusively for 'change of key' in its clinical sense; *die Modulation* and its related forms stand for context, shape, pattern, conduct, all in the earlier sense of the term. Certain difficulties arise, however, when 'modulation' is applied to passages which, in fact, include a key change in the narrowest sense. Nevertheless in the bulk of cases it clearly retains its older generalized meaning.

Insight into Emanuel Bach's differentiated uses of the terms can be gained by comparing two of his passages with parallel passages in Türk's *Klavierschule*,[13] a book modelled in large part on the *Versuch*. Bach writes:

STUDIES IN EIGHTEENTH-CENTURY MUSIC

'A fantasia is said to be free when it. . . changes keys more (*in mehrere Tonarten ausweichet*) than is customary in other pieces.'[14] *Ausweichet* means 'modulates' in the modern sense. Türk in 1789, who used *die Modulation* interchangeably with *die Ausweichung*, but prefers *die Modulation* in this case writes: 'A Fantasia is called free when the composer . . . luxuriates with respect to modulation' ('*In Ansehung der Modulation ausschweift*').[15] Clearly, Bach's and Türk's terms are synonymous and refer to key changes. In another case, however, in which Türk lifts almost bodily from Bach, there is an opposite kind of change. Bach, writing about the accessory, but unnotated accidentals to be used in the performance of trills and their suffixes, says: 'The performer must judge at times from the context' ('*so muss man sie . . . bald aus . . . der Modulation beurtheilen*').[16] Because Bach's illustration is not clearly a change of key, Türk, whose illustrations are also non-modulatory, after borrowing all other considerations literally, changes Bach's *Modulation* clause to: 'A practised player will surely judge . . . also for harmonic reasons' ('. . . *auch wohl aus harmonischen Gründen beurtheilen*').[17] In brief: For Bach, *die Modulation* and *die Ausweichung* had different meanings; for Türk they seem to have been close to identical when they referred to key changes. In the years that separated 1753, 1762 from 1789 modulation had begun to shed its generalized sense and to assume its more modern exclusive one. The double meaning lingered, however, for Heinrich Christoph Koch[18] still wrote in 1802: Modulation is 'the proper and varied conduct of notes generally . . . [and] the leading of notes from the chief tonality into another and back'. However, it was not long before the term assumed its modern meaning; and in German writings, *die Ausweichung* tended to acquire the sense of the English, 'transient modulation'. C. P. E. Bach was far removed from such a distinction.

Before turning specifically to Bach's prescriptions for a change of key, let us examine a few of the many cases to which he applies the various verbal forms of *die Modulation*.

In discussing the recitative, he comments[19] that singers sometimes substitute melodic forms such as those of Example 1a for a written form like that of 1b. The reasons, he writes, may be greater convenience of range

MODULATION IN C. P. E. BACH'S *VERSUCH*

or forgetfulness, the latter, 'because the singer, in memorizing, easily interchanges the ever similar recitative patterns (*Recitativmodulationen*), being more mindful of the underlying harmonies than the written notes'. The sense of modulation, in this case is similar to that intended by Christoph Bernhard, cited earlier.

In another instance, Emanuel Bach, discussing the chord of the seventh, points to a passage in which a three part accompaniment is recommended, 'because the course of the principal part' ('*die Modulation der Haupt-stimme*') 'does not readily suffer a fourth part'.[20] Modulation as 'course' or 'nature' seems clearly indicated here, for if 'change of key' were intended, it would inevitably include the activity of all parts. Basically, the embellished chromatic changing notes are the cause of the difficulty.

Occasionally, the term is applied to a passage in which, from a particularized point of view, a 'change of key' occurs. In discussing the ascending trill, Emanuel Bach suggests that it can be employed with good effect 'when the modulation changes' ('*wenn die Modulation sich verändert*').[21] The passage contains one of the critical factors that Bach

includes under his description of the techniques of key change. Yet, when the various employments of the term are considered *in toto*, it becomes apparent that in the *Versuch*, *die Modulation* relates back to its earlier generalized sense, springing from modal theory. Hence, it is not surprising that it should be applied at times to musical passages that suggest its later exclusive sense.

In his treatment of the Free Fantasia,[22] Bach, using only *ausweichen* along with a few related expressions, turns to a detailed study of the techniques of key change. A new key, writes Bach, should be sought through its major seventh (*semitonium modi*) and a proper accompaniment.[23] Although this cannot be regarded as an epoch-making statement,

STUDIES IN EIGHTEENTH-CENTURY MUSIC

the material that precedes and follows it sheds interesting light on the application of the precept.

Earlier[24] he suggests that a dependable procedure for those of limited ability is to preludize on the ascending and descending scale of a key, employing among other things, 'various thorough bass signatures'. In his musical illustrations, he introduces traditional settings for this 'rule of the octave', but includes others that are somewhat more luxuriant, as in Example 4.

4

Observe the presence of several leading notes. However, Emanuel Bach has made it clear that the scale of a single key is the guide. It would seem that he makes a distinction between inclusive structure and passing, often chromatic detail. The distinction is underlined when his 'various signatures' are compared with the stern diatonic procedures advocated by Rousseau when he prescribes the act of modulation in the older sense. He writes: 'To modulate well in the same tone . . . never . . . alter any of the sounds of the mode; for we cannot, without quitting it, make a diesis [a sharp] or a B flat [a flat] be heard, which does not belong to it, or remove any one that does belong to it.'[25] The difference is striking and further emphasized when Emanuel Bach states that, 'a tonic organpoint is convenient for establishing the tonality at the beginning and end'.[26] The illustrations, although based on widespread practice, might well have been disapproved by the French savant.

5

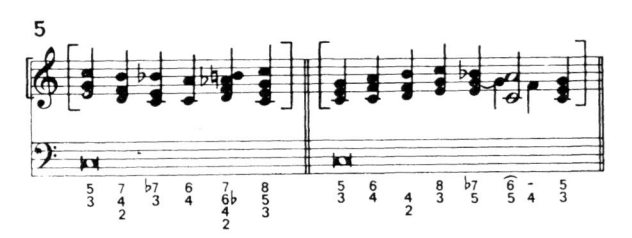

An *Ausweichung* consists not merely of a seeking out of leading tones, but rather of a broad march toward the new key along various chromatic

MODULATION IN C. P. E. BACH'S *VERSUCH*

by-paths. C. P. E. Bach, always strong for a controlled play of fancy in changing keys, writes: 'It is one of the beauties of improvisation when one feigns modulation to another key' ('*wenn man sich stellet . . . in eine andere Tonart auszuweichen*') 'through a formal cadence, and then moves off in another direction. This and other rational deceptions make a Fantasia attractive'.[27] Elsewhere, he speaks of 'a skilful attaining' of the leading note, as well as the need to approach keys 'gradually'. Also, he describes his illustrations as being 'slightly circuitous' ways of changing keys.

All of this suggests strongly that for Emanuel Bach an *Ausweichung* is to be thought of as a long or middle range goal of musical activity, rather than an immediate or transient matter. It suggests further, that *die Modulation* is employed by him to denote many things, including those brief skirmishes with keys while en route to a broadly conceived goal.

The inclusive meaning of an *Ausweichung* is indicated, further, by his statement that when 'one wishes not merely superficially to touch upon (*obenhin berühren*) remoter keys, but formally to reach them (*darein förmlich ausweichen*), it is insufficient simply to reach for the leading tone in the belief that once it is found, the goal will have been attained. . . . The ear must be prepared for the new key by means of intermediate harmonic progressions.'[28]

An examination of one of his illustrations of key change will, perhaps, help to clarify the distinction between *moduliren* and *ausweichen*. He suggests a 'few special ways to come gradually to closely related keys'.[29] One of these is a motion from the tonic to the dominant key. He seems to start off in the wrong direction, striking an F chord, preceded by its

6

applied dominant, threatening to move to a D minor chord, approaching an A minor chord and then one on D, but major, through their respective leading notes, only to settle on the dominant. The *Ausweichung* is the overall change from C to G; the *Modulation* is the actual transition, involving several leading tones. The seeming discursiveness of the route followed is simply a particular fleshing out or prolongation of a firm ground plan. The nature of the plan can be neatly illuminated by superposing

STUDIES IN EIGHTEENTH-CENTURY MUSIC

over Bach's *Ausweichung* an avowedly bare-boned modulation to the dominant written by Max Reger.[30] Reger, in his terms, presents *eine Modulation*; Bach, in paraphrase of his terms, presents *eine modulirende Ausweichung*.

In conclusion and summary, let us turn to an excerpt from one of C. P. E. Bach's compositions.[31] The nineteen bars, coming near the end of the piece, will be presented only in a terse thorough bass outline (Example 8a), since the music is readily available. Suffice it to say that the refrain under examination, having been stated several times earlier in the Rondo, is now repeated in a venturesome rhapsodic guise, embodying much that is chromatic. The first seven chords of Example 8a. illustrate Emanuel Bach's fondness for the diminished seventh chord 'as a means of reaching the most distant keys more quickly and with agreeable suddenness'.[32] Two *Ausweichungen* are thereby carried out, from C minor to F sharp minor, and to E flat minor. The chords from the seventh to the thirteenth bring us back 'gradually' to C minor by means of chromatic *Modulation*, in Bach's usage. The next goal in the plan of *Ausweichungen* is D flat major, reached, again by chromatic *Modulation*, at the nineteenth chord and extended through the twenty-first following which C minor is regained and affirmed by means of its subdominant and dominant chords.

In distinguishing between the meaning of modulation, as a reference to proper, but fanciful musical conduct, and *Ausweichung*, as a reference to inclusive key changing techniques, C. P. E. Bach was pointing the way toward levels of musical meaning. His differentiated usage is the

MODULATION IN C. P. E. BACH'S *VERSUCH*

rough equivalent of the more modern, immediate and intermediate levels of structure,[33] corresponding to Heinrich Schenker's *Vordergrund* and *Mittelgrund*. To facilitate the relating of these to a remote level, Schenker's *Hintergrund*, an inclusive linear-structural analysis of the passage has been subposed in Example 8b.

NOTES

1 Carl Philipp Emanuel Bach, *Versuch über die wahre Art das Clavier zu spielen* (Part 1, 1753, Part 2, 1762, Berlin). All references will be to these editions. An English translation is available under the title, *Essay on the True Art of Playing Keyboard Instruments*, tr. and ed. Wm. J. Mitchell (New York, 1949).

2 Willi Apel, *Harvard Dictionary of Music* (Cambridge, Mass., 1955), entry on Modulation.

3 Max Reger, *Beiträge zur Modulationslehre* (Leipzig, 1903). It had attained its 24th printing by 1952, and has been translated into French and English.

4 Thomas Morley, *A Plaine and Easie Introduction to Practical Musicke* (London, 1597). A modern edition, ed. R. Alec Harman (New York, n.d.) is available. Morley's statements appear on pp. 249 and 261.

5 Matthew Locke, *Melothesia* . . . (London, 1673), as quoted by F. T. Arnold, *The Art of Accompaniment* . . . (New York, 1965), p. 157.

6 Christoph Bernhard, *Tractatus compositionis augmentatus* (1650–1660?), Ch. 2, Par. 8 in J. M. Mueller-Blattau, *Die Kompositionslehre Heinrich Schützens* . . . (Leipzig, 1926).

7 Friderich Erhard Niedt, *Musicalische Handleitung* (Hamburg, 1700), as quoted by Arnold, p. 235.

8 Sebastien de Brossard, *Dictionaire de Musique* (Mont-Parnasse, 1703), entry under Modo.

9 *Ibid.*, entry under *Modulatione*.

10 Jean Jacques Rousseau, *Dictionnaire de musique* (Geneva, 1767). The translation is from the English version by William Waring (London, 1770).

STUDIES IN EIGHTEENTH-CENTURY MUSIC

11 Charles Burney, *A General History of Music* (1776–89), New edition, ed. Frank Mercer (New York, 1957), vol. 2, pp. 98–9.

12 *Versuch*, Pt. 2, Ch. 41, Pars. 6–10.

13 Daniel Gottlob Türk, *Klavierschule* (Leipzig and Halle, 1789). Facsimile edition, ed. Erwin R. Jacobi (Kassel, 1962).

14 *Versuch*, Pt. 2, p. 325, Par. 1.

15 *Klavierschule*, p. 395, Par. 35.

16 *Versuch*, Pt. 1, p. 67, Par. 19.

17 *Klavierschule*, p. 264, Par. 42.

18 Heinrich Christoph Koch, *Musikalisches Lexikon* (Frankfurt am Main, 1802), entry under *Modulation*.

19 *Versuch*, Pt. 2, pp. 317–18, Par. 7.

20 *Versuch*, Pt. 2, p. 118, Par. 13.

21 *Versuch*, Pt. 1, pp. 70–1, Par. 25.

22 *Versuch*, Pt. 2, Ch. 41, pp. 325–41.

23 *Versuch*, Pt. 2, p. 330, Par. 8.

24 *Versuch*, Pt. 2, pp. 327–30, Par. 7.

25 Rousseau, *Dictionnaire . . .*, entry under Modulation, tr. Wm. Waring.

26 *Versuch*, Pt. 2, pp. 327–30, Par. 7.

27 *Versuch*, Pt. 2, p. 330, Par. 8.

28 *Versuch*, Pt. 2, p. 333, Par. 10.

29 *Versuch*, Pt. 2, pp. 331–2, Par. 9.

30 *Beyträge . . .*, p. 6, item 1.

31 The Rondo in C minor, bars 76–94, from the Fifth Collection of *Clavier-Sonaten und Fantasien . . . für Kenner und Liebhaber* (Leipzig, 1785. It also appears in *Four Hundred Years of European Keyboard Music*, ed. Walter Georgii (Köln, 1959)).

32 *Versuch*, Pt. 2, p. 335, Par. 11.

33 *Cf. The Music Forum*, ed. Wm. J. Mitchell and Felix Salzer (New York, 1967), vol. 1 Glossary, pp. 260–8.

[19]

The New Modulation of the 1770s: C. P. E. Bach in Theory, Criticism, and Practice*

By RICHARD KRAMER

M ODULATION, whether expressed in the explosive confrontation between alien tonal fields or in the barely perceptible negotiation between compatible ones, is the abstraction from which the dramaturgy of the Classical style draws its sustenance and vigor. It is not so much that the grammar of modulation in the 1740s was discernibly different from what it would be in the 1780s—although indeed there are differences—but rather that by the 1780s the very meaning of a piece depended so heavily upon the nature of the connectedness and nonconnectedness of its tonal focii, and that event and substance had now so much to do with these kinds of relationships and their repercussions within the piece, that the old definitions of modulation were no longer adequate.

While the decade of the 1770s has been construed as a watershed in the development of the Viennese Classical style, little has been written about the perceptible deepening of style in northern Germany during that decade. The central figure is Carl Philipp Emanuel Bach. Two aspects of his work are investigated here: the one has to do with his music, the other with a somewhat puzzling paragraph added to the final chapter of his *Versuch über die wahre Art das Clavier zu spielen*, Part 2, in the revised edition that was published in Leipzig by Engelhardt Schwickert in 1797, nine years after Bach's death. Indeed, it is the relationship of these aspects of Bach's work that is in question, for the paragraph intimates the theoretical bases of certain modulatory strategies in the music itself.

I

"To keep the costs from running too high, I have had to suppress many examples and useful remarks on the fantasia," Bach wrote in 1762, in the Preface to the original edition of the *Versuch*, Part 2. When

* An earlier version of this paper was read at the annual meeting of the American Musicological Society, Denver, 1980.

that Preface was reprinted in the new edition, Schwickert commented, in a footnote: "The author submitted these additions shortly
before his death. They have been incorporated in this second edition."

Of the five emendations that distinguish Schwickert's edition from
the original, four constitute brief amplifications to technical problems,
and in this they are like the thirty-five supplementary entries included
in Schwickert's revised edition of Part 1, published in 1787. But the
fifth emendation—the only one to affect the final chapter—is different
in kind. It seeks to explore the concept *Modulation*, and in so doing
alters the message of the entire chapter. The relevant portion of the
new paragraph follows here:

> Through good instruction and good example, one can come to learn to
> modulate with originality, pleasingly and surprisingly, in the usual way,
> in a somewhat more remote fashion, and in a wholly distant manner.
> Many examples of these kinds of modulations appear in my keyboard
> sonatas, rondos, and fantasias; in my *Heilig*; and, in particular, in a duet
> from my *Auferstehung Jesu*, in which the listener is surprised in the most
> natural way, without enharmonic artifice. In this duet, which is in D
> minor, there is a modulation through B-flat minor into A minor
> beginning at the sixth change of harmony. To give special expression to
> such altogether usual modulations, one enlists the aid of such means as
> *fermate*, rests, the alternation of high and low register, of loud and soft, of
> various tempos and note values, and a diversity of voices and instru-
> ments, among other things. And if one judiciously applies enharmonic
> artifice, what a wealth of continually new, pleasing, and striking
> modulations offers itself. But as we have often said, these spices must not
> be used too often. The examples under (a) are from one of my rondos,
> and those under (b) are taken from my *Heilig*. They all comprise entirely

> usual modulations. When I played this rondo, I was asked, with regard
> to the third example, "Who but yourself would dare go directly from C
> major to E major?" I replied, "Anyone can and will assuredly do it who
> knows that E is the dominant of A, and that A minor is very closely
> related to C major."
> In my *Heilig*, the arietta closes in G major, and the *Heilig* begins in E
> major. Without the arietta, this beginning [in E major] would have no
> significance. The modulation in the first example under (b) appears three
> times with great effect, although this modulation is anything but new.
> . . .[1]

[1] "Hingegen kann man durch eine gute Anleitung und durch gute Muster dahin
kommen, dass man auf die gewöhnliche Art, auf eine etwas entfernte Weise, und auf

Students of Bach's *Versuch* will recall that the final chapter, following from remarks toward a definition of *free fantasia* and *improvisation*, offers a series of bass motions in which tones foreign to the tonic are gradually introduced; it addresses the special capabilities of the diminished-seventh chord as an implement of modulation and advises upon the varieties of figural diminution requisite to enlightened improvisation. The concluding paragraph is about the elaboration of a written-out improvisation from a figured bass, together with Bach's explication how the plan and the realization are related.[2]

Unlike the original text, the newly interpolated paragraph has been slighted in recent scholarship. William Mitchell excluded it from

---

eine ganz entlegene Art neu, angenehm und überraschend modulieren lernt. Von solchen Arten kommen viele Proben in meinen Clavier Sonaten, Rondos, Fantasien, in meinem Heilig und besonders auch in einem Duett aus meiner Auferstehung Jesu vor, wo auf die natürlichste Art, ohne enharmonische Künste der Zuhörer überraschet wird. Im gedachten Duett aus dem d moll wird, bey der 6ten Veränderung der Grundstimme, durch b moll ins a moll modulirt. Solchen ganz gewöhnlichen Modulationen einen besondern Ausdruck zu geben, nimmt man gewisse Mittel zur Hülfe; z. E. Ruhezeichen, Pausen, abwechselnde hohe und tiefe Lagen, Stärke, Schwäche, verschiedenes Tempo und Geltung der Noten, Verschiedenheit der Stimmen und Instrumente, und a. m. Nimmt man hierzu den vernünftigen Gebrauch der enharmonischen Künste: welcher Reichthum eröfnet sich da, immer neu und immer angenehm frappant zu moduliren! Nur muss man diese Gewürze nicht zu oft brauchen, wie wir schon gesagt haben.

"Die Exempel unter (a) sind aus einem meiner Rondos, und die unter (b) aus meinem Heilig genommen. Sie enthalten alle ganz gewöhnliche Modulationen. Bey Gelegenheit des dritten Exempels unter (a) wurde ich, indem ich dies Rondo spielte, gefragt: wer wird sich ausser ihnen wagen, aus dem c dur gleich unmittelbar ins e dur zu gehen? Ich antwortete: derjenige wird und kann es sicher thun, wer da weiss, dass e von a die Dominante, und a moll mit c dur sehr nahe verwand ist. Bey meinem Heilig schliesst die Ariette im g dur und das Heilig tritt mit e dur ein. Ohne der Ariette würde dieser Eintritt unbedeutend seyn. Die Modulation des ersten Exempels (b) kommt 3mal mit grosser Würkung vor, ohngeacht diese Modulation nichts weniger als neu ist. Man findet sie fast alle Augenblicke. Das erhabene der Anbetung Gottes erforderte einen besondern Eindruck."

For the complete text, see Carl Philipp Emanuel Bach, *Versuch über die wahre Art, das Clavier zu spielen, erster und zweiter Teil, Faksimile-Nachdruck der 1. Auflage, Berlin 1753 und 1762*, ed. Lothar Hoffmann-Erbrecht (Leipzig, 1969), Anhang, pp. 15–16, where two errors in Schwickert's printing of the music examples are repeated: the omission of the double bar between the second and third modulations in Example *a*; and the substitution of a *6* for the flat above the *F* in the third modulation in Example *b*.

[2] Luminous paradoxes reside in the lesson, for Bach's "plan" is as much analytical abstraction as compositional determinant. The improvisation is not only written out but planned. The plan and the realization, conceived simultaneously, conceal a tension between the work and its theoretical abstraction that may be said to invigorate all Classical art.

his English translation of the *Versuch*.[3] And Heinrich Schenker, in his penetrating gloss on the last chapter, omitted it without comment, even while his numbering of Bach's paragraphs accords with the revised text.[4] The omission can be defended, for the new paragraph, made to follow directly upon the discussion of diminished-seventh chords, sits uncomfortably in this context. Bach's lean text, prescriptive and didactic, gives way here to a softer reflection upon aspects of modulation that, on the face of it, have not much to do with the fundamentals of improvisation.

As a document in itself, the new paragraph shrouds its wisdom in text-critical riddles. We want, first of all, to know when it was written; Bach's remarks in the Preface of 1762 and Schwickert's note in 1797 need to be reconciled. Bach refers to passages from three of his own works; these must be identified with greater accuracy and their dates established. And what, precisely, does Bach mean by *Modulation* and *modulieren*?

II

The answer to this last question ought to come easily, but it will not. In a brief essay called "Modulation in C. P. E. Bach's *Versuch*," William Mitchell sought to clarify the differences in meaning between "die Modulation" and "die Ausweichung" according to their usage in the original texts of 1753 and 1762. Mitchell was led to conclude that "for Emanuel Bach an *Ausweichung* is to be thought of as a long or middle range goal of musical activity, rather than an immediate or transient matter. . . . *Die Modulation* is employed by him to denote many things, including those brief skirmishes with keys while en route to a broadly conceived goal."[5] There is surely some truth in this. But the issue is complicated by the very different linguistic conditioning of the two terms. Prior to the 1770s, *die Modulation* seems to signify the quality of change between two or more pitches or pitch collections in any succession, whether or not the succession is

[3] Carl Philipp Emanuel Bach, *Essay on the True Art of Playing Keyboard Instruments*, trans. and ed. William J. Mitchell (New York, 1949). Curiously, a remark in Mitchell's preface (p. viii) alleges: "All of Bach's alterations, additions, and footnotes have been incorporated into the main text."
[4] Heinrich Schenker, "Die Kunst der Improvisation," *Das Meisterwerk in der Musik*, I (Munich, 1925), 9–40.
[5] *Studies in Eighteenth-Century Music: A Tribute to Karl Geiringer on His Seventieth Birthday*, ed. H. C. Robbins Landon in collaboration with Roger E. Chapman (New York, 1970), p. 339.

comprised in a shift between two keys. *Ausweichung*, the substantive, denotes less a quality of relationship than a way of going.

That a definition of *Modulation* needed revision by the early 1770s speaks out from the article "Modulation" by Kirnberger and Schulz in Sulzer's *Allgemeine Theorie der schönen Künste*. Two meanings are distinguished:

> [1] Originally, [*Modulation*] meant the way of handling a given key through its melody and harmony, or the type of chord succession from beginning to end or in a complete *Ausweichung* to another key. [2] Generally, however, one means by it the art of leading melody and harmony from the tonic through other keys by means of appropriate *Ausweichungen*, and from there back again to the first, or principal, key, in which the piece must always close.[6]

The Sulzer article bears witness that earlier nuances of distinction between the two terms had begun to erode, for the two terms had become very nearly synonymous. But if we are to know what Bach intends by *die Modulation*, we must read him without precondition in this regard. The new paragraph means not so much to define modulation as to exemplify it.

III

The passages to which Bach refers, identified here for the first time, are shown in Examples 1, 2, and 3. Beyond their identity, one wants to know something about their position in Bach's work and about their critical reception as well. In these respects, their histories are elaborate.

The *Modulation* from the *Auferstehung* duet had, in fact, been publicized long before 1797. A detailed and generous review of the work, published in the *Hamburgische unparteiische Correspondent* (*HCorr*) in 1778 has this to say about the duet:

---

[6] "[1] Ursprünglich bedeutet es die Art eine angenommene Tonart im Gesang und der Harmonie zu behandeln, oder die Art der Folge der Accorde vom Anfange bis zum Schluss, oder zur völligen Ausweichung in einem andern Ton. [2] Gemeiniglich aber bezeichnet man dadurch die Kunst, den Gesang und die Harmonie aus dem Hauptton durch andre Tonarten vermittelst schiklicher Ausweichungen durchzuführen, und von denselben wieder in den ersten, oder Hauptton, darin man immer das Tonstük schliesst, einzulenken." Johann Georg Sulzer, *Allgemeine Theorie der schönen Künste*, 3rd ed., III (Frankfurt, 1798), 443. The first edition, in two volumes, was published in Leipzig in 1771–74.

Example 1
Auferstehung und Himmelfahrt Jesu, W. 240, from the duet "Vater deiner schwachen
Kinder," mm. 8-22

THE NEW MODULATION OF THE 1770S

557

Ex. 1, cont.

Ex. 1, cont.

Example 2

Rondo in C from *Clavier-Sonaten nebst einigen Rondos fürs Forte-Pinao für Kenner und Liebhaber . . . Zweite Sammlung*, W. 56; mm. 37–47, 68–78, and 105–12

Example 3
Heilig mit zwey Chören und einer Arlette zur Einleitung, W. 217, mm. 47–83. (Trumpets, oboes and tympani are omitted.)

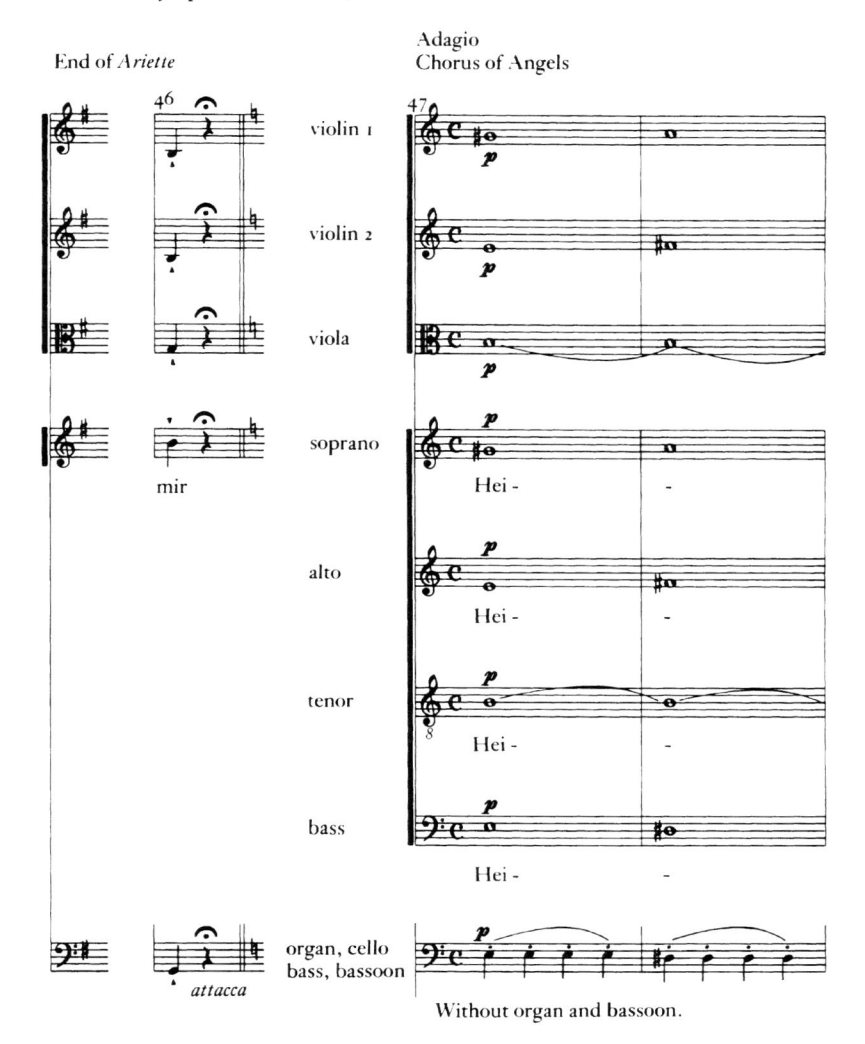

Ex. 3, cont.

Chorus of People

Hei - lig,

Hei - lig,

Hei - lig,

Hei - lig,

Ex. 3, cont.

Chorus of Angels

Without organ and bassoon.

Chorus of People

With organ and bassoon.

Ex. 3, cont.

Ex. 3, cont.

Both Choruses

The duet *Vater deiner schwachen Kinder* is sung by soprano and tenor. It is in D minor. [It contains] a striking *Modulation* in the ritornello from D minor through B-flat minor to A minor in a sequence of two to three measures. As unusual as this is, the ear is yet not in the least offended. But one must understand such processes as *Bach* understands them, if one does not want to blunder.[7]

Here the similarity of this review to Bach's description of the passage is striking and all the more significant in that it is the single instance, in an unusually elaborate review, in which the focus is upon the mechanics of a specific passage. The implications of such a similarity will justify further inquiry.

The modulatory action of Bach's *Heilig* acquired an even wider critical acclaim in the 1770s. The most important early account is again to be found in the columns of the *HCorr*. The study is by Georg Benda, in the form of an open letter dated October 1778. Here is a good portion of it:

I do not wish to tell you anything about Bach's style. You know it and know what this great man, through his genius and fundamental knowledge of harmony, is in a position to accomplish. But this music includes a *Heilig* in whose composition Bach has outdone himself. It is a double chorus, of which the first part is sung by the Angels and the second part by the People. . . . The passage begins in E major—following upon a short introduction in G major [the "Ariette zur Einleitung"]—and ends in C-sharp major, with the simple accompaniment of the stringed instruments. The answer of the People ensues in D major with the greatest force and with the accompaniment of trumpets and tympani. But the Angels repeat *Heilig* as softly as at first. The passage begins in B major and ends in F-sharp major. The chorus of the People answers in G major with precisely the same force and accompaniment as before. Now the Angels sing their *Heilig* for the third time, a passage that begins in F minor and closes in B major, whereupon both choruses answer with all the splendor and power of the accompaniment and begin a passage in C major. . . . In the fugue, one hears the great *Bach* from beginning to end. In the *Heilig*, however, he has assumed a different manner. In this passage he has combined the greatest simplicity with the most profound art. "The Angels," Bach said to me, "must bring to bear no artifice in their song of devotion; noble simplicity must be its principal character."

---

[7] "Das Duett: *Vater deiner schwachen Kinder* etc. wird vom Discant und Tenor gesungen. Es ist aus D moll. Auffallend ist eine Modulation im Ritornell aus D moll durchs B moll in A moll in einer Reihe von 2 bis 3 Tacten, die, so ungewöhnlich selbige ist, dennoch das Ohr im geringsten nicht beleidigt. Aber man muss solche Wege kennen, wie *Bach* sie kennt, wenn man nicht stolpern will." *Hamburgische unparteiische Correspondent* (hereafter, *HCorr*), 1778, no. 43; reprinted, with details altered reflecting various revisions, in *HCorr*, 1784, no. 109, and in Carl Friedrich Cramer's *Magazin der Musik*, II (Hamburg, 1784; repr. Hildesheim, 1971), 256–61.

566   JOURNAL OF THE AMERICAN MUSICOLOGICAL SOCIETY

This concept has been brought to life in such a successful way, that through it, the passage, without chromaticism, evinces an effect the likes of which I cannot describe to you. Note only the key in which the music of the Angels closes, and that in which the music of the People begins.[8]

Bach himself, in a letter to Breitkopf some months earlier, evaluated just this aspect of its harmonic conduct:

This *Heilig* is an attempt to achieve far greater interest and feeling through entirely natural harmonic progressions than is possible with all manner of high-strung chromaticism.[9]

That is very close, in sense and in language, to Benda's understanding of the process. Neither Bach nor Benda will construe the bold

---

[8] "Ich will Ihnen nichts von Bachs Manier sagen. Sie kennen sie, und wissen, was dieser grosse Man durch sein Genie und sein gründliche Kenntniss der Harmonie auszurichten im Stande ist. Aber in dieser Musik kam ein *Heilig* etc. vor, in dessen Composition *Bach* sich selbst übertroffen hat. Es ist ein Doppel-Chor, davon der erste Theil von den Engeln, und der zweyte von den Völkern gesungen wird. . . . Der Gesang fängt aus E dur an, nachdem eine kurze Einleitung aus G dur vorhergegangen, und endigt in Cis dur mit blosser Begleitung der Saiten-Instrumente. Die Antwort der Völker erfolgt aus D dur mit der grössten Stärke und mit Begleitung von Trompeten und Pauken. Abermals wiederholen die Engel das *Heilig* eben so sanft, wie das erstemal. Der Gesang fängt an aus H dur, und schliesst in Fis dur. Das Chor der Völker antwortet aus G dur mit eben der Stärke und Begleitung, wie zuerst. Nun singen die Engel zum drittenmal ihr *Heilig*, und heben den Gesang aus F moll an, der sich in H dur schliesst, worauf beyde Chöre mit aller Pracht und Stärke der Begleitung antworten, und der Gesang aus C dur anheben. . . . In der Fuge hört man den grossen *Bach* vom Anfange bis zu Ende; in dem Heilig aber hat er eine andere Manier angenommen. Er hat in diesem Gesange die grösste Simplicität mit der tiefsten Kunst vereinigt. Die Engel[,] sagte er zu mir, müssen in ihrem Anbetungsgesang keine Künsteleyen anbringen; edle Simplicität muss der Haupt-Charakter desselben seyn. Diese Idee hat den Mann auf eine so glückliche Art begeistert, dass dadurch der Gesang ohne Chromatik eine solche Wirkung hervorbringt, die ich Ihnen nicht beschreiben kann. Bemerken Sie nur die Tonart des Schlusses des Gesanges der Engel, und den Anfang derselben in dem Gesange der Völker." *HCorr*, 18 November 1778, no. 184.

[9] The passage is given in Hermann von Hase, "Carl Philipp Emanuel Bach und Joh. Gottl. Im. Breitkopf," *Bach-Jahrbuch*, VIII (1911), 95: "Dieses Heilig ist ein Versuch, durch ganz natürliche harmonische Fortschreitungen mir weit stärkere Aufmerksamkeit und Empfindung zu erregen, als man mit aller ängstlicher Chromatik nicht im Stande ist zu thun." Hase implies (but does not specify) that the passage is from a letter dated 28 July 1778. Günter Graulich, in the preface to his edition of the *Heilig* in the *Stuttgarter Bach-Ausgaben*, ser. E (Neuhausen-Stuttgart, 1975), claims the letter to have been written in 1776, although he knows it from the Hase article. In fact, Hase conflated two letters here. The sentence in question comes from a letter dated 16 September 1778. I am grateful to Rachel Wade for confirming the dates of several letters whose autographs are now at the Hessische Landes- und Hochschulbibliothek, Darmstadt (hereafter, D:DS).

modulatory inflections between choruses as chromatic inflections. These are relationships of a deeper order. If we cannot know the extent to which Bach may have influenced Benda's hearing of the piece, Benda, in recording at least some exchange between the two of them, encourages us to imagine still more.

And while Benda was struck by the articulation of tonal disparity between the music of the two choruses, he was not the first to respond to this aspect of the piece. Some two years earlier, in a letter dated 11 October 1776, the poet Johann Heinrich Voss reflected upon a performance of the *Heilig*:

> I know nothing by [Bach] that is more daring, nobler, and more overpowering than the music of the Angels and the People (*Heilig, heilig*, etc., etc.). Two choruses, the one soft, the other loud, continually answer one another in the most remote keys—D major upon C-sharp major, and so forth—and close with a fiery fugue.[10]

Again, we must contend with the possibility that Voss's analytical remarks were gleaned from conversation, quite likely with Bach himself. The specificity of the reference, whether or not the insight is Voss's own, illuminates that quality of tonal relationship in Bach's *Heilig* which seems to have struck the sensibilities of his contemporaries.

This is further documented in the two volumes of Johann Friedrich Reichardt's *Musikalisches Kunstmagazin*. In the earlier volume (1782), Reichardt contributed a review of the published score, which had appeared in 1779, describing its events in some detail and with a certain sensitivity to its tonal behavior:

> The Chorus of the Angels continually modulates to more remote keys . . . and the Chorus of the People breaks in with great force in the brighter, more distant of the usual keys, and sustains them. Thus, the first of the Angel choruses begins in E major, moves quickly to F-sharp major, and *closes* with a half cadence on C-sharp major; and the Chorus of the People interrupts in D major and closes in D major; whereupon the Chorus of Angels begins again in B major and closes in F-sharp major. And now the Chorus of the People breaks in again, in G major, and

---

[10] "Ich kenne von ihm nichts kühners, edlers und hinreissenders, als der Gesang der Engel u Völker: Heilig, heilig etc. etc. Zwey Chöre, eines sanfter das andre stärker, antworten sich immer, und in der entferntesten Tonart, auf *Cis dur* mit einmal in *D dur*, u s.w., und schliessen endlich mit einer feurigen Fuge." For the text of just this passage, see *Dokumente zum Nachwirken Johann Sebastian Bachs: 1750–1800*, ed. Hans-Joachim Schulze (Kassel, 1972), p. 303.

568   JOURNAL OF THE AMERICAN MUSICOLOGICAL SOCIETY

closes in that key. Here the Chorus of Angels interrupts once again in F
minor and closes in B major, whereupon the Chorus of the People
reenters in C major and closes there.[11]

Reichardt's infatuation with the piece led him to publish a reduced
score of its central music in the second volume of the *Kunstmagazin*
(1791), with new commentary, rather more reflective and probing:

> That bold sequence of consonant chords, which, in Palestrina's music,
> pierced us with such intensity, is used by Bach only at the transitions
> between the music of the Angels and the music of the People, perhaps in
> order to delineate the great distance between them. Thus, the Chorus of
> the Angels closes at first in C-sharp major, and the Chorus of the People
> begins in D major and closes in the same key; whereupon the Chorus of
> Angels commences in B major and closes in F-sharp major. The People
> begin again in G major, and so forth.[12]

The context of these remarks makes it clear that Reichardt means to
stress the transitional relationships between phrases. The discussion
had begun with an expansive appreciation of a *Gloria Patri* by
Palestrina, whose sequence of triads in root position led Reichardt to
ruminate on the essence of harmony:

> The omitted transitional harmonies, which we ever so diligently supply
> and painstakingly plant out, for us and our critical followers, as
> indispensable little bridges from one branch of the stream to the other—
> these [ellipses] lend an enormity to each step and allow the mind only
> dimly to surmise the path that the harmony has taken. And each
> individual harmony surprises the listener with its full force and strikes

[11] See Johann Friedrich Reichardt, *Musikalisches Kunstmagazin*, I (Berlin, 1782;
repr. Hildesheim, 1969), 85: "Da modulirt nun das Chor der Engel immer in
entfernte fremdere Töne . . . und das Chor der Völker fällt dann gewaltig in den
helltönendern entfernten gewöhnlichen Ton, und bleibt stark. So hebt der erste
Engelgesang in F [*recte* E] dur an, geht schnell in Fis dur und schliesst mit halbem
Schluss in Cis dur, und das Chor der Völker fällt in D dur ein und schliesst in D dur.
Drauf hebt das Chor der Engel wieder in H dur an, und schliesst in Fis dur: und nun
fällt das Chor der Völker wieder in G dur ein und schliesst so. Hier fällt das Chor der
Engel wieder in F mol ein und schliesst in H dur, worauf das Chor der Völker wieder
in C dur einfällt, und so schliesst."

[12] See Johann Friedrich Reichardt, *Musikalisches Kunstmagazin*, II (Berlin, 1791;
repr. Hildesheim, 1969), 57: "Jene kühne Folge von konsonirenden Akorden, die uns
im Palestina [*sic*] so mächtig durchdrang, bat H. B. hier nur bey den Uebergängen
von den Gesängen der Engel, zu den Gesängen der Völker angewandt, vielleicht um
dadurch die weite Entfernung jener von dieser zu mahlen. So schliesst das Chor der
Engel erst in cis dur und das Chor der Völker beginnt in d dur und schliesst darinnen,
worauf das Chor der Engel in h dur anhebt, und in fis dur schliesst. Die Völker
beginnen wieder in g dur u.s.w."

him with doubled strength in that it strikes him unprepared. For us, nearly every consonant chord is simply the resolution of a previously prepared dissonant chord, and thus, in the truest sense, we take delight only in the pleasant gratification of a warily anxious expectation. . . .[13]

That way of hearing Palestrina will strike us as anachronistic, for Palestrina's harmonic language conveys no such sense of omitted but implied harmonies that would negotiate between starkly contiguous root-position triads. But such unmediated chordal successions have a different meaning in the music of the 1770s. To propose of the *Heilig* that the ear seeks to supply preparatory dissonances as a way of mediating between the difficult, ungrammatical harmonic juxtapositions of its two choruses was a shrewd analytical tactic worthy of a theorist with better credentials than Reichardt owned. The models shown in Example 4 must be close to what he had in mind.[14]

Example 4
Two models for the missing harmonies at the ellipsis between mm. 53 and 54

The four *Modulationen* that Bach isolates in his Example *b* do not exemplify the concept *Ausweichung* as it is defined in the *Allgemeine Theorie*. *Ausweichungen*, in that sense, proceed here exclusively within the phrases that the Angels sing. These are the inflected motions toward the dominants on *C*-sharp, *F*-sharp, and *B*. The answers to those dominants—fresh tonics in D major, G major, and C major— dent the syntax: the Angels, evidently, are heard with difficulty. And

---

[13] *Ibid.*, II, 55: "Die übergangenen Zwischenaccorde, die wir immer so geflissentlich hören lassen, und als nothwendige kleine Brücken für uns und unser kritisches Gefolge, von einem Arme des Stroms zum andern so sorgfältig hinpflanzen, die geben hier jedem Schritte eine Riesengrösse, und lassen die Seele nur dunkel den Weg ahnden, den die Harmonie genommen. Auch überfällt jeder einzelne Accord den Zuhörer mit seiner ganzen Kraft, und trift ihn doppelt stark, da er ihn unvorbereitet trift. Bey uns ist fast jeder consonirende Accord nur die Auflösung des auch schon vorher vorbereiteten dissonirenden Accords, und so geniessen wir fast immer nur die angenehme Befriedigung der behutsam gespannten Erwartung. . . ."

[14] Bach had in fact invoked the concept *ellipsis* in this specific sense in the gloss that clarifies the "plan" of the Fantasia in D Major in the final paragraph of the *Versuch*, p.

yet the structure of the piece remains intact, sustained along the lines suggested in Example 5. The Angels respond rather more sensitively.

Example 5
The *Heilig*: a synoptic reading

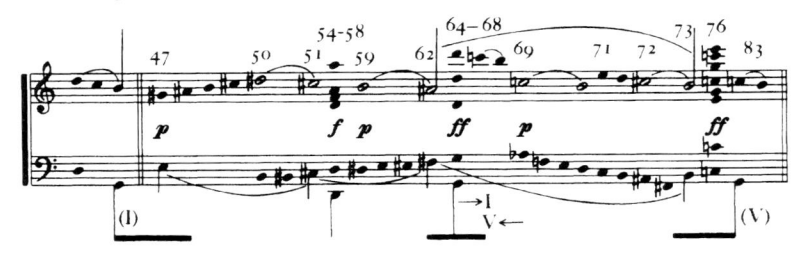

The inflection from a tonic in root position to the semitone above, as the bass of a dominant in first inversion (as in mm. 58–59), will be familiar from the vast expanses of eighteenth-century recitative. Unfamiliar is Bach's play on that convention at the analogous measures 68–69. The ear wants G-sharp in the bass and a dominant in A minor. It gets, instead, A-flat in the bass, rooted to F-natural, a harmony that neither follows easily from G major nor moves logically to the delayed dominant on *E* that we had been led to expect in its place. The relationship is expressed in the third frame of Bach's Example *b*.

How are we to construe this wayward F-minor harmony? Bach seems determined to defend the normalcy of the passage, for it will be noticed that two of the four *Modulationen* given in his Example *b*

---

340. One consequence of elliptic motion in the *Helig*—the de facto fifths between the bass and alto/soprano at mm. 53–54—was not lost on another of Bach's contemporaries. In a letter of 23 November 1784 to Johann Christoph Kühnau in Berlin, Bach wrote: "Since your fifths do not follow immediately upon one another, and the note that mediates between them is neither a passing tone nor a quick note—quick notes in Allabreve are eighths—no one can disallow them. In my *Heilig*, the case has the advantage of the tempo: Adagio. In the Passion [Cantata, W. 233, H. 776], the quarter rest insures that the fifths do not follow directly upon one another." See Friedrich Chrysander, ed., "Briefe von Karl Philipp Emanuel Bach und G. M. Telemann," *Allgemeine musikalische Zeitung*, ser. 3, IV (1869), 187, letter 15: "Da Ihre 5ten [Quinten] nicht *unmittelbar* auf einander folgen, u. die Note, welche sie deckt, *NB* keine durch gehende oder geschwinde Note ist (geschwinde Noten in *Allabreve* sind 8^{tel}), so kann sie niemand verwerfen. In meinem Heilig hat dieser Fall das *Tempo-Adagio* voraus. In der Passion macht die 4^{tel} Pause, dass die 5ten nicht *unmittelbar* auf einander folgen." See also La Mara, ed., *Musikerbriefe aus fünf Jahrhunderten*, I (Leipzig, [1886]), 210.

address the unusual harmonic track of measures 68–70. It is not that Bach protests too much but rather that his defense is insufficient. F minor serves to inflect the antecedent G major as a dominant. That is

Example 6
The *Heilig*: the reciprocal harmonic sense of mm. 68–69

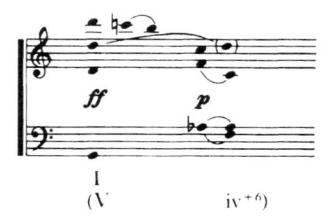

a crucial message: the very first intimation that the great fugue with which the piece will close is to be resolutely in C major. This fleeting suggestion—G as dominant—is encouraged by the residual *D*, which must reverberate through the fermata at measure 68. The Chorus of the People has sung no other pitch for five full measures. It tints the harmony as a kind of *sixte ajoutée*, implicating F minor as a subdominant. But that sense of the thing is countermanded straight away, for the configuration around *F* is now reinterpreted as a delaying of the root *E*; the resolution of *C* to *B* is further delayed to avoid parallel fifths with the bass between measures 69 and 70.

All of this greatly stresses the harmony of measure 69, which, in spite of its articulation as a stable front accent, must be understood as a dissonance—indeed as several kinds of dissonance at once: as a minor subdominant (with subliminal sixth) in C; as an appoggiatura to a dominant on *E*; and, more broadly, as a passing harmony that negotiates between the bass tones *G* and *E*—coincidentally, the very interval that separates the close of the Ariette from the opening of the *Heilig*, represented in the fourth *Modulation* in Bach's example. How, finally, the harmony at measure 69 stands at the crux of the Adagio, at the central turn of the bass motion in the design of the whole, is shown in Example 5.

The significance of these measures is recognized—authenticated, in a sense—late in the piece. Toward the end, the Chorus of Angels, recalling the text of the *Heilig*, interrupts the intrepid motion of the fugue altogether and revives the memory of precisely that difficult *Modulation* at measures 68–71. Without laboring all the subtle ways in which the latter passage plays upon the former, let it do here to note how the discantus forges a phrase out of just those troubling pitches.

Such passages as the one around measures 68–71 touch at the nub of Bach's style. The sense of the harmony at measure 69 is a paradox,

Example 7
Heilig, mm. 173–83

Without organ and bassoon

at once logical and incoherent. The logic has to be wrung out of it. Bach stretches the concept *enharmonic* to its outer limit. And yet because *F* is so distinctly articulated as a root, it sounds alien in its context; even the most sophisticated parsing of voice motion will not explain it away.

This brings us to the crucial issue. Two contiguous harmonies may stand in troubled relationship to each other. Reichardt senses that the strength of such passages lies in the power of ellipsis to imply, and to withhold, explanatory harmonies. How such a phenomenon might generate the large-scale unfolding of a piece, a concept relatively unexplored in the *Heilig*, is central to the Rondo in C.

First, let us be clear that Bach's explanation of the third *Modulation*—"*E* is the dominant of A, and A minor is very closely related to C major"—is evasive, for it tells us nothing about the other similarly articulated but more radically opposed confrontations in the piece; the breach at measures 69–71 is but one example. Here, and indeed in each of the designated *Modulationen* in the rondo, we are surely meant to ponder not the logic of continuity from one harmony to the next but rather the friction between two such elements and all that is implied of their eventual reconciliation.

It was Johann Nikolaus Forkel who, among eighteenth-century critics, seems to have come closest to grasping the significance, for the work as a whole, of *Modulation* as disruptive and generative. His most incisive piece of criticism, an analysis of the final movement of the Keyboard Trio in G Major of 1775, W. 90, no. 2 (Helm 523), recognizes the imperative of remote, enharmonic modulation to justify itself:

> It is not enough to make a bold move. One must know how to do it with assurance and, in addition, how to retreat from it (*wieder zurückzuziehen*) in an acceptable manner. . . . One must feel confidently in control and be master of all possible means, in order to extricate oneself (*herauszuwickeln*) in the best way from a labyrinth into which one has gotten entangled due to boldness; and the listener must not be led to know the difficulties that it has cost to come out of it.[15]

---

[15] Johann Nikolaus Forkel, *Musikalisch-kritische Bibliothek*, II (Gotha, 1778; repr. Hildesheim, 1964), 288–89: "Es ist nicht genug, einen kühnen Schritt zu thun, man muss ihn mit Sicherheit thun können, und sich noch ausserdem mit einer guten Art wieder zurückzuziehen wissen. . . . Man muss Kräfte in sich fühlen, und aller möglichen Mittel mächtig seyn, um sich mit der besten Art aus einem Labyrinthe, in welchem man sich durch Kühnheit verwickelt hat, wiederum herauszuwickeln, und man muss dem Zuhörer kaum merken lassen, dass es Mühe gekostet hat, wiederum herauszukommen." For a discussion of Forkel's essay from a different perspective, see Malcolm S. Cole, "The Vogue of the Instrumental Rondo in the Late Eighteenth Century," this JOURNAL, XXII (1969), 425–55. It seems more than likely that Forkel's analysis inspired August Friedrich Christoph Kollmann to publish the rondo in its entirety, with a running "explanation of the course of its modulation." See *An Essay on Practical Musical Composition, according to the Nature of That Science and the Principles of the Greatest Musical Authors* (London, 1799; repr. New York, 1973, ed. Imogene Horsley), p. 6 and plates 1–5.

Zurückziehen and *herauswickeln*, words that lose some nuance in translation, suggest the playing out of what has at first been heard as inexplicable, even irrational. What Forkel noticed of the "playing out" in the G-Major Rondo is characteristic of all the rondos in the collections *für Kenner und Liebhaber*, and of the fantasias as well. Example 8 shows something of how the *Modulationen* designated by Bach in the C-Major Rondo are, in a manner of speaking, subsumed in a great conciliatory passage toward the end of the piece.

IV

The original question returns. Can we formulate a definition of *Modulation* that would meet the conditions exemplified in those passages that illustrate Bach's text? The *Modulation* in the *Auferstehung* duet is the simplest in concept. It comprises the harmonic conduct of a single phrase whose constituent harmonies are not articulated and do not extend in dissonant prolongations beyond themselves.

The *Modulationen* in the *Heilig* and the rondo are of a different kind. The method of reduction in Bach's examples makes that clear. What we get in each case are contiguous harmonies. These are not in themselves *Ausweichungen*, nor can they be said to stand for *Ausweichungen*. If the *Heilig* and the rondo differ in their response to such events, what they share is a manner of radical articulation that gaps and charges the connection between two unwilling harmonies.

The quality of relationship expressed in these passages is not acknowledged in the definitions of either *Ausweichung* or *Modulation* given in Sulzer's encyclopedia and in writings contemporary with it. *Modulation* is the more flexible term. Bach evidently intends to give it new meaning of the scope and depth suggested in Forkel's study. Unable or unwilling to translate these phenomena into concrete theory, Bach points, simply, to those difficult harmonic couplings whose immediate grammatical sense may need his sanction but which, moreover, represent broader, more significant modulatory strategies. For it will be recalled that each of the *Modulationen* in both the *Heilig* (excepting the remarkable one between measures 69 and 70) and the rondo form articulations. The examples are paradoxical. They are shown to represent coherent harmonic contiguities; but, in fact, they represent moments of formal interruption whose articulation underscores what is intrinsic in a disjunct harmonic relationship.

That, after all, is the fundamental difference between *Modulation* as it was understood before 1750 and as it is understood after 1770. In the Classical style, modulation means tension and formal discord. The

THE NEW MODULATION OF THE 1770S   575

Example 8
(a) Rondo in C, mm. 113–35
(b) The voice leading in mm. 121–28

Ex. 8, cont.

act of modulation is costumed, choreographed, and dramatized in all the ways convenient to the style. The conventions of Classical dramaturgy may have been foreign to C. P. E. Bach, but the gestures of his music are born of the same temperament.

V

When might Bach have written the paragraph under discussion? Not, evidently, shortly before his death, as might be inferred from Schwickert's footnote. For by 1787, Bach's portfolio would include a rich repertory of new music in which the frontiers of modulation are challenged with originality and high purpose. Apart from the big keyboard pieces—the rondos and fantasias in the five volumes of the collections *für Kenner und Liebhaber* that appeared in print between 1780 and 1787—one thinks of the remarkable sets of harmonizations contained in the *Zwei Litaneyen . . . in Partitur gesetzt und zum Nutzen und Vergnügen Lehrbegieriger in der Harmonie bearbeitet*, to which Bach contributed an instructive preface, dated 1785, that speaks to the performance and notation of enharmonics;[16] and one thinks of the setting of Klopstock's *Morgengesang am Schöpfungsfeste* for orchestra, soloists, and chorus, composed in 1783. In light of the accomplishments of these last years, that the curious passage in the duet from the *Auferstehung Jesu* should, nevertheless, have stuck in Bach's mind as one of three models toward a definition of modulation strains all good sense.

It is smarter to suppose the paragraph to have been written between 1778 and 1780. In a postscript to a letter to Schwickert dated 10 April 1780, in which the terms of the sale of both parts of the *Versuch* were described, Bach added: "Should something come out of our transaction, I promise you *in addition* considerable supplementary material to both parts, which I now have in manuscript and shall want sometime to have printed."[17] And the matter was broached again a month later, in a letter dated 19 May: "I am, once more, carefully reading through the supplementary materials that I still owe you, in order to augment them further where it is necessary. Then I will send them to you in a clear, clean copy. You will certainly get them from me soon, for I am an honorable man. Anyway, at this moment you as yet have no need of them, and in good time you will surely get something more carefully thought out and complete than if I had sent my supplementary material along right now."[18] While the manuscript

---

[16] For the text of Bach's Preface, and an English translation, see the edition by Jürgen Leonhardt for the *Stuttgarter Bach-Ausgaben* (Neuhausen-Stuttgart, 1980); and, with some slight discrepancies, C. H. Bitter, *Carl Philipp Emanuel und Wilhelm Friedemann Bach und deren Brüder*, I (Berlin, 1868), 307–10.

[17] "Sollte aus unserm Handel etwas werden, so verspreche ich Ihnen *obenein* noch beträchtliche Beiträge zu beiden Theilen, welche ich im Manuskript habe und einmal drucken zu lassen willens bin, zu geben." The letter is given in Ludwig Nohl, *Musiker-Briefe* (Leipzig, 1867), pp. 68–69.

[18] "Meine Beiträge, die ich Ihnen noch schuldig bin, und die Sie von mir als einen ehrliche Manen gewiss und bald kriegen sollen, sehe ich noch einmal genau durch, um solche, wo es nöthig ist, noch zu vermehren, und schicke sie Ihnen alsdann in einer deutlichen und saubern Copie zu. Jetzt haben Sie solche ohnedem noch nicht gleich nöthig, und mit der Zeit kriegen Sie gewiss etwas mehr überdachtes und vollkommeneres, als wenn ich meine Aufsätze gleich jetzt mitgeschickt hätte." See Gustav Wustmann, "Ein Brief Carl Philipp Emanuel Bach's," *Zeitschrift der Internationalen Musikgesellschaft*, X (1908), 1–4.

material that would serve as the text for the revisions to Part 1 has survived, the original text for the revisions to Part 2 has not.[19] We cannot know, then, whether the manuscript material that Bach mentions would have included the paragraph on modulation or, if it did, whether it went to Schwickert in 1780 or only some years later.[20]

The substance of Bach's text argues that it had been conceived by 1780. Between 1778 and 1780 Bach would have had all three works very much in mind. Entries in the *Nachlassverzeichnis*, a document compiled from information kept and prepared by Bach himself, advocate 1778 as the critical year, for that is the year that Bach assigned to each of the three works under discussion (1777 and 1778 in the case of the *Auferstehung Jesu*).[21]

The dates in the *Nachlassverzeichnis* have a special authority, for the annotations that give the place and date of composition invariably

---

[19] The bookseller Hans Schneider offered for sale a manuscript of twenty-five pages, partly in Bach's hand, and titled by Bach "Beyträge mit Exempeln zu C. Ph. E. Bachs ersten Theils seines Versuchs," bound in with what is described as Bach's *Handexemplar* of the *Versuch*. See Schneider, *Katalogue Nr. 132. Musikalische Seltenheiten* (Tützing, 1968), item 2, and a facsimile of one page from Bach's supplement; the same page is shown in *Early Music*, IV (1976), 385. This same item was offered at auction by Noel Charavay (Paris), 3 April 1925, and before that by Sotheby, Wilkinson, and Hodge (London), 19–21 June 1922, but here it is clearly only the 1787 edition of Part 1 with Bach's autograph corrections and marginalia, and a manuscript appendix of twenty-three pages; see Ernst Fritz Schmid, "Bach, Carl Philipp Emanuel," *MGG*, I, 934. A *Handexemplar* of the *Versuch* can be traced as far back as the auction of Bach's *Nachlass* in 1805. The auction catalogue (copy at Berlin, Deutsche Staatsbibliothek, Mus. Db 313: "Hamburg, gedruckt in der Börsen-Halle von Conrad Müller") lists as items 115–16 "Versuch über die wahre Art das Klavier zu spielen, Berl. [1]762 mit geschriebenen Anmerkungen des Verfassers." Otto Vrieslander, *Carl Philipp Emanuel Bach* (Munich, 1923), p. 181, referred to a new edition of the *Versuch*, "nebst handschriftlichen Nachträgen," ed. Hugo Daffner, then about to be published ("im Erscheinen begriffen") by Bosse in Regensburg. And the article on Daffner by Wilhelm Zentner, *MGG*, XV, 1685, lists the *Versuch* as having been published by Bosse in 1928. But Rudolf Steglich, "Karl Philipp Emanuel Bach und der Dresdner Kreuzkantor Gottfried August Homilius im Musikleben ihrer Zeit," *Bach-Jahrbuch*, XII (1915), 134, n. 15, writes, "Ein weiterer Neudruck von Hugo Daffner nach dem Handexemplar Emanuels ist bei Bosse, Regensburg, erschienen." No one seems ever to have seen it!

[20] For a third letter to Schwickert, dated 27 January 1786, see Dragan Plamenac, "New Light on the Last Years of Carl Philipp Emanuel Bach," *The Musical Quarterly*, XXXV (1949), 565–87; Bach offered the *VI sonatine nuove*, which would be published by Schwickert as a supplement to the *Achtzehn Probestücke*, and issued with the 1787 edition of the *Versuch*, Part 1. There is no mention of revisions to Part 2.

[21] *Verzeichniss des musikalischen Nachlasses des verstorbenen Capellmeisters Carl Philipp Emanuel Bach* (Hamburg, 1790); now reprinted, with annotations, as *The Catalogue of Carl Philipp Emanuel Bach's Estate: A Facsimile of the Edition by Schniebes, Hamburg, 1790*, ed. Rachel W. Wade (New York, 1981). See also Darrell M. Berg, "Towards a Catalogue of the Keyboard Sonatas of C. P. E. Bach," this JOURNAL, XXXII (1979), 276–303.

agree with annotations in just that form that Bach entered on nearly all his autographs. But the autograph of the *Auferstehung Jesu* is undated. In fact, there is good evidence that the work was composed not in 1777–78 but in 1774, for in April of that year Johann Heinrich Voss wrote of hearing a performance of it in Hamburg under Bach's direction. Voss's letter, dated "Sonnabend vor Oster, 2 Apr. 1774," is an especially rich source of information about Bach and is worth quoting here at some length.

> Today the Capellmeister Bach invited me to lunch. I visited him once before and had the good fortune to have pleased him, for I am, as he put it, a German patriot. He is proud to be a German, for they have the only truly serious music. He wants very much to have a musical poet in me; several of my ideas on the usual setting of *Singpoesie* pleased him. This afternoon he leads a performance of Ramler's *Auferstehung*, newly composed.

And the letter continues the next day:

> *Easter Sunday.* . . . At about 11 o'clock I went to Bach. . . . He would rather hear German music praised than his own. He played something for me at the fortepiano that sounded quite like magic. But after the holidays he wants to play for me for an entire evening at his Silbermann clavichord.
>
> Diderot has traveled through town and has written several letters to Bach, asking for the copy of some unpublished sonatas for his daughter, who is an excellent keyboard player. Yesterday afternoon, Bach took me with him to the church gallery, where he performed his new *Auferstehung*. He has composed it splendidly. Afterward, the whole gathering went to the Rabe, a cafe outside Hamburg, where we drank coffee and played billiards. Bach spoke at length about Berlin and his father Sebastian. . . .[22]

---

[22] "Heute hat mich der Capellmeister Bach zum Mittage gebeten. Ich habe ihn einmal besucht, und das Glück gehabt, ihm zu gefallen, weil ich, wie er meint, ein deutscher Patriot bin. Er ist stolz, ein Deutscher zu sein; denn sie haben die einzige, eigentliche, ernsthafte Musik. Er will gern einen musikalischen Dichter aus mir haben; einige Gedanken, die ich ihm über die gewöhnliche Einrichtung der Singpoesie sagte, gefielen ihm. Heute Nachmittag lässt er Ramlers Auferstehung, neu componirt, aufführen.

"*Osternsonntag.* . . . Um elf ging ich zu Bach. . . . Er hört lieber die deutsche Musik loben, als seine. Etwas hat er mir auf einem Fortepiano vorgespielt, das wie Zauberei klang; er will mir aber nach dem Feste einen ganzen Abend auf seinem Silbermannischen Klavier vorspielen.

"Diderot ist hier durchgereiset, und hat etliche Briefe an Bach geschrieben, worin er um die Abschrift einiger ungedruckten Sonaten für seine Tochter, die eine vortrefliche Klavierspielerin ist, bat. Gestern Nachmittag nahm mich Bach mit aufs

The reference to Diderot's journey through Hamburg is significant on several counts. In point of fact, two letters from Diderot to Bach were published in two Hamburg newspapers in 1774, and it is entirely conceivable that Voss knew of Diderot's visit through those accounts.[23] We know that by the date of Voss's letter, Diderot would already have left Hamburg for The Hague; had Bach and Diderot come face to face, it would be reasonable to expect Voss to have mentioned something of their encounter. The reference to Diderot serves, in any case, to confirm the date of Voss's letter and, consequently, the date of this performance of the *Auferstehung*—"neu componirt," as Voss puts it.[24]

It must follow, therefore, that the entry in the *Nachlassverzeichniss* signifies a fundamental revision of the work during the winter of 1777–78. Just how the versions of 1774 and 1778 might differ from one another is quite another matter. The issue is complicated by later revisions, some of which must date from after 5 May 1778, others from after 20 November 1780, for these are the dates of two letters to Ramler in which Bach acknowledges revisions brought to the libretto

---

Chor, wo er seine neue Auferstehung aufführte. Er hat sie herrlich componirt. Nachher ging die ganze Gesellschaft nach der Rabe, einem Lustort vor Hamburg, wo wir Caffe tranken und Kegel spielten. Bach erzählte vieles von Berlin und seinem Vater Sebastian."

The letter is at Kiel, Schleswig-Holsteinischen Landesbibliothek; I am grateful to the staff of that library for providing photocopies of this and the letter of 11 October 1776. The letter is published in Johann Heinrich Voss, *Briefe von Johann Heinrich Voss nebst erläuternden Beilagen*, ed. Abraham Voss, I (Halberstadt, 1829; repr. with a foreword by Gerhard Hay, Hildesheim, 1971), pp. 157–62, but omitting without comment the passage on Diderot, which is evidently given here for the first time.

[23] The letters were published in French in two Hamburg newspapers, *HCorr*, no. 57 (1774) and the *Neuen gelehrten Mercur*, Altona, II, no. 14 (1774), 105 ff. They are given in full in Ernst Fritz Schmid, *Carl Philipp Emanuel Bach und seine Kammermusik* (Kassel, 1931), pp. 44–46, based on transcripts in J. J. H. Westphal's notebook of Bachiana now at Brussels, Bibliothèque Royale Albert Ier, Fonds Fétis II 4133. Johann Christoph von Zabuesnig, *Historische und kritische Nachrichten von dem Leben und den Schriften des Herrn von Voltaire und anderer Neuphilosophen unserer Zeiten*, 2 vols. (Augsburg, 1777), II, 139–41, gave the letters in German translation; see Morris Wachs, "Diderot's Letters to Carl Philipp Emanuel Bach," *Romanische Forschungen*, LXXVII (1965), 359–62. Zabuesnig's German served as the text for new translations into French for the Diderot *Correspondance*, ed. Georges Roth and Jean Varloot, XVI, *Complément, corrections, listes et index général* (Paris, 1970), 49–51.

[24] That Bach should have encouraged the publication of these personal letters may tell us something about his shrewd use of the media—the *HCorr* in particular—to broadcast not only forthcoming performances and publications but reviews and criticism as well. The extent of his collusion in this enterprise is a matter for speculation, but it would be naive to assume that anonymous reviews such as the account of the *Auferstehung* (see n. 7 above) did not to some degree profit from Bach's tuition.

since its printing in 1772.[25] The autograph score and a set of performing parts that contain emendations in Bach's hand reflect these changes.[26] Other alterations, occasionally effecting massive changes in the recitative, were forced upon Bach by the reassignment of performing roles reflecting shifts in the strengths of the voices among Bach's regular group of soloists.[27] Whether the *uralt* layer of the autograph dates from 1774 or from 1777–78 is a question that will evade an answer until more is known of the paper that Bach used in the 1770s and until the perceptible changes in Bach's hand that are evident in the autographs of that period have been chronicled.

Similar problems vex the *Entstehungsgeschichte* of the *Heilig*. The *Nachlassverzeichniss* gives 1778 as the date of composition, and the work was published by Bach through Breitkopf's presses in 1779. But a performance is reported in the *HCorr* of 25 October 1776, and this squares with Voss's account, a few weeks earlier, in the letter cited above.[28] There are grounds for believing the Ariette to have been composed sometime after 1776. The argument rests upon the circum-

---

[25] The letters are given in Friedrich Wilhelm, "Briefe an Karl Wilhelm Ramler nebst einem Briefe an Lessing," *Vierteljahrschrift für Litteraturgeschichte*, IV (1891), 254, 256–57. The letter of 1780 is now in London, British Library, Add. MS 47,843. The letter of 1778 reads in part: "The composition of your beautiful Cantata [*Die Auferstehung und Himmelfahrt Jesu*] brought me much satisfaction. It has had the good fortune to please. Whether it deserves this I leave undecided. Your alterations have merit. Perhaps I can make use of them. But it won't proceed as easily as you believe, dear friend. Perhaps I shall give more preliminary thought than usual before I set to writing. . . ." ("Die Composition Ihrer sehr schönen Cantate hat mir viel Vergnügen gemacht. Sie hat das Glück gehabt zu gefallen. Ob sie es verdient, lasse ich dahin gestellt seyn. Ihre Veränderungen haben Grund. Vielleicht kan ich davon einen Gebrauch machen. So leicht aber, wie Sie, liebster Freund, glauben, wird es nicht angehen. Vielleicht denke ich vorher, ehe ich schreibe, mehr als gewöhnlich. . . .") Bound in with Bach's autograph score (see n. 26) is a copy of the printed libretto (". . . von C. W. Ramler. In Musick gesetzt von C. P. E. Bach. Hamburg, gedruckt von Johann Philipp Reuss [n.d.]"). A single leaf, evidently in Ramler's handwriting, now glued into the text booklet, contains all those emendations that agree with the final edition of Ramler's text. The printed libretto gives the version published in the 1772 edition of Ramler's works; see Karl Wilhelm Ramler, *Poetische Werke*, II (Berlin, 1825), 260–63. I am grateful to Stephen Clark for providing a copy of the Reuss libretto now at the Hamburg Staats- und Universitätsbibliothek.

[26] Berlin: Staatsbibliothek Preussischer Kulturbesitz [= D:B], Mus. ms. Bach P 336, and St 178. Bach's *Urfassung* is a setting of Ramler's original text; this was the version reviewed in the *HCorr* in 1778.

[27] The singers are identified by name in the parts (and, now and again, in the autograph score). For more on this aspect of Bach's work, see Heinrich Miesner, *Philipp Emanuel Bach im Hamburg: Beiträge zu seiner Biographie und zur Musikgeschichte seiner Zeit* (Leipzig, 1929), p. 19 and the appropriate documents in the Appendix.

[28] For the report in the *HCorr*, see *ibid.*, pp. 93–94.

582   JOURNAL OF THE AMERICAN MUSICOLOGICAL SOCIETY

stances of the performance by Bach of a cantata by his brother Johann
Christoph Friedrich for the Feast of St. Michael. On the wrapper of
the performing parts for the cantata *Wenn Christus seine Kirche schützt*,
Bach wrote "Michaelis Quartalsstück 78/84 Nr. 25"—noting, that is,
the dates of performance—along with the names of two of his singers,
Lau and Schwenke.[29] The parts indicate that a *Heilig* was to be
interpolated before the closing chorale, although the music itself is not
specified. This *Heilig* would have been preceded there by an aria to
the text "Herr, wert dass Scharen der Engel dir dienen" by Herder.
From this, Heinrich Miesner concluded that Bach, finding Herder's
text appropriate as an introductory, quasi-liturgical intonation to his
Heilig, composed his own setting of the text, perhaps in preparing the
Heilig for publication in 1778.[30]

That is a compelling hypothesis, and the structure of the autograph score tends to support it: the Ariette and the *Heilig* were written
on paper of two sizes, the Ariette on a single leaf, distinct from the
series of oversize bifolia that were used for the *Heilig* and the fugue.
And, in fact, the special demands that the double chorus and double
orchestra imposed caused Breitkopf some difficulty when it came to
publishing the work.[31]

That the aria must have been conceived later, as an introduction
subordinate to the *Heilig*, was a point argued as well by Carl Friedrich
Zelter. Drawing his inference from the insubstantial quality of the
music, Zelter was led to suggest something about the history of its
composition: "Bach began the work with the *Heilig* as the principal
subject but felt, in the end, that the Chorus of the Angels needed
something mundane as an antecedent, if the intended effect were to
succeed." Even the title was suggestive for Zelter: " 'mit zwei Chören

---

[29] See *ibid.*, pp. 81, 96. The parts are in D:B, Mus. ms. Bach St 266. It has not
been noted, in this connection, that J. C. F. Bach is thought to have passed through
Hamburg in May 1778 en route from Bückeburg to London; see Charles Sanford
Terry, *John Christian Bach* (London, 1929), p. 159.

[30] Miesner, *Philipp Emanuel Bach im Hamburg*, p. 96. But Karl Geiringer, *Die
Musikerfamilie Bach: Musiktradition in sieben Generationen* (Munich, 1977), p. 275, must
be right that it was the brief *Heilig* for one chorus (W. 218, H. 827) that was
performed here, for it is scored for the same forces as the cantata.

[31] See Hase, "Carl Philipp Emanuel Bach und Joh. Gottl. Im. Breitkopf," p. 95.
The autograph score is at Vienna, Österreichische Nationalbibliothek, Cod. 15,517.
Hase speaks of the "Originalpartitur, die noch jetzt im Breitkopf & Härtelschen
Archiv aufbewahrt wird," and that agrees in size and format with the printed edition.
This manuscript, which cannot be the autograph (which came to the ÖNB during the
nineteenth century) is listed as well in "Auswahl von Musikhandschriften des
Archivs," *Der Bär. Jahrbuch von Breitkopf & Härtel auf das Jahr 1924* (Leipzig, 1924), p.
73.

THE NEW MODULATION OF THE 1770S   583

und einer Ariette,' from which one can only presume that this Arietta
is an appendix up front (*ein Appendix voran*) and, consequently, not a
true introduction. . . ."[32]

A valuable insight into the performance of the work has survived
in the correspondence with Breitkopf pertaining to its publication. A
letter from Bach, dated 30 January 1779, speaks to the tempo of the
Adagio, which, in Bach's autograph, is notated allabreve. Bach writes:

> Should the middle movement of my *Heilig*, which is a setting of the word
> "Heilig," be already in print, then this comment, or *Nota*, can be printed
> at the very end of the piece: "Because the performance of Adagio is not
> the same everywhere, this middle movement, the prescribed Allabreve
> notwithstanding, must be performed *very slowly*, and in any case rather
> too slowly than too quickly. . . ." Should the printing of this middle
> movement not yet have begun, then one should give the usual four-four
> signature C in place of the Allabreve sign ₵, and the remark at the end
> will not be necessary.[33]

But since there was time to make the change, Bach's illuminating *Nota*
was suppressed.[34]

Finally, a performance in Berlin in the 1770s provoked a spirited
exchange on the proper tempo of the closing fugue. Johann Philipp
Kirnberger, writing to Forkel in 1779, described a performance in
which the fugue "lasted eleven minutes straight through. I disapproved," wrote Kirnberger, "because the performance was thoroughly ruined. I reported this to Hr. Bach in Hamburg, suggesting that
[the fugue] require no more than five minutes; Bach, in his reply, set
the time at three minutes. But it appears to me that four minutes is the

---

[32] Zelter's undated memorandum is given by Miesner, *Philipp Emanuel Bach im
Hamburg*, pp. 95–96: "Bach hat die Arbeit bei dem 'Heilig' als der Hauptsache
angefangen und zuletzt empfunden, dass dem Chor der Engel das Irdische vorange-
hen müsse, wenn die beabsichtigte Wirkung erfolgen solle. . . . Mit zwei Chören
einer Ariette, woraus schon allein vermutlich wird, dass diese Ariette ein Appendix
voran, und eben deshalb keine wahre Einleitung. . . ."

[33] "Sollte an meinem Heilig der Mittelsatz, welche die Worte *Heilig* hat, schon
gedruckt seÿn, so kan zu Ende das ganzen Stückes folgende *Nota*, oder Anmerkung
gedruckt werden: 'Da die Ausführung des Adagio nicht überall gleich ist: so muss
dieser Mittelsatz, des vorgezeichneten Allabreve Takts ohngeacht, *sehr langsam*,
allenfalls lieber zu langsam als zu hurtig ausgeführt werden. . . .' Sollte dieser
Mittelsatz noch nicht mit dem Drucke angefangen seÿn, so macht man, statt des
Allabreve Takts ₵, den ordentlich vier Viertel Takt C, so ist, hier Anmerkung nicht
nöthig." The unpublished letter is at D:DS.

[34] It ought to have found its way into the commentary of the edition published in
the *Stuttgarter Bach-Ausgaben* series; the editor's observation that "the first impression
and the autograph score correspond exactly" is errant in precisely this detail, for the
autograph continues to show the allabreve sign.

ideal and that a performance requiring eleven minutes cannot be heard without arousing disgust."[35]

The communication from Bach to which Kirnberger refers is dated 16 December 1779: "The fugue in my *Heilig*, by itself, without repetition, which must not be [taken], must take no longer than three minutes."[36] What Bach can have meant by "ohne Wiederholung, welche nicht sein muss" is puzzling, for the score is without ambiguity in that regard. Similarly puzzling, the estimate of three minutes presupposes a brisk tempo (d = 96.67), which would surely have stressed his Hamburg musicians, whose mediocrity is widely confirmed.[37]

Forkel seems to have had the last word. In a postscript to the miscellany of "Neuigkeiten" in his *Musikalischer Almanach* for 1783, he printed the following notice, without clarification:

> P.S. You are correct that the fugue in Bach's *Heilig* . . . makes the best effect when it is done in a lively tempo. But to allow only three minutes for the entire fugue, which is said to be Bach's intention, is, to my mind, rather too fast, especially when one bears in mind that it ought to be church music. I find that five minutes makes neither too much nor too little of the thing; but to need eleven minutes, as is said to have happened in a great and otherwise extraordinary musical city, is abominable and a

---

[35] Heinrich Bellermann, "Nachtrag zu Kirnberger's Briefen," *Allgemeine musika-lische Zeitung*, ser. 3, VII (1872), cols. 441–42: "Die Fuge gerade durch dauerte 11 Minuten. Ich missbilligte es, weil es ganz dadurch verdorben wurde. Herr Bach in Hamburg, dem ich meldete, es gehörte nicht mehr als 5 Minuten Zeit dazu, überschickte mir beifolgendem Brief und setzt die Zeit auf 3 Minuten, mir scheint aber, dass 4 Minuten die beste Art sei; aber 11 Minuten ist garnicht vor Ekel anzuhören." See also Bitter, *Carl Philipp Emanuel und Wilhelm Friedemann Bach*, II, 323.

[36] Bellermann, "Nachtrag," col. 443: "Die Fuge in meinem 'Heilig' allein, ohne Wiederholung, welche nicht sein muss, muss nicht länger als 3 Minuten dauern."

[37] Johann Heinrich Voss, in the letter of 11 October 1776 (cited in n. 22 above), writes of the suitability of the Church of St. Michael for the antiphonal *Heilig*: "Morgen über 8 Tage wird die Musik in der Michaeliskirche aufgeführt, und die beÿden Chöre sollen, wie Bach uns sagte, an zweÿ Ende der Kirche, die recht für die Musik gewölbt ist, stehn." And much the same language appears in a notice in the *HCorr* for 25 October 1776; see Miesner, *Philipp Emanuel Bach im Hamburg*, pp. 93–94. For a description of the church and its important organ, see Charles Burney, *An Eighteenth-Century Musical Tour in Central Europe and the Netherlands*, ed. Percy A. Scholes (London, 1959), pp. 220–21. On the sorry state of the forces at Bach's disposal, see Miesner, *Philipp Emanuel Bach im Hamburg*, p. 15, and Burney, *An Eighteenth-Century Musical Tour*, p. 213. Matthias Claudius, in a letter to Gerstenberg in 1768, reports on a performance "in der neuen Michaelis-Kirche: Die erste Hälfte der Musik war von ihm selbst, sie war aber zu schwach besetzt, in der grossen Kirche Dienste zu tun . . . " (Matthias Claudius, *Botengänge: Briefe an Freunde*, ed. Hans Jessen, 2nd rev. ed. [Berlin, 1965], p. 37).

certain proof that the director of the performance must have little
knowledge and even less musical feeling.[38]

Among the documents pertaining to the rondo, the single leaf that
remains of the autograph score is the most telling. (A facsimile of the
leaf is shown in Figure 1.) It survives because Bach used its blank

Figure 1. Carl Philipp Emanuel Bach, autograph leaf for the Rondo in C, now a part
of Berlin, Staatsbibliothek Preussischer Kulturbesitz, Mus. ms. Bach St 236

[38] See *Musikalischer Almanach für Deutschland auf das Jahr 1783* (Leipzig, 1782; repr.
Hildesheim, 1974), p. 144: "N.S. Sie haben Recht, dass die Fuge in Bachs Heilig . . ."

verso to enter the newly composed horn parts for the Symphony in E-flat, W. 179 (H 654).[39] The horn parts are written on two separate leaves, sewn together to make a bifolium; the verso of the second leaf contains the final thirty-seven bars of the finale of the Sonata in F Major, W. 56/4 (H 269). From the *Nachlassverzeichniss* we learn that Bach composed the sonata in 1780. But it is likely that the sonata had been completed by December 1779, for in that month Bach wrote to Breitkopf of the second collection *für Kenner und Liebhaber*: "The content of these sonatas will differ totally from all my works—for everyone, I hope."[40] And in the letter of 16 December to Kirnberger, Bach added: "Soon I shall speak out with the second collection of my sonatas. May I once again beg your kindness? This collection will be quite different from the first."[41] Publication, again under the imprint of the author through Breitkopf's presses, was evidently completed by autumn of 1780.[42]

The symphony was composed in 1755, again according to the entry in the *Nachlassverzeichniss*. It is only very recently that anyone has bothered to notice that the horn and oboe parts were added very much later and that Bach recorded the change on the title page of the wrapper containing the original parts.[43] These accidental survivors

---

die beste Wirkung thut, wenn sie in einem lebhaften Tempo gemacht wird. Aber nur 3 Minuten auf die ganze Fuge zu rechnen, wie Bachs Meinung seyn soll, ist nach meiner Meinung doch auch etwas allzu geschwind; besonders wenn man bedenkt, dass es eine Kirchenmusik seyn soll. Ich finde, dass 5 Minuten der Sache nicht zu viel und nicht zu wenig thun; 11 Minuten aber dazu zu brauchen, wie in einer grossen und sonst ausserordentlich musikalischen Stadt geschehen seyn soll, ist abscheulich, und ein sicherer Beweiss, dass der Direktor, der das Stück aufgeführt hat, wenig Kenntnisse, und noch weniger musikalisches Gefühl haben müsse."

[39] The symphony parts are at D:B, Mus. ms. Bach St 236. The autograph fragments are not properly identified in Paul Kast, *Die Bach-Handschriften der Berliner Staatsbibliothek*, Tübinger Bach-Studien, 2/3 (Trossingen, 1958), p. 80. I am grateful to Eugene Helm and David Schulenberg for sharing their information on these sources.

[40] Hase, "Carl Philipp Emanuel Bach und Joh. Gottl. Im. Breitkopf," p. 96: "Der Inhalt dieser Sonaten wird ganz und gar von allen meinen Sachen verschieden seyn; ich hoffe für Jedermann."

[41] Bellermann, "Nachtrag," col. 443. The reading in Bitter, *Carl Philipp Emanuel und Wilhelm Friedemann Bach*, II, 300, is corrupt.

[42] Hase, "Carl Philipp Emanuel Bach und Joh. Gottl. Im. Breitkopf," p. 96. Two sonatas and three rondos were dispatched by 21 March 1780, as we learn from a letter to Breitkopf of that date. The unpublished letter is at D:DS.

[43] See *The Symphony 1720–1840: A Comprehensive Collection of Full Scores in Sixty Volumes*, ed. Barry S. Brook, ser. C, Vol. VIII, *Carl Philipp Emanuel Bach, Six Symphonies*, ed. Charles C. Gallagher and E. Eugene Helm (New York, 1982), p. 144, which illustrates the title on the wrapper.

from the autograph of W. 56 help to fix a *terminus ad quem*: the new symphony parts would not have been composed before W. 56 had been seen through the press—by the autumn of 1780, evidently. But it is the dating of the rondo that is to the point here, and in that regard, the juxtaposition of rondo and symphony is of no help.

If the fragment of the rondo is silent on its own dating, it stands as a rare witness to a process of composition that has remained obscure. We may infer from it that as late as the preparation of the autograph— a final autograph, one presumes—the closing music was to have gone differently; just how differently must remain uncertain, for without the control of an *Urschrift*, we cannot know whether the new passage replaces an earlier version of essentially the same music—whether, that is, the passage is a revision of detail—or whether it constitutes a fresh interpolation between measures 134 and 140. If this latter were the case, then measures 134 and 140 were originally contiguous, as suggested in Example 9.

The interpolated passage, whatever it may be thought to replace, speaks to that process of conciliation that Forkel was at pains to describe in his understanding of remote modulation in the Finale of the Trio in G. The articulation of this final, tonicizing statement of the principal theme must distinguish itself from all those disruptive articulations into which the intermediate statements of the theme had been thrust. The passage that I have described above (see Ex. 8) as a conciliatory résumé of those earlier articulations brings the harmony around, finally, to the true dominant at measure 128, prolonged and skewed in the diminished seventh at measure 134.

For all the posturing around the subdominant after measure 128, the dominant itself is rather shortchanged. And the registral positioning of the tritone at measure 134 seems more than normally disposed to reverberate well beyond the reprise at measure 140. But this is a dominant in search of a root. Bach's revision addresses the point and repositions the tritone at measure 139, where the last arpeggio gives us, finally, a dominant in $^6_5$ position. The effect is a rhythmic one, jogging what has seemed an interminable sequence of $^4_2$ appoggiaturas on the strong beats.

The Rondo in C can by no means be reckoned among the more interesting of the thirteen rondos in the collections published in the 1780s. The theme is not a rich one, and its mute profile does not gain from the insipid overtones that C major seems to generate. But the *Nachlassverzeichniss* will have us believe that the Rondo in C was the first of the lot. The point is important, for the order of publication in the subsequent volumes of these collections does not very often

Example 9
Rondo in C, showing a hypothetical early version in which mm. 134 and 140 are contiguous

conform to the order of composition as it goes in the *Verzeichniss*. Six of the rondos were composed in 1778 and 1779, and two of those from 1779 that did not get into Book III (1781) were resurrected for later volumes: one in Book IV (1783) and another in Book V (1785). There is hardly a one whose modulatory strategies are not more striking and subtle. But subtlety is not what is needed here. The Rondo in C exemplifies a new mode of tonal articulation in which fresh areas are struck without prior modulation in any orthodox sense—*ohne Ausweichung*, one might say. The consequences are great. The theme becomes the agent of tonal layering. Its Classical arch gives a certain stability to each of these areas, and, as a result, the rondo unfolds on a scale much grander than any earlier of Bach's works. The implications of such "unexplained" modulation are felt in the form of the piece. Bach must have sensed all of this, and that taste of discovery seems implicit in his little narrative: "When I played this rondo, I was asked . . . , 'Who but yourself would dare go directly from C major to E major?' " We cannot know if the new paragraph was written before any of the other rondos in these collections had been composed, but the novelty of the Rondo in C must have signified something for Bach valuable beyond the more brilliant and profound music to come.[44]

VI

Hamburg in the 1770s, neither an Eszterháza nor a Vienna, compensated for the decline of its musical prowess in a bracing intellectual climate that would invigorate this lively exchange of new music and critical reply. Bach is at its center, the catalyst. His music, never the object of a universal popular awe, did not sweep its audiences away. It spoke more directly to the *Kenner* than to the *Liebhaber*. There is a didactic aspect to the music that sets it apart from even the most complex works of Haydn and Mozart. This quality spoke out even in Bach's private performances, which, one gathers, were rather more like seminars than recitals: the testimonies of, among others, Carl Friedrich Cramer, Matthias Claudius, Charles Burney, Voss, and Reichardt all make the case.[45]

[44] That significance is evident in a letter dated 29 April 1780 in which Bach instructed Breitkopf to open the collection with the Rondo in C ("macht das Rondo aus C dur den Anfang"); that instruction was repeated in a letter of 13 May, in which the order of the entire collection was spelled out. The unpublished letters are at D:DS.

[45] See Cramer, *Magazin der Musik*, I (Hamburg, 1783; repr. Hildesheim, 1971), 36 n., 1252; Claudius, *Botengänge*, pp. 43–45; Burney, *An Eighteenth-Century Musical Tour*, pp. 219–20; Reichardt, *Briefe eines aufmerksamen Reisenden der Musik betreffend*, II

And we learn a good deal about Bach the teacher in a letter dated 15 October 1777 to an unnamed addressee who is evidently Forkel:

> A thousand thanks for your fine, your learned *Programma*! Herr Leister has had it for a long while, in order to review it for the [*Hamburgische unparteiische*] *Correspondent*. To my mind, N.B. in order to educate amateurs, many things may be omitted that many a musician neither knows nor needs to know. But the most important one—analysis, namely—is missing. One selects true masterpieces from all kinds of musical works; points out to the amateur the beautiful, the daring, and the new that is in them; at the same time one shows how insignificant the piece would be without these things; in addition one points out the mistakes and traps that have been avoided and, in particular, to what extent one can depart from the ordinary and venture something daring.[46]

The *Programma* must surely have been Forkel's *Über die Theorie der Musik in so fern sie Liebhabern und Kennern nothwendig und nützlich ist* (Göttingen, 1777), which, as its subtitle specifies, was intended as an invitation ("eine Einladungschrift") to Forkel's university lectures.[47] Very much more than that, Forkel's *Programma* is, in effect, a syllabus for a comprehensive curriculum in music. Or as Forkel puts it: "This, then, is the outline of a musical theory through which, to my mind, the amateur can be educated to become a true and genuine connoisseur."[48] It was this curriculum that would serve Forkel again in the

---

(Frankfurt, 1776), 15–16. For a rich account of Bach's intellectual and social relationships in Hamburg, see Ernst Fritz Schmid, *Carl Philipp Emanuel Bach und seiner Kammermusik*, pp. 27–86.

[46] The letter, without addressee, is given in Bitter, *Carl Philipp Emanuel und Wilhelm Friedemann Bach*, I, 348: "Tausend Dank für Ihr schönes, für Ihr gelehrtes Programma! Herr Leister hat es schon lange bey sich, um es im Correspondenten zu recensiren. Nach meiner Meynung, NB um Liebhaber zu bilden, könnten viele Dinge wegbleiben, die mancher Musicus nicht weiss, auch eben nothwendig nicht wissen darf. Das Vornehmste, nehml. das analysiren fehlt. Man nehme von aller Art von musicalischen Arbeiten wahrhafte Meisterstücke; zeige den Liebhabern das Schöne, das Gewagte, das Neue darin; man zeige zugleich, wenn dieses alles nicht wäre, wie unbedeutend das Stück sein würde; ferner weise man die Fehler, die Fallbrücken die vermieden sind, und besonders in wie fern einer vom Ordinairen abgeht und etwas wagen könne u.s.w."

[47] Forkel's tract is more easily accessible today in the reprint by Carl Friedrich Cramer, with the amended title "Von der Theorie . . . ," *Magazin der Musik*, I, 855–912. Cramer's reprint appeared, evidently, without Forkel's consent; see Forkel, *Musikalischer Almanach für Deutschland auf das Jahr 1784* (Leipzig, 1783; repr. Hildesheim, 1974), pp. v–viii, on the material that Cramer appropriated without Forkel's consent in Vol. I/1 of the *Magazin*.

[48] Cramer, *Magazin*, I, 904: "Die ist also der Plan einer musicalischen Theorie, durch welche nach meiner Meynung der Liebhaber zu einem wahren und ächten Kenner ausgebildet werden kann."

"Einleitung" to his *Allgemeine Geschichte der Musik*, I (Leipzig, 1788), and as the scaffold to the second part of the monumental *Allgemeine Litteratur der Musik* (Leipzig, 1792).[49]

On the face of it, Bach is quite right: analysis as a discipline in itself is missing. What Bach describes has no place in the rigorous taxonomy of Forkel's system, which is about musical *knowledge*: the codification of those properties in which musical grammar and rhetoric are constituted. Analysis, for Forkel, means *Zergliederung*: the work is dissected into its grammatical and rhetorical components. But Forkel's classification is powerless to distinguish the beautiful from the ordinary, the work of genius from hackwork. That is precisely what Bach's empirical, intuitive exercise means to address. And yet Forkel was evidently not insensitive to Bach's criticism, for, if he could find no way to express *analysieren* in his system, he sought, as critic, to put into practice Bach's advice on the teaching of master-pieces. And it was Bach's music that inspired him to his best essays. There are the famous ones on the finale of the Keyboard Trio in G, W. 90/2 (H 523) and the Keyboard Sonata in F Minor, W. 57/6 (H 173).[50] And there is the analysis of the opening phrase from the Rondo in G, W. 57/3 (H 271), to exemplify, in an intentional travesty, a violation of "the good inner relationship . . . or unity of idea necessary to the proper and good construction of a grammatical period."[51]

There is one final confirmation that the teacher in Bach lived on uncompromised until the end. In a poignant letter dated nine months before his death, Bach confided:

I want to write an introduction (*Anleitung*) to composition according to the current times, with all the necessary rules and with the omission of all pedantry. And with that, God willing, I shall close.[52]

[49] The connections between the *Theorie der Musik* and the introduction to the *Allgemeine Geschichte der Musik* were noted by Wolf Franck in "Musicology and Its Founder, Johann Nicolaus Forkel (1749–1818)," *The Musical Quarterly*, XXXV (1949), 591.

[50] For the former, see Forkel, *Musikalisch-kritische Bibliothek*, II (1778), 275–300; for the latter, Forkel, *Musikalischer Almanach für Deutschland auf das Jahr 1784* (1783), pp. 22–38.

[51] See Johann Nikolaus Forkel, *Allgemeine Geschichte der Musik*, I (Leipzig, 1788; repr. Graz, 1967), 40–42.

[52] The full letter is given in La Mara, *Musikerbriefe aus fünf Jahrhunderten*, I, 211–12: "Ich will eine Anleitung zur Composition, mit den nöthigen Regeln und mit Auslassung aller Pedanterey, nach jetziger Zeit schreiben, und damit, wenn mich Gott leben lässt, will ich schliessen. . . ." Ernst Fritz Schmid, *Carl Philipp Emanuel Bach und seiner Kammermusik*, p. 72, n. 5, quotes just this passage; the letter was then in a private collection in Belgium. La Mara proposed Forkel as the recipient, but (as Schmid suggests) the text of the letter is directed to a publisher.

We can only surmise how Bach might have sketched the outline for such an introduction and how compositional practice "according to the current times" might have been made manifest in it. *Modulation* would, no doubt, have figured prominently.

It is tempting to ponder whether the inclination in 1788 to write an *Anleitung* as a kind of last testament was not, in some degree, prompted by the challenge to put in order—to justify in some theoretical program—those great and idiosyncratic works of the final decades, chiefly the keyboard works in the collections *für Kenner und Liebhaber*. The new paragraph in the *Versuch*, for all that it tells us about Bach, signifies more than it teaches. The systematic and thorough treatment accorded such venerable topics as figured bass and ornamentation, whose entrenched traditions encouraged a retrospective view, could not be accorded modulation, for in this endeavor each of Bach's new works probed and explored the concept itself. Composers, however, theorize badly about their own music. That there is a need to do so at all is itself symptomatic of an intuition that the music will withstand the rigorous testing of its coherence.

State University of New York, Stony Brook

[20]

THE ART OF IMPROVISATION

DIE KUNST DER IMPROVISATION
Heinrich Schenker

TRANSLATED BY
RICHARD KRAMER

Our generation has squandered the art of diminution, the composing-out of sonorities [*Klängen*], and, like the fox in the fable, declares sour those grapes which it cannot reach. No longer able to understand the art of diminution bequeathed to us in the teaching of the masters, and the example they set, it turns ear and mind away from a fundamental law with which it can no longer cope, either creatively or in imitation.

This generation has not the slightest inkling that all its despair and impotency, the tormented quest for that which is ever different – different from the art of the master, different even from nature itself – originates simply in the incapacity for the artistic linearization of tonal concepts that are given in nature. It anaesthetizes its incapacity with the gesture of novelty, under the proud and highly suggestive title 'progress'. That became the customary dodge of every reaction from the darkness below, and it remains so today. The stabs in the back which genius must suffer perpetrated at first by a few individuals from below, then multiplied by the masses – simulate a proud revolution, certain of victory. But the perpetrators overlook that genius, unlike emperor or prince, cannot be deposed by the caprice of the masses, that in the eternally aristocratic realm of genius the methods of political revolution are without value. Its revolutions here must remain mere fictions, the imaginary movements of non-professionals, arranged and incited by journalists and book-writers from outside, entirely without effect and outside the true history of the intellect. Finally even this self-induced deafening must fail, for it never transforms incapacity into ability: *Naturam non expellas furca.*[1]

---

[1] [Horace, *Epistles* 1, no.10, line 24: *Naturam expelles furca, tamen usque recurret* (you may expel Nature with a pitchfork, but she always returns).]

And thus it comes about today that from every corner where novelty and progress are 'manufactured', veritable intellectual outbacks, shrieks of a passionate promise for the future resound: this generation would like at the least to stimulate the next towards some decisive artistic novelty, but it feels itself incapable of accomplishing even this deed. If, however, the promise of a deed counts for very little in the political world – revolutions promise much and hold to nothing – how much less do such promises mean in the realm of art!

Thus our generation dwells not even in its own present. It no longer demands of itself the strength to pay its debts to the great masters – and thus the strength to receive the past in itself, which is the presupposition for all virtuous life in the present. Nothing really remains for it but to depend solicitously on the future of the next generation – {12} why ever should it presume to anticipate the work of that generation? – and, in so doing, does battle against an apparition of stagnation. It does not suspect that it itself is the apparition, and that all the effort that it expends to produce something new and to oppose stagnation is not nearly sufficient to rise even a step above the masses.

As the past so often teaches, the few individual representatives of the immutable authority from above remain, and all the more proudly, after the continually repeated reactions of those from below. An authority from above can never be produced from below. As little as the living are able to comprehend death, so little can the spiritually dead comprehend the spiritual life of a genius. And yet this remains to be demonstrated.

★

Music is the living motion of tones in the space given in Nature: the composing-out (the rendering in melodic line, the linearization) of the Nature-given sonority (see *Harmonielehre*, p.281/p.211; 'Freier Satz'; 'Elucidations').[2] The law of all life, the motion which, as procreation, issues forth beyond the boundaries of individual being, penetrates into man in this sonority which Nature has preordained in his hearing. Everything in music is born of this motion, of this procreative force. Yet all procreation is bestowed through the spontaneous grace of life-bestowing Nature. Those whom Nature has sent into the world unfit for procreation: what will they accomplish against her? What does this most wretched of generations, with all its insolence born in delusion and its dogmatically demanding temperament, want in its current alignment against Nature when she has, so to speak, denied it its spiritual loins?

Consequently, it is entirely remote from my thought to oblige the caprice of man when I speak here of the art of improvisation according to the testimony in C.P.E. Bach's theoretical and practical works, and from the examples by Handel (examples which can, of course, be multiplied endlessly). I want only to offer a modest contribution to the art of diminution, which is the principal agent in the free fantasy, and at the very least to alert the ear to the inner laws of diminution in order to protect it from the stagnation induced in precisely those who speak out most loudly against it.

I

Diminution in its entirety surely does not allow of a single theory, for the subject matter is too vast: no theorist could furnish a method in {13} diminution technique for all genres of composition. Accordingly, even C.P.E. Bach is satisfied with a minimum, with the art of diminution in the free fantasy, as presented in his *Versuch über die wahre Art, das Clavier zu spielen*, II, 41.[3] It was the opportunity provided by just this topic that prompted the great master of tone and word to speak out, and he is very clearly conscious of this, as follows from the first two paragraphs of the chapter.[4] They read:

[2] [Here, where Schenker is at pains to depict the phenomenon of music as a metaphor for creation itself, it seems wise to convey the sense of *Klang* as some primordial sonority, preliminary to the notion of 'chord', which allows of no such ambiguity in English, even though the term is often used by Schenker in this specific sense. The lapidary opening sentence of the 'Elucidations' – 'The musical sonority as it exists in Nature is a triad' [*Der Klang in der Natur ist ein Dreiklang*] – encourages this elemental distinction.]

[3] In 'Freier Satz' I undertake to treat diminution systematically. [The topic is addressed in *Der freie Satz*, §§242–83.]

[4] [Schenker seems to have worked not from the original edition of part II of Bach's *Versuch* (1762), but from the authorized revision, published posthumously by Schwickert of Leipzig in 1797 (see

[§1] A fantasy is called free when it contains no regular distribution of bars, and modulates to more keys than is usual in other kinds of pieces which are either composed or improvised in a regular metre.

[§2] For these latter pieces, a knowledge of the entire range of composition is required: for the former, merely a basic understanding of harmony and some rules governing its disposition are adequate. Both types demand natural ability, the fantasy in particular. It is possible that one who has studied composition with success, and has demonstrated his skill with the pen, will nevertheless improvise poorly. On the other hand, I believe that one can always predict with certainty good progress in composition for one who has a gift for improvisation, provided that he does not begin his studies *too late*, and that he writes *profusely*.

Still, I recommend that one read again what Bach says on the elaboration of fermatas (*Versuch*, 1, 2, §9) as well as on the elaboration of cadenzas (1, 3, §30).[5] Although diminution at a fermata or in a cadenza plays a different role than it does in the free fantasy, these explanations are nevertheless of great value for a general theory of diminution.

★

§§3, 6 and 8–11 are concerned with tonal areas in the free fantasy. §3 even advances the notion of a principal key for the fantasy:

A free fantasy consists of varied harmonic passages which can be executed in all kinds of figures and divisions [*Zergliederungen*]. In doing so, one must establish a key with which to begin and end. Although no metre is established in such fantasies, the ear nevertheless demands a certain proportion in the alternation and duration of the harmonies among themselves, as we shall hear further on, and {14} the eye a relation in the note values, so that one's ideas can be written down ...

Bach grasps the necessity of the tonic more pointedly in §6:

When one does not have much time to display one's craft in extemporizing, then one must not venture too far into other keys, for one will have to break off very soon. And yet the principal key must not be abandoned too soon at the outset, nor recaptured too late at the end. At the beginning, the principal key must prevail for a long while, so that

also note 7). In rendering Bach's text into English, I have consulted Mitchell's translation (pp. 430–45) – where ii, 41 is renumbered as chapter seven – but have for the most part translated afresh.]

5   [The term *Cadenz* had a latitude of meaning in the eighteenth century. In this instance, Bach surely means to specify not 'cadence' in its conventional sense, but those elaborated indices of structural significance that would, in slightly later parlance, be classified under the term 'cadenza'. On this distinction, see Mitchell's valuable comment (p.164, note 35).]

one is certain to hear what will follow from it. And one must dwell in it again for a long while before the close, so that the listener will be prepared for the end and the principal key will impress itself in the memory.

Thus Bach insists on a principal key to be used in equal proportion in longer and shorter fantasies alike. And if, like Bach, one takes the scale degrees of the tonic for 'keys' (see below), then one might already extract from §6 a theory of tonality.

§8 is concerned with the interpolation of auxiliary chords that simulate a key. One notes in particular the expressive turn of phrase: 'not truly formal cadences' [*nicht eben förmliche Schlußcadenzen*]. The paragraph reads:

In fantasies where there is ample time to be heard, one may modulate more extensively to other keys, where truly formal cadences are not always required; they occur at the end, and at most once in the middle. It is sufficient for the leading note [*semitonium modi*] of the key to which one is modulating to be present in the bass or in some other voice. This note [*Intervall*] is the key to all genuine modulations and the distinguishing feature of them. When it lies in the bass, the seventh-, the sixth- or the $^6_5$ chord results (a). But it may also be found in dispositions which arise from the inversion of those chords (b). It is one of the beauties of improvisation that, in the midst of a fantasy, one can feign modulation to another key by a formal cadence and then take a different turn. This and other judicious deceptions make a fantasy attractive. But they must not be used to excess, thereby obscuring what is natural.

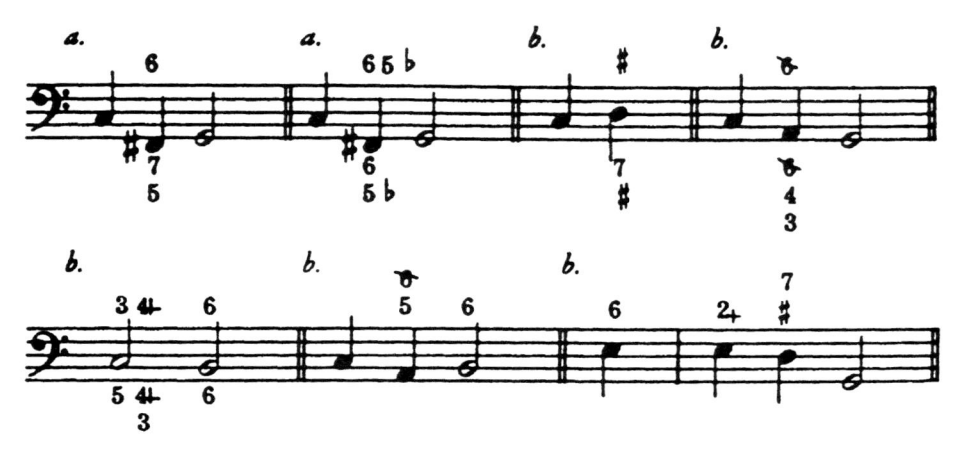

I repeat: when Bach speaks even in such instances of 'other keys', one must not be deceived by his language. The ground-plan of a fantasy adduced by him in §15 indicates clearly that by 'keys' [*Tonarten*] he describes a composing-out of scale degrees; in any case the term is not defined with systematic precision. That is confirmed in the {15} following paragraph, where Bach speaks of 'most closely related' and 'somewhat more remote' keys, which however are designated in the course of the discussion by 'fifth', 'sixth' and so forth. §9 reads:

In a free fantasy one can modulate from the tonic to the most closely related keys, to those somewhat more remote, and indeed to all other keys as well. As little as one ought to undertake strange or frequent modulations to a wide range of keys in strictly measured pieces, a fantasy that adheres to the most closely related keys sounds naïve. As is well known, the closest modulations in the major keys are to the fifth degree with the major third and the sixth degree with the minor third. From minor keys, one moves first of all to the third degree with the major triad and to the fifth degree with the minor triad. When one wishes to modulate to more distant keys, in the major keys this will be to the second and third degrees with the minor triad and to the fourth degree with the major triad. From minor keys, one modulates to the fourth degree with the minor third and to the sixth and seventh degrees with the major third. All the other keys are remote, and can be used with equal effect in a free fantasy, even though they stand at varying distances from the tonic ...

§10 is devoted to chromaticism:

... When one wishes to modulate more firmly to the *more distant* keys, and not merely to touch upon them superficially, it is not sufficient simply to reach for the *semitonium modi* in the belief that one has now arrived where one has wanted to go, and that one may move on at once to other keys. Rather, one must gradually prepare the ear for the new key by means of a few other interpolated harmonic progressions, so that it is not disagreeably surprised. There are keyboard players who understand chromaticism and can justify its use, but only very few who know how to execute chromaticism agreeably, relieved of its crudeness. We note generally, and in particular in the examples given below, that in those exercises in which one begins to stray rather far from the established key, one must dwell rather longer [in the harmonic transition] than in the others ...

Bach demands a more precise justification even in the deployment of chromaticism: not even in the free fantasy will he tolerate the self-deception 'that one has now arrived where one has wanted to go' simply by having seized upon the *semitonium modi*.[6]

{16} In §11 the chord of the diminished seventh is now contemplated:

To arrive at the most distant keys in a yet more concise and nevertheless agreeably surprising manner, no chord is as convenient and fruitful as the seventh-chord with the

---

[6] Perceived from the thoroughly false basic ideas expressed in Reger's *Beiträge zur Modulationslehre* – compare §§7–11 in Bach's chapter on the free fantasy, and *Harmonielehre*, p.445/*p.336* – what a discrepancy in the treatment of chromatic modulation, even on this single point! [For more on Schenker's attitude to Reger's modulation tutor, see *Meisterwerk* II, pp.190–1.]

diminished seventh and diminished fifth, for by inversion and by enharmonic changes a great number of harmonic transformations can be undertaken ...

★

Finally we come to §§13–15 [§§12–14 in the first edition],[7] the most important in the chapter, in which diminution will be treated in its essence. §13 [§12] reads:

The beauty of variety is also felt in the fantasy, in which all kinds of figures and all manner of good execution must appear. Nothing but runs, nothing but sustained or broken full chords, tires the ear. The passions will be neither excited nor soothed, whereas it is precisely to these ends that a fantasy ought to be put to best advantage ...

The expression 'all kinds of figures' here signifies more than it appears to say. Bach expresses it in the demand for an alternation of figures in general, which I designate 'change of diminution'. (See 'Freier Satz' and below, p.? [sic].)[8] A change of diminution of this kind renders important service even in the free fantasy: by antithesis it divides and unifies at one and the same time, and thus serves the unity of the whole as well (see *Tonwille* 2, pp.17 and 36).

What C.P.E. Bach understands by 'all manner of good execution' is to be gathered from the *Versuch*, I, 3, §3:

The elements of performance are loudness and softness of the notes, their touch and velocity [*Schnellen*]; the execution of legato, staccato, vibrato and arpeggiation; sustaining, dragging and pressing ahead. Anyone who uses these things not at all, or at the wrong time, is a bad performer.

One must not seek in Bach's word 'passions' [*Leidenschaften*] what certain aestheticians of the doctrine of affections bring to it. One need only recall part I,

---

[7] [In the original edition of part II of the *Versuch*, 'in welchem die Lehre von dem Accompaniment und der freyen Fantasie abgehandelt wird' (1762), the final chapter comprises fourteen paragraphs (denoted by the symbol §). In the revised edition (1797) a new '§12' is inserted and the final three paragraphs are renumbered 13–15. Schenker clearly had before him a text with fifteen paragraphs. Omitting the new '§12' in characteristic silence, he must have sensed in it an intrusion in the argument of the original text of the chapter.

This very paragraph is the subject of inquiry in Richard Kramer, 'The New Modulation of the 1770s: C.P.E. Bach in Theory, Criticism, and Practice', *Journal of the American Musicological Society* 38 (1985), pp.551–92.

For the present translation, we retain Schenker's paragraph numbering but indicate the original numbering (also used in Mitchell's translation) in square brackets at the start of each of Bach's paragraphs.]

[8] [Schenker seems to have meant to refer the reader to p.69 in *Meisterwerk* I (p.36 of the present translation), where a paragraph on the term *Motivwechsel* concludes with a reference back to p.16. The mark of interrogation is surely an editorial oversight.]

3, §13 to understand that he means by it simply the consequences of a change of diminution: pure musical effects which have nothing in common with the amateurishly misunderstood and so grossly exaggerated ideas of the aestheticians. For Bach, even the individual motives of diminution are really distinct affects, distinct passions, so greatly does he feel their unifying and characteristic properties, and at the same time their contrast to one another. Similarly we read in §29 of the same chapter {17} the sentence: 'Nevertheless one notes that dissonances are generally played louder, consonances softer, for the former emphatically elevate the passions and the latter soothe them.' For Bach, a dissonance even in passing signifies a 'passion' – and from this it follows that in §13 of the chapter on the free fantasy Bach will have wanted to say nothing more than that the creator of a fantasy must have taken pains to alternate motives, in order to produce tension and to transmit it to the listener. Nothing more. And yet how much that signifies may be gauged by the desolate times in which we live, in which even this minimum has become unattainable.

§13 continues:

... When using broken chords one must move neither too hurriedly nor too unevenly (a) from one harmony to the next. Only in chromatic progressions can occasional exceptions to this rule be made to good effect ...

(Compare this to the turn of phrase in §3: 'a certain proportion in the alternation and duration of the harmonies among themselves'.) And further:

One must not arpeggiate the harmony continuously in a uniform colour. In addition, one may at times move with both hands from a low register to a higher one; this can also be done entirely with the left hand, the right hand remaining in its [natural] register. This manner of performance is suited to the harpsichord, for it produces an agreeable alternation of a synthetic *forte* and *piano*. Anyone who possesses the skill does well if he avoids the continuous use of the natural harmonies exclusively, and instead deceives the ear now and then; but if his powers are limited in this respect, a varied and competent performance incorporating all kinds of figures must make agreeable those harmonies which, when played evenly, would sound plain. Most dissonances can be doubled in the left hand. The ear tolerates the octaves that arise when the harmony is thus reinforced. Doubling the fifth, on the contrary, is to be avoided. The fourth, when in company with the fifth and ninth, and the ninth in any case should not be doubled.

To these last sentences it may only be noted that, although Bach does not object to the reinforcing with octaves in the left hand even in dissonances, he always places fifths under the law of obligatory voice-leading.[9] That suspensions of the fourth and ninth may not be doubled follows for Bach from the very nature of the suspension.

{18} §14 [§13] speaks about how diminution, more narrowly defined, may be executed:[10]

All chords can be arpeggiated in a variety of ways, and expressed in fast and slow figures. Arpeggiations of a chord in which its principal intervals as well as those formed by certain neighbour notes are repeated (a) are especially pleasing for they produce greater variety than a simple arpeggio in which the voices are struck one by one as they lie under the hands.

The simple little words 'are repeated' express a significant event. Bach's example a) is to be grasped when one takes as an aid the following illustration, which underlines that diminution:

In Fig. 1a the chords in the left and right hand still leave a gap opened. In Fig. 1b this gap is filled out by the interpolation of a chord in the right hand; at the first and second harmonies these chords comprise an octave, at the third harmony an augmented sixth. This disparity is explained in the contrary motion between $b^2-a^2-g\sharp^2$ in the inner voice and the $g\sharp-a-b\flat$ in the bass (See Fig. 1a). In

---

[9] [Bach, cautioning against doubling the fifth degree, seems to have in mind a doubling of the flattened fifth and the parallelism of octaves that would necessarily follow from such a doubling. Schenker, on the other hand, seems to read Bach to refer explicitly to a proscription against consecutive fifths.]

[10] In all Bach's examples, the additional phrasing marks, dotted slurs, brackets, scale-degree indications and other symbols are my own.

Bach's example, as in Fig. 1c, a descending arpeggiation embellished with acciaccature negotiates between interpolation and principal chord in each instance. The 'repetition' of which Bach speaks refers to the interpolated chords. What art even in this modest application of diminution! Bach perceives an essential distinction between such alterations in the arpeggiations and the simple breaking of chords in an arpeggio (see above).

(§14:) ... In all arpeggiated triads and in passages that can be reduced to a triad one can, for the sake of elegance, approach each interval from the major or minor second below, {19} without permitting these notes to continue sounding. This one calls *arpeggiating with acciaccature* ...

Acciaccature were already apparent in Bach's example a), and they require no further explanation in examples b) and c). But one should take note of the hidden rhythm which, by the interpolation of neighbour notes, now and then insinuates itself in the diminution. Example b) actually sounds thus:

Fig. 2

Great charm often resides in a concealed rhythm of this kind, and under certain circumstances it even assumes significance for the voice-leading.

(§14:) ... In runs the empty intervals of the chord are filled out: with this filling-out one can move up and down in one or in several octaves in proper proportion. When repetitions occur in such runs, as in d),

and, at the same time, foreign intervals are interpolated, as in e),

pleasing variations arise. Runs in which many progressions of semitones appear require a moderate tempo ...

The run shown in example d) is based upon an arpeggiation in several strata
$(1-\flat 7-5-3)$:

Fig. 3

By 'repetitions' is to be understood not only the repetition of the arpeggiation
beginning with c^1 (see the brackets in Bach's example d) and in Fig. 3), but also
the imitation within each arpeggiation of one span, a seventh-progression, by
another, a sixth-progression (see the slurs). The interval of a third between the
individual progressions is filled in with a passing note. Apart from the emphasis
on c, c^1 and c^2 as well as on g and g^1, which occurs automatically, no further
rhythmic articulation enters into consideration here.

{20} The figure at Bach's example e) can be derived from the motive of the
fifth, E♭–A, which is then repeated:

Fig. 4

Accordingly, at the first display of the motive in Bach's diminution the two notes
$e♭^3$ and a^2 rise up from $f♯^2$, which acts like a bass (see Figs. 4b and 4c), while at
the repetition $(e♭^2-a^1)$ the diminished fifth is simply filled in with passing notes.
Note, however, that in the first passage (to the $e♭^3$) $g♯^2$ is intentionally omitted,
for it is surely meant in the first instance to express the prototype of the
diminished seventh-chord; $g♯^2$ appears only in the second passage $(f♯^2-a^2)$.

(§14:) ... In the course of passage work, all kinds of grouping may now and then be
alternated, as in example f) ...

By 'grouping' [*Aufgabe*] Bach means a specific motion in figured bass, in this
instance the succession 5–6 5–6, as in Fig. 5a:

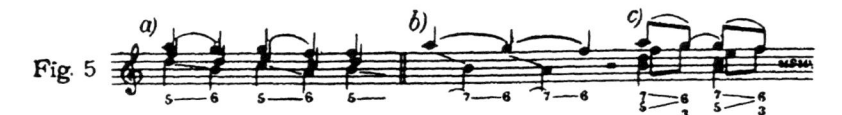

The extensions of the descending scales beneath d^2, c^2 and b^2 (as roots of the fifths) – see Bach's example – are not directed at the production of harmonic intervals to the fifths in question. Rather, Bach simply fills in with passing notes the gaps of a third opened up between the bass notes of the particular sonorities; but he does this in such a way that the passing notes c^2, b^1 and a^1 are developed in special third-progressions, c^2–a^1, b^1–$g\#^1$, a^1–$f\#^1$. The lowest tones – a^1, $g\#^1$ and $f\#^1$ – act as neighbour notes. When they are omitted, one obtains rather the effect of 7–6 7–6; see Figs. 5b and 5c.

(§14:) ... The triad with its inversions can be expressed by one and the same kind of run, and the same is true of the seventh-chord and its inversions. In groupings which contain an augmented second, {21} a progression including that interval is *at times* avoided, as in example g); but in certain figurations it is acceptable, as in h) ...

Bach's word and illustration attest to an exceptionally fine hearing of a parallelism. At g) the arpeggiation bb^1–$c\#^2$ is avoided only because the augmented second does not express the motive of a third (e^2–g^2, $c\#^2$–e^2 and g^1–bb^1), and thus cannot reply in parallel.[11] But if, on the other hand, the diminished seventh is broken into three-voiced chords as in h), then, in spite of the augmented second, it is possible to preserve the parallelism in the last two inversions of the fourth.

(§14:) ... Certain imitations, both in direct and in contrary motion, can be brought into play in various voices to excellent effect, as in example i) ...

---

[11] See J.S. Bach, *Chromatic Fantasy*, bars 21–2 and 31; *Well-tempered Clavier*, I, Prelude in Eb minor, bar 18, a passage discussed in *Tonwille* I, pp.40[–1].

Example i) is concerned with the following:

Fig. 6

The execution displays a fine parallelism in the imitation of the [ascending] seventh-progression c^1–b♭^{1} by the descending seventh-progression d^3–e^2.

★

What energy of musical thought and power of invention are manifest in the following paragraph, which presents the ground-plan and the realization of the free fantasy![12] §15 [§14] reads:

So that my reader will acquire a clear and useful concept of the organization of a free fantasy in related examples of all kinds, I refer him to the lesson [*Probestück*] cited in the preceding paragraph, and to the Allegro to be found on the attached copper plate engraving.[13] Both pieces are free fantasies; the former is interspersed with much chromaticism, {22} while the latter consists *for the most part* of quite natural and usual progressions. The skeleton of the latter, given below, is represented in [the notation of] a figured bass. Note values are expressed as accurately as possible. In the realization, each arpeggiated chord is to be performed twice. When the second arpeggiation is to be taken in a different register in either the right or the left hand, this is indicated. The intervals in the slow, full chords, all of which are arpeggiated, are of a single duration, even though white and black notes had to be set above one another for the sake of clarity, because of limited space. At (1) we observe the sustaining of the harmony in the principal key at the beginning and the end. At (2) a modulation advances to the fifth degree, where one remains for a good while, until the harmony moves to E minor at (x). The three notes at (3), bound together by a slur underneath them, anticipate the following reiteration of the second-chord, which is regained by an inversion of the harmony. The anticipatory motion at (3) is realized in slow figures, in which the bass has been intentionally omitted. The transition from the seventh-chord on b to the adjacent second-chord on b♭ reveals an ellipsis for, strictly speaking, the $^6_4$ chord on b or a triad on c ought to have preceded the second-chord. At (4) the harmony appears to move towards D minor. But with the omission of the minor triad on d at (5), the augmented fourth in the second-chord on c is seized instead, as if one wished to modulate to G major. Nevertheless, G minor harmony

---

[12] In the reprint by [Walter] Niemann (Leipzig: C.F. Kahnt, [1906; repr. 1917, 1920, 1925]), the realization for which the reader of §15 [§14] is most eager is not to be found in its proper place.

[13] [The *Probestück* to which Bach refers is the Fantasy in C minor, the so-called 'Hamlet' Fantasy, published as the final piece (literally, the third movement of the sixth sonata) in the collection issued with part 1 of the *Versuch* as *Exempel nebst 18 Probestücken in 6 Sonaten zu C.P.E. Bachs Versuch ... auf XXVI Kupfer-Tafeln* (Berlin, 1753). For the extensive literature on the piece, see E. Eugene Helm, *Thematic Catalogue of the Works of Carl Philipp Emanuel Bach* (New Haven and London: Yale University Press, 1989), item 75.]

is taken (6), initiating the return to the tonic, for the most part through dissonant chords. The fantasy closes with an organ point.

Here is the ground-plan [see also Plate 1]:[14]

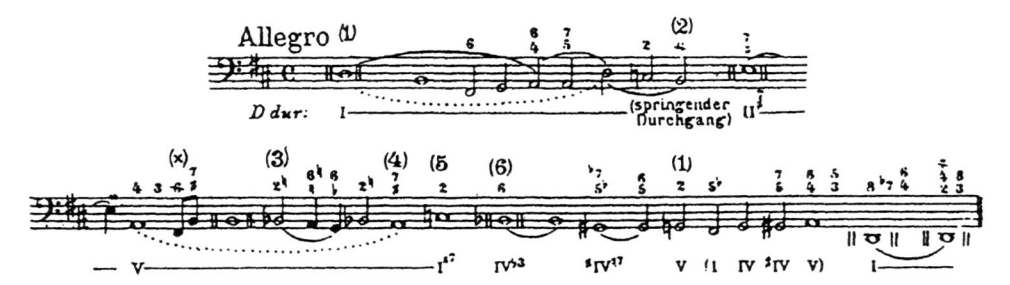

The plan exemplifies a certainty of goal which is given only to genius. Fully conscious of the paths taken, the creative force is mysteriously bound up above all with the Urlinie! Still, so much remains unaddressed in Bach's explanatory language: it is not that the musical facts of the case are falsely represented, {23} but that his language was as yet inadequate to supply the right words to explain the deeper relationships. In order to illuminate and substantiate Bach's plan through the Urlinie and the transformations that spring from it, I submit the following illustration (Fig. 7) – less to rectify Bach's explanation by my own than to clarify what remains still hidden behind his language:

According to Fig. 7a, the bass is comprehended in the fourth-progression D–A, which poses the danger of consecutive fifths (see *Meisterwerk* I, p.149/*p.82*, Fig. 2). For that reason the first fifth in the succession

$$a–g$$
$$D–C$$

is led to the sixth, and following this, to avoid the consecutive fifths

$$f\text{———}e$$
$$Bb–A,$$

a passing seventh is interpolated at $\hat{3}$.

---

[14] [The two representations of the work – what Schenker refers to as *Plan* and *Ausführung* – are shown in Plates 1 and 2, respectively, taken from the original edition of part II of the *Versuch*. Here one might wish to savour Bach's term *Gerippe* ('skeleton'), which has none of the causal implications of Schenker's *Plan* and even encourages the two 'views' of the work as simultaneous and inseparable. It is clear why Schenker will have wanted to privilege the *Gerippe* above the *Ausführung* in a hierarchical sense, but it is unclear why he should have wanted to suggest that the former was actually conceived before the latter.]

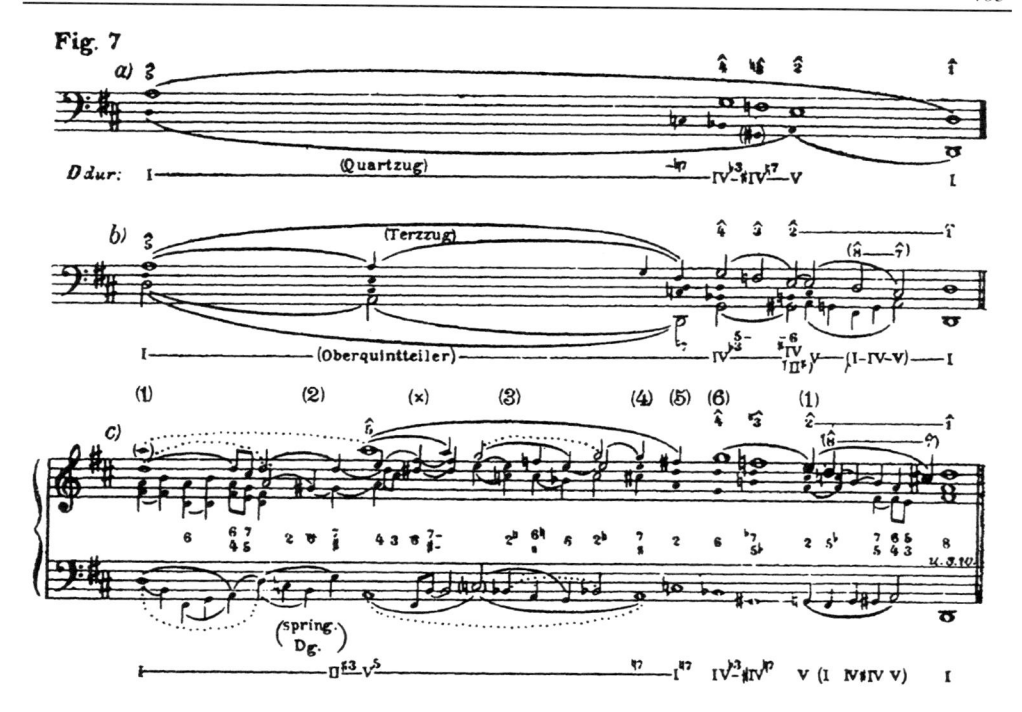

Fig. 7b shows the unfolding of the third a–g–f♯ in the treble, in the service of $\hat{5}$, coupled with a motion through the dominant divider [*Oberquintteiler*] in the bass. At the end of both motions, the seventh ♮7 accrues to the tonic, whose effect is to tonicize the subdominant area (*Harmonielehre*, p.337/p.256). In its further course as well, the Urlinie articulates itself in third-progressions, as if conceived in imitation of the first such progression: the $\hat{4}$–$\hat{2}$ stakes claim to the subdominant area, while the third-progression

$$\hat{2}————$$
$$(\hat{8}–\hat{7})$$

arises from the dominant harmony, where indeed the motion in the bass simulates a cadence.

{24} Further diminution in the voice-leading is captured in Fig. 7c. At (1) – for the sake of comparison, I have retained Bach's numbering (1) to (6) in the sketch – we see what is comprehended in the 'sustaining of the harmony in the principal key at the beginning and the end': the bass moves to the fifth above as a divider, through which the circle of harmonic degrees [*Stufenkreis*] I–IV–V–I is intimated. Against appearances, one must speak here of an ascending fifth-progression, as shown in Fig. 8a:

Fig. 8 {
(diss. Dg.) (kons. Dg.)

but the lower F♯ (shown in Fig. 8b) is expressly sought out in order to obtain a $^6_3$ harmony above the B, instead of the dissonant chord above the passing E. Yet I repeat what I stated above: considering that the results are the same, the difference in the manner of observation is of little importance, which is why it is basically one and the same whether Bach calls this voice-leading a 'sustaining of the harmony' or whether I, weighing the voice-leading more precisely in concept and word, speak here of a division of the tonic harmony D at the A a fifth above, and also of a fifth-progression in the bass to the dominant divider.

If, according to Fig. 7b, the harmony must proceed directly from the tonic to the dominant divider, the inclusion of the harmony on E, in the sense of II$^{\sharp 3}$– V, suggests itself in the prolongation [Fig. 7c]. But a succession of consecutive fifths threatens at the step motion between the triads on D and E (as is seen in Fig. 9a); a 5–6 exchange, with the root omitted, must therefore help (see Fig. 9b).

Fig. 9 {

For Bach, the chromatic g♯ no longer belongs to the 'principal key'. Indeed, it signifies for him a modulation (see §8 in the chapter on free fantasy, quoted above): a 'modulation to the fifth degree', he calls it [in §15]. Accordingly, he places the number (2) precisely above the sixth-chord that generates the chromaticism.

Fig. 7c further represents the dispersal of the third-progression {25} a^2–g^2– $f\sharp^2$ in the treble and the corresponding diminution in the bass. The range of the diminution, which continues as far as (4), aims at establishing the seventh in the dominant chord on A (see Fig. 7b). The bass rises to the minor third of the triad on A, the g^2 in the treble occurring precisely above the C; it then falls back to the root A, and at that moment the V$^{\natural 7}$ is grown to full maturity.

A step-by-step explanation will bring to light all the mystery of this profound and difficult voice-leading. The B between A and C in the bass ought not to be understood simply as a passing note, but rather as the bearer of a harmony in its own right, which does not alter its primary passing nature. Nothing would have been more obvious than to form a seventh-chord ($B_{\sharp3}^{7}$), yet the threat of consecutive fifths demanded that the same means be taken as earlier at the progression from D to E (see Fig. 9). Precisely this chromatic d$\sharp$, which is new in relation to the key of the dominant, will give Bach cause to inscribe it with an (X); see above. The path from $B_{\sharp3}^{7}$ leads more easily to C (quasi V–VI in E minor) than to the C$\sharp$ a whole tone removed. But C$\sharp$ would presuppose the chromatic motion B–B$\sharp$–C$\sharp$ and would moreover force a g$\sharp^{2}$ in the treble instead of the g^{2} which is the goal. Bach clothes this concern in the simple words 'the harmony moves to E minor'. One sees how Bach's word strikes in the direction of profundity without actually describing it in final detail.

But now to the most miraculous event in the fantasy. According to Fig. 7c, the root C was established at the peak, as it were, of the diminution of the dominant, from which point the descent to the root A had to ensue, following the law of the progression $\underline{\text{VII}}\text{–V}^{\sharp3}\text{–I}^{\sharp3}$ in the minor mode, in this instance in D minor:

$$
\begin{array}{ccccccc}
\text{C} & - & \text{B}\flat & - & \text{A} & - & \text{D} \\
\natural\text{VII}^{\flat7} & - & \text{(passing note)} & - & \text{V}^{\sharp} & - & \text{I}^{\sharp3}
\end{array}
$$

(compare with Fig. 19 below and the discussion following it). Thus the composing-out of the harmony on C assumes the form of a third-progression (g^{2}–f^{2}–e^{2}) in the treble and a fourth-progression (C–B$\flat$–A–G) in the bass. Only at this confirmation of the C$^{\flat7}$ harmony does its inversion as a second-chord follow, whereupon the root of the dominant finally returns. And it must not be overlooked that the seventh, g^{2}, undergoes an expressive reinforcement by the third-progression g^{2}–e^{2}. But in the realization, it is precisely this C which falls away, so that the B turns back directly to B$\flat$. Bach was clearly aware of this ellipsis, as follows from §15. (Indeed, if a $^{6}_{4}$ chord on B were supposed in place of the ellipsis, it would yield only a neighbour harmony [*Nebennoten-Harmonie*], while the triad on C, as I propose in Fig. 7c, alludes to the two third-progressions in the bass.)

{26} For the composing-out of the C major harmony in the form of a second-chord occasioned by the ellipsis, Bach finds the poetic words 'anticipate the following reiteration of the second-chord' (see the dotted slur from B$\flat$ to B$\flat$ in Fig. 7c). More emphasis is in fact placed on the second of these second-chords on B$\flat$, as the semitone immediately before the root of the dominant on A, than on the first. Thus I can only repeat here what I have already said more than once: the master's ear creates out of the innermost depth, while his word, though it points in the right direction, lags perceptibly behind without actually losing in beauty as testimony in a significant essay.

At (4) Bach is aware that the species of diminution in the bass (Bb–A) finally induces the expectation of D minor ('the harmony appears to move towards D minor'). In this respect, too, my interpretation agrees with Bach's, for I derive the third-progression C–Bb–A in the bass from the minor (see above). It doesn't matter whether the tonic actually stays in the minor or moves to the major. If, in our example, the tonic triad of the principal key appears to be D major, this only confirms a modal mixture [*Mischung*] with the composing-out in minor that precedes it (see *Harmonielehre*, p.106/*p.84*).

But the root of the tonic is elided – see the (5) in Fig. 7c; the second-chord takes its place. The seizing of the minor third in the subdominant – see Bach's (6) – is the result of this modal mixture (Bach: '... as if one wished to modulate to G major. Nevertheless G minor harmony is taken ...').

Now to Bach's realization of the plan [see also Plate 2]:[15]

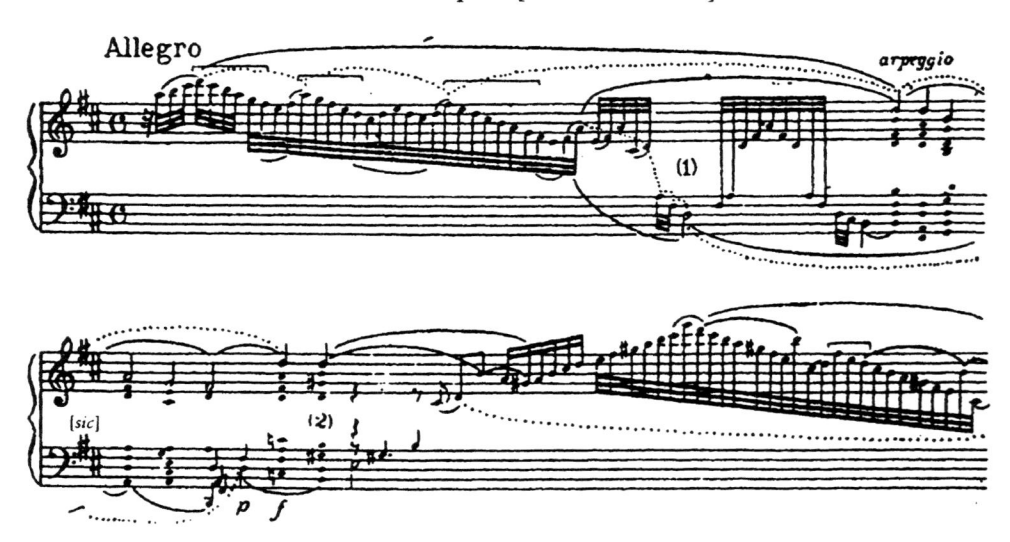

---

[15] [As will be clear from a comparison of Schenker's rendering of the *Ausführung* with Bach's copper plate engraving, the bracketed figures with which Bach cues his explanation to the Fantasy were set in the *Gerippe* but emphatically not in the *Ausführung*. Mitchell, in his English edition of the *Versuch*, takes the same licence, and exacerbates the matter by misplacing Bach's final figure (1) in the *Gerippe* (and necessarily in the *Ausführung*), missing all the subtlety in Bach's suggestion that the 'harmony in the principal key' is heard to reestablish itself towards the end.]

{27} As follows from Fig. 7c, it was the master's intention to establish a² for the first time as 5̂ above the dominant divider (V), i.e. by reaching over [*Übergreifend zu bringen*]. Accordingly, in the treble in the realization, d² holds a position of priority; but Bach holds back even this d² for a while, as shown in the following sketch:

Fig. 10

The illustration shows the outline of an arpeggiation in which d² is not articulated until the very end. In this sense, Bach's auspicious term 'Einleitung' can also be taken to characterize this introductory passage. Smaller arpeggiations

– see Fig. 10b – are built into the larger one (Fig. 10a), so that the task falls to the passage-work in the realization, which veils the arpeggiation as far as a^1, to unite these with successive linear progressions of a sixth, a fifth and an octave (d^3–$f\sharp^2$, a^2–d^2, {28} $f\sharp^2$–$f\sharp^1$); see the brackets in Fig. 10b. The beauty of the realization thus lies in capturing, so to speak, a smaller motive of arpeggiation within the larger arpeggiation and in concealing this relationship with passage-work which, in decisively realizing a goal, nevertheless pretends to wander aimlessly. Bach insists upon a most precise ordering of events even in the diminution of a free fantasy, and only for the sake of 'fantasy' hides it behind the appearance of disorder: in this is constituted the inimitable quality of his art.

A few more details are worth noting. In the passage-work the afterbeat of a trill is attached to $f\sharp^2$; a figure which expresses something like a doubling of such an afterbeat is attached to d^2, whereas $f\sharp^1$ receives only the simple afterbeat. From here on, the arpeggiation is twice embellished with acciaccature and continues unembellished in the end. One notes the rhythmic permutation of e^1–$f\sharp^1$–a^1 at the transition from the passage-work into the arpeggiation: it is enlivened by rhythmic contrast.

In the realization the descending sixth-progression in the treble, d^2–$f\sharp^1$, proceeds in contrary motion to the rising progression in the bass. And here is the [first] arpeggio to which Bach's words refer: 'In the realization, each arpeggiated

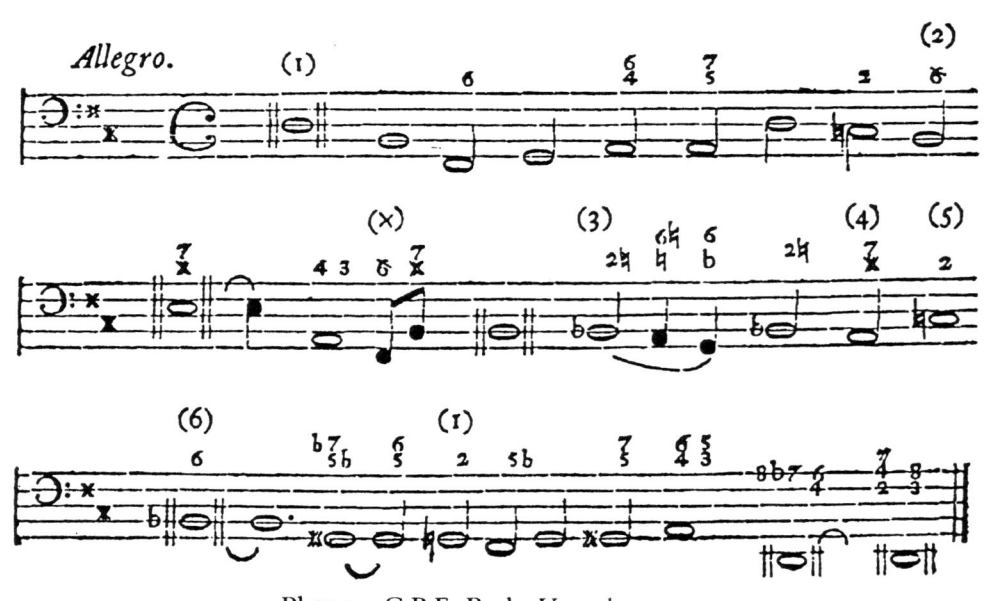

Plate 1   C.P.E. Bach, *Versuch*, II, 341

Plate 2 C.P.E. Bach, *Versuch*, II, engraved plate after p.341

chord is to be performed twice. When the second arpeggiation is to be taken in a different register in either the right or the left hand, this is indicated.' A change of register such as this is annotated with *piano* in the left hand.

The treble seizes d^2 again only at the passing c♮ in the bass (*forte* here because of the chromaticism!), and with this the first register is now regained (see the dotted slur from d^2 to d^2). A glance back over the progress of the treble and the bass shows the fine octave couplings d^3–d^2 and d–D. The bass returns from D to d by an octave leap and compels the treble to leap upwards from f♯¹ to d^2, back to its original register as well. One comes to prize the great value of registral shifts!

The d^2 becomes a seventh above the root $E^{♯3}$; it is then suspended as a fourth above the root A (see Bach's plan). Attention is drawn first of all to the acciaccatura c♯¹–d¹ in the first broken octave; in what follows, passage-work indeed replaces simple arpeggiation, and yet even in the passage-work that acciaccatura asserts itself motivically (see the c♯³–d³ and c♯²–d²). Who would imagine motivic integrity of this sort in the diminution of a free fantasy!

Still more sublime is the beauty of a hidden progression in the voice-leading reproduced in the following sketch:

Fig. 11

{29} An exchange of voices is intended here, leading the seventh, d^2, to c♯¹ instead of to c♯², while g♯¹ in the middle voice is made a note of the treble and is led to a¹. (In the last analysis, the voice-exchange implies that reaching-over by which the $\hat{5}$, a¹ (later a²), is achieved for the first time in the treble; see above.) In the realization, as in Fig. 11a, the motion from d^2 to b¹ is by leap, but from there in a third-progression, b¹–a¹–g♯¹. Now one is able to understand the repetitions in the passage-work, d³–b² and d²–b¹ (see the shorter slurs): these are precisely the first note of the arpeggiation that is shown in Fig. 11a. Since the arpeggiation can escape the ear so easily at the entrance of the $E_{♯3}^7$ chord, it became necessary to keep the memory of it alive during the following extended run. But in the harmony on A, the g♯¹ before the a¹, as well as the g♯² before the a², functions not as an acciaccatura, as it might appear, but as an upward resolution ⌒7–8 as illustrated in Fig. 11. Even the diminution of the suspension ⌒4–3 is motivically prepared (see the brackets [in Bach's realization]).

The following illustration will serve the understanding of the passage at (3) in both the plan and its realization:[16]

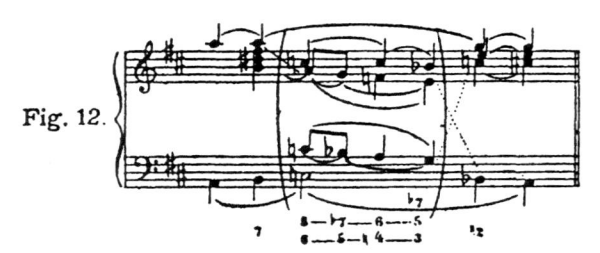

Fig. 12.

The seventh of the harmony on B becomes a sixth in the following harmony on C, which is to be understood as a delaying of the fifth, g (see Bach's *Generalbaßlehre* [i.e. part II of the *Versuch*], chapter 1, §64). In the realization, Bach sets the unfolding of the progression 6–5–♮4–3 an octave lower than is shown in Fig. 7c; he does this in order to hold in reserve the crucial effect of the second, g^2 (above the second B♭ in the bass; see the plan). Moreover, he omits altogether the bass progression B♭–A–G given in the plan, similarly so that {30} the good effect of the second B♭ (with the second-chord) will not be anticipated. In this way the plan announces a voice progression at (3) to which the composer indeed refers in the execution of the fantasy, but which he does not allow fully to materialize! When his words are recalled – '... the anticipatory motion at (3) is realized in slow figures, in which the bass has been intentionally omitted ...' one must pay due homage to the master for this artistic deed, in which the conscious and the instinctive are so intimately mixed. Artifices of such daring belong as well even to the diminution in a free fantasy! How can one imitate them, how can one achieve them?

[16] [Schenker's Fig. 12 addresses what is conceptually the most profound discrepancy between *Gerippe* and *Ausführung*; Bach himself addresses the moment in three illuminating sentences. The 'ellipsis' in the *Gerippe* at figure (3) provokes in the realization a passage that tests the theoretical limitations at this point of greatest tonal remove. In Schenker's representation of the *Ausführung*, the passage is clotted with brackets and slurs, dotted and solid. The decision to place Bach's figure (3) beneath the first c^2 in the unfolding from the dominant seventh on B, by no means self-evident from a superpositioning of the *Gerippe* on the *Ausführung*, is explained in Fig. 12, where a harmony is extrapolated that at once negotiates the ellipsis and sets the slurred bass notes in an inner voice, pointing up the deeper sense in which Bach means that these notes 'anticipate the following reiteration of the second-chord' (*erklären die Einleitung in die darauf folgende Wiederholung des Secundenaccordes*).]

The smaller slurs at (3) in the realization show the inverted genesis of the sonority c^2–a^1–f^1 (see the passing $^6_4$ chord in Fig. 12); the brackets expound a motivic parallelism!

At (5) in the realization, where $f\sharp^2$ concludes the third-progression and g^2 ought to follow (see Figs. 7b and 7c), a detour is taken, as the following illustration shows:

Fig. 13

At (6) in the realization, the detour provides the occasion for a 'slow figure' that descends from d^3 to g^2. Now the ascending arpeggiation $b\flat$–g^2 is interpolated, whereupon follows a more precipitous run, in continuation of the earlier slow figure, which attends as well without interruption to the connection with the next harmony, $G\sharp^{\natural 7}$ – and thus there is no leap in the bass from $B\flat$ to $G\sharp$!

From $G\sharp$ on, the bass produces several octave couplings which are not provided for in the plan.

The realization of the tonic at the close consists in arpeggiations. The gap between the chords of the left and right hands is left deliberately open, destined expressly to be filled by the progression d^1–c^1–b–(g) in the inner voice.

Thus the realization of C.P.E. Bach's free fantasy blossoms from first note to last from the most rigorous artifice of voice-leading, from the most ingenious diminutions which, striking and beautiful in themselves, fulfil all the relationships of harmony and voice, and make them pure.

[21]

Nichelmann contra C. Ph. E. Bach:
Harmonic Theory and Musical Politics at the Court
of Frederick the Great

Thomas Christensen

If musical life at the court of Frederick the Great was constrained by the Monarch's notoriously conservative tastes, the same cannot be said for the music literature of the time. Perhaps it was as an outlet for their creative energies that so many composers in Berlin turned to the writing about music. Whatever the motivation was, the 1750s saw an unprecedented outpouring of journals, encyclopedic treatises, didactic essays, polemical pamphlets, and prolix introductions and prefaces. In Berlin, as Charles Burney noted with a mixture of bemusement and bewilderment, everyone seemed to have something to say on music[1]. These Berlin writings ranged widely over all questions of *Schreibarten,* national styles, aesthetics, performance, theory and pedagogy, and provide telling documentation of the many competing musical forces pulling at German musicians at mid-century. To the well-known works of Quantz, C. Ph. E. Bach, Agricola, Marpurg, Kirnberger, and Sulzer, which Burney noted were "regarded throughout Germany as classical"[2], we may add those by musical writers only slightly less celebrated such as Riedt, Baron, Adolph Friedrich Wolff, Ramler, Krause, Euler, and Reichardt[3].

One author whose voice has been largely lost amidst this literary cacophony is Christoph Nichelmann (1717–1762), who in 1755 published a lengthy treatise entitled *Die Melodie nach ihrem Wesen sowohl als nach ihren Eigenschaften.* Nichelmann is a relatively obscure musical figure today, remembered largely as the second harpsichordist behind Carl Philipp Emanuel Bach in Frederick's band, and a composer of modest talents and conservative tastes who made some contributions to the development of the

---

1 Ch. Burney, *The Present State of Music in Germany, the Netherlands, and United Provinces,* London 1775, Repr. Oxford 1959, p. 205.
2 Ibid., p. 159.
3 A fine anthology of writings by many of these Berlin music critics has recently been compiled by Hans-Günter Ottenberg, along with useful commentary (*Der Critische Musicus an der Spree: Berliner Musikschrifttum von 1748 bis 1799,* Leipzig 1984).

keyboard concerto[4]. But Nichelmann was in fact an important music theorist of his day. With great clarity and forcefulness, Nichelmann staked out a singular position on a number of controversial theoretical and aesthetic issues. To an extent not hitherto realized by musicologists, Nichelmann's ideas resounded through much of the Berlin literature for the next quarter of a century; not the least important consequence of his essay was a bitter polemic it sparked with Carl Philipp Emanuel Bach. No less important, perhaps, was the role it played in disseminating the theories of Rameau and the music of Johann Sebastian Bach. When placed in historical context, then, Nichelmann's treatise emerges as an important missing piece in the colorful mosaic that constituted musical life of the Berlin *Musikkreise* in the third quarter of the 18th century.

In his preface to his treatise, Nichelmann tells us that his work was occasioned by a recent dispute between a "musikverständiger Freund" and another musical writer. We learn in his autobiography that the two combatants were Friedrich Wilhelm Marpurg and Johann Friedrich Agricola. The dispute between Marpurg and Agricola, according to Hans-Günter Ottenberg "led off the round of music journalism in Berlin like a drum roll and would set a tone of polemical intensity scarcely surpassed thereafter"[5]. The issue of contention was that old chestnut of musical aesthetics: the relative values of French and Italian music[6]. For Marpurg, an unabashed enthusiast for French culture, the harmonic richness and graceful melodies of French music were clearly superior to Italian music, with all its vocal extravagances

---

4 The biography of Christoph Nichelmann – gleaned from his own autobiographical essay contributed to one of Marpurg's journals – can be briefly summarized (Fr. W. Marpurg, *Historisch-kritische Beiträge zur Aufnahme der Musik,* I, Berlin 1755, pp. 431–439). He was born in 1717 in Brandenburg. Showing unusual musical promise as a boy, his parents sent him at the age of 13 to the Thomasschule in Leipzig where he studied keyboard with Wilhelm Friedemann Bach and sang under the direction of Johann Sebastian Bach. We do not know whether Nichelmann had only closer contact with the elder Bach, although it is possible given that a number of important Bach manuscripts have come down to us in Nichelmann's hand (see H.-J. Schulze, *Studien zur Bach-Überlieferung im 18. Jahrhundert,* Leipzig 1984, p. 135–145). The great esteem with which Nichelmann held Bach's music will certainly become evident later in this article. In any case, by 1738, Nichelmann left Leipzig and travelled to Hamburg in order – so he tells us – to learn the latest "theatrical styles" under Keiser, Telemann, and Mattheson. A year later he moved to Berlin to study with Quantz and Graun. (Although just how formal or extensive these "studies" were we do not know.) Evidentally, the contacts he made helped Nichelmann to secure in 1745 an appointment to Frederick's band as co-harpsichordist along with Carl Philipp Emanuel Bach, a position he retained until 1756.
5 Ottenberg, *Der Critische Musicus,* p. 8.
6 The polemic occupied several early issues of Marpurg's first journal, *Der Critische Musicus an der Spree* (Berlin 1749–1750). The most important excerpts of their exchange are transcribed in Ottenberg, *Der Critische Musicus,* pp. 83–111.

and harmonic shallowness. Likewise, the precise articulation of the French language was more suited for clear theatrical declamation than was Italian. If Germans were ever to cultivate successfully their own vocal art forms, Marpurg advised, than they must abandon their irrational infatuation with the Italian Opera and study the best French models.

Agricola, being far more obeisant to Frederick's preference for the Italian opera seria, took it upon himself to defend Italian music from Marpurg's attacks. For Agricola, French music was "constrained" while the French language was unsonorous. Most importantly, though, French melodies were "boring and dry." Turning Marpurg's prescription on its head, Agricola held Italian music as the true model for German composers to emulate[7]. Echoing a refrain sung by generations of German musicians before him, Agricola considered that the Italians above all other nations had beautifully combined music and language with "natural ease" leading to a "noble simplicity of melody" ("edle Einfalt der Melodie").

Agricola's favorable assessment of Italian music was one calculated to elicit the sympathy of most Berlin composers. If not all of them shared equally Frederick's enthusiasm for the opera seria, they nonetheless found the Italian *cantabile* vocal art congenial to the reigning galant and emerging *empfindsam* tastes. For both Quantz and C. Ph. E. Bach, the graceful articulation and judicious embellishment of a melodic line was arguably the most essential requirement in their programs for effective composition and performance. Quantz, in advocating a "mixed style" for German composers that combined the best of both Italian and French music, singled out the Italians favorably for their expressive *Singart*[8]. Bach recommended that performers imitate the most skilled singers and strive above all to attain a "Singendes Denken"[9]. In the galant aesthetics, neither excessive ornamentation in the melody nor ponderous and busy harmonic accompaniments could be countenanced, less they detract from the desired "noble simplicity" of melody.

---

7 One of the German composers Agricola mentions whom he believed to have followed his advice was apparently Nichelmann! After listing those Italian composers whose music he held in highest regard, Agricola added happily: "Only recently has a German published some melodious harpsichord pieces in the newest and purest Italian taste" (Ottenberg 1984, p. 88). According to Ottenberg, Agricola is possibly referring to the *Sei brevi Sonate da Cembalo massime all'uso delle Dame* written by Nichelmann and published in 1745 (Ottenberg, *Der Critische Musicus*, p. 367, n. 8). Agricola's identification of Nichelmann's "sangbaren Sätzen" with the "allerneusten und reinesten italiänischen Gusto" may well have been one of the provocations leading Nichelmann to compose his treatise.

8 J. J. Quantz, *Versuch einer Anweisung die Flöte traversiere zu spielen*, Berlin 1752, p. 323.

9 C. Ph. E. Bach, *Versuch über die wahre Art das Clavier zu spielen*, Part I, Berlin 1753, p. 122.

As a fulfillment of these ideals, the pedantic aesthetician, Christian Gottfried Krause, along with the poet Karl Wilhelm Ramler, prescribed a genre
of strophic *Oden mit Melodien* that possessed an "artful, refined, and naive"
melody   supported   by   the   simplest   homophonic – and   ideally
optional – accompaniment[10]. The first collection of such odes were published in 1753, inaugurating the so-called "Berlin Lied School" with contributions by Franz Benda, Quantz, both Grauns, C. Ph. E. Bach, Agricola,
Telemann, and Nichelmann.

It was as a critique of his compatriots's musical prescriptions, then, that
Nichelmann wrote his treatise. He did not so much take exception to their
desire to enhance musical expressiveness. Nor did he contest the beauty and
advantages of a vocally-conceived melody. What concerned Nichelmann
was the best means of achieving these goals. In his view, the many disputa-
tions over *Schreibarten,* national styles, and melodic embellishment and
articulation missed the essential point. For Nichelmann, true musical
expression could only be achieved in one way: through harmony. Despite
its title, it was harmony – not melody – that will be the subject of his treatise.

Nichelmann thus resurrected one of the oldest controversies in musical
literature – the respective values of harmony and melody. (It was also an
issue, it will be recalled, being hotly debated at the same time in Paris by
Rameau and Rousseau.) As far as Nichelmann was concerned, there was no
question as to which side one should take. Harmony, he was convinced, was
an indispensible and universal component in every kind of music, from
every nation, style and time. The composer who wished to write the most
expressive and beautiful melody, then, must first learn how to write harmony, for it is only in harmony that is found the "essence as well as properties" of true melody, as it is expressed in the book's title.

Nichelmann's emphasis upon harmony brings immediately to mind, of
course, Rameau's theory. And indeed, Nichelmann acknowledged Rameau
as the source for many of his ideas. It is likely, though, that Nichelmann
first learned of Rameau through Marpurg who was himself in the process
of propagandizing the Frenchman's thought in his journals. (As we will
soon see, Marpurg became one of the few defenders of Nichelmann's treatise in Berlin.) But much of Nichelmann's preoccupation with harmony
might also be attributed to his generally conservative musical tastes formed
through his studies with – and admiration of – Johann Sebastian Bach.

In any case, the opening of Nichelmann's text is explicitly drawn from
Rameau's acoustical theories. "Music is the science of sound," we are
informed at the very opening of chapter 1. And in chapter 3 we learn that

---

10 C. W. Ramler/Ch. G. Krause (eds.), *Oden mit Melodien,* Part I, Berlin 1753, preface.

"every musical sound [*Klang*] is already harmony," as every tone naturally contains a harmonic series of upper partials. This is a fact attested to by the "newest musical authors"[11]. This naturally generated *Klang,* then, becomes the progenitor of all harmony.

> "All possible music or mixing and combinations of different tones is derived from changes in the organically-rooted agreement of the *Klang.* Thus all and every kind of music is nothing else but altered – or artistically produced – harmonic diversity."[12]

The acoustical origin of every chord could be revealed through the fundamental bass (*Grund-ton*). Because harmony was generated by nature, it had clear etymological primacy over melody. More importantly, it demonstrated that harmony was the key to successful composition, no matter what the *Schreibarten* be. This will be the essential thesis of Nichelmann's treatise.

> "I will try to elucidate [in this work] through reason as well as through examples the following statement: A composer fulfills his duty only in so far as he arranges what is necessary in a composition – whether in general or in unusual circumstances – in such a manner that everything appropriate for his needs is a consequence of the previous impressions of richly perceived harmonies or agreements [that is, those harmonies derived from the natural *Klang*], and that they flow from them as from a spring."[13]

Nichelmann elaborated upon this thesis – sometimes with mind-numbing repetition – throughout his treatise, utilizing fundamental bass analyses to reveal the harmonic structure of dozens of musical excerpts. Nichelmann

---

11 Ch. Nichelmann, *Die Melodie nach ihrem Wesen sowohl, als nach ihren Eigenschaften,* Hamburg 1755, p., 1, 2, 3. – Exactly how much Nichelmann did read of Rameau is not really known; the only two works of Rameau cited in his text are the *Traité de l'harmonie* of 1722 and the *Démonstration du principe de l'harmonie* of 1750. Nichelmann's library, which upon his death passed into the hands of Marpurg, and then to Fétis, contained works by theorists such as Neidhardt, Printz, and Mattheson – all with Nichelmann's own annotations – but none, strangely enough, by Rameau (see Fr.-J. Fétis, *Biographie universelle des musiciens,* 2nd edition, Paris 1873–1875, vol. VI, p. 312). This would support the supposition that Nichelmann learned his Rameau through Marpurg's redactions – except for the fact that his application of the fundamental bass, as we will see, differed so greatly from Marpurg's.

12 "Alle nur mögliche Musik, oder Mischung und Verbindung unterschiedlicher Töne, beruhet auf dieser Veränderbarkeit des Klanges, und der ihr zum Grunde liegenden ursprünglichen Zusammenstimmung; daher ist alle und jede Musik nichts anders, als eine veränderte, oder eine durch Kunst hervorgebrachte mannigfaltige Harmonie." – Nichelmann, *Die Melodie,* p. 4.

13 "Ich will mich bemühen, sowohl durch Gründe, als durch Beyspiele den Satz in sein gehöriges Licht zu setzen: *Daß ein Componist seiner Pflicht nur in so weit Genüge thut, als er das, was sowohl den Haupt- als den absonderlichen Umständen nach, in den Zusammensetzungen nothwendig ist, dergestalt veranstaltet, daß alles nur eine folge des vorhergegangenen Eindrucks solcher vielfalch empfundenen Harmonien oder Zusammenstimmungen ist, die sich vor sein Vorhaben schicken, und aus den selben, wie aus ihrer Quelle, fließen.*"–Nichelmann, *Die Melodie,* p. 14.

must thus be counted as one of the first and most important of Rameau's advocates in Germany, Marpurg notwithstanding[14]. His comprehensive analytic application of Rameau's fundamental bass was the first of its kind in Germany, preceding by some 20 years that of Kirnberger. Indeed, in respect to the sheer quantity and variety of his analyses, Nichelmann's work stands alone in the entire 18th century.

Although Nichelmann wholeheartedly adopted Rameau's fundamental bass and its aesthetic corollaries, he by no means utilized all of Rameau's theory. Most notably, Nichelmann skipped over Rameau's (and Marpurg's) laborious and extensive mathematical and philosophical arguments establishing the minor triad, mode, and dissonance. (He did, however, include a lengthy justification for octave equivalence using many of the same numerical and acoustical arguments Rameau employed in his *Démonstration du principe de l'harmonie*). Nor did Nichelmann feel compelled to systematize harmonic theory within a rigorously deductive and axiomatic hierarchy as did Rameau. His justification for the fundamental bass was more empirical and heuristic than was Rameau's. On the other hand, Nichelmann applied the fundamental bass in a far more rigid manner than Rameau ever had, allowing only root motion by a fifth or occasionally a third, and accommodating the motion of a second or tritone by extravagant use of an interpolated fundamental bass[15].

Finally, to his partial adoption and unorthodox interpretation of Rameau's theory, Nichelmann brought his own aesthetic ideas heavily influenced by the metaphysics of Christian Wolff and German Neo-Platonism.

---

14 The reception of Rameau's theory among German theorists in the 18th century is problematic. Marpurg is typically considered the first disciple of Rameau, although there were earlier theoreticians who seemed to have been partly influenced by the Frenchman's ideas (e.g. Sorge and Hartung). In any case, Marpurg seriously misunderstood – or perhaps deliberately rejected – a number of important elements of Rameau's theory in his early vulgarizations. (One of the most glaring examples being, perhaps, his inflexible invocation of "unterschobne" fundamentals.) Fortunately, not all of Marpurg's misinterpretations contaminated Nichelmann's treatise. While Nichelmann may have been introduced to Rameau's theory by Marpurg, he interpreted and applied it in far different ways.

15 William Caplin has pointed out to me that Nichelmann's interpolated bass differs from Rameau's not only in quantity, but in procedure. Whereas Rameau might (although not invariably) interpolate a descending third between two adjacent ascending scale degrees (e.g. the roots C and D would be mediated by an interpolated A), Nichelmann would interpolate an ascending fifth (C–(G)–D). Rameau's fundamental bass suggests less a temporal root progression that is repressed than a substituted fundamental *par supposition*. Nichelmann obviously took very seriously the idealized proscription against root motion by any interval other than a perfect fifth, and hence he added freely whatever roots were necessary to achieve such connections. His extravagant application of the interpolated bass would not be seen again until a century later in the analyses of Simon Sechter.

Nichelmann believed that all humans are born with an innate understanding
of music:

> "We each carry the seeds of harmony and melody within ourselves through our preor-
> dained love of order and good proportion. And as soon as we are aroused and stirred by
> a musical sound, these begin to sprout and grow."[16]

Nichelmann accepted fully the Baroque doctrine of the *Affektenlehre* – the
power of music to depict and arouse specific passions in the listener, a doctrine intensified in the *empfindsam* aesthetics of Carl Philipp Emanuel Bach.
But for Nichelmann, the means by which such passions may be aroused
– and here is his fundamental point – is through harmonic diversity, what he
called "Mannigfaltigkeit der Harmonie."

> "The cause of the delight that music affords us is due above all to the satisfaction and
> fulfillment of our innate desire for varied and diverse harmony. ... Thus, the first and
> foremost responsibility of the composer is this: that he try to satisfy and fulfill the natu-
> ral hunger of our soul for the diverse harmony we crave. Every composition or musical
> setting must be judged from this perspective. ..."[17]

This becomes the explicit thesis of chapter 43: "Music Utilizes the Variety of Harmony so that Specific Desires and Feelings may be Depicted and
Aroused"[18]. Thus, it was clearly not the ideals of *empfindsam* aesthetics with
which Nichelmann stood in disagreement, rather, the means to realize them.
Let us now turn to Nichelmann's treatise and examine his arguments in
closer detail.

Nichelmann's fundamental point is that there are really only two kinds of
music, differentiated by the degree to which harmony is taken into consideration by the composer. Utilizing terminology which he borrowed from
Wolfgang Caspar Printz, Nichelmann calls these two respective types
"monodisch" and "polyodisch"[19]. Despite their suggestive names, the distinction has nothing to do with the number of voices of a composition,
rather, it is based upon the role of harmony.

---

16 "Demnach tragen wir den Saamen der Harmonie, und der Melodie, schon in uns, in der
   uns anerschaffenen Liebe zu der Ordnung und zu guten Proportionen, und dieser fängt
   an zu keimen und aufzugehen, so bald wir von einem Klange gerühret und getroffen
   werden." – Nichelmann, *Die Melodie*, p. 50.
17 "Der Grund desjenigen Ergötzens, daß uns die Musik gewähret, liegt also vornehmlich
   in der Sättigung und in der Befriedigung des uns angebohrnen Verlangens nach einer
   veränderten, oder nach einer mannigfaltigen Harmonie. ... Die erste, und die vornehmste Pflicht eines musikalischen Setzers, ist demnach diese, daß er die natürliche
   Bedürfniß der Seele, nach welcher wir nach einer mannigfaltigen Harmonie begierig
   sind, zu sättigen und zufrieden zu stellen suche. So ist auch eine jede Composition oder
   Zusammensetzung, aus diesem Gesichts-Punct betrachtet. ..." – Ibid., p. 5.
18 Ibid., p. 101.
19 W. C. Printz, *Phrynis Mitylenaeus oder Satyrischer Componist,* Quedlinburg 1676–1677,
   pp. 3, 76; 131.

In *monodisch* music, Nichelmann tells us, the composer writes a "succession of individual notes or simple harmonies one after another, without attention paid to their coherence"[20]. Because the composer is not sensitive to the logic of tonality, though, the chord succession is either stagnant or arbitrary, while the melody wanders aimlessly. The result is a music which is lifeless; it cannot animate us or satisfy our innate desire for harmonic diversity. We are rather bored by it. The composer may strive to rescue his music with increased ornamentation and passage-work, superfluous rhythmic activity, thickened accompanimental texture, or any number of other compositional devices. But to no avail.

> "The monodist then sacrifices not only the all important property of harmonic diversity, but the gracefulness of the individual voices. He also disappoints the ear desirous of harmony by inappropriately adding together too many notes through his excessive love of harmonic embellishment. The fundamental progression of essential authentic harmonies is thereby either impeded and deferred, or what is the same thing, its nature is contradicted and distorted. [The music] is thus not only incapable of achieving the desired result, but results in cacophony."[21]

The *polyodisch* composer, on the other hand, is fully sensitive to the crucial role of harmony, Nichelmann tells us. In *polyodisch* music, harmony is the dominant factor to which the composer devotes himself. Above all, he strives for a rich and diverse progression of harmony, animated by a lively and changing harmonic rhythm.

> "A *polyodisch* composer utilizes a succession of multifarious harmonies. He tries above all to arrange a progression of different sonorities that are suited to his general as well as specific needs. The cohesion of the individual notes that are based upon these [harmonies] correspond with absolute certainty to the effects desired by the composer through the power of harmony, whether that [harmony] be simple or complex. The melody of such a composer is drawn from these multifarious harmonies, and is fully dependant upon them."[22]

---

20 Nichelmann, *Die Melodie*, p. 15.
21 "Der Monodist opfert also den Zierlichkeiten des einzelnen Gesanges, nicht nur die allerwesentlichste Eigenschaft, die Mannigfaltigkeit der Harmonie auf, sondern er teuschet auch das harmonie-begierige Ohr, durch unrichtige Zusammenfügung mehrerer Töne zugleich, indem er aus übermäßiger Liebe zu den harmonischen Zierathen, den nothwendigen Fortgang der eigentlichen Harmonie entweder gar hemmet, und aufschiebet, oder dennoch denselben, seiner Natur zu wider, verändert, und mithin eben dadurch nicht nur zu der gesuchten Absicht unzulängliche, sondern auch gar falsche Zusammenklänge hören läßt." – Ibid., p. 99.
22 "Ein polyodischer Setzer bedienet sich der Fortschreitung der vielfachen Harmonie, und sucht zuförderst eine solche Folge verschiedener Zusammenklänge zu veranstalten, die sowohl der allgemeinen, als auch seiner vorhabenden besonderen Absicht gemäß ist; und wie er aus dieser die Verbindung einzelner Töne heraus ziehet: so thut diese letztere auch, in Kraft des Zusammenklanges, diejenige Wirkung, so sie der Absicht des Setzers nach thun soll, und thut sie allemal gewiß, sie mag einfach oder vielfach wirken. Der Gesang eines solchen Componisten ist der vielfachen Harmonie unterworfen, und hängt von derselben ab." – Ibid., pp. 20–21.

This last remark is the key to Nichelmann's text – good melody is absolutely rooted in harmony. No melody can be effective that does not cleave naturally to its harmonic origin, but seeks to function independently and compensate for its lack of harmonic support through the addition of passage work, embellishment, rhythmic agition and the like. Nichelmann used a variety of metaphors to describe the melody that fails to relate correctly to a logical harmonic underpinning: It is like a river becoming ever more polluted the further it runs from its source; it is like a boat in water without a mast and sail; it is like hearing the noise of words without understanding their meaning[23]. The title of chapter 47 concisely encapsulates Nichelmann's concerns: "Melody is so much more Beautiful the closer it follows the Progression of Fundamental Harmonies that are appropriate for a given Situation"[24]. Thus, Nichelmann concludes in Chapter 51 ("The Properties of a True Melody"), a melody is expressive only when "in a word, one hears not only a melody of and for itself (that is, essentially alone), but more importantly, as part of the different harmonies from which it originates and of which it is a dependent part ..."[25].

Now, it is important for us to keep in mind that Nichelmann's twofold classification is not based upon any of the traditional *Schreibarten* of 18th-century music. That is to say, Nichelmann does not mean to equate his *monodisch* style with either the galant or theatrical styles, while *polyodisch* music is an implicitly more conservative style – a kind of prima and secunda prattica of the 18th century, if you will. While it is true that a good deal of galant and Italian music did indeed come under Nichelmann's censure as *monodisch*, his categories really transcend any usual division of style or genre.

> "I am not concerned here with any specific style or genre of composition in respect to a prescribed form or desired function. My intention is to present the different ways and means or the different material that the composer may use no matter what the composition is, what the style or genre is, or what its aim be."[26]

We can find both *polyodisch* and *monodisch* compositions in every kind of music, Nichelmann tells us: German, French, or Italian, instrumental or vocal, homophonic of polyphonic, church, chamber or theatrical.

---

23 Ibid., pp. 129, 147, 151.
24 Ibid., p. 111.
25 Ibid., p. 149.
26 "Ich habe es allhier mit keiner Art oder Gattung der Composition in Ansehung einer vorgeschriebenen Form, oder in Ansehung eines dadurch zu erlangenden besondern Entzwecks, ins besondere zu thun. Mein Vorhaben ist, *die unterschiedliche Art und Weise, oder die unterschiedlichen Mittel darzustellen, welche die Componisten überhaupt anwenden, um demjenigen, was bey einer jeglichen Composition, sie sey welcher Art oder Gattung sie wolle, ihre Pflicht ist, ein Gnüge thun.*" – Ibid., p. 11.

The distinction he draws is based rather upon a more subtle but ultimately more significant harmonic element of musical structure which can
only be uncovered through musical analysis. It is this aspect of Nichelmann's work that strikes me as the most original and historically significant.
Through a ground-breaking application of harmonic analysis, Nichelmann
searches for and claims to discover characteristics that cut across traditional
categories of genre, national origin, and style. Let us now examine a few of
Nichelmann's musical analyses to see how his theory works in practice.

After a lengthy and largely abstract discussion of his twofold distinction
for the first 31 chapters of his text, Nichelmann proceeds to offer some
musical examples illustrating the *polyodisch* and *monodisch* approaches,
respectively. It is telling that the very first example he chooses here is by
Johann Sebastian Bach – the Sarabande to the *French Suite in E major,*
BWV 817[27] [see example 1 a]. Nichelmann proceeds to praise Bach's use of
harmony in the first eight measures of the piece, finding it satisfyingly rich:

> "Within the space and limit of precisely eight measures this setting contains not only a
> sufficient quantity and variety of chords so that the natural activity of the soul may be
> sustained through sufficient diversity of harmony, thereby fulfilling the primary and
> most universal function of music, but the differing harmonies are also suited to the spe-
> cific plan [of the music] and appropriate for this [purpose]."[28]

Nichelmann refers with particular approval to the expressive use of the
mediant harmony and the well directed harmonic and rhythmic motion to
the half cadence. Implicit here – as in the rest of his text – is a clear preference for a fast harmonic rhythm with frequent modulations. To clarify his
discussion, Nichelmann then provides a kind of harmonic reduction of
these eight bars, which is in essence a realized fundamental bass [see example 1 b]. This is incidentally a good instance of Nichelmann's unorthodox
use of an interpolated fundamental bass. Note for example in measure 2 the
addition of an E in the bass so as to mediate the motion from A major to B
major.

---

27 Nichelmann will quote and analyze a number of other Bach compositions in his treatise,
    including two cantata arias and the Kyrie to the Mass in B minor. (The relevant passages
    and analyses are reprinted in: H.-J. Schulze, ed., *Dokumente zum Nachwirken Johann
    Sebastian Bachs* 1750–1800, Leipzig 1972, pp. 96–103.) These analyses are not only the
    first of their kind, they constitute the first published citation of this music anywhere.
    Nichelmann's important contribution to the Bach-reception in Berlin in the 18th century
    has recently been explored in Schulze, *Studien zur Bach-Überlieferung*, pp. 135–145.

28 "Denn es hat diese Zusammensetzung, in dem Raume und dem Umfange einer abge-
    messenen Zeit von acht Tacten, nicht nur der Anzahl nach genugsam verschiedene
    Accorde, um die natürliche Activität der Seele, durch genugsam-mannigfaltige Uebersein-
    stimmungen, zu unterhalten, und mithin den Haupt- und allgemeinen Zweck der Musik
    dadurch zu befördern; sondern die verschiedenen Zusammenstimmungen sind auch
    dem besonderen Vorhaben gemäß, und schicken sich für dasselbe." – Nichelmann, *Die
    Melodie,* p. 59.

After citing the Bach example, Nichelmann goes on to provide additional excerpts of *polyodisch* music, including a *Sinfonia* by Carl Heinrich Graun (N. 34), two *Air de cour* by Michel Lambert and Lully (Nos. 19 and 86, respectively), an *Ode* by Telemann (No. 80), an opera seria aria by Hasse (No. 83), and the opening *Kyrie* from Sebastian Bach's *Mass in B minor* (No. 95). Later in the text, he adds some additional works by Handel and Hasse to the list of *polyodisch* music that he feels are deserving of emulation[29]. The diversity of these examples underscore how Nichelmann does not necessarily equate *polyodisch* music with a specific style or nationality. Many of his approved excerpts represent unequivocally the most progressive musical tastes of the galant and theatrical styles, yet still satisfy his demands for sufficient harmonic diversity.

On the other side of Nichelmann's harmonic coin, we are offered a number of illustrations of *monodisch* music. Again this has nothing to do with the country of origin, genre, or *Schreibart*. *Monodisch* music can be found anywhere and anytime, indeed, even by *polyodisch* composers when they become lazy, indulgent, or inattentive to the demands of harmony. To demonstrate his distinction, Nichelmann selects numerous examples of *monodisch* music that he subjects to close and critical scrutiny. He will then take it upon himself to rewrite the given excerpt in a *polyodisch* setting – retaining the same basic harmonic and melodic plan as much as possible. Nowhere does he identify the composers for any of his *monodisch* excerpts, and apparently a number of them were of his own creation. Yet of those examples that I have been able to identify in Nichelmann's text, well over half of them are the work of musicians associated with Frederick's court[30]. It seems that Nichelmann was able to find all the *monodisch* music he needed for his critique right in own backyard. With a bull-headedness stemming from a brazen ego or just simple evangelic zeal, Nichelmann quotes and then pro-

---

29 Ibid., p. 168.
30 Of the 40-odd works Nichelmann cites, I have been able to identify about half. Of these, Johann Sebastian Bach, Carl Philipp Emanuel Bach, and Carl Heinrich Graun are cited four times each, while Micheal Lambert, Lampugnani, Argicola, Telemann, Hasse, Lully, and Nichelmann himself are cited once each. The specific citations are as follows (using Nichelmann's own example numberings:) J.S.Bach # 14 (15), # 21 (23–25), # 84 (85), and # 95; C.Ph.E.Bach # 29 (30–33), # 38 (39–40), # 47 (48, 77), and # 72 (73–74); Graun # 34 (35), # 93 (94), # 96 (97), # 99 (100); Lambert # 19; Lampugnani # 52 (53, 67); Agricola # 58 (59, 70–71); Telemann # 80; Hasse # 83, Lully # 86; and Nichelmann # 111 (112–117). (The first example number in each citation refers to the original composition given in Nichelmann's text, while the numbers in parentheses refer to his analyses or recompositions of the same work.) The remainder of the unidentified excerpts are almost all from Italian opera serias, and may well be by either Graun or Hasse – the two operatic composers whose music Nichelmann was undoubtedly most familiar with in Berlin.

ceeds to castigate excerpts from Carl Philipp Emanuel Bach, Carl Heinrich Graun, Hasse, and Agricola, and then rewrite them. Obviously our theorist was not the most diplomatically astute of men.

One of the first such excerpts is given in example 2a. This virtuosic passagework is typical of many Galant concertos, and could have easily been written by someone like Quantz. Indeed, in a writing that we will soon examine in detail, Carl Philipp Emanuel Bach claimed that the work was in fact a Flute Concerto by Quantz, although Nichelmann insisted that he made it up himself. Whatever its origin, Nichelmann finds the passage repetitive and "superfluous"[31]. Nichelmann's complaints are not so much directed at the specific harmonies used – which he analyzes in example 2b – rather in how they are deployed. The incessant repeated notes of the accompanying voices – the so-called "trommelbass" – are rhythmically monotonous and do not relate at all to the melody which is itself just an empty exercise in arpeggios and scales. Nichelmann then rewrites this excerpt using the same harmonic progression given in example 2b, but transposing it into a four-part counterpoint in *gearbeiteter Stil* seen in example 2c. (The bottom line is not a sounding part, but the fundamental bass.) Nichelmann finds his revision more *polyodisch* since he feels the harmony is better projected by voices that are more rhythmically and melodically animated.

Nichelmann continues in this fashion for the rest of his treatise, that is to say, for another 100 pages and another 40 *monodisch* excerpts, each of which he will quote, criticize, and then rewrite. Nichelmann's criticisms cannot easily be generalized here, nor can his prescriptions for *polyodisch* writing. Depending upon the music, he will substitute the specific harmonies used, accelerate the harmonic rhythm, add some modulations, vary the phrasing and text setting, simplify the melodic embellishments, or add counterpoint to the accompaniment. In most cases, Nichelmann attempts to stay within the composer's intended *Schreibart*. (The transmutation of style in example 2 is somewhat of an anomaly.) The following selected examples from Nichelmann's text will illustrate the wide variety of his concerns and solutions.

In example 3a, it is the slow harmonic rhythm that bothers Nichelmann. The harmony is totally "enervated" as made clear by the drawn-out fundamental bass given in the bottom line[32]. Worse, the elaborate diminution in the descant results in a "quantity of excessive figures and ornamentation." Nichelmann's solution in example 3b solves the problem by radically con-

---

31 Nichelmann, *Die Melodie,* p. 39.
32 Ibid., p. 36.

tracting the harmonic rhythm, eliminating the diminution in the descant, and transforming the basso continuo into a more contrapuntally-independent line.

Example 4a gives the opening theme of the *Concerto in D major* by C. Ph. E. Bach (H 414; W 11). It is difficult to imagine that Nichelmann could find so much wrong in just these two seemingly innocuous measures. Yet he finds the harmony too stagnant and rhythmically repetitive, leading to an effect both "unpleasant and loathsome"[33]. The revised version seen in example 4b corrects this through the simple use of alternating dominant and tonic harmonies.

A more substantial example considered by Nichelmann is seen in example 5a. Here we have a typical example of the "aria di bravura" so favored in the opera seria. It is unambiguously in the most elaborate Italianate theatrical style, one typical of the Venetian school represented by composers like Galuppi. But this is not why Nichelmann criticizes the setting. Rather, it is that the melody is too jagged; it jumps around in "inappropriate trumpet-like progressions." Moreover, it is awkwardly phrased without any clear direction or shape. All this is because the underlying harmony is so badly worked out. The opening harmony stagnates on the tonic over the monotonous *trommelbass.* Thereafter, we find only a constant repetition of the tonic and dominant that soon becomes "unnatural and unpleasant"[34]. Nichelmann's resetting of the text attempts to preserve the flavor of the original version but with a more varied and better directed harmonic plan, a more independent accompaniment, and finally a smoother and more regularly shaped melodic line. This is seen in example 5b.

A frequent complaint by Nichelmann concerns inappropriate text setting. In the numerous opera seria arias and odes he cites, he claims the music evinces little relation to the affections depicted in the text. In the *Aria Cantabile* in example 6a, for instance, Nichelmann concedes that the music is "not unpleasant. ... How often haven't we been amazed by the performance of [this aria] by a formerly well-known singer through the variety of inflections and arpeggiations of her pleasing voice and dexterous tongue?"[35] But, he adds, this has little to do with the subject of the text which concerns pain and remorse. This is because the harmony never modulates and consists only of a tonic and its two dominants. In no way can such a simple harmonic setting convey the idea of "remorse and sorrow." Nichelmann's solution, as we see, is to introduce some poignant chromatics on the word "per-

---

33 Ibid., p. 75.
34 Ibid., p. 94.
35 Ibid., p. 114.

dona" – the expressivity derived, of course, from the new harmonic changes underlying these chromatics [see example 6 b].

In example 7 a, Nichelmann criticizes the deemphasis of the crucial word "sento" by virtue of its placement at the bottom of a descending leap in measure 2[36]. Further, the literal repetition of the last phrase which creates the typical ABB thematic structure so common to opera seria arias of the 1740 s[37] deprives the melodic line of any clear direction and weakens the sense of climax. Finally, the gay accompaniment and *trommelbass* employing the cliche ascending bass line leading to a cadential 6/4 contradicts the text subject of anger and revenge. Example 7 b is Nichelmann's correction of these perceived faults, including a fundamental bass analysis of the new harmonies.

Nichelmann makes much the same criticism concerning example 8 a – from Graun's opera *Ezio* (1754) – as he did with example 7 a. The *trommelbass,* jagged melody, and stilted phrasing all must go, he tells us[38]. Nor apparently should the crucial word "tradimento" be repeated, rather it should be saved for the end of the line. We might question, through, whether Nichelmann's lyrical reworking of the music in example 8 b expresses any more effectively the notion of "fury" and "betrayal"!

Lest we think that it was only Metastasian texts which can be mis-set, Nichelmann offers a correction of a cantata aria by J.S. Bach, "Ich bin vergnügt," BWV 84 [Example 9 a]. In words reminiscent of Scheibe's well-known critique, Nichelmann reprimands his revered teacher for putting too much art and effort into his setting – "alzugrosse Kunst" he calls it[39].

Bach's over-elaboration in the melody, Nichelmann complains, is unnecessary and detracts from the expressivity of the underlying harmony. In example 9 b, Nichelmann simplifies the melody, creating a line more "noble, simple and natural." He concludes from all this that even the greatest of composers can succumb to *monodisch* tendencies.

It is worth repeating here that Nichelmann is not recommending any one style or genre as better-suited for *polyodisch* music, rather, that in whatever style one writes in, the harmony is appropriately utilized, and the melody and accompanying voices conform to this harmonic underpinning correctly. Certain kinds of harmony, accompaniment, and melodic embellishment are appropriate in an opera aria but not in a church cantata.

As a final example, I would like to consider an *Ode mit Melodie* written by C.Ph.E. Bach for Krause's 1753 collection and subjected to especially

---

36 Ibid., p. 106.
37 E. Weimar, *Opera Seria and the Rise of the Classical Style,* Ann Arbor 1982, p. 33.
38 Nichelmann, *Die Melodie,* p. 141.
39 Ibid., p. 129.

detailed criticism by Nichelmann. In his text, Nichelmann cited and harshly
condemned a number of the songs contained in this collection – to which it
should be recalled he himself also contributed. Among the composers
receiving his censure besides Bach were Agricola and Carl Heinrich
Graun[40]. As usual, Nichelmann would first quote an excerpt from the
respective setting, analyze why it was unsatisfactory, and then offer his own
improvement. For reasons which were probably as much political as artistic,
Nichelmann found Bach's odes particularly distasteful. And here a historical digression is in order.

It is crucial for us to keep in mind that throughout his tenure, Nichelmann was in constant competition with Carl Philipp Emanuel Bach. Contrary to most histories that describe Nichelmann as "second harpsichordist"
behind Bach, the American musicologist Douglas Lee has shown that
Nichelmann was not at all subordinate in his position to Bach; they were in
fact co-equals[41]. Indeed, according to account books, Nichelmann actually
received a higher salary than did Bach – a point of no small irritation for the
latter. In the confined and competitive atmosphere of Sanssouci, it was
inevitable that a high degree of tension would thus exist between the two
harpsichordists attempting to curry the favor of the King. It seems quite
plausible, then, that Bach's well-documented dissatisfaction with his position in Berlin was in no small part due to his rivalry with Nichelmann. The
animosity that must have existed between the two became apparent in the
lengthy and invective attacks Nichelmann made upon one particular ode of
Bach's with a text by Nikolaus Giseke: "Die Küsse" (H 673; W 199/4). It is
one of the longest and most intricate of the collection, atypically through-
composed with an unusually elaborate accompaniment.

This ode will be the centerpiece of Nichelmann's critique, and to which
he will return repeatedly in his book. Indeed, no other work of music
receives such detailed analysis and categorical condemnation. Nichelmann
corrects the faults he perceives in the song by completely resetting the
poem. The resulting recomposition is by far the longest of Nichelmann's
examples, taking up three full plates.

As it is not feasible here to consider all of Nichelmann's criticisms in
detail, I shall only point out the highlights of his discussion. To begin with,
Nichelmann lodges his by-now familiar complaint that the music lacks suf-

---

40 The songs cited by Nichelmann were "Amint," "Die Küsse," and "Trinklied" by Bach
(H 673–5; W 199/4–5, 11), "Ja Liebster Damon" by Graun, and "Willst du diesen Raub
nicht strafen" by Agricola.
41 D. Lee, *The Instrumental Works of Christoph Nichelmann,* Ph.D. diss., University of
Michigan 1968, p. 31.

ficient "Mannigfaltigkeit der Harmonie"[42]. This is evident already in the very first three measures where Bach is content to repeat the tonic [see example 10 a]. Asks Nichelmann, "Who does not sense here the complete absence of a progression of harmony or fundamental bass and the resulting monotony?"[43]. A simple change to the subdominant in measure 3 as in example 10 b, Nichelmann suggests, would improve the setting vastly. (As before, the bottom line is not a sounding part, but the fundamental bass analysis.) He then proceeds to castigate Bach for his negligent setting:

> "What was the reason that the composer burdened us with this awful and boring mono-tony instead of lively, contrasting harmony? Could it be that he believed he had dis-charged his duty with this setting through a specific succession of single notes by them-selves in a single voice without any attention paid to the harmony or thought to satisfy-ing our hunger for diverse and multifarious harmony?"[44]

Nichelmann also condemns Bach's setting of the words "Die Alten, lehrt er mich" in mm. 16–18 shown in example 11 a. Bach's three bar phrase, claims Nichelmann, is awkward and stifles the natural coupling of the text with the next phrase, "die pflegten auch zu küssen." There is no need for the awkward pause in measure 18, which both interrupts the harmonic flow as well as unnaturally emphasizes the word "mich". The result is that the text meaning is "obscured" while the harmonic progression lacks "life and movement"[45]. It would be better, as Nichelmann illustrates in example 11 b, to contract the first phrase into two measures, thus allowing the music to continue uninterrupted.

Similar problems of text setting are pointed out and corrected through-out the piece. Indeed, there is hardly a measure kept intact by Nichelmann. He criticizes virtually every aspect of Bach's music: the unnatural break-ing-up of phrases, poor metric placement of words, a jagged melodic line, a badly conceived accompaniment, and always a lack of attention paid to the harmony. After one particularly egregious passage Nichelmann remarks: "It is thus certain that the necessary balance between the differing parts within the whole is disrupted; the measured movement of harmony is uneven and

---

42 Nichelmann, *Die Melodie,* p. 116.
43 Ibid., p. 85.
44 "Was war aber die Ursache, daß der Setzer, statt der uns erquickenden verschiedenen Harmonie, uns mit dem aus der Monotonie entstehenden Ekel und Ueberdruß belästi-get? Etwa was anders, als weil er glaubte, sich der, bey dieser Zusammensetzung ihm obliegenden Pflicht, durch eine für sich selbst, und ohne Absicht auf Harmonie, bestim-mete Folge einzelner Töne, in einer einzelnen Stimme zu entledigen, ohne darauf bedacht zu seyn, unsern Hunger nach einer mannigfaltigen vielfachen Harmonie zu stillen?" – Ibid., p. 85.
45 Ibid., p. 118.

jagged ["hockerigt"], thus [making the] entire piece difficult to sing and even more difficult to listen to"[46].

Another aspect of Bach's song that offends Nichelmann is the illogical tonal disposition. Nichelmann divides the music into five phrases consisting of, respectively, 15, 27, 28, 22, and 13 measures. In all but the last phrase, the cadence is on a non-tonic triad. This is tonally disproportionate, complains Nichelmann, as the tonic is prevented from being clearly established. The final cadence upon Bb is a surprise to the listener and unsatisfying as a close. To remedy this, Nichelman chooses to recapitulate the opening tonic theme again, thus creating a kind of Rondeau form. He admits this causes problems in terms of the text. (He had to extend and repeat the last stanza of the text superimposed upon the music from the opening.) But his primary concern, he lamely explains, is with the harmonic structure and melody[47].

Now, it is not hard to imagine that Bach would have been less than pleased by Nichelmann's treatise. Not only did the upstart harpsichordist insolently condemn a wide spectrum of Bach's compositional output, he had the audaciousness to rewrite it! Further, Nichelmann presumptuously cited Johann Sebastian Bach as corroboration for his ideas. But surely if anyone was to appeal to Johann Sebastian's practice with any authority, it would be his son! Bach's indignation can be well-imagined.

Of course, Carl Philipp Emanuel was not the only one whose toes were stepped upon. Nichelmann's captious essay was guaranteed to stir up a hornet's nest. Among the many musicians who critically responded in one way or another to issues raised in Nichelmann's treatise may be mentioned Ernst Gottlieb Baron[48], Friedrich Riedt[49], Johann Adam Hiller[50], Johann Friedrich

---

46 Ibid., p. 119.
47 Ibid., p. 122. – We must keep in mind that it was not the genre of the ode itself that Nichelmann was contesting – he did, after all, contribute to the same collection in which Bach's appeared. Yet there was an undeniable discrepancy between Nichelmann's aesthetics and Krause's prescription of a proper ode that deemphasized harmony in favor of a singable – and optionally *a cappella* – melody. A comparison of Nichelmann's four settings contributed to the Krause collection show that, indeed, he did use comparatively a faster harmonic rhythm and more adventurous chromaticism that the other settings in the publication, including Bach's. Also, his accompaniments were more intricate and independent that was recommended by Krause.
48 *Abriss einer Abhandlung von der Melodie: eine Materie der Zeit,* Berlin 1756.
49 "Betrachtungen über die willkürlichen Veränderungen musikalischer Gedanken bey Ausführung einer Melodie", in: *Historisch-kritische Beyträge zur Aufnahme der Musik,* II, 1756, pp. 95–118.
50 *Wöchentliche Nachrichten und Anmerkungen,* II, Leipzig 1767, p. 65.

206   Thomas Christensen

Agricola[51], and Abbé Vogler[52]. Even writers outside of Germany such as the Swiss theorist Jean-Adam Serre took disparaging note of Nichelmann's treatise[53].

But undoubtedly the most direct and vehement rebuttal to Nichelmann's treatise was found in a small 16-page pamphlet dated July 1, 1755, and entitled *Gedanken eines Liebhabers der Tonkunst über Herrn Nichelmanns Tractat von der Melodie,* written under the pseudonym of "Caspar Dünkelfeind." Now, the identity of this "enemy of conceit" has never been established for certain. Some scholars such as Wade[54], and Lee[55] have suggested that Carl Philipp Emanuel Bach himself might have penned the pamphlet, while Eitner ascribes the work to a Georg August Leopold[56]. Given a fresh rereading of this pamphlet in light of the musical examples which I have been able to identify in Nichelmann's treatise, I think there is now a preponderance of evidence establishing that Bach was indeed „Caspar Dünkelfeind". The vituperative anecdotes and direct personal criticisms made by Dünkelfeind reveal him to have had first hand knowledge of Nichelmann. And certainly as we have seen, Bach had more reason than anybody else to be offended at Nichelmann's criticisms, the most acerbic of which seemed to have been directed at his music. The indignation and passion with which Dünkelfeind defends Bach's music from Nichelmann's charges suggests unequivocally that we are dealing with the wounded and aroused ego of the composer. Nichelmann, himself, as we will see, had no doubt that Bach was indeed Herr Dünkelfeind. This short pamphlet, then, is really a new and important document clarifying Bach's professional and aesthetic position in the mid-1750s, and suggests the impetus for certain ideas which would be elaborated in Part 2 of his *Versuch* in 1762.

---

51 "Beleuchtung von der Frage nach dem Vorzuge der Melodie vor der Harmonie" (1771), in: *Magazin der Musik* II, 1786, pp. 809–815.
52 *Betrachtung der Mannheimer Tonschule,* vol. I, Mannheim 1778, p. 1.
53 J.-A. Serre, *Observations sur les Principes de l'Harmonie,* Geneva 1763, pp. 63–64.
54 R. Wade, *The Keyboard Concertos of Carl Philipp Emanuel Bach,* Ann Arbor 1981, p. 2.
55 D. Lee, *The Instrumental Works of Christoph Nichelmann,* p. 46.
56 R. Eitner, *Biographisch-Bibliographisches Quellen-Lexikon,* 2nd edition, Graz 1959, vol. VI, p. 142. – The attribution to Leopold is hardly likely given that Leopold – according to Gerber – was born on October 17, 1755. On the other hand, Eitner's suggestion that Leopold – and hence probably Dünkelfeind – was in fact a penname for the organist and theoretician, Christoph Gottlieb Schröter (1699–1782) is plausible, given that Schröter spent most of his working life in Nordhausen, the place of publication for Dünkelfeind's pamphlet (Schröter's lengthy figured bass treatise was finished in Nordhausen in 1754, according to the Preface, although not published until 1772). But it would seem out of character for Schröter to take issue with Nichelmann's thesis, given that he was himself an outspoken proponent of Rameau's thesis, and in his *Deutliche Anweisung* argued passionately for the primacy of harmony in a manner identical to Nichelmann.

In his assessment of Nichelmann's treatise, Bach does not mince words. Throughout these 16 pages, Bach heaps unrelenting sarcastic and abusive criticism upon both the treatise and its author, and racks his vocabulary to come up with enough derisive adjectives with which to describe them. The treatise is labeled variously as "obscure", "pretentious", "scholastic", "wretched", "dry", and "boring". Nichelmann is described as "pedantic", "vain", "unscrupulous", "a barrel-organ composer", a "hypochondriac", a "visionary", a "charlatan", and a "plagiarizer". Complained Bach, "He only took what others found beautiful and made it worse ... There is an envy and hatred in his writings towards the richness of other men's ideas; he would rather that everyone think dryly and simple-mindedly ... He reveals an aversion to the great refinement in today's musical taste"[57]. Didn't Nichelmann have anything better to do, asks Bach, then to criticize and presumptuously try to "improve" the works of composers more talented than he? Bach suggests that Nichelmann would have done better to look at some of his own keyboard sonatas and spend as much effort improving those as he did with the examples in his book[58].

Cutting even deeper, Bach goes on to accuse Nichelmann of pilfering and "shady-dealing" ("Schleifhandel"). Some of Nichelmann's compositions, he darkly suggests, are actually the work of others. But this is not surprising, he continues. Testifying to a personal animosity in their relationship that must have long predated this polemic, Bach writes: "To be sure, we are used to this writer and his works of musical plagiarism. One must endure him with patience, as neither the most polite nor the sternest of admonishments have helped."[59] Bach goes on to claim that Nichelmann's unscrupulousness runs so deep that he did not even trust his own copyist to leave his home with his manuscripts lest Nichelmann find and steal them for himself![60]

---

57 [Caspar Dünkelfeind], "Gedanken eines Liebhabers der Tonkunst", p. 3.

58 In point of fact, Nichelmann did precisely that. In one section near the end of the treatise, Nichelmann took the opening of his own harpsichord sonata in G minor (# 1 from the first collection of 6 published in 1745) and criticized its lack of harmonic motion (p. 170). He then offered several revisions of the opening, employing a faster harmonic rhythm and his favored technique of invertible counterpoint.

59 "Gedanken eines Liebhabers der Tonkunst", pp. 2–3.

60 Bach's wrath here may have something to do with Nichelmann having copied and made numerous annotations and corrections some time in the early 1750s to the performing parts of Johann Sebastian Bach's Harpsichord Concerto in D minor (BWV 1052) based upon holograph copies by Agricola and C.Ph.E. Bach (see H.-J. Schulze, ed., Johann Sebastian Bach: Konzert für Cembalo und Streichorchester BWV 1052, Leipzig 1975, pp. vi–vii). Schulze (Studien zur Bach-Überlieferung, p. 143) suggests this would indicate that a cordial relation existed between Nichelmann and Bach, at least initially. But it is equally plausible that Nichelmann's transcription was undertaken without the knowledge or approval of Carl Philipp Emanuel, a possibility eluded to in this passage.

Bach next launches into a vigorous defense of his ode "Die Küsse" and an equally scathing attack upon Nichelmann's resetting. Bach begins by taking issue with Nichelmann's injunction against repeated notes and points out that such a procedure is a legitimate and well-tested compositional device. He notes further that Nichelmann himself used repeated notes in his melody. Asks Bach sarcastically, "Does the composer forget his own rules or does he believe that he alone possesses the right to defy them?"[61]. Bach is also happy to correct several voice-leading mistakes in Nichelmann's setting including a number of hidden parallel fifths. Bach sarcastically assures the reader that this must be a printing error, as no competent musician could overlook so obvious a mistake in such a simple two-part aria, and especially one meant to correct the errors of others[62].

The major complaint Bach voices concerning Nichelmann's treatise is that it does not fulfill its promise of instructing the reader how to write and judge a good melody. Bach analyzes the opening of the text chapter by chapter and finds it all superfluous. What, for instance, do acoustics and metaphysics have to do with melody, Bach demands to know?[63] Music is not a sciene of vibrations and mathematics – it deals with notes put together by a composer. And here Bach propounds a radical empiricist position:

> "The musician looks at [music] from a totally different perspective; he experiments and formulates rules on how different tones must be combined in order to please the ear. This has as little to do with mathematics as it does with physics. The rules of composition are drawn neither from physical laws nor mathematical calculations, rather they are determined by the judgement of the ear."[64]

Bach clearly shows he understood the acoustical premises of Rameau's theory, for he acknowledges the existence of harmonic overtones in most (although not all!) vibrating bodies[65]. But he rejects that this has anything

---

61 "Gedanken eines Liebhabers der Tonkunst", p. 3.
62 Ibid., p. 13.
63 Ibid., p. 5.
64 "Der Musikus siehet sie von einer ganz andern Seite an, er untersuchet, und bestimmet durch Regeln, wie verschiedene Töne zusammen gesetzt werden müssen, wenn sie dem Gehöre gefallen sollen. Mit der mathematischen Untersuchung hat er eben so wenig zu thun, als mit der physikalischen, und die Regeln der Setzkunst sind weder aus physikalischen Grundsätzen noch aus mathematischen Rechnungen hergeleitet; sondern die Grundsätze, daraus sie hergeleitet werden, sind die Empfindung des Gehörs." – Ibid., p. 6.
65 Bach's critique here resembles those articulated by two contemporaneous scientists whose work he may well haven known: Leonhard Euler and Daniel Bernoulli. Euler was the premier member of the Berlin Royal Academy of Sciences at this time, while Bernoulli was a frequent contributor to the Journal it published. Both Euler and Bernoulli had recently pointed out in both published and private writings that not all vibrating systems contained a uniform family of harmonic upper partials; many such overtones were non-harmonic. They concluded that Rameau should not use such an acoustically

to do with the practice of music. How can such a phenomenon tell the musician, for instance, how to resolve a seventh chord?[66]

As for Nichelmann's distinction between *monodisch* and *polyodisch* music, Bach is a bit more charitable. He acknowledges that composers have always tended to employ differing degrees of melody or harmony in their music. But, he continues, no composer uses exclusively the one at the expense of the other – or at least no good composer would. Invoking the metaphor of a painting, Bach reminds his reader that a picture has both light and shadow, and the best painters use both effectively[67]. Likewise, then, a good composer uses both harmony and melody. It is ridiculous to think that anyone would simply write a succession of chords or notes one after the other arbitrarily, as Nichelmann accuses[68]. On the other hand, Nichelmann's total subordination of melody to the harmonic structure of a piece is pedantic and pernicious, complains Bach. Harmony by itself without the animation of melody lacks any "fire, spirit, and life"[69].

This was a theme, it should be mentioned, to which Bach returned in Part 2 of his *Versuch* published in 1762. There, he repeatedly pointed out the necessity of conceiving both the melody and harmony simultaneously. Neither could be separated, as they together constituted the musical piece[70]. Nonetheless, the ideal composition and performance in Bach's view still needed to be conceived vocally, for without the "singendes Denken" he prescribed, all music would be lifeless. As if to illustrate the fallacy of Nichelmann's harmonic emphasis, Bach ended the *Versuch* with a discussion of the Fantasy. A series of chord progressions were provided in figured bass. He then showed how a skilled composer could improvise over the progression – that is, give it different "melodies" – and produce totally new and contrasting effects. A similar aesthetic may well have impelled the publication in 1760 of his 6 keyboard sonatas *mit veränderten Reprisen* (H 136–9, 126, 140; W 50). (Although to be fair, it should be pointed out that elsewhere Bach took the opposite approach; that is, he harmonized a single chorale phrase in nearly 100 different ways [H 871; W 204].) Furthermore, Bach's advice to the would-be accompanist in Part 2 is coupled with amusing but cutting caricatures of a harpsichordist who commits unpardonable gaffes in voice-

---

heterogeneous phenomenon as his principle of harmony (see Th. Christensen, "Eighteenth-Century Science and the *Corps Sonore*: the Scientific Background to Rameau's Principle of Harmony", in: *Journal of Music Theory* 31/1, 1987, pp. 23–50, esp. pp. 34–38).
66 "Gedanken eines Liebhabers der Tonkunst", p. 6.
67 Ibid., p. 14.
68 ibid., p. 15.
69 Ibid., p. 14.
70 C. Ph. E. Bach, *Versuch einer Anleitung ...*, Part II, Berlin 1762, pp. 212, 243.

leading, indulgent interpretations, improper decorum, and general poor taste in performance. These are so vividly described that one wonders whether he had a particular villain in mind – perhaps his rival accompanist Nichelmann?[71]

Bach, then, saw little of redeeming value in Nichelmann's treatise. He consoled himself with the thought that it was so badly written that at least no one would bother reading it all the way through, let alone understand any of it[72]. Its appearance was nonetheless lamentable as it would surely bring shame to all musical authors and the everlasting suspicion of book publishers. Bach ended his comments with this stinging slap in the face:

> "This should be sufficient to convey the ideas to be found in this book. The author expends much unnecessary energy in criticizing with much finickiness, obscurity, and confusion the mistakes of inexperienced beginners, any one of which could be recognized by a competent teacher and corrected through experience. ... We would above all like to offer this friendly advice to the author: Instead of writing books which will prove to be as unsuccessful as his compositions, it would be better [for him] to play pretty barrel-organ trifles that do not require so much dexterity. ... We heartily regret that his effort was insufficient to raise himself as high as his smug self-complacency."[73]

The pamphlet then concludes with this satiric couplet:

> "Sey nie dem klugen Rath Verstandiger zuwider;
> Doch suche *nimmermehr* ein Lob für deine Lieder."
> [Never spurn the sound advice of the wise;
> But nevermore seek praise for your songs.]

To answer Bach's charges, Nichelmann issued – as was the custom of the day – a counter-pamphlet entitled "Die Vortreflichkeit der Gedancken des Herrn Caspar Dünckelfeindes über die Abhandlung von der Melodie ins Licht gesetzet von einem Musick Freunde". He was quite clearly stung by Bach's sharp rebuke, although it seems naive of him to have expected anything less. He begins his pamphlet by expressing surprise and dismay at the invectiveness of Dünkelfeind's diatribe. What, he wonders out loud, did he do to so arouse the ire of this author? Nichelmann then confesses that several friends had tried to persuade him that Bach was in fact the author of

---

71 Ibid., pp. 268 ff.
72 "Gedanken eines Liebhabers der Tonkunst", p. 16.
73 "Dieses mag vor diesesmal genug seyn, einen Begriff von einem Buche zu geben, worinnen der Herr V. sich viele unnöthige Mühe giebet, mit vieler Aengstlichkeit, Undeutlichkeit und Verwirrung einen Fehler ungeübter Anfänger zu tadeln, der schon einem jeden von seinem Lehrmeister gezeigt wird, und sich durch mehrere Uebung verliehret. ... Wir wollen bey dem allen dem Herrn V. wohlmeinend rathen, anstatt des Bücherschreibens, womit es doch so wenig als mit seinem Componiren fort will, sich lieber mit der Abspielung eines sanfte leyernden Stückgens, wozu nicht viele Geschwindigkeit erfordert wird, abzugeben. ... Wir bedauern herzlich, daß ihm seine Kräfte nicht vergönnen, sich so hoch zu erheben, als seine Selbstgefälligkeit es ihm eingiebt." – Ibid., p. 16.

this pamphlet. Barely concealing his sarcasm, Nichelmann claims that he finds this difficult to believe, as his critique was not made out of ill-will or spitefulness, and Bach should certainly know this.

> "But so great is my respect for the merit of this man, that I wish to allay any suspicion of partisanship when one honours me by having the true and authentic meaning of my words understood, without having them – as it often happened – be grossly misinterpreted."[74]

The first issue Nichelmann wishes to clear up is Bach's charge of plagiarism. This is a "shameful lie", Nichelmann indignantly replies[75]. He points out later in the pamphlet that two of the examples quoted in his treatise that Bach attributes to Quantz were in fact his own compositions[76]. Nichelmann does admit, though, to using the harmonic progessions of other composers. But, he quickly adds, that hardly constitutes plagiarism. It depends more on how the given progression is elaborated[77].

In the rest of the pamphlet, Nichelmann refutes Bach's many charges, although his arguments for the most part are a mere repetition of ideas already stated in his treatise. He repeatedly protests that Bach misunderstood or misrepresented his intentions. Nowhere, for instance, did he ever claim he would provide a prescription for the writing of a beautiful melody[78]. Nor did he ever deny the importance or beauty of melody. Bach, Nichelmann complains, clearly did not see the distinction he was drawing between *monodisch* and *polyodisch* music. As to the specific criticisms Bach made concerning parallel fifths in Nichelmann's resetting of "Die Küsse", Nichelmann claims that a "certain skilled Capellmeister" believes that such ascending false fifths are permissable at times[79].

As if to throw some sand back into Bach's eyes, Nichelmann selects some new compositions of Bach for criticism – this time the 18 *Probestücke* in 6 Sonates published as a supplement to Part One of Bach's *Versuch* in 1753 (H 70–75; W 63). It seems as if Nichelmann couldn't resist taking yet a few more swipes at his rival's music. He points out how Bach uses the same cadential figurations and motives over and over throughout these pieces,

---

74 "So groß aber auch meine Hochachtung gegen die Verdienste dieses Mannes ist, so gewiß hoffe ich dennoch den Verdacht einer Partheylichkeit zu entgehen, wann man mir die Ehre erweiset, meine Worte nach ihrer wahren und eigentlichen Bedeutung zu nehmen, ohne ihnen, wie es öfters zu geschehen pfleget, einen falschen Sinn anzudichten." – Nichelmann, "Die Vortrefflichkeit" (n.p., n.d.), pp. 1–2.

75 Ibid., p. 3.

76 Ibid., p. 7.

77 Ibid., p. 5.

78 Ibid., p. 8.

79 Ibid., p. 14.

resulting in "boring", "impoverished", and "empty" music[80]. Nor can Nichelmann resist mentioning the striking similarity between the third movement of the last sonata – the so – called *Hamlet-Fantasy* – and a "well-known Prelude by a Thuringian Country Schoolmaster"[81].

We can see that there was clearly no love lost between the two harpsichordists. The results of this polemic are not surprising. Although there was probably always a good deal of tension between the two harpsichordists, it must have risen to unprecedented levels after their war of words erupted into the open. Furthermore, Nichelmann could hardly have endeared himself to the other members of Frederick's band with his impertinent criticisms and corrections. Virtually the only contemporary of Nichelmann who had anything positive to say about his treatise was – not surprisingly – his fellow Rameau enthusiast, Marpurg[82]. Thus he must have found himself in a lonely and unbearable position. In late 1755, Nichelmann petitioned for and was granted his release from Sanssouci. Whether this action was taken on his own volition or he was pressured into doing so we do not know for certain. But clearly Nichelmann realized it would be impossible to continue to stay on. After his departure, he wrote no more theoretical tracts and did not publish any more music; he was for all practical purposes ostracized by the Berlin *Musikkreise*. His remaining days were spent desperately seeking some kind of employment to sustain himself, ultimately without success[83]. He died bitter and impoverished in 1762.

But the feud between Bach and Nichelmann did not end with the latter's death. As I have already pointed out, parts of Bach's *Versuch* published in 1762 can be read as a continuation of his polemic with Nichelmann. There is another consequence of their feud, I think, which is perhaps not as obvi-

---

80 Ibid., p. 4.
81 Ibid., p. 4.
82 F. W. Marpurg, *Historisch-kritische Beiträge*, I, pp. 438–439; II, p. 268.
83 We have two poignant letters from Nichelmann written in early 1756 to his former teacher in Hamburg, Telemann, and an organist named Johann Conrad Schwalbe from Weißenfels, informing both of his recent release form Sanssouci. In his letter to Schwalbe, Nichelmann speaks cryptically of "compelling reasons" for leaving his post, while to Telemann, he wrote that although we would not bore him wih a "lengthy explanation" concerning the reasons for his departure, such a decision he assures would obviously not have been undertaken "without pressing reasons." He pleads for help from both men in finding a new job, "all the better," he tells Schwalbe, "if I could be so lucky as to find employment *out of town*" [my emphasis]. Obviously, nothing came of Nichelmann's supplications. Presumably the on-set of the Seven-Years War was not an auspicious time for musical job-seeking in Prussia. (Letter to Telemann dated Feb. 2, 1756, and transcribed in: H. Grosse/H. R. Jung, eds., *Georg Philipp Telemann: Briefwechsel*, Leipzig 1972, no. 49; Letter to Schwalbe dated March 31, 1756, and transcribed in "Christoph Nichelmann – ein anderer verschollener Thomasschüler", in: *Signale für die Musikalische Welt* 38 [1866], p. 634.)

ous, but nonetheless is important for historians of theory. And that is Bach's well-known repudiation of Rameau's music theory. Until Nichelmann's treatise came along, it does not seem that Bach knew very much concerning Rameau's theory. For that matter, it is not clear that he ever did master any of it. (His only comment concerning Rameau in his pamphlet was one rejecting the Frenchman's definition of melody[84].) Yet Nichelmann's aggressive promotion of Rameau was apparently enough to turn Bach into an ardent opponent of the Frenchman's theory.

Thus, in later years, when Bach was called upon to resolve a dispute between Kirnberger and Marpurg over the value of Rameau's theory and its relevance to Johann Sebastian Bach's teachings, Carl Philipp Emanuel replied that neither he nor his father subscribed to Rameau's views, indeed, they were entirely "anti-Rameau"[85]. But there is no evidence to suggest that J. S. Bach was aware of Rameau's theory. More importantly, though, there is no unbridgeable theoretical chasm separating Bach's counterpoint and Rameau's theory, as Kirnberger's own fundamental bass analyses of Bach's fugues would ironically show[86]. The polarity Carl Philipp Emanuel sets up, I suspect, was motivated more on political than theoretical grounds.

Fortunately, as time passed and the dust settled after these polemics, German theorists began to recognize that the question of the priority of melody or harmony and its numerous theoretical spin-offs was moot. Even Agricola, the defender of Italian music and translator of Tosi's famous vocal treatise, could admit by 1771 that melody was neither superior to nor independent of harmony "since from the perspective of the composer, melody and harmony are of equal value"[87].

Nichelmann was obviously a conservative voice in a time of musical change. From his point of view, the lack of harmonic activity in the galant style, and the mannerisms of the musical *Empfindsamkeit* contradicted natural and eternal requirements of musical composition, ones ideally realized in the music of the High Baroque. Yet Nichelmann was not simply a stubborn reactionary in the mold of Buttstett, Fux, or Spieß. He recognized that styles were irreversibly changing; he, himself, contributed to this develop-

---

84 "Gedanken eines Liebhabers der Tonkunst", p. 15.

85 J. Ph. Kirnberger, *Die Kunst des reinen Satzes in der Musik*, vol. IV, Berlin 1779, p. 188.

86 That Kirnberger could consider himself as the opponent to Rameau's theory in his polemic with Marpurg when in fact he was much closer to it than was Marpurg is telling evidence that the understanding and dissemination of Rameau's theory in Germany in the later 18th century was almost hopelessly clouded by nationalistic and political factors. As long as Rameau was only known to Germans through contentious – and in important ways, ill – formed interpreters such as Marpurg and Nichelmann, there was little likelihood that his ideas would receive a widespread or favorable audience.

87 J. F. Agricola, "Beleuchtung von der Frage …", p. 811.

214   Thomas Christensen

ment, after all. Nichelmann's singularly important insight, I think, was the realization that harmonic richness and logic need not be incompatible with the goals of galant melodiousness or *empfindsam* expressiveness. It is true that he was not always able to reconcile these elements in his own music and recompositions of his colleagues'; for all their logic and undeniable harmonic clarity, they were a bit too predictable and square; they lacked both the grace and the *elan* which were such essential components to the galant and *empfindsam* styles. Yet neither Bach nor Nichelmann could have suspected that their positions were not as far apart as their polemic suggested, and that their respective ideals of "Mannigfaltigkeit der Harmonie" and a "Singendes Denken" would find a brilliant balance in the not too distant future in the music of the Viennese classicists.

Acknowledgements

An early draft of this article was read on October 15, 1987, at the annual meeting of the American Musicological Society held in New Orleans. The initial research was undertaken at the *Institut für Musikforschung* in West-Berlin during the Spring of 1986 and was supported by a generous post-Doctoral research grant from the *Deutscher Akademischer Austauschdienst.* For their help and advice, I am also grateful to Douglas Lee, William Caplin, Reinhard Strohm, Rachel Wade, and Anne-Katrin Krätschmer.

Musical Examples

Example 1 a

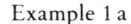

J. S. Bach BWV 817

Example 1 b

Nichelmann contra C. Ph. E. Bach 215

Example 2 a

Example 2 b

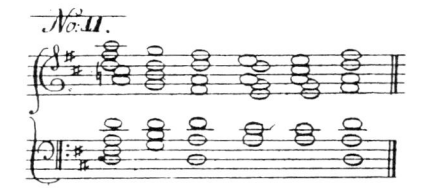

Example 2 c

216   Thomas Christensen

Example 3 a

Example 3 b

Example 4 a   Example 4 b

C.P.E. Bach H 414; W 11

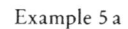

Example 5 a

Example 5 b

218   Thomas Christensen

Example 6 a

Example 6 b

Example 7 a

Example 7 b

Nichelmann contra C. Ph. E. Bach   219

Example 8 a

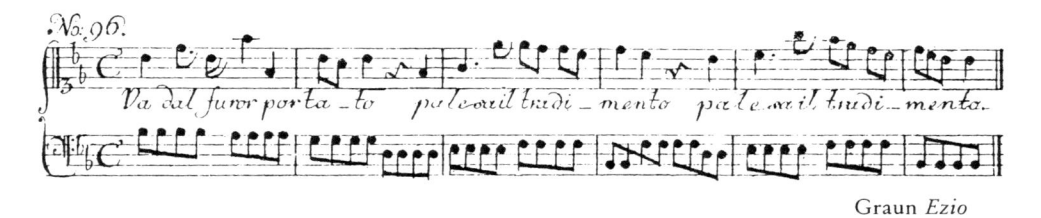

Graun *Ezio*

Example 8 b

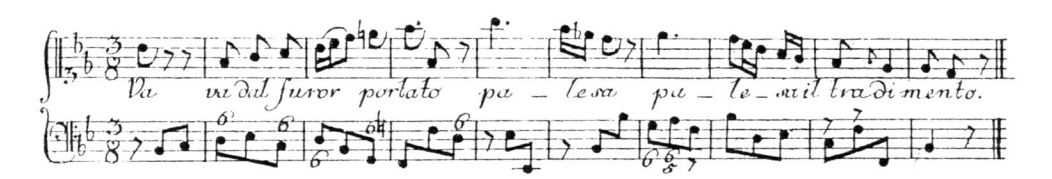

Example 9 a

(BWV 84)

Example 9 b

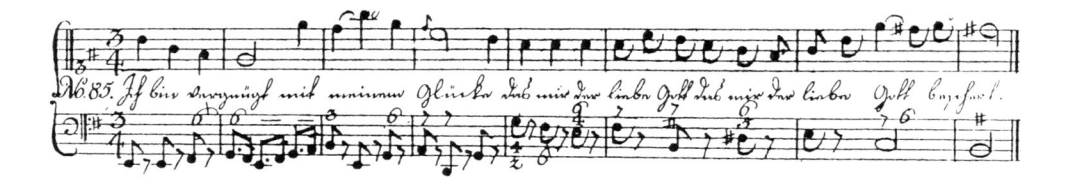

Example 10 a

Example 10 b

Example 11 a

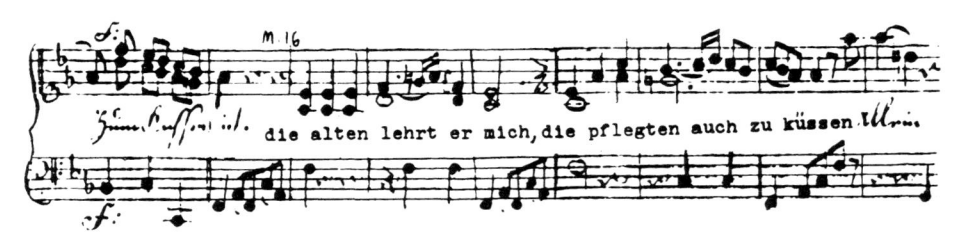

Example 11 b

Part IV
Performance and Reception

[22]

"Our old great favourite": Burney, Bach, and the Bachists

Christopher Hogwood

The reception history of C. P. E. Bach's music has been, from the eighteenth century to the present day, very much a matter for Germans in German; Cramer, Forkel, Reichardt, and Schubart are names to be balanced against Bitter, Miesner, Vrieslander, Suchalla, and Ottenberg. For relief for and from this monoglot approach, a collection of English names from the circle of Charles Burney can provide an alternative linguistic and aesthetic angle; certainly, their reactions help to preserve the immediacy of a new musical discovery from foreign parts, and demonstrate the hardy critical attitude of the true musical *Liebhaber*. Burney's entertaining and graphic description of his 1772 dinner with C. P. E. Bach is too often quoted to require repetition here. But in his other notes (many unpublished) and private correspondence, Burney fills in the picture of the way the average (and that included the amateur) listener appreciated C. P. E. Bach's music. From him, and even more from his major correspondent Thomas Twining, we get not only the sense of excitement and discovery with each new publication but also the reasoning underlying their enthusiasm, their rapid succumbing to what they diagnosed as *Carlophilipemanuelbachomania*, and, on occasion, their bafflement with the later styles of their hero.[1] Additionally, Burney's writings help us to understand C. P. E. Bach in relation to the surrounding European musical culture; his notion of a "Bachist" is a useful tool with which to evaluate how far contemporary German keyboard culture had been colored

Thanks are due to The British Library, the Beinecke Rare Book and Manuscript Library (Yale University), Lars E. Troide (The Burney Project, McGill University), Fr. Alvaro Ribeiro, SJ, Alexander Bauhart, Ralph C. S. Walker, Darrell Berg, Tobias Plebuch, Derek Adlam, Stephen Rose, Heather Jarman, and Guillermo Brachetta. An earlier version of this essay appeared in Bernard Brauchli, Susan Brauchli, and Alberto Galazzo, eds., *De Clavicordio IV, Proceedings of the Fourth International Clavichord Symposium, Magnano, 1999* (Magnano: Musica Antiqua a Magnano, 2000).

[1] The Twining correspondence is primarily to be found in the British Library, Add. MSS 39929–36. Some, but not all, of the passages quoted are in *A Selection of Thomas Twining's Letters 1734–1804*, ed. Ralph S. Walker (Lampeter: The Edwin Mellen Press, 1991). Burney's letters are immaculately transcribed and annotated in Alvaro Ribeiro, SJ, *The Letters of Dr Charles Burney: I, 1751–1784* (Oxford: Oxford University Press, 1991).

222   *Christopher Hogwood*

by C. P. E. Bach's example, as well as a way of highlighting repertoire that hitherto has been undeservedly neglected.

I

Charles Burney's admiration and hunger for Bach's music is well expressed in a letter to Christoph Daniel Ebeling (November 1771), the writer and historian who was later to collaborate on the translation of Burney's *Italian Tour*, and who had recently sent Burney a copy of his *Versuch einer auserlesenen musikalischen Bibliothek* (1770). Burney writes:

Mr C. P. Bach, who stands so high in my opinion, that I should not scruple to pronounce him the greatest writer for the Harpsichord now alive, or that has ever existed as far as I am able to judge, by a comparison of his works with those of others, & by my own Feelings when I hear them performed . . . Grace, Fancy, Feeling & clearness, are to me superiour to all other merits. There are Times for shewing learning & contrivance; but I think the best of all contrivances in music, is to please people of discernment & taste, without trouble. A long & laboured Fugue, recte et retro in 40 parts, may be a good entertainment for the Eyes of a Critic, but can never delight the Ears of a Man of Taste. I was no less surprised than pleased to find Mr C. P. E. Bach get out of the trammels of Fugues & crowded parts in which his Father so excelled. Domenico Scarlatti did the same at a Time when a Fugue followed every passage like its Shadow. They both struck out a style of their own. Scarlatti's full of Enthusiasm fire & passion, Bach's every thing, by turns, that music can express.[2] I am extremely curious to see some of C. P. E. Bach's vocal Music. If you can get me the church music mentioned in your Essay, & any new Harpd Pieces of that Author, I shall receive [them] with great pleasure.

The most unbuttoned and entertaining sequence of letters is Burney's private correspondence with the Rev. Thomas Twining (the oldest son of the tea-dealing family) in his country parish of Fordham near Colchester. Scholar, translator (later nicknamed "Aristotle Twining" by Fanny Burney in recognition of his translation of that writer's *Poetics*),[3] and musician, Twining was an enthusiastic amateur performer on the keyboard and violin. He was allowed to read much of Burney's writing before publication, assisted him with his commentary on ancient authors, and offered exact, and sometimes blunt, criticism. Burney in return relayed items "musical &

---

[2] In his *German Tour* Burney points out that "both were sons of great and popular composers, regarded as standards of perfection by all their contemporaries, except their own children, who dared to explore new ways to fame." In *Dr Burney's Musical Tours in Europe: being Dr Charles Burney's Account of his Musical Experiences*, ed. Percy A. Scholes, 2 vols. (London: Oxford University Press, 1959), II: 220.

[3] Ibid., I: 260.

newsical" from London, and advised Twining of fresh repertoire available in town, especially for his newly acquired "Piano forte." In one such letter, of 21 January 1774, Burney wrote to Twining: "But for Instrumental music, are you much acquainted with that of the Hamburgh Bach – of Haydn – Vanhall – Ditters – Hoffmann[4] &c? – their compositions never consist of *Notes* et *RIEN que des Notes*..." In a response to Burney on 13 October 1774 Twining reports about the state of his piano, and his interest in Emanuel Bach:

A warmer room has, in part, restored my P[iano] F[orte] to the use of its faculties... I had a most comfortable musical week here, with my friend [The Rev. Mr Hey of Cambridge]. You will respect his taste when I tell you, that he is charmed with Em. Bach, even thro' my imperfect scrambling, & tho' not at all used to him. I played: he sat with his hands over his eyes in a corner; & I heard him muttering at all the right places – We played Vanhall together & he was much pleased with it... For my part I find the *Carlophilipemanuelbachomania* grow upon me so, that almost everything else is insipid to me. I thank God I shall next week have two sets of him...

A year later Twining's enthusiasm for C. P. E. Bach was undiminished, and he writes to Burney on 31 October 1775, obviously after correspondence that took in Pythagoras and Greek music:

I'll be hanged if I think it *was* so absurd of you to be so *melancholy* about music not mending the heart. when I said that, I was a critic, – a thing of ice. Now I have been playing Emanuel on my Piano forte, and am ready to swallow the largest Pythagorean bolus you can give me. For this reason; – & because

&c Q.E.D.[5]

I throw down my glove; – tell me that anything in music can be more delicious than the *fall* upon the 2d. chord, – or any other possible arrangement of that chord, half so sweet, so balmy, (so God knows what) – & chuse your weapons, & your place! – I feel the ηθος, the *moral* effect of it this minute.

Clearly in a missing letter Twining asks Burney's help in fingering a tricky passage, for in response Burney allows himself, for the first time, to be critical of the occasional ungratefulness of Bach's writing, writing to Twining on 16(?) November 1775:

---

[4] There is keyboard music by both Leopold and Johann Georg Hoffmann (see the Breitkopf Catalogues).
[5] From *Sechs Sonaten* ("Erste Fortsetzung") 1761, Wq. 51.4: Sonata 4/ii, Largo e sostenuto, mm. 1–2 (with omissions); Twining draws his glove beneath the second chord.

O! – the awkward scrawls you wish to have fingered. – where are they? – aye – here they are – what queer toads! – yet they are Bach's – would one not think they were written by a man who had never laid his hand on a keyed instrument? . . .

But Twining's hunger for C. P. E. Bach continues, and he replies to Burney on 3 December 1775:

I have an eager, craving appetite about me for that man's music, that I never felt for any other. There they [a set of Concertos] lie upon my Piano Forte with the red tape about them; I shall play with them as a cat does with a mouse for this week, before I eat them . . .

Burney responds with musical greetings on Christmas Eve in a typical doggerel poem entitled "Noel" with the lines:

> May the friends whom you see
> To love Music agree
> And ceasing to laugh
> May they call for a Bach . . .

Meanwhile Bach's music was also a regular feature of the Burney household; Fanny Burney, in a letter to Samuel Crisp (2 March 1775) speaks of entertaining the Italian soprano Agujari:

After Tea, we went into the Library, & Hetty was prevailed upon to play a Lesson of Bach of Berlin's, upon our Merlin Harpsichord. It was very sweet, & *she* (Agujari) appeared to be *really* much pleased with it, & spoke highly of the *Taste* & *feeling* with which she (Hetty) played. Mr Burney sat down next. They all stared, as usual, at his performance.[6]

Samuel Crisp himself, the disappointed playwright and lifelong friend of the Burneys, preferred his "favourite pieces of Bach of Berlin, Handel, Scarlatti" to the "clang of horses and hounds." According to Fanny,

the love of music, in Mr Crisp, amounted to passion; yet that passion could not have differed more from modern enthusiasm in that art, if it had been hatred; since, far from demanding, according to the present mode, every two or three seasons, new compositions and new composers, his musical taste and consistency deviated not from his taste and consistency in literature: and where a composer hit his fancy, and a composition had filled him with delight, he would call for his favourite pieces of Bach of Berlin, Handel, Scarlatti, or Eckard, with the same

[6] *Memoirs of Dr Charles Burney 1726–1769*, ed. Slava Klima, Garry Bowers, and Kerry S. Grant (Lincoln: University of Nebraska Press, 1988), 77–8. Hetty (Esther, Charles Burney's daughter) subscribed to Bach's *Sechs Claviersonaten für Kenner & Liebhaber* I (1779) and presumably acquired one of her father's twelve copies of the fourth collection (1783).

Burney, Bach, and the Bachists   225

Plate 9.1 C. P. E. Bach, *Claviersonaten mit einer Violine und einem Violoncell zur Begleitung*, Erste Sammlung (1776), p. 18

reiteration of eagerness that he would again and again read, hear, or recite chosen passages from the works of his favourite bards, Shakespeare, Milton, or Pope.[7]

One of the most extended descriptions of the new music and a detailed account of the effect of Bach's modulations comes in a letter from Twining to Charles Burney on 29 November 1776. It is replete with musical examples, and demonstrates an analytical expertise which was very possibly more prevalent in the amateur musical circles of England at this period than we allow ourselves to imagine. Here is enthusiasm backed by reason:

Pray, did you ever see or hear any thing more charming than the Rondeau in the 2d. of those new *Clavier-sonaten* of Bach's?[8] [See plate 9.1.] More touching simplicity without triteness or *fadeur* in the *Motivo*? more elegance of variation? more relief

[7] *Memoirs of Doctor Burney*, ed. Madame d'Arblay [Fanny Burney], 3 vols. (London: Edward Moxon, 1832), I: 51–2.

[8] *Claviersonaten mit einer Violine und einem Violoncell zur Begleitung*, 2 vols. (Leipzig, 1776–7), Wq. 90.2. Burney was listed as a subscriber (and presumably agent) in these sets: "Herr Burney, Doctor Musices in London, auf 12 Exemplare." The "Rondeau" was much studied: Forkel analyzed it in his

& contrasts of all sorts? a more bold & masterly sweep of modulation – the ear often beautifully surprized, never shocked? Did you ever hear any thing that more fairly reminded one of Milton's

       — many a winding bout
       Of linked sweetness long drawn out;

than the passages that lead back to the original key in p. 16

♪ & p. 18, ♪

& the passage from G to D in the first page? But I do think the getting into E♭ (p. 18) & out of it, is one of the most beautiful & *artful* strokes I ever saw. Only see how he manages it, to make it pass smoothly upon the ear. First comes the chord of Sixieme superflue, very naturally. The traitor! he never means to resolve it in *that sense*. A pause upon E♭, unaccompanied, *alone*, prepares the ear for the transition, from its propensity to take every single note it hears dwelt upon any time, for key-note. Not content with *this* preparation, he very artfully changes the bass accompaniment of the subject, retains the chord upon which he paused, availing himself of the *equivoque* of temperament, & by this means giving it a *resolution*, tho' in another sense; whereas had he not flung in that ♪ the chord wou'd have had no regular resolution, & the ear wou'd not have been so smoothly *filched* over the gulph. But see what a charming timidity in the modulation, – *pianissimo*, – upon tip-toes, – biting it's lip, & hardly venturing to fetch it's breath – in the 3d bar, it can bear it no longer; – starts wildly, but still gracefully, out of the perilous path, & after running, without once looking behind it, this 5 bars of delicious *égarement* finds itself once more at home & calmly & comfortably resumes the subject. The thing gives me all these ideas; – I can't help it! If I'm a simpleton you must tell me so. Now, by way of variety, I'll find a little fault. I don't think Bach succeeds well in his accompaniments, especially of the Allegros. They are in too many notes – too *responsive* – not *nourishing*, & smooth & sostenuto enough: – too much in the old Organ Concerto way. – Then he is now and then a little *fogrum* (example p. 6 ♪ says the harps. –

♪ answers the fiddle.) &, for him, old fashioned as he is in the Concertos you sent me last winter. Can you account for his going backwards thus sometimes in his later compositions? From that perfect elegance & high finish he had got to in the lessons with his own graces I thought there would be no "vestigia nulla retrorsum." Sure somebody, (whom God forgive!) must have told him that he must accommodate, & vulgarize, & have made him put himself out of his way? However, everything he does abounds in fine fancy & uncommon passages; he can't go on long like other people. I know nothing so *amusing* as the *first cut up* of his things; nor any food of the kind that keeps fresh & sweet so long. My chaps run pails-full of juice at the 6 *easy* & *charmg.* lessons you say Bremner is to publish . . .

Musikalisch-kritische Bibliothek, 3 vols. (Gotha, 1778–9), II: 281ff.; and in August Frederic Christopher Kollmann's *An Essay on musical harmony* (London, 1796) it served to illustrate "improper rondo" form.

Burney, Bach, and the Bachists 227

P.S. P.16 of Bach's Rondeau – ♪ – will you give me leave to do those sprawling contre-sevenths with 2 hands, or not? 'Tis easier so, but perhaps will not render the slurs so well?

Not all music was within Twining's grasp however, and on 24 January 1777 he writes after a disappointing assault on the music of Eckard, which had been highly recommended by Burney:

I was not acquainted with Eckard before, you characterize him well. Tough indeed! When I cast my eye upon the last lesson, & saw it as black as an Undertaker's ticket, I was frighten'd; but when I saw *con discretione*, O, ho! said I; if discretion will do, I am discrete enough; and down I sate to play it; but soon I found it the most indiscrete thing I ever did in my life. He swims above the common level; the first lesson I like much. But after all, I had rather have made the first movement of Bach's first lesson, than the whole set of Eckard's. I know nothing more graceful & pleasing; nothing quear or *recherché*, yet the cast of the whole remote from anything common. His endeavouring to make them easy, has, especially in the slow movements, produced some *unpleasing vacuities* of sound, as you somewhere say. But all together, 'tis a charming set & the playability makes it particularly valuable to us *gentlemanly* bunglers. But what a proof they afford of his taste & invention. Do you think any other man, confined to the same simplicity, – indeed, for the most part to 2 melodies, such as might be performed by 2 single instruments, – cou'd have done anything like it? Nothing so hard as to *invent* melody; nothing so easy as to throw *dust* in the ears by the jingle of chords, & Harmony ready invented to one's hand. Upon a *harpsichord*, this support of harmony, batteries, & *poddlediddle* basses &c seems necessary, at least in movements that are not rapid. The Pianoforte will bear simple melody much better, to be sure. But even here, I find myself always supposing the instrument only a good sort of *simulacrum* for 2 instrs. of more perfect expression, or 2 voices. I continually catch myself singing when I play E. Bach's music. – a key'd inst. that can sustain & vary a tone is a great desideratum that still remains to be supplied. [Twining goes on to discuss Burney's duets, said to be the first for the medium of four hands, but then mentions:] Bach, I find, has been at it. My friend Hey heard two ladies play a duo of his lately . . .[9]

I never longed to see & hear anything so much as that MS Sonata of E. Bach, you talk of . . . Why, in spite of E. Bach's curls & *tutical* divisions *now & tan*, in his Harps. things, I must say that his runs of semiquavers are frequently full of uncommon fancy, & like those of no other writer for the instrument. For instance, I think the first movement of the 1st Clavier Sonata ♪ charming. But these things will serve to talk about. I am all obedience, as to the septenary passage; I wish my *hand* was as obedient to *me*.

---

[9] Twining is possibly thinking of J. C. Bach's duets, though these were published in 1778.

228   *Christopher Hogwood*

Twining also manages to be simultaneously tactful and honest about Burney's own compositions when he mentions his *Duets*, writing on 28 July 1778:[10]

> I have to thank you for your cuddling lessons, & the new set of E. Bach. I lament that I have nobody to take half a stool with me. I seem to like your 2d set still better than your first. In Bach I find, as usual, in his later things, charming places, with fits of antiquity, & caprice. The Andantes in yr. set are less good than common with him. He has run into cramp, equivocal modulation, made more equivocal, & less intelligible to the ear by his leaving *jours* for the accomps., which seem as if they were scarce worth gutting his harpd. part to make room for.

Nevertheless, Twining was still exerting himself to get copies of everything he could directly from Germany, since the letter continues:

> I did commission Mr. Schultz to write to E. Bach for as many of his works as he cou'd get together, except what I already had, of which I gave him a list, wth the first bar of each set, for fear of mistakes. I have not yet heard from him, & so can say nothing to Bremner yet. [To Burney's suggestion of returning copies of Bach's music that he had ordered but had failed to sell in England, Twining was firmly opposed.] Why, the music I have of E. Bach eats neither oats nor hay, nor costs me anything but house-room. What a contempt that man must have for the musical gusto of us English!

On the back of the letter is another cry for digital assistance:

Finger, finger! – the 2d. bar laughs

It clearly took Burney some time to reply to this appeal, and five months later (19 December 1778) Twining again bemoans his unruly fingers:

> I am glad E. Bach is coming out [i.e., publishing] again; & thank you for putting my name in a way to be germanized – oh – & for the fingering: I had utterly forgot that I had set you to that task. *Pour cette fois*, I am a clever fellow, & the light of nature has not been a dark lantern to me. I had finger'd, & played the passage *exactly* as you have figured it. But before I did it in uncertainty; now I feel firm, & *know* there is no better way. I can get very well to F♯; but the worst is that dog of a fore-finger, knowing that he is to touch E after F♯, thinks he may as well go to it at once, & let the calling at D♯ alone – It *feels* very like shifting a finger from one key

---

[10] In 1777 Burney had published *Four Sonatas or Duets for Two Performers on one Piano Forte or Harpsichord*, with a second set following in 1778.

to the next; which we great *Digitists* & *Doigtists*, you know, hold to be *anathema, maran-atha.*[11]

Now, however, a more perceptible disillusionment begins to tinge the correspondence; the name of Haydn is more frequently invoked – as the natural successor to C. P. E. Bach, but also as his replacement in their affections. Even here, however, there is a note of embarrassment hinting at what later became an open stance – that a preference for C. P. E. Bach indicated superior taste: "Dr J[ohnson] criticizes [the poet] Gray, as a common Organist wou'd criticize Em. Bach," writes Twining to Burney on 10 October 1781.

Parenthetically, Thomas Gray was perhaps a more suitable choice in this context than Burney realized, since the poet, writing to William Mason from Cambridge, had shown that he too was partial to Bach, though oddly finding in him "the best Italian style":

Send for six lessons for the piano-forte or harpsichord of Carlo Bach, not the Opera Bach, but his Brother. To my fancy they are charming, and in the best Italian style; Mr Neville & the old musicians here do not like them, but to me they speak not only music, but passion. I cannot play them, though they are not hard; yet I make a smattering that serves "to deceive my solitary days," and I figure to myself that I hear you touch them triumphantly.[12]

"Charming" is also the rather automatic adjective with which Burney sidelines Bach once more in his next letter to Twining (10–12 November 1783):

I pack up in the Parcellina, a new set of Em: Bach's Pieces – chiefly Rondeaus – with many new *kicks*, & *detours* – But he seems reduced to *recherche* & caprice in order to be new – & to say the truth, his Eleve Haydn seems to have given him the *go by*, on his own ground. However, the great Man frequently appears, & there are charmg. things par-ci par-là in this collection.[13]

Once Burney had succeeded in his long-term plan of attracting Haydn to England, these transferred loyalties can be found more openly in his letters to other correspondents. Writing to Mrs. Chambers on 3 November 1797,

---

[11] A curious half-Greek, half-Aramaic phrase, used as a form of imprecation in the seventeenth and eighteenth centuries.

[12] Letter dated "1763," *The Correspondence of Thomas Gray and William Mason*, ed. John Mitford (London: Richard Bentley, 1853), 314. The words in quotation marks are cited from a sonnet by Mason. Both the first and second sets of *Sechs Sonaten mit veränderten Reprisen* (Wq. 50 and 51) were issued by John Walsh in 1763, but Gray is clearly referring to the first collection, *Sei sonate per cembalo...* (advertised in the *Public Advertiser*, 25 April), rather than *A 2d set. Sei sonate per cembalo... Opera seconda* (advertised in the *Public Advertiser* on 15 October, i.e., after this letter was written). See William C. Smith and Charles Humphries, *A Bibliography of the Musical Works published by the Firm of John Walsh during the Years 1721–1766* (London: The Bibliographical Society, 1968), 30.

[13] This collection is presumably Bach's *Clavier-Sonaten und freye Fantasien... für Kenner & Liebhaber* IV (1783), twelve copies of which Burney subscribed to.

Burney appears to complain of excessive chromaticism in Bach; he mentions that the young composer Steibelt "was a scholar of our old great favourite Emanuel Bach. But he is no imitator of Haydn, or even his Master. His melodies are always elegantly natural, and his rage for *half notes* is much tempered by better resources."[14] In a letter addressed to Charles Butler on 23 August 1798 with a present of seven sets of sonatas by Bach (a duplicate set meant for Miss Butler), the process of recension is complete, and C. P. E. Bach has become a necessary historical stepping-stone to the more universal Haydn:

> Whoever studies the productions of this author will discover him to have been the model of the admirable Haydn, particularly in writing for the P[iano] F[orte] & indeed in Bach's compositions we may sometimes see the germ of many of Haydn's comic strokes & what may be called his musical bons mots. Modulation too had been greatly extended by Em. Bach before it was quite unchained by Haydn. I mean not however, by any means, to diminish the just title wch. H. has to originality of wch. he has more perhaps in Melody & effects. Bach wrote well only for one keyed-Instrumts. H. has furnished every instrument worth cultivation with productions in its true genius . . .[15]

A second, largely unpublished source of evidence from Charles Burney, as indicative of his literary techniques as his musical opinions, is to be found in the notebooks that he kept in preparation for writing his entries in Abraham Rees's *Cyclopaedia* (1802–20), now part of The James Marshall and Marie Louise Osborn Collection, Beinecke Rare Book and Manuscript Library, Yale University. "Materials towards the History of German Music and Musicians 1772" (Osborn Shelves c 100) contains many references to C. P. E. Bach and his associates.[16] The Notebook, although dated 1772, contains alternative assessments, often with later alterations and interlineations up to 1788. A sequence of the salient passages will speak for itself, and in cases where the same material has been recycled by Burney in print, even the diplomatic changes and grammatical polishing are intriguing. Where Burney has left alternatives, these are transcribed, separated by a slash. Superscripts, e.g. Harp[d], have been brought to the line; interlineations and omissions are let into the line, and some relevant deletions have been included struck through.

In the entry entitled "King of Prussia" Burney comments:

---

[14] Robert Müller-Hartmann, "Two Unknown Letters of Charles Burney," *Journal of the Warburg and Courtauld Institutes*, 3 (1939–40), 161–4 (at p. 162).

[15] Signed autograph letter (draft), Osborn collection. Burney first wrote: "Bach wrote well for keyed-Instrumts," then interpolated "only" and "one"; possibly only the first insertion was intended.

[16] Thanks to Alvaro Ribeiro and Alexander Bauhart for their assistance with these sources.

He had certainly great professors abt. him, tho' he never was partial to C. P. E. Bach[,] the greatest musician of them all.[17]

[p. 21, after "Kirnberger" on a page entitled "List of Eminent German Musicians living in 1772"]

C. P. E. Bach, Chapel Master to Princess Amelia, Abbess of Quadrisburg & Music-Director at Hamburg, whose merit is beyond all praise, whether he is considered in the light of a learned, an Elegant, an inventive Composer; or a neat, expressive, & perfect Performer; in every one of these Particulars he surpasses all his Cotemporaries as much as if he possessed no other excellence. Always original, bold & masterly in his writings, he lets nothing escape from his pen, without stamping upon it the mark of his peculiar Genius, wch. is easily discoverable in some bold stroke of modulation or new & graceful trait of Melody. In short, both as a Composer & performer, I shd. not a moment [p. 22] hesitate giving him the first place among all the writers for & performers on Keyed Instruments that had ever existed.

Complaints have been made against him for being sometimes trop recherché in his Modulation & Melody, & generally, too difficult for moderate performers. but easy & difficult are relative Terms. his Compositions are calculated for great players &

[continued on p. 30 as an "addition to C. P. E. Bach's Character. p. 22"]

& cultivated Ears. & as he seems to have passed by all his Cotemporaries in refinement, it is possible that his Passages & Style may be rendered familiar to posterity, tho' this age, pede Claudo,[18] in vain attempts them.

[added later]

This prediction made in 1772 has been since fulfilled – in the works of Haydn – Geo. Benda of Brunswick, Pleyel, &c.

[This next section was later erased by Burney]

Those who accuse him of being whimsical & Fantastical shd. remember that his Pieces are so rich in Invention, taste & Learning that each line of them wd. wire draw/cut into slices & furnish more genius than is to be found in a whole page of many other Compositions that have been well recd. by the Public, where whole bars, nay Lines & even Pages frequently contain nothing but meer Notes without design or meaning.

[p. 22]

Charles Fasch, {son of the Church composer, of whose works see list in Breitkopf[†]} Musico di Camera to the K. of Prussia at Berlin, seems by his compositions

---

[17] Osborn Shelves c 100 p. 12.

[18] In full "pede poena claudo" (Horace, *Odes* III/32), of the punishment that limps after the crime.

232   *Christopher Hogwood*

to have been possessed of a great Hand, with Taste & Invention. His Style resembles much that of ~~the great~~ C. P. E. Bach, with whom he resided at the Court of Berlin, a considerable time. They used to wait monthly upon his late Prussian Majesty, alternately as Chamber Musicians to that Prince.

† I am hardly enough acquainted with his work to speak of them with Cognition, but from what I have seen . . . seem to have been possessed of great fire & original Genius. His style is that of Vinci, polished, correct & elegant. His melodies natural, grateful and charming and Harmony correct & pure. But in variety of subject . . . in accompts. [he] was not only far inferior to Handel but to many younger composers. He died at Berlin 1759.

[p. 31. Added later to the entry on Fischer]

When he quitted Dresden he went to Berlin, & continued a Month with his Majesty of Prussia, with whom he played, constantly 4 Hours, alone, each Day. This last Circumstance was occasioned by an offence having been given by C. P. E. Bach – who in going from Potzdam to Sans Soucy, had been so frightened by the bad Road as to exclaim to one of the Household, on his Arrival, in rather strong Terms, tell our [orginally "your"] Master, sd. he, that no Honour or profit will be a sufficient Compensation to us for such dangerous Service, & unless the roads are rendered less hazardous we (speaking in the Name of the whole Band) can come here no more. It is true the roads were very bad, & it is as true that Bach was extreamly frightened in passing them. but Cowardice sometimes in desperate Situations gives a degree of Courage in remonstrance to wch. the greatest Heros are not in possession. For Bach's boldness in this particular not only surpassed that of all his Brethren, but of all the Generals & real Captains in the Prussian service, none of whom however they might have wished it, had the audacity to Complain of this Dangerous pass ere they could arrive at Sans Soucy, a situation in all Countrys & at all Times of difficult access! – the Consequence of the Transport wch. had escaped Bach, was disgrace & banishment from Court for a considerable Time.

[p. 33, in a discussion of Müthel]

Müthel. I know not his Country [inserted later "he is listed at Riga, & was Scholar of J. Sebastian Bach."] nor have I ever seen any of his Compositions except 2 Harpd. Concertos printed at Riga: but so full of Novelty, taste, grace & Contrivance are they that I shd. not hesitate to rank him among the first geniusses of the present Age. his Style resembles that of C. P. E. Bach, & like his it abounds with difficulties & passages wch. to Common performers & hearers may seem trop recherché – & his accompts. too, like those of the great Bach, require performers equal to himself – wch., in fact, is Expecting too much – it is requiring an army of Generals, instead of Subalterns under one Leader. When Bach lived at Berlin he cd. have a great performer to every part he chose to write† – but as no other place in Europe can boast the same advantages, it was rendering his Concertos <u>Local</u>, & utterly impracticable elsewhere.

† or at least he cd. like his R. Master place an able commander at the Head of each Corps.

[added later]

His duet for two Harpds. or Piano fortes, is one of the finest and most Masterly compositions I have seen, but so difficult that two performers able to execute it with precision will seldom be found in the same place.[19]

[p. 36, in the entry on Georg Benda]

George Benda, Chapel-Master to the D. of Gotha, at Altenburg, Brother of the preceding. his Compositions for the Harpd. are new, Masterly, & learned; but his fondness of singularity will, by some, be construed into Affectation. indeed such perpetual Disappointments to the Ear, can only be supported in the works & talents of the great Bach, where they seem to flow from Nature, whereas in all Others they have the appearance of Art & Labour. The Wildness of a Scarlatti [originally "Bach"] & the peculiarities of a Bach are but the Ebullition of Genius. These animated & firey Flights are cold & vapid when produced either by study or Imitation.

[p. 58 under "Marpurg" and a discussion of the fugue subjects quoted in his writings]

It is remarkable that of all the subjects given of Sebastian Bach, there is hardly one that is pleasing or easy to work; he seemed to think difficulty the chief merit of music. whereas those of Handel, without being common or barren, are all natural & striking. Those of Emanuel Bach are too recherchés & full of taste to admit of answers without Confusion, difficulty, & extraneous modulation.

[p. 94]

Sebastian Bach
Qu. When did he die?
This Musician was so fond of Polyphonic Music & full harmony that besides a constant & active use of Pedals, he is said to have had a stick (some say a short Tobacco-pipe) in his mouth, by wch. he put down such notes as neither feet nor Hands cd. get at.

[later addition]

---

[19] One must recall here the accounts of performances in the Burney household by his nephew Charles Rousseau Burney with his cousin-wife Esther which were "heard with great applause." Percy A. Scholes, *The Great Doctor Burney*, 2 vols. (London: Oxford University Press. 1948), II: 37.

234   *Christopher Hogwood*

Review his works. Speak of his admirable <u>Credo</u>. Pieces in all the 24 keys for the manual exercise of his Son C. P. Em. of his great reputation while his style continued in favour, & the reverence for his works & name to the present time.

[p. 105]

If Haydn has ever looked up to any great Master as a model, it has certainly been C. P. Em. Bach: the pauses; bold modulation; rests, free use of semitones, and unexpected flights of Haydn remind us of Em. Bach's Early works more than of any other composer. He has however surpassed his Model in facility, the knowledge of instruments & invention; freaks, caprice, & even buffoonery sometimes seem natural in Hayd. wch. in the works of others wd. appear downright Caprice & affectation. Em. Bach used to be censured for his extraneous modulation, crudities, & difficulties; but like the hard words of Dr. Johnson, the public by degrees grew reconciled to them; & now, every Germ. composer takes the same Liberties as Bach, & every English writers [sic] uses with impunity the language of Johnson.

Osborn Shelves c 97 p. 48 (reverse pagination) has the following reference:

Fischer says he [C. P. E. Bach] has the peculiar & unaccountable Power of affecting his hearers even to Tears upon the Clavichord, his favourite Instrument . . . C. P. E. is as original as he is learned & refined; his favourite Style is pathetic tho' occasionally he has no want of uncommon Fire. But his powers of Expression are unrivalled by any Performer on Keyed Instruments that I have ever met with in any part of Europe. these powers been so much tasted & so deeply felt by his Countrymen that he may be called as much a Reformer in the music of Keyed Instruments as his Countrymen John Hus, Jerome of Prague, or Martyn Luther, were in religion. indeed he has proportionally more followers among musical practitioners, than the religious reformers among their Sectaries. Catholic, Lutheran & Calvinist; all have adopted his Doctrines or received some of his Tenets. All the German players of Keyed Instruments aim at Expression more than Brilliancy or feelings (the Chief objects of former Harpd players) & all greatly prefer the Clavicord or Piano Forte to the common Harpd as infinitely more favourable to their present Style.

Osborn Shelves c 101: "Remarks on Sr. J. Hawkins's General Histy. of Music 1776" contains one reference (p. 246):

The delicate, refined, & original style of C. P. E. Bach, though universally imitated in Germany, has never been sufficiently known or familiar in England to supply food to predatory professors. It therefore forms no Æra in this Country, though it occasioned a memorable revolution in the Harpd. & Piano forte Music of his own.

In the carefully expurgated *Memoirs*, Burney's daughter summarized the Doctor's admiration for C. P. E. Bach with none of the doubts that he had expressed privately to Twining: "Amongst his German correspondents, Dr. Burney ranked first the super-eminent Emanuel Bach, commonly known by the appellation of Bach of Berlin; whose erudite depths in the science, and exquisite taste in the art of music, seemed emulously combating one with the other for precedence; so equal was what he owed to inspiration and to study."[20] This chimes well with the German view that Bach was an *Originalgenius*, and essentially inimitable, though there might be worthy attempts and a strong and beneficial influence to be derived from his seriousness. Reichardt stated that "the style of each composer may be more or less original; there is only one Bach, whose style is utterly original and utterly his own."[21] But this party line, and Fanny's later anodyne résumé of her father's real feelings, hide the more disquieting questions that were being asked; even Dr. Burney had been compelled to mention in his *Musical Tours* that "complaints have been made against his pieces for being *long, difficult, fantastic*, and *far-fetched*."[22]

The Abbé Vogler advanced the same query more slyly in 1780, asking: "How do the two great keyboard players Carl Philipp Emanuel Bach and Alberti from Rome compare with one another?" ("Wie verhalten sich die zwei großen Clavierspieler C. P. E. Bach und Alberti von Rom gegen einander?"). His essay describes the "merits of a worthy gentleman grown old in the outmoded system" (patently C. P. E. Bach), whom Vogler hopes "would introduce into his style more sentiment, more daintiness, more simplicity, and less artificiality (which, it must be said in his defence, the somewhat dry Northern taste still demands). By simplicity we mean not only that the notes should be straightforward, but also the key-scheme: there should be a balanced arrangement of all foreign keys around the principal key, variety within tonal unity, etc."[23] The fictional young spokesman continues: "Maestro, your taste is incorrect; you prefer artifice, you wish to be learned, and forget to be simple; conspicuous in all your music is the anxious quest for uniqueness, for novelty, the desire to say something never said before; in this way you pay too little attention to the formal concept . . . Here, for example, you have written a piece in A minor which, instead of establishing the main key of the work at the outset, starts with four beats in A minor followed by four beats in G minor. What a way to begin, what a curious kind of music!"

---

[20] *Memoirs of Doctor Burney*, II: 326.

[21] Johann Friedrich Reichardt, *Über die deutsche comische Oper* (Hamburg, 1774), 15.

[22] *Memoirs of Doctor Burney*, II: 218.

[23] Georg Joseph Vogler, *Betrachtungen der Mannheimer Tonschule*, 4 vols. (Mannheim, 1778–81), III: 151ff.; trans. from Hans-Günter Ottenberg, *Carl Philipp Emanuel Bach*, trans. Philip J. Whitmore (Oxford: Oxford University Press, 1987), 142.

In England the new wave of enthusiasm for the music of J. S. Bach, much trumpeted by Samuel Wesley, led to some unnecessary belittling of his children. Wesley wrote to the organist Benjamin Jacob on 2 March 1809:

By the way I have had the loan of many *exercises* of his [J. S. Bach's] for the Harpsichord, which are every Whit as stupendous as the Preludes and Fugues . . . the very quintessence of all Musical Excellence. It's droll enough, that amongst these is inserted a beautiful Air which is published along with a sett of Emanuel Bach's Lessons, and which I saw at Bath: I am very much inclined to think that this Son, like many others, made but little scruple of robbing his Father; and that he was not concerned for his Honour seems plain enough by the vile and most diabolical Copy that he gave Dr. Burney as a Present and from which the latter was wise enough to judge of and damn his Works (as he thought), but the Phoenix must always revive.[24]

Understanding and appreciation of the development of C. P. E. Bach's compositional methods and their importance to later composers did not improve over the next half-century: even Carl Friedrich Zelter, the Director of the Berlin Sing-Akademie, could pen this misguided and depressing report, dated 14 May 1825:

His otherwise vigorous humour, filled with the joys of life, he soon began to indulge, and his music became more lightweight; he adapted his style, and thought to pander to the musical amateur by applying himself to lighter tasks.

In the process he gradually lost more and more of his former admirers, Pr[incess] Amalie, Kirnberger, Marpurg, Krause, etc., without attracting new friends for his new style; his late works may be called his weakest, since they show little trace of Bach's seriousness, or uniquely personal touch, which, however, he was unable to set aside entirely. His Hamburg works, then, are an unhappy compromise, for the composer, perhaps, more unsatisfactory than for anyone else, and thus did he depart this world.[25]

On balance, an equally sad but more objective postscript is offered by Dr. Burney himself in his will of 1807, where he simply writes: "My Collection of music, printed and manuscript, I wish to be sold by auction. It was most of it good in its day, though now some of it is out of fashion . . ."[26]

From Burney's standpoint, the most important innovation of the later C. P. E. Bach for Haydn and eventually Beethoven – the control of tonal

---

[24] This was a manuscript copy of Book 1 of the *Well-Tempered Clavier*. See *Letters of Samuel Wesley to Mr Jacobs*, ed. Eliza Wesley, 2nd edn. (London: William Reeves, 1878), 22.

[25] Quoted and translated by Hans-Günter Ottenberg, "Bach and Carl Friedrich Zelter," in Stephen L. Clark, ed., *C. P. E. Bach Studies* (Oxford: Clarendon Press, 1988), 185–216 (at p. 209).

[26] *Catalogue of the music library of Charles Burney sold in London 8 August 1814*, facsimile ed. Alec Hyatt King (Amsterdam: Frits Knuf, 1973), viii.

organization within free surface writing – was outside his time-frame. As he stated, his opinion was based on *published* keyboard music, of which the real glut came during the period in which he issued the four volumes of his *History*, from 1776 to 1789. The relatively simple structures of this earlier C. P. E. Bach, where the surface stitching is more important than the fabric, lend themselves to easy imitation. The conceits that Burney observed in Benda, Fasch, Reichardt, and Haydn can be traced back to more than one example from C. P. E. Bach, usually readily available in print, and created more by gesture than construct or balance. Interestingly, it is Twining who seems to have been more conscious than Burney of the underlying tonal design that rendered the language of harmonic rhetoric possible; he is very aware of the effect of Bach's tonal-expressive subtleties within melodic lines and in the larger structure, which for us suggests a hypersensitivity to the musical implications, as well as the manner of performance, of this kind of expressive composition.

Although modern analysis might bridle at the idea, it is likely that the choice of instrument became increasingly important, and distorted critical appreciation: Twining's lack of access to a clavichord may well explain his lessening enthusiasm for C. P. E. Bach's later repertoire, just as the public fell away from an output that was so instrument-specific. The figure presented by late C. P. E. Bach to his contemporaries was less revolutionary and more "inconstant" and "capricious" than we would like it to be, while his influence as a keyboard technician and teacher was admired for a rationality of expression more calculated than we might feel compatible with the Romantic image of the inspired improviser. But in practical terms he advanced the acceptable "average" keyboard technique with demands for rapid octaves, extreme dynamics, cadenzas, and all the "clatter" of toccata figuration, plus complex and precise ornamentation, which in itself laid a wider field open for his successors. Most importantly, he constantly presented keyboard works, and especially the sonata, as a serious receptacle – even his "leicht" publications were both issued and reviewed as original and important statements. As Rochlitz put it (in Mozart's mouth), "Nowadays one doesn't do *what* he did. But as for *how* he did it – there he is without peer."[27]

II

In his *History*, Burney claimed that from the middle of the eighteenth century the "elegant and expressive" keyboard music of C. P. E. Bach

---

[27] Quoted in Heinrich Miesner, *Philipp Emanuel Bach in Hamburg: Beiträge zu seiner Biographie und zur Musikgeschichte seiner Zeit* (Wiesbaden: Sändig, 1929), 45.

was imitated "so universally in Germany by writers for keyed-instruments, that there have been few works published for them since, which are not strongly tinctured with his style; those of Wagenseil, Schobert, and Schulz excepted; but Geo. Benda, C. Fasch, Fleischer, Ernst Benda, Reichardt, &c. &c. are strong Bachists."[28] Burney's concept of the Bachist, though ranging into circles far distant from C. P. E. Bach himself, offers intriguing insights into the extent of Bach's influence, actual and perceived, in the late eighteenth century. For Burney, in the light of his later disenchantment with C. P. E. Bach, a Bachist must be one who copies, develops, or derives from Bach's earlier styles; in the case of a comparable "original genius" such as Haydn, Burney modifies the term to "successor": "If Haydn has ever looked up to any great Master as a model, it has certainly been C. P. Em. Bach: the pauses; bold modulation; rests, free use of semitones, and unexpected flights of Haydn remind us of Em. Bach's early works more than of any other composer."[29] All these characteristics are apparent in Bach's first printed sets (Prussian Sonatas 1742, Württemberg Sonatas 1744, and the *Probestücke* of 1753), and several of Burney's "Bachists" had also appeared in print before 1760 when the first volume of *Sonaten mit veränderten Reprisen* was issued.

Modern commentators have expanded on Burney's catalogue of internal evidence to take in Bach's later style, combining it with historical association in their hunt for Bachists. The first ring of "Bach descendants," as they are termed by William Newman, includes Hässler, Rust, Müller, Vierling, Forkel, and Gruner and represents as much the posthumous influence of J. S. Bach as a conscious imitation of C. P. E. Bach.[30] Nevertheless, certain "Bachist" features (and specific clavichord techniques, which were certainly not a feature of J. S. Bach's style) color their productions and even their titles declare allegiance: the presence of "varied reprises," for example, can be taken as a direct tribute (e.g. Rust's *Sonata in F* [Czach no. 18], Löhlein's *Sei sonate con variate repetizioni per il clavicembalo*, op. 2 [1768], the fifth of Binder's *Sei sonate* [*c*. 1776] or the third movement of Sonata III in Reichardt's 1776 *Sei Sonate per il Cembalo*). The technique of "veränderte Reprisen" became a basic component of Haydn's system of musical extension (especially in the final rondos of his keyboard sonatas and the slow movements of string

---

[28] Charles Burney, *A General History of Music from the Earliest Ages to the Present Period*, 4 vols. (London: author, 1776–89), IV: 591.

[29] Osborn Shelves c.100, Notebooks, 104, and, with slight changes, *A General History*, IV: 596.

[30] William S. Newman, *The Sonata in the Classic Era* (Chapel Hill: University of North Carolina Press, 1963), 579ff.

quartets), and in an open spirit of imitation we find Leopold Mozart writing to Breitkopf (6 October 1775) on behalf of Wolfgang, asking "whether you would care to publish clavier sonatas in the same style as those of Herr Philipp Carl Emanuel Bach with varied reprises."[31]

Additional criteria proposed by Pamela Fox include "similarity in type and application of ornaments, dotted rhythms, *all'unisono* writing, diverse figuration techniques, avoidance of Alberti bass, greater harmonic depth and variety, and an enriched texture."[32] Fox lists a large number of keyboard composers "associated with the C. P. E. Bach style": J. C. F. Bach, C. S. Binder, F. G. Fleischer, J. N. Forkel, N. G. Gruner, C. F. S. Hägemann, J. W. Hässler, J. G. Müthel, C. G. Neefe, J. F. Reichardt, F. W. Rust, J. A. Scheibe, F. Seydelmann, J. N. Tischer, D. G. Türk, E. W. Wolf, and H. O. C. Zinck. Darrell Berg adds to this list E. Benda, G. Benda, J. G. Eckhard, C. F. C. Fasch, J. W. L. Hertel, C. G. Richter, and J. C. Reichardt; she mentions Binder, but separately from the Bachists.[33] Other writers have advanced a variety of individual candidates: Marian Stecher's *XII Variationen nebst I. Rondo fürs Clavier oder Forte-piano . . .* op. 6 has been read as a compliment to Bach, Emanuel Aloys Förster's early sonatas are said to be in his style, and Johann Friedrich Hugo Dalberg's solo sonata, op. 20 (1804) ends with a finale "returning, surprisingly and refreshingly, to the free fantasy of Emanuel Bach"[34] – a *stylus phantasticus* that few writers dared imitate. Alexander Reinagle's American sonatas "follow closely in the footsteps of Ph. Em. Bach and the early Haydn without being void of individuality" according to Sonneck.[35] Other proposals come from Newman and include C. W. Glösch, who wrote *6 Sonatines* (1780) "influenced by C. P. E. Bach," N. G. Gruner, whose two sets of sonatas (1781, 1783) include *Bebung* and develop C. P. E. Bach's style without being slavish copies like those of Forkel, and C. W. Podbielski, whose sonatas are reported as being "very much in the style of C. P. E. Bach's sonatas," although "he stemmed indirectly from J. S. Bach."[36]

This last proviso is salutary. With the growing awareness of the importance of C. P. E. Bach's father in the last years of the eighteenth century,

---

[31] *The Letters of Mozart and His Family*, ed. Emily Anderson, 3rd edn. rev. (London: Macmillan, 1988), 265.

[32] Pamela Fox, "The Stylistic Anomalies of C. P. E. Bach's Nonconstancy," in Clark, ed., *C. P. E. Bach Studies*, 105–31 (p. 130 n. 76).

[33] Darrell M. Berg, "The Keyboard Sonatas of C. P. E. Bach: An Expression of the Mannerist Principle" (Ph.D. diss., SUNY Buffalo, 1975), 72n.

[34] Newman, *The Sonata in the Classic Era*, 576.

[35] O. G. Sonneck, *A Bibliography of Early Secular American Music* (Washington: the author, 1905), 13.

[36] Newman, *The Sonata in the Classic Era*, 582, 779.

"Bachist" underwent a change of meaning and came to indicate the ripples of influence radiating directly from Johann Sebastian. Kollmann's famous "sun-flower" of leading German musicians allocated the central triangle to "Joh. Sebast. Bach" alone; around the triangle are "J. Haydn, Haendel, C. H. Graun"; the first layer of petals (from the top) consists of "Emman. Bach, Mozart, Kozeluch, Van Hall, Gluck, Reichardt, Schulz, Naumann, Schwanenberger, Hiller, Pleyel, Georg Benda, Rolle, Telemann," and the second (from the top) of "Seidelmann, Abel, Fis[c]her, Stölzel, Pisendel, Quantz, Hasse, Albrechtsberger, Forkel, Fleischer, Haessler, Türk, Wolf, Ditters."[37] C. F. D. Schubart supported this pedigree, referring to people who did not accept the preeminence of J. S. Bach as *Modeinsecten* – fashion-insects,[38] but Haydn was less happy with Kollmann's scheme: "He was gratified to be placed next to Handel and Graun, but rather more critical of Joh. Seb. Bach being the core of the sun, inferring that all true musical insight emanated from him."[39]

The following are preliminary thoughts that do not constitute a watertight "Method for Finding Bachists," but rather an exploratory mapping operation, undertaken in the hopes that not only new connections but also new repertoire may be brought to light. Such a general assessment of the parameters by which to establish circles of influence and appreciation around C. P. E. Bach should draw attention, in the case of composers, to repertoire that cannot reasonably be overlooked by anyone trying to place Bach and his keyboard music in perspective. However, the names, qualifications, reservations, and selected examples are listed below (as lawyers would say) "without prejudice."

Bach's pupils were both composers and performers, and it was as difficult for the eighteenth-century commentator to separate the two functions as it is for us. It is hard to disentangle composition from performance in Burney's judgments, and indeed it is a symptom of the unique integrity of C. P. E. Bach's style that the one often stands for the other. Delivery was not seen as a secondary characteristic for analysis here, and in Bach's case, more than with any other contemporary, it was closely bound up with the rhetoric and promulgation of an esoteric thought process. Obviously, all those who

---

[37] Reproduced in Hans-Joachim Schulze, ed., *Bach-Dokumente III: Dokumente zum Nachwirken Johann Sebastian Bachs 1750–1800* (Kassel: Bärenreiter and Leipzig: Deutscher Verlag für Musik, 1972), 587.

[38] Christian Friedrich Daniel Schubart, *Ideen zu einer Ästhetik der Tonkunst* (Vienna: Degen, 1806 [though written in the 1780s]), 101.

[39] F—l., "Anecdoten," *Allgemeine musikalische Zeitung*, 2/5 (1799), 103. Reprinted in *Bach-Dokumente III*, 587.

passed such a judgment announced themselves as belonging to the select group who had actually heard C. P. E. Bach play in person, and of these, most were enthralled more by his *extempore* performances than by printed notes.

Bach's pupils may not have ended their careers writing in his style but must at least have begun with sympathy for both it and the clavichord. Among this group one might even include those who tried to become pupils, but failed: Schulz, for example, who later learned from Kirnberger (although Burney feels him to be a "non-Bachist"), or Weyse and possibly Vierling. Johann Carl Friedrich Rellstab, we are told, intended to study with Bach but didn't – probably for the good, considering their later inimical relations over publishing. A stray remark from Burney is our source for the otherwise unnoticed fact that Daniel Steibelt "was a scholar of our old great favourite Emanuel Bach."[40] Zinck, in the preface to his *Sechs Clavier-Sonaten*, noted that he had been a singer under Bach in 1768, and he would have been familiar with at least the first three volumes of *Kenner und Liebhaber* sonatas before he published his own set of sonatas in 1783.

E. W. Wolf describes himself in his autobiography as a Bach associate whose aesthetic compass was firmly set by his encounter with Bach – "everything that I can achieve at the Clavier in his style and in mine I owe to those happy hours"[41] – and the admirable introduction he added to *Eine Sonatine, Vier affektvolle Sonaten, 13mal variirtes Thema . . .* of 1785 makes a worthy supplement to Bach's instruction in the *Versuch*.[42] But a clear demonstration of surface versus structural imitation emerges from the comparison of his keyboard works with Bach's; while Wolf could absorb the cosmetic side of Bach, he preferred the simpler and more symmetrical forms of classical writing.[43]

Jan Ladislav Dussek, who was a pupil in Berlin and visited Bach again in Hamburg in 1783, both composed and played in the style of Emanuel Bach more than any other, according to Burney who engaged him to teach his son in London in 1789.[44] Justus Theodor Rauschelbach, another Bach pupil,

[40] Müller-Hartmann, "Two Unknown Letters of Charles Burney," 162.
[41] Ernst Wilhelm Wolf, *Auch eine Reise aber nur eine kleine musikalische in den Monaten Junius, Julius und August 1782* (Weimar, 1784), 43.
[42] See Christopher Hogwood, "A Supplement to C. P. E. Bach's *Versuch*: E. W. Wolf's *Anleitung* of 1785," in Clark, ed., *C. P. E. Bach Studies*, 133–57.
[43] See Vera Funk, *Klavierkammermusik mit Bläsern und Streichern in der 2. Hälfte des 18. Jahrhunderts* (Kassel: Bärenreiter, 1995).
[44] Letter to Fanny Burney, 2 October 1789 (Yale collection). Cited in Kerry S. Grant, *Dr. Burney as Critic and Historian of Music* (Ann Arbor: UMI, 1983), 201, 343 n. 119.

242   *Christopher Hogwood*

complimented his master in the title of his *Zwey Grosse Clavier-Sonaten für Kenner und Liebhaber* (1790); he also played "in the Bach manner" according to the *Musikalische Real-Zeitung* (1790, col. 135). Johann Friedrich Wilhelm Wenkel (1734–92) although officially a pupil of C. W. Müller, was helped by both Kirnberger and C. P. E. Bach. (For a fuller listing of pupils, see the names marked with * in the Appendix.[45])

Bach's working colleagues, at one remove from his pupils, formed a closer bond with him as a composer than might be expected from the acrimonious assessments of Burney; composite collections of variations were not unusual – the pasticcio set based on "Ich schlief" (MS, D-B 30201) was the product of Bach, Marpurg, and Kirnberger (1761), while the "Clavierstück mit Veränderungen" in *Musikalisches Allerley* (pp. 190ff.) plus five extra variations in *Vielerley* (1762, pp. 113ff.) are identified by Westphal as being by Agricola, Steffani, and Carl Fasch as well as Bach. Kurt von Fischer has analyzed the interdependence of these variations and a set on the same theme by Neefe (1774); Bach himself, in his *Nachlaß-Verzeichnis*, said that where necessary the theme with its Italian variations was "Germanized" ("Die Ariette selbst, mit ihren italienischen Veränderungen ist, wo es nöthig war, verdeutschet"). Helm takes this to mean "notated according to German convention," but Fischer, by comparing it with Fasch's rendering, points out the addition of lombardic rhythms, appoggiaturas and the alternation of duplets with triplets, all symptoms of the surface complexity that typified the Berlin style.[46] Bach also contributed a recitative to the cantata "Die mit Tränen säen" by Fasch, in much the same way as he adapted and expanded the cantatas of Georg Benda. To this list of working colleagues one might add his off-duty friends in the Monday Club, one-off visitors such as Galuppi, and even the dedicatees of his character portraits.[47]

In his capacity as editor, Bach would not have readily included composers inimical to his principles in collections such as the *Musikalisches Allerley* (1761) and *Musikalisches Vielerley* (1770); in *Tonstücke für das Clavier vom Herrn C. P. E. Bach und einigen anderen classischen Musikern* (1762) he added

---

[45] See also Tobias Plebuch, "Veräußerte Musik. Öffentlichkeit und Musikalienmarkt im Zeitalter Carl Philipp Emanuel Bachs" (Ph.D. diss., Humboldt-Universität Berlin, 1996), 56–7.

[46] Kurt von Fischer, "Arietta variata," in H. C. Robbins Landon and Roger E. Chapman, eds., *Studies in Eighteenth-Century Music: A Tribute to Karl Geiringer on his 70th Birthday* (London: Allen and Unwin, 1970), 224–35.

[47] See Darrell M. Berg, "C. P. E. Bach's Character Pieces and his Friendship Circle," in Clark, ed., *C. P. E. Bach Studies*, 1–32.

music by Nichelmann and Kirnberger. (Is it possible that the anonymous final Piece VI in this volume is also an overlooked work by C. P. E. Bach, since it reverts to a C clef like his opening Sonata in the collection?) As a subscriber himself, Bach supported the *Sechs kleine und leichte Sonaten fürs Klavier oder Fortepiano* (1788–91) of Breitkopf's chief proofreader, Siegfried Schmiedt, though guardedly; his intention to recommend the sonatas "if I only know first their spiritual parentage," suggests some "anxiety of influence" in his attitude to developing styles around him.[48] Bach was a subscriber to W. C. Bernhard's *Ein Praeludium und Drey Sonaten fürs Clavier* (1785),[49] and he also features in the subscription list of Gruner's *Sechs Sonaten für das Klavier*, op. 1 (1781). Of F. S. Sander, Bach said "this young man has fire, has genius," but, alas, his name does not appear on the subscription list of Sander's 1786 *Sonatinen*.[50] Even Bach's requests for portraits to add to his extensive collection yield composers such as F. G. Fleischer and J. G. Schwanenberger, for whom one could suspect he harbored some admiration.[51]

One presumes that the publishers of C. P. E. Bach's music, and the middlemen involved in sales, were sympathetic to (as well as commercially hopeful of) the Bach style; Franz Anton Hoffmeister, for example, not only published Bach, Türk, and Petri among others, but wrote keyboard music himself (twenty-one sonatas are mentioned in *New Grove*). The circle of musicians who acted as agents for Bach's publications includes E. W. Wolf, F. Horn, J. F. Gräfe, N. G. Gruner, C. M. Wolf, J. F. Hering, J. G. Hoffman, F. W. Schilling, and C. Transchel. Conversely, Bach, in his capacity as an agent for other composers, accepted fourteen copies of E. W. Wolf's *Sei sonate* (1774).[52] (Wolf was later asked to succeed Bach in Berlin but turned the offer down.)

Publications and unpublished works carrying a dedication to C. P. E. Bach, or similar sympathetic titling, include B. Fritz, *Anweisung, wie man*

---

[48] Letter to Breitkopf, 28 July 1786, in Stephen L. Clark, trans. and ed., *The Letters of C. P. E. Bach* (Oxford: Clarendon Press, 1997), 250. The term "anxiety of influence," first devised for literary influences by Harold Bloom, has been given a musical context by Peter Williams in his "Is There an Anxiety of Influence Discernible in J. S. Bach's *Clavierübung I*?" in Christopher Hogwood, ed., *The Keyboard in Baroque Europe* (Cambridge: Cambridge University Press, 2003), 140–56.

[49] See letter to Breitkopf of 15 April 1785 in Clark, *Letters*, 227.

[50] Ernst Suchalla, ed., *Carl Philipp Emanuel Bach: Briefe und Dokumente. Kritische Gesamtausgabe*, 2 vols. (Göttingen: Vandenhoeck & Ruprecht, 1994), III: 1690.

[51] See letter to J. J. Eschenburg, 1 December 1784, in Clark, *Letters*, 218.

[52] See letter to Breitkopf, 2 April 1776, in ibid., 93.

Claviere . . . stimmen könne (1756), C. G. Neefe, *Zwölf Klavier-Sonaten* (1773), E. W. Wolf, *Sechs Sonaten* (1775), C. F. S. Hägemann, "Clavier Versuche" (1777), F. W. Marpurg, *Fughe e Capricii* (1777), C. F. W. Nopitsch, "Die sieben Namenbuchstaben Carl Filip Emanuel Bach . . . ," D. E. von Grotthus, "Rondo, 'Freude über den Empfang des Silbermannschen Claviers'" (1781), J. P. Kirnberger, *Anleitung zur Singekomposition* (1782), C. R. H. Ritter, "Versuch einer Sammlung . . ." (1786), J. E. Rembt, *Sechs Trios für die Orgel* (1787), and C. D. Krohn, *Sechs Klavier-Sonaten* (1789). (For full titles of works cited, see the Appendix.) A Mecklenburg manuscript source of Albrechtsberger's fugue on B–A–C–H (op. III) states that it was composed in 1753 when he was seventeen ("Composta dal Giovanni Giorgio Albrechtsberger 1753 demnach vom Verfasser in seinem 17. Lebensjahre ausgearbeitet"); with its intimations of Mendelssohn's style, it is more likely to have been intended as a tribute to C. P. E. Bach, who had just published his *Versuch*, rather than to his father, who was already three years dead. There is also a "Fantasie über B–A–C–H" in Johann Friedrich Christmann's *Elementarbuch der Tonkunst* (1782–9), obviously directed to C. P. E. Bach, since there are four pieces by him included in this manual. It has even been suggested that Mozart might have been paying deliberate homage to Bach in his keyboard Menuett K. 355 in D major; the tell-tale theme B–A–C–H can be found at the beginning of the second half, and the most recent dating suggests that the enigmatic piece was probably written in the year following C. P. E. Bach's death.[53] If this is true, it follows Mozart's similar tribute to J. C. Bach, whose death in 1782 he marked by quoting a theme from his overture to "La calamità de' cuori" in the second movement of the piano concerto K. 414.

The phrase "Kenner und Liebhaber" is now so firmly connected with C. P. E. Bach's six-part collection that it is too easy to assume a resonance when it occurs in other contexts. H. C. Schnoor's *Musikalisches Blumensträuschen . . . den Kennern und Liebhabern gewidmet* (n.d.), J. N. Forkel's *Über die Theorie der Musik, insofern Liebhabern und Kennern notwendig und nützlich ist* (1777), Rellstab's *Clavier-Magazin für Kenner und Liebhaber* (1787 – a collection that included Fasch, Haydn, Naumann, Reichardt, Schulz, Zelter, and many other suspected "Bachists") – and Becker's two publications of 1788 and 1790, both designated "für Kenner und

---

[53] See Peter Schleuning, "Mozart errichtet ein Denkmal: Das Menuett D-dur KV355," in Hanns-Werner Heister, Karin Heister-Gech, and Gerhard Scholz, eds., *Zwischen Aufklärung und Kulturindustrie: Festschrift für Georg Knepler zum 85. Geburtstag*, 3 vols. (Hamburg: Bockel, 1993), I: 83–94 (p. 83).

Liebhaber," may have been intended to compliment Bach, although they could as well have functioned in a more conventional (and pre-Bach) sense.[54] The *Anthologie für Kenner und Liebhaber der Tonkunst* published by Bossler in 1789 contains few Bachists in its complement of composers; however, we do find there a mention of C. P. E. Bach's *Anfangstücke für's Klavier . . . betreffend von J. C. F. Rellstab* (p. 153).

At the farthest horizons of influence might be the parents who optimistically gave their sons names such as Karl Philipp Emanuel [Pilz] or Carl Immanuel [Engel], but in the middle distance are the more serious professed admirers such as Johann Kaspar Lavater – "your admirer and worshipper" as he described himself in his first letter to Bach[55] – who analyzed Bach's features in his *Physiognomische Fragmente*; Gerstenberg; P. C. Kaiser; J. H. Voss; Junker; Grotthus (the recipient of the Silbermann clavichord); the collector Johann Jacob Heinrich Westphal; the Itzig family in Berlin; Baron van Swieten in Vienna; the composer Eckhard in Paris, who claimed that Bach's music was his only source of instruction; similarly Johann Hässler and musical historians from Burney and Forkel to the neglected John Stafford Smith, who was given J. S. Bach's copy of the *Ulm Gesangbuch* by C. P. E. Bach in Hamburg in 1772. Musical journalists such as Carl Friedrich Cramer and Hans Adolph Friedrich von Eschstruth were busy promoters of Bach in their published criticism; Eschstruth even wrote an unpublished (?lost) biography of C. P. E. Bach.

A form of unwitting inclusion in the C. P. E. Bach circle occurs with false attributions, those pieces by other composers which are accepted in manuscripts as being by Bach. In this category we find, for example, composers such as Johann Heinrich Rolle, whose Allegro in G (from *VII Suites per il Cembalo Solo, c.* 1763) is included in a sequence of C. P. E. Bach character pieces now in Gotha (D-GOl, Mus.2.o.21 a/3, Fasz. IXbis). Platti (op. 1 no. 5), Georg Benda (*Sei Sonate*, 1757), and Türk (*Sechs Sonaten*, 1776, nos. 2, 3, 4, and 6) are paid the same unconscious compliment,[56] and a manuscript copy of Benda's 1757 collection is attributed to Bach in Gotha,

---

[54] The term had already been used by Krieger, J. S. Bach, Kauffmann, and others. On the eighteenth-century distinction between *Kenner* and *Liebhaber* see Erich Herbert Beurmann, "Die Klaviersonaten Carl Philipp Emanuel Bachs" (diss., Georg-August Universität [Göttingen], 1952), 78–80. See also Erich Reimer, "Kenner-Liebhaber-Dilettant," in Albrecht Riethmüller, ed., after Hans Heinrich Eggebrecht, *Handwörterbuch der musikalischen Terminologie* (Stuttgart: Franz Steiner Verlag, 2000).

[55] Letter from Johann Kaspar Lavater to Bach, 13 May 1775, in Clark, *Letters*, 82.

[56] See Ulrich Leisinger, *Die Bach-Quellen der Forschungs- und Landesbibliothek Gotha* (Gotha: Forschungs- und Landesbibliothek, 1993), 45–6.

together with four sonatas by Türk (*Sechs Sonaten* 1776, nos. 4, 6, 2, 3) also
passing as Bach's.[57]

In Dresden, Sächsische Landesbibliothek, MS Mus. 3107-T-1a, a reverse
compliment occurs when six sonatas all attributed to Benda turn out to be
nos. 1–5, copied from his 1757 collection, followed by a Sonata 6 which
is C. P. E. Bach's Wq. 65.14/H. 42 (though Helm does not mention
this source). Christoph Ernst von Boineburgk openly admits of his collection of *Polonoisen* (MS, Gotha) that one polonaise is C. P. E. Bach's,
but that Bach approved also of his own efforts in the genre: "when I
played [my] Polonoise for the Hamburger Ph. E. Bach he expressed his
approval, [but] he was then a very decrepit man, and I took my leave."
More such leads are to be found in the "Spurious" sections of Eugene
Helm's catalogue of C. P. E. Bach's works, some of them more credible than
others.[58]

Helm's catalogue also includes a listing of early prints that contain
music by C. P. E. Bach alongside music by other composers (pp. 235–6).
This casual association of Bach's music with that of others can be a convenient gauge of the "Bachist" tendencies of his associates and can be extended
to manuscript collections and literary contexts where Bach and his music
are measured against his contemporaries: some come out of the encounter
well, and may be allowed as Bachists ("Bach and [Georg] Benda distinguish
themselves by means of a great and noble style, in jest and seriousness,"
according to Reichardt),[59] while others emerge less happily. Hiller, in a
scathing review of the "inharmonious jangle" (*unharmonisches Gepolter*) produced by Manfredini in St. Petersburg, asks "aren't the works of [Emanuel]
Bach, [Georg] Benda, Wagenseil, Kunz,[60] Binder, and other German masters known in Russia?"[61] Karl Benda (Franz Benda's son) and Karl Fasch
were said by Reichardt to be the only true successors to C. P. E. Bach and
Georg Benda,[62] although he admitted elsewhere that Binder "plays in the
Bach style with great delicacy and refinement."[63] Adolph Carl Kunzen, on
the other hand, played "zwar nicht in Bachischer, doch in guter Manier"

[57] Ibid., 63.

[58] See E. Eugene Helm, *Thematic Catalogue of the Works of Carl Philipp Emanuel Bach* (New Haven and
London: Yale University Press, 1989).

[59] J. F. Reichardt, *Musikalisches Kunstmagazin*, 1 (1782), 87.

[60] Can he mean Kunze, or Kunzen?

[61] "Sollten denn in Rußland die Clavierarbeiten eines Bach, Benda, Wagenseil, Kunz, Binder, und
anderer deutschen Meister nicht bekannt seyn?" *Wöchentliche Nachrichten und Anmerkungen die
Musik betreffend*, Zweites Vierteljahr, part 17 (21 October 1766), 131.

[62] Reichardt, *Musikalisches Kunstmagazin*, 1 (1782), 25.

[63] Johann Friedrich Reichardt, *Briefe eines aufmerksamen Reisenden die Musik betreffend*, 2 vols. (Frankfurt, 1774–6), I: 121.

and was "noch beßer auf dem Flügel und Clavier, wie auf der Orgel gefiel" according to Johann Wilhelm Hertel.[64] Again, the performing similarities seem to outweigh the composing differences.

The major investigative writers of this period were, like Burney, conspicuously alert to the difference in status between "successor" and "copyist" – influence versus imitation. In the *Allgemeine deutsche Bibliothek* Johann Friedrich Agricola approved Christian Gottlieb Neefe for his serious studies of Bach but also complimented him on not succumbing to "servile, forbidden imitation."[65] Johann Hässler was another Bach "Nachahmer" identified in the pages of the *ADB* – an opinion confirmed by Hässler himself in his autobiography. In a letter he described his meetings with C. P. E. Bach and Bach's approval of his *Ariette mit 30 Veränderungen*: "as I am a particular devotee of Kapellmeister Bach in Hamburg, I made a journey there last summer in order to hear from him direct whether I was performing his works properly and whether I might dare to make known to the musical world those pieces that I produced for him. I was fortunate enough to meet with his approbation."[66] Hässler later claimed to have passed on technical hints to both Türk and Rust.[67] Reichardt, however, noted while reviewing Hässler's *Sechs Sonaten* (1776) that the composer had lifted several passages (not itemized) from C. P. E. Bach's music,[68] and underlined the hazards of becoming too excessively dependent on a single model (an inbuilt danger in Bachism). An even more barbed critique is aimed at Forkel's *Sechs Klaviersonaten*, suggesting that he borrowed from Bach and then forgot whose the music was – "Give me a Häßler any day" is the reviewer's plea.[69] This may appear to create a category of the "unintentional" or "subliminal" Bachist, although Charles Burney was sure that Forkel's "borrowings" from Burney's *General History* were conscious and deliberate.

In terms of performance influence, the most widely recommended technical advances that derived from Bach involved the "Bachische Applicatur,"

---

[64] *Johann Wilhelm Hertel: Autobiographie*, ed. E. Schenk (Graz: H. Böhlaus Nachf., 1957), 50; see also Arnfried Edler, "Zwischen Händel und Carl Philipp Emanuel Bach: zur Situation des Klavierkonzertes im mittleren 18. Jahrhundert," *Acta musicologica*, 63 (1986), 180–221 (p. 199).

[65] Johann Friedrich Agricola, *Allgemeine deutsche Bibliothek*, 22/2 (1774), 525–6.

[66] Although this letter to Breitkopf (23 July 1772) would seem to imply C. P. E. Bach's approval of the enclosed *3 divertimenti vors Clavier allein nebst einer Ariette mit 30 Veränderungen*, these do not appear to have been published. Quoted in Christopher Hogwood, "The Inconstant and Original Johann Wilhelm Hässler," in Bernard Brauchli et al., eds., *De Clavicordio III*, *Proceedings of the International Clavichord Symposium* (Magnano: The International Centre for Clavichord Studies, 1997), 151–220 (167, n. 45).

[67] Ibid.   [68] In *Allgemeine Deutsche Bibliothek*, 35/1 (1778), 172–4 [misprinted 114].

[69] *Litteratur- und Theaterzeitung*, 2/2 (5 June 1779), 23.

the system of fingering that he promoted in the *Versuch*; even reviewers noted the importance of observing the fingerings suggested in his published music.[70] Kirnberger made open use of the system during Bach's lifetime in his *Clavierübungen mit der Bachischen Applicatur . . . Sammlung*, 1761–6, although neither he nor later advocates of the Bach system used the principle of larger figures for a change of hand position (e.g., 3–5) that Bach demonstrates in the *Versuch*. After Bach's death, editors such as Rellstab with a didactic catalogue made increasing reference to the Bach fingering system (see Appendix). As late as 1804 the "Bachische Applicatur" was in evidence when C. G. Tag published *Sechs kurze und leichte Parthien für kleine Anfänger im Fortepiano oder Klavier mit darüber gesetzer Applikatur und einer Ausführung der Manieren nach Bachischen Grundsätzen. Erste Sammlung*.

While the fingering system was the section of Bach's *Versuch* which had the widest application, later keyboard methods and performance texts leaned on his writings in general; these include B. Fritz, *Anweisung* (1756), M. J. F. Wiedeburg, *Selbst informirende Clavierspieler* (1765), J. C. C. Töpfer, *Anfangsgründe* (1773), C. Schmidtchen, *Kurzgefasste Anfangsgründe* (1781), J. J. Klein, *Versuch* (1783), G. F. Wolf, *Kurzer . . . Unterricht* (1783), Ricci-Bach, *Méthode* (1786), E. W. Wolf, *Musikalischer Unterricht* (1788), and J. C. Kaye, *Kleine Clavier Schule* (1820) (see Appendix for full titles). In addition, numerous composers borrowed from Bach the so-called "Bach ornament," the *prallender Doppeltrill* or *Doppelschlag* (≈), which was already accepted as a "Bachism" during his lifetime; Niels Schiørring, a Bach pupil, added handwritten comments to his *Kirkenmelodier, for Claveer . . .* (1781) and *Choral Bog* (1783) about the ornament and its appropriateness in chorale settings, and C. F. D. Schubart described it as a feature devised by Bach: "Bach was the first to introduce dynamic shading to the clavichord; he invented figures, trills, turns and numerous other ornaments at the clavichord."[71] Those composers who used or discussed the ornament at all frequently are marked with § in the Appendix. But its use is by no means definitive; an identical effect, though differently notated, is intended by Thomas Arne, whose English sonatas of 1756 are one of the closest and earliest approaches to the Bach style outside Germany:

---

[70] See the review of Bach's *Claviersonaten mit einer Violine und einem Violoncell zur Begleitung*, vol. II (1777) [Wq. 91/H. 531–4] in the *Hamburgischer unpartheyischer Correspondent* (1777), reprinted in Ernst Suchalla, ed., *Carl Philipp Emanuel Bach im Spiegel seiner Zeit: Die Dokumentensammlung Johann Jacob Heinrich Westphals* (Hildesheim: Olms, 1993), 117.

[71] Schubart, *Ideen zu einer Ästhetik*, 178.

while Søren Sønnichsen in his 1812 tutor proposed a resolution of the ornament very different from that recommended by Bach. Both are listed in the Appendix, though in parentheses.

The decline from influence to imitation and thence to parody was a gradient that enthralled the eighteenth-century aesthetician, and its stages can be seen in the variety of Bachists and their product. The various senses of "imitatio" range from paying homage, through assimilating and building upon a model, to aping a predecessor or simply borrowing without interest. In the volumes with dedications to Bach listed above some authors undoubtedly pay homage, while the lesser-known figures may simply be seeking to travel on C. P. E. Bach's coat-tails. Often harsh criticism is justified, but one critical slander of Bach himself deserves rebuttal. In October 1784 the *European Magazine, and London Review* led with an article on Haydn claiming that

amongst the number of professors who wrote against our rising author was Philip-Emanuel Bach of Hamburgh (formerly of Berlin); and the only notice Haydn took of their scurrility and abuse was, to publish lessons written in imitation of the several stiles of his enemies, in which their peculiarities were so closely copied, and their extraneous passages (particularly those of Bach of Hamburgh) so inimitably burlesqued, that they all felt the poignancy of his musical wit, confessed its truth, and were silent.[72]

The sonatas implicated in this malicious thrust were Hob. 36–41 and 42–7 (published as Opp. 13 and 14). Eventually, when the article was republished in German in Cramer's *Magazin der Musik* in 1785 – with the editorial comment: "Lie upon lie"! – Bach felt compelled to reply and declare the accusation to be untrue.[73] However, given the wide readership of both magazines, it is illuminating to note which passages in Haydn the anonymous author felt would be widely accepted as parodying Bach's "capricious manner, odd breaks, whimsical modulations, and very often childish manner, mixed with an affectation of profound science" – a summary of defects not so far removed, we may note, from the complaints of Burney and Twining. Haydn's true feelings, reported by Griesinger, were that on first coming across the *Prussian Sonatas*, "I did not leave my clavier until I had played right through them; whoever knows me well must realize that I owe very

---

[72] The full text is reproduced in H. C. Robbins Landon, *Haydn at Esterháza 1766–1790* (London: Thames and Hudson, 1978), 496–7. See also A. Peter Brown, "The Earliest English Biography of Haydn," *Musical Quarterly*, 59/3 (1973), 339–56.

[73] C. F. Cramer, *Magazin der Musik*, 2/1 (7 April 1785), 585–94; *Hamburgischer unpartheyischer Correspondent*, no. 150 (20 September 1785), reprinted in Suchalla, ed., *Briefe und Dokumente*, II: 1099–1101.

250   *Christopher Hogwood*

much to Emanuel Bach, that I have industriously studied and understood him." To clinch the argument he added bluntly, "Emanuel Bach once paid me a compliment on that score himself."[74]

Burney made specific exception for certain composers he considered "non-Bachists," and in fairness this category should be continued. To Wagenseil, Schobert, and Schulz we could add his later reference from Osborn shelves c 100 p. 56: "The Abbé Sterkel has not travelled through Italy for nothing; his Harpd. pieces, though not very hard [?] or consonant with harmonical rules, are full of spirit, taste & fancy. & he has not only collected all the vocal flowers of the greatest opera singers of the recent times, but scattered them liberally through his works . . . His pieces, though not very original, are less tinctured with Bachism and Haydenism than those of his countrymen who have not visited Italy." Sterkel, who arrived in Italy with nothing but "a miserable clavichord"[75] was criticized by Cramer for having "the nerve to reject [C. P. E.] Bach's excellent Essay and disparage his compositions, without his being able to play the easiest Bach sonata acceptably . . . his [own] sonatas are for the ladies."[76] On the whole (and despite Thomas Gray's pronouncement) the non-Bachists can be identified by increased Italian leanings; ever since the 1770s much of the public had favored the "Modeschönheiten der Neu-Italiäner" – "Rutini, Galuppi, Schobert, Abt Fischer, Heyden"[77] – and were drawn to that transparency (some would say flimsiness) that Nietzsche later identified in Mozart's music as deriving from "a belief in the South."

The following list integrates the various categories of Bachists outlined above, as a starting point for more substantial research. In the case of those composers not yet well represented in modern editions, a selection of keyboard titles has been added; besides forming a preliminary repertoire basis on which to judge the assets of the Bachists, this may also encourage players to move away from the exclusive concentration on C. P. E. Bach that characterizes too much research as well as too many recitals.

---

[74] "da kam ich nicht mehr von meinem Klavier hinweg, bis sie durchgespielt waren, und wer mich gründlich kennt, der muß finden, daß ich dem Emanuel Bach sehr vieles verdanke, daß ich ihn verstanden und fleißig studirt habe . . . Emanuel Bach ließ mir auch selbst einmal ein Kompliment darüber machen." Georg August Griesinger, *Biographische Notizen über Joseph Haydn* (Leipzig: Breitkopf & Härtel, 1810), 13.

[75] According to Norbert Hadrava; see John A. Rice, "Stein's 'Favorite Instrument': A Vis-à-vis Piano-Harpsichord in Naples," *Journal of the American Musical Instrument Society*, 21 (1995), 30–64 (p. 33).

[76] C. F. Cramer, *Magazin der Musik*, 2/1 (1783), 574.

[77] Review collected by Johann Jacob Heinrich Westphal, cited in Suchalla, ed., *Carl Philipp Emanuel Bach im Spiegel seiner Zeit*, 101.

[23]

WHEN DID THE CLAVICHORD BECOME C. P. E. BACH'S FAVOURITE INSTRUMENT? AN INQUIRY INTO EXPRESSION, STYLE AND MEDIUM IN EIGHTEENTH-CENTURY KEYBOARD MUSIC

BY DAVID SCHULENBERG

The question posed in my title presupposes that the clavichord was indeed the favourite instrument of Carl Philipp Emanuel Bach, the second son of Johann Sebastian. I do not intend to dispute this; I do, however, wish to inquire into what exactly it means to say that Emanuel Bach favoured the clavichord; on what evidence this view is founded; and at what point in his life he indeed adopted it as his preferred instrument.

In saying that the clavichord was Bach's favourite instrument, I imagine that most of us have in the backs of our minds Charles Burney's account of a private performance by Bach on what Burney described as 'his *Silbermann clavichord*, and favourite instrument'.[1] Several other documents support the view that this particular instrument was indeed Bach's favourite and one on which many of his most distinctive compositions had been written (see appendix). But does that mean that he wrote those pieces specifically for performance on this clavichord (or on clavichords like it), to the exclusion of other instruments? Had he always favoured this type of instrument, and if so for what types of music and for what performance situations: only for solo practice, or also for private chamber music and even for informal concerts and musical 'academies'? The famous Silbermann clavichord was probably a double-strung unfretted instrument with a relatively wide dynamic range and compass, a type of instrument that came into widespread use only in the course of Bach's long career; when and how would Bach have acquired his mastery of its distinctive performance technique, and at what point did this come to be reflected in his writing for keyboard instruments? Another way of formulating the question is to ask when Bach began to participate in what Derek Adlam has described as 'the development of a new clavichord aesthetic'.[2]

First let us consider the verbal documents that testify to Bach's use of the clavichord for any purpose. These are listed in the appendix. As is immediately apparent, the documents are few in number and mostly quite late, from Bach's last two decades at Hamburg, and they provide no clues as to when Bach might have adopted the clavichord as his favourite — not

---

[1] Charles Burney, *The Present State of Music in Germany, the Netherlands, and United Provinces, or: The Journal of a Tour through those Countries, undertaken to collect Materials for a General History of Music*, 2d ed. (London, 1775; facs., New York: Broude, 1969), pp. 269–70.

[2] 'The Importance of the Clavichord in the Evolution of the New Musical Aesthetic in Eighteenth-Century Germany and in the Development of the Fortepiano and Its Repertoire', *Magnano Proceedings I*, p. 248.

38   DAVID SCHULENBERG

even a suggestion that he might have been brought up on or once preferred another keyboard instrument. Fortunately, we already have clear indications of Bach's predilection for the clavichord in volume 1 of his *Essay on the True Manner of Playing Keyboard Instruments*, first published in 1753.[3] The *Essay* is curiously reticent on certain basic issues, such as the precise nature of keyboard touch, the exact manner of temperament, and above all the choice of instrument for specific compositions. But in it the clavichord is clearly Bach's favoured instrument for solo practice and instruction; it is, moreover, the most demanding instrument, the one 'on which a keyboard player can most conveniently be judged'[4] and on which one learns a sensitive touch. Even so, the harpsichord remains his instrument of choice for accompanying and directing large ensembles, and players are urged to own both harpsichord and clavichord and to play 'on both instruments all sorts of pieces interchangeably'.[5]

The fortepiano, although often the focus of modern studies of Bach's *Essay*, plays a comparatively minor role in it, especially the first volume. But the oft-encountered claim that Bach criticised the fortepiano does not withstand a careful reading. He merely notes that its 'touch [*Tractierung*] must be carefully worked out' and that on it it is difficult to play certain ornaments.[6] In the second volume, published in 1762, Bach praises the instrument's 'undamped register' and expresses a preference for fortepiano and even clavichord when a particularly refined accompaniment is desired.[7] The two instruments differ chiefly in the fortepiano's incapability for *Bebung* and the *Tragen der Töne*, for reasons that Daniel Gottlob Türk later explained more fully: in both techniques the key is given additional pressure after being struck.[8] Like *Bebung*, the *Tragen der Töne* was thought to produce an intensification of the sound while avoiding what Türk calls the 'odious raising of the pitch';[9] John Barnes has offered an explanation for why this technique produces an audible effect on the clavichord.[10]

Although the *Essay* leaves little doubt that Bach preferred the clavichord for teaching and study, the work leaves it unclear whether Bach, on the one hand, considered the clavichord the proper instrument for particular pieces of music or, on the other, simply considered it a useful tool for private practice and study. Prior to the date of the *Essay* we have only indirect witnesses to his use of the clavichord. Thus in seeking the origin of Bach's preference for the clavichord it is necessary to examine the music itself and its sources.

---

[3]   *Versuch über die wahre Art das Clavier zu spielen*, 2 vols. (Berlin, 1753–62); English translation in one volume by William J. Mitchell as *Essay on the True Art of Playing Keyboard Instruments* (New York: Norton, 1949). References to this work will be through volume, chapter, and paragraph numbers of the original German edition (the chapters are renumbered in part 2 of the English translation).

[4]   *Versuch*, i.introduction.11.

[5]   *Ibid.*, i.introduction.15.

[6]   *Versuch*, i.introduction.11, i.2.3.36. Donald H. Boalch, *The Makers of the Harpsichord and Clavichord 1440-1840*, 2d ed. (Oxford: Oxford University Press, 1974)], p. 46, translates the related word *Tractament* as 'workmanship' in Bach's letter of Nov. 10, 1773, to Forkel. He is followed in this translation by Stephen L. Clark, ed., *The Letters of C. P. E. Bach* (Oxford: Clarendon Press, 1997) in his translation of letter 46 (p. 43). But Ernst Suchalla, ed., *Carl Philipp Emanuel Bach: Briefe und Dokumente: Kritische Gesamtausgabe*, 2 vols. (Göttingen: Vandenhoeck & Ruprecht, 1994), 1:354, understands *Tractament* here as 'die Art der Übertragung des Tastenanschlags auf die Saite zur Erzielung einer besonderen Tongebung.'

[7]   *Versuch*, ii.41.4 and ii.introduction.6. The word *Register* probably refers to something like a hand-stop that lifted all the dampers, not a permanently undamped portion of the keyboard compass as on the upper strings of a modern piano.

[8]   *Versuch*, i.3.20; Türk, *Clavierschule oder Anweisung zum Clavierspielen für Lehrer und Lernende* (Leipzig and Halle, 1789; facs., ed. Siegbert Rampe, Kassel: Bärenreiter, 1997), p. 20ff.

[9]   'häßliches Uebertreiben des Tones', *Clavierschule*, p. 293ff.

[10]   'Coupling Between Clavichord Unisons and Its Effect on Tuning', *Het Clavichord* 2/3 (December 1989): 4–5, cited by Peter Bavington, 'Keylever, Tangent, and String: A Preliminary Analysis of Clavichord Touch and Action', *Magnano Proceedings III*, p. 82.

Joel Speerstra has enumerated the bases on which arguments can be made for the use of a particular instrument in a particular piece.[11] The presence of *Bebung* markings is an unambiguous indication for the use of clavichord, but these occur in only a few of Bach's compositions.[12] Hence scholars have had to rely on the presence or absence of dynamic markings, keyboard compass, and any verbal titles or inscriptions accompanying the music, as well as the more subjective analytical criteria also mentioned by Speerstra. But the very difficulty that we have in determining the intended or optimal medium of a given work suggests that such enterprises may be somewhat misdirected. In undertaking them we may be operating on the basis of peculiarly twentieth-century assumptions about music and composition — in particular, that composers have always shaped pieces for specific instruments, and that the harpsichord and the clavichord are therefore each uniquely suited to particular compositions.

In fact, pieces that we might regard as variously appropriate to the organ, the harpsichord, and the clavichord often mingle in no particular order within eighteenth-century anthologies. Both manuscripts and printed editions often employ generic designations for keyboard parts that leave the intended instrumental medium uncertain. In other cases, different sources often employ differing instrumental designations for the same composition.[13] Clearly, players throughout the century used whatever instrument was available, for all manner of music. This seems to have been as true for Emanuel Bach as for his father, among the older generation, and of Haydn and Mozart, among later ones. Needless to say, this poses an added difficulty in determining when Bach adopted the clavichord as his favourite instrument.

The great majority of Bach's keyboard works preserved in manuscript bear the inscription *per cembalo solo* or the like. This is true for both autograph and apograph manuscripts, including the authoritative copies made by Johann Heinrich Michel for the composer and his family around the end of Bach's life. In modern Italian the word *cembalo* is generally understood to mean specifically the harpsichord, but, as Darrell Berg and others have noted, for eighteenth-century German-speakers it often had a more generic significance, referring to any stringed keyboard instrument.[14] For example, the title page of Bach's first significant publication, the six 'Prussian' sonatas issued in 1742 with a dedication to the newly crowned King Frederick (Wq 48), designates them as being *per Cembalo*.[15] Yet, many movements from the set employ three levels of dynamic markings as well as musical gestures which I will describe as being particularly suitable for the clavichord.[16] By the 1760s, Bach was regularly indicat-

---

[11] 'Towards an Identification of the Clavichord Repertoire Among C. P. E. Bach's Solo Keyboard Music: Some Preliminary Conclusions', *Magnano Proceedings II*, pp. 43–4; the article is followed by a table listing the proposed instrumental assignment of each of Bach's keyboard sonatas (pp. 62–81).

[12] Notably in the sonata in F, Wq 55/2 (H. 130), written expressly for Bach's Silbermann clavichord according to the review of 1779; and the *Abschied* rondo Wq 66 (H. 272). Erich Herbert Beurmann, *Die Klaviersonaten Carl Philipp Emanuel Bachs* (Ph.D. diss., Georg-August-Universität, Göttingen, 1952), p. 92, lists thirteen sonatas as containing *Bebung*: nos. 48, 61, 64, 77, 79, 85, 92, 121, 133, 136, 140-1, 145 = Wq 52/1, 63/1, 63/4, 62/20, 70/1, 55/2, 52/2, 54/4, 55/3, 56/6, 59/1, 61/5, and 65/49 (H. 50, 70, 73, 120, 133, 130, 142, 206, 245, 270, 281, 287, and 298). In all but two cases, however (Wq 55/2 and 63/4), the sources for these works available to me show repeated notes or *Tragen der Töne*, not Bach's distinctive *Bebung* marking. I have consulted the facsimiles of eighteenth-century sources reproduced in Darrell Berg, ed., *The Collected Works for Solo Keyboard by Carl Philipp Emanuel Bach* (1714–1788), 6 vols. (New York: Garland, 1985).

[13] For example, what were published as organ works appear elsewhere as sonatas or concertos for 'clavier' or 'cembalo'; see Darrell M. Berg, 'C. P. E. Bach's Organ Sonatas: A Musical Offering for Princess Amalia', *Journal of the American Musicological Society* 51 (1999): 484–7.

[14] See Berg, 'C. P. E. Bach's Organ Sonatas', p. 479 n. 7.

[15] Facsimile in Berg, *Collected Works*, 1: 1.

[16] Speerstra, table, p. 62, overlooks the presence of pp alongside p and f in this collection.

ing diminuendos and crescendos, as well as accents, through the use of closely spaced fortes, pianos, and even mezzofortes, in works that still bore the heading *per il Cembalo solo*.[17]

Similarly, the German word *Clavier*, although often used by Türk and other younger writers with the specific meaning of 'clavichord', does not usually have that significance for Bach. At least from the time of the *Essay* onward, when Bach wishes to specify the harpsichord he usually employs the word *Flügel*; for the clavichord he uses the term *Clavichord*. Similar distinctions occur in the writings of Johann Nicolaus Forkel,[18] as well as in the German translation of Burney's *Musical Tours*.[19] Hence the titles of Bach's publications that include the word *Clavier*, from the *Essay* and the so-called *Reprisen-Sonaten* of the 1750s and 1760s to the late collections of pieces *für Kenner und Liebhaber*, do not necessarily refer specifically to the clavichord.

Even where eighteenth-century documents make a clear distinction between the various keyboard instruments, this is rarely in the context of specific pieces or individual musical scores. When this is the case, it may be because the instrument in question is something rather exotic, such as the bowed clavier invented by the Berlin maker Johann Hohlfeld in the early 1750s, for which Bach wrote the Sonata in G, Wq 65/48 (H. 280).[20] But there is little in the sonata that seems distinctive to such an instrument, and possessors of the music were obviously expected to play it on whatever instrument they happened to own.[21] As Berg has shown, the same is true of most of Bach's pieces disseminated as organ works. These occasionally employ musical tropes that might have been identified with older organ music, such as a moderately contrapuntal style with chains of suspensions in the upper voices.[22] But they rarely demand anything specific to the organ, such as long sustained tones or pedal notes.

The title pages of the last five of the collections *für Kenner und Liebhaber* indicate that the rondos, contained therein alongside sonatas and fantasias, are 'fürs Forte-piano'.[23] These pieces were evidently a novelty, introduced after the first volume, which contained only sonatas. The rondos incorporate lengthy sections comprised of arpeggiated passage-work; Bach might have thought the latter particularly appropriate to the fortepiano (especially, perhaps, when played without its dampers). Another novelty, probably intended for performance in a public concert, was Bach's double concerto for harpsichord and fortepiano,

---

[17]   See, e.g., the autograph of the sonata in E-flat, Wq 65/42 (H. 189); the autograph, although probably not a composing score, appears to be close in date to the original composition of 1765 (facs. in Berg, *Collected Works*, 4: pp. 162–7).

[18]   *Ueber Johann Sebastian Bachs Leben, Kunst und Kunstwerke* (Leipzig, 1802); contemporaneous English translation in *The New Bach Reader*, ed. Hans T. David and Arthur Mendel, rev. Christoph Wolff (New York: Norton, 1988), pp. 419–82.

[19]   *Carl Burney's der Musik Doctors Tagebuch seiner Musikalischen Reisen*, trans. Christoph Daniel Ebeling and Johann Joachim Christoph Bode, 3 vols. (Hamburg, 1773; facs., Kassel: Bärenreiter, 1959).

[20]   The *Bogen Clavier* is specified in the title of Michel's manuscript copy (facs. in Berg, *Collected Works*, 4: 223), and in the entry for the work in Bach's estate catalogue (see below).

[21]   Bach reportedly played Hohlfeld's instrument in a court concert in 1753 (Berg, *Collected Works*, 4: xxi). The sonata was composed thirty years later (thirteen years after Hohlfeld's death), suggesting that at least one example of the instrument still survived at that time (none is now extant). A few passages, such as an implied crescendo and diminuendo on sustained quarter notes (second movement, left hand, bars 14-15), might have been particularly effective on a bowed clavier.

[22]   As Berg notes, 'C. P. E. Bach's Organ Sonatas', pp. 506–7.

[23]   This is the usual reading of the title, as also assumed by, e.g., Adlam in 'The Importance of the Clavichord', p. 247. Taken out of context, the syntax of the full title may appear ambiguous to a modern reader: *Clavier-Sonaten* [or *Clavier-Sonaten und Freyen Fantasien] nebst einigen Rondos fürs Forte-Piano*. Indeed, Beurmann understood it as referring solely to the fortepiano ('Die Klaviersonaten', p. 88). But in other titles the word *Claviersonaten* is self-sufficient, not requiring a qualifier ('for the fortepiano'). It is true that the phrases 'einigen Rondos' and 'fürs Forte-Piano' were printed on different lines and in different type sizes on the title pages of the first two of the volumes in question (Wq 56 and 57; see Berg, *Collected Works*, 2:291, 2:327). But in the last three volumes the two phrases appear on one line and in the same type, clearly set off from the remainder of the title (*Collected Works*, 1:123, 2:369, 2:411).

Wq 47 (H. 479).[24] Its autograph calls explicitly for *Fortepiano* alongside the harpsichord. Yet even this work, one of Bach's last, makes only a minimal stylistic differentiation between the two instruments (in the last movement, where each has distinct thematic material).

Thus, titles, dynamic indications, and other seemingly objective indices are of limited value for our investigation, even when coupled with stylistic analysis of the music itself. A further difficulty arises when we attempt to establish a chronology for Bach's adoption or development of a 'clavichord aesthetic'. An authoritative list of Bach's compositions was published after his death in the catalogue of his estate, known to scholars as his *Nachlassverzeichnis*.[25] This document provides dates and places of composition for most of Bach's surviving works, including early ones from his student days at Leipzig and at Frankfurt an der Oder. Exceptionally, it describes most of these early works as having been *erneuert*, that is, 'renewed' or 'revived' at Berlin during the mid-1740s. But surviving sources of these pieces rarely indicate which version they transmit: the original Leipzig and Frankfurt versions or the 'renewed' ones from Berlin. Moreover, it has become clear that after the 1740s Bach continued to revise these pieces, as he also did many other works for which the *Nachlassverzeichnis* provides no indication of the existence of alternate versions.[26] It would seem, then, that the use of the expression *erneuert* implied something more than a routine revision — that the early works underwent some sort of profound transformation when Bach revised them at Berlin.

Scholars have held differing views as to the survival rate of the very earliest versions of these works. I suggested in 1987 that what were thought to be early versions were in some cases Bach's 'renewed' versions of the 1740s; my reasoning was that in most cases the supposed early versions differed from the later ones only in small details, such as the addition of a few ornament signs in the revised version.[27] This view was supported by Wolfgang Horn's argument, based on the provenance of the sources, that almost none of the original versions remained extant. Horn concluded that 'in most cases the original versions of the early sonatas listed in the *Nachlassverzeichnis* are lost; the only certain exception to this is the Sonata WQ 65/7 (H. 16)'.[28] Horn's pessimistic findings have been somewhat modified by the subsequent identification of early versions for a number of works; in each case the style of the newly identified pieces supports the idea that Bach indeed transformed them when he 'renewed' them at Berlin.

As an example of one of these, let us consider the Largo in E minor that occurs in late manuscript copies as the second movement of the Sonatina in G, Wq 64/2 (H. 8). The latter is one of six early sonatinas that Bach revised at least twice, at one point exchanging each of the slow middle movements from one work in the set to another.[29] Thus a slightly different, presumably earlier version of this Largo occurs in two manuscript copies as the second move-

---

[24] Public performances of Bach's keyboard concertos using both harpsichord and fortepiano are included in the list of concerts provided by Christoph Gugger, 'C. Ph. E. Bachs Konzerttätigkeit in Hamburg', in *Der Hamburger Bach und die neue Musik des 18. Jahrhunderts: Eine Veranstaltungsreihe anlässlich des 200. Todesjahres von Carl Philipp Emanuel Bach 1714–1788*, ed. Hans Joachim Marx (Hamburg, 1988), pp. 176–85; see also the corresponding entries in Suchalla, ed., *Briefe und Dokumente*.

[25] *Verzeichniß des musikalischen Nachlasses des verstorbenen Capellmeisters Carl Philipp Emanuel Bach* (Hamburg, 1790); facs., ed. Rachel Wade, as *The Catalog of Carl Philipp Emanuel Bach's Estate: A Facsimile of the Edition by Schniebes, Hamburg, 1790* (New York: Garland, 1981).

[26] See, for example: the critical commentaries for the seven sonatas in: *Carl Philipp Emanuel Bach: Keyboard Sonatas, 1744–1747*, ed. David Schulenberg, Carl Philipp Emanuel Bach Edition, I/18 (Oxford: Oxford University Press, 1995).

[27] Review of Berg, *Collected Works*, in *Journal of the American Musicological Society* 40 (1987): 110–11.

[28] *Carl Philipp Emanuel Bach: Frühe Klaviersonaten: Eine Studie zur 'Form' der ersten Sätze nebst einer kritischen Untersuchung der Quellen* (Hamburg: Karl Dieter Wagner, 1988), p. 271.

[29] According to the *Nachlassverzeichnis*, all six sonatinas were composed at Leipzig in 1734 and *erneuert* at Berlin ten years later.

42 DAVID SCHULENBERG

ment of the Sonatina in E minor, Wq 64/4 (H. 10). Berg included both sonatinas in her facsimile edition of Bach's keyboard works, designating one as a 'later' and one as an 'early'
version.[30] But an even earlier version of the movement was identified in 1993 by Ulrich
Leisinger and Peter Wollny; it occurs as the second-movement Andante of a previously
unknown Sonata in E minor [Example 1].[31]

Example 1: C. P. E. Bach, Andante in E minor (second movement of Sonata in E minor),
from Hamburg, Staat- und Universitätsbibliothek, ms. ND VI 3191
(facsimile in Leisinger and Wollny, 'Altes Zeug von mir', p. 145)

Like several other very early compositions by Bach, this one seems simple, almost
rudimentary, in its polyphonic texture of two voices, like an instrumental sonata or aria with
continuo accompaniment. This aspect was eliminated in the renewed version, which also discarded the double bar at the centre. Most striking, however, is the transformation of both

---

30 Berg, *Collected Works*, 3:144–7 and 3:153–9.

31 ' "Altes Zeug von mir": Carl Philipp Emanuel Bachs kompositorisches Schaffen vor 1740', *Bach-Jahrbuch* 79 (1993):
144–5 and 156–63. The first movement of this sonata is an early version of the first movement of Wq 65/5 (H. 13); the
third movement corresponds with that of Wq 64/4 (H. 10).

melody and accompaniment through a process of variation and embellishment, to the point that one can hardly recognise the two versions as the same piece of music [Example 2].[32]

Example 2: C. P. E. Bach, Largo in E minor (second movement of Sonatina in G, Wq 64/2 [H. 8]), from Staatsbibliothek zu Berlin, Mus. ms. Bach P 775; facsimile in Berg, *Collected Works*, 3:146

The 'renewed' version retains the harmonic and melodic skeleton of the original; hence the revisions are superficial in a technical, analytical sense. They are nevertheless crucial for performance, especially in regard to the instrument on which one might prefer to play the piece. Even the earliest version is, of course, playable on the clavichord, which makes possible not only expressive dynamics but such refinements as the use of *Bebung* on one or two 'long affetuoso notes', as Bach prescribed.[33] But only in the later versions does one find cer-

---

[32] Example 2 is from the 'later' version in Berg, *Collected Works*. This differs only in the presence of a few additional embellishments and ornament signs from the 'early' version in the same edition. Berg has analysed Bach's revisions in a number of other early sonata movements; see Darrell M. Berg, 'Carl Philipp Emanuel Bachs Umarbeitungen seiner Claviersonaten', *Bach-Jahrbuch* 74 (1988): 123–61.

[33] Such as the c^2 in bar 10; see *Versuch*, i.3.20. Staccato notes under slurs, possibly indicating the *Tragen der Töne*, appear in bars 11 and 25, but as in several later pieces — e.g. Wq 52/1 and 52/2 (H. 50 and 142) — the note values in question

tain musical gestures and textures that, as I will explain shortly, I take to be clearly and relatively exclusively idiomatic to the clavichord.

The same types of gestures and textures introduced into the 'renewed' version of this movement occur as well in works whose first composition dates from the early and mid-1740s. Indeed, at almost the same time as the 'renewal' of this sonata, Bach was also composing some of his most distinctive original works. Among these are several sonatas which, in a 1775 letter to Forkel, Bach described as having been written in the spa town of Töplitz on a clavichord with a short octave (see appendix). This does not mean that Bach intended them expressly for such an instrument; indeed, an instrument with a short octave would probably be inadequate for most of Bach's surviving works. Rather, Bach seems to have been indicating to Forkel that despite the limitations of this small instrument, probably intended for travel, he was still able to compose some exceptional pieces on it. Indeed, the six pieces described in the letter may have included the extraordinary Sonata in G minor, Wq 65/17 (H. 47), and its somewhat comparable companion in C, Wq 65/16 (H. 46).

Among the three pieces that can be securely identified as having been composed at Töplitz is the B-minor Sonata Wq 65/13 (H. 32.5).[34] It also happens to be one of just three sonatas composed in the 1740s that survive in autograph.[35] If, then, we can identify features in any of these sonatas as specifically idiomatic to the clavichord, we can tentatively date Bach's serious involvement with, if not preference for, the instrument at least as far back as his early years in Berlin.

Indeed, the B-minor sonata contains a number of such features; these are in addition to its use of what Speerstra has termed 'melodic dynamics' — markings within a phrase that require an instrument capable of flexible dynamics, such as the clavichord.[36] At several points, the first movement employs slurred figures of diatonic and chromatic quarter notes extending over two measures. Particularly notable is the passage in bars 5–6, where both hands have such figures in contrary motion; the right hand, moreover, contains the same figure in parallel sixths [Example 3].

---

seem too small for the *Tragen der Töne* to be effective, and it is unclear to me what the written articulation means. Possibly the slurs are merely the copyist's way of collecting the notes into groups of six.

[34] This is one of three works listed in the *Nachlassverzeichnis* as having been composed at Töplitz; a partially autograph manuscript score (in Staatsbibliothek zu Berlin, Mus. ms. Bach P 359) is dated 'Töplitz, 26. Junij 1743'. The identification of the other sonatas mentioned in Bach's letter to Forkel has been debated; see Schulenberg, ed., *Keyboard Sonatas*, p. 110.

[35] The others are Wq 65/16 in C (H. 46) and Wq 65/24 in D minor (H. 60). A fourth sonata, Wq 65/19 (H. 49), must be discounted; although the *Nachlassverzeichnis* dates it to 1746, its autograph was written in the 1780s and in its extant form the sonata must date from late in Bach's life (see Schulenberg, ed., *Keyboard Sonatas*, pp. 127–8). Autographs of three earlier sonatas can also be dated to the 1740s: Wq 65/2 and 65/7–8 (H. 4, 16–17).

[36] 'Towards an Identification', p. 47.

WHEN DID THE CLAVICHORD BECOME C. P. E. BACH'S FAVOURITE INSTRUMENT? 45

Example 3: C. P. E. Bach, Sonata in B minor, Wq 65/13 (H. 32.5), first movement, from Staatsbibliothek zu Berlin, Mus. ms. Bach P 775; facsimile in Berg, *Collected Works*, 3:260

Similar gestures appear in other works from the same decade.[37] A true legato is difficult enough to achieve on a keyboard instrument lacking a damper pedal; harpsichordists today often employ over-legato to this effect, but the presence of parallel thirds or sixths within one hand makes it difficult to apply this technique to both voices. Such gestures are more practicable on the clavichord, where the absence of a sharp plectrum attack and the possibility of voicing individual notes of a chord through dynamics makes it possible to disguise non-legato attacks. This strengthens the impression of legato in such passages, especially when the instrument has good sustaining powers.

Another telling gesture is the use of sustained melodic tones against accompaniments comprised of moving or repeated notes and chords, as in bars 13–14, 41–5, or 76–7. No conventional stringed keyboard instrument can effectively sustain a long melodic note against shorter ones of the same dynamic level, particularly in slow or moderate tempos. On the harpsichord (or organ), if the accompaniment contains chords it can be difficult to avoid producing accents in what are supposed to be subsidiary voices, on weak beats within the measure. Such textures, on the other hand, can be negotiated on the clavichord through the dynamic shading of each note in the texture and, in addition, the application of *Bebung* on the sustained melodic notes.[38]

Both types of gestures might have been suggested by the homophonic textures of early eighteenth-century *opera seria*, which furnished an obvious model for the singing style of *galant* instrumental music, including Bach's. *Opera seria* was introduced to Prussia on a large scale with the inauguration of the royal opera at Berlin in 1742, one year prior to Bach's composition of the B-minor sonata. But it would have been familiar previously to members of Frederick's court, including Bach, through visits to Dresden and the participation of Italian singers and other virtuosos in the concerts that Frederick sponsored at Ruppin and Rheinsberg prior to his succession. Moreover, the music of Johann Adolph Hasse and other Dresden composers is found in the 1725 *Clavierbüchlein* of Anna Magdalena Bach, where it evidently formed part of the pedagogic material used for Sebastian's children.[39]

The early Andante in E minor already contains apparent echoes of the Hasse style, such as the descending slides in bar 3 and the falling sixth in bar 5. But although this movement and others like it — including much of the pedagogic repertory in the 1725 *Clavierbüchlein* — already sounds plausible on the clavichord, it does not contain anything that can be said to demand the instrument in the way that the revised versions do. To be sure, its thin two-part texture, which is found in many of Emanuel's early sonata movements — and in Sebastian's inventions — is arguably less effective on harpsichord than clavichord. But it lacks the types of gestures described above in the B-minor sonata, which reflect not just the style of Hasse's melodies but the varied orchestration and dynamic flexibility that are increasingly typical of *opera seria* from the 1730s onward.[40]

If indeed Bach's development of a 'clavichord aesthetic' took place around the start of his Berlin period, then it coincided with other important developments in his compositional style. In the period beginning around 1740 Bach not only produced such innovative sonatas as those of the Prussian and Württemberg sets but was also making astonishing developments in

---

[37] For example, the E-major Prussian Sonata, Wq 48/3 (H. 26), first movement; the Sonata in B-flat, Wq 65/20 (H. 52), third movement.

[38] A modern pianist would likely use the damper pedal as well, not only to help sustain the melodic tones but to prevent a repeated-note accompaniment from sounding dry or cold — a danger unlikely to arise on quieter eighteenth-century instruments.

[39] The 1725 *Clavierbüchlein*, now Staatsbibliothek zu Berlin, Mus. ms. Bach P 225, was later owned by Emanuel Bach. The Polonaise in G, BWV Anh. 130 (no. 28 in the manuscript), is from a sonata by Hasse.

[40] Not only does the early Andante lack all dynamic indications, but it contains few harmonic or rhythmic events that might imply some sort of dynamic contrast.

the area of the keyboard concerto. Indeed, the twenty concertos of the 1740s must be considered his most important works of the period, constituting perhaps the most profound contribution to the genre before Mozart. Like Bach's solo keyboard music, his concertos of the 1740s show an increasing flexibility of dynamics and texture, often using melodic, rhythmic, and accompanimental patterns present as well in contemporary *opera seria*.

Presumably the solo parts of the concertos continued to be played on the harpsichord, at least through the 1740s. But in these works the orchestra provides dynamic effects which therefore need not be projected by a keyboard instrument playing alone. Moreover, alternation between soloist and ripieno provides an element of dramatic dialogue that also need not be present within the solo keyboard part. Apparent imitations of such effects are already present in harpsichord and organ pieces by J. S. Bach, and they continue in those of Emanuel. Indeed, the 'renewed' version of the E-minor Andante contains several *forte* interjections (bars 12, 18, 20, 22) reminiscent of ripieno outbursts in Bach's concertos.[41] But these intrusions of a 'terraced' approach to dynamics are less expressive of a true clavichord aesthetic than are the subtler effects described previously.

The trend toward greater flexibility of texture and dynamics in composition is reflected in the apparent movement in Bach's environment toward the use of what John Koster has termed 'expressive claviers'.[42] Some three years after his use of a small clavichord at Töplitz in 1743, Bach acquired his famous Silbermann instrument.[43] King Frederick was acquiring fortepianos as well as a 'Clavier' from Silbermann at precisely the same time,[44] and Sebastian Bach, who visited the court in 1747, apparently acted as an agent for Silbermann during the same period.[45] Thus it is no surprise that by the early 1740s Emanuel was writing in a keyboard idiom very different from that of his father, one that can be effectively employed on the clavichord.[46]

This keyboard idiom already included many of the expressively quirky rhythmic and melodic gestures that give Bach's later and better-known solo keyboard music its distinctive flavour. More than anything else, it is this sort of keyboard writing, such as is already strongly hinted at in examples 2 and 3, that today defines Bach's personal style and the mid-eighteenth-century 'clavichord aesthetic'. But Bach's solo keyboard music contains far greater variety of affect and musical style than is found in my first three examples. The last movement of the B-minor Töplitz sonata is a fiery Allegro di molto reminiscent in character of some of Bach's most impassioned keyboard concertos of the same period, alternating between a slashing arpeggio in its *Hauptmotiv*, chromatic drum basses, and dotted rhythms. Other sonatas, such as the G-minor one of 1747 (Wq 65/17), conclude with equally dramatic virtuoso movements. If the lyrical opening and middle sonata movements shown in examples 1–3 indeed represent aspects of a 'clavichord aesthetic', then the same must be equally true of these final movements.

---

[41] I described Bach's insertion of similar orchestral passages into the solo passages of his concertos in 'C. P. E. Bach Through the 1740s: The Growth of a Style', in *C. P. E. Bach Studies*, ed. Stephen L. Clark (Oxford: Clarendon Press, 1988), pp. 222–3.

[42] 'Pianos and Other "Expressive" Claviere in J. S. Bach's Circle, Part One', *Early Keyboard Studies Newsletter* 7/4 (October 1993): 1–11.

[43] According to Baron Grotthuss's letter of 1781, Bach had then owned the instrument for thirty-five years; see appendix.

[44] See: Mary Oleskiewicz, 'The Trio in Bach's Musical Offering: A Salute to Frederick's Tastes and Quantz's Flutes?', *Bach Perspectives, Volume Four: The Music of J. S. Bach: Analysis and Interpretation*, ed. David Schulenberg (Lincoln: University of Nebraska Press, 1999), pp. 98–9.

[45] As documented by a sale receipt from 1749; see *New Bach Reader*, p. 239 (no. 262).

[46] Or the fortepiano — but the latter can be ruled out as a usual choice for contemporary performers, probably including Bach, for reasons summarized by Adlam, 'The Importance', pp. 247–8.

When Bach played for Burney in 1773, the latter of course noted Bach's mastery 'in point of *expression*'. But Burney added the important comment that 'he [Bach] possesses every style', illustrating this with the fact that Bach played for him from his recently published set of six keyboard concertos (Wq 43, Hamburg, 1771).[47] Burney does not say explicitly that Bach played the latter on the clavichord. But other accounts from the same period make it clear that Bach was accustomed to playing virtuoso music of a highly extroverted nature on the clavichord, if not in public concert halls then at least before small gatherings in his own home.

In the mid-1770s Bach published three collections of keyboard trios (Wq 89–91). These are described on the title pages of their German editions as *Claviersonaten* with the accompaniment of violin and cello — 'piano trios' in modern parlance, but evidently as flexible in their scoring as solo 'clavier' music of the same period.[48] An anonymous review, published in 1777 at Hamburg, describes Bach's performance of pieces from one of these collections on his 'clavier' by Christian Ernst Friederici, accompanied by a muted violin and a cello 'played with discretion'.[49]

As in other so-called accompanied keyboard sonatas of the period, the two string parts are indeed subsidiary to the keyboard and can be omitted. Indeed, the last sonata of the set (Wq 91/4 = H. 534) survives in an alternate version for solo keyboard as the Variations with Varied Reprises, Wq 118/10 (H. 259).[50] In its predominantly lyrical, expressive style it conforms with what many would regard as an idiomatic 'clavichord aesthetic'. But the quick movements from all three sets of keyboard trios tend to be in a lively virtuoso style comparable to that found in the opening movements of Bach's concertos, symphonies, and other works of his Hamburg period composed for public consumption [Example 4].

The same is true of the *Sechs leichte Claviersonaten* (Wq 53) published in 1766, one of which Bach played for the writers Gotthold Ephraim Lessing and Matthias Claudius two years later on his Silbermann clavichord (see appendix). Alongside stereotypical 'sensitive' (*empfindsamer*) movements, the volume contains symphonic opening allegros (Wq 53/6 = H. 183) and concluding prestos resembling those in his Hamburg concertos (Wq 53/4 = H. 182).[51]

Evidently, then, Bach and his admirers found nothing in this music that was unidiomatic to the clavichord. To be sure, this is not a type of music that seems to *demand* the clavichord — no more so than does the early Andante in E minor. But the fact that this type of music could be played adequately — no doubt more than adequately in the hands of a Bach — demonstrates an important point about the mid-eighteenth-century clavichord and its repertory. Although we tend to emphasise the 'expressive', that is to say the lyrical and quiet aspects of the mid-eighteenth-century clavichord, these qualities were already present in much older instruments.

---

[47]   Burney, *Present State of Music in Germany*, pp. 271–2. The keyboard part of Wq 43 includes cues to the violin lines in the ritornellos, thus facilitating its use for performance on unaccompanied keyboard.

[48]   In the English edition of Wq 89 (London, 1776), the keyboard instrument is specified as harpsichord or pianoforte.

[49]   'ein mit Discretion gespieltes Violoncell'. The reviewer was clearly on close terms with the composer; he may have been Joachim Friedrich Leister, identified by Richard Kramer as the likely author of other reviews of Bach's works. See 'The New Modulation of the 1770s: C. P. E. Bach in Theory, Criticism, and Practice', *Journal of the American Musicological Society* 38 (1985): 580.

[50]   The sonata consists of a single movement, a set of variations on an Andantino in C, Wq 116/23 (H. 249). The latter was the first of a set of *Sechs leichte Clavier-Stückgen* composed at Hamburg in 1775, two years prior to the keyboard trio.

[51]   Like 'easy' sonatas by some other eighteenth-century composers — such as Mozart — the set in fact makes significant demands on both player and listener.

Example 4: C. P. E. Bach, Sonata in C, Wq 90/3 (H. 524), first movement, from *Carl Philipp Emanuel Bach's Claviersonaten mit einer Violine und einem Violoncell zur Begleitung, Erste Sammlung* (Leipzig, 1776)

The larger, unfretted ones that came into widespread use during Bach's lifetime were distinguished in part by their capacity for greater volume and ease in the playing of rapid passage-work and ornaments in all keys — in short, dramatic virtuoso playing of a type that might previously have been thought appropriate only to the harpsichord and the organ. Hence, although writers such as Burney, Türk, and Bach himself tended to extol the clavichord and its music for their lyrical or 'expressive' qualities, it may in fact have been the 'inexpressive' features of the new instruments that made it possible for them to become favourites of musicians such as Bach. Such instruments could now be used for 'every style', as Burney put it — symphonic and concerto-like display passages in the latest fashion, as well as music whose singing or rhetorical qualities placed it in a clavichord tradition extending back at least to the suites of seventeenth-century German composers such as Froberger and Buxtehude. What is more, the same piece could now not only alternate suddenly between very different styles; it could do so smoothly as well. Both possibilities had to be available to keyboard players if they were to achieve dramatic effects equal to those of accompanied recitative and aria in the latest *opere serie*.

The case of Emanuel Bach and the clavichord presents many of the classic issues in the relationship of organology to performance practice. Did the composer write his music for specific instruments? Does the music contain concrete, identifiable elements that are clearly and incontrovertibly suited to one instrument over another? Whether Bach's innovations in his keyboard sonatas of the 1740s were product or cause of his adopting a new type of instrument is one of those chicken-and-the-egg questions that cannot be readily answered.

50   DAVID SCHULENBERG

But during that period Bach was certainly gaining an intimate familiarity with new types of 'expressive claviers', including clavichords, by Silbermann and no doubt other makers. At the same time, his compositional style was undergoing a substantial change, at least at the surface of the music. We might surmise that the new types of instruments were becoming available to Bach at a critical time in his development as a musician. In them he found a medium that overcame the disadvantages of such instruments as the clavichord with a short octave that he disparaged in his letter to Forkel. It was now possible for solo keyboard music to combine all of the dramatic, expressive, and virtuoso effects that harpsichord and strings together could create in his concertos of the same period.

Still, like his predecessors, Bach continued to compose most of his keyboard music without directing it exclusively to any one type of instrument. This may have been due in part to commercial considerations; music that was flexible in respect of instrumental medium could enjoy a broader market than that which was not. But it may also have reflected an aesthetic of variety — one that transcended any 'clavichord aesthetic' that also may have influenced Bach's development at one time or another. Bach may well have had a 'favourite' instrument, but, as with his father, his musical nature was far too broad-spirited to permit its confinement to any single medium or style.[52]

Example 4 (cont.)

[52]   This essay contains material orginally written for an article commissioned by Igor Kipnis. Although the work in which that article was to have been published never appeared, I am grateful to Mr. Kipnis for having sparked my interest in the subject. I am also grateful to André Larson, director of America's Shrine to Music Museum, for facilitating my research for this paper in the museum collection.

APPENDIX:
DOCUMENTS RELATING TO EMANUEL BACH'S USE OF THE CLAVICHORD

Documents are listed in chronological order. 'D' refers to the numbering of documents in Suchalla, ed., *Carl Philipp Emanuel Bach: Briefe und Dokumente: Kritische Gesamtausgabe*, which gives full bibliographic citations.

- 1743. Trip to Töplitz; composes six (?) sonatas on a clavichord equipped with a short octave (see under 1775 below).
- 1746. Bach acquires his Silbermann clavichord? See under 1781 below.
- 1752. Part 1 of Bach's *Versuch* published; implies preference for clavichord, at least for instruction and solo practice.
- 1767, September 28. Bach, letter to Breitkopf (D 47), mentions the latter's packing an unspecified instrument to send to Bach in Berlin (?).
- 1768, October. Letter, Matthias Claudius to Heinrich Wilhelm von Gerstenberg (D 68), reports Claudius's having listened alongside Lessing to Bach playing the Silbermann clavier; he describes the instrument as 'the famous little Silbermann clavier' (*das kleine berühmte Silbermannsche Klavier*) with a compass up to e^3 and its tone as 'bright, ringing, and sweet' (*ein helle, durchdringende, süße Ton*), but without exceptional strength in the bass or an unusually soft, 'flattering' upper register (*keine außerordentliche Stärke im Baß, keinen außerordentlich sanften schmeichelnden Diskant*). Bach twice played three movements 'expressly written for this clavier', adding embellishments the second time, as well as one of the sonatas from Wq 53 (*Sechs leichte Clavier-Sonaten*, Leipzig: Breitkopf, 1766).
- 1773. Burney's *Present State of Music in Germany* published, including an account of Bach's performance on 'his *Silbermann clavichord*, and favourite instrument' at home, before a few guests (identified in Bode's translation; see below). Before dinner Bach 'played three or four of his choicest and most difficult compositions', afterwards 'many other things', including 'his last six concertos', i.e., Wq 43 (*Sei Concerti per il cembalo concertato*, Hamburg, 1772).
- —, Volume 3 of the German translation of Burney published, containing additional details about Burney's visit as well as Bach's autobiography.
- — November 10. Bach, letter to Forkel (D 142), mentions his preference for Friederici's over Barthold Fritz's and Johann Adolph Hass's clavichords, on account of their *Tractament* and octave stringing in the bass.
- 1774, April 2–3. Johann Heinrich Voss, letter to Ernst Theodor Johann Brückner (D 159), mentions Bach's promise to improvise (*vorspielen*) on his Silbermann clavichord for a whole evening after the upcoming Easter holiday.
- 1775, February 2. Bach, letter to Forkel, mentions having composed six sonatas in 1743 while at the spa in Töplitz, using a clavichord with a short octave.
- 1777, October 10. Review in *Hamburger Correspondent* (Suchalla, *Briefe und Dokumente*, 1: 632–3) reports Bach's playing the accompanied sonatas of Wq 91 on clavichord with muted violin and cello 'played with discretion' (*ein mit Discretion gespieltes Violoncell*).

- 1779, July 31. Review in *Hamburger Correspondent* of Wq 55 (Suchalla, *Briefe und Dokumente*, 1: 763) states that Bach wrote the second sonata of the set (= H. 130, composed at Berlin, 1758) expressly for his Silbermann clavichord. On the latter, the 'Schwebungen' (i.e., *Bebung*) indicated in the first movement sound with astonishing strength (*Kraft*).
- 1781, September 30. Letter, Baron Dietrich Ewald von Grotthuss, allegedly to C. P. E. Bach (D 411), reports buying Bach's Silbermann clavier and that Bach had owned it for 35 years. Also claims to have wished to see the instrument for fifteen years, i.e., since he was a boy of 14 — confirming that the instrument was 'famous' (see Claudius's letter of 1768).
- 1789. Bach's estate catalogue (*Nachlassverzeichnis*) published. Includes five-octave clavichords by Heinrich Wilhelm Jungcurt and Friederici; nearly all his Hamburg works were composed on the latter.

[24]

Performers Remarks

Miklós Spányi

Concertos Vol. 1 (Djursholm: Grammofon AB BIS CD–707

Aspects of Performance – The Choice of the Solo Instrument

In performing Carl Philipp Emanuel Bach's keyboard concertos, we encounter a lack of information on two extremely important points. We do not know:

1) for what kind of solo instrument(s) these works were composed; or

2) on what kind of instrument they were performed in the 18th century.

The inscription of the keyboard parts: 'cembalo' does not tell us much. According to latest researches 'cembalo' could mean *any kind* of keyboard instrument, sometimes even just 'manual' in organ music. This word does not define any special instrument.

In all probability C.P.E. Bach knew and used many different keyboard instruments. He was always very open towards new ideas in instrument building and greeted them enthusiastically – he even admired a curious invention called the 'Bogenclavier'. One of his best friends, the instrument builder Christian Gottfried Friederici, was himself an ingenious inventor of keyboard instruments.

In his music C.P.E. Bach focused on a few central genres. Beside solo keyboard music, the keyboard concertos form the most important group of works in his output, and they span nearly all his life: he composed his first concerto in 1733 at the age of 19, and the last one in 1788, the year he died. In between, he performed concertos regularly, most probably on many different sorts of instruments: harpsichords, fortepianos, tangent pianos, organ as well as the popular combination instruments of the time (e.g. harpsichord and fortepiano combined in one instrument), as well as a number of other keyboard instruments which we may know only from written sources – types which disappeared long ago.

We might not say the composer did not have any special instrument in mind when composing a piece. However we cannot rule out the possibility that he may have seen opportunities to perform them on different instruments as well. This was the normal attitude of the period, and very likely, that of C.P.E. Bach as well. Thus the modern interpreter has great freedom; everything which serves the music is permitted.

Unfortunately, the choice of good copies of historical keyboard instruments is still very restricted at present. We have far fewer different possibilities than the contemporaries of C.P.E. Bach. We can only choose the best possible instrument for certain pieces from the instruments currently available – following objective historical arguments as well as many subjective, personal ones.

For the early concertos I have chosen a large harpsichord. In my opinion these works sound very well on such an instrument, making full use of the very rich sound of the alto-tenor register. However, I wanted to avoid the use of the French and Flemish models so 'common' today, as it is rather uncertain whether or not C.P.E. Bach ever had anything to do with these types. Also a technical problem may arise when using such harpsichords: the rich middle register is frequently too dominant compared to the treble, which is, nevertheless, the leading voice in this music.

I finally found the ideal instrument for these pieces in the workshop of Michael Walker. It is a copy after Hieronymus Albre Hass, the original being preserved in the collection of the Brussels Conservatoire. The instrument has clearly accentuated treble, a very strong but warm sound, the attack of the tones being clear but still soft, giving the instrument a certain singing character so typical for German clavichords of the time. The rich disposition of the harpsichord (lower manual: 16', 8', 4'; upper manual: 8' and 8' nasal, these two plucking the same strings at two different points; harp stop ['Lautenzug'] to the upper 8' and the 16') allows many combinations of colours. The presence of a 16' stop is a peculiarity which was however, more typical in German harpsichords than has long been presumed. This stop gives a fantastic depth and power to the overall sound of the instrument and can be used very colourfully in different combinations. This harpsichord encourages the player to use varied registration: the total number of combinations is (theoretically) close to 50.

The Epoch of C.P.E. Bach and 'Empfindsamkeit' was not a period of dogmatism in music and performance. The most important thing was to express different feelings, if possible a great number of them. This harpsichord serves this aim very well.

Vol. 5 (Djursholm: Grammofon AB BIS CD–785, 1997)

Performer's Remarks: Silbermann and the Fortepiano

In some 18th century German sources Gottfried Silbermann is mentioned as the father of the fortepiano. Later, priority was given to Bartolomeo Cristofori, who was said to have 'invented' the fortepiano towards the end of the 17th century in Italy. Only the most recent investigations have dared to contradict existing opinions by saying that neither Cristofori nor Silbermann was the inventor of the fortepiano, but that they were merely ingenious instrument makers, whose work marked the culmination of a long process of development begun much earlier. Indeed, more or less obscure sources have been found mentioning instruments with hammer action from as early as the 15th and 16th centuries, but lack of more concrete information, and, especially, the absence of surviving instruments from these early centuries makes further investigation extremely problematic. It can be stated with certainty, however, that fortepianos were built and used long before the 18th century. The former belief that the fortepiano became known only in the last quarter of the 18th century can be forgotten for ever, and performance of earlier music on the fortepiano should be taken into consideration very seriously.

Gottfried Silbermann (1683–1753) is among the best-known German organ builders of the 18th century; he built more than 40 organs, and his stringed keyboard instruments were also very much appreciated: clavichords, harpsichords and fortepianos. According to research by Konstantin Restle, Silbermann must have experimented with different types of hammer action even before he became acquainted with instruments built by Cristofori. Cristofori's fortepianos were probably not entirely unknown in Saxony: it is supposed, for example, that the Italian composer Antonio Lotti, who worked in Dresden between 1717 and 1719, had brought such a 'hammer harpsichord' with him to Dresden, where Silbermann could see and investigate it.

True enough, the known fortepianos by Silbermann have an action based on that of Christofori's fortepianos, but it is adapted to a very heavy case, resembling that of the German harpsichords. Silbernmann's fortepianos were praised for their beautiful sound, solid quality and durability. Though musical taste was rapidly changing, there is evidence that at least some of Silbermann's fortepianos were still in use as late as in the 19th century!

Searching for suitable instruments for our recording of Carl Philipp Emanuel Bach's keyboard concertos, I came across a copy of Silbermann fortepiano (presently the only one known to me), built by the Antwerp instrument maker Jan van den Hamel. This instrument has a very clear, but somewhat fluty tone, which blends beautifully with the string instruments, and on which, despite its rather soft volume, concertos can be beautifully performed. The clearly tinkling sound of the upper register (resembling little bells) comes through the sound of the orchestra and makes even the fast passages audible. Its touch is relatively heavy (an aspect criticized by some contemporary sources), but it allows the very safe playing of fast runs and ornaments.

Vol. 9 (Djursholm: Grammofon ABBIS CD–868)

Performer's Remarks

1762 was a very important turning-point in Carl Philipp Emanuel Bach's output for solo keyboard instrument and orchestra. After a hiatus of seven years, during which he composed just a single keyboard concerto (the opening piece on this disc), Bach again began to compose new works in this genre. In this year too, he composed the first pieces in an entirely new genre for keyboard instrument and orchestra, the so-called *Sonatinas*. And 1762 also marked a new turn in revising and re-composing his earlier keyboard concertos.

What gave C.P.E. Bach this new impulse to turn again to the keyboard concerto? One plausible explanation – as Jane Stevens points out elsewhere in this booklet – is that the revitalization of concert life in Berlin after the Seven Years War led to Bach having to face the challenge of presenting to the public new compositions with a leading keyboard part. There is, however, another possible explanation. About 1760 Bach must have had access to some new kind of instrument. One obvious sign of this is the use of a larger keyboard range up to f^3 in nearly all of his concertos and sonatinas as well as in chamber sonatas with obbligato keyboard composed in and after 1762. Earlier he used a keyboard range that was common on German instruments with e^3 as the highest note; the compass, for example, of fortepianos by Gottfried Silbermann, which Bach used during his Berlin years.

We may presume that the newcomer was a more 'modern' instrument. In the works composed after 1762 Bach's keyboard writing changed essentially and we may well wonder what sort of instrument he had in mind. Historically it would be right to think of a harpsichord, an instrument in use until the end of the eighteenth century. Bach's new keyboard idiom, however rather indicates some kind of early piano. His keyboard writing became more 'pianistic' around 1762. The sonatinas composed between 1762–65 contain the most pianistic passages that Emanuel Bach ever composed. In these works the keyboard part is less soloistic than in the concertos, often introducing no thematic material, and it is incorporated in the whole texture in such a way that the 'solo' instrument often 'accompanies' the orchestra with virtuoso passagework. This, combined with a very refined instrumentation, especially the sensitive use of the flutes and *con sordino* strings, requires a keyboard instrument which blends ideally with the other instruments. Only a dynamically flexible instrument, i.e. a piano, is capable of fulfilling these requirements. The robust and majestic harpsichord is absurd in this rôle.

As I pointed out earlier in this series, we may assume that Bach already preferred the fortepiano (or its relatives such as the tangent piano) to the harpsichord for performances of his concertos before 1762, and we find vague indications of this in the music itself. The fact that Bach's keyboard changed so radically around 1762 indicated that he had come into contact with an instrument which differed from the pianos he had known earlier. This style of change is still more conspicuous in the concertos revised after 1762: comparing them to their earlier versions it is interesting to see how Bach modified the keyboard texture in order to make it more flexible and 'piano-like' and to accommodate it to the ideals of the (presumed) new instrument.

The present disc contains C.P.E. Bach's last concerto composed before the turning-point of 1762 (the concerto in E flat major, H.446/W.35), two sonatinas composed in 1762 and an earlier concerto (C minor, H.407/W.5) from 1739, which Bach thoroughly revised in 1762. In this way the disc tries to give an idea of the opening of a new era in Bach's concerto output. On coming discs we also intend to present 'new' concertos, composed in or after 1762, mingled with the sonatinas of the same period as well as with concertos presumably revised after 1762. In most cases we have no direct evidence of the revisions. One unambiguous sign of a revision after 1762 is the use of the larger keyboard range up to f3. In the scores, on the other hand, there are many signs of later erasures and additions. Variant versions also survive in different manuscripts, which verifies the hypothesis of late revisions. In cases where no indications of different versions or revisions are to be found, we can suspect a revision from Bach's keyboard writing: whenever an earlier keyboard concerto displays elements in the keyboard part which are similar to Bach's concertos and sonatinas from after 1762 and seems to require a piano-like instrument, we can be assured that the work underwent some revisions, most probably after 1762.

Exactly what instrument Bach encountered around 1760-62 we do not know, and at the moment we cannot find any documentary evidence in the history of the early German piano either. We can only try to find a keyboard instrument which harmonizes with Emanuel Bach's music. For Bach's concerto output after 1762, I have decided henceforward to use the tangent piano, already introduced on three previous discs in this series. I do this with the conviction that that required harmony between the music and the instrument can be achieved on and by the tangent piano. It is not impossible, either, that Bach would have seen and used such an instrument, and the tangent piano is closely related to other types of early pianos as to both sound and touch. The opening work on this disc, the concerto in E flat major (H.446/W.35) from

1759 also survives in many manuscripts as an organ concerto. The work was revised at some later time by Bach and this version (performed here), with its richer embellishments, seems to fit better to a stringed keyboard instrument. For more detailed information concerning my choice of the tangent piano in both of Bach's 'organ concertos' see my remarks to the previous volume. Many passages of the concertos and the sonatinas seem to require a special effect of the early piano: the raising of the dampers. This effect, praised by many contemporary sources, may be rather unusual to many listeners. I shall discuss it in more detail in the next volume of the series.

Vol. 17 (Djursholm: Grammofon AB BIS CD–1687)

The Hamburg Dilemma

The history of instruments and their development is never completely linear. Despite the fact that the fortepiano became more and more popular during the 18th century, it did not succeed in overshadowing the harpsichord until the very end of the century - indeed, never were so many harpsichords built during the 1770s, which seems to indicate that the rise of the fortepiano also provided an impetus and a challenge to the builders of harpsichords.

In the second half of the 18th century Hamburg already looked back on a long and remarkable tradition of organ and harpsichord building. Though the local harpsichord output gradually became less significant, the harpsichord itself did not. It remained a popular and important member of the keyboard family in the North German regions and numerous instruments were imported, mainly from England where the most 'modern' harpsichords of the period were produced.

In moving from Berlin to Hamburg, C.P.E. Bach left an environment very open towards experiments with new instruments and arrived in a slightly old-fashioned musical community with its own strong traditions, including a love for the harpsichord. Bach must have seen this as a challenge. As soon as he had settled down he began to give concerts, and he continued doing so until the last decade of his life. A considerable number of Bach's public performances have been documented in the Hamburg press. From these we can see that Bach often performed on the harpsichord but he is also mentioned playing the fortepiano (both solo and in concertos). The average Hamburg *bourgeois* was ready to be introduced to the modish fortepiano but retained and kept using his beloved harpsichord.

This ambivalence towards the choice of instruments may have been a constant factor during the whole of Bach's Hamburg period. Should the famous *Double Concerto for Flügel and Piano-Forte,* Wq 47, be seen as one of its consequences? That is so far only a speculation. Against this background, however, I was not very surprised to find how much Bach's first two Hamburg keyboard concertos differ in style. The *Concerto in E flat major,* Wq 41 (H469), is one of Bach's most pioneering and experimental achievements in the concerto genre, combining elements of the traditional concerto with features of his own *Sonatinas* from the 1760s. It is a 'modern' work, intended for both connoisseurs and the wider public, and with a very fine instrumentation – with independent flute and horn parts as well as two viola parts – that enfolds the solo keyboard in the accompanying ensemble in a near-Mozartian way.

Though the work could be performed on a good harpsichord, my feeling is that its supreme refinement can be conveyed even more effectively by using a more 'modern' and expressive instrument: the tangent piano, an earlier member of the piano family. Bach's next work in the genre, the *Concerto in F major*, Wq 42 (H 470), is a much more traditional work in every respect: it follows the traditional formal concerto design and uses a more conventional musical language. Although it is playable on fortepiano or tangent piano, I have found the keyboard part to be most convincing and resonant on the harpsichord. A more traditional work composed for the more traditional keyboard? This seems to be a very plausible explanation and I have therefore opted for the harpsichord on this recording.

Bach mentions the *Concerto in C minor*, Wq 31 (H 441), in a letter as having been 'one of my showpieces' ('eines meiner Paradörs'). He thus performed it regularly, most likely also in Hamburg. With its slow movement imitating an operatic *recitativo accompagnato* it belongs to the most personal works in Bach's œuvre. Its solo part reflecting Bach›s most personal thoughts and requiring fine shadings and dramatic contrasts, lends itself excellently to being performed on early pianos. In consequence, the tangent piano is used in our recording.

Name Index